Long Time Passing

Vietnam and the Haunted Generation

Other Books by Myra MacPherson

THE POWER LOVERS

Long Time Passing

Vietnam and the Haunted Generation

MYRA MacPHERSON

DOUBLEDAY AND COMPANY, INC.
GARDEN CITY, NEW YORK, 1984

ISBN: 0-385-15842-4
Library of Congress Catalog Card Number 82–45258
Library of Congress Cataloging in Publication Data
MacPherson, Myra.
  Long time passing.
  Bibliography: p. 643
  Includes index.
  1. Vietnamese Conflict, 1961–1975—United States. 2. Vietnamese Conflict, 1961–
  1975—Psychological aspects. 3. Vietnamese Conflict, 1961–1975—Influence.
  I. Title.
  DS558.M32 1984   973.923

*For yesterday's youth, the Vietnam Generation,
and for Leah and Michael and all of today's young.
May past not be prologue.*

Contents

Part I
Long Time Passing

"Where Have All the Flowers Gone?"

BY PETE SEEGER

Where have all the flowers gone?
Long time passing. . . .
Where have all the soldiers gone?
Long time passing.
Where have all the soldiers gone?
Long time ago.
They've gone to graveyards, every one.
Oh, when will they ever learn?
Oh, when will they ever learn?
Where have all the graveyards gone?
Gone to flowers every one.
Oh, when will they ever learn?
Oh, when will they ever learn?

Prologue

THIS BOOK LOOKS AT ONE FACET OF THE PROFOUNDLY COMPLEX Vietnam War—the generation that came of age then. The ones who went and the ones who didn't: the men who were asked to fight the war and what they did about that decision—and how that long-ago youthful move shaped their lives; the women who were exposed to combat as nurses in Vietnam and those who saw combat on the streets and campuses of America.

Many of the disparate voices of that generation come together here. In essence, they were the foot soldiers in both armies. Those in Vietnam were far removed from the manipulations of the policymakers who put them there. Those on the streets or striking on campuses were equally removed from the manipulation of the most flamboyant and incendiary of their leaders who— thrust into prominence by the media and caught up in factions and ego power trips—muddied the public's perception of the movement's many faces. And there are also voices from that vast army who made few moral commitments on either side and were simply swept up by the times.

Perhaps the Vietnam veteran would have stayed forever a stranger to me had I not watched *Friendly Fire* on television in 1979. Like many, I had subconsciously avoided revisiting that war during the seventies. I had read none of the many excellent books—*Dispatches, A Rumor of War, Friendly Fire, To What End, Fields of Fire, Winners and Losers, Fire in the Lake, Going After Cacciato. . . .* I had studied none of the moving psychological studies, such as *Home from the War* or *Strangers at Home*.

Then I watched Carol Burnett, with the burned-out stare of a stricken mother, playing Peg Mullen, the Iowa farm woman who lost her son to "friendly fire" in Vietnam. What stayed with me was the scene with her son in the airport, saying goodbye, hovering, buying the magazines, trying to say something cheerful for the last time. I cried, transferring my thoughts to my own nineteen-year-old son and all those other sons who are eighteen and nineteen. President Reagan now sends a new generation of soldiers into for- eign lands, some of them to their deaths. I see those faces—the new, young generation, all peach fuzz and teenage acne—and now I finally know what those mothers of the sixties felt.

At the end of *Friendly Fire,* a ticker tape sentence marched across the bottom of the TV screen: HONOR VIETNAM VETERANS' WEEK. I started up from the sofa in cold anger. Some mythical "they" were at work.

They're at it again. They're eulogizing, glorifying another war, I thought. I had nothing but contempt for such hollow holidays. As satirist Mark Russell says, "Every Memorial Day we honor our war dead by going to the beach and staying drunk for three days." I felt as if some superpatriots were trying to gloss over the pain and agony, trying to make Vietnam an "acceptable noble cause" for a new generation. Another Memorial Day on which to mythologize about the glories of dying in war. I was not thinking of the veteran.

But then curiosity took over. Vietnam. I wanted to *know.* I had not truly thought of it in years. And so I suggested a series on veterans for the Washington *Post.* I met Lonnie Sparks, whose only dream of glory was to work in the Chevrolet plant in Muncie, Indiana. Both legs are gone. He plays in wheelchair basketball tournaments, shoots pool, can't work. He uses his arms to get in and out of the wheelchair, slides his body along the grass as he plays with his two daughters, born since his return. I met Eddie, who lost a leg, and Steve Zardis, who thinks he is dying of the insidious aftereffects of Agent Orange. I met Tom Vallely, who in 1971 threw his medals at the Capitol— along with thousands of other Vietnam Veterans Against the War—and who is now a Massachusetts state politician. None of these veterans was whining; they told me things I had never realized about their lives after their return. That was in 1979. I did not get a chance for full-time research on my book until 1981.

By that time I was stunned at how the public's awareness of Vietnam veterans had changed dramatically in less than two years—from 1979 to 1981. Still, there was resistance to the veteran, as well as to reliving the war.

This book seeks neither to prove the rightness or wrongness of the war nor to refight old ideological battles but to illuminate the effect of the war *as it was* on the generation asked to fight it. In so doing, however, ideology and attitudes toward government policy come into play constantly. Sometimes their arguments are simplistic, sometimes profound. Whatever the view, it is the truth as they perceive it about a cataclysmic time in their adolescence that, in large part, shaped the men and women they are today.

To this day, many veterans feel an indescribable rage that they, for so long, seemed to be the only Americans who remembered the war's suffering and pain.

I was unprepared for the defensive recoiling of many other Americans— who do not yet want to hear what this generation has to say. "Why on earth would you want to write a book about *that?*" was not an uncommon question when I first began my research four years ago. "I don't want to read a book about a bunch of whiny vets," was the comment of a World War II combat officer. The mention of delayed stress invariably led to indignant moralizing about the horror in *all* wars. Have you read about the Civil War carnage, the cauterizing of stumps with irons while the patient was not anesthetized? The Battle of the Somme? The Bataan Death March? The only group free from such comparative judgment seemed to be the Vietnam veterans. As one said, "The only war you know is the one you were in." And that is what they speak to.

Vietnam was the most divisive time of battle in our country since the Civil War. It was the third most pivotal experience in this century—following the Depression and World War II. Its consequences are still being felt in our foreign policy, our troubled economy, in a haunted generation, in the new generation faced with possible new Vietnams, and in our hearts and minds. And yet because we lost many refuse to face its monumental importance.

There are several binding themes; I have risked repetition to allow for many to express their variations on them because these generalizations are central to how people view their *specific* lives and actions in the aftermath of Vietnam. Each time, the elaboration explains something about the person speaking.

Among these themes is the pervasive frustration of combat veterans who felt they lost friends and were wounded in a war they either could not or were not allowed to win. Some grasp the domestic and geopolitical reasons *why* this terrible war was conducted as it was; others do not. Some respond from deep emotional wounds, with no ordered arguments, but I have let them talk because, in the end, their perception is what matters.

Another theme, encountered in every veteran I have ever met, is searing anger at their homecoming—of being shunned, of having to expunge the most indelible year from their lives, of having to become "closet" vets. And for many there is the depression that comes from the feeling that it was all a waste.

Among the men who didn't go, the range is wide—from guilt or sheepishness over how the veteran was treated or guilt for the less-than-honorable way in which many ducked the draft to an earnest defense of their actions, sometimes with sixties' rhetoric intact.

We hear from exiles who fled the country, men who chose jail, those who bought or faked their way out, and those who were simply passed over.

All of their decisions shaped their lives in ways that some as yet do not comprehend. They—and their families, friends, intimates—speak from deep wells of pain and private memories, from conviction and confusion, from joyous as well as scarring experiences. In all, over 500 people were interviewed, including historians, sociologists, psychiatrists, as well as members of the Vietnam Generation.

Today generational divisions are not even along so simple a line as those who went and those who didn't. A Vietnam veteran who returned vehemently antiwar has more in common, for example, with a former dedicated resister than he does with a veteran who champions the "rightness" of the war.

The echoes of Vietnam can be heard in debates over supporting right-wing Central American regimes, troops in Lebanon, the invasion of Grenada. Once again those arguments are breaking down along the lines of right and left among veterans who strongly supported our presence in Vietnam and those who didn't.

Vietnam was a swirling, ever-changing place that in itself defies a simple common shared experience. Veterans who saw heavy combat and those who saw little do not speak the same language. Nor do those who went in 1964, when the country was moving through the long twilight of cold war containment, have much of a bond with the reluctant draftee who went to a hot and futile war in 1970. "Everyone wants to capsulize Vietnam," sighed one former helicopter pilot who works with veterans, "and they just can't."

Simply trying to get a handle on Vietnam statistics is a frustrating shuffle through a paper maze of conflicting numbers. Experts disagree on how many saw combat and how many were in transport units. They even disagree on how many actually were sent to Southeast Asia.

For several years government statistics about the number of Americans who served in Southeast Asia ranged from 2.8 million to 3.2 million. However, recent reports and analyses of persons on active duty have led to a larger figure. Of the approximately 9 million Vietnam-era veterans, 42 percent—or 3.78 million—served in the war zone during the eleven years of United States participation. The war zone is defined as Vietnam, Laos, Cambodia, and adjacent sea and air space.[1]

Systematic underreporting of who was serving in the Vietnam theater at the time of the war accounts for the discrepancies. In this book the larger numbers are used when referring to those who served in Vietnam.

Vietnam was a multiphased war that produced vastly different impressions as changed political atmosphere in America brought changed military strategy over there. A lingering, subtle, and insidious indifference is directed at the men who bore the brunt of this lost war. Among intellectuals and shapers of policy, there is residual condescension, although it is no longer fashionable, a minimizing of the thoughts and remembrances of young foot soldiers. After all, what did they know? They were only there. Never mind that they have a poetry and depth of their own, that their experiences can electrify far more than armchair participants who mouth their "if you wills" and "so to speaks" and dredge up all those polysyllabic cover words like "harassment" and "interdiction" for the killing that took place.

"Every soldier exaggerates and lies—including me," chuckled a World War II combat hero friend of mine by way of warning. And one colonel warned incoming troops that it would take them years to sort out all that they would see and feel. And even then maybe they would not understand. Still, no matter how small their deadly terrain, no matter how narrow their focus, their stories build, in many instances, to remarkable insights about that war, how it was fought, and what happened to those who returned.

These portraits are veritable cascades—subjective remembrances and opinions. A comment of Virginia Woolf applies.

"When a subject is highly controversial . . . one cannot hope to tell the truth. One can only show how one came to hold whatever opinion one does hold. One can only give one's audience the chance of drawing their own conclusions as they observe the limitations, the prejudices, the idiosyncracies of the speaker. . . ."[2]

"In their remembrances are their truths," wrote Studs Terkel of the men and women chronicled in his book on the Depression, *Hard Times.* "This is not a lawyer's brief nor an annotated sociological treatise. It is simply an attempt to get the story of the holocaust known as the Great Depression from an improvised battalion of survivors."[3]

And so speak these voices of the sixties generation—my "improvised battalion of survivors." It is my hope that those on both sides will listen to one another and, in so listening, will begin to understand their differences.

And those differences are complex and volatile. For every nongoer who sometimes thinks badly of the less-than-noble way he avoided the war, there is a soldier who blames himself for having gone. For every resister who takes pride in not having gone, there is a soldier who takes pride in his service. And many times the emotions are ambiguous and mixed. The same veterans who can look back a decade, and now take pride in their service, can also feel the war was wrong. Other veterans cannot even fathom why people their age protested. And some protesters cannot fathom why someone would have chosen to go.

Expressing their diverse feelings is important. I am continually amazed at those on both sides—the ones who went and those who didn't—who told me they were speaking of their experiences for the first time. Maybe in their coming together, some of the past can be laid to rest.

Above all, this is a generation in transition. Their sense of history will change ten, twenty years from now. But there is enough distance, now, for a beginning.

Enough distance so that we can begin to erase our collective amnesia over the Vietnam War.

Enough distance so that we can begin to heal the wounds of our nation's most troubled decade of war.

1 Two Soldiers

THE PATROL PICKED ITS WAY THROUGH JUNGLE SO THICK THAT BY noon it was dark. A dead, midnight kind of darkness. Fifty men threaded their way. The first ten began to cross a river. The soldier walking point touched something with his boot. It was not a twig, not a root, not a rock. It was a trip wire to oblivion. In an instant the wire triggered a huge, fifty-pound Chinese mine. There was an enormous roar, like the afterburner of a jet, as it exploded, instantly ripping the point man apart. Shrapnel flew for yards.

Tom, six feet tall and slim, at nineteen already developing a characteristic slouch, froze, hunched his shoulders, and, in a flash, caught the scene forever in his mind: the face of one buddy disintegrating from the explosion; others walking their last steps and falling, bones sticking white out of flesh sheared off at the hips. Some bled to death, coating the ground and mud and leaves with their last moments of blood, before the medevac choppers could come. Some were caught in the river. Tom always remembers the river, running red "like Campbell's tomato soup." Those that weren't hit screamed in panic. Those that were screamed in pain.

Tom's first thought, as always, was of Chuck. He whipped around and saw Chuck lying immobile, staring, with the most startled look Tom had ever seen on his face.

Tom wasn't sure what was causing it—Chuck's breathing or his heartbeat —but *something* was causing it. Every few seconds, a fountain of blood gushed from a wound in Chuck's chest. Tom knelt and, with trembling fingers, grabbed a compression bandage, a thick cotton square with the bandage tied to it like a scarf. He wrapped one, two, three around Chuck's chest, pulling tight. The pressure held back the gush, even though blood seeped out around the borders—a brilliant red Pop Art pattern—but the bandages held.

Only then did Tom feel something sticky on his left arm. He felt down around his elbow. His hand came back bloody. A chunk of shrapnel was lodged there. Someone quickly bandaged his arm.

There was no time for anything but frantic, adrenaline-charged action. The jungle growth was so thick that they had to hack fiercely at the bamboo, its sharp ridges ripping their skin, before the medevac helicopters could come in. The choppers took the seriously wounded—the ones with no legs, the ones with gaping chests. And the dead. More than fifteen of the men were dead or seriously wounded.

The rest would simply have to walk out of there.

Only later would Tom and Chuck have time to think that magic was with them once again. They almost always walked point—one checking for snipers and grenades and booby traps, the other following right behind with compass and map.

They had been walking point all morning. Just five minutes before the explosion, the captain had decided to rotate his troops. Had they been walking point, they would have been dead.

For those left in the jungle, the terror of the next hours would rival the horror of the mine going off. They were in the kind of war America's youth fought without end in Vietnam—an unceasing guerrilla war with an enemy seldom seen. A kind of war perfected by the VC . . . a kind of war that to this day brings shaking nightmares to many veterans . . .

"We had to move off the trail and chop our way out—*every step of the way,*" remembers Tom. "The reason we got blown up, to begin with, is that we walked on the trail."

The jungle was steaming—as if the sky was not the sky at all but a giant bell jar encasing some monstrous greenhouse. The men gulped for air, but suffocated in the humidity. Sweat and blood stuck fatigues to backs, arms, legs. No one knew if the mine was a prelude to an ambush. There was always the certain knowledge that the Vietnamese knew that jungle like the back of their hands, that they could walk it blindfolded at night.

Something as ominous as a lurking enemy *was* at hand: hundreds of grenades, lightly attached by thin, invisible wires, festooned the jungle growth like deadly hidden ornaments on a tree. The least snag of a foot would trip a wire, pull the pin, and the spoon would fly off. Just brushing against a tree could set the grenades off. After what they had seen, there was enormous fear. With each step, they waited for the sound of an explosion, a scream of pain. It took four hours to go 500 yards. "Every twenty feet you would run into another booby trap," recalls Chuck. "The options were either to go around a grenade, once you spotted it, or try to disarm it, stick the pin back in if you could. There were some guys that shouldn't have messed with them and did. They got their arms blown off."

Tom's voice shakes. "We just prayed we'd get the hell out of there." Some men would get very, very quiet. Some would cry. Everyone could feel the gut panic. "All you could do was hold to the back strap of the one in front when it gets that dark. You couldn't keep spirits up, couldn't talk loud for fear the VC were around."

Tom's eyes grow distant. "It was one of the most terrible times."

Chuck is thirty-seven now, Tom thirty-five. In 1980 they came together for a singularly compelling reunion. There were disagreements and raised voices as they sifted through the endless maze that was Vietnam, but through it all there was a palpable, protective, and unshakable love. For Chuck and Tom have known each other a long time.

Tom's earliest memory of Chuck: the two of them sitting on a dusty curb in their jockey shorts in a small Nebraska town. Two little boys talking with some friends as early morning summer sun washes the Nebraska sandhills. A woman comes out and tells them, "For land's sake! Go in and put some clothes on." Tom, age three, toddles in after Chuck, age five.

Tom and Chuck are brothers.

Chuck leans back in his leather chair near the spitting and hissing fire on a cold Washington evening in the early eighties. His artful wood- and brick-renovated Capitol Hill townhouse is one of ordered comfort: books as straight as sentinels on their shelves, firewood in neat stacks, a gleaming wax floor, a single rose in a bud vase. Teddy Roosevelt, Chuck's favorite President, stares pugnaciously from an old-fashioned oval frame on one uncluttered wall. President Reagan and Vice-President Bush adorn a painted plate on the mantel.

Chuck pops beers to ease the stories along. Sentences begin with "I don't know if I ever told you this, Tom . . ." and "Chuck, remember that Navajo Indian? 'Chief' we called him . . ."

Thomas L. and Charles E. Hagel, sons of Nebraska, volunteered to go to Vietnam and requested to serve with each other. The closest they ever hoped for was to be in the same division of about 35,000 men. For reasons still unclear to them, they were placed together in the same twelve-man squad. For ten months they ate and drank and slept and watched friends die together. They saved each other twice and sent five Purple Hearts and two valorous unit citations home to their mother.

Chuck and Tom were eagerly sought after for Officer Candidate School because of their basic intelligence and Army test scores. The thought intrigued them—until they found out that the extra time in training would not count against their time in the service. In Vietnam, as casualties grew daily, they both made sergeant anyway. "Attrition," says Tom caustically.

Chuck was in country sixty-five days before Tom, stationed with the 2nd Battalion, 47th Infantry Regiment, 9th Division, at a base called Bearcat. When Tom arrived, the weekend of the pivotal 1968 Tet Offensive, he was sent farther north.

Chuck's letters home were filled with concern about where Tom was sent.

"Dear Chuckles," Tom scrawled eventually. "Well, by now I suppose you're wondering what in the hell happened to me. I am in what amounts to a recon squad and securing force. When we move to the DMZ, I'll really be busy. I'd just as soon be with the 2/47 [Chuck's outfit: 2nd Battalion, 47th Infantry] as here. The CO is really a prick. Well, take it easy and I don't know when I'll be seeing you next . . ."

A month later Tom wrote home to a younger brother, Mike, that his request for reassignment to Chuck's unit had been accepted. "Sweet Mother should feel a little better . . ."

In the back of his mind, Tom always thought that if he went to Vietnam, the Army would send Chuck home. It was a promise, he claims, that the Army made to him. "Chuck was the hope of our family," says Tom, looking at his brother. "Also, I knew Chuck. He's gung ho stuff, the type of guy who would screw around—Mr. All-American Kid—and get himself killed."

Chuck smiles softly at his younger brother. "You should have *known* I would never have gone home no matter what they said." Tom agrees. "I realize now neither one of us would do it. The one who got out would end up with an ungodly feeling of guilt if something happened to the other."

The thought of something ungodly happening was beyond their understanding. Nothing is as invincible as youth. That is how, from time immemorial, countries have gotten youths to do the fighting. "We were the 'Fighting Hagel Brothers.' No harm could come to us."

In one month with the 5th Cavalry, in some of the bloodiest days of Vietnam, Tom had already seen heavy fighting. "There were hard-core NVA up there. Everybody was just getting blown away constantly."

Chuck looks over at Tom, a silent message passing between them. "I went to the general and asked if I could get Tom down with me and Tom did the same thing up there. So we're both doing our thing at the north and south ends of Vietnam. In the meantime—I don't know if I ever told you this, Tom—but I got orders to be sent to the 25th Division!"

Now, thirteen years later, Tom is hearing for the first time of their near-miss.

"I've never understood this," says Chuck. "I was on the truck leaving Bearcat, not knowing how in the hell I was going to tell Tom where I was—and you can imagine the sinking feeling in my stomach. All I knew was that they said, 'Pack your bag. Grab your rifle. Get your ass on that fucking truck.' The truck got out to the gate and was stopped by an MP. The MP walks around with a list on his clipboard and he says, 'Is there a Private Charles Hagel on the truck?' I said, 'Yeah.' The first thing I thought was that something had happened to Tom. 'Get down here, Private Hagel. The captain wants to see you. Bring your bags.' The truck leaves. What in the *hell's* going on? I think. So I go in and report to the captain. He says, 'You're staying here.' I've never to this day known how that happened. And the next week Tom shows up."

Vietnam—America's most unpopular, most divisive, and longest war—created its own San Andreas Fault in the hearts and minds of Americans. The cracks and fissures continue to spread and divide. *The only war America has ever lost.* That phrase has been a drumbeat to rev up the bellicose and a cautionary counsel to those who felt we should have never moved into that unknown land. Vietnam is still debated in bars and boardrooms, in homes on

Main Street, in Georgetown drawing rooms, and in the Pentagon's war colleges. Passion and acrimony lie not too far beneath the surface; with a lost war, speculation over "what went wrong" never dies. Revisionists worry away at the facts and conjectures of the past as a cat worries a half-dead mouse. Divisions are so deep that some are still unclear. A class war that deeply divided a generation also divided the veterans.

Yes, it was the first war we lost and no nation can easily absorb such a defeat whole. Bill Mahedy, a former chaplain who has worked with troubled veterans, calls Vietnam an "undigested lump of life. It simply won't go down." It was like a great family neurosis and, as happens in such situations, someone has to be blamed. The cruel irony is that we chose to make the soldiers who fought that war the scapegoats.

And they, too, came home torn and confused and divided over what they felt. Ideological and intellectual mind skirmishes of historians, scholars, and critics of Vietnam do not begin to touch the depth of searching for right answers these young men went through. How they viewed that war, its aftermath, what they were doing there, why we didn't win: these are deeply significant barometers as to how they have coped, both with their experiences and the reactions of an America that didn't want to be reminded. An America that didn't want to look closely at what happened in Southeast Asia or in our raging streets and campuses in the sixties.

There is no way to capsulize Vietnam. There were as many Vietnams as there are veterans. A war of many confused policies that spanned several administrations has no monolithic character. And so, the Hagel brothers take on a certain fascinating significance. After all, they were *there* together, at the same time and in the same place during the bloodiest year of all. They breathed Vietnam together. And how do they see it? Chuck thought it a noble cause. Tom thought it a rotten waste. Chuck returned a conservative Republican, comfortable with a top Veterans Administration job in Reagan's administration until he quit in dissent over VA Administrator Robert Nimmo, who later resigned under pressure. Tom calls himself a socialist, teaches law at a university, and is deeply cynical about politicians. Chuck believes you have to put the emotional troubles of Vietnam behind you. Tom does too, but finds it a great deal harder to do so. Chuck believes we were saving peasants from communism and has no guilt. Tom believes we slaughtered and maimed for nothing and the guilts are many. Vietnam, of course, did not shape them entirely; there were other forces, other family dynamics. But Vietnam solidified their beliefs. They were brought closer together by Vietnam—and yet remain ever-distanced by it.

Chuck, the adored, eldest son of a World War II patriot, went over a believer. He remains one to this day. For seven months he was deputy director at the VA—the very target of disillusioned and angry Vietnam veterans. "Though I have great difficulty with how the war was conducted and, even, whether we should have been there, I still truly believe this to this day: we were trying to do what was best for the people of South Vietnam." Tom also went a believer. Six months after he was in Vietnam, his disillusionment became—and remains—rock-bottom deep. The second of four sons, he was inherently more ripe for dissent than Chuck. He felt deeply rejected by his father—who was consumed by his devotion to firstborn Chuck. His older brother was the star football player Tom watched from the sidelines. Tom remembers the fights with his father, the vain attempts to get him to notice him.

Theirs was a hard-scrabble childhood. Their father worked as a trouble-shooter for lumber companies—helping to salvage flagging businesses, then moving on. Chuck and Tom were children of the Nebraska sandhills, rolling grassland too arid for farming which was used for ranching. For years they knew only the life of small towns, a thousand people or less. Ainsworth, Rushville . . . They rode horses in the wilderness. They would fall asleep listening to the bawling of cattle in the pens by the railroad tracks a block away; the windows would rattle when trains went by. There was no central heating and when winter came, with its freezing and whipping winds, every-one would huddle by the kitchen coal stove.

The second floor was large, dormerlike, and the family raised chickens next to the boys' bedrooms. Tom remembers the warm hatchery lights, the round fuzzy yellow balls cheeping as dawn came.

Tom smiles a satisfied smile of memories. "The sandhills had a very bleak beauty. Some of my strongest memories are of its bigness and freedom." In minutes he could walk out of town, down trails freed of houses and cars, walking for miles, searching for water snakes and turtles. His childhood gave him something that Eastern city youths never had and he can't help a touch of smugness. "You can always get the education, absorb the sophistication—but *they* can never go back and get what we've got. It gave me a good balance for the realities of life."

The Hagels were like many of the men who went to Vietnam from Middle America. While they were not among those who automatically assumed they would go to college, they also grew up in a land of superpatriots. Dodging the draft was unthinkable. Tom speaks of the dodge used by many upper-class youths—getting a psychiatrist to write an exempting letter. *"That* kind of maneuver illustrates the class difference. In my environment that would have never crossed anyone's mind. In my town we didn't even *have* a psychiatrist."

Their father took enormous pride in his own military service. From their earliest days the boys remember the meetings in their home of the backslap-ping VFW and American Legionnaires and their old men's service caps, with patches and medallions commemorating past units and campaigns, hanging on the hallway rack.

Both sons see in their father a bitter version of the idealistic believer in the American Dream, for whom the dream was but a mirage. "Dad was naïve enough to believe in the 'American ethic'—if you worked hard and kept your nose clean, that *alone* got you ahead," says Tom, a caustic edge to his voice. "He was ill-treated by the man he worked for and refused to see it."

There remains some of the wistfulness of a left-out second child. "Fat Chuck was a 'carbon copy' of my father. Dad was amazingly handsome, charming. He looked to Chuck to become everything he was not. It was a burden, but Chuck *never* rebelled. In my opinion, once you get *used* to seeking and getting everyone's approval, it's like a drug. You want to keep it. He was the classic All-American Perfect Son."

The brothers look as different as they are. Chuck is fair, blue-eyed, with wavy hair billowing into blow-dried perfection. Although a half inch shorter than Tom, he is bigger, barrel-chested. Neat, ordered, controlled Chuck Hagel: the small monogram crisp on the shirt, the house immaculate, the smile charming yet slightly studied. Tom is dark, with straight hair and a slightly drooping mustache. He slouches comfortably in corduroys and turtleneck and tweed jacket. He talks with emotion and candor as his brother, protective of his own political turf, shoots wary looks. Tom's smile, which is less frequent, reveals dimples and some of the carefree spirit he knew in the long ago before Vietnam.

Tom, the clown, seeking the attention he didn't get from his father, saw more school corridors than classrooms. He always had a keen intelligence; his brother freely says he is the smartest in the family. "I am probably one of the few people in America who ever read the encyclopedia from A to Z," says Tom with a laugh. "Every time I got kicked out [of class], I would go to the library and read the encyclopedia on my own."

Mimicking the nuns—doing a ten-minute routine on the ones that fell asleep—was Tom's major gift. He questioned much in religious class. "The nuns said that other religious books contrary to Catholic philosophy were wrong and we had a *responsibility* to destroy those arguments. That struck me as crazy. We were told that those who weren't Catholic would go to someplace like 'limbo.' It sounded like more fun than heaven."

It was firmly suggested he leave parochial school. Public school—and his self-taught encyclopedic course—came next. Tom sought approval, not at school but at work. A strong work ethic was instilled early; before they were ten, the boys packed ice in an ice house for two cents a bag, filled potato sacks in potato cellars.

His last year and a half in high school, Tom worked from four to midnight in a factory. "It seemed more real. None of this chickenshit stuff we were doing in high school."

But Tom was popular, had his own friends apart from Chuck's, discovered girls and lost his virginity when he was not quite thirteen. He laughs. "There wasn't a helluva lot to *do* in those Nebraska hills!"

Chuck had dutifully gone on to college but had also found his fun in fraternity life. After two years of nomadic wanderings to three colleges, the Army seemed a good bet. Tom joined his brother in the service the day he graduated—barely—from high school.

The Hagel brothers look amazingly untouched by the war, although shrapnel still floats in Chuck's chest and Tom's back is dotted with little scars and darker, pitted spots.

Years later, little metal reminders of Vietnam have their way of working their way out of the system. One night recently, Tom woke to find one side of his neck, near his ear, severely swollen. Doctors found a chunk of metal—war's remains—covered with calcium.

They had several close calls, had seen enough horror to last a lifetime, and returned with a special reverence for life and rage to make up those lost months. Chuck tends to minimize any adjustment problems. He has quite erased them all. He found no hostility. "People in our town welcomed you with open arms." Then, on reflection, Chuck says, "The more I think back on it—the more I question how minimal my readjustment was." After the first six months, Chuck simply disappeared. He rented a little house in the wilderness and "just holed up there. I barely saw anybody for a year, except in my classes. I maybe had two, three dates in the whole year. It was the strangest thing, so out of character for someone like me. Then I woke up one morning and said, 'Okay, enough of this. It's time to get back into society.' It was my way to do it. I have tremendous sympathy and understanding for the veterans who seek help in the Vet Centers today. I just happened to be more disciplined."

Tom, on the other hand, flew into emotional, crying rages. He slid into deep depressions, heavy drinking, and debilitating guilts "about all those people we slaughtered." The drinking was, in part, to stop the nightmares, but they came anyway. Some were recurring—in color. Even the smells, the burning fires, and the burning flesh returned in those dreams. And always, the eyes.

The collectible prizes of that war were the dead, stacked like torn dolls for the body count—that Strangelovian measurement for "victory" in a war of "attrition" and "containment" that had no fixed goals for winning. Television footage in those days showed American soldiers heaving bodies into piles as officers marched by for review. What is striking, viewing those film clips today, is the very *ordinariness* of it all. Officers strut proudly, smile even, at a day's work well done. If you look closely, though, the young soldiers seem robotlike as they stack the pile.

"Everybody dies with their eyes open," says Tom quietly. "The eyes get bloodshot and dark circles form real fast." He repeats, almost in wonder, "It just takes a little time for the circles to come." Tom could never get over the feeling that all those staring, dead people were looking directly at him. "It was almost accusatory. That bothered me a lot then."

In Tom's dream—which still comes at times—he is standing in an open field, a little after sunrise. Everything is green. Nobody is holding him, yet he can't move. "All these people, with their Vietnamese eyes, walk past, just staring at me. They're walking past, dead."

Tom, talking in his sleep, tossing and turning, has awakened the women with whom he has slept. They repeat the next morning what he has said.

It is apologetic, repeated over and over, and he is talking to those rows and rows of walking dead people: "I'm sorry. I didn't mean to. I'm sorry."

Tom gives a little shake of his head, as if trying to rid himself of his memories. "To this day, one of the reasons people don't have guilt feelings is that we were taught—and taught *well*—*not* to think of them as human beings. They were slopes—gooks—not people."

For Chuck there are no guilts. The important thing is to forget it all and get on with his life; not to wallow in Vietnam is his repeated message. Tom says, "I've seen him break down. I *know* we share some nightmares. He has just suppressed them so deeply. But he's going to have to walk through the valley sometime."

Chuck denies any denials. Tom smiles, doubting still. "Denial is a wonderful psychological tool."

After Tom was wounded the second time, he was reassigned to a noncombat role as an information specialist. On one mission he was to take pictures of an assault. "Armed with a camera and a cheap little .45 with about seven rounds in it," he laughingly recalls.

It was the Fourth of July, 1968. He went in with an assault against hardcore NVA in a village. "They 'softened up' the area," he says, bitingly using the term for air attacks. Then the ground troops went in. "Shooting started immediately. One thing you never do is walk around a bunker of theirs without dropping a grenade in. You don't know if anyone's in there. Well, the squad I was with didn't do it and, once our back was to them, they just opened up. A rocket grenade went off. It burned my leg." There was shooting and pain and madness. When Tom looked around, he saw that "the entire platoon had thrown down their rifles and run. Someone regrouped and brought them up. Their platoon sergeant was killed. The next in rank happened to be me."

Tom took a carbine off a dead North Vietnamese soldier and they made the assault. "Jeez, we had a *total* incompetent of a first lieutenant. Blond, crew cut, couple of years of college, All-American Boy type. Couldn't read a map! The incompetence of that stupid son of a bitch. We're collecting all the NVA bodies and this woman walks out of a hooch. He just shot her dead. She just walked out and looked at us! She didn't have anything in her hands. No guns or *anything*. He was from here to there and could see her," says Tom, gesturing twelve feet to the end of the sofa. "Some women we've killed *had* web gear and ammo pouches, but she didn't have any. And he just killed her."

No one said or did anything; they were busily collecting the kill. The fighting was over and an observation helicopter was coming in. Then a sniper with an AK-47 shot down the helicopter. It dropped like a rock into the middle of a river. The men in the helicopter floated to the top. "This goddamn sniper starts killing them in the river as they're swimming. Like ducks in a barrel. You're watching this and you can't believe it's happening. So I took the rusty M-1 I got off a dead NVA. That's what I killed the fucker—excuse me—with. He was in a little mound inside this real heavy stuff, nipple [Nipa] palm that grows around the rivers. I snuck up and this guy was just cranking away. He had a thirty-round magazine. I couldn't believe it. It scared the shit out of me. The guy turns around and I shoot him. It was just so immediate."

In the next few minutes, the insanity of the war came together for Tom Hagel. "It was the only atrocity I ever witnessed and, since it was on dead bodies, I don't know if you can call it that. But it wasn't your grunts," he says, clenching his teeth, "it was *officers.* Three helicopters let down and all these sucky-faced colonels with all their shiny shoes and shit got off.

"The officers went to the bodies and started taking off watches for souvenirs. These were ranking officers! Majors, colonels. I just couldn't believe it. I thought, What in the *fuck* are these guys doing?

"Then one of the majors ordered an ARVN with him to *cut off the fingers* on a couple of these bodies so they could take their rings; after someone dies, they start swelling, especially in that heat. We were all hurt, exhausted, and they were joking, shooting the shit, and cutting off fingers to take rings."

The assault was written up in a national news magazine. It was mentioned in the worn hometown paper that tells of Tom Hagel receiving his Bronze Star. There was, of course, no mention of the trophy taking.

That attack earned Tom his third Purple Heart.

A few days later, Tom wrote his brother, Mike, eleven months younger. It was no hymn to the glories of battle. The urgency comes through, still, reading a letter written in 1968:

"Dear Mike: I hope you will forgive me for dismissing with the niceties, but what I have to say is important. We received your letter today, informing us of your military status. Your letter was not too clear, so we do not know what your exact status is. First of all, I want to say that I respect your decision—whatever it is. It is just that joining the Army at the time of the Vietnam crisis is rather foolish. *This war is completely immoral. We are losing more every day.* Chuck will probably pat you on the back and have nothing for you but praise. He is still living under the illusion that the United States is 'all-good' and 'all-righteous.' This of course is false. If you have signed your papers, good luck and God help you."

Chuck recalls today, "I just stayed out of it. If Mike had asked me, I would have said it was his decision. Mike was so distressed that he 'wasn't doing his part' that he went down and volunteered to go. My mother damn near died. He went to Omaha for the physical. They wouldn't take him; he had a bad knee. He's very conservative. I always felt that he feels funny he did not go."

On the bottom of that faded letter there is a large P.S. It is scrawled the length of one page, from brother Tom to Mike.

"P.S. You don't have to go into the Army to have my respect.

"To the day I die, I will be ashamed that I fought in this war."

Chuck thinks three things helped him adjust better than Tom. "I was a little older. At nineteen and twenty-one, that age difference is very important. Plus I had some college and could rationalize all this a little better. And finally, like I said, it was easier just because of what I believed. 'If America was involved, then it's right.' I'm a believer—always have been—in the idea that whatever cards you're dealt are the ones you've got to play with. And there's no point in whining. I went about trying to get my life in order and not reaching back into what happened. I don't have these same problems that Tom has about guilt and these emotional feelings."

In fact, the stories have been so long buried that there are, astonishingly, mutual moments that the Hagel brothers had not ever shared over the years. Tom is hearing, for the first time, in his brother's home, exactly how Chuck saved him fourteen years before.

It was late in the afternoon and they were in the last of several APCs (Armored Personnel Carriers), lumbering steel-plated behemoths called "tracks." They were on their way back to an old Michelin rubber plantation after an unsuccessful search of a village. The enemy watched and, when it looked as if they could get the last track, they opened up. A command-detonated mine went off underneath Chuck and Tom's track with a horrendous blast. Chuck was soon in flames, his left side burning, his face a mass of bubbles. Both eardrums were broken by the blast. Tom was concussed and unconscious.

"I thought he was dead," recalls Chuck. "I started throwing everybody off the track. With all the ammunition we had, it would just blow. I grabbed Tom and he was just dead weight."

"Is that how I got out of there?" Tom interrupts.

Chuck tugged and threw Tom off, then landed on top of him, just before the VC opened up on them with machine guns. They were shielded in part by the huge burning track. GIs in the tracks up front heard the explosion and returned fast enough. "If they hadn't, it would have been all over. They would have either killed us or taken us prisoner."

It seemed like hours to Chuck before they got back to the rubber plantation. His scorched face was bubbled and blistered; the pain was nearly unbearable. When Tom woke up in the plantation, he groped around and immediately hollered to the medic for Chuck. "He's right here," said the medic, "in the bunk next to you."

Letters home during wars take on a reality all their own. The Hagels were not the first to write letters to mother softened with a protective veil. Mrs. Hagel could have been reading her sons' version of *The Hardy Boys Go to Vietnam:* "Dear Mom," writes Tom, "Don't have a heart attack. Yes, it's me again. Two letters in a row." The first paragraph is all aglow about the awards they received that morning for performance in combat. "There will be a National Defense [Award] coming along—but they only had one, so the other we'll get one of these days."

Then, in a quick throwaway, he adds:

"Well, I guess that it is time to tell you that we'll be sending two more Purple Hearts home. Now, take it easy. Here's the story.

"We were called up to surround this village. Well, everything was all right until we ran over a mine. When it went off, Chuck was burned on his left arm and left side of his face, which is *completely* healed and *no scars.* I got burned on both arms by the powder and the explosion blew me off the track, thus giving me a concussion, which is *completely* healed. So no sweat when you get the next set of Purple Hearts."

Chuck vied admirably for the casualness award when he described the *first* set of Purple Hearts, received after the booby trap exploded during that panicky search and destroy mission through the jungle. After four pages of talk about their new colonel's "asinine policies," great praise for brother Tom, thanks for a care package that contained meat spread and Valentine suckers, Chuck wrote: "It's time now for another episode in 'Surprise Surprise.' I hope you haven't received anything from the Army as yet. But (oh yes, light a Camel, get a cup of hot coffee, and then sit down) your two sons have earned a distinguished medal, the Purple Heart. Now, now, please stay calm! It's more of a joke than anything. Let me explain . . . yesterday, as we were conducting a search and destroy mission through some of Charlie's favorite 'parks,' we ran into one of his ingenious homemade booby traps, constructed with *our* [U.S.] material. They were Claymore mines." Chuck reported fifteen wounded and did not mention the dead to his mother. "*ALL* Tom and I got was: 1. Tom got a pellet in his elbow (which was easily popped out). 2. And I got a pellet in my chest (which was no problem). But they couldn't get it out, so they left it in. It's between two ribs and will *never* cause any problem. So, you see, it was nothing!" Lots of italics and capital letters. "*Do Not* Worry! We're both in great shape! We could have got the same thing with a pin hole. *So No Problems!* No sweat!" The only reason he told her was because he didn't want her to hear it from the Department of the Army, Chuck wrote. Then he added a theme that threads throughout his letters. "We were two *very, very, very lucky* young men. The only way to explain it is that we're being watched over from *Above.* . . . We've had *too* many close calls. So it's out of our hands. The Good Lord, the Saints, Dad . . . everyone is working overtime for us. . . . Now, Dearest Mother and brothers, I hope everything is understood!"

Death was given the same quick treatment. "Now for some sad news," wrote Tom in another letter. "Do you remember us saying something about E—— from Columbus? Well, last night I was talking to him and messin' around until they had to go on patrol. Well, last night some VC snuck up on them and killed four and wounded four. Bad! E—— was killed! Well, take it easy. Your number-two son, Tom."

Today, years later, Tom remembers with finite detail the soldier from his hometown who was killed.

"I found his body. The whole top half of him was blown off by an attack. He was cut clear in half. I recognized him 'cause his face was untouched. Here he was, cut in two, and just a matter of hours before we were bullshitting around. Someone I knew in high school. He had a Hawkeye camera. I cleaned out his footlocker and sent it home. . . ."

For all their close calls, the brothers bear no obvious marks of that war. Neither needed skin grafts after their track blew up. Except in the summer, when the sun flames Chuck's face beet red, there is no disfiguration.

Still, as he remembers the incident, Chuck finally loses some of that preciously gained control. He downs his beer, jiggles one leg up and down, and talks almost as if in a dream. "That night the pain was so intense, I'll just never forget it. You don't know how bad you're burned, what you'll look like. I lay there and I thought, In my whole life, if there's anything I do, it's going to be to try and stop wars."

Chuck's way to stop wars is to embrace the "peace through strength" buildup Reagan advocates. "We must ensure a very strong defense posture, a strategic balance; that's the only way to ensure not having a war."

Tom, on the other hand, worries over the saber-rattling rhetoric of the Administration and feels the defense budget is out of sync with what should be spent on domestic social programs. "Either we will become *more* of a police state or we'll start putting human needs first. I came back from Vietnam very much dedicated to social change. I vowed that never will I do anything to direct my energies toward 'taking.' It was a sense of guilt. You have to pay back. I owe a lot to mankind."

When Chuck left Vietnam, Tom had two months to go. They avoided an emotional farewell. What they remember most is that Chuck's empty jeep blew up the night he left, one of those good omen jokes to laugh about when they are old and gray. Chuck gave Tom a hug, then walked out of Bearcat, not looking back. "I never had a moment's rest until Tom got out. He was an absolutely remarkable soldier, much better than I, almost too much for his own good. So brave. He never had any concern for his own safety. So I worried for him. I couldn't relax a second until he was safe."

Tom's last two months, spent out of combat, were blurred in a drunken haze.

"He was starting to worry about reentry. Here was this brilliant guy who barely got through high school coming back to a system and society he wasn't sure about," says Chuck.

The brothers have mellowed over the years. Disagreements over Vietnam used to end in shouts and near-blows. "We could *never* get away from it, sooner or later we'd be arguing it all over," recalls Chuck. One time Chuck chased Tom out of the house. "We'd walk right up to the line 'I'm *never* going to talk to *you* again.' But we were scared to death about what we would say to our mother."

Yes, they have mellowed, but today the arguments are just as endless—and futile—as they probably will always be. This is not just true at the Hagels; the war still rages in other living rooms and forums and in books and wherever Vietnam is relived and reargued.

Chuck shakes his head. "We should have held out, supported the South longer. We could have *maintained* South Vietnam."

"Then why did the people *hate* us so much? You could see it in their eyes, you could smell it."

The brothers go at it, warming up to a decade-old struggle to force each other to think otherwise.

"They have *no* choices now," protests Chuck.

Tom starts in, "And what were *we* doing? We weren't murdering any?"

Chuck starts to anger. "What do you mean *murder?*"

"Remember New Year's Eve, everybody getting drunk and shit—at Bien Phuc? Remember the corner bunkers had fifty-calibers? They just burned down the fucking village."

"So what is your point? What about the invaders? Nobody ever told me why the *North* was in the *South* to begin with. It just wasn't the North Vietnamese—it was the Soviet Union and China giving them all the hardware and all the . . ."

"We didn't give 'em a comparable part of the hardware?"

"It was *not* the people's choice!"

Tom jumps up. "If the North had invaded with *no* support from the South, they would have lost."

"That's not true."

"Oh, *shit!"* says Tom.

They argue about Northern troops coming down by the hundreds, about the VC hiding their food and ammunition, about villagers helping. Tom says they wanted to; Chuck says they feared reprisals.

"I'm not saying the North Vietnamese or the VC were humanitarians; they were sleazy sons of bitches. But you've got people in Operation Phoenix admitting selective assassinations," counters Tom.

Chuck agrees. "There was *some* of that. I don't know of any war in the history of mankind . . ."

"All I'm saying is we did the same thing. We were winning 'hearts and minds,' right?" Tom asks caustically. "What was the name of that alcoholic Southern son of a bitch sergeant we had? He was so drunk that night out there near the orphanage. *Remember the orphanage,* Chuck? We got hit real bad that night. That sergeant was so drunk and so pissed off that he crawled up on that track and *opened up on that orphanage with a fifty-caliber machine gun."*

Chuck starts to protest and Tom waves him off. "Chuck, *you were there!* Down at the bottom of the sandhill."

Chuck says incredulously, "Are you saying that he *slaughtered* children in an orphanage?"

"I don't *know* if he did"—Tom's voice is strangled—"because *none of us went in to check.* But I know that he opened up on that orphanage. Just rained on it."

Chuck protests, "In any war, you can take any isolated incident . . ."

They move back to abstracts. If only the harbors and supply routes in the North had been bombed earlier, argues Chuck. Tom says it would have made no difference. The Vietnamese had been invaded for thousands of years and were in it for the long run. . . .

And so it goes.

Tom finally says, "It all seemed so senseless. We'd kill and they'd kill and it didn't mean anything." His voice is ominously soft; he speaks of a knowledge he wished he had never known. "And both of us were *very, very good at killing.* The whole process we were good at. We were amazingly proficient at it all. In firefights we'd shoot hundreds and hundreds of rounds and after we'd walk a hundred yards and see hundreds and hundreds of bodies. Women and children. For the longest time, that was about the only thing that bothered me. We found women with lots of ammo on and then it didn't bother me as much. But there were all the others. And they *didn't* have guns—because we saw them after. Remember I mentioned 'softening up' an area?" The sardonic smile never touches the sadness in his eyes. "A Cobra gunship spitting out six hundred rounds a minute doesn't discern between chickens, kids, and VC. Sure, there were lots of atrocities on their side. They were capable of incredible cruelty to one another. That was always my argument. Let *them* deal with themselves.

"Of course, it's more 'antiseptic' when we kill. We didn't come in cutting arms off living people. We just decimated square miles from up in the sky. And napalm. If it doesn't burn you to death, it just cuts all the oxygen out of you. I don't see a qualitative difference."

Tom sighs. "We make such a bad practice of picking allies. They feed us all that bullshit and then we support tyrants in Guatemala, Chile, El Salvador. We are taught the evils of communism—and there's Nixon embracing China —which is an okay step forward but, meanwhile, guess where American boys were? Still being killed in Vietnam 'stopping communism.' "

Unlike some veterans, Tom feels no animosity toward those who didn't go. "Why should you blame them for seeing that it was nothing but a goddamn slaughter at the end of the road?" Still, he raged at the antics of the less committed. Outspokenly antiwar when he returned to become a college student at Omaha, Tom felt such anger after attending a peace rally that he wrote a letter to the editor: "Probably—or *hopefully*—10 percent were what might honestly be described as concerned. The rest, some dressed in their 'regulation' hippie uniform, were far too busy in the social-recreational activities. I was particularly impressed by the individuals who verbally attacked 'this filthy, capitalistic system'—and then got into their Corvettes and drove off to rage in their fraternity houses.''

Chuck doesn't think twice about those who didn't go, he says. However, his mouth clamps so tight that veins show on his neck when he thinks about those who went to Canada or got out through some ruse. "I'm not going to hunt them down. They've got to live with their decision. There was a *noble* way out—if they believed. For example, I have three very good friends who wouldn't go—and they were conscientious objectors. Two were over in Vietnam as *medics.*"

The pain in his brother's eyes is unconcealed. Tom thinks about his deep rage for the system—if not the individuals—that deferred the privileged. But Tom cannot discuss the abstract. He is remembering men he once called friends. "I don't give a shit about 'the best and brightest.' I give a shit about human beings.'' Tom looks away, swallowing hard. "I saw some *beautiful* human beings over there. They were never going to be the heads of some corporations—but they were *good goddamn* human beings. And they got *slaughtered.*"

Chuck and Tom share a cherished understanding for the fleeting ways of life. They embrace it with every moment's breath. This is a legacy many veterans share.

Many veterans found strength and maturity the nongoers do not possess, but most feel this was gained at a frightful price. "I lost a certain part of my life—my perception of what makes me *me,*" says Tom. "And I don't know if I'll ever get it back. Sometimes I can be so goddamn *cold* about things. I just can't feel anymore."

It is a complaint of the soul, far older than the warriors of Vietnam, transcribed and recorded through the ages by those who went to battle as boys and returned old.

"I don't believe in blaming your whole life on that war—but it had *nothing* to do with the survival of our country," says Tom. "When someone can give you a justification for something that bothers you, you feel all right again. Chuck bought the justification. He feels real comfortable—and I don't. I can live with myself now, but in earlier years I couldn't.

"The main thing I'd like to get across is that not everybody was hard-core and blind who was in Vietnam. There were people like me who felt we were on a conveyor belt and helpless to stop it.

"And we were deeply hurt."

Tom's voice becomes intense. "I have consciously stayed away from groups of veterans. I do not spend a lot of time talking to them. But the ones that I do stumble across are crying in their hearts. For them, for a long, long time, it will be there. There will be that crying in the night."

2 The Generation

THEY ARE IN THEIR THIRTIES NOW. MEN WHO CAME OF AGE IN THE sixties and left their homes, left their families, left their youth nearly as soon as they had acquired it. Left their youth—and their innocence—in the jungles of Vietnam. More than 3 million went. Nearly 58,000 never returned. Those who did were never quite the same. Above all, their experiences made them forever different from a vast other Army—those who stayed home.

In 1963 Vietnam was still one of those far-off spots on a map of Southeast Asia. Most Americans didn't even know where it was. But in the ten long years to come, their sons would go . . . and go . . . and go. . . .

They came from Middle America. They came out of the Appalachian hills. One was a tall, lean mountain boy named Bobby Joe. His county does not have one single stoplight. His home is North Carolina hill country, where men have first names like Edgel and Hoover, where tobacco fills the hollows, where rhododendron bushes grow as tall as oak trees and are called a more beautiful name—mountain laurel.

Bobby Joe looks down from his mountain home and points to a blanket of emerald green far below. "Grew up poor as Job's turkey in that holler over yonder." The first time Bobby Joe ever left the mountain was to go to Vietnam. The first time he ever got into a plane was to jump out of it—in parachute training school. His two brothers also went to Vietnam. For generations the South has given up its young to war. A grandfather went off to World War I, to someplace in France that Bobby Joe cannot pronounce.

Today Bobby Joe, a former Green Beret, refuses to talk of Vietnam. "H'it were just one of them things I reckon I'd like to forget." His mountain face, sun-lined from the tobacco fields, handsome, with a sharp, chiseled nose, loses its expansiveness, closes down hard.

"Next time they get me off'n this mountain, I'll have to be throwed off or go in a pine box."

They came out of urban streets, out of ghettos, North and South. They got their notices when they came home from the night shift at Ford or the day shift at Bethlehem Steel. They stopped their tractors in Iowa and came in for the noon meal and there would be those official telegrams filled with artificial friendliness: GREETINGS . . .

In Vietnam there were Cherokees from Oklahoma, Poles and Slavs from Pittsburgh steel mills. The soldiers were not from Berkeley, Harvard, Princeton, or Yale.

The jungles were filled with Fighting Irish from enclaves such as South Boston.

Irish Catholic patriotism—"We went to kill a Commie for Jesus Christ and John Wayne"—placed its special, sad stamp on Southie. Out of a population of 34,000, 25 sons died in Vietnam, 15 of them marines. The casualty numbers for Southie are simply "incredible" says James Webb, who commanded a platoon of marines filled with Southies and "rebels," as the Southerners were called, and came home to write about it in his acclaimed novel *Fields of Fire.* "It's about twenty times the national ratio," Webb said. "If every community had the same ratio of men killed, there would be 250,000 dead marines."

Today, conversely, men who were across town from Southie at Harvard during the sixties often offer a smug statement of class, occasionally tinged with sheepishness: "I don't know anyone who went."

Well over a quarter of a million youths—303,652—were wounded in Vietnam. Eddie, from South Boston, was still in his teens, just nineteen, lying in a Boston hospital, the bedclothes smooth and flat where a leg should be, when Cardinal Cushing bent solicitously over his bed. "How did you lose your leg, son?"

Eddie, sick of the whole business, replied, "I lost it in a crap game."

By the mid-sixties the racial and class inequities of the Vietnam War were scandalous. General S. L. A. Marshall, the noted military historian, commented, "In the average rifle company, the strength was 50 percent composed of Negroes, Southwestern Mexicans, Puerto Ricans, Guamanians, Nisei, and so on. But a real cross-section of American youth? Almost never."[1]

In 1965 blacks accounted for 24 percent of all Army combat deaths. As black leaders publicized the plight of blacks in Vietnam, the Defense Department reduced the minorities' share of the fighting—to 16 percent in 1966 and 13 percent in 1968.[2]

Eldson McGhee was one of those blacks. He was in the Atlanta Federal Penitentiary for a decade before being paroled in 1982. For McGhee, the Army was his Harvard. His family proudly threw a party for him when he left for Vietnam and displayed his uniformed picture everywhere in the house. "My mother always thought I was going to make something of myself through the Army," says McGhee drily, talking in a corner of a prison visitors' lounge. McGhee was injured in Vietnam and—like thousands of others —soon learned of morphine's blissed-out pleasures. He became addicted to morphine, then turned to heroin. Back home, he took part in a robbery to support his habit and was jailed.

When McGhee returned from Vietnam, he had three months left in the

Army. His job was to drive another wounded veteran—an officer—on his special, unforgettable missions.

Into the ghettos and up the side roads of Southern hamlets they went. It was bad enough in sunshine, but McGhee especially hated it when it rained and red clay colored the fenders of the car blood red. Everyone knew why the green Army car was coming when it moved up the street and stopped in front of a house. Sometimes it would be fifteen, twenty minutes before McGhee and his officer could get out because the mothers would come. They would come and start beating on the car, beating on the windshield, screaming, hating McGhee and his officer, shouting "No no!", their faces ugly in grotesque distortion, not wanting to let them out, until friends would come, put their arms around the mothers, and pull them away.

McGhee and his officer were coming to tell them that their sons were dead.

The young black man from Atlanta and the stiffly starched white officer shared a closeness of pain and sorrow. McGhee on heroin, the officer on painkillers for his war-crippled leg. But the heroin and the painkillers dulled only the physical pain. Sometimes they would drive around the corner, out of sight of the grief they had just left, and cry.

More important than the celebrated generation gap, an intragenerational gap occurred on a grand scale in the sixties—an emerging clash of contemporaries that Vietnam only served to fuel. There were, for example, those termed "proponents of renunciation" by Harvard University professor Seymour Lipset and Earl Raab, executive director of the Jewish Community Relations Council in San Francisco. They were not only college youths but the elite of that population. Caught between security and status derived from their families and a desire to find their own status, they were "freer to act without concern for consequences . . . *in between engagements, so to speak.*" In their detached and advantaged position, isolated on campuses, they were able to roam in like-minded masses, ferreting out inconsistencies and imperfections of society, able to denounce the war with total certitude. The mass media tended to portray them as "the cutting edge" of this generation. However, a less publicized right-wing element emerged—among those working-class youths who went to state colleges for "practical" rather than enlightening reasons and among the nation's young steelworkers and cops. What propelled them, too, was anger, a sense of displacement. "For them, racial integration is part of an organized effort within which agents of government, the mass media, and even the church are conspirators," commented sociologists William Simon, John Gagnon, and Donald Carns. Thus they, too, became antiestablishment.[3]

George Wallace became a hero to many of these men in 1968. And when college students taunted the working-class cops, all hell broke loose. Police frustrations—from overt attacks in slum neighborhoods to being called "pigs" by students—hardened their New Right posture. From these ranks many Vietnam soldiers came and returned.

A third group was the bulk of black youth. "All polls indicate that at least three quarters of 'embittered' black youth are appalled, not by the system but by their failure to get into it."[4] Over and over black veterans have told me that it was this desire to buy into the system that led them to Vietnam. Racism in the Army led to deepening conflicts.

And finally there were all those young men in the center who drifted into Vietnam with little or no thought or, on the other side, stayed out by taking advantage of the system but were otherwise uninvolved.

While the media focused on antiwar youth, polls indicate that those *under* thirty consistently supported the war in larger percentages than those over thirty. In fact, those over forty-nine showed the strongest disapproval throughout the war than any other segment of the population.[5]

By late 1967 a plurality of Americans had concluded that the United States had "made a mistake" in committing combat troops to Vietnam. However, polls show that overall American opposition to the war was not, as often presumed, "pro-peace." "This sentiment was often analyzed wrongly," wrote Southeast Asian expert Stanley Karnow. A November 1967 poll indicated that, while 44 percent advocated complete or gradual withdrawal, 55 percent wanted a *tougher* policy. The attitude was we were in error to have gone in— but once in we should either win or get out.[6]

The Vietnam Generation remains a divided generation; there are no imminent signs of reconciliation.

An estimated 27 million relatives of those who went were deeply touched by Vietnam. They were the poor and the blue-collar prosperous who populated Middle America. And then there was another nation, a more privileged nation, torn by Vietnam as well, but, in most instances, left with far fewer personal wrenches. A 1965–66 survey discovered that college graduates made up only *2* percent of all draftees. One congressman studied 100 inductees from his northern Wisconsin district and found that not one came from a family with an annual income of over $5,000. A 1970 Harvard graduate tallied his 1,200 classmates and counted only 56 in the military, mostly in cushy stateside or noncombat jobs. Just two went to Vietnam. By contrast, 35 men from the Harvard class of 1941 *died* in World War II and hundreds more saw combat.[7]

In the sixties and early seventies, 27 million men came of draft age. They, along with 26 million women, formed an enormous demographic bulge identified forever as the "baby boom generation." For most of those men, Vietnam caused a generation-wide scramble for survival. Of the 27 million draft-age men, only a third served at all and only about 10 percent of those 27 million went to Vietnam. Still, the war was to divide them, sear them, wound them, and would ultimately leave lasting scars. Some of those scars are raw and visible—such as the thousands of physically and psychologically maimed veterans. Other scars are indistinct and blurred, such as the quiet guilts of many who dodged the war and painfully acknowledge more than a decade later their feelings about the other men who went in their places. Other young men who were poorer, less privileged, less educated, less aware, or simply believed that their duty to their country was to go.

The draft was no luck-of-the-draw blind fate. Instead, it worked as a Darwinian instrument of social policy. "The fittest—those with background, wit, or money—managed to escape. Through an elaborate structure of deferments, exemptions, legal technicalities, and noncombat military alternatives, the draft rewarded those who manipulated the system to their advantage."[8]

However, those who would indict the generation of nongoers as cowards should look instead to the system which deliberately "channeled" the generation by providing excessive exemptions and deferments for the more privileged. After World War II, the problem for the federal government was how to reconcile the myth of an egalitarian youth with the reality of manpower requirements. (This was compounded by the massive size of the baby boom generation.)

"Those who avoided service in the Vietnam War were doing exactly what was *expected* of them when they sought and held on to deferments with some uneasiness or outright guilt," argued Tom Alder, a Yale Law graduate who founded the *Selective Service Law Reporter* in 1967, when he was thirty-four and long past draft age. Throughout the war he compiled a massive report of Selective Service cases and decisions for lawyers and draft counselors. "The idea was to make the country feel better about the inequity of a limited draft by evoking a guilt reaction from men who believed they had 'used' the system to avoid service." For many, that meant taking the deferments, finding the loopholes, and remaining quiet. But the formula backfired when men, made to feel guilty about their decisions, threw their sense of unfairness and guilt onto the war itself and marched in the streets.

"The case *against* the war was too substantial, almost from the beginning, and it is ludicrous to say that the student movement was founded solely on an aggregate of personal fears and aversions to physical risk," noted Alder.

For the first time, it was chic and righteous in influential and power circles not to go to war. Avoiding Vietnam was more of a badge of honor than going. Approximately 60 percent of draft-age males who did not serve took positive steps to avoid it, through legal and illegal means.[9]

"The best and the brightest" started that war, but they did not send their sons.

Millions of young men bought themselves out by paying the tuition to stay in college. Doctors willingly wrote letters attesting to enough physical and psychological problems as to suggest a whole generation of weak, halt, and lame.

For some who resisted, the war truly was immoral. For many others, their purely selfish decisions were only cloaked in rhetoric. One Republican lobbyist, comfortable in a $500 suit in a palatial Georgetown house, brags about avoiding the war. "I pled a hardship case—drove down in my brother's Mercedes." Would he talk for this book? "If I am not named," he says sheepishly.

For some who didn't go, there is a minor, nagging sense of disquiet. Others vehemently deny guilt. "How could anyone feel guilty about not going to that war?" asks a congressman's son. "Vietnam was a *mess*. Besides, it didn't fit into my career plans." He was deciding this even as his father got haranguing phone calls from Lyndon Johnson to keep Congress in line on the war. A Princeton graduate and high-priced corporate lawyer says, "I feel sorry others did not have my benefits, but I certainly feel no guilt."

For some there is a defensiveness and lingering hostility toward veterans— particularly among the youngest of the generation who, by the time they came of age, were steeped in antiwar rhetoric. One young television producer said, "I have *no* pity for those veterans. They were either fools or they wanted to go. Anyone could have gotten out."

He is wrong, of course. That so many chose dissent, however, underscores the peculiar pathology of living through a war that few understood; a war conducted in subterfuge, a war that never had the commitment of the country, a war that had no clearly defined military objectives, a war that was never even declared a war. Vietnam divided father and son, intellectual and hard hat, hawk and dove, peacenik mother and John Wayne father. It created a changed mood in America—which may have lasting consequences. Vietnam scored the conscience of the nation. It has affected attitudes toward national defense, toward the acceptance of discipline and service, toward patriotism and what that means, toward government and the veracity of our leaders.

Protest started on the campuses but, by 1969, blue-collar America was also crying "Enough." They were the ones who watched the flag-draped coffins come back to their towns. In one Gallup poll of Middle America, a staggering 55 percent said they personally knew someone who had been killed or wounded in Vietnam. One in five thought the war was being lost and only 8 percent believed that the United States and South Vietnam were winning. *And a vast majority—70 percent—felt that the nation should have kept its sons at home.* Interestingly, there was almost a total absence of *moral* arguments against the war from blue-collar America. Despite four years of violent antiwar protest, this group voiced a heavily pragmatic opinion. It was reflected in the comment of a New York City housewife who wanted the United States out of Vietnam because "There's nothing to be gained."[10]

Vietnam tore away any remaining myths or innocence the generation possessed about war and warriors. And so the Vietnam veteran was either reviled as an unwelcome relic of an unwanted war—or treated with shattering indifference. That hapless homecoming would scar thousands of veterans for years. The veteran was the loser of our only lost war. "The left hated us for killing," commented one deeply troubled veteran, "and the right hated us for not killing *enough.*"

There have always been nonwarriors—from the rich who bought their way out of the Civil War to the conscientious objectors of World War II—but never was there a time in our history to equal the massive dissent of youths toward fighting in Vietnam.

The special negatives of Vietnam should never be forgotten when examining the motives of those who chose not to go.

Still, there is one major indictment of the antiwar movement. Draft counselors, doctors, lawyers, and students, for the most part, ignored the Eddies of South Boston, the Bobby Joes of Appalachia, the Eldson McGhees of Atlanta. Some in the resistance argue, accurately, that many of the ghetto and blue-collar brigades would not have listened anyway. And there were the dedicated who tried against all class obstacles to explain options to the poor and ignorant, often in vain. But the majority did not try. Draft dodging was mainly for the privileged.

Instead, hundreds of thousands of men who would have been rejected as mentally and physically substandard for peacetime service were marching off to Vietnam. "Project 100,000" was a Great Society brainchild, a manpower program whose ostensible purpose was to provide military training and discipline for America's disadvantaged youths. The military took some with an IQ of 62. Meanwhile, as these youths—eventually more than 350,000—filled the quotas, America's finest were staying in college, joining the reserves, plotting ways to get out of going.

Former aides to Robert McNamara, who instituted Project 100,000, insist the motives were honorable—yet, certainly the program provided political advantages for President Johnson. By the systematic, deliberate drafting of those with marginal minds and lives, the President was able to avoid the politically incendiary action of ending student deferments or calling up the reserves.

Few of the promised remedial programs materialized and the low-quality recruits were rarely offered special help. Labeled "the Moron Corps" by fellow soldiers, they were commonly abused and disparaged.

Meanwhile, the reserves were afforded special treatment. Michael Kramer, a journalist, says of his reserve training days, "They kept us in a special barracks—so as not to 'contaminate' the regulars with our antiwar views. There was such leniency that you could distinguish our barracks by the smell of pot wafting out when the door was opened. The Army just wanted us quiet and out of the way."

Those who now call for reinstituting a peacetime draft would do well to remember such inequities of the Vietnam-era draft—which have their parallels in the Civil War's rampant draft avoidance. In the first years of Vietnam, deferment for postgraduate study was allowed, swelling the ranks of nongoers until such deferments were ended in 1967. The growth in student deferments was phenomenal. The total number of all student deferments grew by *900 percent* between 1951 and 1966.[11]

Today there is a distasteful irony at play. Some of those clamoring for a draft were violently antidraft back in the sixties—when they were of age to go —men such as antidraft leader Sam Brown or draft dodgers such as author James Fallows. Their newfound dedication to the draft enrages many, including veterans, who see a standing stockpile of young Americans as one less deterrent to getting the United States into another war. "If they've got 'em, they'll use 'em" is the cynical view of many antiwar veterans. They, particularly, are shocked that those who sat it out and are geriatrically safe in their mid- to late-thirties now urge a draft on a new generation.

Veterans are divided over the draft. Some are for it as the only fair way out of the inequitable volunteer Army. Others are military-oriented and feel we need a stronger force. Others favor a draft to restore a sense of commitment beyond self.

Still others—including blacks and Latinos who were drafted the last time—are sending another message. They tell high school youths about a war that is ancient history to them; today's nineteen-year-old was three at the time of the 1968 Tet Offensive.

One black veteran I know wears a beret and dark shades, vestiges of his Black Power days, and preaches in Harlem high schools that the draft is mass genocide. Blacks are disproportionately filling the all-volunteer ranks. He knows that it is "economic conscription" and that as more social programs are cut and jobs grow scarce, more eighteen-year-old blacks will be forced into the service. Yet he believes a draft would simply force more of them to go.

The blue-collar and ghetto soldiers of yesteryear cannot forget who went the last time.

Pinball machines buzz and *ding-ding-ding* along with Bruce Springsteen on the jukebox in Manhattan's West End bar, near Columbia University one cold spring night in the early eighties. In the late sixties, all was unrest there—sit-ins, occupying deans' offices, marches, demonstrations, freaks versus pigs, Mark Rudd stomping around, making his nonnegotiable demands as many professors caved in with a chorus of *mea culpas.*

Angel Almedina—"Just call me a spic from Harlem, honey"—sits with a group of Vietnam veterans. Two young men, with bookbags and peach fuzz, drink beer a few feet down the bar. The Vietnam veterans suddenly look very, very old.

"For the next war," says Almedina, nodding to the college students, *"he* don't go and *he* don't go." Then he looks across the counter. "The guy making the pizza, *he* go; the guy in the kitchen washing dishes, *he* go."

The argument for the draft is a good one: if everyone has to go, senators' sons and bank presidents' sons, maybe the country will be slower to move into another involvement.

"But hey, man," says one black vet, "it just ain't gonna happen." He speaks from deep cynicism and deeper memories: "The ones with pull ain't gonna go."

I know hundreds of Vietnam veterans now. I have seen them in Vet Centers and on their jobs and in their homes and in their bars. I have listened to their mothers and fathers and wives and children. I have cried with some and laughed with others. Got drunk with some, smoked grass with others. Yes, I know them now.

But in the sixties, in my world of Washington, I knew not *one.*

No parents or friends I knew got those terrible telegrams: WE REGRET TO INFORM YOU. . . . Or heard from an Eldson McGhee messenger of death. No one I knew came back with a leg or an arm or both missing—or blind.

My older friends, instead, had children "crashing"—how arcane that term now sounds—in their recreation rooms or basements, home from college, surrounded by the sweet smell of marijuana.

The hair, so long, in ponytails, and wearing faded, patched jeans—*their* special uniform. The guitars, the songs of peace and love. Crashing and then marching off to the war of the streets. "Drug-gutted flower children" Norman Mailer called them.[12]

Much has been written about the self-indulgence of that generation. Many plead a special cynicism, a negativism—the residue of seeing death, destruction, deceit on a grand scale; a childhood filled with violent death—Martin Luther King, Jr., John F. Kennedy and Robert F. Kennedy; Vietnam and Kent State and Jackson State; Watergate.

Such generalizations hold some truth, but I find that it is only a certain segment of that generation that has been so microscopically examined by the media, by society. These are yesterday's protesting children; the upper middle class, the well-educated, success-oriented families' kids. And, yes, some of them truly show an insensitive lack of commitment to anything but themselves.

"We were just so special," say many of the sixties, by way of wistful explanation. They were, indeed, treated that way by the Selective Service decision makers.

During World War II, America's campuses were emptied of males. By 1944 the male college population was less than one third its prewar level. World War II created a "brain drain" that gave the country pause. The bright were needed more as scientists and teachers and corporate executives than cannon fodder, argued special interest groups. The engineering and medical professions, educators, and, of course, the National Student Association lobbied for student deferments. They were greatly expanded following World War II.

It was a callous concept but one that parents of the college-bound during Vietnam understandably clung to. Had my son been of age then, I have no doubt that I would have clutched the student deferment like a life jacket. (Vietnam and the draft certainly had a salutory effect on college enrollment. In one study, 20 percent of college youth mentioned *avoiding the draft* among their three most important reasons for entering college.)[13]

And yet is someone who glides through college as a class privilege *truly* a worthier national commodity than someone whose coal miner father could not afford college? And are people who didn't *choose* college *at all* of less value? Among the most tragic tales of Vietnam are those wounded veterans who had been struggling blue-collar youths in college but who had to drop out for lack of funds, knowing as they did so that they were trapped into going to Vietnam.

Complex and confusing emotions and reasons were the motivations for being on either side of the barricade; there was nothing as simple as patriotism versus not serving in a war they couldn't support or cowardice versus getting killed for nothing.

The antiwar movement was characterized not only by altruism but by hypocrisy and intolerance as well. Some candidly indict themselves—as they have gone from dope-smoking trashers of deans' offices to three-piece-suit, conservative investment bankers. A favorite comment of many, recalling the era, is: "Protesting was a great place to get laid, get high, and listen to some great rock."

Garry Trudeau, creator of "Doonesbury," half-jestingly described his college days in a 1979 graduation address to the University of Pennsylvania: "It was as a sophomore that I first became acquainted with the vagaries of the U.S. Criminal Code. My main interests were, in order of priority, a steady supply of recreational drugs, a 2-S draft deferment, and overthrowing the Nixon administration. In pursuit of these, I became, at least in my own estimation, the model of lawlessness. My specialty, like that of every other undergraduate of the day, was civil disobedience."

It was that mix—intelligence and smart-ass irreverence—that so often inflamed Middle America's parents whose sons were going instead to Vietnam.

In that nation Trudeau exemplified, a mother today speaks for many. "But *my* son was *magna cum laude!* He was my only child. I could *not* let him go," she says, vehemently recalling her successful struggle more than a decade ago to keep him safe from Vietnam.

I wonder if her grief could have been any more than John Sexton's. He is a gentle Kentuckian who left the hills for the mind-breaking monotony of Detroit's auto plants.

He watched *his* only son go off to Vietnam. John Jr. was captured by the Viet Cong in August 1969 at age nineteen. Sexton was chained and lived in a hole in the ground for twenty-six months. I met him at age twenty-three in 1972, back home in Warren, Michigan. His story of death and pain seemed bizarre and remote as his Thunderbird raced in sunlight down concrete highways that seem both the soul and the sinew of Detroit.

Sexton's once-powerful body was old and wasted. Before Vietnam, he lifted weights, got his chin split with a beer bottle in a fight, ran track, bowled, played baseball. At twenty-three, shrapnel remained in his face and legs. Bomb fragments had torn into his right eye and left it blind. Most of his right elbow was blown off and his arm was fused—he can never bend it again. He has a herniated disc and a bad esophagus. Malaria attacks came in the night. So did the headaches from the concussion, caused by the deafening pound of mortar fire.

Sexton had only two more weeks to go when the armored personnel carrier he was riding in was ambushed. He was shot in the head and "felt the warm blood pouring down my face." The Viet Cong carried him deep into the jungle, his blood wetting the canvas stretcher. For two years and two months, Sexton never talked to another American. He lived in a four-by-eight-foot shelter in the ground, where he was unable to stand erect. At night, when he was shackled, he could hear *them*. They would scurry and *scritch-scratch* their way in the hole, come close, somehow sensing Sexton's helplessness. He could *feel* them and not be able to do anything about it; mice, digging in, *crawling* through his hair. He went months without a bath. It was a "constant struggle" not to lose his mind. He thought at times of "just giving up and dying."

In those two lost years, Sexton went to a place in his mind where few people go. There were not just hours or days but months of loneliness and despair. He returned with a special reverence for life, mixed with a gnawing dissatisfaction. There were bursts of nostalgia for the aimlessness of his youth, but Sexton knew he couldn't go back to it. And yet he didn't know how to find a new world. He was never a "studious-type person . . . I always depended on my body." He could no longer do the demanding manual jobs his friends could, but he could not concentrate on schooling either. "I just feel so wasted."

I shall never forget his father, staring with sad and loving eyes at his son, summing up with wrenching clarity, bad grammar and all, what happened to boys like John Sexton. "I used to think, My Johnny is too young for that war, it can't last that long—but he growed right into it."

Could that mother who spoke of not letting her son go have felt any worse? Her son burned his draft card, was preparing to go to Canada, but was disqualified anyway due to poor eyesight. The word "brilliant" is stroked like a talisman in his mother's conversations. "I knew those kids who protested. They were brilliant students, not your basic shleppers. The *crème de la crème*. They were supported in their cause by their professors. They had deep, deep feelings about the immorality of the war. You have to understand. These people were very sensitive. They marched and got teargassed and my home was a haven for those kids and I scraped up the money for the bail. And I felt as patriotic as if I had a Gold Star in the window!"

For some who went, Vietnam was seen through the supply officer's world or Saigon's safer streets. The distant rolling thunder was war and someone was being killed or maimed—but not them.

In the field, "Better him than me" was the war-toughened shrug of many when they heard of another dead. Only years later did they begin to tell of the frustration and pain of being impotent to help dying buddies, the heavy depression of survivor guilt, the emotional lobotomization.

"I seen so much I just forgot how to cry," one veteran said. "I can't cry about anything ever. And I can't get close to anyone ever."

Many medics and nurses suffer terribly from remembered feelings of helplessness. "When I went into the field, the first casualty was a marine, about nineteen years old with his legs blown off, and he said, 'Doc, Doc, I'm gonna live! You're gonna save me, aren't ya, Doc?' And I said, 'Yeah, yeah babe, you're gonna live.' And then he dies in my arms, so I cried and there was nothing I could do but go to the next guy that was hurt, and then the next guy, and then the next . . ."[14]

Some veterans can never get over seeing friends killed—or killing. For others Vietnam was, quite simply, the most exciting time in their lives. Those in combat were as brave and courageous as soldiers of other, "acceptable" wars. Many returned strengthened by the ordeal. Some veterans still speak with disgust of those who "got off on killing." (The men I have met who tell of the "thrill" of killing are rare.) For still others the war meant discipline and growth. Some are torn between conflicting emotions—a belief in the worth of military life but disgust with its end result for them, Vietnam.

For most there is still enormous ambiguity about the experience of battle. Its terrors, anxieties, and bereavements mingle with the thrill of comradeship, the excitement, the brilliance of red tracers, the deafening noise of mortar, the indescribable horror *and* exhilaration. One West Pointer, Tom Carhart, speaks of the "hard-on I would get in battle." A veteran, now a journalist, talks of the terrible nostalgia that washes over him for something he so hated at the time. Even those who found the war a tragic, shattering waste and wore peace symbols on their helmets know a sense of honor in doing their own job well, in helping others to live, in having survived.

Nearly 58,000 died in Vietnam or are still missing. As war goes, those numbers are far less horrendous than the slaughters of all-out battles in the Civil War, World War I, or World War II. On the first day of the Battle of the Somme, 60,000 British fell in the trenches; 21,000 had been killed, most in the first hour of attack, perhaps in the first few minutes.[15] More than 24,000 marines were killed or wounded on Iwo Jima in World War II.

Yet, in human terms, Vietnam's dead and wounded were indeed tragedy enough; grief compounded by the national sense of guilt and defeat, grief compounded by the sense that it was all for naught, grief among veterans that there was no expiation for war's often hideous measures for survival.

Veterans are not monolithic. They came back hawks, they came back doves, they came back just plain apolitical. There are former Black Panther vets—and Ku Klux Klan vets. They are in prisons and in executive suites. They are professors and cops, poets and politicians, truck drivers and musicians, plumbers and artists, rich and poor. Many think the war an immoral waste. Others think that the only thing wrong with the war was that "We weren't allowed to win it."

My Lai's Rusty Calley has his beer-drinking defenders in working-class bars—as well as detractors. Some ex-marines would go to El Salvador tomorrow. Others would *"drive* my kids to Canada if there's another one like Vietnam."

Some went to fulfill the John Wayne visions of their World War II fathers. A son of a Maryland plumber said, "I told my father I was thinking of going to Canada. I turned to walk out of the room. I saw my father, his head in his hands, sobbing at the kitchen table. I had never seen him cry before. I knew then that I had to go."

Some were wildly gung ho. "I saw them World War II movies," one told me. "I thought war was glorious, I thought it was glamorous. Why didn't someone tell us different? Why didn't someone tell us? War is *shit!*"

I have found many Vietnam veterans to be the most gentle, compassionate, and nonjudgmental people I have met; often, on an emotional caring level, a cut above those who didn't go. On the other hand, as one veteran said, "Some of us were pure shits when we went there and pure shits when we came back." There are psychotics and wife beaters and drunks and sadists and just plain "mean mothers." There is one major distinction unrevealed in bare, cold statistics. The phrase "drop out" doesn't tell the full story. An overwhelming number—especially those who became successful after returning from Vietnam—were high school or college dropouts who merely didn't have their lives together then. The mid-sixties was hardly the time for adolescent confusion about goals.

Nongoers were no more monolithic than the veterans. There were dedicated resisters who went to jail and those for whom Vietnam was, ultimately, just a minor blip in their lives. There were those who never had to face a test because they never got drafted and those who took deliberate steps to avoid the war. Although hawks defended the war, it wasn't only the liberal who avoided Vietnam. Thousands of conservative Republican sons charted a successful course to corporate success by coolly evading the war.

Some of the privileged starved themselves to flunk induction exams. Some paid $2,000 for artificial braces; the law provided an exemption for anyone under orthodontic care. (This is a reversal of the nineteenth-century Russian serfs, who were given to knocking out their front teeth, with which soldiers bit the old musket cartridge, to avoid conscription).[16]

Faked homosexuality was a major dodge. Some simulated ulcers by drinking their own blood and then throwing up during their examination. A few resorted to self-inflicted wounds, such as cutting off a part of the thumb. (Soldiers, particularly since the development of antiseptics, have resorted to self-inflicted wounds, such as shooting oneself in the foot. Part of gung ho patriot lore is that everyone prior to the Vietnam Generation marched eagerly to war. This is pure mythology.)

Today many in the generation at first insist that they bear no one ill will on either side. And some veterans are indeed best friends with those who did not go. Yet, after hours of conversation, the qualifiers often appear. A Princeton graduate who was a Navy officer clenches his teeth when he talks of his roommates who didn't go and are now further ahead in their careers. "One got out because he said he was *deaf* and now he's a highly successful *reporter* for a major magazine!"

A veteran tells how he proudly marched in antiwar rallies and thinks that anyone who escaped that war was lucky. But after a few beers he says, with a grin, "I always thought those college kids in the marches were a bunch of assholes." With the condescension of someone who was there, he adds, *"They didn't even know what they were protesting. We did."*

Many nongoers still regard their escape as an inalienable class right.

At the height of the war, a vicious polarization existed among returning veterans and campus students. Students saw mangled vets and shouted, "Baby killers!" (In one survey, a full one third of returning combat vets said they received direct unfriendly treatment from their nongoing peers.)[17]

A familiar bumper sticker decorated working-class bars—white peace symbol marching across a black background with the words: FOOTPRINT OF THE AMERICAN CHICKEN.

Viciousness was matched by viciousness. Protesters spat at and taunted soldiers. Cops in Chicago and hard hats on Wall Street brutally beat students until blood ran. At Quantico, recalls Jim Webb, the day after Kent State, a cheer actually erupted when an enlisted man wrote on the blackboard: KENT STATE 0, NATIONAL GUARD 4. Meanwhile, Fred Downs, who lost an arm in Vietnam, was walking across another campus. A student noticed his hook. "Get that in Vietnam?" he asked. Downs replied, "Yes." The student sneered. "Serves you right."

The stock answer then—and clung to today by many—was that the war was so wrong that anything they did was justified.

David Morrison, a conscientious objector, seems embarrassed at what, compared to others of the generation, was a small loss—a loss of carefree dalliance. Taking off from college, bumming around the country, trying some unconventional form of education was a luxury the sixties generation could not afford without the specter of Vietnam. Morrison never did and there lingers a wistful regret. Tim Noyes did drop out of college and was working at being discovered on Broadway when the Army, instead, discovered him. He became a helicopter pilot and came back troubled for several years. In his mid-thirties, Noyes is in Hollywood, still trying to be discovered.

Atlantic Monthly editor James Fallows, in a much-cited *mea culpa (Washington Monthly,* October 1975), details how he exploited the system in the sixties. With a "diligence born of panic," Fallows starved himself and barely made the cutoff for an "underweight" qualification.

He nodded eager assent when the doctor asked if he had ever contemplated suicide. The doctor deemed Fallows "unqualified." At first came elation, then "the beginning of a shame that remains with me to this day."[18]

As the Harvard contingent left, a bus arrived with the working-class boys of Chelsea. They did not fake their color blindness tests or starve themselves or carry envelopes of freedom from their doctors.

Fallows told me, five and a half years after he wrote that article, that for a great number of well-motivated young men, those years meant an anguished choice between alternatives which were "hateful" and "wrong," no matter which you finally took. Fallows feels that perhaps those who made more of a stand for their beliefs feel the least guilt, a view I concur with after hundreds of interviews. "The time," he concludes, "was hard on everyone."

Hardest, of course, on those who went to war or chose prison, exile, or desertion.

Parents of the Vietnam Generation were often left achingly bewildered. Parents of veterans sometimes grew to share their sons' guilt for being, often unwilling, participants in the war. Parents of those who went to Canada felt the slurs and hostilities of neighbors and were forced to defend their sons' choices.

For those who went to Canada, it was not the cowardly vacation in a neighboring land that some of their detractors depicted.

One of the greatest fears for exiles was a death in the family.

When Jack Colhoun's mother was dying of cancer, friends openly castigated her son's decision to stay in Canada. A parent becoming seriously ill was the ultimate concern of many who crossed the border. Colhoun thought that his mother, like her mother before her, would live into her nineties. Shortly after Colhoun fled to Canada, his mother became ill. If anything happened, he was *not* to come home. Exiles had been warned. The FBI kept their lists, even read obituaries and staked out funerals of family members of exiles. Colhoun realized he was truly a fugitive.

"My mother decided she preferred me free to write or call her, than to be in the United States in jail," Colhoun recalls. In her last months, they became closer than ever. Colhoun wrote daily. He never saw her in the last years of her life.

Colhoun lived in exile for ten years. Today he works out of a Capitol Hill townhouse, writing screeds for left-wing publications. A tiny nub of a ponytail rests at the back of his neck.

He seems frozen in amber, a specimen of another time, still pursuing the same course. One afternoon Colhoun was on the phone, giving marching orders for an antidraft demonstration, 1981 style, at the Pentagon. He spoke cautiously about notifying the press. "We don't want CBS there until we can guarantee a crowd." The year 1981 was not the time of marchers, several thousand strong. War and the draft still seemed distant threats to most. About forty showed up.

For years the quickest way to start a fight among veterans was to mention amnesty for exiles or deserters. But now many veterans feel that these men paid more of a price for their beliefs than they originally suspected. Especially the deserters.

Colhoun said, "Many of the veterans are poles apart from me on the war. We can't talk about *that*—but we understand we both did something for our beliefs." Dean Phillips, a lawyer who gave up his student deferment out of revulsion for the unfair draft laws and enlistment, agrees, "We both made a sacrifice—but not those assholes who sipped sherry at Harvard, denounced the 'system' while staying safe and sound with the deferment that system allowed them, and awaited Daddy's allowance check."

Above all, what the veteran, the exile, the deserter, the ones who went to jail feel most deeply is a sense of lost *time.* They speak often of losing friends, losing limbs, losing time while their nongoing counterparts moved into careers. In Korea and World War II, college graduates went to war. I know World War II veterans who grew up studying the Talmud and listening to Brahms and ended up toting rifles on Iwo Jima. Professors, politicians, journalists, and businessmen now in their early fifties saw duty in Korea. After the wars, since so many had gone, there was less catching up to do.

On a freezing sunlit January Inauguration Day in 1961, John F. Kennedy electrified a nation with his message that America would "pay any price, bear any burden" for freedom.

Today I wonder if he truly knew just how much patriotism he inspired in young American boys—boys who were thirteen or fourteen or fifteen when he was assassinated in 1963. His words carried a special message for them. How often I was to hear a certain kind of veteran repeat the words—the ones who went in the earliest days of Vietnam, the ones who eagerly enlisted, the ones who *believed.* Over and over they repeated it, these men in their late thirties now: "Ask not what your country can do for you. Ask what you can do for your country. . . ." Always they say it with a sense of emotion, as if it were a message meant for each alone, like the lyrics of a love song. It is, they say, the single most memorable sentence of their lives. It propelled many of them into Vietnam, a war that was still in the future for most Americans on November 22, 1963. All Americans remember where they were, what they were doing when they heard the news that Kennedy had been shot. At the White House, mourners began to arrive immediately, the blankness of incomprehensive shock on their faces. At 6 P.M., as the skyline deepened behind flags flying at half-staff, almost 2,000 rimmed the fence in quiet vigil.

The faces changed constantly. Businessmen and secretaries at 5 P.M. were replaced by men in slacks and women with curlers in their hair at 1 A.M. College boys sprawled on the face of the statue in Lafayette Park. Couples held hands. A man walked back and forth cradling his sleeping baby. The utter silence was eerie. At 3 A.M., workmen draped the black bunting. At three minutes to four, two priests walked up the curving driveway. At 4:25 A.M., the word " '*Tenshun!*" crackled from the portico porch. The gray ambulance moved up the driveway. Mourners saw the flag-draped casket from the back window. An honor guard lifted the coffin and carried it through the North Portico doors, draped in black crepe. Jacqueline Kennedy, still in her pink, blood-spattered suit, leaned on Robert Kennedy's arm and moved inside.

A day that no one's heart could forget had come to an end.

Almost six years later to the day, one quarter of a million Americans marched past the White House in one of the largest demonstrations ever held in the nation's capital. And 40,000 participated in the "March Against Death" that same weekend. It began at twilight on a Thursday in November 1969. Seven drummers—beating a funeral roll—stepped toward the White House and the Capitol. Behind, single file, came the marchers—each one wearing a hand-lettered placard around his neck bearing the name of a GI killed in Vietnam. They cupped their hands over lighted candles, protecting them from the Potomac's icy wind. In front of the White House, each marcher called out the name on his placard and then moved on toward the Capitol. They marched to a row of twelve pine coffins. At 8:39 P.M. Mrs. Judy Droz, a twenty-three-year-old war widow from Missouri, dropped the first placard into the first coffin. It bore the name of her husband, Donald Glenn Droz, a Navy lieutenant killed in Vietnam on April 12, 1969. She snuffed out his candle.

They would come for the next thirty-eight hours—maxi-coated college girls, veteran dissenters with granny glasses and knapsacks. By night, by dawn, they came, their candles bobbing and flickering. And still they came, slowly, past the TV cameras, past the drums beating out their mournful cadence.

They were not all young. There were middle-aged housewives and well-dressed businessmen. One man with a Pentagon ID pass pinned to his coat said, "I am here because I am against people dying."[19]

The year before, 1968, was filled with that tragic, terrible list of events—Robert F. Kennedy killed; Martin Luther King, Jr., killed; Chicago's bloodied Democratic Convention; Vietnam and more Vietnam; Tet, My Lai.

The unanswerable question is what kind of escalation would there have been had John F. Kennedy lived. That question, like so many about Vietnam, belongs to the land of ifs, to be pondered by historians and scholars for years to come.

I am, instead, exploring the reality of what happened to the generation asked to fight. I come late to this questioning. My lateness is matched by millions who, as I did, chose to rip a whole violent decade from their calendar of memories, rather than face it.

In some ways I quite simply sat out the war. Like everyone in the United States, I felt that Vietnam was benumbing, confusing, deeply troubling. My friends who were over there, however, were not young fighting men but correspondents.

I knew none of the pain of a child lost to war or to drugs or to an alien world of rebellion or to jail or to Canada.

We who graduated from college in the latter part of the fifties barely missed Korea, were too old for Vietnam, not old enough to have children threatened by Vietnam.

Largely, adolescents of the silent fifties had never been forced to choose sides. And then along came the sixties.

A few weeks after Kennedy was killed, I married. By the following November, my son was born. I was not learning personally nor agonizingly about those strange places—Mekong Delta, Chu Lai, Hue, Phu Bai, Pleiku—like thousands of older mothers. I was learning about colic and diapers and that amazing vulnerability that comes with being a parent. Two years later, my red-haired baby girl was born. I was a journalist, yet had grown up with all the traditions of the fifties. Even though I rebelled enough to have a career, it seemed only natural to become a total mother in a period that coincided with the most crucial years of the sixties. Other mothers were marching for peace, committing themselves. But I was not.

I did cover some of the antiwar demonstrations. I remember the New Mobe headquarters filled with the young, helping to plan the largest protest ever in the history of our country—millions across the nation. I remember Richard Nixon ignoring those millions of voices. I sympathized with their aims, but was troubled by the arrogance of many in the movement; the looks of contempt for those outside their world. Stewart Alsop, revisiting Yale, his alma mater, in 1969, expressed a similar thought: "Collectively, these kids are not very attractive, with their attitudinizing and their inadequately fertilized facial shrubbery. But individually, they have a genuine idealism, a sort of searching innocence, and also a kind of good-hearted nuttiness which is very appealing."

Millions of us in this country lived through Vietnam as distant viewers.

This remembered complacency still rankles veterans.

America's foreign policy was sowing the seeds for such apathy and uninvolvement years before. "We all share in this stigma of general apathy in this question-mark war. How can these men be expected to cheer over a war that has never been officially declared, a war from which their return is marked by no homecoming ceremony or other public recognition? Can you blame our troops for low morale? They are dying and shedding their blood in a hopeless war while they are forgotten at home."

These remarks were not about Vietnam; they came from an address delivered by Donald Johnson, an Iowa American Legion commander, on April 8, 1953.[20] Korea was our slow slide into Vietnam. As one general, Eugene ("Mike") Lynch—who served in our three most recent wars and returned from Vietnam violently opposed to that one—said, "We won World War II, tied Korea, and lost Vietnam."

There were no riots against the Korean war, in part, because America was just coming off the win of World War II. Still it was unpopular and polls showed widespread discontent. Had it lasted as long as Vietnam, there would surely have been extreme dissension. (While the Korean veteran did not get his homecoming parade, he was not reviled nor did he suffer under a grossly inequitable GI Bill as did the Vietnam veteran. The Vietnam-era GI Bill enacted in 1966 was $100 a month, actually $10 less than the Korean GI Bill. Nor did he face the hostility of would-be employers who feared hiring a "dope-crazed killer.")

Vietnam was our first living room war; the daily barrage did much to turn people against it. Still, somehow watching the war every night on TV both shocked and numbed at the same time. In a personal sense, it was like a nightly docudrama for those who had no firsthand involvement. As the war worsened, people even began to subliminally ignore what they were seeing nightly on their TV sets, just as they would ignore the returning veteran later.

In some ways, the sixties would have been an insane, radical time, with or without Vietnam. POWs who were away for even two years lost a whole culture. When they left, they were wearing brush cuts. They returned to see men with shoulder-length hair. When they left, women were wearing bouffant hairdos and above-the-knee dresses. They returned to braless women in thigh-high micro-minis. There were unisex clothes and massage parlors and topless waitresses.

The counterculture, the Beatles, and the gurus spoke to America's children. America's industries were eager to please the young because they were the ones buying records, clothes, stereos, and cars. Children of the affluent were leaving the "claustrophobia" of their parents' $200,000 suburban homes, with their swimming pools and their stereoed bedrooms, to live ten abreast in cockroach-infested communes. Timothy Leary's "Turn On, Tune In, Drop Out" philosophy provided just the right touch of mindless irresponsibility for many. Walking through Georgetown today, I remember the sidewalks that were nearly impassable in the sixties. Barefoot youths with dirt-blackened feet sprawled, stoned, on the sidewalks, strumming guitars or panhandling along Wisconsin and M. Their fathers had made it bigger than any other previous generation. Prosperity was *now*. More young people than ever were going on to higher education. Many of the privileged belonged to a group who—for the first time in America's upwardly mobile history—could not automatically expect to do *better* than their parents. Even as they disabused all those trappings of success, the knowledge that they just might *not* be able to do as well as Daddy ultimately left many feeling lost. In spite of that feeling, today, many of those who occupied deans' offices now occupy boardrooms, macrobiotic diets have given way to Julia Child, communes to luxury condos.

"I saw an old friend, he's the same as he was then—the long hair, working on causes. He seems like he just hasn't moved on," said one New York woman executive. "It was embarrassing."

"Relevance" was of monumental importance, but the ironies were constant. As Martha Ritter, a Harvard graduate, wrote in 1981, "We won the opportunity to study black history," but "few real-life specimens were around for firsthand observation." Instead, they were dying in disproportionate numbers in Vietnam.

It seems inevitable, looking back, that the sixties, filled to bursting with those young people, would have exploded in some rebellion after the silent fifties. Civil rights marchers braved clubbings and water hoses and police dogs to sit in for racial equality. The Free Speech Movement had begun; Students for a Democratic Society (SDS) made its debut in 1962. Students were demanding often constructive change on America's campuses.

With Vietnam, the smoldering sixties blew up into incendiary proportions.

The year 1968 was a turning point and 1969 followed wildly behind. Woodstock and the Manson murders, moratoriums and the first tales of My Lai, the death of Ho Chi Minh and the wonder of the first moon walk.

Pop psychology polarized the world into "freaks and straights" and black was beautiful. Violence raged in the streets—sixty Weathermen captured, three of them killed in Chicago. Black students with guns took over the student union at Cornell. Police with nightsticks swept through student mobs at Harvard Yard. Columbia University was in the throes of the spring SDS offensive.

It was a year of mass movements. Some 528 million humans around the world, from Panama to Prague, watched as Neil Armstrong placed his 9½B lunar boots on the moon. Lured by music and some tribal pull, nearly half a million young people from across the country descended on a 600-acre dairy farm in the Catskill village of Bethel, New York, the site of the Woodstock festival. For one week they formed an instant city; the roars after the songs scared even veteran rocker Joe McDonald of Country Joe and the Fish. Country Joe sang his "I-Feel-Like-I'm-Fixin'-to-Die Rag" at Woodstock, but its nihilistic message also became one of the most popular songs among young draftees and enlisted men in Vietnam.

> *And it's 1,2,3, what are we fighting for?*
> *Don't ask me I don't give a damn*
> *Next stop is Vietnam*
> *And it's 5,6,7, open up the Pearly Gates*
> *Well there ain't no time to wonder why*
> *Whoopee we're all gonna die*

The sixties' reluctant warriors bought the patterns of the "youth culture": language, hairstyles (to the extent that they could get away with it), drugs, peace medallions, antiwar literature, antiauthoritarian protest against "straight" lifers. Many infantry men formed a military underdogs' rebellion against the military establishment.

Says one former GI about Country Joe's "I-Feel-Like-I'm-Fixin'-to-Die Rag": "It gave me the ultimate vent to all those feelings of idiocy and lunacy about the whole war. . . . I was forcing myself to be 'reasonable' about the war—you know, to find the middle course and say, 'Okay, you people didn't say you wanted the war, but we might as well do our best. . . .' But I was really feeling that it was crazy and idiotic and I wouldn't allow myself to express that. I guess when I heard the 'I-Feel-Like-I'm-Fixin'-to-Die Rag,' I really just let it all hang out. . . ."[21]

In 1969 smoldering blue-collar rebellion was felt across the land. A Gallup poll of middle-income blue- and white-collar workers (who made up three fifths of America) suggested they were more deeply troubled about their country's future than at any time since the Depression. And blue-collar workers, much more than the rest of Middle America, were convinced in 1969 that prosperity was passing them by. They were beset by "a futile war abroad, a malignant racial atmosphere at home, unnerving inflation, scarifying crime rates, the implacable hostility of much of the young."[22]

There were ugly voices, the beginnings of the punitive Moral Majority as they hunted for scapegoats. Blue-collar and middle Americans felt angry and threatened as they watched their professed ethos of premarital chastity and respect for parents mocked by the young.

But the major and worst frustration for these working people was Vietnam. Their sons had died and had been wounded by the thousands. By the summer of 1969, President Nixon, after six months in office, was promising a steady pull-out. August saw the lowest weekly figure for death in Vietnam since that January. In that dispassionate, inanimate world of statistics, the government reported "only" 110 dead that week. In one magazine, Nixon's pull-out announcement ran next to a picture of four soldiers, their faces contorted in fear, holding a wounded comrade, crouching, waiting for the dust-off chopper. A major of the 1st Air Cavalry Division responded to the word from Washington about a combat lull: *"Bullshit!* We are still very much in the business of finding Charlie and zapping him." A company commander of the U.S. 9th Division concurred: "It doesn't matter a tinker's damn what they say in Washington. It's a matter of our survival. . . ."

The men in Washington would have to continue to struggle to survive until the last troops came home. That would be four long years later.

3 A Different War

IT IS DIFFICULT TO UNDERSTAND THE SPECIAL PROBLEMS OF VIETNAM veterans without knowing what made that war different. "War is hell" and "Killing is killing" are clichés certainly based on reality. After all, the horrors of combat in Erich Maria Remarque's *All Quiet on the Western Front* or Stephen Crane's *The Red Badge of Courage* or James Jones's *The Thin Red Line* find their parallels in the tales of Vietnam.

In many ways Vietnam veterans, repelled by the absurdity of dying in Vietnam, identified with the searing recollections of those who fought in the senseless slaughters of World War I more than they ever did with their fathers of World War II: "What am I doing here? We don't take any land. We don't give it back. We just mutilate bodies. What the *fuck* are we doing here?" cried one GI in Vietnam. "We are indifferent. We are forlorn like children and experienced like old men. I believe we are lost," cried one soldier in *All Quiet on the Western Front.* In the woods of France several World War I German soldiers tried to comprehend why they were dying there—"What exactly is the war for?"—just as GIs in Vietnam would ask years later the same question.

There are, however, specific differences between Vietnam and other wars.

First, the antiwar element is paramount and cannot be stressed too often. It is the unique facet that colors every aspect of the Vietnam experience. In this past "decade of denial," veterans were the scapegoats. When they finally speak of coming home, they recount still wrenching memories. Whether successfully readjusted or troubled, hawk or dove, college graduate or high school dropout—they remember. The neighbors and relatives who did not want to listen. The people who moved away from them on planes. In a major study by Louis Harris in 1980, nearly half of the younger veterans (47 percent) recalled that when on leave they were not "always proud to wear my uniform to public places."[1] Even in Middle America, where antiwar stigma was missing, there were older men who would preach to them of wars they had *won.*

The problem was especially acute for the thousands—often high school or college dropouts—who returned from the horrors of war driven to succeed and who encountered ridiculing antiwar professors and nongoing peers on campuses. Now there is some meager measure of reconciliation; some who used to taunt them at Army camps and airports—the students deferred taunting those less privileged draftees or those who felt compelled to serve their country—admit guilt and shame. Still, those memories haunt veterans. In interviews with hundreds of veterans—from the most successful to the least well-adjusted—I have yet to find one who did not suffer rage, anger, and frustration at the way the country received them.

Above all, indifference, hostility, and denial allowed no catharsis for the veteran. That is why the phrase "No homecoming parade" is much more significant than the simple cliché it has become. Many veterans of past wars say they, too, were soon forgotten. As civilians began to ignore them, former soldiers viewed their homecoming as "Welcome our boys back" hollow claptrap. Yet they did, collectively, benefit from that returning warrior's welcome with its symbolic cleansing that offered both respect and expiation.

From ancient times, there have been elaborate rituals for purifying and returning the warrior to society.

In the *Aeneid,* Virgil ascribes these words to Aeneas:

> *In me it is not fit, holy things to bear,*
> *Red as I am with slaughter and new from war;*
> *Til in some stream I cleanse*
> *The guilt of dire debate and blood in battle spilt.*

American Navajo Indians have long recognized the need to cleanse the warrior. After battle, they paid homage to their enemies and made reconciliation with their spirits. American Indian veterans in World War II went through such tribal rituals.

Ticker tape parades and the generous GI Bills of the past were forms of absolving the soldier of anything he may have done in the course of battle, as well as signs of societal commitment, the recognition that "You did it for your country."

All of this was absent after Vietnam. Societal indifference was a form of punishment instead; this was symbolized in the punitive attitude toward everything from meager GI benefits to unconcern for Vet Centers or Agent Orange studies. "In past wars, symbolically, through cleansing acts, society *shared* the blame and responsibility by saying, 'We sent you off to do this for us.' Victory banners, medals, and parades were ways of recognizing the tasks they did in the country's name. Vietnam was not 'in our name,' " said Jack Smith, an ex-marine and psychologist. "The responsibility and blame was left on the heads of the guys who fought it. They were left to sort out who was responsible for what."

Sharing has not been easy for those who protested our involvement and felt it was not "their war." But that is what veterans and those who work with

Vietnam's delayed stress victims feel must be achieved to reach that catharsis. "They want the country to say, 'God, it was a mess—but we can acknowledge that and then go on,' " said Smith.

Going on is what it is all about for the survivors of Vietnam, the majority of whom have adjusted successfully, have found pride and strength in their service, no matter what their feelings on the war. Most are understanding of the estimated 500,000 to 700,000 still suffering from delayed stress.

The Vietnam Veterans Memorial, dedicated in November 1982, was not only to honor the dead but for the living, "for the guy who has been stigmatized and needs that cleansing," said Hubert Brucker, standing by the wall one spring day in 1983. A former Army lieutenant, Brucker saw heavy fighting at Dak To in 1967. He cannot forget a final, horrific farewell to men who had been his friends. "We were there three days, couldn't get the helicopters in. The bodies were rotting in the sun. They got this cargo net. There must have been thirty bodies. As the cargo net swung back and forth, fluid and blood sprayed down from the sky. Arms and legs were falling out. . . ." Some would have combat veterans keep such nightmares to themselves. But wars are not marble monuments and dress uniforms. For Brucker, as well as many others, being forced to hide those memories by an unsympathetic public took its toll. Now a successful businessman, Brucker said, "Some of us have made it, but a lot haven't."

It was not just the homecoming that caused problems for many veterans. Revisionists and veterans who supported the war do not like to hear of the many veterans who feel a guilt about Vietnam, but one VA study shows that 33 percent of the younger veterans (those in the Vietnam Generation age group) expressed a sense of shame or guilt about Vietnam—at the same time expressing pride in their individual performance. The study concluded that the representation of veterans as being consumed by guilt is a myth—pointing out that two thirds reject the statement "It is shameful what my country did to the Vietnamese people." However, when you study *only* the young, who comprise the Vietnam Generation, the numbers change dramatically. Only 7 percent of the older veterans said they were not always proud to wear their uniforms while home on leave, as opposed to nearly half of the younger veterans.

Similarly, younger veterans far more often expressed guilt or shame—33 percent to 16 percent, respectively. The study concluded that "A sense of guilt or shame about Vietnam is fairly common among younger veterans. It seems highly unlikely that similar attitudes would be found among veterans of any of America's earlier wars."[2]

Another major point differentiates Vietnam from past wars. Vietnam-era veterans of the Vietnam Generation, now in their thirties, "are decidedly negative in their assessment of American involvement in the Vietnam conflict," concluded a major 1980 study. However, "above age forty-four [in 1980] a clear majority of Vietnam-era veterans believe that their country did the right thing in getting involved in the fighting in Vietnam." Moreover, the difference in generational attitudes carries over in how they regard their own service. While 90 percent of Vietnam-era veterans say they are glad to have served their country, that number drops sharply to 64 percent among men in the Vietnam Generation. An ambivalence and sense of duty courses through these answers however. No matter how they felt about the war, two thirds of Vietnam veterans who were in the war zone said they would serve again.[3]

"If my own postwar experiences and those of other veterans I've talked to are typical, the main unresolved problem is guilt, a triple burden of guilt," wrote Phil Caputo, author of *A Rumor of War.* "There is the guilt all soldiers feel for having broken the taboo against killing, a guilt as old as war itself. Add to this the soldier's sense of shame for having fought in actions that resulted, indirectly or directly, in the deaths of civilians. Then pile on top of that an attitude of social opprobrium, an attitude that made the fighting men feel personally morally responsible for the war, and you get your proverbial walking time bomb. . . ."[4]

Other veterans, who felt the war was right or did not participate in acts that bothered them, do not manifest such guilt reactions—but they can feel stress nonetheless. As one psychiatrist and veterans' counselor said, "*Antiwar* veterans are troubled because they experienced Vietnam as an atrocity and believe they did terrible things to the Vietnamese for no good reason. *Pro-war* veterans feel that our government and our military betrayed them for cynical purposes by sending them over there and not letting them win."

In considering both the generation gap of the 1960s and the sense of profound patriotism that prompted many to enlist, the timing of Vietnam must be stressed. In many ways the young men of that generation were destined to be marked by their fathers' World War II memories. The war of their fathers was history's anomaly; America's one black-and-white, good-versus-evil war of the twentieth century. And it was *the* war that touched and motivated the Vietnam soldier, the war they heard about from infancy, not the more recent, murkier, and far less glamorous Korea. Had Vietnam come later—had the fathers of a Vietnam Generation been *Korean* veterans—perhaps that reflexive blind patriotism would have been less strong. Conversely, many young men who chose not to go to Vietnam had to battle the heartbreak and anger of fathers who remembered a time of simpler choices, when you went to war without question. Only years later would some reconcile with their sons, recognizing in retrospect that Vietnam was different.

Lines of combat were blurred. It was a war of intense guerrilla fighting, as well as major battles with NVA forces, but seldom conventional frontline maneuvers. Veterans themselves go through a litmus test of who was and wasn't in combat. Purists scoff at the cushy world of Saigon posts, while some who were in base camps argue that without front lines all were adversely affected by the fear of attack.

"Complete safety was always relative in Vietnam and therefore combat paranoia was endemic," comments Clark Smith in *Strangers at Home.* Others argue that less than one out of three who served in the war zone saw action. Yet another study theorizes the opposite: "Exposure to at least moderate levels of combat was the rule, not the exception, in Vietnam."[5]

Being in the rear was no protection against rocket attacks or emotional wounds. To this day, nurses and medics remain shattered by their memories of the dead and dying and wounded. Men who served as grim accountants of the dead in graves registration and never fired a shot were profoundly affected by their nightmare task of filing the dead.

For the combat soldier, relentless guerrilla warfare caused isolation and months of jungle combat with an unseen enemy. Above all, the soldier did not know who the enemy was. The farmer by day was the soldier by night; the smiling mamasan was often a Viet Cong sympathizer. Soldiers in the field lived in a constant state of nervousness. No civilian could be trusted.

In heavily Viet Cong-controlled territory, killing civilians was hardly unique; many, including children, were armed enemies. The dehumanizing endemic to warfare had begun in boot camp when GIs were taught to "waste gooks and dinks."

In order to make civilian death acceptable, "the mere gook syndrome" prevailed. Phrases were invented to take the place of death. Instead of someone being killed, he was "wasted." (This inventiveness is common in war. In *All Quiet on the Western Front:* "When a man dies, then we say he has nipped off his turd. That keeps us from going mad; as long as we take it that way, we maintain our own resistance.")

In World War II it was Japs and Nips; in World War I it was Huns and Krauts. When an enemy was "wasted" in Vietnam, he or she was "merely a gook anyway." After seeing buddies led into ambush by villagers, after seeing them slaughtered, many soldiers retaliated. *Breaker Morant,* the brilliant Australian film about the Boer War, in its way does more to explain Vietnam warfare than an overblown extravaganza such as *Apocalypse Now.*

"It's a new kind of war, for a new century," says Australian officer, Harry ("Breaker") Morant, just before he is executed for killing civilians who had mutilated his best friend. Boers invented a new word for the men and women civilians wearing no uniforms, who stealthily and persistently fought the enemy: "commando." "They are people from small towns, they shoot at us from paddocks. Some of them are women, some of them are children, and some of them are missionaries," says Morant.

The rules of war did not apply: "We fought the Boer the way *he* fought us."

Sixty-five years later, the same issues as those in *Breaker Morant* were examined at many trials of Vietnam soldiers: in a remote guerrilla war, where the enemy wears no uniform and plays by no rules, where ambiguous orders come from deskbound officers remote to the realities of that kind of warfare, where does combat end and murder begin?

Seventy-one Americans were convicted of murdering Vietnamese noncombatants. Thousands more tell of having to fire on villages or of not being sure who they killed. The most extreme case was that of Lieutenant William

Calley, convicted of systematically rounding up civilians and gunning them down by the score. Many veterans insist My Lai was an aberration, others say it was not. Other cases were more ambiguous, conflicting, and, ultimately, heartbreaking for many of the young grunts who were, truly, "following orders."

Another difference was the attitude of the public toward Vietnam's carnage. Daily television coverage was in stark contrast to the highly censored coverage of World War II. For example, the first published photo of a dead American World War II soldier was not until 1944—a warrior face down in the sands of New Guinea. In this war, Americans were treated to pictures of Vietnam marines of the "Zippo brigades" torching hooches, sending out napalm's fiery flare. Many Americans, viewing such grisly realities of war from the remoteness of their living rooms, concluded that the men in Vietnam were somehow morbidly different from those warriors of the past. This is, of course, untrue.

Americans, steeped in the worst of Vietnam's war—the atrocity trials, the hamlets leveled—knew far less about the marines, for example, who risked their lives to help Viet Cong-surrounded villagers.

The hatreds of war are difficult to understand when viewed from the safe morality of civilian life. Listen to Anne M. Auger, a former nurse in Vietnam: "The only time I've ever felt hate and rage enough to murder was when I was expected to treat an injured NVA [North Vietnamese Army soldier] who had just *killed* several GIs. I couldn't go near him, or touch him, or treat him because I knew without a doubt that I'd put my hands around his throat and *strangle* him. This intense emotion scared me to death." Now, a decade later, she says, "I'm *still* scared of experiencing it again. I had tremendously conflicting thoughts: 1. I *hate* this man. 2. I want to *kill* him. 3. I'm scared of these overwhelming and almost uncontrollable feelings. 4. I am a nurse: I vowed to help *all* sick people. 5. I must be worthless as a nurse because I can't bring myself to help this patient—and worthless as a human being because I want to kill another."

This from a good Catholic young woman.

"War changes men's natures," says the lawyer, pleading for the three soldiers in *Breaker Morant.* "The barbarities of war are seldom committed by abnormal men. The *tragedy* of war is these barbarous acts are committed by normal men in abnormal situations. . . ."

Off the field of battle, back home, soldiers have time to reflect. After World War II, sleepless nights and doubts came to young men once taught "Thou shalt not kill."

However, public attitude played a major role in expunging traumatic memories. Dr. Jack Ewalt, the VA's chief psychiatrist, counseled World War II veterans. They spoke of nightmares, of bombing villages and knowing they had killed civilians. Dresden and countless lesser horrors lingered. But everyone was telling them that they were heroes. Buying them beers at the club or tavern. Small town car dealers saved the best cars "for the boys when they came home." Pretty young women were hugging them in the streets. If they ever hinted that they might have done something wrong "over there," they were bathed in the approval of home. Ewalt marks this as a major, significant difference for Vietnam veterans. "Those poor suckers were taught to fight and then yelled at for it."

Unrelieved combat was another significant difference. In World War II, the Marine "Battle Cry" Division was in the South Pacific for three years—but in combat a total of six weeks. Tarawa was described as a seventy-nine-hour, brutal, mad moment in history. But those who made it out, as James Webb, author of *Fields of Fire,* said, "could go down to Australia. They could get drunk, get laid, could refurbish, could become human beings again." (In Europe, however, some troops spent long periods of time under battle conditions.) In Vietnam, although some soldiers saw almost no action, many in the Marine Corps operated continually—often in the field for eighty days at a time.[6]

A major anger comes from the betrayal veterans feel at the government for the kind of war they were asked to fight—a war of "attrition" with no fixed goals for winning. Hills were taken at great cost of lives and then abandoned. There were free-fire zones where you could kill everything—and zones where you couldn't kill at all.

In San Diego, Larry refuses to give his last name. He skirts every issue, plays verbal games for hours. Then at 2 A.M. he pounds at my hotel door to tell me he is sorry and then disappears again. Larry is brilliant, with two master's degrees collected since his return from Vietnam. He can talk in scholarly flights of fancy with the former chaplain who works with him at San Diego's Vet Center. Yet he is able to sustain only marginal jobs, such as selling fish or being a short-order chef. Larry never removes his dark sunglasses. "I'm getting better," he says with a soft smile. "I used to wear hats all the time."

After much patient waiting, there is, finally, one small breakthrough to Larry's feelings. He talks of Khe Sanh and how the Marines took it and held it for days and how friends were killed there. "And *then* they *abandoned* it. *Those fuckers abandoned it!* We took it, we won it, we died there, and then those fuckers abandoned it. That's what our lives meant to our government."

Disillusionment with the country's leaders runs deep. In one major study, 76 percent of the Vietnam veterans agreed that "Our political leaders in Washington deliberately misled the American people about the way the war in Vietnam was going."

Above all, body counts became a perverted measurement for victory. They were often inflated, faked, or served as an incentive for further, needless killing. The common saying was: "If it's dead, it's VC."

Vietnam grunts and groundpounders tell terrible, demoralizing stories: about officers pushing for success in the form of more body counts, of charging on when there were no goals anyone could possibly understand.

Jack McCloskey, a wounded and decorated veteran leader of the San Francisco Vet Center, says that body counts haunt veterans to this day. "They would set up competition. The company that came in with the biggest body count would be given in-country R and R or an extra case of beer. Now, if you're telling a nineteen-year-old kid it's okay to waste people and he will be *rewarded* for it, what do you think *that* does to his psyche?" Over there it was orders. Now, years later, they're reflecting on it.

The warriors of Vietnam were among America's youngest. The average age was 19 as opposed to 25.8 for World War II.[7] "What did I need with shaving equipment?" wondered one marine when they handed it out at the Marine Corps Recruit Depot at Parris Island. "I was only seventeen. I didn't have hair under my *arms,* let alone my face."

Psychiatrists and sociologists who have studied the Vietnam veteran see their youth as fundamental to understanding why many feel emotionally bereft. At a time when they should have been freeing themselves from parents, making career choices and early attempts at sexual intimacy, learning about *themselves,* adolescence essentially stopped for them. Teenage warriors in Vietnam were denied that "psychological moratorium" of adolescence; the unreal reality of war halted a natural progression of youth to manhood. "Forming a coherent sense of ego identity" at this point is "paramount" to that growth, wrote John P. Wilson, one of the foremost authorities on Vietnam veterans.[8]

There are precedents, of course, for sending the young. The Civil War, as it raged on, took youths barely out of grammar school—and other countries, ravaged by battles on their own soil, have also had their "War of Children." Remarque, in *All Quiet on the Western Front,* tells of the unspoken thoughts of Paul, saying farewell to his mother on his last leave.

"Ah! Mother, Mother! You still think I am a child—why can I not put my head in your lap and weep? Why have I always to be strong and self-controlled? I would like to weep and be comforted too, indeed, I am little more than a child; in the wardrobe still hang short, boy's trousers—it is such a little time ago, why is it over?"

Paul of 1918 and the teenagers of Vietnam were kindred youths.

Something new was tried in Vietnam—fighting the war in one-year hitches, creating "short-timer's mentality." Various phrases were invented for the remaining length of time in the country. A "one-digit midget" was so "short" that he had anything under ten days left.

The idea behind the one-year tour was to make fighting in Vietnam more palatable.

World War II soldiers, once assigned to a fighting unit, could look forward to release from danger only through death or wounds or, hopefully, a cessation of war. This resulted in a sensation of "endlessness" and "hopelessness" so depressing and widespread in its effects that it eventually prompted the high command to institute fixed one-year terms of combat battle. Thus began the controversial "Vietnam Year."[9]

While some World War II veterans called Vietnam soldiers "candy asses," sissies fighting one-year hitches, the experiment proved disastrous in many cases. The prospect of leaving as your year came to an end created enormous tension and fear. Soldiers would do anything to keep from fighting in their final days. Leaving created both joy at going home and a conflicting "survival guilt" as buddies were left behind.

This was the first war in which drugs were plentiful—especially in the later stages. Keegan writes that alcohol has long been "an inseparable part both of preparation for battle and of combat itself. Alcohol . . . depresses the self-protective reflexes and so induces the appearance and feeling of courage. Other drugs reproduce this effect, notably marijuana; the American Army's widespread addiction to it in Vietnam, deeply troubling though it was to the conscience of the nation, may therefore be seen, if not as a natural, certainly as a time-honored response to the uncertainties with which battle racks the soldiers."

James sits in the Coolbreezes restaurant, just a few blocks from the Congress that long ignored special legislation to aid Vietnam veterans. He is seeking help at the Vet Center across the street. "I wasn't on nothin' when I went there, but in Vietnam you had a choice: getting high on hard drugs or hard liquor. Heroin was plentiful, falling out of trees. You see someone get blown away and, hey, you smoke some OJs [Opium Joints, of very strong quality] and, hey, man, that's cool."

Many came home addicted—including the all American farm boy. A Harris survey in 1971 showed 26 percent of Vietnam veterans had used drugs after returning from the war, about 7 percent had used heroin or cocaine, about 5 percent had used heroin. Some 325,000 Vietnam-era veterans had taken heroin since being discharged. One New York City Mayor's Office for Veterans Action estimate: between 30,000 and 45,000 Vietnam veterans in New York are heroin addicts. Of those who saw heavy combat, 24 percent have been incarcerated for a crime, often drug-connected. While some went to Vietnam from backgrounds of violence, many returned from Vietnam changed for the worse, vainly trying to support a drug habit. The voice of a white veteran: "Where did I get hooked? Nam. Why Nam? Cheap stuff, good stuff. Why Nam? I'll give you one word: 'despair.' Now that's a big word, it's damn near the biggest word I know. I got hooked for jollies, to ward off the despair."[10]

It was a loner's war of isolated, private little battles; companies and squads, platoons and five-man teams. No Ikes. No Pattons. "A dirty little war," the saying goes. And it was a loner's return. Unlike other wars, they came home not on troop ships where they could wind down, decompress, be together. They went alone and came home alone. And with the mind-wrenching suddenness of jet-age from here-to-there, from Nam to the world.

From firefight to front porch in thirty-six hours. After all these years, many veterans still shudder at the unbelievable suddenness of it all. "I was killing gooks in the Delta and seventy-two hours later I'm in bed with my wife—and she wonders why I was 'different,' " says one warrant officer. No one both-

ered to examine the incredible psychological trauma this jet return to civilization often created.

And so they came home. Some were eager to embrace the antiwar movement of their peers, growing their hair as fast as they could. Others were
driven to make up for lost time. Some were "still in Saigon"; one veteran, an
eventual Walpole Prison inmate, recalls bivouacking in fatigues and boonie
hats and combat boots with his veteran friends in a Boston park, unable to
move on from their nomadic killing days in Vietnam. Some truly put it all to
rest, as if Vietnam was some distant thing that happened to them. Others
appeared to have put it all behind, only to erupt in anger or violence years
later.

An insidious erosion of self-confidence began for men and women in their
early twenties who had been given enormous responsibility beyond their
years: captains of companies in charge of the life and death of comrades;
college dropout intelligence officers handling networks of agents with the skill
of those many years their senior; nurses in emergency rooms who literally
became assistant doctors in terrible on-the-job crisis training; medics who
learned much about medicine and death and dying.

In many, the confidence to cope in the most difficult of situations was born
in Vietnam. In other wars such skills were rewarded on return. The Vietnam
veteran found that to many doing the hiring his experience was as meaningless as the war. A former helicopter pilot and successful lawyer today recalls
a prospective boss who asked him to take off his coat—to see if there were
any needle tracks on his arm. An intelligence officer who got his master's
degree on return couldn't get a job, so he tended bar in Washington where he
would slip his résumé to influential customers. They all advised him—especially State Department officials—to X out Vietnam. A medic whose emergency room experience more than qualified him for a stateside hospital job
was turned down as soon as the administrator learned he picked up his skills
in Vietnam. "I could see in his eyes that I wouldn't get the job when I
admitted I had been in Vietnam," he said. "It was all accusatory." A nurse
who had saved many lives—had operating room authority beyond her years
—came back to the rank and file of the Walter Reed Army Medical Center
and was given bedpan duty. For years many veterans were underemployed,
working at jobs far beneath their capabilities.

While there is nothing new to ex-soldiers' complaints about being left behind or overlooked, Vietnam, once again, was different in its "we-they" confrontational nature of postwar competitiveness. Vietnam veterans comprised
such a definite minority of their peers that they were both isolated and alienated from the mainstream of their generation who stayed behind.

Time blurs how completely the two themes—the war and the antiwar
movement—dominated the media in those days. One group not explaining

the war was Vietnam veterans. An overwhelming number told the public *nothing* on their return. Not even their parents and close friends.

Their very silence, in fact, profoundly told much about that war and our government's policy. It was a war that was "psychologically illegitimate," to use the term of Dr. Robert Lifton, who wrote one of the first studies of returned Vietnam veterans.

When they did speak out, the two earliest voices came from opposite ends of the political spectrum. The POWs who returned with tales of torture remained for the most part steadfast to our involvement in Vietnam and became accidental heroes in a war that crowned very few. The other group came to the Capitol in 1971 to fling their medals, to protest—Vietnam Veterans Against the War. America learned from this remarkable demonstration. *For the first time in this country's history, men who fought a war marched to demand its halt.* More than 1,000 came. They were mostly the grunts of that war. They spoke of a corrupt South Vietnamese regime, of lack of support by the South Vietnamese Army, of obliterating villages in order to "save" them, of the falsification and glorification of body counts. Many came in wheelchairs and on crutches. Still, they were denounced as fakes by the same Administration that would be disgraced a few years later by Watergate.

They ripped the myths away and many did not want to hear. "My parents told me that if I turned in my medals that they never wanted anything more to do with me," wrote one VVAW member. "That's not an easy thing to take. I still love my parents."[11]

They were dismissed by many—including hawkish veterans—as a fraction of a minority. Yet, years later, I have heard the same views from many veterans who never joined a group but sat silently, only to speak out finally, a decade later. On the other hand, those who supported the war felt that the media didn't want *their* voices. "Early in 1970, I still thought what we were doing was right. I would go on talk shows and no one wanted me to talk like that," said Chuck Hagel. Men like Hagel feel that the media only wanted veterans who would recant.

For years the traditional veterans service organizations wanted nothing to do with Vietnam veterans who had lost their war. In turn, the young band of veteran rebels ridiculed the VFW and American Legion beer drinkers as a bunch of "puss guts."

"The very words 'American Legion' make many of us shudder," wrote Tim O'Brien in 1974. "A place to go to play bingo, to wallow in pride and self-congratulation. But we have no victories to celebrate till we die; we did not win; *our* war, it is said, was not a just war. We are loners. Loners and losers."

Today 750,000 Vietnam-era veterans belong to the 2.7 million-member American Legion and over 500,000 to the 1.9 million-member VFW. The recent dramatic turnabout in attitude by the traditional service organizations is looked on with a cynicism endemic to many Vietnam veterans. "I know why they want us, why they're wooing the hell out of us," says Angel Almedina, who runs a Manhattan Vet Center. "It's because the old farts are all dying out—and they need the money for dues."

A turning point for veterans began in January 1981 as they watched the nation's extravagant euphoria over the return of the fifty-two hostages from the American Embassy in Teheran. Suddenly, all over the country, veterans were expressing rage at the contrast between the hostage homecoming and the silence and hostility that greeted them a decade earlier.

"The return of the hostages stands as the single most important event to benefit Vietnam veterans," contends Robert Muller, a paralyzed former Marine lieutenant and director of Vietnam Veterans of America.

Veterans' adverse reaction to the hostage homecoming welcome startled a complacent country into recalling the *non*homecoming Vietnam veterans experienced. And enough time has passed so that people were able to begin listening. They found that the inequities in treatment of the Vietnam veteran were outrageous.

Many of the minorities and unskilled, promised a trade by the Army, face chronic unemployment today. Wounded veterans were saved in the field often to live a half-life at home; unemployment for them was more than 20 percent. GIs returned when times were hard and jobs scarce. "Veterans' preference" was often not enforced and even then was being challenged as unfair to women by feminists. For Vietnam veterans, because of inflation, the GI Bill was greatly inferior to that for World War II and Korean veterans.

There is a pervasive myth that Vietnam veterans are crybabies, asking for special programs—such as readjustment counseling centers—not afforded past GIs. But, in fact, there was extensive treatment available for World War II GIs who returned with war neuroses. Congress eagerly passed laws after World War II providing psychiatric counseling, both federally administered and community-based.

By contrast, Vietnam veterans sought help for years. It took Congress a full decade after they had returned to fund a handful of readjustment centers—and this is in an era when psychiatric help is widely recognized and practiced.

After Vietnam, Congress, mirroring the public's attitude, treated the veterans' special needs with consummate indifference. Once again, the divided generation played a major part in that response. World War II veterans often capitalized on their war records to win elective offices. However, the vast majority of congressional members who comprise the Vietnam Generation were the ones who *didn't* go. In 1981, of the eighty-two members born since 1942, only a handful had any service. Just five saw combat. (A half-dozen more joined them in 1982 when they were elected to the House.) For years there was no Vietnam veteran constituency pushing for readjustment counseling or Agent Orange studies.

A few years ago, Agent Orange was so unfamiliar to most that when veterans complained of lack of treatment for symptoms allegedly caused by the defoliant that rained on Vietnam some thought they were saying, "Asian Orange." After years of ignoring the issue, in a turnabout, Congress unanimously passed a bill in 1981 calling for preferential treatment in the VA of those who feel they are Agent Orange victims. (The "Catch-22"—there always seems to be one—is that the VA had next to nothing in the way of treatment and is staffed with people who resist the idea that there are any problems due to Agent Orange exposure.) Today Agent Orange remains an incendiary issue that the government prefers to duck.

In 1974 the Educational Testing Service, Princeton, New Jersey, reported that our national newspapers—and the editors and journalists who staff them —had decided that veterans did not make "good copy." One Washington editor said, "Veterans are not sexy. Who cares?" In 1946 popular magazines printed over 500 articles about veterans. In 1972 they printed fewer than 50.

Books on Vietnam were not selling in the seventies. This was not unique. For example, the great literary outpourings about World War I—moving and enduring accounts of man confronting death in battle—did not come until a full decade following the war. It is perhaps only at a distance that people can read of such horror.

Still, there may be another reason why the Vietnam veteran was generally buried by the mass media. Most Vietnam Generation reporters and writers in the mid-seventies were not the ones who went. I have known editors, whose sons went to Harvard and protested the war, totally unconcerned with stories about veterans. Today there are the beginnings of change. Both the public and the press seem to want to understand better what the veteran is all about. And more and more veterans are moving into positions of power in business, politics, and the media.

Today, as veterans are becoming more vocal, more listened to, there is one disturbing backlash. In their attempts to deny, to prove that they have no problems or to *remove* themselves from any taint, some veterans vociferously attack other Vietnam veterans who seek psychological help or remain antiwar.

As just one example of how statistics are used by groups to prove differing points of view about veterans, conservative members of Vietnam Veterans Leadership Program (VVLP), who seek to change the image of veterans and cast Vietnam as a noble cause, emphasize that two thirds of the men who served in Vietnam enlisted. That figure is misleading. Studies and individual interviews show that time and again, men enlisted *after* they were drafted or with the draft breathing down their neck, in the hopes of getting a better assignment.

The VVLP also contends that volunteers accounted for 77 percent of combat deaths in Vietnam. If they take the *Army* statistics alone—without adding the Marines, more than 90 percent of whom enlisted—the view drastically changes. In 1969 Army draftees were killed in Vietnam at nearly double the rate of nondraftee enlisted men. Draftees comprised 88 percent of infantry riflemen in 1969, while first-term regular Army men comprised 10 percent. The remaining 2 percent were career Army men. Over five years in which Americans were engaged in combat through March 1970, draftee casualties ran 130 per 1,000 as compared to nondraftee casualty rates of 84 per 1,000. At that time, William K. Brehm, Assistant Secretary of the Army for Manpower and Reserve Affairs, said, "We couldn't come anywhere near the 5,000-man level [of men with hard-core combat skills] a month without the draft."[12]

Today the media are blamed—for sensationalizing, distorting, or wanting to make veterans a new pitiable crowd. One veteran railed in a letter to the editor about the "liberals" whose "intent is to turn us into another welfare constituency. Your best bet, pity the vet. 'We are heroes' only if we express our guilt."

Veterans shewdly point out that many of the psychiatric and sociological studies of veterans are conducted by men their age who didn't go. Some do have an antiwar bias to protect that undoubtedly skews some of their findings. "The men who fought in Vietnam are being looked upon as victims, often by the very sort of people who reviled them—liberal columnists, actors and actresses, academics, the usual crowd who need some oppressed group to pity and champion," wrote Caputo. "Unfortunately, some veterans are falling into this sentimental trap. Having been denied the laurels due victorious heroes, they are clutching at the sprigs of sympathy offered the victim. . . . Most veterans, though, reject this course."[13]

While I understand the anger that Caputo, a Marine combat veteran, feels, I think he is painting an incorrect picture of America's response to veterans. If anything, I see not pity but still far too much indifference.

In 1980 a survey on public attitudes toward the Vietnam War conducted by Louis Harris and Associates indicated overwhelming public support for veterans. The public felt the war was a decided mistake, but did not hold the warriors responsible for either the war or its consequences. What is more, the public's feeling toward those who actually served in Vietnam was, after the fact, "especially warm"—and *on a par with their feelings toward veterans of World War II and Korea.* Asked to name the two or three most important aspects of the war on Americans, 33 percent cite harm done to veterans. The most striking of the public's *volunteered* statements about the effects of the war focus on the price paid by veterans. There is a high level of concern, in terms of both direct effects (death and disability) and indirect effects (being badly treated by the rest of society and having employment, psychological and family problems). Blacks are much more likely than whites to cite concerns for veterans (44 percent to 32 percent), as are women more likely to than men (37 percent to 28 percent). Researchers detected a growing sympathy for veterans. Thus, while 49 percent of the public felt in 1971 that "Veterans were made suckers, having to risk their lives in the wrong war in the wrong place at the wrong time," that number jumped to fully 64 percent in 1980.[14]

Veterans may bristle at people having "sympathy" for them or feeling they were "made suckers" in a war that went bad, but there is little indication that these attitudes translate into "pity."

However, giving lip service to concern in an attitude survey does not translate on a large scale into active support for veterans' programs or benefits.

America needs to cure itself of the post-Vietnam syndrome—so often attributed only to veterans. The way to do that is by "reconciling the schism created by the war," writes Caputo. That schism he sees between "moral conviction, as represented by those who *resisted* the war—and service, as represented by those who *fought* it."

That goal cannot be met by reopening the "tired old Vietnam debate between right and left. . . . President Reagan's attempts to conceal the ugliness of the war under the cloak of a 'noble cause' are as suspect as the left's attempts to present it as a crime on a par with the Nazi invasion of Poland."[15]

His point is a good one. However, I have found in countless interviews that it is important for everyone to walk through his beliefs on that war—not for the sake of debate but for catharsis. Only then can they better understand one another.

Ideological and political arguments are more than just historical musings for most veterans. They go to the heart of their sense of alienation or, at least, separation from others.

Both veterans and the American public-at-large strongly cling to the comforting view that we could have won but that "Our troops were asked to fight in a war which our political leaders in Washington could not let them win." Forty-seven percent of the public agree—and 72 percent of the Vietnam-era veterans do. Moreover, of those who saw heavy combat, the number jumps to 82 percent. The country and the veterans remain deeply divided on this central issue, however. Some 37 percent of Vietnam veterans believe that they were asked to fight in a war we could *never* win. (The American public percentage is roughly the same, 38 percent.)[16]

Today, as the country turns more to the right, as hundreds of billions are being spent on what many analysts view as useless weaponry, right-wing revisionists are trying to turn Vietnam into a "noble cause." Some veterans scoff at the idea: "You can't sell bullshit twice." Others feel revisionism has considerable appeal to a country still licking its wounds. We seem to be a nation overly willing to forget—even as we barely take the time to try to comprehend our last sad little war.

Vietnam and its generation are too important for the country to ignore. Vietnam was a turning point. Reverberations of Vietnam will be felt by society for the next fifty years, as the Vietnam Generation moves, once again, into a position of prominence. By sheer numbers alone, they will move on to become tomorrow's leaders and followers. They, of course, present no single voice, but they are a large voting bloc; politicians who can capture their majority will derive a strength in numbers.

"The shaping experiences for this next generation of American leaders were the civil rights struggle and the war in Vietnam—or, more precisely, the effort to end the war in Vietnam," wrote David Broder in *The Changing of the Guard.* Broder theorized that tomorrow's leaders were forged largely in the antiwar movement. Veterans feel—and rightly so—that they have been unwisely overlooked in such a judgment. Already there have been battles for political appointments between nongoers and veterans. A Senate hearing over the appointment of Tom Pauken, now director of Action, is a case in point. Pauken, a Vietnam veteran, was in Army intelligence. There was a legitimate question as to whether a former intelligence officer should run the agency that oversees the Peace Corps—long vociferous in its attempts to protect itself from any CIA involvement. However, Pauken and his forces charged that his antagonists were "antisoldier." The other side—composed of Senate assistants of the same age who had *not* done any service—scoffed "Hogwash." However, the "we-they" antagonisms were palpable. After all these years, both sides had difficulty understanding the realities of the Vietnam years that the other tried to describe.

How this generation is going to play out is an imponderable, however, worth exploring. The questions are many. As the country turns more to the right politically and militaristically, what role do the Vietnam veterans play? The VFW and American Legion of the past have long pushed right-wing causes. Will the Vietnam veteran, as he grows older, be different than those of past wars? Will the divisions ever heal?

At least for now there seems to be one legacy. America's upper middle class did not fight the Vietnam War. Its working class may be tomorrow's defectors. The lessons of Vietnam veterans—unemployment, psychological problems, health problems—are cruel, a far greater deterrent, some believe, than any incentives the government can push for signing up a whole new generation for the next big one.

Many of today's skeptics, concerning United States involvement in other countries, are Vietnam veterans and their families. Efforts to reinstate the draft, our huge defense budget, military advisers in Central America, marines dying in Lebanon and Grenada, hard-line attitudes toward Russia, talk of "winnable" nuclear wars make the lessons of Vietnam as current as tomorrow's headlines. This time the disaffection may well come from the blue-collar world. Middle-class parents of teenage children, facing unrest in the world, may not have the less privileged bailing them out the next time—no matter how "immoral" the next conflict might seem. A draft would surely have to be more equitable than the last.

Working-class youths now share a cynicism with their Harvard counterparts. A shiny silver-and-blue Air Force recruitment poster hangs on a subway wall in working-class Dorchester. The poster is as marred by graffiti as those outside Harvard Yard. JOIN THE AIR FORCE AND SEE THE WORLD beckons the slogan. Across it, in black, is scrawled: AND DIE YOUNG.

Already, nearly half a million young men have not registered for the draft —a felony that could mean five years in prison or a fine of $10,000. And 25,000 who have registered have signed a declaration that they will apply for conscientious objector status if a draft is enacted according to antidraft groups. A federal survey of high school seniors in 1981 revealed that 30 percent would try to avoid compulsory military or civilian service if drafted. By 1984, however, the Reagan era had produced a new enthusiasm for the military. Still, that legacy of the sixties—a fear that tomorrow's youth may be asked to fight another unfortunate war like Vietnam—makes many veterans cautious. They relay that caution to their younger brothers and nephews. They regard themselves—and are—among the most patriotic of American patriots. But what many have said signals not the death of that patriotism in their hearts and minds but the death of *blind* patriotism.

The Vietnam War will not go away. Veterans are moving from their sackcloth-and-ashes victim status toward a new militancy. It takes on bizarre forms at times: the bikers, arms ladened with tattoos, in camouflage fatigues, shouting in Senate hearings for their rights in 1981, were tragicomic.

They invoked memories of the most outrageous black militants of the sixties. They were almost ineffective and an embarrassment to those veterans who had made constructive legislative change through years of hard, quiet work. A quiet militancy shows in Vietnam veterans who have made it in the professional world and are now forming networks to further advance other veterans.

It showed in the contentiousness of the air traffic controllers' strike in 1981. One negotiator pointed out that PATCO's ranks were filled with Vietnam veterans. "These veterans were militant to begin with," the labor official said. "Most of them are combat veterans. They have longer hair, they wear Levi's. They think nothing of confronting their supervisors." Vietnam is a big part of their attitude today, he contends, "the bad treatment they got, the unpopular war. They're the ones pushing guys like me into the line."

At first blush, the militant Vietnam veteran often seems an anomaly. His vaguely counterculture attire—the mustache, the beard, the hair over the collar—belies, in some cases, a conservative political ideology. Meanwhile, those who never had to go through basic training have moved into establishment Brooks Brothers suits and sport haircuts in that crisp 1930s look.

Government and management in the future are probably going to have to deal with this Vietnam veteran phenomenon—as they test the waters and fight for what they feel is their due in the aftermath of Vietnam.

As the baby boom children grow into their early forties, the grab for bigger and better brass rings will escalate. Some observers predict that misunderstandings and hostilities left over from the sixties may give that competition a cutting edge. Many a veteran, for example, feels a deep satisfaction at besting some yesteryear draft dodger in today's job market.

Ron Simon, a lawyer who now works for veterans' benefits, went to Harvard, protested the war, but came from a working-class background. "I had a lot of resentment against those rich kids." He feels that attitudes still fall along class lines. "There are a lot of sixties' radical chic protesters who are corporate junkies, sitting out in the suburbs, smoking dope and still thinking they are radical because they opposed Vietnam. A lot of their identity is tied up in that, as if they are somehow 'different' from all the other achievers. They're *conservative* on every issue, for Christ's sake, but they've got this vague identity with the 'oppressed people,' left over from the sixties. I think they have a guilt, but they hide it and still hate veterans—or have a continuing distaste for them."

The divisions are not necessarily divisions of animus. Rancor has faded on both sides. For some the division lies solely in the fact that they experienced a vastly different adolescence. They have been denied shared memories. This is, to some extent, true in all wars. A World War II clerk in the Pentagon certainly had no commonality of experience with a marine on Iwo Jima, but there was a shared common goal.

There are all kinds of permutations of friendship today; draft dodgers and veterans are roommates, women who protested the war are married to veterans. A cultural affinity and shared attitude comes with being a part of the same generation—until Vietnam surfaces and then old differences collide.

Some nongoers say they feel embarrassed and awkward about talking to veterans. Yet, in my experience, even veterans who believed they were mistreated or that we could have won seek no revenge.

Veterans, for the most part, simply want to be recognized as having made great personal sacrifices in good faith. That is definitely one quality they share with veterans of previous wars. Acknowledging it is long overdue.

4 Southie and the Rebels

CERTAIN AMERICAN COMMUNITIES HAVE TRADITIONALLY SENT THEIR sons to war in disproportionate numbers. Linked by patriotism and, often, by poverty, the small town Southerner and Northern urban Irish have long regarded it their duty to go to war.

A few years after the Civil War, the South began to construct its marble memorials to the "Lost Cause." Slender shafts topped by tall soldierly figures became the resting place of many a pigeon in village squares, large and small, south of the Mason-Dixon line.

On into the turn of the century, old Confederate survivors would gather and warble in quivering voices, "I'm an unreconstructed rebel!" Still, their ancestors would fight fiercely as part of a united nation—from San Juan Hill to Hamburger Hill. "It gave us no pause to put our men into uniform. . . . Not even when Southern boys boarded transports to go to foreign battle-fields," wrote Katherine Lumpkin, the daughter of a Confederate soldier, at the time of World War I. Patriotism flourished mightily in the South as soldiers from nearby camps glutted their streets.[1]

The spirit continued on into Vietnam—although more reluctantly—and beyond. In 1980 eight men met dramatic deaths in a flaming inferno in the Iranian desert during the abortive attempt to rescue the hostages. Six of the eight were from the South.

Decade after decade the South has given up its young to war. For the poor, military life was a way up and out; for the middle class and the elite, military academies were citadels of respect and honor. Even when Vietnam tarnished the military in many eyes, to die for God and Country was a Southern, flag-waving, honorable sentiment. They were often called "rebels" in Vietnam and some flew their Confederate flags on their tanks. Some were bigoted and dumb and mean. Some were gentle and bright and brave. And they were all over Vietnam.

Their twangs mingled with the sharp accents of the Massachusetts Irish—who also went in disproportionate numbers from such places as South Boston—"Southie."

One cool, sunlit September Sunday in 1981, Southie unveiled a monument—the first monument in the country to be dedicated to the memory of Americans who died in Vietnam with official recognition from the President of the United States and all five branches of the military.

Donnie Turner, Jr., twelve, with his scrubbed altar boy's face, placed a wreath beside the black granite monument in honor of the father he never knew.

His father's history is slim—played football in the Boston Park League, graduated from high school, and then died in Vietnam. His mother Donna became a widow when she was barely old enough to vote. She watched as her son laid the wreath and several thousand friends and neighbors clapped. The sun caught her tears; they glinted like diamonds, coursing down her cheeks.

Widow's weeds came to the young through all wars; Gold Stars were in the windows on such Southie streets as Marine Drive—named following World War II, when every son on that block automatically joined the Marines. Upper-class communities around Boston sent their sons to college and Canada during Vietnam. Southie's working-class sons went to war—as usual.

"Those guys went to Andover for finishing school; we went to Parris Island. It put the finishing touch on the Southie macho mystique," said Thomas Irwin, director of the Boston Police Department planning division and one of the five veterans who spent three years working on the memorial.

Southie's dedication day was one of those Norman Rockwellian scenes—absent from the landscape in the sixties—bands and Marine brass, babies in strollers, and old men in lawn chairs; morning church services and wakelike partying late into the night. Chiseled on the monument: IF YOU FORGET MY DEATH, THEN I DIED IN VAIN. The war itself was not being championed. Over and over, priests and pols, parents and veterans spoke of honoring individual patriotism and loyalty, of honoring the dead, not the war itself.

These are the descendants of Irish immigrants who left their homeland when the potatoes rotting in the fields caused half a million Irish to starve to death by 1847. The Vietnam veterans grew up on tales of Ireland—and in Southie today donations to aid Northern Ireland are plentiful. Raised to be patriotic to the country that gave their ancestors a home meant even going to a war that most felt made little sense.

Southie is a community suspicious of outsiders. There are the bigoted and the pinch-minded, consigned to poverty because they do not put much store in education. And there are others, gentle and caring, and those who have made successes of themselves. Theirs is a clannishness turned ugly at the sight of intruders—as in the volatile, screaming seventies' fight against forced busing. They feel they are misunderstood by the outside world and the press. Still, it is the peculiar paradox of this tightly knit neighborhood that, for all its insularity, it sent so many of its sons 12,000 miles away to a remote and foreign field of battle. It was what you did for a country that gave your great grandmother, God bless her, a roof over her head. The war dead were like family. "In Southie everybody knows everybody. Your grandparents came over on the boat with your friends' grandparents. If your ma got sick, it was automatic 'Come on over for suppah,' " says George Landers, a Vietnam-era veteran.

Eddie, a marine who lost a leg in Vietnam, is fiercely protective of Southie. "We're a fantastic community—Cardinal Cushing came out of South Boston, Speaker of the House John McCormack came out of South Boston. And if our country calls, we're there."

The list of Southie's 25 dead traces the war's history—a huge, terrible bulge in the statistics, when grief came hard and often. More than half—14 of them—died in 1968 during the murderous Tet Offensive. Those 25 deaths spread across many lives—aunts, uncles, cousins, brothers, sisters, grandparents, mothers, and fathers. More than 250 relatives were there to honor those 25.

And so, on the day of the memorial, veterans hung together for old times' sake with their friends from the "cornah." You played baseball together and you got in fights with other gangs and you went to war together. The scene at the monument: thumping drums, Marine band spit and polish, gleaming Corfams and teenage acne, several thousand people clapping. It was a welcome the men, some 200, had never known. Some wore Sunday suits, others work clothes. As they marched through that swirl of noise, the veterans were suddenly four abreast—marching in cadence, remembering it by rote from a long ago time. Some brushed away tears.

Eddie is one of those men who went from Southie; Jerry is one of the men who went from Alabama. They are neither typical or atypical. But the Eddies and the Jerrys are important, for they tell us something about the kind of men who went to Vietnam in *large* numbers and what happened to them. Eddie returned more antiwar than most marines and many Southie veterans. Jerry returned the hard-core anti-Communist he was the day he was drafted. Ideologically far apart, both are bitter blue-collar relics who wear their disillusionment like cloaks.

During the Southie parade, Eddie hung back, far removed from the park's center, standing with his slender wife and two freckle-faced children. It was a different Eddie from the one I had met two years before. In 1979 he was lying on his bed with one leg of his blue jean trailing into soft, flat emptiness below the left knee. I have seen so many of them now, those corduroys and jeans, empty from the knees down—pieces of unfilled material, like pairs of pants on an ironing board, soft and limp and ending in nothing.

Yet there he was, standing tall in the park with his Jackie Coogan visored cap shoved at a cocky angle. His is the jaunty, rolling, side to side gait of a sailor—rather than that of a man whose leg was blown off. Eddie propelled himself on his wooden leg with a furiousness of purpose.

"I saw the old woman that blew my leg off. It was a command-detonated mine. I saw her! When I got hit with the mine, it took the leg, then we got hit with the ambush. I was crawlin' on fire with the willie peter [white phosphorous]. *Just me and a buddy. Everyone else was dead. This one VC come up on me and he looked at me.* Looked *at me. And he shot me in the knee. And I killed 'im. That's what bothered me. If I shoulda. That's the nightmare I have always. He shot me in the knee.* Deliberately. *He looked me right in the face. He had me—and he didn't blow me away. Why didn't he just blow me away? 'Cause I blew him away right afterwards. I feel guilty that he didn't kill me. You know what I mean? I don't feel guilty that I killed him. This fool guy give me a second chance—and it cost him his life."*

It is Eddie's lasting nightmare of Vietnam, that November day when he lost his leg, one of thousands who would lose their legs before they were out of their teens. The pain of third-degree burns on his face and excruciating skin grafts are muted now by Eddie's black humor. Skin from his buttocks was grafted onto his face from the crease by his nose to his hairline. When Eddie gets in an argument, he grins wryly, touches his cheek, and says, "Kiss my ass."

For several days in 1981, Eddie wandered through his hometown and his memories—moments undiluted, even by more than a few beers.

There were irreverence and clarity, wit and bitterness, sorrow and joy in his stories. Remembrances of welfare days, the Job Corps, and the Marines, the excruciating pain of the leg and the burns and skin grafts and the hospital, the crazy antiwar days as a GI in an elite university, the downers of unemployment and stress. The world of a young man with a very bright mind born into a nonintellectual life of poverty.

Eddie was born in the waning days of Mayor James Michael Curley's rule. Boston had just built public housing in South Boston for the Irish poor. Eddie's mother was determined to get into that project. She took Eddie with her to see the mayor and she exposed the neck of her infant son and everyone looked at this red mark that was decorating his neck. "Ach, and do you see what the rats do to pooah innocent little babies? Would ya look at that mahk?" she asked. The family was whisked into the project. The story was handed down through the years and always brought a laugh—for the marks on Eddie's neck were accidentally caused by the zipper of a snowsuit in a hasty zip-up.

Southie produces more priests, nuns, and servicemen than any other community of comparable size in America. Growing up tough is the only way to grow up in Southie. In the old days it was mostly fists; now there are knives and guns and dope in the projects. There is an old saying in Southie; you grew up to be either a priest, a cop or a crook—and some families had all three.

There are the devout, who wouldn't miss daily mass—and there are the loan sharks and leg-breakers, who enforce the unwritten laws of that other world, a *Friends of Eddie Coyle* subculture.

A friend, whose father had a fifth-grade education and who became a successful journalist, explains the order of life in Southie. "The tribal thing is very strong." He is a gentle man, but recalls how "You *had* to fight. It was just a rule of the corner. If you read, if you thought deep thoughts, you had to keep it to yourself. Just had to beat the shit out of someone to survive. And the Army or the Marines were an extension of the corner. The young served because, to some extent, the *system* made them serve. They served because of the discipline of the church. If you were a Catholic, you believed in the mysteries. You accepted them on blind faith." One of those acceptances was a blind loyalty to defending the country.

Eddie pulls the car up near his old project home. Row upon row of flat-roofed, low-slung brick apartments. There is no grass; it is brown dirt in May. There are boarded-up windows. MIKE 'N MARY inside a chalk heart is scrawled on one wall. NIGGERS SUCK—the statement of eighties' racism that decorates Dorchester subways and downtown Boston billboards—is scrawled nearby. Playing children have a County Cork timelessness to their look—round, beautiful faces of freckles and red cheeks and large blue eyes and red hair—giving a lie of innocence to their surroundings. Some sniff glue at nine and by twelve are into heavy drugs. A friend of Eddie's now works to stop the flow of drugs into Southie's housing projects. "Nobody gives a damn because it's here. If it was in Wellesley, it would not be going on," says Eddie. "If it was at *City Point* [a better section in South Boston], it would not be tolerated.

"Some of the best days of my life was here," says Eddie, looking at the project. "That's where Timmy and Kevin lived. They're cops now. When I was on punishment, I'd lower a fishing rod from my bedroom window and my buddies would pass cigarettes up." His eyes sweep the windows. "The first time I ever got lucky was up behind them windows over there. With Coleen."

There is wistful recall of more stable times when his father had a good job with a machinery manufacturer. "He wore a coat and *tie* to work," says Eddie, still with some awe—and they lived in a home of their own outside the project.

Eddie leafs through a photo album. He picks seven out of twenty-eight in his fourth-grade class he knows for sure went to Vietnam. Several were wounded. "One guy's an alcoholic, one's doin' okay, and two are dead."

Eddie's childhood was not without turmoil. His parents fought for years and finally, when Eddie was thirteen, they were divorced. When his father left, the family moved back into the projects, Eddie trundling possessions in his little wagon.

Eddie soon joined the Job Corps and was in the Midwest with other street toughs when a fight broke out in the cafeteria between blacks and whites.

During the brawl, Eddie and some friends ducked out and headed for Detroit. He spent the $100 Job Corps pay on clothes. Black silk shirt, black iridescent sharkskin pants, black suede shoes with Cuban heels, white tie, black leather jacket, and black stingy brim hat. All dressed up, "Like Dillinger," he recalls, laughing.

Any shades?

"No shades." The pause seems a sad one. "No shades. I had beautiful blue eyes in them days."

Eddie returned to South Boston, essentially a runaway. He lived in a hallway in the public housing project, would go to a nearby gas station in the morning to wash his face and hands, and then go to school. When you are a runaway, it is not the time to hook school. You need the school lunch.

He couldn't wait to join the Marines. Eddie was typical of many who went into the Corps seeking a home. A family. Success. Adventure. He came back antiwar, confused, unhappy, troubled. Twelve friends signed up the same day in 1967. "We came back disciples. Most of us are against the war." The fathers, he feels, often maintained the same prewar hawklike mindset. "But some of us kids changed."

At the time, though, he was seventeen and invincible. Eddie *knew* what war was all about. He had seen John Wayne leading his men gallantly in war film after war film, the embodiment of guts and glory, in a darkened theater rich with the smell of popcorn. Eddie was hardly original in his devotion to the gravelly voiced monotoned heroics of an actor who never got any closer to real combat than Hollywood and Vine. As Sergeant Stryker in *Sands of Iwo Jima,* Wayne's personality became merged with the character and Americans found a man who personified the ideal soldier, sailor, or marine. More than twenty-five years later, his military image continued to pervade American society and culture. References to Wayne and his film-made image appear in virtually every book about Vietnam.[2]

It was sickeningly different in real life. Eddie became a demolitions expert who performed the grim ritual of disarming dead American soldiers who had been booby-trapped. "You had to disarm them—because everything was booby-trapped—in order to send the bodies home. We were behind the infantry. We'd go in and soon spot everyone dead. They always left someone just about to go. That scared hell out of us. If you tried to move 'em, if you got too emotional about what you saw, if you grabbed a guy too quick"—Eddie snaps his finger— "he'd be gone." Blown up as he watched, helpless.

"I knew I was gettin' out of there—if I had to kill every one of 'em. But I was a coward. I was gonna kill 'em out of fear." Eddie laughs. "I don't believe in heroes. They felt so guilty about us being there, they gave medals out like candy. Everybody come home lookin' like Georgie Patton. I told one reporter the truth and he didn't believe me. They wanted to write what a big hero I was. A buddy was still on fire and I carried, I crawled with him twenty-five feet. It had nothin' to do with heroism. It was because I did not want to be alone. Everybody else was dead and I was sittin' there cryin'." Eddie spaces his words for emphasis. "And . . . I . . . did . . . not . . . want . . . to . . . be . . . alone.

"The reason I can talk about it now is because I don't believe it anymore. I cannot picture me crawlin' around the rice paddies with a helmet on. It just cracks me up. The whole thing was silly. I remember gettin' mad at myself. Yellin' at myself as we got shot at, 'Are you happy now? Is this what you want? Is it real enough for you now, buddy?' Nobody wanted to know the truth. The truth is, we were kids. We had lieutenants, for cryin' out loud, who still wet the bed. You couldn't get a full grown man to do it. Me, today, wouldn't go."

Eddie is spent by his story and suddenly the voice falls. "It shoulda been called the 'War of Children.'"

Boot camp scenes: some men, of more sheltered backgrounds, remember boot camp with distaste—for the vulgarities, the sadism they feel is masked in the time-honored ritual of teaching discipline and manhood. Eddie thought it all quite amusing and loved the Marine Corps.

"Move it! Move it! Move it! All I want to see is assholes and elbows!" the sergeant bellowed at the disgorging busload at Parris Island. Eddie, half drunk, started laughing. "I'm an *elbow!*" he bellowed back. The marine glowered. "One of them smart alecks. We'll straighten you out."

Eddie remembers the shaved heads, the drill instructors taking pictures out of wallets, saying, "Who is this *whore?* Who is this *pig?*" and it would be a recruit's mother.

"They break you down to absolutely nothing. Parris Island is a science. When the bullets start flying—because of Parris Island—you don't panic so much. The only thing you know is to follow the squad leader."

An aunt, Eddie recalls with a sigh, "called me! How she got through I'll never know."

Eddie seriously hoped someone was dead in his family—because if somebody *wasn't* dead he was in deep trouble. In boot camp, where they were trying to break the recruits into manhood, a phone call from such a relative was a distinct no-no. Eddie hung up. The drill instructor asked with fake solicitousness "Anyone dead?"

Eddie considered lying but knew he'd need a death certificate to get out on leave. He said no.

"The instructor stuffed me in a wall locker. I was bouncin' around in there for thirty minutes." He held nothing against the instructors. "They had seen marines die. They were doing their best to keep you alive." Loyalty to the Marines was everything. One of his instructors would light two tiny flags— the American and the Marine—at the same time. "What are you gonna do?" he asked one recruit. Without hesitation, he passed up the American flag and put out the Marine Corps flag. He passed the test.

"We didn't have your West Pointers, we had *men*. And when marines charge and scream, you can't hear the people gettin' killed beside ya. In an ambush, the Army used to turn around and dig in. And get their ass whipped. The Marines went straight at the gun." Eddie paused. "We'd lose a third. But it's better than *everybody.*"

Still, in another mood, Eddie bitterly remembers a gung ho officer who "sent us into the biggest *massacre.* We took 80 percent casualties. He wanted to take that goddamn hill that had been taken *before* I got to Vietnam."

Nothing captured the flavor as well as Michael Herr's *Dispatches:*

> *The belief that one marine was better than ten slopes saw Marine squads fed in against known NVA platoons, platoons against companies, and on and on, until whole battalions found themselves pinned down and cut off. That belief was undying, but the grunt was not—and the Corps came to be called by many the finest instrument ever devised for the killing of young Americans . . . entire squads wiped out (their mutilated bodies would so enrage marines that they would run out "vengeance patrols" that often enough ended the same way), companies taking 75 percent casualties. . . . And the grunts themselves knew: the madness, the bitterness, the horror and doom of it. They were hip to it and, more, they savored it. It was no more insane than most of what was going down and often enough it had its refracted logic. "Eat the apple, fuck the Corps," they'd say. They got savaged a lot and softened a lot, their secret brutalized them and darkened them and very often it made them beautiful. It took no age, reasoning, or education to make them know exactly where true violence resided.*
>
> *And they were killers. Of course they were: what would anyone expect them to be? It absorbed them, inhabited them, made them strong in the way that victims are strong, filled them with the twin obsessions of Death and Peace, fixed them so that they could never, never again speak lightly about the Worst Thing In The World . . . And naturally, the poor bastards were famous all over Vietnam.*[3]

Eddie was one of those marines who was in the Central Highlands, during the bloody days and nights of 1968, for seven months, until a little old lady detonated a land mine. He was up there with the other baby-faced kids with hard messages on their helmets: BORN TO LOSE; BORN TO DIE; BORN TO KILL; HELL SUCKS. One photo of Vietnam shows a stack of helmets of the dead. On the top helmet, in white paint, is scrawled: WHY ME? Eddie put a bull's-eye on his helmet. A faded telegram pasted in his scrapbook tells about his lost leg and "second- and third-degree burns on the hands, arms, and face," burns on 60 percent of his body, and how he was not expected to live. Next to it is a letter from one of the friends who remained behind: "We got the lady who blew you up."

Eddie was given an American flag because they thought he had died. "I did die. I know it, for a few minutes. I felt comfortable and content, in another world. I was in a coma like, but I could hear the nurses sobbing, 'He's only a baby.' The priest started doin' his mumbo jumbo and I wanted to yell, 'Get away from me!' I was an altar boy and I knew he was giving me the last rites.''

For months life was a morphine and Demerol haze, but through it all Eddie knew he had lost something precious in Vietnam—an extraordinarily common loss among many veterans—a sense of caring. Now he was suffused with an unfocused violence.

He comes up with a classic Catch-22 phrase. "Everyone became a little nutty over there—in order to save your sanity. I seen marines dismembered. You're with a guy one minute, talking about his girl or somethin', and the next he is blown up, next to you, all over you. To kill just takes a piece out of you. I remember standing around in a village, all of us laughin', just laughin' our heads off while some villager is dying. We were animals. You can't believe this is you, but it is. There were a lot of little My Lais, believe me. I never found people who got off on killing. I know people who were involved in atrocities, but they never got off on it. It was a spur-of-the-moment thing, where they had just killed someone who was close to you. Everyone in the village would deny the enemy was there and then maybe you'd just kill somebody.

"When you come home you feel like everybody you touched turned to shit. I forgot how to cry. I just buried my best friend in 1979 and I couldn't cry. I knew how before I went to Vietnam," says Eddie plaintively. After thirteen years, the dam broke, finally, in 1981 when a son was born. His first tears, this time of joy, in over a decade. They were long, hard years—hospitals and school, odd jobs and fights, Brownie Scout leader and loving father, a readjustment that still goes on but has vastly improved.

His anger and violence alienated him. "When I was in the hospital, I did crazy things. Burned my brother with a cigarette 'cause he wouldn't get me a beer. Threw urinals at the nurses. I was nervous and depressed. I was loaded up on Demerol for nine months. When they tried to taper me down, they'd say, 'Hey, we think this kid's addicted.' Those fools! I *knew* this kid was addicted.''

His nervousness, after months of guerrilla warfare, lasted for years. "I still can't pass out in bars like I used to—I'm that paranoid." Sometimes his depression so enveloped him that he stayed in bed for days on end.

Rage, rather than pity, got him through. "You were better off with your anger. My friends were cruel. Stole my crutches. The best friends in the world. They didn't pamper me."

During a family crisis when the doctors refused him leave because he was so ill, men in the ward took only half their medication and squirreled it away for Eddie to use during his breakout. They stole a pair of crutches and scratched together $26 for his bus ride home.

"When a cousin got married, I did the most heroic thing I ever done. I stole out and had to go down that aisle with no leg—on crutches—just months after I was back. They had a chair for me, but I said no and knelt for forty-five minutes on one knee."

Eddie's next stop was an elite Northern liberal arts college. "I had no business bein' there," he says with a deep chuckle. "I had to carry a dictionary in my back pocket, just to understand the conversations."

They must have been incredibly raw and obvious intruders, the young blacks and whites, some of them veterans, who, like Eddie, came on campus as part of an Upward Bound program in 1970, right at the time when the university was an SDS stronghold.

The hilly tree-shaded campus in Waltham, Massachusetts, was going through "unrelieved nightmare of student disruption and growing faculty unrest." This institution of academic excellence was described as a "veritable wunderkind among American colleges." It became one of the first major universities to admit substantial numbers of educationally and financially deprived black and white students. In 1969 seventy black students took over one building for eleven days. Whites joined them and a relentless pursuit for unmet demands was under way—through vandalism, class disruption, and intimidation of students and professors. In the spring of 1970, the National Student Strike Information Center—a clearing house for information about protest activities around the country—was set up there. The notion that the university became a breeding ground for violent radicals spread after a student, an ex-student, and another, deeply involved in the strike center, were allegedly involved in a bank robbery, terrorist activities, and a killing. One of the arrested stated they belonged to a radical group that had declared war on America.[4]

Into that maelstrom limped Eddie, among a handful of Vietnam veterans and some inner-city blacks for a remedial program.

"All the sudden, the professors built their classes around us. They were trying to discuss intellectually a war." The laugh is derisive. "You know, to discuss logically an illogical situation. One buddy, Bobby, was trying to explain about Vietnam and why all the tragedies had happened. And he says, 'Well, the gooks come over the hill . . .' "

The professor admonished him for calling Vietnamese "gooks."

"Bobby was a pisser. He says, his voice full of wonder, 'That's what we call 'em! They were just "the gooks." They were the enemy.' And he got laughed at." He adds, "They used to laugh a lot because we didn't have the vocabulary of the kids from Scarsdale.

"Some of those kids were real radicals. They wanted me to sell guns to them! I said, 'I don't sell guns.'

"The kids had all their flags flyin'. They had their Black Panther flags flyin', they had their peace flags flyin', their NLF flags flyin'.

"I was totally against the war, too, and I never bothered anybody's flag, but the more they pushed left, the more the other guys had to push right. They used to get on us—and some of the Israeli students—about what it was like to kill. And they called me 'baby killer.' I had nothing against the kids who resisted and went to jail or Canada. They did what their conscience told them. Who was the hero in that miserable war? But I didn't think these college kids had a right to say things to me when they didn't even know what 'antiwar' was. Anybody who has ever seen war would be antiwar or you're not a human being."

One day on campus, Eddie told a student to take an American flag patch off the seat of his jeans. The student said he was against the war. "So am I," said Eddie, "but there's other ways of doin' it. A lot of mothers that raised kids until they were eighteen don't have no kids anymore. They only got flags. That's all they got left of their kids." The student apologized.

Some of the student radicals were livid about Eddie's American flag that flew from his window high on the hill—the flag the marines gave him when wounded.

"They said it was against the law to fly an American flag twenty-four hours a day unless the flag is illuminated. I said, 'Okay, you sons of bitches.' I went out and bought the biggest floodlight you ever saw. All that night this sucker blazed. You could see it all over Waltham.

"That got 'em even madder. I came back from class one day and found my flag ripped down off the window, with coffee, urine, and louies on it." Louies? "Spit. I'm sorry. I should translate."

After the flag was trashed, Eddie's crowd bribed some keys to the room of the student ringleader, creeped in at night, held him down, and gave him a haircut. "It's pitch-dark and we had half his hair gone before he even woke up," says Eddie, laughing at the remembrance of "this silly-lookin' thing with half his hair to his waist, the other cut off to the ears."

Today the flag forms an unconscious montage to war in his bedroom, folded neatly beside the rifles and the crutches.

The wooden leg goes up and down on the gas pedal, a leg as hard and unyielding as a baseball bat, encased in argyles and loafers. Eddie was on his high school track team. (The Irish of Southie took pride in being star athletes who beat other city teams.) Sometimes he dreams that he is running in Columbia Park again. "I still want to feel the wind blowin' through my hair. In the Marines I could run forever. I used to think that someday there would be a medical breakthrough and they would come out with a better prosthetic. Then the day my son was born, I said, 'Well, it may not be me, but another Eddie is gonna go runnin' in Columbia Park.' "

He drives to his small house in a working-class town outside of Boston. Bikes and trucks are in a corner of the dining room. On one wall, Eddie's one daughter smiles in her first Communion photo, with veil and tiara. His son stares from a snapshot at his first-year birthday cake—made by his father. Cowboys and Indians play on the icing. One day the ex-marine taught his daughter's friends "how to fold the flag," he says solemnly.

The front door bursts open; his daughter Mary is home from school.

"Great news, Dad!" Eddie puts his arm around her and studies her report card. Six B's and two C's. "Alllllright!"

Her father's handicap has not always been easy for Eddie's daughter. "Mary goes crazy with the fighting when the kids tease her about me hopping on one foot." If there is a school activity, such as ice skating or roller skating, her father automatically refuses to go. His son, in imitation, hopped before he could walk. His daughter feared that when she grew up she would automatically lose a leg.

For years after Vietnam, Eddie had a hard time adjusting. A job with the Post Office didn't last long. "They had me unloadin' bags off trucks. I had a letter from the hospital sayin' I should have a sittin'-down job, but the supervisor didn't do nothing about it. I slammed him up against a mail chute once and got fired for 'bad attitude.' "

There were years of several painful leg operations and recurring sessions with less-than-understanding VA authorities. "I have to go in for reevaluation —to see if my leg is still worth 60 percent disability. I keep telling 'em, 'It ain't gonna *grow.*' All we want is our benefits. We gave them those years to kill us and if we made it back they promised us certain things. I never know when the leg is gonna act up on me—and I would end up fired—so I have to keep the disability. Sometimes my burns flare up. Sometimes my emotions. I just see a lot of tragedy out there that could be avoided. I see 'em lying and gearin' up for this, that, and the other thing. We're gonna kill our youth again over in the Middle East if we're not careful," said Eddie, two years before marines on the peacekeeping force were killed in Beirut.

Yet, for all the turbulence of these post-Vietnam years, Eddie feels, "If I had come from any other place except Southie, I wouldn't be as well-adjusted. They refused to make me feel sorry for myself. We're a proud, proud community. You could be a kid from the projects, blown up and hurt, and there would be Speaker McCormack, gettin' in touch to help right away.

"My kids and my wife had a lot to do with getting rid of bitterness. You need a wife, someone there all the time, even when you're being a jerk. My wife stuck with me long enough to let me grow out of it."

What would you have done if you had not gone to Vietnam?

"I probably woulda been in jail, gotten in a little juvenile trouble. But I would have ended up a success. I woulda been a police officer, working with juveniles."

I am surprised when I ask Eddie how he sees himself ten years from now and he answers, "Happy."

"If I had a turning point, it's when I went down to the monument for the Vietnam reunion in 1982. I met two guys I had not seen since Vietnam. That was the most positive feeling—the love the veterans still had for each other. The hugging and the kissing and, hey, these are not the kind of guys who go 'Disco Duck.' I hugged more guys than Liberace that day."

He joined some service clubs, mainly to work for Vietnam veterans' benefits and to present a voice for peace. "I've decided to get involved, to make sure it doesn't happen to another group of veterans again. I got nephews to worry about now."

As for his own life, Eddie feels, "If the attitudes had been the same fifteen years ago about Vietnam veterans as they are now, things woulda been different. I woulda finished college. I majored in sociology and wanted to work with troubled children. I could relate to them. I did real well in courses where I didn't have to write. If I coulda passed my papers in on a cassette, I woulda done fine."

Eddie is deeply concerned for the young poor who go into the service today "for their first pair of shoes and three squares a day. I'm tired of seeing the youth singled out for no good reason, no good war.

"We didn't have one person over there who actually had anything personal against the Vietnamese. I knew they weren't comin' down the streets of Southie."

Eddie feels there is much ambivalence about war, not only in Southie but in America. "The whole country's immune. They never seen a war, never smelled a war. That's one thing I'll never forget. The place reeked of death. If parents had ever smelled it, they wouldn't let their kids go to that war or any other unnecessary war.

"In Southie there are some who to this day can't understand why we're complaining, who don't understand how meaningless it was. If you took a poll, you'd probably find that the only thing shitty about that war was that we lost it.

"I feel sorry for the mothers of the guys who died in Vietnam. You can't tell 'em it was a waste 'cause they can't bear to hear that. We should be like Jon Voight in *Coming Home,* telling them that war isn't glorious."

Eddie hopes enough veterans who feel like he does will speak out. "I still think the kids are going to talk to their older brothers. When we talked to the older generation, they told us about World War II. Now I just think, whether they bump into a veteran that is shooting junk in Harlem or what, they're gonna hear 'The government didn't do nothin' for me, man.' Or if they talk to a Vietnam veteran who's made it, he's gonna say, 'Watch out and listen before you go.' If it was another war like Vietnam and my son wanted to go to Canada, I'd drive him.

"My kid brother asked me what the war was all about," says Eddie. "I told him, 'Nothin'. It was a waste. They're still asking in Washington what it was all about.' So he says, 'But you got all blown up,' and I says, 'Yeah.' "

The pause is a long one.

"I told him, 'If you can remember that, then maybe I wasn't a waste.' "

I thought of Eddie as I drove one day down dusty country roads in rural Alabama: there are white-framed churches and deeply furrowed land and, sometimes, drunken-leaning, weathered shacks, instant reminders of the photographs in James Agee's *Let Us Now Praise Famous Men.*

Eddie could not say enough about the Southerners he met in Vietnam.

"That war couldn't be fought without Southie and the rebels and the blacks and the Indians. The rebels were great. I loved 'em. Used to drive 'em right out of their minds. At night we'd be sittin' around and some of 'em were still fightin' the Civil War—and I'd say, 'General Pickett was a faggot.' "

I had been in the South for several days and talked to veterans who are now professors, lawyers, businessmen—and some who have sought adjustment counseling. One of the leaders of a Southern Vet Center told me that most of the men he knows have been deeply wounded by the war. I argued that perhaps he has a distorted view, just as psychiatrists often do, because of his job. I was determined to find a good old boy on my own. I wanted to find the sort of veteran who, the right-wing patriots assured me, were "out there" in large numbers. Someone who was proud of his service and had no problems.

I opened the door of a small town fire department station. Six men stared. I cleared my throat. "Uh, I'm writing a book on Vietnam veterans and I just wondered if any of you had gone or knew anyone who did."

"Jerry did. He's downstairs. Jerry!" yelled one. "There's a woman wants to talk to you about Vietnam."

Jerry agreed to talk but not to use his last name. We sat for hours in the basement of the fire station on a quiet afternoon when no one needed the fire engine.

Jerry stretched back in his fireman's uniform and black boots. His hair waved off his forehead in a pompadour and his sideburns were long, halfway down his cheek. The politeness of his Southern upbringing is an endemic part of his personality as Jerry recounts his story.

He grew up in one of those blink-your-eyes-and-you've-missed-it farm towns and graduated from high school in 1964 at the age of seventeen. "Needless to say, with Vietnam going and the draft popping about like popcorn, I couldn't get a job. They knew I was goin'. I managed to land one job, general flunky in a nitwit little book company long since out of business."

Jerry, a reluctant candidate for war, was drafted at the age of eighteen and a half. "Tell you the truth, ma'am, I wouldn't never join the Boy Scouts."

Had he thought of college? "That's when I made my terrible and worst mistake. My father had long since been dead, but my mother was lucky enough to put back for college. I was a typical nitwit boy, knew all the answers, wanted to see the big city life. I needed the big pickup. College wasn't it.

"I grew up not knowing anything, really," Jerry says with a shrug. "It was hard work on the farm and I didn't understand the opportunity. I'd give anything if I could have it all back—with the knowledge of what I know now. In that day, there was more brotherhood than there is anymore. So when ole John Doe, say, was threw off at the junior rodeo and broke his leg, you cared. We worked sunup to sundown, but it seemed we had more time then." Jerry picked a guitar in high school and lettered in sports, "although I wasn't no

Joe Namath." Southern men have a way of startling listeners by using a predictable macho phrase—and then softening it with a perfectly gentle one. Elvis Presley and Marty Robbins, to Jerry, "had the prettiest voices of the men."

The first hint that Jerry was not going to be easy about Vietnam came next. Vietnam veterans are "kinda in a 'gap' group," he said. "World War II and Korea vets got no use for us. Our youngsters got no use for us. That war was a joke. Who are we? Just a bunch of bums who didn't have sense enough to run. We were brought up to serve our country. After three months over there, we knew it was a goner. I was at my sister's when I got my letter. Sure enough: 'Merry Christmas, how de doo, your friends and neighbors have selected you.' When you're that young, you don't give a hoot. Like goin' hikin'. You don't know what's ahead and you don't give a damn. You had guys like me that thought it was the worst thing you ever went through and then you had those gung ho kinds that would fight rattlesnakes in Mexico."

He remembers basic training at Fort Benning and his eyes stretch wide, recalling: "A breach into reality I never suspected. A horrible shock. Having to say 'Yes, sir' and 'No, sir' politely to people you couldn't stand—and then the physical demands."

Jerry's home was back off the highway on a dusty road, deep in Bible Belt country, with little old country stores and Kudzu vines choking trees and hard scrub pine. In his day it was a wilderness where blacks lived in one area, whites in another, and everyone went to segregated schools.

"I guess I never knew one and I don't really know any today. You say you're from Alabama and some automatically say, 'Ku Klux Klan,' and then you got some good 'uns that didn't think that way. It's agitators and Communists what's caught us in a mess today. All your school mixin'. See, you got your agitators in both groups. You got your 'honky' there and you got your 'nigger' here. Stirrin' it up for the rest of us who just want to be left alone. They haven't corrected the quality of education; what they're doing is destroying."

As for basic: "They trained us to kill without it bothering you and to do it under command without a question. Trained to kick butts and take names later. I was mad at everybody. Mad at the people that sent me, but then I was there and, sure enough, if someone shoots at me, I'm gonna get mad. You find out right quick this ain't playin'. You have in the back of your mind a sense of hope that it's not really all that bad and then you're dumped there. Hatred at my own government." All these years later, Jerry said that as if the revelation pains him. "I don't think anyone who sent us over there had any regard for anyone. It was all based on economy. The waste was unbelievable. You could have fed millions of people on what they threw out. You'd take over an area and leave behind jeeps, tools, clothes, foods by the millions of dollars. What kinda nonsense is that? Things they put in the paper was all ridiculous. You'd read about a particular battle and it didn't even sound like the same place, what they were feeding the public."

Jerry trained at Fort Benning, then Fort Sill, Oklahoma, learning how to man heavy artillery. He was in a howitzer battalion, one of those few units shipped overseas together with their equipment. He was in the DMZ for thirteen months, throughout 1967.

I ask him what happened in those thirteen months. He pauses for a long time.

"There are not enough pages in a book. The nearest thing to hell I lived through. I thank the Lord every day I have limb and life. The things I saw at that age. I feel some of the other wars were worse in force and yet, on the other hand, this was worse because of realizing it was a joke. We were over there losing friends and they were dying for nothin'. Other wars, they had a sense of pride when they stood the flag. These idiots said, 'Pull out!' What a joke. There was a front; in World War II and in World War I there was a line. In Korea they come across a zone. In Vietnam it was altogether different. It wasn't planned to be won or lost. There was no front, just a rice paddy and a bunch of people hoeing and the next thing they're all shooting at you."

Jerry is one of those who wants to believe that all America had to do was blast 'em hard. "Couple of bombers and, wham, there wouldn't be such a thing as war." He is not alone. Many educated militarists believe that without constraints, conventional forces could have leveled the North.

The irony is that Jerry, Bible Belt religious, deeply anti-Communist, who wanted to bomb them to smithereens, talks like the most cynical leftist of the sixties' antiwar movement. It was, he says, all just "economics" and greed of the military-industrial complex. "They didn't have any intention of ending that gravy train. Soon as you took a hill, they turned around and ordered you elsewhere. You turn your back and those little idiots were up the hill again. Lay in a hole and eat dried rice for a whole week just to kill a little ole GI. So we shoot everything flat and move on. If we had gone over to save them from communism and done it, I would not be bitter today, I sure wouldn't. But for that idiot [Nixon] to say we ended the war with peace . . ." There is disgust all over his face.

I ask if he thinks there is anything worth fighting for today. Jerry straightens up, slaps his boots on the floor, and looks as if he has been asked the most insane of questions. "Of course I do! My homeland, my children's right to be free against an idiot like Hitler. Against all Communists. Why of course I believe in a war such as that. But I do not agree to the most powerful country goin' into such a mess as that one was. We shoulda blowed 'em off the end of the sea. That's what makes me so proud of nothin'. I saw them people with nothin'. They didn't have a lot of bread, just a grass hut and dirt floor and maybe an old throwaway can from the military. I felt sorry for them. Now they're under communism. And what about all the people maimed and the guys what died? And their *families?* Somebody owes them something."

No matter what some historians say about Vietnam. No matter the theories that we could never have won—without massive land troops and casualties beyond the endurance of this country—or theories that we should not have been there, Jerry is a student of experience. What embittered him is not some abstract interpretation of what went on but his perception from the field. Ideology aside, there are few veterans who lived through heavy combat who do not feel they were hamstrung in their operations. The stress of guerrilla warfare remains, like a drumbeat, in their memories.

"They was like backstabbers—get you anyway they can. The stress and what-all of that, it was just too much at one time. Too much at that age. You had no peace within your body for thirteen months. You couldn't even relax to go to the bathroom. Weeks and weeks, not able to relax, no rest, no sleep." His voice takes on the tenseness all these years later. Then his head snaps up and there is fire in his eyes. "And then what was galling was that, on R and R you're still in a foreign country. The people hated us so much on R and R. Throwin' rocks at the bus. Taiwan. I was so unused to crowds, people, groups. I didn't grow up like that." Suddenly Jerry is talking in the present tense, as if still there. "Here you sleep, drink, and bathe with ever' national-ity, ever' kind of person. And you're only eighteen. You see a war picture and it wasn't what it was. I wasn't watchin' war pictures much growing up in-nyway. Mostly Roy Rogers."

Jerry emits a long sigh. "I tell you, it was like taking an earthling and throwin' him into space. War, machinery, people, killing, noise and stuff. Your first kill, you just can't believe what you done. 'Oh my God, I hit a village!' " Jerry suddenly whirls, flicks out his arms quick, as if holding a rifle. There is an unerring, sure, quick professionalism to the charade motion. You know veterans are not faking the movement. "You gotta put a stop to a bee that is stinging you, but after, it's such a shock you never forget."

Could some soldiers handle killing easier?

"Say you come out of a ghetto and grow up some macho-type bully or you're nothin' but backwood scum—maybe. Hell, they saw killin' at the moonshine hill ever week. And say you see people, mothers and fathers who are alcoholics, fighting day and night. I suspect they had less problems. In our platoon we had maybe one, two what weathered it a whole lot better'n most. They was generally older and had prior military experience. You thought they were bein' there because they wanted to be. You don't find any drafted against their will that come out in very good shape. Now my brother-in-law's brother is one of them guys. He was a helicopter gunner and don't nothin' bother him.

"Guys like me, growin' up with old teachings and values, one of those old country guys. Sure 'nough, nothing crossed my mind except treating others as you would have 'em treat you. I was never in no unit where wild stuff took place.

"Now I saw and was with the Third Marines. We'd make rendezvous at Camp Carroll. Them guys, as far as I was concerned, was crazy as a bat. We set up two batteries of our battalion base camp for the Marine position and for us to give 'em fire support. Some of them marines had ears. As far as I'm concerned, anyone tote an enemy's ears in his pocket is weird. Them kids is nuts. There'd be not but three of twenty left—and them comin' in singing. Two of 'em tote one and the rest of 'em all dead and they come in singin' the Marine song. Now to me that is dumb.

"We would go into Khe Sanh. A network of ratholes and nothin' but a joke either. We'd be there two, three weeks, lose half the people, fight, fight, fight, and then they pull us out and those goddamn gooks would be right back."

Jerry says, "I'm a faithful admirer and lover of people like Patton and MacArthur. If you'd left 'em alone, there wouldn't be no communism. I'm not condemning the idea that it would take a war to stop communism. I'm not informed enough to render a judgment on El Salvador. I'm only cautious because of what happened to me. If I was eighteen years old, I'd go right over there. But let's not go playin' politics. If we're gonna do it for economic reasons, let it at least be known."

Jerry, Bible Belt Baptist to the core, is a student of the Good Book and feels that mankind is bringing a lot down on himself. "I'm not just waiting on doomsday, but it's wrote in the Book. It says earthquakes in diverse places, turmoil, and bloodshed, all kinds of deviations of sex, greed, and bloodshed all over, and you just look around. Mount St. Helens, earthquakes in Italy, wars everwhere, nuclear bombs at everbody's disposal. You got so many little countries now with so many big ideas. Arabia, you talking about the most nomadic people, what do they know about democracy? They are wild people and, all a sudden, here they are with jillions of dollars and, in a sense, dictating to the most powerful nation in the world."

Coming home was its own nightmare for Jerry. What was it like when he was short? With only a few weeks to go? He produces the first smile in two hours.

"Scared smack slap to death. Ten times more cautious, if that was possible. Fearful, remorseful for the ones you know had a whole year to go and would never probably make it, but gratified that you was almost out. I was nervous as a cat, even until I landed in California. The last thing any military man said was, 'Do not put VIETNAM on your bags or your clothes. There's likely to be little old ladies in the terminal who will want to kill you.'" He looks stunned to this day. "He told us, 'People will hate you.' And they did! It like to kill me.

"There's no way to describe the contempt for everyone I saw. I just made a beeline for home."

Was he treated better in the South? "I was disturbed at some of the things they did at the university, but, as a matter fact, most people was sympathetic and mad as I was. They saw it was just a raw deal for us—in terms of money, taxes, the kids who had to fight it, and theirselves. The fact that they did not never intend to win. That's what I'm still mad about. That we were sold down the damn drain."

Jerry went to a junior state college for eighteen months. "Of course, I didn't broadcast I was a Vietnam veteran. You know, when I was growing up, I trusted you 'til you proved I couldn't. Vietnam reversed that. Now I don't trust someone 'til they prove I can. It was your arts and sciences where you met your troublemakers. As a matter of fact, the football players championed us. They just wanted to kick those troublemakers' butts completely out of school. Them protesters! Biggest majority was a bunch of nitwits. Overeducated. They were programmed and agitated into it by Communist teaching and then you takin' them drugs you just ain't the same. In the unit, you could recruit you up a bunch of folks. Eight would be smokin' pot and, in another section, eight would be drinkin' beer. And some would fall together more. In my group we drank beer. We didn't know what pot was. To this day, when someone says 'Coke,' I think they're talkin' 'bout Coca-Cola."

As Jerry remembers, he becomes very fired-up about the students and begins to view them with monolithic contempt. "They was more subject to this propaganda stuff. They want to shoot us down for going. I hate 'em. I hate 'em for selling out our own freedom. If they don't like it, go to Russia. I couldn'ta went to college knowing I was ducking out of my duty for my country."

What about trying to heal the wounds over Vietnam? What about amnesty?

"That's as gross a thing as I can see. Now, let me ask you, how would you feel if you son was killed over there?" Because of the pardon, he refused to call Carter by name or refer to him as President. "That man was from the South and he let Southerners and everything we think of for ages get tore down by what he does. He doesn't show anyone the South can produce capable men."

However, like many veterans, Vietnam and their experience has softened them on the next generation. "My son, he ain't going to go to El Salvador or any of that junk. My buddy, his son's eighteen, he had a son afore he went and he's real worried too."

It took Jerry a long time to adjust after Vietnam. There was a broken marriage, college when he was too nervous to study, odd jobs for about three years.

"That marriage. That was another horrible mistake from the beginning." How did you meet? Jerry looks puzzled. "Seems, as I recall, someone had a Tupperware party and she happened to be there. Never had no compatibility. We didn't know what the word meant.

"As far as girls went, I warn't no open-minded or rough-and-ready guy in a big school. I was just a big zero. I didn't know nothin' about girls. Now I know it's shared. As much to please her as you. Oh, I'd had that first little ole puppy love and cryin' all night and all, but let's face it, manhood-womanhood, the very idea that a wife should be your best friend, lover, companion, and everything—I had none of those ideas. When I learned about making love, I met a prostitute; same old junk, all that rent-a-lady business. What is that? That's nuthin'."

Jerry met his second wife in June of 1980. He married her the next month. She is young, with a round face and her hair flipped back in blow-dried Farrah Fawcett fashion. They live in a tiny home far into the country with their young son—a home that is sparsely furnished, with handmade book-case, TV, religious pictures on the wall, and the Bible predominantly dis-played. "First time I ever met one of the other sex who thought like myself. She was raised like me. I don't like going out dancin'. I get more enjoyment to go out in the woods, hunting odd plants. She is what I grew up lookin' for. I was thirty-three before I managed to find it."

Jerry worked fourteen months for the Police Department. He never wor-ried, as some veterans did when they first joined the police force, that he might be trigger-happy. "No. I hated it so much. It bothered me so much to do it. First place, it isn't in God's law, except in self-defense. I do like deer huntin' and ducks, but I do it to feed the family, not sport huntin'. I condemn anybody that does that."

By 1981 Jerry had worked eleven years at the fire department, the job he wanted when he took the police job and waited for an opening. I remark to him that, for all his rage, he came out of it well—good wife, good job. There was obvious stability to his life.

"Yes, I remember right well when I come to the fire department.

"It was just about the time I had my nervous breakdown."

The unexpected words profoundly startle. Jerry tries to shed some light on his problems.

"This is brotherhood," he says, looking around the fire department. "A group-type, pull-together situation. I was here one day and just come un-glued. Shaking all inside. Wanted to cry. I went to my captain and he said I had to see a doctor. They ordered this test. It got so bad that ever' time my heart beat, I just knew it was fixin' to quit."

What was wrong? Jerry just looks straight ahead, shrugs. "I was just goin' nuts. I'd be walking down a road and just start cryin' like a baby. Just all lonesome inside."

This was years before delayed stress was identified as a syndrome of emo-tional disorder and applied to Vietnam veterans, years before readjustment counseling Vet Centers. Like many veterans, Jerry blamed his feelings all on himself. He never considered Vietnam the problem.

Nor did the doctors. "They never asked you much questions. Wouldn't talk about Vietnam and they never asked me nothin' about it. I still don't feel that I care to talk about it. I asked the doctor, 'What's the matter with me?' and he said, 'Your mind is not resting, night or day. Your subconscious mind is not at rest at all.' I was just wore out. Woke up tireder than when I went to sleep. I don't think they ever diagnosed the problem."

Jerry spent over $2,000 of his own money, was subject to inhumane shock treatments and the easy cop-out of hospitals who treat patients with emotional problems. He was kept sedated on debilitating and depressing drugs.

An anger wells up when I hear Jerry's story. The obtuseness, the downright stupidity in the way troubled veterans were treated a decade ago, is one of the greatest indictments of our society, the medical profession in general, and the VA in particular. Jerry and countless veterans may have had minimal problems if, earlier, they could have talked over their frustrations about the kind of war they fought and the attitudes of this country toward it and them. At a time when veterans needed it not quite so desperately, coming home from a popular cause as World War II, there was more acceptance and enlightenment that "our brave boys" might need help. Women's magazines, such as *Ladies' Home Journal,* guided wives, mothers, and girlfriends on "how to treat them." But the Vietnam veteran, defeat's greatest orphan, had to go it alone.

Unlike the negative—and incorrect—image that most veterans who seek help are using Vietnam as an excuse, Jerry was among the overwhelming silent majority who refused to blame his war experience. And no one helped him to see otherwise.

How did he get better?

"I really don't know. All I can tell you is, after they gave me shock treatment and all, it didn't make no difference. I never did and still don't have faith in psychiatrists. I'm as dumbfounded and madder than when I went to them."

Jerry says softly, "I might be near death inside, but I'd hide it from you. Just hurtin'—and not knowin' why."

In part, the acceptance of his colleagues went a long way to help. "They didn't make a big joke out of it. You got to figure that is amazin' in a sense. I work with guys here either too old or too young for Vietnam. Very few that's my age. But they just took and understood and didn't ride me."

He seems, mostly, haunted by the killing—particularly since he cannot justify it in his mind with any of the reasons that would make war acceptable for him.

"I tried to beat it for over three years by myself. I didn't even know what or who I was fighting." He speaks of anxiety, of nightmares. "Horrible things. How do you shoot a kid? A thing like that? It don't bother me to slaughter cattle. But you talking about humanity. They have a soul. Somebody's going to have to answer for that. My mother carried me to a Baptist church from the time I was this high," he adds, as a parenthetical explanation of his deeply religious sense of "Thou shalt not kill."

"I guess the worst was to lose a lot of my real close friends. You was much closer over there, even to a black. Of course he was from the South. Went to a different school, but he had that basic God-and-man, brotherhood, you-don't-lie, same country-type upbringing.

"My best friend from Texas—his name was Jerry, just like mine. He was my same age. We were like brothers. Planned to visit and we would have. He was rural. All our ideas was the same. Two kids who know nothin' about life, settin' in a bunker talking. I get up and left and, thirty minutes later, there wasn't nothin' left of him to send home. It took a direct hit from a forty-millimeter Russian-made rocket." His thoughts tumble in one jumbled sentence. "Knowing what you know and were, you hate your government and what it done to you, and then knowing the people back home hate you, and then callin' his momma and dad and knowing only them and you was all that cared for him. That's the awful thing."

How did he mentally cope with it all at the time?

"I really don't know. If I knew the answer to that, I'd be a psychiatrist. I reckon I just went numb. And the rest of you learn to pull together more."

Others withdrew. "We had a pitiful case of a guy slitting his wrist to get sent home." Did he? "Course not. They sewed him up, sent him back, and he was useless to hisself and to us, too."

"What was so bad," Jerry mused, "it was over a girlfriend—not a mother or wife or nothin'. He was from New Jersey. He wanted to be home with her and he just couldn't—or wouldn't—conform.

"He was just in love with a little ole gal and wasn't going to leave her."

Jerry has no idea how his life would have turned out had he not gone to Vietnam. At times he feels trapped in his job. He makes $18,500 a year. "Not near enough, but eleven years is too much to dump or throw away. I've flowed with the time and adjusted to these fellas. I've faded into being with something, stayin' with something. But I've got a curious mind in a sense. There's all kinds of things I'd like to try—woodworking, welding, electricity —and yet, I like knowledge. I'd like to teach, if I had anything I could teach."

He is fascinated by archaeology, likes gardening, likes to play the piano and guitar. "I'd give anything to be out West on a cattle ranch."

I wonder how often Vietnam wells up in his mind these days.

"It's beginning to pass," he says. "Like a first sweetheart. That's the only way I can look at it. It's like a broken leg you got years ago and it still hurts. But it's a long while ago."

His wife has given him a measure of peace.

"She has real compassion for what happened to me. Nobody seems to care except my wife. But she looks upon it as what it should have been."

Jerry stares across the empty firehouse, his brown eyes as wistful as his voice, wistful for the heroics of a time he never knew.

"She looks at it," he says softly, "as if I had fought in World War II."

Part II
Draft and Protest

"Hey, Mr. Draft Board"

BY DAVID PEEL

Hey, Mr. Draft Board,
I don't want to go.
Hey, Mr. Draft Board,
I don't want to go.
There's a war in another land.
We go to fight for Uncle Sam.
We are America—so strong
We don't know the difference from right or wrong.
Hey, Mr. Draft Board,
I don't want to go.

1 Draft Board Blues

IT WAS MAY DAY, 1971, A YEAR AFTER FOUR STUDENTS LAY DEAD IN Ohio and two died at Jackson State. Tens of thousands of protesters, mostly young, mostly students, swarmed into Washington. Antiwar protest had become a spring ritual, practically a part of the curriculum. This time they were in Washington to "shut down the government." Pot wafted from smoking campfires in West Potomac Park where protesters bivouacked. By dawn they sat ten deep, blocking every Justice Department entrance. Whooping, chanting, cheering, they took over the east steps of the Capitol. Chicken droppings were thrown on the Pentagon. Fire hydrants were turned on, spraying water into streets. Garbage cans were thrown into intersections. Cars were pushed from parking places to block streets. Connecticut Avenue near Dupont Circle was a vast trash land. At Connecticut and K, demonstrators held hands and danced, clogging the intersection.

Government workers en route over bridges either cursed or tolerated them. Then came the assault landing. Smoke grenades guided Chinook helicopters carrying 82nd Airborne troops onto the Washington Monument grounds. The bridges—14th Street, Memorial, Roosevelt, Key—were conduits of clogged humanity. Demonstrators, citizens in cars, and soldiers. Four thousand soldiers in all. Four thousand more were on standby. Hundreds and hundreds of police moved in. More than 10,000 demonstrators were arrested—a record even for protest-prone Washington—and herded into makeshift pens at Robert F. Kennedy Stadium. Middle-class parents, by now weary of the ritual, went down to find their children.

It was the madness of it. Never before in our century had there been such furor over going to war. For years the draft had been the cornerstone for the antiwar movement. "Hell no, we won't go!" and "Stop the draft!" chants roared from thousands of young throats. Many who opposed the war saw the draft as a convenient political tool, others also had a self-interest in wanting the draft halted.

May Day did not grind the government to a halt. It was, instead, one of the last-gasp efforts of a waning movement. In early spring of 1970, the Vietnam

Moratorium Committee shut its central office in Washington. The era of mass peace demonstrations was over, they decided. (Cynics would say that, now that Nixon had moved to a lottery system, now that there was talk of ending the draft, students felt less personally threatened and with that came a remarkable tamping down of concern for napalmed Vietnamese. Activists recall a different reason—discouragement. They had demonstrated by the millions and still the war did not die.)

But then came the ferocity of campus reaction across the country to Nixon's Cambodian invasion and the killing by National Guardsmen of four students at Ohio's Kent State University and the shooting deaths of two more at Jackson State.

In the dormant eighties, it is startling to look at the pictures of Kent State —like stumbling over some ancient frieze. A mob of guardsmen, bayonets pointed and rifles loaded, kneel as if ready for combat, facing an NLF flag-waving Kent State student in old fatigue jacket, trailing hair, and headband. In the next frame, students kneel beside Jeff Miller, dying, his mouth open, a thick ribbon of blood trailing along the pavement.

Allison Krause, nineteen, was walking with her boyfriend to class. Her high school graduation photo, the one that stared from national magazines and newspapers, suggests pre-sixties' formal—flipped-up shoulder-length brunette hair, a single strand of pearls on a dark sweater. The deaths of Allison and the other three students were senseless tragedies in a violent time. They were anything but militants. Allison, a liberal arts major, earned good grades, worked summer jobs, helped retarded children. She opposed both violent protest and the war—one of millions across the country who straddled a center line of moderate protest.

On the day before the shooting, Allison passed one of the National Guardsmen. A flower was stuck in the barrel of his rifle. Allison smiled at him. "Flowers are better than bullets." She was not among those who threw rocks and pieces of cement and the standard epithets at the guardsmen hurling tear gas.

At her funeral Allison's father stood by in bitter anger. "May her death be on Nixon's back." The President had called protesters "bums" and Krause's daughter "resented being called a bum because she disagreed. Is this dissent a crime? Is this a reason for killing her?"

And a neighbor: "You have no idea how this has brought the whole thing about the war and campus dissent home to this neighborhood. If someone like Allison is killed, my God . . ."[1]

Kent State shocked the country and created striking turning points. Some movement moderates, who had for some time been disturbed at the shift to more violence—violence of the Weathermen, for example—pushed for more peaceful confrontations. Others began to simply walk away. For other Americans who had held back, Kent State fostered a need to speak out as nothing else in five years of street rage had done. That one could get killed, that there were no blank cartridges on that campus signaled an end to the carefree aspects that coexisted with the clubbings and tear gas of student protest.

In the days immediately following, Kent State and Jackson State rocked colleges across the country—some into more violence, others into seeking more peaceful solutions. One of the ugliest battles took place on the already scarred battleground of the University of Wisconsin. A two-day slug-out with police left scores of injured students. Countless universities were shut down. Ronald Reagan, California's governor then, shut down all twenty-eight four-year campuses for four days—retreating from a vow to keep the schools open "at the point of bayonet, if necessary."

On other campuses, Kent State unified disparate faculty and students. Different universities played out what seems, in the eighties, an incredible Russian roulette game of how to proceed with higher education. In the midst of strikes, suspensions, lockouts, and reopenings, it was hard to know who favored what or why. But a new coalition of moderates, who had always been there but had stepped back from confronting radicals, felt that enough was enough. At Harvard, SDS leaders headed 500 students toward the ROTC building. But this time moderates stopped the rock throwers. At MIT, the chairman of the music department, Klaus Liepmann, spoke at a faculty meeting for the first time in his twenty-three years at MIT. "In Germany great masses of people, notably the intellectuals, remained passive. . . . I feel it is our duty as intellectuals and artists to speak up and to act now." Liepmann got a standing ovation. For the first time, the MIT faculty joined its students in condemning Nixon's war policies.

In 1981 a critically praised TV dramatization of Kent State was a resounding ratings dud. No one wanted to remember yet. Denial once again. At the time there were middle Americans who had bought heavily into Spiro Agnew's rhetoric and lumped all protesters with the anarchists and bomb throwers that existed in some of the leadership. They seemed hardened to the tragedy. "You mess around enough and you get what you deserve" went the sentiment. The most cynical view of all made the newspaper rounds: it was just one bunch of draft dodgers fighting another. (The National Guard was long considered a safe haven from the draft, as was, of course, college.)

Today, among some, there remains a residual discontent that so much was made of Kent State. A monument was erected to four—but what about the millions who went to Vietnam and those who were killed and maimed, asked parents of some who died in Vietnam before they got their own Vietnam Veterans Memorial in 1982. The divisions, buried, run deep. But there were many, many others who felt Kent State forced people to focus on what was wrong with what they viewed as America's miserably misguided Vietnam policy.

Historians for years to come will be assessing the importance of the not-so-nonviolent peace movement. The war continued for three more years following Kent State. A man named Sam Brown, in the late sixties, stood at the center of a movement most students thought romantically exciting. He led antiwar forces, mobilized demonstrations. He was one of their young; listened to on network news; the darling of antiwar columnists. In the late seventies, Brown mused over those days with Washington *Post* columnist Haynes Johnson. Some acquaintances remembered him as a smooth opportunist riding the antiwar movement. He had no real power back then, he said. Moreover, he regarded the antiwar movement as substantially a failure. Death and destruction brought to them from Vietnam via the media did more finally to end the war, he thinks. By 1981, working within the government, Brown said he had spent a number of years "incorrectly opposing the draft."

It is a thought echoed by many antiwar males. Now in their mid-thirties, in hindsight and free from such responsibilities, they vociferously champion the draft for the young. They seem to see no hypocrisy now that they are safe from the call to arms. As Sam Brown, the elder, now says, "All of us owe some obligation to society."

There was only one other time in our history when the country was so massively torn over the draft. Draft was born, bloody and riotously, in the Civil War. The war had been struggling on with volunteer troops before conscription was imposed in 1863.

During the Vietnam War, antidraft sympathizers sought parallels with the Civil War antidraft riots. There were both similarities and differences. One obvious parallel was the class nature of the draft. The draft was baldly inequitable during the Civil War and only slightly less so during the Vietnam War. During the Civil War, a rich man could buy his way out by purchasing a substitute—$300 in the North, up to $600 in the South. A hundred years later, a college student could stave off the draft by buying his way into a college student deferment. There were myriad loopholes that the rich or clever could find in both drafts.

However, there was one major difference. Those who chose to fight the draft during the Civil War were the poor, not the country's campus elite and middle class.

There was another glaring difference—if one accepts the broad premise that many in the anti-Vietnam movement believed that war was immorally racist. Much of the Civil War antidraft rioting stemmed from opposite racist feelings of America's downtrodden newly immigrated. They saw no reason to fight for blacks or to end slavery.

New York City, for example, harbored a vigorous strain of pro-Southern and anti-Negro sentiment among the poor and the rich—including what has been termed a "near-psychotic hatred" among the copperheads. New York's predominately Irish slum dwellers, who led the mobs in four days of bloody rioting, were notoriously hostile to blacks and adverse to abolition. They were joined in sentiment by New York's mercantile and maritime businessmen, long made rich financing and shipping the Southern cotton crop.[2]

Yet there were many other complex social reasons besides racial prejudice for such mass obstruction to the draft—party feeling, disgust with the "incompetence" of the Lincoln administration, belief in the hopelessness of sub-jugating the South, outrage at being forced to enter a service, anger at the rich man's war with its immense frauds and profiteering.[3]

It would be very hard to find a more botched endeavor than conscription in the Civil War. Fanning the already considerable working-class resentment was the most obvious and scandalous provision—the ability to buy out of the war. Such class discrimination led to bloody riots and the slogan: "Rich man's money and the poor man's Blood."

The result was chaos. In the North, a male could become permanently exempted by hiring a substitute, whether he died or deserted the next day—which many did. The Confederate draft was an even greater fiasco. Unlike the Union law, large classes of citizens were exempted—railway employees, newspapermen, lawyers, school teachers, druggists. It was a draft dodger's paradise: schools were established without any pupils and newspapers with-out readers, while drugstores sprang up everywhere.

The worst exemption was the excusing of plantation overseers at the rate of one overseer for every twenty slaves. The "20 Nigger Law," as it became known, set poor whites in the South at the throats of rich plantation owners and overseers.[4]

Resentment swept the country. In 1863 New York mobs roamed out of stinking, filthy tenements to smash draft enrollment offices—looting, burning, killing. Enrollment officers in those days had the unenviable job of searching out draft-age men in their communities. Many an officer never made it home. They were shot in Wisconsin and they were shot in Ohio and Pennsylvania.

There was so much paranoia and suspicion of cheating that during the choosing of names, a blind man in Philadelphia was recruited to draw the numbers out of a drum. Even though blind, he was still blindfolded.[5]

In the end, about 46,000 draftees and 118,000 substitutes (only about 6 percent of the Union force) were pulled in by conscription. However, the draft was nonetheless considered a major contribution to the Union success by some historians. Its existence stimulated enlistments, since volunteers re-ceived a bonus for joining and draftees did not.[6]

Some historians believe that Confederacy draft exemptions and substitu-tions (coupled with massive desertion) was an important reason why the South lost.

Despite dire remembrances of the Civil War, the draft was an unmitigated success in World War I. There were no substitutes or buying of exemptions. World War II is viewed as the one just war in this century; accounts leave the impression that every eligible male raced down on December 8, 1941, to enlist. However, 66 percent of all who served were draftees. Ultimately, 10 million men and women were inducted into the Army, Navy, Marine Corps, and Coast Guard.[7]

Korea began with reserve or National Guard units made up of World War II veterans. Men up to thirty-five and as young as eighteen were called up,

some 1.5 million men in all. Another one million who were likely to be
drafted decided to enlist.[8]

A more representative share of the population had a personal stake in
Korea than Vietnam. However, the inequities of the Vietnam draft have their
roots in Korea, when the student deferment came into existence. During
Korea, however, a student was generally spared only until the end of his
current semester—and then only if he was carrying at least twelve semester
hours. Proponents of a peacetime draft today sometimes imply that such
peacetime duty is a way of life in America. This is not true. The first peacetime draft came after prolonged debate, one year before Pearl Harbor. It was
reinstituted in 1948, a few years before Korea. The only time the country had
a prolonged peacetime draft was in the years between Korea and Vietnam.

The draft call up for Vietnam began as slowly as the war crept up on
America. The first American was injured on October 2, 1957. The first American died on July 8, 1959. Troop strength reached 4,000 in 1962; 12,000 in
1963; and 23,000 in 1964. A massive jump came in 1965—125,000—and
again in 1966—358,000—even though, as David Halberstam pointed out in
The Best and the Brightest, there were already grave doubts among some of
President Johnson's advisers that we could win. Doubts that were well-hid-
den from the American public. By 1967 troop strength reached half a million
—a level that remained fairly constant through 1969 and then slowly began
to taper off.[9]

As the war progressed, the draft led to riots in the streets, clubbing, tear
gassing, bloodied heads. Older people, reared on American patriotism,
watched in dismay as some of America's youth hoisted NLF flags, cheered on
the VC, and chanted, "Ho ho ho, Ho Chi Minh is going to win!"

Some of this was mindless camp following. Others were true Maoist sympathizers. Others held a romantic notion that North Vietnam was pure and
only the American-backed Southern regime was bad. There was enough
heated rhetoric about the imperialist aggressions of America to fill several
dirigibles. Through the lens of television, one could easily view swirling
crowds and conclude that all of America's young were filled with such em-
phatic notions. This, of course, was not so. There were many ambiguities and
torn emotions. No one in the movement thought the South Vietnamese Government was any good, but neither did that mean that the North was automatically championed. Some pragmatically opposed the war on the grounds
that we couldn't win. Many men today state over and over the impact of
watching war's death and destruction on television—and deciding that they
would look out for number one. The war was not for them, regardless of any
reason.

The blue-collar workers and the lower class seemed compelled to go, sometimes because they thought it their duty, sometimes because they saw no way
out.

On America's campuses, the prevailing view was the opposite. "It is just taken for granted that every male is planning draft avoidance as carefully as he is planning his career," wrote George Reedy after touring college campuses in the sixties.

His view is consistent with large numbers of Vietnam draft avoiders I talked with today. "The concept that there is an obligation to fight for the country is alien to student intellectual life," wrote Reedy. Anyone viewing this as a "deterioration in moral fiber" was "quite wide of the mark." A more valid appraisal, he felt, was that "society had failed to convince its youth that there is any connection between the military establishment and the values of Western civilization." The older generation has either lost its capacity to explain the realities of national life, he wrote, or *"has adopted mistaken policies which cannot be explained."*[10] That is quite a hedge, and yet it was quite an admission, considering. George Reedy just a few years before had been the troubled and beleaguered press secretary to Lyndon Johnson.

Two older men—shaped in earlier times—became involved with the young men in the sixties. Their remembrances are many. One saw both the young who died in battle and those who were on campus. The other knew almost exclusively the student world. They both live in Washington now. One is an editor for *Penthouse* magazine. One is a priest.

The phrases tumble out crisply, little capsuled slogans of the war these years later—tumble out despite the three martinis, the chain-smoking of Winstons. U.S. Marine Colonel William Corson (ret.), his eyes staring and compelling, looks remarkably like Peter Finch in *Network.* "I thought it was fucking *madness.* The objective was to *outstay* the enemy. That's too costly. If it costs ten Americans to kill one VC, then, goddamn it, you won't win. . . . It was search and destroy and 'Get the last little bastard.' . . . And that absolutely *superfluous* adjective—*favorable* body counts! Somehow these deaths are justifiable because we managed to kill more that day than last. . . . When both strategy and tactics are flawed, you have *no* winnable war. . . ."

Corson wrote a blistering book, *The Betrayal,* about our policy in Vietnam. The young men who died, in part because of that policy, he cannot forget. A slum child from Chicago who grew up to learn the ways of Indochina, Corson knows a lot of secrets. He was a CIA agent in the earliest days of Vietnam. Disillusionment turned Corson into a causist. His cause was to keep as many marines and as many Vietnamese peasants alive as possible. He started a village pacification project based on freeing peasants from the grips of both the VC and Saigon.

Corson cannot forget his soldiers of Vietnam. There was the black from Detroit, called "The Cobra," with three Purple Hearts, who volunteered to stay in the village. His talent was mimicry; he had an ear for languages. "He picked up Vietnamese just like that. Some guys stopped to visit one day and they see this black kid from Detroit and these two Vietnamese listening to his every word." Corson's friends wondered, "What the hell is going on?"

"You are seeing a case in domestic relations," replied Corson. " 'The Cobra' is going to grant a divorce."

When "The Cobra" was killed in a firefight, the entire village came to mourn. For years, when most didn't want to remember men like "The Cobra" or the war, Corson edited a column on veterans' problems in *Penthouse* magazine. A shrewd move, yes, because many *Penthouse* readers are veterans. But a caring move, too.

Men like "The Cobra" were on Corson's mind when he returned from Vietnam, wrote *The Betrayal,* and "became a 'messiah' for some of those college kids. I was asked to speak at the University of Kansas. I was going to be their banner—a colonel who wrote of *betrayal.*

"One student shouted, 'Are you against the war?' after I had spoken in just that vein for an hour and a half. I said, 'Yes—for a variety of reasons I thought I'd made clear in the last hour and a half.' "

The student shouted defiantly, "Well *we're* gonna make it end."

Corson looked at the gym filled with long-haired young men and something snapped. "No, you're not!" yelled the colonel. "You can end this war in ninety *days* if you chose so. Do any of you have the balls to do it? In your hip pocket you should have in your wallets a card. It's called a draft card. And it's stamped with 2-S. The government didn't automatically confer that deferment. You can turn that 2-S *back* and then you become 1-A." The students were looking at one another. Where was all this leading?

"And *then* you become a 1-A and you move to the top of the list, my friends. And at the draft they ask you to step forward; they don't *command* you to. If you do *not,* my friends, that's an act of disobedience. Now, if fifty or a hundred or two hundred and fifty thousand of you do that, it's all over.

"If you believe in it, *that's* what you do!"

Corson drains his martini, chuckling.

"I was practically run out of there on a rail."

What *would* have happened if Johnson or Nixon *had* been faced with thousands upon thousands of students risking jail, rather than keeping their deferments? As it was, the 250,000 who defied the law in some way did clog the judicial systems. Some theorize that it brought the Selective Service operation —if not the war—close to a standstill.

Others, like Tom Alder, an expert on the Selective Service System, feel that draft avoidance, prosecutions, appeals, and protests never threatened to dry up the monthly quota of draftees. "What opposition did do was to force the hasty design of a 'Vietnamization' strategy in the Johnson administration, which Nixon executed." It is an unknown equation, but, if there had been a truly massive movement—if even 20 percent more had turned in their deferments—it seems possible that it would have ended the war.

Father Timothy Healy, President of Georgetown University, settles into a pleasant ramble through theology and war and youth. He defends the large numbers of caring and dedicated antiwar students he knew. Father Healy was at City University of New York (CUNY) during the war. The actual numbers of students participating in demonstrations were about 8 percent, he feels, but "there was deep, deep sympathy for those participating." This was not an elite Ivy League crowd, but sons of blue-collar workers who had struggled hard to get to college. "There was profound opposition to the whole notion of the Vietnam War."

I tell Corson's story to Father Healy. If they really cared, why didn't they do what Corson and some of the resistance leaders exhorted them to do, turn in their student deferments?

"I think that's unfair. That's asking them why they didn't act adult and adopt a means to an end. The reason they didn't get very good at a means to an end is because they were nineteen.

"At first the war was not a closed issue. It *became* one under the corruption, mismanagement, lies. We saw so many lights down so many tunnels and so often they turned out to be the lights of a locomotive. We were really with the kids. *Hundreds* of us went down, appeared before draft boards.

"We were there to talk about C.O.'s and the question would be: 'Is this kid sincere?' A lawyer said, 'You know, it's very difficult, this job we have to do. To try to decide these questions.' And I said, 'Yeah, it's an obscene law. There's that lovely line: "I will not open windows into men's souls." That's what you're trying to do. I'm trying to help you do it. I'm embarrassed and you're embarrassed and we're all trying. . . .' "

Father Healy remembers the scene. "You walk in and there's a long table and at the end is the chairman, looking faintly embarrassed. A good Roman Catholic businessman and I'm a priest in a Roman collar. And there's a lady who is absolutely set that the kids had to go. There is just no *touching* her. And a lawyer, who is Jewish. You *know* he's reachable with a moral problem. And then you try to talk, try to read their minds."

Did he ever fudge it, speak for youths whose beliefs he thought might be questionable?

"I've got an old-fashioned ruling. Unless you've got hard evidence to the contrary, you take what people say about themselves as true. This is their *perception* of truth. The kids who went *through* this process and really fought for it were the ones who really had reflected. I remember they asked me once, 'Does this kid take part in protests?' And I said, 'Yes.' " Father Healy, a good actor, pauses for effect. " 'In three protests he's been a *marshal,* trying to keep the kids in line.' "

Father Healy tried to keep his temper, facing that draft board, but he had just seen the hard hats beating youths on Wall Street. "I can remember saying, 'What do you think of a democracy where we beat up our children with clubs and staves because they're saying something we disagree with politically? Since when have we settled our political differences with physical violence?'

"The most terrible 'we-they' was the Columbia student-cop confrontation. Upper-middle-class WASP and Jewish kids yelling down at lower-class cops

—Irish, Italian, Jewish, black—and calling them unbelievable names! Kids have the most imaginative insults. What their wives were doing while they were on night duty. You know. You could just see this slow boil and the cops got loose on those kids and just beat the hell out of them. The officers weren't *there.* That was a real failure of police command."

Like many of the religious protesters, Father Healy was against the war but felt nothing but concern and compassion for the soldiers. "I can remember my 'learned colleagues' in a bull session, bitching about Spellman supporting the troops in Vietnam. And I just exploded. 'You don't go out and tell eighteen- and nineteen-year-olds in battle, "Look, this is a highly dubious enterprise you're engaged in. You might be killed and that's unfortunate, but don't expect any thanks." You don't *tell* kids that. What do you want in a letter from home when you're in a war? You want a letter that says, "I love you." That's the principal thing. And then you want to hear about your aunt's false teeth and the cat did this and this happened to the car.' "

And Healy thinks of the nineteen-year-olds he knew on campus and also defends them. "It's the age at which you get wrapped up in your own contemplation. They kept saying, 'Why can't the world be perfect?' 'Why can't we have love?' The ones who did it on drugs, well, that's one form of reality. There was a *deep* strain of self-indulgence. Kids who didn't addict themselves to something often still had this *terrible* romanticism: 'If we just really will it, then we won't be in an imperfect world.' They, too, were doomed to failure.

"But there were lots and lots of others who were sincere and dedicated. And they were right."

For millions in a generation bursting with millions, it was not all desperate choices. They just followed the flow. It is astounding still to find an inbred sense of class. Over and over, men who avoided the draft have told me they *knew* they would find a way to get out of going to Vietnam.

In wide, sweeping classifications there were three types—the avoiders, the evaders, and the resisters who took a stand.

The avoiders took a certain mental gymnastic's delight in beating the system—finding legal escape routes and loopholes and dodges. They rejected out of hand the idea of evading (going to Canada) or resisting (going to jail). Many of today's lawyers began their indoctrination into oral arguments as they poured over draft laws for loopholes. The Selective Service directives and induction guidelines were well-thumbed and memorized. They could quote the exact page that had to deal with bad knees or high blood pressure. The avoiders faked homosexuality and faked craziness, much in the larky spirit of beating the government at its own game. One French-kissed an inducting officer. And then there were extremes. One man I know cut off his finger. Others knew only a quick moment of terror after the lottery was instituted in December of 1969 and then breathed easy for the rest of the war with a high lottery number. From that time on, Vietnam was something that happened to someone else.

To point out that someone poorer or less aware was going in their stead—to a war that couldn't adequately be explained—was hardly an inducement for millions of avoiders. "Containing communism" in Vietnam did not seem the first—or last—step in keeping them out of San Francisco Bay.

Now, years later, no matter how they felt about the war, there are various reactions among avoiders to their methods of getting out. For some, there is a blotting out of any feeling about that period. Or there is outright denial of any residual concern about their actions. Guilt—or at least sheepishness—is, however, not uncommon, particularly for those who devised some scam not to go. A number of men react similarly when they start to tell how they got out of the draft. There is often a measure of class arrogance—an amused smile on their face, as if they are about to tell a joke. Then they often will pause and ask to remain anonymous. They are not exactly proud, they say, of what they did. Their stories seem to tell it all—equally so, their desire not to certify their actions with their names.

The climate in the sixties, however, made draft dodging not just acceptable. In their crowd it was *honorable*. Beating the draft was a status symbol.

(In one study, fully 60 percent of those who did not go said they took active steps to ensure that outcome.)[11]

Many of the 16 million who did not serve at all were just lucky. Others did nothing more than exercise their legitimate rights under the law—through student deferments, physical exemptions, becoming C.O.'s. Nationwide enrollment during those years suggests that male college enrollment averaged 6 to 7 percent higher than normal because of the draft. When deferments for graduate schools were dropped in 1968, the Harvard *Crimson* published an outraged editorial about how "unfair" this was to students. Divinity schools then became popular draft shelters. David Stockman will never convince anyone—either his nongoing peers or veterans—that he was at Harvard Divinity School for any other reason. If time ran out, you could teach school, another deferment (10 percent of a Notre Dame survey admitted the draft influenced such career choices). From 1963 to 1966, you were deferred if married. During those years, there was an immediate 10 percent rise in marriage rates for twenty- and twenty-one-year-olds. One of every eight husbands in the Notre Dame survey admitted that they married as a means of avoiding the draft. And three of every ten fathers in the survey said the draft influenced their sudden desire for fatherhood.[12]

When college—that sequestering sanctuary—finally ended, the dodge was really on. Abusing one's body was a small sacrifice for almost a million men who manipulated their health to avoid the draft. Some athletes deliberately reinjured old joints. Some students jabbed forearms with pins to fake a heroin problem. Gaining or losing weight was a common ploy. One University of Michigan football player ate three large pizzas every night for six months, gained 125 pounds, and flunked the physical. Others starved themselves. One student ate six dozen eggs and got an exemption for excessive albumin.

There were enormous support systems within the community of doctors, lawyers, and clergy. "Anita Stevens, the New York psychiatrist, do you know her?" asked one artful dodger, Bruce Landerman. "She wanted to hold a party for all the guys she got out. She would have had to hold it in Madison Square Garden."

Publishers churned out "How To" books on draft avoidance that became dormitory staples: *The Draft and You; Representing Clients Under the Selective Service Law;* numerous books labeled, simply and ominously, *The Draft.*

David Suttler's *IV-F—A Guide to Draft Exemptions* was a small treasure. Suttler reprinted the entire section of the examination (acceptable audiometric hearing levels, how much limitation of motion of the upper extremities you needed to be disqualified, etc.). The book included Suttler's unmistakable biases: "A man who murdered as a civilian is unacceptable to the Army, which trains men to kill. A convicted arsonist cannot be inducted for shipment to Vietnam, where American soldiers burn villages. In short, the citizens whose demonstrated talents indicate the greatest potential are summarily rejected by the military."

Some potential draftees were astonished to find kindred souls among examining military doctors, many of whom were themselves dragooned into service during Vietnam.

"This doc was going on about Muskie and I could just *tell* he thought he was the greatest," said one Washington political consultant. "I thought, What the hell? I told him I was a speechwriter for Muskie. I was working for *McGovern!* But he loved it. That night I ran into Gene McCarthy and told him how I got out. He said, 'Way to go.' "

In 1971 Pentagon computers divided into groups the millions of young men who evaded service by taking advantage of loopholes in the law. In 1968, 6.8 million were in college—about half of them males—and thousands more were granted deferments for the duration of the war. Those with various occupational deferments jumped 124 percent from 220,012 to 491,998. Dependency deferments jumped 11 percent from 3,776,117 to 4,194,756. ROTC, considered a refuge, did have its share who went. From 1965 to mid-1970, 101,882 men received ROTC commissions. Forty percent were assigned to combat duty.[13]

The avoiders are, by far, the largest group in the Vietnam Generation who did not go to war. They bought into the very system many of them professed to despise by going along with the discriminatory rules that favored the privileged. But what was the very "in" thing back then is seldom spoken of with pride today. Many who pulled a ruse to get out do not want their names on their stories, which in itself speaks volumes.

It is not difficult to find these people. They are all around you. Try asking your own friends or acquaintances.

They just might tell you their own stories.

2 The Chosen

JOEL GARREAU (PRONOUNCED GAIR-O), THIRTY-FIVE, WAS THE FIRST
male ever granted conscientious objector status from his Pawtucket, Rhode
Island, draft board. That was in 1969. Garreau's world was overwhelmingly
blue-collar and his draft board had been shipping young men off in waves for
years. Unlike draft boards in upper-class communities, it had not seen the
likes of a Garreau.

There were, ultimately, only 172,000 Vietnam-era C.O.'s. It was an infinitely harder route than many of the dodges used by millions of other draft-
age males. It involved planning and preparation and a fair measure of religiosity and sincerity. (One Samoan was exempted by his California draft board
because he sincerely believed that if he killed anyone, his pagan god would
cause a volcano to erupt.)

During Vietnam, there were more categories of conscientious objectors
than in previous wars. Jehovah's Witnesses and Quakers and other sects who
opposed fighting on religious grounds were joined by thousands of young men
who questioned the morality of the Vietnam War but did not belong to traditional C.O. sects. As the war progressed, the Supreme Court upheld C.O.
cases for moral and philosophical—personal "religious"—reasons if the
points were well-argued and seemed sincere. Garreau is representative of this
group.

Garreau went about getting his C.O. status as if preparing for a doctoral
thesis on church history, ethics, and morals. It was *not* going to be easy. His
first nemesis in his pursuit was the Selective Service board clerk—a woman.
(Coincidentally, many men of the Vietnam Generation comment on the
women draft board members. They often felt that, for some inexplicable reason, the women were relentlessly vigilant—often to the point of being punitive—in halting any escapes through the gaping loopholes that existed.)

Garreau's board clerk told him flat out that he would never make C.O. He
was Catholic. Garreau, she said, belonged to the "War Church."

"That was her phrase, 'War Church.' She was Catholic. Everybody was."
Garreau laughs when he recalls that his chances with the full board hardly

seemed better: "five French-Canadian Roman Catholic American Legion-naires; average age, sixty-five."

Armed with a genius IQ, Garreau went about proving his case. Being smart—or at least having a smart lawyer—was essential if you were going to maneuver in the labyrinthian maze of C.O. didactics.

Garreau applied for C.O. status when he registered at the age of eighteen. He did not have four full years of college student deferment waiting. By the time he was eighteen, Garreau, having skipped a grade, was already a junior in college. He spent most of his college time wondering what to do.

"I sure as hell wasn't going to go to Nam. It wasn't anything about 'third world solidarity.' It just seemed a real punk's game." Later, he would see the war as morally wrong, but at the time, "I saw no point in getting my ass shot."

Garreau searched for ways to accomplish this mission. He was one of thousands consumed with the thought of avoiding the war. Such obsessions took hold in the late sixties. Once only marginally concerned with Vietnam, males at Harvard who no longer had graduate school deferments to look forward to, for example, became "desperate."

"We were like the man about to go into the gas chamber . . . the walls slowly but inexorably closing. . . . To be *always* talking about 'the war' was no longer the sign of an eccentric," wrote Harvard student Steven Kelman. The soul-searching and sudden hard-core antiwar stance was caused, in many cases, not by "our oft-praised idealism and sensitivity—those traits which we frequently and stupidly believe we are the first generation in world history to possess. It was something close to self-interest . . . nothing to be ashamed of —but nothing to become a self-righteous self-proclaimed guardian of morality over either."

Castigating the self-righteousness that swept Harvard that summer, Kelman wrote, "People who even six months earlier had supported government policy in Vietnam were now shrieking like banshees gone berserk . . . at anyone who didn't absolutely agree with them on the war, now that the threat of going seemed more personal. Harvard tolerance stopped at the Mekong's edge."[1]

Garreau even toyed with joining the CIA. "It was considered a way to at least stay out of the Army." His roommate was in Navy ROTC—"a way of getting out."

Neither of those routes seemed quite compatible with Garreau, who had hair past his shoulders. In his entire adult life, Garreau has never seen his lower lip or chin. He has only a dim memory of ever shaving what passed for hair in his early sweet-sixteen days.

There lingers a satisfying recollection. "The beard pissed off my parents at the time." Which, of course, was one of the major goals in the sixties. Much has been made of "hair" and its place in generational protest—with good reason. "That told everybody who wanted to know about 90 percent of where you stood on any given issue. That was a *statement.* In some places in Indiana [where Garreau went to Notre Dame], you couldn't get served with long hair and a beard."

I first met Garreau when he was twenty-one and came to the Washington *Post* as a young, hotshot layout editor. I noticed the freckles, the beard, the intense giggle, but mostly the flowing red hair caught in a ponytail and Garreau's distinctive nervous mannerism. As he read copy, he constantly twisted curlicues into his mane. Today Garreau is the author of a successful book, *Nine Nations of North America.* To his delight—and some amazement—he out-talked William Buckley on "Firing Line" in 1981. There was Garreau—in suit and tie, red hair beginning to bald, and neatly trimmed, beard well-clipped—sparring with the columnist. When Garreau was a teenager at the barricades, Buckley was flailing college administrators for laxness against such demonstrators, accusing college presidents of being "made out of Cornell jelly"—a reference to the capitulation to the demands of blacks who took over the Cornell student union with guns. There was a diabolical gleam in the eye of Garreau, old protester and C.O., as he sat with Buckley. There is, however, more empathy in Garreau today now that he too is past thirty, a mellowing from those days when Garreau viewed the world with an arrogance of youth and intellectual privilege.

"Special." That is the one word an extraordinary number of Garreau's generation use to describe themselves. "Special." It is a curiously enveloping sixties word, not used by those who came of age before or after. "There was always the 'specialness.' A thought drilled into me—and which scarred me for life—was that we were 'the best and the brightest.' I did terrible in high school—but at the same time I was getting these King Kong SAT scores in the high 700s. The lowest I ever scored on an IQ test was in the 160s. I was always aware of being some freak of nature. It was so direct: 'Here's your potential, you're special,' and all that."

The difference was particularly obvious in Pawtucket, population 80,000. Garreau's parents were first-generation American; his family goes back to 1670 in Quebec. Garreau spoke only Quebeçois until he was six. Garreau never got along particularly well with his father, a furniture salesman. "My father would not look out of place in an asbestos mine in Quebec. He was very nonverbal. But, having said that, he had some osmosis, some level of communication that had nothing to do with verbal expression. He could sell a million dollars' worth of furniture."

There are many layers, minigenerations within the mass labeled "the sixties generation." Garreau refers often to the "most dominant" aspect of growing up for him—skipping a grade in grammar school.

As a result, Garreau was in on the first wave of major change. Like many of the era, he was struck by the dramatic difference in the freshman class of 1965 and the class immediately preceding it. The class of '64 followed orders, held to more traditional college concepts. For example, many of the college graduates of 1963 and 1964 went to Vietnam without much thought, as officers. It was just a natural extension of their ROTC training and of the dominant spirit of John F. Kennedy.

Garreau's class at Notre Dame was on the cutting edge of change, the demarcation point. "We were much more rebellious of authority than the class immediately ahead. The standard response of the time was: 'If you think I'm weird, wait until you see my little brother.' "

Political reasons helped spark the abrupt shift to rebellion. Members of the class of 1964 were still believers in John F. Kennedy's "Ask not what your country can do for you" call to service. The summer of their graduation, however, saw the Gulf of Tonkin incident and the subsequent congressional resolution, which gave Lyndon Johnson the green light to escalate the war dramatically. The very next class, 1965, was facing the stark reality of Vietnam, as Johnson quickly began to step up the pace of troops to war.

Garreau went to an elite Catholic high school, La Salle Academy, in nearby Providence. His poor grades made Harvard, his first choice, inaccessible. Garreau hated Notre Dame. "Sheer parochialism and narrowness. Politically sleepy." Garreau was among the more radical, although he laughs at that definition compared to those on more activist campuses.

His voice still holds a bit of wonder, as Garreau says, "The year we enrolled was the *first* year we didn't have compulsory mass. We still had 10 P.M. *curfews!* You weren't allowed to see girls at all except on weekends. And a girl in your *room!* That was three years down the pike. The attitude of not taking any shit was standard at places like Berkeley and Harvard, but not at Notre Dame."

Still, there were enough fellow rebels at Notre Dame—"about forty hardcore and a coterie of fellow travelers up to a couple hundred"—and more would follow in the years to come. "The mood, the feeling, was simply there —all over the country."

The "why" of that rebellion is still emotionally—if not intellectually— inexplicable to many who were not a part of that generation. All the collective reasons—from permissive parents to Vietnam, that incredible galvanizer, to sheer numbers—played a part.

"In hindsight we all knew it was the 'pig in the python' [the description used for the massive baby boom that didn't digest easily into society]. As I said, 'the best and the brightest' was rammed down our throats. How nineteen were turned down for every *one* accepted at good colleges!

"They preach that you're privileged and you start believing it. We had no reason to believe it wasn't true." In effect, since they were considered so "special," many deduced that it was their privilege to stay alive. "If all this is true about us being the future of the goddamn country, then the attitude was: 'Now *wait* a minute. You want *us* to be cannon fodder?' "

Nor was the idea of "specialness" reserved for the intellectual cream. Benchmarks of "specialness" were all over. How much taller they were than the previous generation. How much this, how much that. How much more money they had to spend. In 1964, 3.7 million baby boomers celebrated their seventeenth birthday—a million more than the year before. Teenagers were spending $12 billion a year. It was *discretionary* spending—not durable goods purchases of items such as washing machines. Teenagers spent $12 million a year in lipstick, accounted for 55 percent of *all* soft drink sales, 53 percent of *all* movie tickets, and 43 percent of *all* records sold. Teenagers spent staggering millions on toiletries—hair cream and mouthwashes and deodorants and lipsticks and zit remedies. Purdue polled 2,000 teenagers in 1964 and asked them what was the gravest problem facing American youth. One third knew without a doubt. Acne.[2]

In the single decade of the sixties, the numbers of young people aged 18–24 expanded by an unparalleled 8,559,000—more than in the rest of the century put together. As push came to shove over the war, the baby boomers in college felt an exultant safety in numbers. "We're right at the center of everything," said one. "It's us. We're right in the center, reading about ourselves in the newspaper. It's youth. Everything is youth and *us.*"[3]

Yes, they read those stories and—tragically, for some who never grew beyond those years—believed them.

Still, there were cult characteristics that cannot be explained by size alone. Ideas and attitudes seemed caught by the wind, traveling across the country in a strange dialect that only the tribe could understand. Drugs were daily influences for millions, not just on college campuses or urban high schools but in backwater towns like Fort Bragg, California. The 5,000 inhabitants tended to be simple people, descendants of the two-fisted-drinking fishermen and lumbermen who settled the town in the 1880s. In the winter of 1969, parents were stunned by a staggering statistic. A large majority—75 percent—of the 550 high school and junior high school students were on drugs. Not just marijuana, but speed, LSD, Demerol. Some fourteen-year-olds were trying a new improvisation—mainlining alcohol. The prettiest and most popular, "the best and the brightest," were among those so zonked that one teacher commented, "I'm the only one alive in the classroom." Some parents seriously thought of setting up roadblocks to halt the flow of drugs from San Francisco's Haight-Ashbury district. The school couldn't expel the drug users—there were too many of them. Finally, two former hard-core junkies started Awareness House, reaching the teenagers with their own experience and a combination of the then-fashionable est and Synanon techniques. The parents were the outsiders throughout. Drugs *were* the true generational unshared experience. Parents, in their own day, may have cut classes or made out in backs of cars or gotten drunk, but they hadn't tried speed. A doctor at the time could have been speaking for the masses when he spoke of Fort Bragg. It was an "exclusive kid phenomenon. Kids turn other kids on. Keep it a secret from parents . . . separating themselves from parents and other authority figures."[4]

Not one factor easily explains the phenomenon of their music, movies, and mores. By the late sixties, music was a common bond, linking many of Vietnam's citizen-soldiers with their nongoing counterparts.

"Vietnam and our generation changed 'wine, women, and song' to 'drugs, sex, and rock 'n' roll,' " said a former helicopter pilot.

For Joel Garreau, the effect of music on his political attitudes came easily. He was in a high school band and listened keenly to the protest lyrics of Bob Dylan and Joan Baez, memorized their albums, and could do three hours straight without a repeat. "There was true meaning to 'The Times They Are A-Changin'.' Bewildered parents should have listened to the *words.*"

An interesting parallel is posed by Todd Gitlin, an early SDS leader, between the violence in sixties movies and youth's growing rebellion. *Bonnie and Clyde* was no mere story of a couple of 1930s gangsters, ripped apart by police bullets in long and lingering detail by Arthur Penn's direction, according to Gitlin. "The spirit of *Bonnie and Clyde* was everywhere in the movement—and in the larger youth culture surrounding it." Peter Collier, in *Ramparts,* wrote that *Bonnie and Clyde* "speaks to" the generation. Then, with that self-indulgence of their time and stretching all credibility, he continues, "It is about *their* life, about the cops beating on their heads and the inertia they have to wade through." Peckinpah's *The Wild Bunch* was contorted by the Berkeley tribe into a "revolutionary film." It showed "You have to pick up the gun."[5]

All this was matched by the bloodshed, divorced of meaning or cause, shown nightly on TV: the battered remains of marines after Tet, the pain and horror in the eyes of Vietnamese women clutching their children. Violence was literally everywhere—on nightly news and in pop culture.

"These films were part of an edgy, apocalyptic culture," wrote Gitlin. The movies, the music, the drugs, the "fuck you" flamboyance of underground papers; all thrived in and reproduced an apocalyptic, polarized political mood. It was exciting to be a part, to be swept up by all this, especially if you were a student from a family where affluence had eased away all possible personal confrontation.

As Garreau remembers, "We were *power.* You couldn't use your banana republic tactics on us without us screaming 'rebellion.' "

Something else was going on in college circles—a flip-flop of the John Wayne off-to-war hero. The pariahs of earlier wars—those who chose not to go—were sex objects in the sixties. To be sure, this was largely only in their own sphere, but to them it was the only sphere that counted. (Negative polls across Middle America at the time toward draft avoiders were later matched by the outpourings of acrimony in 1977 when President Carter pardoned draft evaders.)

To charge the police and be routed by tear gas, to defy God and Country and your local draft board was, in itself, a rite of passage for many. Fathers tried to taunt their sons into haircuts—what respectable girl would be seen with a boy who looked like a *girl* with his hair down to his shoulders? The boys merely smiled their secret smiles—they were getting more than Dad ever got in his entire life.

Garreau does a Woody Allenesque replay of his dramatic leave-taking from Notre Dame to return to Rhode Island for his shoot-out with the draft board. "My girl saw me off. *Big* kisses! It was like those old movies about going to war," he says with a laugh. "It was considered more daring to *not* go to war. It was *dangerous*—at least it was perceived that way at the time. I was ready to go to *jail!* I'm not holier than thou, but it just didn't seem right to go to the doctors and lawyers and get off on a lie. Or," he says disgustedly, "this business of going to Harvard Divinity School when you didn't really mean it."

Garreau thought jail might be a distinct possibility. There was enough bloodshed in the history of Catholicism—the Crusades, the Inquisition—to make his draft clerk's charge of "War Church" a perfectly legitimate argument.

Garreau's draft board members were among thousands across the country who were mistaken about the rules for C.O. status during the Vietnam War. In 1965, a few years before Garreau faced his board, Daniel Seeger, a New York pacifist, said he wasn't going to war. His case began the unraveling of draft enforcement. In a landmark ruling, the Supreme Court overturned his Selective Service conviction. Seeger's draft board, like most, granted C.O. status only to Quakers, Mennonites, Jehovah's Witnesses, and other pacifist sects. Seeger did not belong to any such sect, nor did he believe in God. The Supreme Court held that he still qualified for a C.O. exemption—leaving the clear implication that anyone with a sincere *personal* "religious" opposition to war could be a C.O. The key was to make a sincere claim that one opposed all wars regardless of religious background. It was the first major Selective Service decision issued by the Supreme Court since World War II. The draft system was ill-prepared and ill-disposed to change—and many would-be C.O.'s were wrongfully denied C.O. status.[6]

Garreau knew nothing of the Seeger case as he marshaled his arguments with a diligence unapproached in any classroom studies. "It was very chic for faculty members to be antiwar, but when I actually had to find *out* about this, 90 percent of them evaporated. It was too much like work," he said caustically. "I will always remember the 10 percent who were willing to sit down in the dusty stacks and say, 'This is what you need to know about the early church.' "

The former Cub Scout who once sold doughnuts door-to-door did the same mindless canvassing of neighborhoods to find support. He wrote 125 letters to people who knew him and the draft board was flooded with nearly 70 favorable letters. Garreau was an Eagle Scout with a marksmanship merit badge. "It never did come up, but I was prepared to twist it into the argument that knowing how to shoot just indicates the depth of my knowledge and the horror of what shooting can do."

For his draft appearance, Garreau made the consummate compromise. He

left the beard untouched but *cut his hair.* Twice. He dusted off a suit left over
from high school graduation. As he dressed for the occasion, Garreau
couldn't help think about the irony. Here he was, going for a C.O. and
forming points of moral theology at a time when he had stopped going to
church. His defection came after a summer's night on the beach with a girlfriend. "I realized, as a result of that night, I had a lot to confess," he says,
laughing at the memories of a Catholic boyhood. "Then I realized that I
wasn't sorry—*and* that I would do it again at the next opportunity. So what
the hell would I confess? And so I quit."

Although many draft-age men knew well the term "C.O.," most felt they
couldn't qualify. Draft counselors advised: "Sit down and think about why
you are against killing people in war. Write down short sentences or ideas [for
instance: love . . . brotherhood . . . peace . . . equality . . . personal
responsibility]." They were advised to let their minds work freely; perhaps a
good C.O. case could be formulated.[7]

Armed with his twenty-page thesis, Garreau was well-prepared for the
draft board. The day of his review, Garreau sat outside in the hall with his
father and a lawyer. The draft board lured him in on a pretext of "Could we
see you for just a minute?" Garreau went in alone.

The questions began:

"Would you fight against Hitler?"

Garreau knew that was a trick question. "If you said yes, then *bam* you
were off to Vietnam." And yet, how could you say you would *not* fight against
Hitler?

Garreau drew a deep breath and faced them. "That's a hypothetical question I can't answer. I wasn't born then. I would like to think World War II
was brought about by as big a mistake as this one was." He was getting
wound up and launched into the importance of nonviolent solutions to global
problems. By then, he believed it. He spouted the logic of nonviolence, from
Tolstoy to Gandhi.

He laughs at the ironic figure he presented—preaching about *not* being
violent as he pounded his fist on the table and shouted in a manner that could
hardly be termed nonviolent. *"Look!"* he shouted to the board. "If we'd spent
the same amount of money on how to wage *peace,* we wouldn't be there in the
first place. We've got to worry about fixing these problems *without* going to
war!"

He fell silent. The board members said, "Okay, thank you." Garreau said,
"That's it?" The board members said, "That's it." Only then did Garreau
realize that *that* was the hearing for which he had been prepping for months.

Back at Notre Dame, panic sank in. After days of waiting, Garreau's hands
shook as he opened the Selective Service envelope. His classification had been
changed to 1-0. He was safe. What if it had been 1-A? "I would have gone to
the induction and when they said, 'Take one step forward,' I wasn't going to
do it."

In retrospect, Garreau recognizes that the little social dance he went through had far more to do with getting his C.O. than his beliefs.

"I always thought I'd write an essay, '101 Reasons Why Joel Garreau Got His C.O.' The one hundred and *first* was whatever I believed. That was the *last* reason as far as the realities of the draft board. Where it all got decided was within Le Foyer Club [the bastion of local pols and influence makers]." There they would talk about Garreau: "This kid is serious about this. He's really putting us on the spot." The editor of the local newspaper, a former summer boss, was pushing for Garreau. His father was a respected business-man. The way was greased.

Garreau tried to talk some of his working-class friends in Pawtucket into resisting—with little luck. He remained an active foot soldier in the move-ment. Earlier demonstrators speak of the street confrontations as going off on their own crusade, jousting with the system. "In the beginning, it was scary as hell. You might be expelled and lose your deferment. At that time there was no safety in numbers."

General Hershey, in 1965, in fact, tried to instigate punitive reclassification for protesters after thirty-five University of Michigan students staged a sit-in at the Ann Arbor draft board. His "club of induction" met with national disapproval. Authorities were faced with troubling political ramifications; the image of massive arrests as "The whole world was watching." Despite the polarized attitudes in the country about demonstrators, it was still a ticklish dilemma. For every person who thought, They should be sent over, that's what they deserve, others would see a "repressive" police state action.

"Clearly, they were in a bind and we exploited it for all it was worth," said Garreau. "We were yelling 'totalitarianism' and 'fascism' and they were going to respond by expelling us? They would have *proven our point* and they couldn't."

This is not to say that arrests did not occur. In 1969 police and national guardsmen were called in on at least 127 campuses, sometimes for weeks on end. More than 4,000 were arrested in campus protests from January to June. At least an additional 1,000 were expelled or suspended. Leaders immediately roared that this made them instantly eligible for the draft and Vietnam. New administrators, imposing this tougher stance, were castigated for "signing a death warrant."[8]

Garreau was on the fringe of the 1968 Chicago riot and left early when the head bashing began. He saw enough to recognize that the confrontation was, in part, "real class warfare. Lower-middle-class Irish cops and all these mid-dle-class and upper-middle-class kids generally provoking them. Of course," he adds hastily, "it wasn't enough provocation to justify what happened, but, in benefit of hindsight, I can now understand what set the cops off. We kids were basically saying we were nonviolent, that we didn't swing at anyone, that we didn't start the fracas. But you can argue that violence can be done with your *mouth.*" As street rage became more violent, protesters were given advice on how to attack *verbally.* Words like "motherfucker" out of sweet-faced coeds or casting aspersions about a policeman's mother were pointedly guaranteed to set the police off.

Once again, as in all areas of Vietnam discussion, there were many shades of gray—not only the variegated factions within the movement, but in the antiwar movement's overall effectiveness. For example, viewers drew widely different conclusions from the Chicago riot. Antiwar and movement sympathizers were everlastingly horrified by police violence, while the right accused the networks of bias and rallied to the police.

For huge numbers of people in the middle—Americans who were not personally involved or concerned with Vietnam—Chicago shattered past complacency as they watched the bloody beatings. Although cameras caught mostly youth, nearly a third of all civilians injured seriously enough to be hospitalized were over twenty-five. The *Walker Report* (the 1968 report by the National Commission on the Causes and Preventions of Violence) detailed a Chicago police squad gone berserk, citing "ferocious, malicious, and mindless violence" and enough "gratuitous beating" to convince the investigators they had witnessed a "police riot."

Still, "for an overwhelming majority of white Americans, seeing was not believing," write sociologists Ida and Jesse Frankel in a forthcoming book on inter-age conflict. Even those who presumably shared their goals saw the "kids" getting what they deserved. "In one survey, almost 70 percent of antiwar whites giving an opinion do not think 'too much force' had been used by the police. Most frequent response of whites who took clear 'dove' positions—nearly 40 percent—was that 'not enough force' had been used to suppress the demonstration," write the Frankels (using information from the sixth annual presidential election survey conducted by the University of Michigan's Survey Research Center).

Prejudice and concern of TV viewers witnessing the head bashing were confounded by ignorance of the counter-violence from within.

Movement leaders charged for years that the FBI had infiltrated their ranks. They were believed by those who sympathized with them and called paranoid crackpots by those who didn't. However, ten years after the fact, CBS news attributed to *Army* sources the claim that "almost *one* demonstrator in *six* was an undercover agent."[9]

I remember aides to the late Senator Hubert Humphrey, trying to defend his backing away from the fracas. "Those weren't nice little flower kids," said one of his aides, his face contorted in disgust. "They threw feces and urine in the hotel lobby. They were *awful.*" The lingering question is just how much was done by whom—FBI provocateurs or extremists who charged the movement with inflated rhetoric and militancy.

Todd Gitlin, the former SDS president who became disenchanted with the movement's increasing violence, wrote that, no matter, "Provocateurs by themselves cannot explain everything; provocateurs must move in a movement that tolerates their wild talk and wild action. The movement's own incendiaries—rhetorical and actual—colluded in a self-defeating system of rising rhetoric, rising militancy and theatrics, rising publicity, rising government repression, and presumably rising provocation."[10]

By 1970 the resistance had splintered, leaders had battled, causes had diffused. Garreau was one of the many followers who became disillusioned. He covered the SDS convention in Chicago in 1970. "They were heading off in a direction I thought was complete bullshit. The Weathermen had surfaced. That had nothing to do with where *I* was at. At that point, *they* seemed to have little to do with Vietnam." The ultimate fascistic irony was the SDS treatment of the First Amendment at that conference. They confiscated tapes, cameras—and threw out the press.[11]

The moderate approach remained, significantly, the majority antiwar alternative. Most students were never committed to far-left Communist doctrine or Weathermen violence laid down along with opposition to Vietnam by the most extreme leaders. They were not, in fact, followers for long. They were not there to build a new anticapitalistic world. Motivated by a more single-minded guiding cause—self-interest *(and* a secondary but genuine belief that the war was wrong)—their revolutionary fervor faded along with the draft.

C.O. was one deferment that carried a penalty of sorts—a required stint at alternate service if you were classified 1-0; considered opposed to war in any form. The bravest were those who faced the horrific nightmares of being medics in Vietnam. They were classified 1-A0; objecting to bearing arms but not to noncombatant service. Garreau had three choices—counselor for disturbed children in Anchorage, Alaska; counseling Rosebud Sioux Indians in Rosebud, South Dakota; or program director at an Ohio State mental hospital in Cleveland. His lottery number was 206 and by August of 1970 they were up to number 195. "They were going up thirty or forty numbers a month. I was sure I was going to get it. But then it stayed there for the rest of the year! They froze the call-up at August level. At 195."

If they had introduced the lottery earlier, how would that have affected you? "If I had known I had number 365, I would never have gone to all the trouble of being a C.O. The day I found I didn't have to go, that was *the* day that my life changed. At age thirty-five, I can still say that is the pivotal day in my life."

When Garreau walked out of Notre Dame, he landed a job that would stun most college graduates today. "If I walked in the door *today* with the credentials I had in 1970, I couldn't get a job at the Washington *Post.* All I had going for me was that I could do layout and copy editing in a hurry, with flair." He also had his youth going for him. This was an era when national papers and magazines genuflected before youth. They gave them columns on social themes of interest to their peers—from rock concerts to women's rights to their attitudes on politics. Sections called "Style," "Portfolio," "Living" burgeoned. "They are no longer exciting," believes Garreau. "They have no *raison d'être.* They came and went."

Something else came and went. Their youth—although critics of the sixties generation feel that a special immature self-indulgence, an all-too-youthful "arrested development," remains. Garreau doesn't buy the pejorative. He prefers to call it the Peter Pan Syndrome.

"We did change in predictable patterns. We have gone for marriage and 2.4 kids and mortgage payments in bucolic suburbia. You can concentrate on that —but I consider it truly remarkable how we continue to carry so much freight in terms of those old sixties' values."

He launches into a comic routine about his decade-long bout with encroaching maturity and materialism. The first chink in the we-will-not-be-like-our-parents armor came when Joel and his girlfriend found that living together just wasn't quite right. They got married and bought the house. Then came the landmark, over-the-cliff moment. *They bought a $1,000 couch.* Garreau had once vowed that he was never going to own anything he couldn't carry off in an hour. Then that was amended to never owning anything that he couldn't carry in a *knapsack.* Then, well, nothing he couldn't put in his car.

"By the time 1976 came along," he says with a slight sigh, "it took two and a half vans to move." Still, there was a small comfort; he had kept faith with the vow in principle. "The stuff I owned was your hippie-dippie furniture." Then came the $1,000 "real grownup's" couch. There simply was no return. "I dropped into a bottomless depression for three months. It was just the next classic cop-out. First came the marriage depression, followed by the mortgage depression, and then the buying-the-couch depression. With marriage I gave up the ability to quit tomorrow and do the *Easy Rider* number, which was up to then considered a completely reasonable and viable option."

Members of his generation were hardly the first—or the last—to feel such commitment panics, but a well-developed fear of commitment does seem to be a common denominator among many. "Whenever you make a commitment, you cut off an option. To this day, I go through a certain zen; the day I feel I couldn't quit and go to some paper in Wyoming and make $15,000 and be happy, that's the day I'm looking to shoot myself."

Children touched a nerve with Garreau. "I waiver all the way up to 'neutral'—and then I think, No way am I going to have kids." His wife wants children, the biological clock is clicking away. Like all the other avowals, one suspects that Garreau may move into the world of fathers some day. (Statistics show the fastest-rising birth rate is among women above thirty.)

Garreau insists that many in his generation who have moved into business or politics or journalism are still purer than many in other generations. "In journalism, for example, I see a generation of ambitious guys who will do *anything.* They are in their early forties. Then there is a sharp demarcation. In our age group you get people who went into the system after all, but there are still all sorts of things they wouldn't do to get ahead. Like, if it means having to start going to the right parties and meeting the right people and generally doing things I swore I wasn't going to do." I protest that his generalization doesn't hold up. We banter back and forth, naming people we know who fit neither mold.

Garreau insists he and many others cling to some coda for living from the sixties. "All things considered, given the money I make, it would be unusual for someone a little older to live the way I do. I'm not what you'd expect some junior executive, an editor on a major paper, and the author of a book to be like. I grow 80 percent of my food and live in a log cabin in the foothills of Virginia."

I mention others in his generation who have moved slickly, ambitiously into traditional patterns. This includes the inevitable mention of David Stockman. *"He's* a draft dodger. I understand that the first priority was staying out of that war, but I find it despicable that he did it out of a sense of aggrandizement. I give more credit to the guys who went to Canada than the guy who gave $1,000 to the shrink. And deserters really put it on the line."

Our conversation recalled one I had had just a few days previously. It fascinated me to see the vast sweep of intense feelings, the old acrimony lying not too far beneath the surface about how one avoided the war. A newspaper friend of Garreau's, who went to Vietnam, heatedly argued that those who went to Canada or deserted were the "worst. They left their country." A product of his age of cynicism, he was surprisingly tolerant of those who stayed student-deferred or faked ailments or bought their way out with sharp lawyers. "They were buying into the *system.* If the system said they could get away with it, if the system gave them those dodges, then, okay, man. I didn't say they weren't *punks*—but they were doing what the system said they could." Another colleague, who didn't go to Vietnam, couldn't understand. "I don't see *how* you *couldn't* give credit to the ones who went to Canada. That was an act of belief."

Garreau is one of many who instantly conjures up a list of sixties' wrecks who never made it into the eighties. "Those of us who were experimenting with new ways of living and new ways of thinking were being sent out on long patrol by our generation, just as certainly as the grunts in Vietnam were sent out on long patrol by the Army. Some of us didn't come back at all."

Some were lost to drugs. Others found more exotic dead ends. "There were some golden boys in my high school," Garreau recalls. "One, who went to Harvard, is now in Southern California, heavily into transcendental meditation. In fact, he called me when my book came out and it became clear in the conversation that he took the idea of actually levitating pretty seriously. Another was arrested for impersonating a member of Brzezinski's National Security Council at a Navy base. He was the Ivy League geopolitical hotshot. We used to joke that he had no ambition for the Presidency—because the Presidency didn't hold enough power for him."

Finally Garreau assesses Vietnam and what his C.O. decision did to him. "It forced me to adopt an entire lifestyle and world view consistent with what I said I believed in the course of becoming C.O." The threat of Vietnam also forced Garreau to stay in college. "I guarantee I would not have lasted four years otherwise. So it changed my life, in that sense. And probably for the best. I probably would have split for the West Coast—and would now be doing God knows what."

3 The Maimed

THE LEFT HAND IS TUCKED OUT OF SIGHT AT FIRST, UNDERNEATH THE
table in the restaurant. The right hand stirs the coffee, stabs the air in gestures. His fingers are long, slender. At one point, Gene leans his head on his
left hand in reflective pause and it looks as if the third finger—the "wedding
ring" finger—is merely bent back, hidden by his thick dark hair. A closer
look reveals that it simply is not there at all.

In 1970, after receiving his draft notice, Gene stood in his kitchen for an
hour. Then, taking a deep breath, he spread his left hand on the counter,
tucked the other fingers back, took a hatchet, and chopped off his finger.

"I was a draft counselor. I knew the rules. It had to be two knuckles on
either one of these fingers," says Gene, holding up his hands. "And this was
the most expendable." He wears his wedding ring on his pinkie.

Gene cut off his finger as a protest statement, as well as to get out of
fighting in Vietnam. At the time, he viewed it as a symbolic gesture. He
carries the self-maiming with him forever. Conflicting thoughts intrude about
what he did as a youth. Even looking back, with some chagrin of a man in his
mid-thirties, Gene isn't at all sure that—the way he viewed his options—he
would have done it any differently.

When tales began to emerge of Vietnam veterans with psychological problems, there was a tendency to paint them as having a predilection to mental
instability. The idea that their problems could come from combat stress or
from their pariah position in society was resisted. They *had* to stem from
troubled home lives or because they came from that lower economic and
intellectual rung of America's ladder. Much work has been done by sociologists and psychologists to counter that myth, but it persists. Not often exposed, however, are the idiosyncratic deviations on the part of those who did
not go. Those who were lost forever in the movement or the counterculture or
to drugs. Or, like Gene, lost in a quest to prove something noble in their
manner of not going. Nearly every person I've talked to who was in college in

those days can recall some friend who had serious trouble coping, some to the point of suicide.

For Gene, patterns of melancholia and depression, coupled with dreams of martyrdom, merged with the turbulence of the sixties. The war pushed him over the edge and led to his ultimate defiant act. His darker side was masked by the flashing smile of an intelligent overachiever. When asked what he wanted to do with his life as a teenager, his response was "To be a lawyer." If anyone asked what kind, he answered, unhesitatingly, "A rich one."

Gene's cheekbones are deeply etched, set off by long sideburns. The smile is still incandescently boyish. Gene was always, even as a child, confronting "the duality in me. Growing up, I was 'cute' and, then, often called handsome. I wanted people to see another part of me. That sense of not being perfect."

Gene, who teaches psychology and works with troubled people today, was drawn to the profession in part after years of therapy and trying to understand himself. Gene's childhood was "very stable, very secure. My father was a chemist; my mother stayed home and tended to the children." However, he now recognizes that there were some seeds for his underlying doom-and-gloom view of the world. "My mother was depressed a great deal. Her own mother died when she was three—and her whole life was a sense of grieving and yearning for her mother. I felt her moods in that way.

"Clinically, there is a way of looking at 'hysterical' men in terms of their depressed mothers. [Hysterical men he described in terms of heightened self-importance, overseriousness, lack of distance, sense of enormous importance attached to their deeds.] Ernest Hemingway has been used as an example." Gene switches from talking like a classical observer to himself. "What I did about the draft was *not* the end of Western civilization as we now know it," he says drily. "That sense of martyrdom was just kind of pissed away in a rather ridiculous act of self-maiming. I remember a friend said something then that later impressed me. 'Goddamn it, Gene, what are you doing? The draft is not that fucking important. Nobody cares.' "

Still, what continues to lurk in his mind is this: "If faced with the same circumstance, I'm not sure I wouldn't do it again. In that act—in its total absurdity and ridiculousness—I still was placing a great value in *something.*"

His words laced with self-indulgent jargon, Gene alternates between emotionalism and clinical detachment—as if he is studying himself as a specimen.

In his work boots, L. L. Bean blue-and-white-dotted sweater, and tan corduroys, Gene looks very much a part of the eighties. Like many men his age, he seems fascinated to return in conversation to the sixties.

Was Vietnam a pivotal change for him?

"I certainly felt swept up in events. I went through a lot of changes." He seems content about one thing. "I would not have been a very happy lawyer."

Gene grew up Catholic and was influenced by "two strains in the Catholic church—the crusader, warlike one and another of martyrdom." It was the latter that intrigued him. "The whole emphasis on martyrdom and the heroic nature of that. The nuns would read about Tom Dooley. What enthralled me was *not* that he was anti-Communist but that he was a *hero."* (This was before the world knew that Dooley was a CIA informer.)

"So, in me, there was a very strong impulse toward martyrdom, heroism, doing the right moral thing. And the whole myth of the warrior *was* very crucial to me. I remember in college, we were on some trek through some mountains. I did some kind of daring leap over some rocks and I told the rest of the guys to follow me. One said, 'Fuck it, man. We'd love to have you in our platoon. We just don't want you *leading* us.' "

They sensed in Gene a thirst for reckless victory at any cost. Had Vietnam been something he believed in, Gene feels he might have become precisely that kind of glory-seeking warrior.

A turning point regarding Vietnam came the summer after Gene graduated from an Eastern establishment Catholic university. Dissent there was relatively muted. Gene was one of the first on campus to wear a "McCarthy for President" button in 1967. "But I was not a politico. I was not a Communist or Maoist. I never joined any party. Mostly, I felt a sense of outrage in a religiously moral way. As I got closer to induction, I needed to reconcile my own ideas about the enormous injustice and cruelty of war. The first time I really felt that way was when somebody showed me some pictures of children that had been napalmed. It was a very painful point."

Gene began to question whether or not he really wanted to go to law school. By now he was twenty-three and had been successfully student-deferred since he was eighteen.

Gene became a draft counselor at a Quaker house. "It was mostly middle-class kids, coming in and wanting to get out. As I studied the laws, I just realized how class-biased the draft was." Gene had a very low lottery number, 62, and by the fall of 1970 he knew his days were numbered.

"How I chose to get out became very crucial for me, as to who I was and how I wanted to think of myself. I wanted to make a very personal witness about the draft. I wanted to get out in such a way that anyone could, regardless of class."

Why not go to jail, as a martyr's statement?

"Heyyyyy," he says with a wide flash of even, white teeth. "I was falling in love, man. I didn't want to go to jail and have my woman visit me in jail. And besides, I didn't want *them* to interrupt my life."

Canada was equally ruled out.

"I could not stand the whole notion of being exiled. I knew a man from Colombia who occasionally talked of being exiled. I had a good friend from Yugoslavia. His family fled as the Nazis were burning down the door." As Gene listened to their sense of displacement, he decided not to leave the country. "A helluva lot of my friends went that route, but I feel a very deep identity with America. I kept thinking, This is my country, goddamn it. Those sons of bitches in the government are not going to push me out."

One fall afternoon, Gene got his draft notice in the mail. The week before his induction, Gene took a deep breath—and walked into the kitchen.

"I was a Christian soldier—and if I wasn't going, I had to get out of it in some soldierly way."

Sally, his girlfriend then and wife now, waited in the living room. Gene was not drunk or stoned, nor did he inject his finger with Novocain. He insists that he was in such a transported state that he felt no pain. He had to chop twice to sever the finger. Then he calmly went to the hospital to have it sewn up. There is a tuck and a slight indentation where the surgeon pulled the skin together. "I imagine I was in the same state as going into battle, the same psychodynamics. The body can produce enough adrenaline."

I argued that the actions of people in battle or heroically saving someone's life stem from necessity, while he had *chosen* to do something painful to himself.

"You're still thinking as if I had choices. I had convinced myself I had no choice—and told myself, 'You gotta do it.' "

And so you thought your act was a badge of honor and courage?

"Oh, absolutely."

The story is told simply, with little bravado and yet no embarrassment. At times Gene looks slightly agitated, his brown eyes look away, or he once again tucks the left hand out of sight.

Does it ever trouble you now?

"Oh yeah." Dazzling smile. *"That's* part two. I ain't twenty-three any-more." He shakes his head. "There are small ironies about the whole thing. Until the age of twenty-three, I didn't do much with my hands. Since I, uh, did 'it,' I found out I'm an artist with my hands." Gene completely renovated his house in his changing neighborhood of Spanish, blacks, and young whites. "In some spooky way, amputating that finger unleashed a lot of energy in my hands."

For a while, as he studied psychology, Gene made a living as an electrician. Many of the good old boys and blue-collar men his age who worked with him thought he had cut his finger in a construction injury.

His mouth clamps into a thin line. "I let them think that. As you can imagine, I'm pretty reticent." Gene agreed to talk for the book only after assurances of anonymity. "That was in part just to preserve my privacy—and partly a sense that I did not want to touch all those feelings again. I've been reading history and it's been very comforting to me that you had draft resist-ers in World War I and II and Korea, but there were clear reservations that I had about this *specific* war. I most clearly felt we were on the wrong side. If we lived in a country like El Salvador, I would join the rebels."

When Gene went to the hospital twelve years ago to have his finger sewn up, he did not tell the surgeon what he had done. "I was 'interfering with the draft.' It could have had criminal implications." When he went to his draft physical, his moment of exhibitionism came. He shoved his hand in the face of a horrified sergeant.

He said to Gene, "There's easier ways to get out of the draft, buddy."

How do you feel about it now, after all these years?

The pause is a long one.

"Part of me feels very proud of it. And then there's another part of me. . . ." Gene starts again. "I can't help but ponder, over and over, How did it come about that I did something so maiming to myself? I think it's not so much shame—more just a sense of reticence. It's a window into some deep and passionate feeling that I wear all the time. It's there all the time. At the time, it felt great. A permanent tattoo, this badge." He stifles a wry laugh. There is anger as he speaks of himself in the third person, that the decision of "that twenty-three-year-old—the son of a bitch" could so alter his life.

It is important to recognize that his choice came not just from the antiwar cause. "I carried a sense of doom-and-destruction. My years of therapy helped me deal with depression and hysteria. In a sense, I see things in black-and-white cosmic terms and I lose my sense of humor about them. That can be either a stifling hindrance or enormous power. With cutting off my finger, it was both. It evoked enormous passion in me—and it also permanently crippled me." He continues, "I *amputated* something about me." Then bluntly, *"Cut . . . it . . . off."*

Gene says he has rarely felt hostility from men his age, including veterans who find out what he did. "It's very evocative."

Do they see you as chicken?

"No. It's macho! It impressed the shit out of a bunch of guys I've been working with at Lorton [Prison]. Rapists and murderers. And for veterans, it presented a paradox. They could not call me a coward—they *would have* had I gone to Canada. The irony to me is that doing that, leaving my country, would have hurt me more. . . ."

The pause is a long, reflective one. "What I did was very important for me to do. To be brave. The Hemingway aspect: 'You're going to get screwed, but you need to carry on with bravery.' "

Members of his family and those close to Gene have felt more resentment of his act than strangers, as well as understandable sorrow.

Sally "sometimes regrets that she didn't confront me more with what I was doing. At the same time, she wished to support me."

Have you told the children?

For the first time, there is real agitation as Gene talks of his children, aged five and three. He clips off the conversation. "We've had some rather skittish conversations. I told them I would tell them later."

While moving through the sixties, Gene cast off many of the old traditional values and then eventually modified them. He and Sally lived together for four years, went through "couple's therapy," and were known to one and all as man and wife. But they never did get married. "Although we really did want to join," says Gene—in absolutely tortured jargon—"the ongoing generation of people who bind together." So they invited all their relatives and friends to a "ceremony" where there were no priests, no saying of vows. "But my parents called it a marriage."

Growing up in the sixties made it difficult to mature, Gene feels. "There was such *enormous* emphasis on youth and being young—in society as a whole and, in particular, with the left-wing urban liberals. Youth was very crucial and giving up one's youth was a major concern. I've talked with my parents about how they felt growing up and they seemed dumbfounded that we thought that way. They said, 'We never thought of it that way.'"

In some ways, Gene appears to be still struggling with growing up and chasing out the special demons of his life. He became a fanatic runner, jogging up to ninety miles a week. Then he wrote an article in a local paper about the woes of fatherhood, of being tied down, that was singularly lacking in humor and the height of self-indulgence. He is a vegetarian: "It's not going to save any animals from being killed, but it's a way of expressing some spiritual value, the depth of my values."

Finally, Gene ponders the question "How did Vietnam and growing up in the sixties affect you?"

"I found that it forced me and everyone else I knew to reckon with how cruel and insane the world is. There was such prosperity that, had it not been for the war, we all might have been isolated. . . ." He sings a line from the song "Woodstock" about the generation being "stardust" and "golden." "We would have been much more materialistic and so forth than we are."

What about the professed idealism of those days? Has that carried through?

"Idealism doesn't have much substance. The force and power of idealism usually come from self-interest." He sees as universals "a desire to be well-fed, secure, and loved—and preserving something of value."

We talk of those who railed against capitalism in yesteryear and are furiously competing in that same market today. "I think you're taking the myth too seriously," he says. "Those people are in the myth of idealism—but on the other side of it. A cynic is nothing more than a person who feels there still ought to be idealism. I don't see the polarities. I see it as two faces of Janus, just different sides.

"*If* something can be done to make things better for people, that's nice, but it's not the controlling value now. What's important to me is to be a father, husband, healer, a person involved in the American life in the twentieth century. That's what I sense most of the people in their thirties are like now." He makes about $30,000 and "would like to make more."

Is there any lasting legacy of Vietnam and the sixties?

Gene shrugs slightly. "It will be forgotten. Maybe it will be remembered for a while, until we all die. To me, the number-one threat to the world is that the Soviet leaders are getting very, very old—those who remember what World War II was about. How millions upon millions of Russians died. How the battles were on their land in Europe. When the old die out and the new don't know what war is all about, then I will be concerned.

"Leaders in this country are very irresponsible. We have never had war in our country in this century.

"We do not," Gene says—his left hand, now, after two hours of talk, resting casually on the restaurant table—"have a reference point for the horrors of war."

4 Hawks and Doves

THEY BOTH WERE AMONG THE IVY LEAGUE'S BRIGHTEST; THEY both were exempt from service for medical reasons; they both ended up in government in the State Department. There the similarity ends. One was a hawk, the other a dove.

As foreign policy experts—one for Carter, the other for Reagan—they took diametrically opposite views of how we should deal with repressive governments and their human rights—or lack of human rights—policies.

Vietnam was remembered more and more in the eighties as our escalation in Central America passed from the headlines into the consciousness of America. Poll after poll showed that the vast majority of the citizens had no stomach for another war like the last. The controversy and concern mounted as Reagan proposed millions more in aid, sent troops for "exercise" maneuvers in Honduras, ran a "covert" operation in Nicaragua, put marines in Lebanon, invaded Grenada, and continued to alarm with his hard-line rhetoric.

Both the hawk and the dove formed their present foreign policy positions during Vietnam. Elliott Abrams was the rarest of species—an outspoken hawk at Harvard, class of 1969. The year of the takeover of University Hall, the police, the strike.

"I always felt that refusing to go to classes was an extraordinarily odd way of making a political protest," says Abrams sardonically.

Amherst graduate Steve Cohen, on the other hand, is representative of those men who were deeply committed to the peace movement. His antiwar activism took on paramount importance in his life, more so than for most. Still, he embodies the kind of students who believed strongly in trying to end the war and felt that dedication to antiwar work absolved them of guilts or conflicts that came with their student deferment.

Abrams remained fervently faithful to our involvement in Vietnam and uses the outcome there to dot his many arguments for our continued "containing communism" presence in Central America. Carter populated his administration with antiwar advocates from the sixties. Reagan has found, instead, doctrinaire conservatives like Abrams. A devoted neoconservative and fervent anti-Communist, Abrams is Assistant Secretary of State for Human Rights and Humanitarian Affairs.

His view of today's foreign policy was shaped vastly by Vietnam. "It always seemed to me that the so-called NLF forces, the Buddhists, were in fact not going to take over, but rather that the Communists were going to take over. The notion that if the United States would just leave, the killing would stop was unbelievably foolish. That's why I like to make Vietnam analogies when discussing El Salvador. If the opposition wins in El Salvador, the Castroite forces will take over."

But what of the view that Vietnam was not our cause to be involved in? That our presence there created such death and devastation? That the outcome was inevitable, that a "win" "was too costly politically"?

Abrams vehemently puts forth all the revisionist arguments: "One need not believe wholeheartedly in the domino theory to say, in fact, that 'If the United States pulls out and abandons South Vietnam, there will be a Communist government in the South and Laos and Cambodia will fall as well.' That's exactly what happened. What *nobody* quite predicted was the extent of the bloodbath that took place in Cambodia. We never claimed then that *all* the opposition in the South was Communist. What we *did* claim was that the Communists had the guns and that they would take over if the opposition won. And that is what happened and all the Buddhists and all the Catholics and all the labor leaders and the intellectuals—the ones we used to hear about being in the opposition—are *dead* or they are in jail or they are in exile."

Abrams launches into a lesser-of-two-evils worldview of support for authoritarian countries. The larger evil is always communism.

"Anybody who does not think South Vietnam was 'freer' under President Diem or Thieu than it is now is crazy." He argues that Nicaragua was "freer under Somoza than it is today." He sees "a steady march toward totalitarianism" in Central America. "If there is one thing that unites them, it is that they're getting Soviet support and Cuban support. At what point do we stop this nonsense and realize that they do not *want* a free society? We're not *pushing* them into the hands of the Soviets? They're leaping into it because that is the kind of society they *want.*

"There is no problem in pointing out enormous failures in American policy. For example, Somoza. Not only is it indefensible morally, it is foolish politically to support a government that doesn't have the support of its people. *But,* that said, I think the fallacy of the left argument is that people end up in the Soviet camp only if and when we push them into it. Did we push Mao into it? Castro or Ho Chi Minh? There *is* such a thing as a Communist. The average government in the world is pretty rotten and repressive—right and left. There is just no evidence with respect, for example, to the Sandinistas, who *proclaim* themselves Marxist-Leninists, to think, Well, really, they're Democrats or nationalists who turned sour on America. Any more than this is true about the North Vietnamese. Carter *welcomed* the Sandinistas. His administration gave them $125 million in aid and tried to work with them and they *jumped* into the hands of the Russians.

"I find it a very odd notion of human rights or morality to be *indifferent* to the victory of Communists. As in Vietnam. Real-live, genuine, Communist party-type Communists who will absolutely destroy liberty in that country! How it can be in the cause of human rights for *that* to be the end result is the question the left has never been able to answer for *me.*"

Abrams brushes aside widespread church-based attacks on our policy of supporting the repressive El Salvadoran government.

"It seems the churches are making absolutist moral judgments and closing their eyes to some very difficult moral questions about 'Who is the other side?' and 'What fate do we have in mind for these people if the opposition wins?' "

The sixties' peace movement had a large impact—in Abrams's view, a negative one—on the conduct of current foreign policy. "Opposition to Vietnam was infused with a sense of morality. They were the 'good guys.' That business of the opposition being more moral and progressive than the people the United States Government is supporting remains with us and is one of the central problems of American foreign policy still."

Abrams belongs to a conservative chorus that has never ended: that we could have won in Vietnam if we had mined Haiphong Harbor earlier and bombed the dikes. All that bombardment—three times the tonnage dropped on Germany and Japan in World War II—was not "strategic" enough. "I believe the Christmas bombing is what ultimately forced them to negotiate. It was not inevitable that they win, any more than it was inevitable that North Korea beat South Korea. And if it would have required a few thousand American troops stationed there for years in order to prevent this *unbelievably damaging* American defeat, then I think most Americans would have been willing to do it. We had *business* being there, just as we have business being in Central America to resist the expansion of communism."

Abrams said much of the same at Harvard in the mid-sixties. He purses his lips into a satisfied smile. "We were the ones who were the counterculture in a place like Harvard. I was at Adams House and every night somebody would get up with some antiwar speech. Of course some of us would get up to make a reply. I remember the night I got up to speak—and everybody hissed *before* I spoke. I thought, Now you've really made it."

Abrams has a flat, almost prissy, automaton-precision manner. It is softened in person by a less intense demeanor, but he remains ready to pounce, like a champion debater. He seems never swayed by doubts, governed by unrelenting absolutes.

Abrams feels that his Harvard colleagues remain hopelessly misguided and "unwilling to reach the logical conclusions" of the evils of communism. "I do think, for the most normal reasons, that most people didn't want to go to

Vietnam or into the Army. It was a *huge* interference, if you had graduate school or a career or marriage planned. In addition, nobody wanted to get killed. I think, for the students who did not want to go for all those *personal* reasons, there was a psychological reaction: 'Either I am a coward or I'm unpatriotic—*or* the war is indefensible.' So which is it? Nobody wishes to conclude that 'The real reason I don't want to go to Vietnam is that I'm afraid to get shot.' It *must* be that Thieu is a corrupt dictator."

Abrams himself did not go to Vietnam or into the service. He applied for OCS (Officer Candidate School) but was turned down because of a bad back. Abrams has "often asked myself" why he has never wavered on an absolute approach taken so young.

"It was never possible for me to believe in the 'Hate America' campaign that was popular in the sixties. Spell America with a 'k' and all that. Also, I went to a very progressive, very left-wing high school in Greenwich Village from 1961 to 1965 [Elizabeth Irwin High School]. Everybody was already into marijuana, SNCC, SDS, antiwar, sandals. When I got to college and everybody from Scarsdale was discovering this 'new great lifestyle,' it put me off. I had been through it. It was not an expression of individuality or dissent, but rather just another form of conformity."

Through marriage Abrams joined a coterie of neoconservatives—former liberals who abandoned their past allegiances with a vengeance equalled only by the drunk-turned-teetotaler. His mother-in-law is Midge Decter, who recoiled from her own intellectual-liberal-Jewish parenting. She extrapolated from the experience of those around her to blister the sixties generation and their parents in *Radical Children, Liberal Parents*. She is married to Norman Podhoretz, the once-liberal editor of *Commentary,* now steeped in conservatism, who has added another tome to the Vietnam revisionism, *Why We Were in Vietnam.*

Decter's book "did not spring up from an ideology. It came from raising four children and seeing how it works," says her son-in-law. "She became a stricter mother with each successive child.

"The parents of most in my generation had essentially given them the view that they could do what they want. That is, I think, part of the reason the poor old deans in the sixties got chopped up. They were the first people who had ever said to a lot of middle- and upper-middle-class kids, 'No, you can't do that.' Some of them retain the old rhetoric and some don't, but nobody believes in that crap anymore—'no limits, no orders, no discipline.' Everybody has learned the hard way that you cannot live that way," says Abrams.

"When it comes to the *real* test—how to live your life and raise your kids—everybody has either openly or tacitly acknowledged that all that sixties propaganda was mostly garbage."

Another voice who remembers that time presents a more moderate view. "They weren't all spoiled brats *then* and they aren't all IBM salesmen now.

Some were incredibly bright, moved a lot of people, were dedicated then, and remain so today."

David Halberstam, author of *The Best and the Brightest,* was talking about those in the youth brigade who impressed him in the sixties. One of them was Stephen Cohen, who Halberstam met as an intense twenty-two-year-old working on Eugene McCarthy's 1968 Presidential campaign.

Cohen is in his late thirties but looks older. He is balding; there is gray in his curly beard. There is a reflective, professorial quality about him. Deeply touched by his youthful involvement in the peace movement, Cohen remains faithful to causes. He is involved in antinuclear work and in trying to fend off some of the damage that many Americans feel Reagan's policies are inflicting upon the poor, elderly, and disadvantaged. A major successful battle was the 1982 fight to defeat the Administration's proposed tax exemption for segregated schools.

Cohen was at Amherst, graduating two years ahead of Abrams at Harvard. From 1966 to 1972, he was a part-time student and full-time antiwar activist and peace candidate organizer. After Amherst, he was "technically enrolled" in Harvard Graduate School and then Yale Law School. He was one of those brainy students who could show up on campus three weeks before exams, cram on high-potency vitamins and black coffee, take the tests, pass—and go back out organizing. He now teaches at Georgetown University Law School. In the Carter administration, Cohen was on the State Department policy planning staff on arms control and was Deputy Assistant Secretary for Human Rights.

His message is in marked contrast to fellow Ivy Leaguer Abrams who followed him into the State Department.

We talk of the hawkish quick-fix, early-on selective bombing argument for winning in Vietnam. "Look, you know you can say the moon is made of cheese, but it's not. There were only two things that would have made them cave. One was a *massive* land invasion of American troops, one to two million at a time—and thousands more dead. Or two—nuclear weapons.

"The things that happened—Cambodia—all these things are horrible. But what could we have done to prevent it? To have had a Korean situation; that would have caused so much suffering and killing, it would have been impossible."

As for El Salvador, "There is no 'centrist,' there is no *middle* in that country, even if there *was* substantial land reform. Reagan compares the guerrillas of El Salvador all the time with the Sandinistas. They are not democratic, but they are not monolithic either. Opponents of Reagan would do a lot of good to admit that the opposition leadership *is* Marxist. The choice is either a horribly repressive government, the way it is now, or a Marxist-totalitarian solution," Cohen contends. "The major questions are: What is the cost of changing things? Can we make it better? At what cost?"

One of the many sobering aspects of Vietnam is that the "either-or," "right-or-wrong" concept didn't work. There were strong social and moral claims to be made against the government we created and maintained, but we also learned that those claiming to be a populist alternative were hardly flower children. Still, clearly reacting to the Vietnam debacle, Cohen opposes U.S. intervention against Marxist-oriented guerrillas and particularly favors keeping our hands off Central America.

"Insist on no Soviet military aid, no Soviet advisers, but indicate tolerance for a Marxist form of government. The idea that there is a new set of dominoes necessarily going to topple is incorrect," he says. "They probably *will* have a Marxist-totalitarian government in El Salvador and we should say, 'No Soviet troops or aid, but *we* will extend to you what aid you need.' "

Cohen buys an appeal to economics, rather than a military approach, in Central America. "If we can get along with Yugoslavia, Rumania, People's Republic of China, for God's sake why not Central America? Whether they are Marxist or not, they are desperate for economic ties with the West. The Soviet's economy is terrible. We should encourage the French, Germans, and other Western countries to get involved in development there also.

"But Reagan has created this mythology that Cuban support is critical. What we're likely to see is not troops but American planes or ships used to blockade Nicaragua." He sighs. "And that could escalate into larger conflicts."

Cohen's reasons for opposing Vietnam had their origin in world events that occurred before he was born. "I cared so deeply about Vietnam because I am Jewish and I cannot forget the Holocaust. I couldn't understand the lack of protest. The lesson I derived was; 'If your country is doing something wrong, you've got to try to change it.' I remember a quotation: 'To be silent is to lie.' I tried to live my life by that. Vietnam, *of course,* was not the equivalent of the Holocaust, but we were killing a helluva lot of people."

Cohen grimaces about those who hoisted the NLF banner. "Och! They [the other side] were as bad or worse, certainly no better. You don't glorify these people. That prolonged the war, I think."

In his senior year at Amherst, Cohen worked tirelessly for Allard Lowenstein in what became the "Dump Johnson" movement, then worked for McCarthy. His life was chaotic, intense, driven. For months he went three or four days at a time without sleep.

He spoke out on campuses wherever he could, not in moral terms but pragmatic ones. The war was a civil war; there was a nationalist element to it; the cost was out of proportion to winning it; there was government duplicity.

By that time, Cohen had an ulcer and was 1-Y. "If I had wanted to, I think I could have gone, despite the ulcer. I took advantage of it and have some guilt. I rationalize in two ways. One, I did work all that time committed to ending the war. Second, I would have refused induction, I believe. I would *not* have gone into the reserves. But I thought if I had taken the stand and gone to jail I was not going to be doing any good politically."

Ironically, he later says, "Had there been *no* student deferments or loopholes, the war would have ended a lot sooner. Those deferments and loop-holes neutralized the opposition of the middle- and upper-class parents."

Cohen feels that there are two major facets about Vietnam that Americans have not faced.

"The people who were for the war have not faced up to the moral issue of what we were doing there. To say that the 'other side was doing it too' does not make it right for America."

The second is a harsh indictment of what he considers the self-defeating actions of many in the peace movement. He feels these actions prolonged the war.

"I fought hard against associating lifestyle issues—drugs, rock music, sex —with the peace movement because they so alienated and turned off people who would have been genuinely against the war. Students generally made a fundamental strategic error by not continuing the 'Clean for Gene' appeal to the middle class."

Cohen looks pained even now as he remembers the factionalism and in-fighting before the October 1969 Moratorium. He was with the pragmatics who wanted to broaden the base and were pushing for housewives, concerned businessmen, and laborers to join. "Sam Brown and I had a vicious brawl on what direction we should take. Another group—remember the Mobe [New Mobilization]? The more radical? Well, they had this list of nine demands on a whole area of things. God, I can't remember—'Free the New Jersey Eight,' 'Equal Rights for Gay Senior Transvestites,' what have you," he says wryly. He adds, "Some of the demands were quite reasonable—but they weren't to another class of people."

Cohen and others, such as labor activist Carl Wagner, had succeeded in doing what the peace movement had not. They had gotten Walter Reuther and the UAW leadership on their side. Reuther and his group offered to march—which would have had dramatic appeal and an effect on the rank and file whose sons were going to war—if the Moratorium expressed only one demand: withdrawal from Vietnam.

The fights in the Mobe and Moratorium headquarters raged, according to Cohen. Mobe leaders were insistent. They were not going to drop their other demands. Cohen and company argued that Reuther and the UAW were tak-ing a political risk as it was. The Mobe argued that they were not taking a risk. "Besides, what did they matter?" they asked. Union leaders were out of touch with the rank and file anyway. In the end, Sam Brown and his larger-based Moratorium sided with the Mobe.

"Six months later, Sam Brown came to me and said, 'You were right. We should have taken your course.'" Cohen saw a pivotal chance ruined. "I was traumatized. The *one* thing we had been working for was to get the blue-collar on our side.

"Laying aside the tactic of *massive* draft resistance—which no one could persuade enough kids to do—the war would have ended a year or two earlier had the movement *not* adopted radical tactics," Cohen believes. Just at the time when polls showed many in the public were opposing the war, "That realization collided with one violent disruption after another on campus. The Nixon administration was able to present itself as reasonable and moderate in contrast to the students. That prevented a crest we had reached earlier from recurring.

"The movement was many things. There were the New Left, the Rennie Davises and that junk, but there were many moderates who were effective, who unfortunately didn't get the media attention."

Cohen sees complex psychological reasons for what he terms the "acting out" participants in the peace movement. "A strong motivating force for many in college was political guilt. People in better universities felt guilty about coming from affluence and guilty about people starving in this country. They felt guilty about their stereos and nice life—which they *didn't* want to give up. But, believe me, there was a tremendous amount of guilt that people were poor—and that they also were the ones going to Vietnam. That guilt led to looking for an easy, quick catharsis. They got it by yelling 'pig' at a bunch of cops, trashing windows. When you look at it now, what did anyone hope to achieve by breaking windows? There was catharsis in adopting a lifestyle opposite to the establishment."

Impressions are the warp and woof of much of the conversation, views, and theories about the sixties; no ordered, controlled study will ever tie those threads together in some scientific sampling. I ask Cohen why he feels so certain of his guilt-catharsis theory.

"It's my instinct," he says with a smile. "I've worked an awful long time in politics and I have an instinct about what motivates people. There were so few people going to jail at that time that it seemed such a politically futile act," he argues. "There was no point in going to Canada. And the way to assuage my guilt was *not* to go fight in a war that was so morally wrong. Sure, self-interest motivated a lot in the movement, but my answer to that is 'So what?' The real question is would they have gone if America or America's interest had been threatened? I believe they would."

His friends from the past remain active today—working for ratification of SALT II and the nuclear freeze and are involved with local social issues.

"For some, Vietnam did create a political conscience. They're still at it. They're just not all that visible. They've got mortgages and families, but they're still doing things."

The legacy for a generation?

"That's hard. The people I know are in a privileged position. I can't tell how it affected the lives of those who fought and were maimed by it. For those in my socioeconomic class, it was easy to avoid service and we were really no more than inconvenienced. By 1969 there was no way anyone with a good lawyer would be inducted."

There remains one vast division in the generation. No one, not even the most dedicated—although they now decry the way the veteran was treated—

shows any inclination to push for veterans' causes. "They should get whatever benefits veterans usually get," says Cohen, "and that Agent Orange stuff is outrageous." What about helping with delayed stress or Agent Orange? "You decide what you want to work for on the basis of what interests you, what you can relate to." Unfortunately for veterans who need help, the war experience is just not in most activists' frame of reference.

Cohen's personal legacy? "I benefited from it because I got involved in political experiences I wouldn't have had for ten to fifteen years. It's a perverse outcome. The war was so horrible in terms of what it did to this country and to Vietnam.

"But I don't think I paid any real price for it."

5 The Scams

THE MAN SPRAWLED ON THE GRASS EATING A KNOCKWURST IN A Washington, D.C., park is far removed from the despairing view of life that Gene, who chopped off his finger to avoid the military, embodies. He writes—often humorously—for a living. He is short and stocky, but has the leftover moves of a good tennis player. He learned, with easy grace, the gyrations of rock in the sixties because dancing was fun and he smoked dope because it was fun and he got laid because it was fun. His curly hair is beginning to thin about a clown's face—large nose, large mouth, gray-blue eyes that get a manic glimmer when he's thinking whimsical thoughts. He enjoys a heightened sense of irreverence, without being mean. There is an intriguing mix of shyness and a cockiness left over from his New York City youth.

"George," refusing to go on record with his story, starts into his how-I-got-out-of-the-Army shtick:

"It is 1970, sixty men about to take their draft physical, all from suburban affluent towns. *Everybody* is high. I mean, *stoned outta your mind* just to go for the physical. Every single one, bar none, is at least a senior in college. Nobody there with your eighth-grade education. Everybody's got a manila envelope—the shrink notes, the X ray of bad knees, bad eyes, bad legs. You name it. *Much* of it is fake. *Nobody's* goin' in. The guy in front of me is six feet tall and weighs 117 pounds! He's been waiting for this day. Went from 140 to 117. That's *his* scam. Now I am gonna get out. There is *no* question! This is why I don't want my name on this. It sounds real awful today—but I decided I'm going to get out by being *crazy*. I get this fancy note from this Boston shrink. His name has gotten around to everyone. For sixty bucks, I get the note. It says, in essence, that if you send *this* guy, you shoulda surrendered six months ago. I have no idea if he is antiwar and I don't give a shit. I just want my note to pad my act.

"My act is this: I'm not going to take off my pants. And if they force me to, they're gonna find out I don't have on any underwear. I am going to make them believe I am doing weird things. I carry three rolls of toilet paper and a copy of the *I Ching* and a teddy bear in this duffle bag. I am all ready with my dreams. I am going to say, 'I dream of cloud formations and they always look like unicorns and they end up fighting and I wake up and I've eaten my pillow!' I am willing to do anything! I am trying to be a thorough asshole: 'Ah, don't you want to see what's in my duffle bag, Sarge?' "

The sarge takes one look at George, stifles a yawn. He's seen it all. A whole battalion of "M*A*S*H"-style Klingers had come through. "That's all right, son," is his calm answer to everything George tries.

George thinks to himself, The fucker isn't going to let me go through my rap! He just has the whole thing wired. If I say, "Blow it up your ass," he will say, "That's all right, son."

The laugh is infectious as George flips over a paper and reads about Jerry Rubin, yesteryear's Yippie, trying to make it in the eighties on Wall Street. "Rubin always was a phoof—but he was *our* phoof. Nobody took him seriously—but he was reassuring to the kids who felt comfortable being on the *fringe* of protest. He was saying, 'Hey, you don't have to take this seriously. It can be fun.' He stands for nothing much, sure, but wasn't that always the case? Hey, I mean, Jerry Rubin is the kind of guy who would go on Monte Hall dressed as a pizza."

Like many of his generation, George remains struck by the monumental social change that seemed to happen overnight in the sixties and shaped their lives with stunning swiftness.

"Up until 1964, I was told to obey my parents, obey my teachers, go to college, plan my life. Then came this great change. By September 1965, it was 'Do anything you want to do. It's okay.' I recall it as a time of enormous freedom. *Everything* changed—all attitudes toward power figures, authority figures. Respect for authority truly broke down. In college we were just against *anything*. And, mind you, this was not Harvard. I went to a state school. These were not rich kids, but if you took a yes or no on Vietnam, it would have been 85 percent no."

Because they thought it was immoral?

"I don't know why *they* did, but it was to save my ass. I was always troubled about this immoral business, this 'Ho ho ho, Ho Chi Minh.' If you were South Vietnamese and your country was being invaded, you wouldn't think it an 'immoral' act to go out and fight."

We talked about the theory that the sixties generation was shaped by tragedies—from John F. Kennedy's death through the never-ending Vietnam. "That's all crap," says George. "It *wasn't* all depressing. That's a real easy thing for sociologists to do. The idea that we don't believe in anything because of all the crap that happened in our day. It wasn't all death and destruction. You ask anybody and he'll say that one of the great times was the protest movement: staying up all night, getting high, listening to good rock, finding some girl—and acting in protest. Just one of the college experiences—like 'Social Contact, 101.' Some of my friends didn't believe in much of anything. They were on the periphery of the protest movement. The ones that went along for the ride. And everyone was beating on us to 'believe in something.' "

Like many writers, George has an observer's, rather than an activist's, personality. "In every generation, say, 30 percent believe in some one thing. Five percent, at the most, believe *very, very strongly*. That's the way it was about the war. Five percent. Then the depth of belief trickles down from there. A helluva lot of guys just did not want to get killed."

What about all the talk about civil rights, the urgency for "black studies," the unfairness of life for blacks in America—sixties' staple of white-middle-class rhetoric on injustice. What was the attitude about blacks and poor going?

"Rough break," says George.

Did you think about it?

"No. I didn't think about it worth a damn. When you're focusing on yourself, your own problems, you're not thinking about anyone else's. I didn't think of them and I don't think they thought of me. I mean, I believe in civil rights, equality, and all, I just didn't want to get my ass shot. I could tell you that my consciousness was torn by that—but I'm not going to lie. It was not in my plan to go and die. I didn't attach any great metaphysical thing to it. I just *wasn't gonna go*."

That kind of assurity is echoed, all these years later, by many college-educated men. "I don't feel sorry for the guys who believed in it, who volunteered to go. The ones who believed in it all the way through, more power to them. They did what they wanted to do and I did what I wanted to do. I don't see how they can get pissed off at me or vice versa." His voice becomes softer. "I do feel *real* bad about the people who went who didn't want to go and were drafted."

George muses slightly about the war. "The domino theory, in retrospect, is in part true and so we were wrong and they were right. And yet the other point is it didn't all fall—and *that* was supposed to put our lives in ruins. The Commies would be at San Francisco Bay."

His face brightens, a young man nurtured on black humor. "Hey, look at all the benefits! All these great Vietnamese restaurants."

We had been talking about Vietnam and his generation for many months. Beneath the joking, I noticed a barely discernible avoidance of discussing Vietnam veterans. I asked George if he saw any guilts among men in his generation. "I just think the Vietnam veteran got a terrible, terrible, raw deal."

I found it hard to understand why protesters reviled them.

"I understand. *Anything* military was fair game. That kind of response was germane to a very small percentage who exist in every generation, who really had nothing but blind vision on the subject. You had to remember the knee-jerk social conditioning of the time. The first time I heard of a Vietnam veteran who came back and became a cop, I thought, That figures. Be a *pig*—

come back from Vietnam and get your gun!" George felt no vehemence to-ward veterans but felt they were light-years removed from his world. He was one of those who ignored them.

When I ask George what he thinks about them today, there is no joking.

"My guilt is that I see these guys walking around who went. I didn't go. I don't blame them for getting pissed off at me. The most important thing I feel about all this is wishing we all could become *friends.* But down the line, at the day of reckoning, the difference is he went and I didn't.

"That split was forever a divider. As time goes on, it becomes less and less important that you went or didn't go. Five years ago, it was the biggest division in their lives and ours. Now it's *one* of the divisions. Less obvious. Less a division. But our lives are forever changed.

"Sure, the social class divisions would have always been there. A New York Jewish kid didn't have that much in common with an Irish inner-city Boston kid. Nothing at *all,* say, with your common rural shitkicker from Valdosta, Georgia.

"Maybe the division is not insurmountable. I believe that most of the peo-ple . . ." He stops. "Well, *some* were too dumb not to get out, but most who went simply didn't know how to get out. In the main, the average IQ of those who went to Canada or became C.O.'s or found a way out were higher than those who went." George stops, as if embarrassed. "But what the fuck does that mean? I know a lot of high IQs who don't know what the fuck's happen-ing anymore."

For all of the cultural differences George would have found at boot camp, there is a sense of having missed a chance to grow beyond his stereotype of Valdosta "shitkickers" and South Boston Irish. "I envy the camaraderie. I envy the *experience*—if they could have guaranteed me it would have been just the sharing and the camaraderie *and not the killing.* I envy my father. To this day, he has a certain part of his heart reserved for this buddy stuff, for his infantry buddies from World War II."

George stretches his legs and there is this look of chagrin as he watches three teenagers walk through the park, ghetto blaster to their ears, listening to the Police and the Go-Go's, shattering the sedentary sedateness of govern-ment workers on a noon break.

There is wistfulness for times past as he laughs. "I remember my father saying in the sixties, 'How can you listen to that music? I can't even under-stand the words.' Well, *I* got to be thirty and *I* can't listen to this new stuff and *I* don't know the words." His music, once the stuff of protest and revolu-tion, is now billed on radio stations as "mellow adult contemporary rock 'n' roll." The Beatles, Simon and Garfunkel, even the Rolling Stones have been Muzacked into dentist office and elevator treacle.

"I look at the mirror and I look at my disappearing hairline. I guess every generation becomes its parents. The only thing that saves us is that it is always with slight differences."

George has a close friend, another writer, who went to Vietnam and came back thinking it was all a mistake. "Still, I get real silent with him on the subject of Vietnam. There's *nothing* I can say to him about it."

He picks up a blade of grass and twists it over and over. Then George begins a confessional, so out of character that I look to see if he is serious. He is.

"I envy those guys for having gone—*so that they never have to apologize for it.* I apologize every day of my life to them. If I ever have a child, how can I take a stand militarily? What can I say?" The way he got out, rather than the actual fact of not going, bothers him. "Had I done it differently . . . well, it's not something I'm proud of because I'm not one of those in the 5 percent who believed in something. I have a *conscience,* but I don't have beliefs."

In 1970, when George got his draft notice, whatever idealism or belief propelled young men to go were pretty well stripped away by the harsh realities of what was happening in Vietnam. Television made young men in New York very aware of what was happening to young men in Pleiku. "Guys your age were getting their legs blown off in places you'd never heard of." It made them aware of the botched policy. Critics were everywhere. And television gave draft-age men an immediacy with kindred souls around the country who were protesting. "We had a choice. We didn't *have* to go. We could pull some kind of hustle and it was 'okay.' "

Although George feels "reasonably guilty" about his hustles, he is quick to add, "If you think I'd have felt better about myself had I *gone* and got shot at, the answer is *no!* But if there was some other way to have served my country, I would have much rather have done that."

Why didn't he try for conscientious objector?

"I felt it was very hard to get a C.O. Besides, I would have had trouble being honest about that, about religious beliefs and such."

He pauses. "There are some people who had conscience and belief and made some sacrifices. Then there were the vast majority of us in the middle with no beliefs. That's who, twelve years later, I feel sorry for."

1970: The Army officer looks down at the sixty stoned souls who had all taken the written test. He asks with studied innocence, "How many of you have graduated from high school?" George and all the rest shoot up their hands. "How many of you have or are about to graduate from college?" All hands go up. "Then why is it, gentlemen," the officer thunders, "that none of you seems to be able to pass the very elementary test for the Army?" Stoned silence. The officer's voice rises: "Gentlemen, I will keep you here for the rest of your natural lives until you pass."

They take the test again and all pass. Hysteria—fake and real—takes over, recalls George. "The guy next to me was shouting, 'Get me a gun. I want to kill Commies!' Another was shouting, 'I have my X rays!' I failed my ear test, my eye test, found a guy with diabetes, and dipped my paper into his pee. I deliber-

ately found the one guy with diabetes! I checked off every disease, including cancer and homosexuality."

The emaciated self-starvation victim is right in front of George, on the scales. George peers over and sees the officer writing down a higher number. "Say, Sarge, he's only up to 117!" The sarge answers, "That's all right, son."

Finally George faces the doctor. He looks at George's psychiatrist's note. He sighs. "Son, we get fifteen letters a day from this guy. There ain't nothing wrong with you and this ain't gonna get you out."

"Come on, Doc, I'm fuckin' crazy."

The doctor looks through him. "You just ran your bluff. It's over."

George looks at him, forces himself to look the doctor in the eye. "Look, okay. We both know I'm not crazy. I just don't really want to go. My parents are old and my dad was in World War II and I'm the only son and I don't want to go."

The doctor stares a good while. Finally he sighs, writes something on a sheet of paper, and sticks it in an envelope and seals it. "I do this once a day."

"Thank you."

The doctor shrugs. "It happens. Give it to the last guy on the desk."

George hands it to the last man, who opens it, looks up, and says, "I'm sorry."

George walks out. A few weeks later, his classification came in the mail: 4-F.

"God only knows what was on that paper!" he muses today, getting up from the grass to walk back to work. "To this day, I don't know. It must have been *something* for that guy to say, 'I'm sorry.' Every so often I think about getting my records and finding out—but I know I'll never do it.

"I don't want to open up that whole period again."

David Orgel got his draft greetings in 1970 and quickly found himself at his preinduction physical, in with the "bad knee crowd." They were the ones with X rays and notes from their doctors and old knee injuries. "There were about fifteen of us. They had us crawl around. We were walking on our knees, trying to fall on our faces naturally. And then this officer shouts, 'Okay, you guys with bad knees are *in.*'"

There was stunned silence and then a roar of protest from the fifteen. The officer shrugged. "Yesterday I let 'em all *out.*"

It was, Orgel knew, the luck of the draw; the whim of an officer who had seen it all, day in and day out, scam after scam. Suddenly, Orgel felt panic. This was *it*. Orgel had read in some book that doing isometrics while your blood pressure was being taken could raise it. With an inventiveness born of complete fear, Orgel sat on the edge of his chair, squeezed his buttocks tight, grasped the underside of the chair with his left hand, clenched his right arm tight, and concentrated pulling up with his left as they took his pressure. His blood pressure shot up.

"I'll never forget the guy saying, 'Okay, you found a way.'"

Orgel was supposed to have his blood pressure checked in a few days, but the induction center allowed his own doctor to monitor it. Orgel returned to William and Mary and headed first for the college library. "I got a book on *How to Lower Your Blood Pressure*—and did all the opposite things. It said don't smoke, so I smoked four packs a day. It said don't drink wine, so I drank wine. I was doing Kools and Ripple at 7 A.M. and 6 P.M., just before they took my pressure. I was a mess. I had to go for three days of checks at the infirmary." Orgel managed to keep his blood pressure up.

Today Orgel, in his mid-thirties, feels he would have gotten out anyway. "I would have done *something*." He seems astounded that anyone would have guilts about the manner in which he got out. "Hell no, I didn't have guilts, nor did I think of anyone else going! I was getting close to graduation. I didn't see squeezing my ass and holding onto the edge of a chair a matter of class privilege."

A friend, Bruce Landerman, went to school in New York City. Many friends were seeing sympathetic psychiatrists.

"It was just a sense of urgency I felt. The Army?!" recalls Landerman. "I wasn't even a *Boy Scout.* The smart always survive. We were kinda lucky. We had options." Landerman remembers his first session with the psychiatrist. Do you like girls? Landerman makes a long face, in remembered imitation. "Well, I haven't really noticed them much." Do you belong to any groups? "Well, I'm really kind of a loner." Landerman started going to group therapy to establish a pattern of believability. "Hey, it even *helped* me!"

Neither Landerman nor Orgel were active in the peace movement. Still, growing up in those days, Orgel believes, "made us more politically aware." Landerman adds, "We were much more group-oriented. Everyone now is out for the bucks." They are both in real estate and the mortgage insurance business and view the "group-oriented" sixties as "just another section we added to our lives." Why have they not continued in that vein? "Just too many options, too many choices."

Both say they would not have minded some form of alternate service had it been available.

They try to recall their feelings about the veterans when they began to return. "I hope I wasn't among those who blamed them for being there," says Orgel with a slight shrug.

"That's as bad as blaming *us* for taking advantage of the system."

The Republican lobbyist, back when he was a law school graduate, tried everything. He tried to get a psychiatrist's letter. He tried unsuccessfully to get a *hardship* deferment—arrogantly arriving at the hearing in his brother's new *Mercedes XL.* The chairman of the draft board was also arriving—in a beat-up Chevrolet. "I ducked down in the Mercedes," he recalls. He went to the dentist; thought he'd get artificial braces, but finally rejected that idea. He was working for the government and he tried to get them to say his work was essential. Finally he remembered his childhood eczema. His letter from the dermatologist did the trick.

Today he is an influential lobbyist, a daily dealer among conservative Republicans—the kind who never took kindly to draft dodgers. Bruce Caputo, the former New York congressman, was a 1982 conservative Republican candidate for the Senate. It was discovered during the campaign that Caputo *had faked a war record.* Said he was a Vietnam era lieutenant. In fact, he had worked in the Pentagon as a civilian—quite a cushy out in the sixties. But times had changed and revisionism was in the land. For conservative Republican candidates in 1982, having fought in Vietnam has a certain caché. Hence Caputo's mythological record.

The Republican lobbyist for conservative causes doesn't tell anyone his war history either. "When anyone brings it up, I mention the Merchant Marines. Actually, I was in the Merchant Marines for one summer. So I let them think that's where I was."

The lobbyist is nearing forty, tall, lean, impeccably dressed with steel-rimmed glasses, pinstripes and suspenders. He has the requisite Georgetown address, an office filled with diplomas and plaques. He has been all over the political map—worked at HUD under Nixon and in the Justice Department during the Carter administration. He campaigned for Carter and thought he might hit it big when Carter came to town. "I had the good sense to have as my patron saints Peter Bourne and Smith Bagley," he says with a laugh. Bourne and Bagley were short-lived in Carter's inner circle.

Still, he did all right with his good job at Justice and he campaigned for Carter in 1980. Now he seems at ease with the Republicans and suggests that he is at ease with whomever holds the power. He hands over a speech he had just given, faithful to the Republican economic dogma. "I was whoring a little bit—but essentially I believe it."

I had agreed to not use his name, but had hopes of changing his mind. I had little success. "You've heard my story. I'm not exactly *proud* of it—but I have no guilt whatsoever." Still, he insisted on anonymity.

"We all live in different times."

The son of a prosperous New York lawyer, he took his student deferment as a matter of course, then got married, had a child, and went to University of Virginia Law School. One by one his deferments melted as the rules changed and he graduated.

"Here I was, a husband and a father. I didn't want the disruption in my life. I opposed the war, not morally but because it was a stupid war. I had no real concern about Vietnam—I felt I would *not* be on the front lines. I observed the war only as someone who had lived in Washington. There were National Guards in the streets of Georgetown! I could see it was tearing the country apart."

Applying for hardship status, the lobbyist argued that "Going to Vietnam would have terrible traumatic effects on my wife and family." The draft board didn't buy it. The lobbyist went to one of the street clinics that had sprung up in Georgetown in the sixties, trying to get a letter from a psychiatrist to bolster his argument that going to service would traumatize his wife.

"You don't go to your *regular* shrink for *that.*"

The clinic was filled with "kids with VD, kids on drugs."

The lobbyist told the psychiatrist, "Look, I'm not going to bullshit you. It would really help if I could get a letter from a psychiatrist for the draft board that going in the service would have a terrible effect on my family. It's not for *me*—I don't want you to say I'm crazy. It's for my *wife.*"

The psychiatrist didn't believe him. "To this day, he probably thinks I was using the draft story as some *pretense* to talk to him about something else!"

Next, "A bunch of us at HUD tried to get them to say our jobs were essential. The deputy general counsel was very much a hawk and got pissed off at all of us.

"Finally I am panicking. My preinduction physical is coming and I don't have any letters. You *don't* go to Fort Holabird without papers."

The lobbyist thumbed the Selective Service regulations as if panning for gold. There it *was,* under "Skin and Cellular Tissues, causes for rejection," right between "dermatitis herpetiformis" (viral skin disease) and "elephantiasis or chronic lymphedema" (swelling of extremities). "Eczema." "I knew a marine who had eczema and it got so bad in the jungle he couldn't walk. I got a doctor to write that I had been treated for eczema as a child."

The day came, a cold, miserable day in February. He picked up the bus at North Capitol Street. "The crowd was made up of your basic D.C. population and all of us smart-ass lawyers.

"*Every* white person had a letter and some of the blacks. Some had bulging briefcases!" the lobbyist recalls. "All I had was my scrawny little letter."

The lobbyist noticed that the other line was shorter and figured the doctor was funnelling people through faster. He switched lines. The doctor read his letter, skimmed through the manual, found eczema.

The lobbyist was indefinitely deferred to continue therapy. "I was 1-Y, which meant, 'We don't need you unless all hell breaks loose.' I couldn't believe it!"

Do not look to the lobbyist to remember his experience and thus necessarily caution future involvement in the affairs of other countries. Yesterday, to him, was long ago. "I believe it probably makes more sense to jump into El Salvador than Vietnam." He would have another generation do what *he* would not. Now, he says, "I probably missed something. I think student deferments were a mistake. I do not oppose the draft."

He has a son, aged eight. "It would probably do him good to go in the service. I would do everything possible to see that he went in, but that his life was not in danger. That's just a parental response. I think it would be a good exposure to people who have not grown up like we have."

He believes in a "strong combat-ready force to assure that we don't have to use it."

And if that weren't sufficient to deter aggression?

"I certainly don't know." Then, with a peculiar aplomb indigenous to some who speak with mindless casualness about such horrors, he adds, "I don't think it's beyond the realm of possibility that we might use tactical nuclear weapons."

6 The Reserves and National Guard

CLIFF GIBBONS CAME OF AGE IN A CLOISTERED EPISCOPAL BOYS' prep school in Charlottesville, Virginia, where he always felt isolated from reality. The preppies were being groomed for Harvard or Yale or Princeton. "Nothing less than Duke." It was not taking with Gibbons. "I had no intention of spending my college days in some snowbelt tundra," he recalls with his slight Southern drawl. Gibbons wanted to be back home in Florida. "I hung around with a pretty fast crowd. Partying a lot, doing some dope and lots of beers. We'd go catch Jimi Hendrix and think, This is way-out."

In 1966 Vietnam came into Cliff's consciousness earlier than for some sixteen-year-olds, despite his prep school isolation and his preoccupation with having fun. Gibbons's father Sam was—and still is—a prominent Democratic congressman. When the family got together, there was always intense talk about what was going on in Washington.

And Cliff was forming some negative thoughts about Vietnam "as a result of TV and newspaper headlines." Most in the media were not against our involvement then, "but they were *covering* it. I was always wondering, Am I going to be going there? If I had been a fifteen- or sixteen-year-old girl, my attitude most likely would have been 'Who cares?' But I could see those helicopters and the body counts and the *blood* on that color TV set.

"The greatest conflict between me and my parents began in the summer of 1967. I was an eleventh-grader. All my friends were pretty much against the war. We were not the kind you would categorize as Marine grunt material. It was 'What's this all about? What's communism? Who's the enemy?' I never came in contact with people who had those 'Our country, right or wrong' black-and-white opinions."

As the war escalated, so did the battles around the dining room table. Cliff confronted his father in shouting debates. His mother finally set rules. They were not going to talk about Vietnam at the table.

There were several dimensions to Sam Gibbons's support of the war. For one, he was a Democratic congressman loyal to the support-your-President ethos. Lyndon Johnson was trying to run the war on the cheap, escalating our involvement but not raising taxes, still wanting to keep the money flowing for his Great Society programs. Gibbons, on the Ways and Means Committee, was a valuable ally and Johnson had few peers in the stroking department when he needed something.

In the summer of 1967, Cliff was enjoying sailing and fishing and an easy, hell-raising teenager's life. And he would answer the phone and sometimes it would be the White House calling.

There was always a certain caché in running down the beach and hollering, "Dad, the President wants to talk to you!" And his father would get up from cleaning the fish, wipe the fish scales off his hands, and go talk to the President of the United States. Cliff, fascinated, would sit and listen. Mostly, it would be about Johnson's domestic programs and then there would be one of those sentences, "By the way, we got this military program bill coming up—hope you're with us."

Cliff's father had a special feeling for the military. He was a genuine World War II hero. "He fought so many battles, survived all that, and came out with a sense of duty. This war was a really big turning point in his life."

Before Vietnam, Cliff took pride in wanting to emulate his father. He used to wear his uniform jackets, play with his medals. The night before D Day, June 6, 1944, his father parachuted behind enemy lines. When the movie *The Longest Day* came out, Gibbons took his son to that. It was a big event for Sam Gibbons. It brought tears to his eyes. He had lost half of his friends in that invasion, "shot right out of the sky."

It probably never crossed his mind that his son would refuse to go to war. "We would argue and debate—him out of his past experience and me arguing what significance that had with going to Vietnam. I'd *volunteer* it after a while. 'This is *not* my bag. This is not something I want to get into!' Knowing his background and feelings, it was like putting a barb in him."

The calls from the President merely heightened the polarization. "Even if he is the President," Cliff would shout, "I think he's dead wrong!"

Cliff thought even then that there was "too much conflicting information. Just total chaos of information, numbers. Who's doing what to whom? And the answers were never that good. Kids were getting killed and essentially it still was 'What the hell are we doing here?' I'd ask him and *he* didn't know either. None of 'em knew. All you'd get was 'The President supports it and we're behind it.'

"The military was a very influential lobby on the Hill. They did it with a style the older members are accustomed to. They would go on all these trips —to see the hardware. He went to Fort Bragg and there were these spectacular military displays. Dad described how some Green Beret bit off the head of a rattlesnake. One of those survival things. Showed how macho these guys were."

Cliff Gibbons was not alone, among the sons of congressmen, in his feelings about the war. As the war progressed in endless, sad fashion, as *Life* magazine filled its pages with the faces of 250 killed in one week, the questions were asked. Just how many children of "the best and the brightest," of the men on the Hill were going?

A 1970 report showed that 234 sons of senators and congressmen came of age since the United States became involved in Vietnam. More than half— 118—received deferments. Only 28 of that 234 were in Vietnam. Of that group, only 19 "saw combat"—circumstances undescribed. Only one, Maryland Congressman Clarence Long's son, was wounded (twice, in the same leg). This was the closest the 535 members came to any personal grief as a result of the war. No one on the House Armed Services Committee had a son or grandson who did duty in Vietnam. Student deferments were shared by sons and grandsons of hawks and doves alike. Senators Burdick, Cranston, Dodd, Goldwater, Everett Jordan, and McGhee had sons who flunked the physical—two each for Cranston, Goldwater, and McGhee. Barry Goldwater, Jr., was doing "alternate service" in the House of Representatives.[1]

Senator Albert Gore, Sr., risked the wrath of his Tennessee constituency by speaking out early and loudly against the war. His son, now a congressman, felt an obligation to go to the war he detested so that his father's position would not be compromised. He served his year in Vietnam, in the infantry— and is now an impressive voice on the Hill for arms control.

Today Cliff Gibbons, thirty-one, is a lawyer and Washington lobbyist. He is tall and handsome in banker's gray suit, white starched shirt, tasteful striped tie, hair waved back. There is slickness in his superpolite Southern charm— the easy, noticing compliments and smile. There is an advantage to being unfailingly polite and well-mannered, Gibbons knows, and yet the politeness and compliments are so deeply ingrained that they are, in part, also sincere.

In the sixties, Gibbons played that charm to the hilt, dropping by the local draft board, jollying the nice little lady clerks. He imitates his style, sliding into a smile and exaggerated accent: "Hi, how yew doin'?" He explains, "It was all a matter of numbers. If they can assign a face and a name to it, so much the better."

Did he use his father's influence?

Cliff recoils. As a politician's son, he knew well the conflicting roles, the public front versus the private reality. "I avoided that like the plague! I *never* wanted anyone to know we disagreed. I never wanted it to come off in a public display as a lack of unity."

Cliff went to the University of Florida but was taking only twelve hours instead of the fifteen that ensured a student deferment. Cliff found a "cooperative education" program that allowed him to combine college and a part-time job and still retain the student deferment. The program had another advantage. It took him five, rather than four, years to graduate, thus extending his deferment another year.

The irony is that Gibbons worked with the Capitol Park Service. Along came one of the big demonstrations and guess who was helping to keep the peace in his Smokey the Bear hat and uniform?

"I sympathized with the people and felt so alienated because I was in uniform." Walking back from the Washington Monument, Cliff suddenly heard a group of guys behind him screaming, "Hey, motherfucker, you and all those goddamn motherfucking cops."

"They were bombed, long-haired. I wanted to say, 'Hey, I'm on your side.' This one guy got next to me and started spitting on me and screaming at me. I ran down the block."

Later that night, Cliff was sent to the Lincoln Memorial. "We didn't have guns or anything. We were just figureheads to protect the marble."

Demonstrators planned to camp out all night at the Memorial. Cliff was inside a booth. "All of a sudden, a barrage of cops with helmets and sticks came in and I heard the *thwunk* of sticks on bodies. Broken bottles were flying against the Plexiglas of this booth I'm in. Then they rolled out the tear gas." His voice rises. "It was an *incredibly* frenzied atmosphere."

As the tear gas rose from the floor of the Memorial, Cliff looked up and saw youths being beaten through the haze as lights shone on Abraham Lincoln. He thought, "What the hell am I doing here? This country has gone mad. I ripped off my tie, pulled off my hat, ducked out of that booth, and raced out of there. My sympathies clearly were with the protest movement."

The final straw came when he went back to the University of Florida that year. With its flat campus and one of the first to have ramps, the university became a magnet for the handicapped.

The Vietnam War was delivering up its wounded. "There were all these men in my peer group, all disfigured and screwed up. Veterans." Cliff would hear the sound of motorized wheelchairs. He imitates that eerie *eeeeeeuuuuuwww* sound that signaled their presence. "They'd bump into the desk," he says, grimacing. "I'd see these poor guys coming."

Did he ever talk to them?

"Good God no! I was embarrassed. What do I say? How do I react? Me, free and easy, on my skateboard? I felt more than ever like being removed from it. *I was not about to come back like they were.*"

Did Cliff have any guilts about them, about staying out?

"I had absolutely no guilt whatsoever. It began to politicize my feelings. My body and using it was a high priority—swimming, skiing. I decided, 'I'm not going to go through this kind of hell. I'm not going to sacrifice a part of my body to something that I don't believe in at all.' "

A decade later, Gibbons is sipping a vodka in Charley's, a Georgetown spot heavy with a prosperous, young after-work crowd. Frank Pfifer, Jr., a lawyer with the subcommittee on trade, of the Ways and Means Committee, joins us and quickly swings into his own reactions to Vietnam.

Frank went to Columbia, became active in protests. He sees no hypocrisy in fighting for the rights of neighboring blacks by opposing the expansion of Columbia University—yet letting these same blacks fight the war. The big takeover came when students opposed the university building a gymnasium in the surrounding black neighborhood. White upper-class students marched into Harlem carrying signs that said NO GYM CROW and KEEP COLUMBIA OUT OF HARLEM. It seems safe to say that no students carried signs that said KEEP HARLEM OUT OF VIETNAM. ("I felt so far removed, culturally, from those who were going," Pfifer now remarks.)

In fact, Gibbons and Pfifer are slightly defensive about their privileged status during the war. At first, Frank Pfifer practically denies class was a factor in the Vietnam drama. "I'm neutral about the class differentiation," he says, catching his reflection in the bar mirror and smoothing his thick dark hair. Cliff interjects, "What Frank and I did was find *legitimate* avenues to avoid going."

"A lot of the others," says Pfifer, "didn't comprehend the issues."

"I never thought of the others," said Gibbons. "I didn't care about them. If they wanted to go to college, there were plenty of state colleges and enough programs to get them in." What if they *had* to work? "They could come up with fifteen hours a week, going at night."

How did Vietnam affect their direction in life?

Pfifer got a high lottery number and rested easy although, he says, "Vietnam activated me. I wouldn't have been that aware otherwise." He worked for liberal politicians and was "basically antibusiness." That has changed. "Now that I'm on the trade subcommittee, I've discovered private sector initiative and so forth."

Says Gibbons, "I don't think it affected my direction at all. I was grade-A meat—but just in time Mel Laird got up and said, 'The draft is over. We're going to an all-volunteer Army.' So I graduated, sat on the beach that summer, and went to law school."

His personal legacy? "I learned there's more than one way to skin a cat. Playing within the system—and beating it."

"Everyone I knew was against the war. On the other hand, a reserve unit was respectable. Everybody knew it was a way of not going to Vietnam," says Darcy Bacon, the wife of an Ivy League graduate who was in the reserves.

Lyndon Johnson—scourge of the campuses, the man the youth brigades would eventually drive from office with their peace candidate, Eugene McCarthy—was, in fact, the very man who made the reserves such a safe haven for the baby boom elite.

Calling up the reserves would have blown it all, providing not only manpower but evidence that we were really going to war—and that we would have to pay a price. The military dogged Johnson, asking for a reserve call-up, but Johnson did not want to telegraph such heavy war signals to the American public. He feared his critics would seize on the call-up as a sure sign of all-out war and that, eventually, this would cost him his Great Society programs. And, as the peace movement grew, he knew it was politically expedient to pacify the vocal factions from whose ranks the reserves were, by and large, drawn.

One way to beat the system, by using the very military they ostensibly abhorred, was to "join up"—for safety.

As the war grew increasingly unpopular, the reserves and the National Guard became prized sanctuaries. Over one million Vietnam-era males became guardsmen and reservists. Even as early as 1966, a Pentagon study found that 71 percent of all reservists were draft-motivated; the National Guard claimed in 1970 that as many as 90 percent of all Guard enlistments were draft-motivated. At the end of 1968, the Army National Guard had a *waiting list* of 100,000. In 1971—a time of shrinking draft calls—the Guard was 45,000 *under* strength. A Pentagon official labeled guardsmen and reservists "Sergeant Bilkos—trying to look brave while making sure that someone else does the fighting." They were better-educated, more affluent, and whiter than their active forces peers. The National Guard and reserves became such a dodge for professional football players that if there had been a call-up there scarcely would have been a football season.

While they made more of a sacrifice than those who dodged, reservists and guardsmen found their duties minor inconveniences necessary to avoid Vietnam. They had a four-to-six-month active duty obligation, yearly summer camps, and monthly unit meetings over a six-year period. Training was haphazard and much less rigorous than that for active forces. During Vietnam, a small percentage of reservists went to Vietnam; the rest of the guardsmen and reservists were called upon strictly for domestic service—natural disasters, urban riots, and antiwar fracases.[2]

A reserve unit was indeed the place for a college graduate to sit out the war. Of the 1,040,000 guardsmen and reservists, only 15,000 went to Vietnam. Nearly one million (973,000) were never mobilized. In 1968 to 1970, 28,000 *more* college-trained men entered the National Guard or reserves than were *enlisted or inducted into all active forces combined.*[3]

Even on campuses where ROTC (Reserve Officers Training Corps) was reviled, many students joined up, reasoning that if they had to go it was better as an officer, with a possible cushy assignment, than a draftee. "I belonged to a 'subversive' outfit at Duke called ROTC," recalled Art Harris, a journalist who now often writes sympathetically about veterans. "My dad told me he had spent too much money on me to have me become Vietnam cannon fodder." He recalls the antiwar furor over ROTC as something of a joke. "The antiwar students would lay down in front of us [during ROTC drills] and throw tomatoes." After the demonstration, however, "we'd all go out and have a beer together."

As the war continued and protest mounted, the scramble for safe berths intensified. Family connections, bribes, and pull were used to get at the top of waiting lists. "My husband applied to a couple of officer's programs, but they were full," recalls Darcy Bacon. I register surprise. I thought officers were in such demand. "Well, it wasn't an *infantry* program," she says, rolling her eyes. Her husband's reserve civil affairs unit was "a very academic unit. A lot from Harvard Law—bright, talented, and interesting." Her husband, now a journalist, had a master's in business and journalism and was a weekend clerk-typist in the reserves. "He got into his uniform at 7 A.M. on Saturday— and got out of it as soon as he came home on Sunday. They had the short haircuts, the whole thing. It was not fear that led him to the reserves. He wanted to be doing something interesting with his life. It wasn't just Vietnam, it was the whole concept of the Army." Bacon knows one friend from Amherst who didn't make it. "He had one month to go. He graduated on June 1, 1968, and could not get into an intelligence unit until July 1. In that one month, he was drafted. He was killed at Hamburger Hill." The Bacons knew people who tried gimmicks to flunk their physicals, but "It wasn't in our friend's nature to do that. Nor my husband's. If he had been drafted, he would have gone.

"The war was part of my life but, considering how many died and how many lives it tore up, I was incredibly untouched. Those who went—that was something we *never* had any questions about. Looking back, there should have been questions asked. People just blocked out who was going. It's very hard to shed all the layers; the luck of being born privileged, born bright. McNamara came to the Amherst graduation in 1966 and he was struck by the fact that the brightest people were already wearing peace armbands. All the *summas,* practically all the *magnas.* He asked my husband what was it that made the brightest at a place like Amherst feel that strongly that the war was wrong."

In 1963 Michael Kramer went from Great Neck, Long Island, to Amherst. The Kramers were liberal Republican in a world more liberal than they. When he was eight, Mike wore an IKE button. Most everyone he knew was for Stevenson. Great Neck was predominantly Jewish, liberal, and supported the civil rights movement avidly. Martin Luther King, Jr., was a regular visitor.

Kramer's generation grew up during the cold war, hiding under school desks during air raid drills. Bomb shelters were a national mania.

Kramer found Amherst politically uninvolved, compared to large state universities. "It placed such a premium on scholarship and dispassionate thinking. The elitist schools were second to the more melting pot state universities, like Berkeley and the University of Wisconsin."

Kramer's old girlfriend, a high school cheerleader, was going down an activist path at the University of Wisconsin.

"She became a card-carrying Communist and later a Weather leader." They soon fell out over politics. "Once out of bed, you had to talk—and there we were, screaming at each other. To her credit, she stayed with her beliefs."

The war hit home when Kramer was at Columbia Law School and he began to see the rush to avoid service. "Some split for Canada. A bunch of us got in the reserves or National Guard. There was a long list. A lot of guys were bribing people—$100 bribes—to put your name at the top of it." Kramer, after thorough and arduous canvassing, found a slot in the Albany reserves. He looked up all the armed services units in the phone book, went to all of them, and filled out all the applications. "They were in fat city—getting the college-educated kind of recruit they never had before." Kramer recalls his search for safety as a "nuisance, interruptive. I didn't feel like going to Canada. If drafted, I would have gone—and I would have counted on my intelligence to keep me off the front line.

"I was against the war but not violently. I was using the rules to beat the system. Of all the people I know who went to Canada, no one took it seriously that he couldn't come back. There was this feeling that, at some point, everyone would come to realize it was a terrible war and they could come home. Going to Canada wasn't regarded as breaking a meaningful law. It was like speeding."

Although Kramer was in a medical reserve unit, he never felt they would be called up. "All I can remember is the disruption. I had to go to Albany two Thursday evenings and one weekend a month. I would leave law school; take the bus to Albany, which took three hours; go to the meeting; and take the bus back. It was a real annoyance. Then I went to basic training and after that I could transfer to a unit close to home."

Training of reserves was rather an afterthought in a war that was getting its fighting men elsewhere. "Some had been in units two years and had not gone to basic training. The regulars, the draftees, filled all the basic training spots."

At Fort Jackson, they were all in basic together—draftees, enlisted, and reserves. The reserves were distinguished from the rest by the ER (Enlisted Reserve) prefix. There was never hostility or contempt from the others. "At least they never *expressed* that. It was 'Oh, you're lucky.' We felt no animosity. Even the guys who were not bright said, 'I tried that but couldn't get in.'

"We college graduates were considered a potential antiwar threat, although it was never stated. We were given jobs that had as little contact as possible with other soldiers. A sergeant once told me this was policy." Kramer became a night truck dispatcher. "The only problem was that trucks never left that motor pool at night. I had no contact with *anybody.*"

His barracks resembled some unit out of "M*A*S*H." "Tremendous amounts of dope-smoking. We were removed from everyone. The Catch-22 for the Army was that we were harmless; there were no rabble-rousers among us. No real serious antiwar discussions at *all.*"

The last day of basic stays forever in Kramer's mind.

"I think the dreaded number was 11-B-30. You were going on for another eight weeks of advanced training, depending on your MOS [Military Occupational Specialty]. They read out the code that told you what you were going to be. 11-B-30 meant infantry. When you heard that, man, you knew the kid was just fucked.

"It was all so patently clear the kids who were dumb were going. They were the most inarticulate. There was an overwhelming sense that the slower, poorer kids who didn't test well were getting that 11-B-30.

"All I can tell you is my experience, but the *best* reaction from those guys was a stunned stare. Kids broke down and cried the minute they heard that number with their name. It was just awful. Besides feeling guilty, you knew this guy sitting next to you had a chance of *dying*.

"Even if you didn't know them personally, it was just enough to see their faces. You couldn't say anything. You just didn't know what to do.

"You just looked away."

7 Game of Chance

THEY CAN'T ALWAYS REMEMBER THE NUMBER, BUT THEY ALWAYS remember the moment.

It was December 1, 1969, and the country was going, for the first time during the Vietnam War, to a lottery selection of draftees. Across the country, in dormitories and fraternities and bars, they watched television as small plastic capsules were drawn from a giant fishbowl in Washington. A man's fate rested on his date of birth and his last name. This determined the order of the calls. First came the drawing of 366 dates of the year (February 29 had to be included, even though it did not occur every year). The second drawing picked out the twenty-six letters of the alphabet. Those born on September 14 were first, those on June 8 were last. "J" became the first letter drawn and "v" the last. In other words, if you were nineteen, you were born on September 14, and your last name was Johnson, you were in deep 1-A country.

Michael Hurd was nineteen and at Wesleyan University in Connecticut. His birthday was September 14. He sprang to his feet and hurled his chair through the TV set at the Beta Theta Pi fraternity house. Harvard senior Nat Spiller, too nervous to watch, played Ping-Pong. His roommates kept score. He found his birthdate was number four. In other corners of the country, the lottery defied all odds. At Stanford University, Tyler Comann's birthday had come up *first*. His roommate, Charles Thulin's, was *last*.[1]

While the lottery was obviously no respecter of one's educational and economic status, it was barely more equitable than the draft. Those privileged who came up at the top of the list merely began a nationwide scramble for deferments and dodges. Draft lawyers were charging $500 and finding easy loopholes. ("If you can prove that your wife is on drugs or that she is seeing a shrink and she needs you, you can usually get out," said Norman Zalkind, one of the most active of Boston draft lawyers in 1970.[2])

The armed service was drafting about 250,000 annually at the time. The first third drawn were virtually certain to be called, those in the middle had a fifty-fifty chance, and those in the last third—barring a national emergency—were home-free.

For that last third, life began to change. Some thought of dropping out of school. "One reason I'm at Stanford is to keep out of the draft," Thulin said at the time. "Now I can take some time off and not worry." Others with high numbers sought ways to get out of ROTC programs.

Those in the antiwar movement worried—with good reason—about the lottery's effect on activism. "People who are free seem self-satisfied," remarked one high-number nineteen-year-old.

For some with high numbers, there was more than relief. The sense of guilt that had dogged them vanished. As one Harvard student, Mitchell Jacobs, said, "I feel a lot less guilty. Now I can look at guys my age who didn't go to college and say that I had to go through the same drawing that they did."[3]

One of the editors of Harvard's *Crimson,* James Fallows, got a low number. An English major at Wesleyan, Eugene Legg, got a high number. Their fate and their subsequent actions still pursue them.

Eugene Legg's number was 269. He joined the top one third—the four million who made it out with a high number. To this day, having that decision taken out of his hands by chance "always clouds my thinking. I remember in '65 it was always assumed I would go. I romanticized it."

Legg, always competitive, had driven himself at Landon, a sports-oriented private school in Washington. Life and attitudes were drastically different at Wesleyan. "When Huey Newton escaped, that's where he stayed for almost seven months."

Legg "went to all the rallies," but was not a conscientious resister. As dissent heated up, he couldn't understand the breakdown in civility. "What good is spitting on a college professor going to do for a kid getting napalmed in Vietnam?"

Legg felt uncomfortable relying on rhetoric and tried to study the pros and cons of Vietnam. It took him overly long, he feels, to come to a gut conclusion he had embraced in a distant, intellectual way—that the war was wrong. Even when Nixon went into Cambodia, Legg found himself thinking, He's got to know something I don't know.

When did he think it was really senseless?

"Probably when it was safe to. I remember telling myself it was important to understand the issues, but I realize what a great rationalization that was for not doing something! It's like going to a strip joint for a sociological study on how others watch strippers. Again, that's personal revisionist hindsight. I hope it wasn't that, but really I was two years behind the times.

"The night of the lottery, everybody sat around and drank a lot of beer. One guy in the fraternity got number one. Everyone had all these figures in his head. After it got past two thirds and my birthdate hadn't come up, I didn't listen anymore.

"I still believe that I wanted to go, in a way. Still, that high number makes me think that what I feel about wanting to go may not have been genuine—

because I was safe." There was a familial obligation not to go. Legg was the last male in his family.

"I have guilts still. I have friends who went and some who died. You live with that constantly."

When lives are personally touched, the guilt, understandably, is more lasting. Legg cannot forget Buddy Kupka, a star athlete in high school. "He was killed almost immediately. People apologize for the war, but that doesn't bring him back to life. I went through stages. It was sad—but he died for his country, outrage that it happened to him, then how worthless it all was. I still have this measure of 'had-I-gone-instead' guilt. He is—was—just a wonderful person. I considered him to be far more valuable than I. He was wise and good and talented and he befriended all of us.

"I think a guilt feeling some of us have is that we should have made more of a conscious effort. The ones I admire the most, besides Muhammad Ali—I thought he was the best—were the kids who went to jail or actually left the country. At least they were not hypocritical to stay in a country they 'wouldn't fight for.' "

Legg decided to teach, in part out of guilts about avoiding service; it was his form of alternate service.

"I feel now that if I had thought about it more, I would have—or should have—gone. Not for the country, but for the kids who went and those mothers of the ones who didn't come back. If all the resisters had gone, think of all the brains that would have been there," he says with a slightly facetious laugh. "We might have helped end it faster. I could have enlisted, but my rationale—and I realize it was a weak one—was that familial obligation. So I went into teaching. It wasn't to avoid the draft. It wasn't something I was going to do for two years and quit when I was twenty-six and safe. I felt the ones who did that and didn't care about teaching were all assholes. It was to teach forever."

Legg acknowledges that his inherited money gives him the freedom not only to teach but to teach in private schools, where the pay scale is generally less than in a public school system. Still, Legg brings a rare sense of caring and dedication. He dresses sharply, almost in that 1930s well-creased manner, has reddish-blond hair and regular-featured good looks, and a slim, straight nose. His students like him for his quick wit and respect him for his exacting courses. Legg, in turn, goes the extra distance—whether writing extended criticism and encouragement in the margin of English essays or hamming it up in the school's talent night show.

In his mid-thirties, he is no longer certain, however, that he will teach forever. After teaching for two years, Legg read Ken Kesey's *Sometimes a Great Notion*. He thought striking out "would be a really neat thing to do." He became a logger out West. There was an element of macho and danger and it also appealed because it fit the back-to-the-earth ethos espoused at the time. "I hated the idea of a commune. It seemed so passive. This didn't."

While it was "definitely a rite of manhood passage," says the Eastern-reared Legg with a laugh, his reason for logging is the same reason he may not stay with teaching.

"My feeling was—and still is—try to do everything before you die."

We talked about the embarrassment that comes over some of that generation when they recall their sixties' behavior. The laugh is rueful. "I think the sixties was all prolonged adolescence. You're embarrassed in the same way you are after you reached puberty. You don't know what it was that made you do some of the things you did. All you knew was you couldn't stop it." It was a time when antiwar rock stars "paved the way for social conscience."

Legg feels the antiwar movement and the climate provided an "acceptance and enthusiasm for the women's movement," but he also saw a darker side for women. "I'm convinced you could meet a virgin in 1980 who was a whore in 1968. There was a license for that in the sixties. In a way, it was so much more demeaning to women than when they were pedestaled. All this stuff about a 'sexual revolution' was such a farce. The sexual revolution, as far as many males were concerned, was grounded in nothing except getting laid. For a male, there is nothing you'd like to start faster than a 'sexual revolution.' "

He realizes that today's young are getting no historical lessons about Vietnam in most high schools. "It is still too close to us to be able to teach it."

How does he feel history will ultimately view the ones who didn't go?

Legg pauses and thinks for some time.

"I think they'll call us 'passionately hypocritical.' "

There is another pause.

"I think it's true, too. Unfortunately."

Jim Fallows has come a long way since the fall of 1969 when his secure world came crashing down around him in the form of number 45 in the lottery.

Fallows, a Harvard senior, was tall and skinny. Heretofore less than remarkable attributes, he now seized upon his basic configuration as true salvation. At six feet one inch, Fallows starved himself down to an underweight disqualification of 120 pounds.

They were quite a crew, the boys from Harvard and MIT who showed up at the Boston Navy Yard in the spring of 1970 for their preinduction physical on what had become known as "Cambridge Day." Some wore red armbands and chanted the familiar "Ho ho ho, Ho Chi Minh is going to win!" (Draft counselors had informed them that disruptive behavior was a worthwhile political goal.) Instructions for the intelligence test were drowned in a chorus of boos and hoots. "Twice I saw students walk up to young orderlies—whose hands were extended to receive the required cup of urine—and throw the vial in the orderlies' faces. The orderlies looked up, initially more astonished than angry, and went back to towel themselves off," wrote Fallows in 1975.

I still see red over that description of the privileged behaving so outrageously vile to orderlies, young men who certainly had none of their class privilege. Where are the urine throwers today, I wonder, and what do they feel?

To his credit, Fallows spares no one of his class, himself included. Nor does he gloss over the tunnel vision they brought to their opposition.

Fallows subscribes to a view that to many seems obvious today—the true way to have shortened the war was for the deferred privileged to "be drafted or imprisoned en masse."

Because they were not subject to the suffering of their "inferiors," their parents opposed the war in a "bloodless, theoretical fashion," he argued in 1975. "As long as the little Gold Stars kept going to homes in Chelsea and the backwoods of West Virginia, the mothers of Beverly Hills and Chevy Chase and Great Neck and Belmont were not on the telephones to their congressmen screaming, 'You killed my boy!'; they were not writing to the President that his crazy, wrong, evil war had put their boys in prison and ruined their careers." That knowledge is so painful that denial exists to this day among many members of the peace brigade and their parents.

At the time, it was even more denied. "How little of this phenomenon we at Harvard pretended to understand," wrote Fallows. In fact, their failure to address egregious class discrimination made them quiet co-conspirators with the "war machine" they so detested. (It is likely that Johnson, Kissinger, Nixon, and other government leaders, cynically saw the value of keeping them deferred, out of the Army and, thus, out of the way. The uproar they were creating would have been mild compared to their response to losing their student deferments.)

The denial of class privilege coincided with an astoundingly incongruous set of beliefs—that by withholding their excellence and resisting the war machine on the streets, they were really stopping it all. The view was "reassuring," wrote Fallows, "for it meant that the course of action which kept us alive and out of jail was also the politically correct decision." Of course, the "basic fraudulence" was that "General Hershey was never in danger of running out of bodies. . . . With the same X-ray vision that enabled us to see in every Pentagon sub clerk, in every Honeywell accountant, an embryonic war criminal, we could certainly have seen that by keeping ourselves away from both frying pan and fire we were prolonging the war and consigning the Chelsea boys to danger and death. . . . Of course we were right to try to stop the war. But I recall no suggestion . . . that it was graceless, wrong of us, to ask the Foreign Service officers to resign when we were not sticking our necks out at the induction center. . . ."

Today Fallows, an *Atlantic Monthly* editor and champion of the draft, feels that as a college antiwar advocate he participated in the "historically harmful" move to get ROTC off campus and now champions the draft. He has written an award-winning book on defense. He "honestly feels no taint—and some admiration—for those who went." His past clearly colors his present-day thinking: he still gets "dirty coward" epithets for his published siftings through that past.

A black veteran, also a writer, caustically said, "Fallows has gotten a lot of mileage out of his 'self-flagellation' in print. No one would have known who he was otherwise. I find it reprehensible that he now makes big bucks off his 'guilts' then. He's got it both ways."

Fallows was included in a Washington *Post* book, *The Wounded Generation* —interviews with seven men who did and did not go to Vietnam. At the book party, Fallows seemed distant from the bonhomie of the many veterans present. The "we-they" tables were turned. "Veterans in groups make me know how the first black enrolled at Mississippi must have felt," he says.

One of Fallows's veteran friends tried to explain the gulf of resentment. "Veterans faced situations that had permanent effects. We resented those who never had to cope with permanent consequences."

Fallows gets a little testy at the criticisms leveled at him. "To those who would judge me as a person, I have a minor query. I wonder why people think I would choose to get involved in a subject if I did not think it important, particularly when it is about something I obviously cannot come out well in. I can understand my being called a hypocrite, but *exposing* myself to that charge is a form of showing my faith. The background which I have chosen to lay out may make the argument [for the draft] more compelling, even though it may make me a less appealing character."

Fallows's resounding guilt is for not taking more of a stand. "The greatest failing was not putting ourselves on the line. I should have refused induction and gone to jail." This is hindsight. "In those days, it was correct to do what you thought was reasonable."

Three times he returned his draft card as a mass protest. "Three times I got issued a new one." He was never prosecuted. "The government's attitude was in keeping with the student deferment—making it very easy to *not* take a direct stance. Most human beings will not push things to that degree. There was some individual soul-searching, but you also have to consider the rules that were set up and the way human behavior will function within those rules."

Fallows remains true to his opposition of our Vietnam involvement.

"What the revisionists spend most of their breath on knocking down is an argument that never had much credence in the larger community of protest— that the war was totally immoral, there was no shred of good intentions at all in going there, that it was only for profiteers. I'm happy to concede that there was some mixture of proper impulses that got us in there. But that does not change the fact that very quickly that balance between means and ends was skewed. Another argument is that we abandoned the South to the North. We could have stayed indefinitely only if we were a different nation than we are. Russia can stay indefinitely in Afghanistan. We can't stay with something that gives us so remote a conception of national interest. The major argument about the evilness of the North—which is a true argument—changes the case only if you had the romantic idea in the sixties that the North was better than the South." (Fallows said he was among those on the *Crimson* who argued against the editorial that called for support of the NLF.)

The lasting reason for not being there, according to Fallows, was that we could not come out ahead. "It was an untenable situation." What of the argument that the true historical tragedy was the North Vietnamese take-over?

"Not all tragedies are within our power to prevent."

It is hard for Fallows to answer the question, "What did Vietnam do to your generation?"

"I have such a distorted view of it. By my own actions, I have made it part of my daily life."

He, in fact, cannot leave that theme long in his writings. He remembers, when he became Carter's speech writer, right-wing papers running pieces about the draft dodger in the White House. "I think it plays a larger part for me than for most in my category."

There are, however, tangled residues of the era. Fallows says he has "come to understand and feel fully at peace with and respect a sense of duty to country that does influence those people in the military."

He also sees in a number of his contemporaries "this yearning to show that they are 'real men.' If that's a result of an unexpressed, unthought-out sense of anxiety of not having gone, I think it's dangerous. I don't think my emotions are governed by that. I don't know anyone who has changed his views about the rightness or wrongness of the war—but for some there is this feeling that a normal way station on the route to masculinity has been missed. I would fear romanticizing things to an opposite degree, but as a generational distinction, it's probably true that the ones who went—who had to cope with permanent irreversible situations in the personal sense—were strengthened and became mature through that experience."

He thinks long over the question of how history will finally examine the ones who didn't go.

"It's a good, hard question. The revisionist period is beginning now—the feeling that we looked entirely too kindly on the peace movement and entirely too negatively on the ones who went. People have to recognize that the movement made a difference on the conduct of the war. It was an important political fact the Administration had to cope with."

Ultimately, Fallows feels, the brigade who opposed the war may not be judged as having been right or wrong but regarded as an historical fact—as simply "having been."

8 Confessions

In 1981 a young poet named Michael Blumenthal wrote a New York *Times* Op-Ed confessional. The avalanche of emotional mail that followed demonstrated that Vietnam was far from a dead issue. Blumenthal learned that to speak out, even all these years later, was at some peril.

Blumenthal wrote how he, in 1969, spent three weeks "deliberately inhaling canvas dust from the sewing tables at a tent factory in Upstate New York. I was merely another college graduate evading the draft. . . . I was attempting to revive a childhood history of bronchial asthma that, I hoped, would keep me safely at home, morally and physically untainted."

Blumenthal succeeded, along with thousands of "my well-educated, middle-class friends," in never entering the service. "What it was precisely that most of us 'believed'—if anything—seems increasingly unclear. Our 'thinking' was a vague coalescence of fear, self-serving idealism, search for identity, and (in all too few cases, I think) genuine opposition to what almost everyone now agrees was a misbegotten, morally indefensible war. For most of us, the logic was hardly Aristotelian: we first decided that we wanted out, then *why.*"

Blumenthal thanks "my gods that I didn't go to Vietnam. Given a like situation again, I'd still do my best—though, I hope with a bit more moral integrity—to avoid it. What many of us then 'believed,' largely out of fear and narcissism, we now believe out of conviction. . . ."

Then came the ambivalence that haunts him today. "I don't much care for imposed discipline. I don't like regimentation. I detest uniforms. I am afraid of guns and squeamish about blood. But, as I 'survey' friends and acquaintances who have served, I notice something disturbing that makes me want to rethink the issue.

"To put it bluntly, they have something that we haven't got. It is, to be sure, somewhat vague, but nonetheless real, and can be embraced under several headings: realism, discipline, masculinity (kind of a dirty word these days), resilience, tenacity, resourcefulness. . . . I'm not at all sure that they didn't turn out to be better *men,* in the best sense of the word.

"There is something missing in my generation of hypersensitive, *'untainted'* men. . . . There is, I now believe, something to be said for the dose of 'realism' that serving in the armed forces (but not in a war, I would hope) gives a man (and a woman, I suspect). It has to do, I think, with camaraderie, with shared purpose, with self-transcendence. . . . It has to do with learning that life involves more than being concerned with—indeed, being obsessed by —our own skins."

Blumenthal's nostalgia seemed, in part, a poet's questing wistfulness for any unknown experience. It was also a search for tidy answers for his uncertainties of today.

Not having that Army experience "may have to do with everything that follows: with having a family, with making commitments, with knowing what it means to sacrifice, with being an adult (another dirty word these days).

"Maybe," he concluded, "short of violating one's most deeply held moral principles, serving in the armed forces or, for that matter, being in a war isn't the greatest tragedy that can occur in life."[1]

A new current of thinking that can only be called "Viet Guilt Chic" comes from some of yesterday's draft dodgers and avoiders. If not a trend, it seems, nonetheless, to have become a staple of columnists or writers having a bad day. From the sanctity of fast approaching middle age, they write of their guilt for avoiding the war, making money off these *mea culpas,* appearing on the "Donahue" and "Today" shows to confess all. Now most of them champion a draft for today's young men. Some remain opposed to American intervention in Vietnam—but a disturbing number of this group either never *were* against the war in Vietnam or now, with no personal threat at stake, see it in America's interest to step up its involvement in global hot spots.

Christopher Buckley, when nineteen and a student at Yale, carried a letter from his doctor to his Army physical. The letter told of his childhood asthma. He shuffled along, "trying to look wan and faintly tubercular." Buckley was rejected. Twelve years later, he stood at the edge of the crowd, watching the dedication of the Vietnam Veterans Memorial. As a nearby marine in ceremonial dress began to weep, Buckley felt like an "intruder" and left.

At the time of the dedication, I had written in the Washington *Post—* remembering the massive antiwar demonstrations that had occurred near the site of what was now the memorial—that there was a meager measure of reconciliation. "Some who used to taunt homecoming soldiers at Army camps and airports—the student-deferred taunting those less-privileged draftees or those who felt compelled to serve their country—admit guilt and shame." I meant guilt and shame for their treatment of the returning soldier, but Buckley requoted that sentence in a September 1983 *Esquire* article and applied it to his guilt for having "missed Vietnam." He points out that "80 percent of the Vietnam Generation did not participate in the dominant event of their time. About 6 percent of the males saw actual combat." Buckley wrote of a friend who confessed disappointment at never having been gassed at demonstrations "because then it would have been my war too." Another friend's "war story" was taking large amounts of LSD before his physical.

Buckley's confession: "I didn't watch my buddies getting wiped out next to me. And though I'm relieved, at the same time I feel as though part of my reflex action is not complete. I haven't served my country. Haven't faced life or death. I'm an incomplete person. . . . It's guilt at not having participated. At not having done anything." Buckley's sense of what it takes to become a man seems to be senseless violence: "I blew up neither physics labs in Ann Arbor nor Viet Cong installations." What about resisting and going to jail or saving a dying buddy in the jungles of Vietnam? Certainly far more appropriate symbols of growth. "I just vacillated in the middle," he continues. "Now I know I should have gone, if only to bear witness."

Chicago *Sun-Times* columnist Bob Greene followed suit with his own confession that he was "more concerned about not being shot than the morality involved in killing Asiatics" and that he worries about being less manly than those who went.

Most combat veterans, who remember their dead and maimed friends and remember the horrors as well as the romance of war, find such armchair anguish loathsome—except for some on the right who see such recanting as bolstering their noble cause sentiments.

A maddening hypocrisy is that some who confess today weren't even *against* the war *then.* For someone else, that is. I assumed after reading the Buckley article that he had probably given lip service at least to being anti-war, thus defying his conservative columnist father William Buckley, who staunchly defended the war while his son ducked out. But no.

Were you against the war?

"No. Not at all. I was sort of *quietly* for the war." How did your father feel about you not going? "I had dinner with him that night. It was my birthday and I think he was very grateful. He went through a war. I'm an only son. Even if I had been drafted, there was no chance —probably—that I'd be sent to Vietnam. It was September 1971.

"I didn't consider myself a draft dodger. That letter was not a lie," said Buckley, although his article points out that his letter contained the "worrisome" detail that his asthma attacks occurred "up to age sixteen." He continues, "They *chose* to disqualify me. What it boiled down to was my *spiritual* sense of having dodged it."

In his "heart of hearts" Buckley believes in a draft for today's youth, "but I think my actions forever disqualify me from the luxury of voicing my opinion. I have ducked out of a war."

Politically, Buckley, thirty-one, had some slight influence as a speech writer for Vice-President George Bush and conceivably could have more in future Republican administrations. He favors much of our intervention in foreign lands. Like many of his friends, he tends to be a "fairly robust anti-Communist."

The veterans he knows "seem as though they would be head and shoulders above us in a crisis." He acknowledges a danger in such "unproductive hero worship" of the men once despised on campuses—although none of these guilt-ridden that I know of have lifted a finger to work on veterans' issues. Buckley made a few half hearted attempts to do something for veterans by trying to volunteer at the VA, but seemed to view the veterans as largely in need of remedial help. "I offered to teach English or writing or something mildly useful."

An earnest sort, Buckley followed up our interview with a letter. "I hope you won't think me too bizarre or too guilt-ridden a Catholic, but for the record I have to say that in the matter of volunteering for the Vet Centers, they didn't have their act together, but neither, really, did I. The first time the guy stood me up for my appointment. The second time I saw that he did not have a clear idea of how to use me, so I never went back. My point is that I *should* have gone back and made it work. To have written about commitment in the *Esquire* piece and to have ducked out as I did was hypocritical.

"I hope I'll be committed enough to pull a tour of duty at the Memorial [as a volunteer for people needing assistance in finding names on the wall]."

Buckley feels he is in a minority with his guilt, but adds, "It's been a long time since I've run into anyone who was proud of the fact he didn't go or who bragged about how he got out. That has disappeared—certainly at the cocktail party level."

Such outpourings as Buckley's stir anger in those who were sincerely antiwar, as well as veterans and their relatives. Wanting to save oneself from a war as confusing and misguided as Vietnam was an honest emotion. Many agonized over it. The anger rightfully should be directed at those who cloaked that self-interest in overblown indignation, lecturing the world self-righteously about "immorality." Those—and the ones who railed against the establishment but assiduously took advantage of every loophole it offered—seem more specious as time goes on.

Buckley in 1983 and Blumenthal in 1981 were immediately blasted for their comments, just as Jim Fallows was when he first spoke of this guilt feeling in 1975.

John L. Hess, a World Wall II veteran who lost a nephew in Vietnam, summed up the essence of disgust in a letter to the editor of *The Wall Street Journal* (September 27, 1983). He spoke of Greene, Buckley, and Fallows. "I've got news for you, boys. It's not too late. They tell me Uncle Sam is involved right this minute in nineteen wars. They're nearly all guerrilla-type actions where a volunteer might manage to take a hand. So take your pick. If it's the Vietnam connection that grabs you, there's a fine border war going on with Cambodia. If you prefer Beau Geste and the desert, there's Chad. For savannahs, there's Angola; for jungles, Central America; for both urban and mountain warfare, there's Lebanon. And lots more. Ask your travel agent. I eagerly await your response. But I'm not holding my breath."

Hess, who saw "long and bad action in World War II," added that he felt the majority of combat veterans regarded those who did not see combat as "just lucky." As for Vietnam, "Nobody in my family is proud of what our country did over there. We were dragged in to save the Viets from the Chinese Reds, so we were told. Millions died and now the same Chinese are our buddies. Nobody in my family . . . ever blamed you for not serving in Vietnam. [Now] you urge that young readers not make the same mistake you did. Well, if that's the way you feel about it, then go. But don't send other boys to war just to prove your manhood."

In 1981, as soon as he read Michael Blumenthal's column, Murray Polner, author of one of the earliest books on Vietnam veterans, *No Victory Parades,* let fly with a blistering retort. It contained some of the smoldering anger I have felt while interviewing yesterday's evaders who now blithely endorse the draft for another generation of young. It is especially hard to hear this from them, after spending any time with veterans who will never walk again, or never see again, or ever think clearly again through their remembered haze of horror.

"A self-confessed draft evader, Michael Blumenthal obviously knows nothing about military service or war, though he counsels younger men that 'serving in the armed forces or, for that matter, being in a war isn't the greatest tragedy that can occur in life,'" wrote Polner. "Aside from his chutzpah and hyprocrisy, Blumenthal can resolve his personal mid-life crises by enlisting immediately in the military service of his choice. They'll take him until the age of thirty-five."

Then Polner scrawled at the bottom of his typed letter, "Found your Op-Ed piece appallingly amoral and wanted you to know, since *I* served in the Naval Reserve *and* the Army and wrote a book about Vietnam veterans *and* another on exiles and resisters. Shame on you for suggesting that *now that you're safe* it's okay for nineteen- and twenty-year-olds to serve!"

From Connecticut came a response from a veteran of Korea who received a Bronze Star. "I have always wondered how I would have felt if I had succeeded in avoiding the draft for the Korean War. I did not succeed. . . . I will tell you what you missed in war: 1. Brutality of humans against humans, worse than animals. 2. Discrimination by Koreans against Koreans. Blacks against whites. Officers against line officers. Men against women. Total debasement of humans. Vulgarity that one cannot even dream up. 3. Corruption in the armed services that makes Watergate look like child's play. 4. Forget patriotism at the front. Lots of patriotism at headquarters because they cranked out all the lies about the progress of war. 5. Life up front in Korea was like being in Siberia in winter. Cold enough to make your wounds freeze. 6. Death. Constant image of death. Death in the wrong sounds (bombs, grenades, rockets, stabbing, gunfire, machine gun, mortar, choking, shrapnel, burning flesh)." And then followed: "Realism, discipline, masculinity, resilience, tenacity, resourcefulness, camaraderie, love of your birthplace, fondness of your past, loyalty to your group, believer of the future, of tomorrow." And *then* followed by: "Never stop learning or studying." And finally: "Never trust a politician." He concludes: "Did the Army make me a better human? I have always wondered."

A male of Blumenthal's generation wrote from Rhode Island: "It seems a shame that . . . your imagination couldn't have stretched a bit further than the military as the object of your privation. Certainly the official organ of destruction is the wrong beneficiary of your frustrated camaraderie. What about the Boy Scouts? Astronauts, construction work, exploration—aren't these more worthwhile avenues for bonding men together than peril of survival? . . . The possibility for war waxes in yearnings such as this. . . . Is it not obvious that Russian aggression and military growth are responses to American hawkishness; cold war activity is a self-inflicted tumor whose pathology is Pentagonian thinking."

On the other hand, Blumenthal was applauded by a World War II veteran. "We take great pride in having served and those of us who survived in one piece (a major consideration) feel we gained a great deal of maturity. We also feel that those who have not served have not seen the whole parade. . . ."

And some nongoers wrote that they too felt they had missed something.

A mother, whose father and husband were marines but whose son starved himself out of the Vietnam-era draft, seemed on both sides at once. "Having known so many C.O.'s, I know that many were incapable of standing up for anything. Others were true.

"Surely our Constitution isn't ever going to stay safe and sound without the true objector and the true soldier—who decides each war on its merits."

A Texan wrote: "You are a sensitive man and I commend you for your very candid thoughts. Anyone that is thirty-three years old can easily recall the summer of 1970. I was drafted and it made me upset and bitter. . . . As they say, I got to travel. Straight to Vietnam. . . . At this time, I just cannot get it out of my mind. I cannot forget how father was turned against son, young against old, and how favored traditions were ignored or forgotten. . . . I gave my best efforts to avoid the situation. I think that this is our nature. I believe that I am a better person because of my Army experience . . . I believe that we were trying to help other people in the world fight off the yoke of oppression and that Jane [Fonda], Joan [Baez], and Abbie [Hoffman] have done a lot to make us feel guilty—and this still bothers me. . . . War is always bad; I hope that none of my children find themselves in the same pitiful dilemma that we faced. But I also hope that they will listen to me instead of people like Jane, Joan, and Abbie. . . ."

A man from Massachusetts shared the same view of our involvement in Vietnam, but not the same largesse for Blumenthal: "Now that you are safely past the draft age, there apparently is some dim perception that the military exists to defend and protect the interests of the citizenry-at-large and their values. Since you now have some stake in a secure future, it surely must seem only fitting that not too many people dodge the draft *this* time around. . . . Of course, it is still necessary to maintain the illusion of the superior morality of the Khmer Rouge. Ignore their three to four million hapless victims. Otherwise, you might start to feel pangs of guilt and self-doubt—that would never do for one with the highly developed moral sensitivities of the sixties. And those vulgar boat people! They just don't understand that all you wanted to do was to 'Give Peace a Chance'! . . . Let's not forget the asthma! No doubt, you've informed your insurance carrier of your self-induced malady. That would relieve the rest of us from paying for your future respiratory treatments with our premiums. Or does your sense of 'Fair is fair' require that we also carry that burden for you?"

Interestingly, women came down the hardest on Blumenthal. A letter from Brooklyn: "Self-preservation and the refusal to die in a senseless war are not bad motives to start with—and there was a camaraderie on which to build. Maybe *you* didn't go far enough. Who are these former soldiers you talk with? The ones suffering from Agent Orange? The ones with guilt feelings for the atrocities which were committed? The ones who resisted the military from within? The poor and/or black soldier who would have experienced 'real' life —if by that you mean *suffering—without* the war? . . . You are also falling into the danger of counseling acts for which you cannot take the conse-quences—the 'old sending the young to war.' "

Another woman from Great Neck wrote that many young people sought ways to develop resiliency and realism—"backpacking, serving in outlying posts in the Peace Corps, working on construction gangs, etc.—but want no part of character training that includes the brutality of learning how to kill. . . . It seems quite smug of Mr. Blumenthal to preach from his now-safe perch. . . . Has he any answer to those whose lives were cut short or who have been physically and/or emotionally disabled for life because they were unfortunate enough to be in the armed forces at the time of a war?"

And yet another female wrote that he should seek the qualities he felt he missed in contexts other than war—working in communion for clean air, to clean up toxic wastes or for peace. Otherwise, "I will have to think too much canvas dust got into your brain."

For some Vietnam veterans, Blumenthal's admission was seen as a begin-ning in an attempt to breach a gap. One former marine emphasized that the young man who has killed needs the support of "ritual expression" of accep-tance, he wrote. That denial of such a human need—"a national purging of sorts—is at the root of the Vietnam veterans' problems." When the marine returned from Vietnam, he attended a small rural college "deep within John Birch territory. . . . Eighteen of us veterans organized the first protest after Kent State. With a few exceptions, our *non*veteran peers declined to partici-pate after a few sniper threats were phoned to the school. We felt frustrated at our inability to convince the other students that self-transcendence, truth in purpose, risk, and sacrifice were necessary."

Blumenthal, drinking cappuccino in a Washington restaurant, reached for his file of letters. He seemed sobered by the reactions he had stirred. "In some way, the generation was *filled* with victims. Absolutely! We still haven't gotten over the polarized view of a time when you were 'for' or 'against' the war.

"It's such a complicated subject, but everybody struggles with some rites of passage. Historically, for thousands of years, one of the rites of passage has been some kind of military one. I feel that I and a lot of my peers have, in lots of ways, remained children. Selfish. Veterans who saw combat were responsible for others' *lives.* I continually see in those people something I don't have."

Blumenthal seems to possess a writer's curiosity, of wanting a deep experience, in part, in order to create from that experience. "Three of the poets I most admire were all World War II bomber pilots—Howard Nemerov, Richard Hugo, and William Meredith."

Blumenthal repeats what I have heard from other nongoers. Because it was Vietnam and not a "better" war, "we were all cheated out of having a meaningful experience in the military."

I put the question from those replies to him. What about absolving that sense of "something being missed" by a camaraderie in sharing, in helping others? "It's true. I don't have any excuse. I'm not into community organizing, doing something for the poor. Everyone is self-involved now and there is an emptiness in that."

What about those who ask, "If you missed so much, why don't you enlist?"

"It would have had to have been at that young age, that rite of passage."

What happens when you meet a Vietnam veteran?

"I am tremendously *curious.* I want to know what it was really like to be there. I have a close friend who is scarred for life. He was a platoon commander. He's very pacifist. Reads Zen."

Blumenthal looked back to the days when many who didn't go treated veterans as objects of derision, both for having gone and for having killed.

"Those guys showing up on campus with their short hair! It was just not cool to be seen with them. There was an intolerance of the sixties and I still fight against it. I have a residue of that kind of judgmental thinking. I don't believe there *ever* was a period more conformist than then!

"I think one of the problems of the sixties was this tremendously romantic and stupid view of human nature. I would be willing to bet a disproportionate amount of wife beaters, child beaters, guys getting into brawls are *not* veterans."

It is easy to see the child in Blumenthal, in his mass of curly hair, his blue-eyed face that looks still untouched—or "untainted"—by life. He grew up in Manhattan's Washington Heights, the son of Jewish immigrants. "I thought German was the national language," laughs Blumenthal. His father was a hardworking retail furrier. His son would be the first in the family to graduate from college.

Being "swept along by peer pressure" was a large part of college for Blumenthal. "My roommate's best friend took LSD when he brushed his teeth in the morning. It was like a vitamin. But, even then, there was only a small group of freaks. A lot were into grass. I smoked dope only a few times. It was just my German-Jewish upbringing."

Like many of his generation, Blumenthal mentions the "radical change between the sexes. We were the first generation to really discover, en masse, birth control." The acceleration of sexual freedom brought an acceleration of life beyond the ability of some to keep up with it.

"The richness—I hated it—the kind of arrogance of the generation. It's an arrogant age anyway, adolescence, even in the best of times. In the worst of times, it's accelerated.

"What disturbs me about the war is, even though we were right, we really didn't mean it. Some of the committed, like the Berrigans, they're constants, genuine and real. Their participation came from real conviction, not peer pressure or an egomaniacal chance to leap into something, like a Jerry Rubin."

Blumenthal feels that many of his peers are vaguely embarrassed about their present goals and ideals. "A lot feel some sort of guilt because they want the money, the split-level house, and yet still want to cling to something. They go get the MBA and the house—but attached to the house is an organic greenhouse and that makes them feel better."

Like so many who did not take a strong stand, Blumenthal seems among the most uncertain about past actions. Still, he contends, "The sad people are the ones who are still idealistic. One guy I know is into some Jesus movement, works with hungry people, street people, bails them out of jail. I really admire and envy him—it takes great guts to do that. But it is sad. I myself feel torn between an 'acquisition' kind of life and a more idealistic kind."

Washington power circles are always populated by those who desire to be with the prevailing sentiment. David Stockman renounced his University of Michigan antiwar activist days when he became Reagan's OMB budget director. He quickly set about slashing programs that Democrats had set up to aid, among others, the poor, the elderly and Vietnam veterans.

A "fanatical Goldwaterite" during his high school days in a Michigan Republican farming community, Stockman says he was led down the primrose path by a "Brooklyn, Jewish, socialist, atheist" professor who challenged Stockman's assumptions and "left me skeptical about everything I thought." The natural questioning rebellion of many a freshman was "intensified by Vietnam. The war just drove that traditional sophomoric struggle to a much more intense, active level. It was sort of easy for me to be convinced by the anti-Vietnam stuff since I had been convinced all that other stuff was wrong too."

He has dramatically changed his views on Vietnam. "Then I thought there was no U.S. interest involved. Now I think there was in the abstract. Then I thought it was an entirely indigenous nationalist uprising. Now I think it was exploited from Hanoi. The way we conducted it and managed it was a mistake—but not because it was wrong to be there."

Stockman's retreat into divinity school is largely viewed as a draft dodge. Stockman contends, "My primary motive was that I did want to study theology—the secondary is that it did give me a deferral. I'm not going to argue with anyone. I just know how I recollect it." He admits that "Once I went to divinity school, I never worried about the draft that much." He remained there until 1970. By then, the lottery was in existence and his number was "well over 300." A summer job with Congressman John Anderson became full-time. There was no return to divinity school. Stockman, who insisted his primary motive was to study theology, reluctantly concedes, however, "Had the lottery not come through, I might have felt differently [about returning]."

The New Republic, left-wing in tone in the sixties, now embraces much of Reagan's foreign policy. Its publisher, James Glassman, recalls his days of writing antiwar tracts for the Harvard *Crimson.* Much of his "political and moral instincts" then stemmed from the "immaturity" of youth. "I was a little cavalier. I had this moral objection to this particular war. I probably don't even know what I meant by 'morally' then. I don't feel guilt, but I'm embarrassed by the lengths my friends and I went to to get out. Migraine headaches, certified by the doctor," Glassman says with a slight laugh. "We exhibited a kind of political and moral blindness. Other guys were going, for God's sake! I knew there was something wrong [about deferments], but I never went beyond intellectual realization."

There was power in being against the war in Ivy League universities. "We were so special and had an *adult* support system, especially in universities, with all these professors pandering to you," says Glassman, who was there at the height of protest, graduating in 1969. "None of us would have gotten away with this if we didn't get the support of all these people we were disparaging. We were never at risk. We sat in against a Dow Chemical recruiter and everyone was 'put on probation'—and this meant you couldn't be an officer in a college organization. About a month later I was up for managing editor of the *Crimson* and another guy was up for photo editor. We made a deal—we could be managing editor and photo editor but couldn't get our names on the masthead."

Today Glassman says, "Vietnam was a war we should never have fought, but I don't feel now that it was a massive moral error. Now I believe the VC and NLF were wrong and we were right to support the South Vietnamese. Vietnam couldn't be any more of a puppet state than it is now." His absolutist view is now on the other side. "In El Salvador, we should get rid of the rebels and stabilize the regime that is there." He recognizes that civil wars and foreign policy, despots versus Marxists, are much more complex than his student's eye view. Still, says Glassman, "If they were both equally bad, I would choose [to support] the right-wing bad guys over the left-wing bad guys. More of my pals are close to the *New Republic* position in foreign policy; the drift is a little more to the right. But I have no idea if that is true of the majority [from antiwar days]. Probably not."

We talked about those from the generation who were lost to drugs or eschewed a materialistic lifestyle. "I don't know a single peer who is like that. Some postponed becoming normal conformist adults. It took some longer to become socially integrated capitalists," he says with a laugh. "I think I'm a born capitalist." He recalls that some wandered on the outer edges for a while, "trying to adhere to a different lifestyle that didn't last long. Some of them returned to law or med school six years later. Like many, I postponed my own adulthood. There is a lack of commitment among many, who are immature, still trying to keep all their options open."

After listening to some of these men, there is an impulse to cast every sixties campus "revolutionary" as a secret conservative neocapitalist who didn't know what he was saying back then. However, many were dedicated then and remain so today, and tell their stories in succeeding chapters. I would wager that the amount of commitment to causes today is in direct proportion to the amount of commitment back then. Many sixties activists are now quietly working for local community organizations, are involved in such issues as consumer and utility battles, and campaign for progressive candidates.

"For every one of them [the Stockmans or Glassmans who have changed their views], you will find an Ira Arlook, head of the Ohio public interest campaign, which helps consumers, or a Lee Webb, head of the conference on alternative public policy," said Andrew Spahn, an aide to Senator Alan Cranston in his 1984 presidential campaign. "Many activists don't use the word 'anticorporation' today, but they're trying to direct corporations toward more democratic forms. It's all just being done more quietly." Spahn is a staunch defender of Tom Hayden and Jane Fonda and tries to deflect criticism that their Campaign for Economic Democracy (CED) is nothing more than a self-serving organization that provides a base for Hayden's political ambitions. "There are a lot easier ways to move ahead than to build local organizations all over the state."

Fonda remains the point woman for many veterans who hate her for espousing pro-Hanoi sentiments during the war. "It's moderating, but there continues to be violent hostility," says Spahn. "Tom has done a lot in terms of veterans benefits in California and the CED political director is a Vietnam combat veteran with shrapnel in his back. Jane helped raise money for the boat people." She is, however, remembered more for refusing to support a Joan Baez ad decrying Hanoi's repressive tactics and the plight of the boat people. "Jane was not contesting the status of the government [now in Vietnam] but the larger picture. She felt that Joan, unintentionally, was a useful tool for the cold-warrior pro-defense interventionists."

Spahn, twenty-nine in 1983, is among the last in his generation who faced the draft. He refused to register, and devoted his time and energy to encouraging others to resist as well. He views his political work as consistent, continuing to push for liberal and progressive aims, and is "committed to grassroots organizations."

Spahn remained active in antiwar work as an eighteen- and nineteen-year-old, long after the mass of students had given up. Like many who worked tirelessly in the antiwar movement, Spahn feels he paid a price. "I wouldn't trade it, but there are times—particularly when I look at the young people moving up around me—when I feel, 'God, if I hadn't wasted those years on unfocussed anger; had not dropped out for a while.' I have not progressed in the establishment definition of progress. I feel I gave up a great deal, in terms of my life."

Michael Blumenthal sifted the legacies. "Everybody's life was, in part, derailed. Whether you went, tried to get out, or what. I had a friend, now a psychiatrist in Pittsburgh. He taught in Harlem as his way out. He absolutely hated it; his life was in *danger*. It took him years to get where he wanted.

"Lots got off the track and never got back. There was so much upheaval and confusion. Trying to grow up, pursue serious intellectual growth, and sort it all out was very difficult. It really got in the way of my education. There is that confused search for identity anyway and layered over that was this larger story of what was going on regarding Vietnam."

After graduating, Blumenthal taught in upstate New York and finally brought some activism into his life. He preached antiwar views to a school that was a socioeconomic mix—professors' children and IBM executives' children and the townies "who wanted to be cops and car mechanics." Blumenthal felt free to speak because "I was acting out of my own individual beliefs, away from peer pressure. It's ironic—only then did I have moral feelings against the war." After teaching out of guilt, partly, Blumenthal taught emotionally disturbed adolescents in a mental institution. Cornell Law School came next, then a job with the National Endowment for the Humanities. In 1982 he was writing for Time-Life Books.

He is unmarried and is as confused as many in his generation about personal commitments. "Never having had the experience of community—whether in the Army or otherwise—has made me a very bad sharer and very self-centered."

Blumenthal's poetry is good; he has won national awards.

> *Contrition*
> *is something we are born with—*
> *the easy grief of sacrifice, the goose down*
> *of regret and apology. Some nights,*
> *the voices of all we've failed to help*
> *gather like moss at our feet and our steps*
> *grow treacherous and slick, pentameters*
> *of unrest and longing. But once,*
> *in a dream, I met a man*

who took me with him everywhere in a suitcase
of emptiness. Each night, in a new town,
he'd open it and close it, open
and close it, the way toucans open
their beaks with a longing for insects.

Air, he said,
was how he took the world with him,
everywhere. And now, still silly
with irreverence and youth, I take air
as the measure of all grace, a hand
that rises to bless all things equally—
soot, crabgrass, you, and me.
And I find justice in the evenness
of wind, how it rises
like a perfect skater over the ice
to fill the suitcases of old men
and carry the warm kisses of lovers
from place to place, and how it falls again
over the darkening night
into the quiet, airy stillness of the world.

9 Impressions

IT IS HARD TO SORT AND SIFT THROUGH THE AMBIGUOUS AND CON-flicting feelings that come after listening to the stories of the avoiders. Some of them are sensitive and romantics still. They have transferred that romanticism and idealism into a vague yearning for a lost experience, that "maleness" of going to a "right" war.

Some on the other side called them heroes. "From the time I entered the military, it became increasingly obvious that the heroes of this war were those who fought it in the streets of American cities or in the courts or in the jails or by leaving the country rather than lend their support. Certainly there are distinctions among them. . . . But the distinctions are *irrelevant.* Whatever the personal cost, all of them—exiles, deserters, and resisters of every stripe—answered to the call to fight in a senseless war with the most appropriate response—an outright refusal."

Arthur Egendorf, Jr., a Vietnam veteran who served in military intelligence in Saigon, wrote that in 1972.[1]

In 1981 Egendorf was among the team of sociologists, psychiatrists, and psychologists who conducted the most far-reaching study to date on the effects of Vietnam on veterans.

Obviously, Egendorf represents the most charitable response. More recently, he has spoken in favor of mending the generational breach in a manner that champions military service. "The idea of service is important. This country needs to believe in service. Moral ideals are important, too. There is no reason to keep them separate."[2]

Thousands of other veterans, however, can still barely contain themselves when the subject of avoiders comes up. Many thousands more fall somewhere in the middle. In a major 1980 attitude survey, Vietnam-era veterans' attitudes toward their peers who demonstrated against the war or avoided the draft by leaving the country are particularly cool.[3]

The most reflective see a danger in the nostalgia expressed by those who never experienced the real thing. Men like Tom Hagel, who took years to sort out his experience, cautions against such thinking. It is one thing to feel guilty about letting another class go to war in one's stead, he argues, and quite another to overly romanticize war itself.

It is a concern I share. Will such doubts lead to a knee-jerk acceptance of the military and, ultimately, war as a rite of passage for the next generation?

All my interviews with avoiders contain variations on a certain theme. First, there is a necessity to "set the record straight," to let the world know that their dissent was often a personal fear or a conformist, running-with-the-tide response—in addition to feeling the war was stupid and/or immoral. Another theme, shared by their women counterparts, is a sense that it took them longer to grow up than other generations. And another is a sense of confusion still about how the generation will play out.

Most fascinatingly, there is almost universal allegiance to a draft among yesteryear's dodgers—a *fair* draft—for a younger generation. I am astounded —and often angered—at their aplomb. There is seldom a moment of chagrin at asking another generation to do what they were unwilling to do.

Their argument is always that the all-volunteer Army either isn't working or that it is grossly unfair. It is heresy to suggest that—at least in peacetime— the all-volunteer Army serves as an achievement center for men who might not have made it elsewhere. Men who most certainly would be back at the bottom of the ladder if the middle and upper middle class were added to the mix. *"That* is pure elitism," some say with disdain, ignoring their own actions during the sixties. Perhaps, but, I argued, no one in the admittedly inequitable all-volunteer Army is fighting and dying at this point—as they were in the sixties when these men were *not* going.

In a matter of months, that thought was sadly outdated. Marines were dying in Lebanon and Grenada. I winced as I saw their fathers and mothers, once again the faces and accents of Middle America, captured in grief by television.

Even Joel Garreau, a conscientious objector in the sixties, wants a draft. I argue that there is a certain hypocrisy in their view, now that they are safe themselves and are still too young to have the emotional tug of draft-age children. Garreau's reason is one espoused frequently—peace through draft.

"It's ironic, but I think the way we could fight Reagan militarism is to fight for the draft. As a conscientious objector, I don't *really* want the draft. What I want is the balloon going up that is associated with the draft."

A draft would galvanize and scare influential parents into fighting the buildup of militarism—or so the argument goes. However, this view seems to overlook the salient point that there *was* a draft during Vietnam and it was outrageously abused by the privileged.

Also, if there is a *peacetime* draft and it is dutifully honored, how do a collection of young military men then legitimately dissent if the country decides to get involved in another questionable venture? "There's a built-in political calculation," says Jim Fallows. "The likelihood of using such force— if it's a bunch of the current guys, whose parents are not going to complain— is greater. There is more of a brake on that happening if the middle class sees a personal peril. I compare it to busing. If the editorial writers and judges had had children in those schools, the busing policy would have been different from the beginning."

For now, the memory of Vietnam is, in part, responsible for some caution. In 1982 Gallup polls, taken during the spring, 89 percent opposed any involvement in El Salvador—an undreamed-of figure during the Vietnam escalation. At that time, the likelihood of President Reagan pushing an incendiary draft seemed dubious.

I point out to Fallows that it is particularly galling to many that the men who escaped the last time would be untouched by a draft today. "Since I'm preaching all these things about the draft," he says with a smile, "I would have to make some gesture of enlisting if it came through."

What about enlisting now?

"That would serve no purpose, other than to showboat. The concept of the volunteer Army is the appeal to each individual. It would be to my individual cost and benefit not to go in.

"In the ideal world, a draft would include men in their thirties"—Fallows uses a curiously benign phrase to describe the ones who avoided going—"the ones who were 'passed over.' " He also acknowledges that "in the practical world" it would be the young called upon once again.

I was searching for an explanation of why these men speak as they do. Jack Smith, a psychologist and former combat marine in Vietnam, says, "Vietnam profoundly forced a decision on a generation. If we look at delayed stress as sorting out blame and responsibility and coming to grips with it, then some degree of this is working its way through yesterday's draft dodger who talks about championing the draft today. That is one way of saying, 'You shouldn't have let me get away with what I did, but I can't tell you up front.' At the same time, that stance also serves to *deny* the lessons those of us learned from Vietnam. Jim Fallows writes in the abstract about putting together a fair Army the 'next time around'; he is still buying into the war mythology. His views were never altered by the *reality* of *war that we saw.* On one level, he seems to unconsciously criticize the position he took—and on another level, he denies the atrocity of what happened."

I am no adherent to that hobgoblin "consistency," yet the belated concern of avoiders for an egalitarian Army is worrisome. It is a strange, unsacrificing form of expiation. So, too, is the more cautionary advice they often give—to judge "the next one" on its merits. Not every confrontation has to be as "immoral" as Vietnam. Or now they confess a certain error in their youthful judgment of what was immoral. One draft dodger argued recently that there were merits in getting militarily involved in the Middle East. "Oil *is* important," he said. Many more buy the domino theory as applied to Central America. These are different times, is a repeated theme.

It is difficult, as well as unfashionable, among many from the Vietnam Generation to argue against the draft these days. After all, the absence of a *fair* draft in the sixties is one of the central premises of this book, as well as a problem for this divided generation. If the upper and middle classes had been subjected to a more personal threat with a fair draft, I agree that their influential parents would have brought political pressure to bear in far larger numbers and far more emotionally. A fair draft might have ended the war sooner. Charles Mohr, the New York *Times* correspondent who was wounded covering the battle of Hue, argues that "The reason Nixon and Kissinger—with their *incredibly* flawed policy—were able to hang in there, in my opinion, was because the middle class was not emotionally involved. I thought his policy was immoral—it was a plan of slow defeat, there was no way Vietnamization was going to work. And so we got some 22,000 more men killed." [The Vietnam Veterans Memorial lists 22,615 dead or missing after November 1968, when Nixon was elected on a secret plan for peace.] "He would *not* have been permitted to get away with that policy if the cannon fodder had not been from Weeping Willow, Nebraska, and the ghettos. If those had been 22,000 kids from Yale who had to get killed so that Nixon wouldn't have an embarrassing, quick defeat, well, it just wouldn't have been tolerated."

I accept that, but I do not buy the follow-up argument: that a fair draft in *peacetime* is the way to ensure no more Vietnams.

In fact, the peacetime draft made it easier for the government to move into Vietnam. An Army was already in place. Reagan can invade Grenada, keep a force of Marines in Lebanon, supply Central American countries with military assistance, but he does not have enough manpower in the volunteer Army to greatly widen conflicts on the order of Vietnam. That is why I agree with those who are antidraft. Having to reinstate the draft—with full debate in Congress and the country—would be a deterrent, a trip wire to cross before a President could wage another Johnson-style war.

However, Tom Alder, a lawyer who founded the *Selective Service Law Reporter* during the sixties, warns that while not having a draft is still a deterrent, "it is nothing like it was in the early seventies. In the late seventies, induction regulations were changed with virtually no congressional oversight and were issued in 1981. The regulations implement a plan called the Emergency Manpower Mobilization Procurement System. The Defense Department wanted it. The President still has to have the authorization to induct restored by legislation—but if there is a rallying to the flag and popular groundswell, this could all happen in a very short time. The Pentagon, in planning to use those regulations, has had two exercises in which they have gone from emergency to first induction in thirteen days. They assume that the one-line bill to restore the draft—all it takes—will pass the afternoon the President asks for it."

Where *does* the dissenting soldier go if he is drafted in peacetime and *then* chooses to disagree with whatever skirmish the Administration may deem desirable? I am always reminded of the blindness of those in the peace movement who shouted at soldiers to "desert." There is a story that Jane Fonda encountered a soldier outside one of the military camps and exhorted him to desert. "That's fine for you to say, ma'am," he politely drawled. "But tomorrow you can go back to Hollywood. If I desert, it's Fort Leavenworth [Prison]."

That the draft would keep a cap on future involvements is hardly a certainty. These *are* different times. The more hawkish elements in power seem to be trying to convince enough people that a win somewhere would erase the shame of Vietnam. Or, at least—mindful that many Americans seem justifiably wary of using the "No more Vietnams" argument in all instances— blunder into some mistaken show of strength.

Relying on Congress to stand fast is risky—if their caution and cowardice in last fall's showdown on the War Powers Act is any indication. Despite heated debate that rang with remembered anguish about the Gulf of Tonkin, the members gave Reagan everything, including the right to keep marines in Lebanon for eighteen months. In a matter of weeks, he was sending an unusually large fleet of warships to the Mediterranean, following the suicide terrorist attack that killed 241 marines.

At the moment, public sentiment remains cautionary, although there was overwhelming applause for his invasion of Grenada last fall. Given Reagan's "voodoo power over the American voter," as columnist Mary McGrory put it, will that caution last?

Men coming of age today are beginning a downward crest. There will be a far smaller pool from which to pick *and* to dissent than there was in the sixties. This generation simply will not have the clout of numbers. And, until the baby boomers have teenagers of their own, they will not have the same emotional involvement.

Where, in fact, *would* yesterday's avoiders come down on the possible confrontations of tomorrow? Would the ultimate irony be dispassionate acceptance of another Vietnam "on its merits"? That, of course, assumes some unlikely knee-jerk acceptance of government policy from a generation that feels, even more keenly than any other segment of the population, a post-Vietnam loss of confidence in political leaders and institutions. Still, I feel that the numbers who would take to the streets would be meager. They are not, in any proportion to their size, activists, for example, in today's antinuclear movement.

There should be more talk of *peace* than of a *peacetime draft.* The nongoing draft advocates could learn from some of the hardened and wary antidraft veterans. The very inequitable history lesson the nongoers offer seems to have favorably seared the public's conscience. If there has to be a next time, no class group should again be so spared. I, too, am haunted by the possibility of America's own version of its serfs and vassals—the black and poor who comprise the all-volunteer Army—bearing the brunt again.

I would be dishonest if I did not admit that self-interest motivates some of my concern on the draft. I have two children of draft age. It is easy to say the military would do them both good. I wouldn't mind the discipline, if only to see neat teenage bedrooms as an end result. And my older son says he would easily accept some form of alternate service.

Yet I am haunted by the phrase of some of the antidraft veterans: "If they've got 'em, they'll use 'em." Given Reagan's macho diplomacy and his ability to smooth-talk the public, I do not want that standing Army in place —for anyone's son.

In the sixties, some of the pro-Marxist leaders who rallied the students felt nothing but contempt for them. Carl Davidson, one leader, wrote "draft resistance tables in the student union building—the arrogance of it all. We organize students against the draft when the Army is made up of young men who are poor, black, Spanish-American, hillbillies, or working-class. Everyone except students. How can we be so stupid when we plan our strategies? Students are 'oppressed.' Bullshit."[4]

The same exemptions they clung to when it meant their own lives would "obviously" have to be waived in the future, the nongoers say with self-righteous certainty. It will be a long time, I hope, before such an inequitable system again will be allowed. However, I also fear *any* draft. The government should not have that large a standing Army; it's a simple theory, but it gnaws nonetheless—"If they've got 'em, they'll use 'em."

One way to assure that today's youth pays its dues to its country—something that many of the sixties generation now feel they not only *escaped* but *missed*—is to have some form of universal service that helps others and doesn't entail being trained to kill. It has an easy ring of sacrifice and duty. However, many counter that, in a country this size, such universal service is too expensive and cumbersome to administer.

The irony is, we don't need that many bodies. "We didn't then and we don't now," said Garreau. "How are we going to fund all these kids for two years of universal service? That would break the bank."

Of course. That is, unless there is another war.

Part III
Still in Saigon

"Still in Saigon"

BY DAN DALEY

Every summer when it rains
I smell the jungle, I hear the planes.
I can't tell no one I feel ashamed,
Afraid someday I'll go insane.

All the sounds of long ago will be forever in my head,
Mingled with the wounded's cries, and the silence of
the dead. . . .

'Cause I'm still in Saigon.
Still in Saigon.
Still in Saigon in my mind.

1 Post-Traumatic Stress

TOM HAGEL DULLED THE DAYS AND NIGHTS UNTIL HE COULD LEAVE Vietnam. Dulled them with alcohol and grass, zombieing out in his base camp job. "They would bring beer by the pallet load—forty or fifty cases—and you would get blind. For next to nothing you could get a pound of the best dope in the world."

What distinguished Tom's and other Vietnam veterans' drinking and pot-smoking is that the stories are seldom remembered with humor. Jocular war stories, the light side of battle told by veterans of other times, seem remote to Vietnam. Anxiety and numbness seem the strongest remembered emotions.

"It used to drive me nuts, the waiting," recalled Tom. "Instead of being sharp, you'd be lulled by fatigue and a false sense of security and then, all of a sudden, hell would break loose. The chipping, chipping away at you. You could never get your hands on it. Half the time you didn't even see anything." Pause. "Until you'd find the bodies. The anxiety did more *psychological* damage than the nature of the wounds." Hagel, like so many veterans, returns again and again to the anxiety. "They could booby-trap *everything*. A cigarette package—anything—and leave it around. There was unbelievable terror of everything booby-trapped. Sometimes the terror is so deep-set you simply *cannot* remember. It comes back in nightmares."

Drinking dulled the terror and frustration and guilt and it dulled something else. Already, at twenty, Hagel sensed an awful knowledge about himself. The knowledge that he would remember the excitement and, yes, the power of killing; the knowledge that he would remember it much later—and not want to remember it that way.

"I really believe there is no greater opportunity for tactile evidence of a sense of power than to get the M-16 working at full tilt. [There was a sixties phrase for it. Putting the weapon on automatic—"on rock 'n' roll—and letting it go."] There are two types of power. The power to create—and the power to destroy. We found that power to destroy in Vietnam. I know women don't understand it, but I don't think it's necessarily 'macho'—or male versus female. I couldn't understand it if I hadn't gone, hadn't seen it, experienced it. Right now, I can't adequately explain it."

It is understandable why Tom cannot explain his feelings today—far removed from the warrior mode of another time. From dragon slayers to crusaders to modern day's "most decorated genuine war hero," the warrior has always laid claim on our emotions. Aristotle described and condemned the glorification of the socialized warrior: the Scythian custom that "No one who had not slain his man was allowed to drink out of the cup" passed at the feast. In America's frontier days, the body count was notched on the gun barrel. Britain, with its long history of colonialization, produced generations of military men—often scholars and poets—who knew no greater exhilaration than the call to arms.

"To reach the desired psychological state, the socialized warrior has always required an initiation process, a symbolic form of death and rebirth," noted psychiatrist Robert J. Lifton in a celebrated study of veterans. "In that rite (now called basic training), his civil identity, with its built-in restraints, is eradicated—or at least undermined—and set aside in favor of the warrior identity and its central focus upon killing."[1]

Lifton, who decries the "tenacious pseudomythology" of warrior heroism, concentrates on war's searing aftermath—from Hiroshima survivors to Vietnam veterans. His strong antiwar stance is grist for those who feel his bias distorts his conclusions. Lifton and other observers of the Vietnam veteran often describe them as alienated.

Alienation can exist in veterans of all wars, but with Vietnam veterans it seems heightened. A remarkable fact is that from earliest studies of Vietnam veterans to the most recent there echoes a sameness. "Not one of them— hawk, dove, or haunted—was entirely free of doubt about the nature of the war and the American role in it," wrote Murray Polner after interviewing more than 200 veterans while the war was still in progress. "Never before have so many questioned as much, as these veterans have, the essential rightness of what they were forced to do."[2]

I found much the same feeling years later.

Lifton found, in his studies, that "The predominant emotional tone about the war is all-encompassing absurdity and moral inversion." Although there were full-scale battles with the NVA, many GIs fought the unseen enemy. There was no "script" within which "armies clash, battles are fought, won, or lost, and individual suffering, courage, cowardice, or honor can be evaluated," he wrote.

There are mutilations, absurdity, evil, degradation, and unspeakable suffering in all wars and the returning warrior carries much of this within him forever. For many, war is the one soul-shaking experience of their lives. Audie Murphy, World War II's much-decorated hero, once said that a man never gets over his war experiences; the inner conflicts remain. Wilfred Owen wrote of dark and bitter war guilt in poem after poem about World War I.

Coming to terms with war experiences, however, was especially hard for the Vietnam veteran. Purpose and significance were murky—even for hawks. Revisionism does not dispel the awful truths: massive obliteration of a country and its people in order to "save" it. In Vietnam one underwent the "ordeal" or test of the warrior without the redemptive possibility of "holy validity."

This is why some veterans sift over and over again the merits of the war, clutching at or violently rejecting "noble cause" straws, seeking answers, seeking comfort, seeking to place blame elsewhere. Where that blame justifiably belongs is with leaders who devised and strategized this war but somehow they have escaped the tainted scapegoatism of the veteran. Kissinger and his like cavort in the highest circles, are assured of media and political camp followers, and generally cleanse themselves in self-justifying memoirs.

"It was left to us to do the shit" is the way one veteran described the war. The desensitization, frustration, and rage engendered by guerrilla warfare —with the revolutionaries indistinguishable from the rest of the population— were abetted by instructions from boot camp on to "kill gooks." The overt impression was that all gooks were fair game, that napalm and aerial bombardment by the ton on one and all were "justifiable."

Vietnam was not alone in its nightmarish qualities. Probe a veteran who saw combat in World War II or Korea and you will often find evidence of atrocities or, at the very least, war's brutalizing dehumanization.

One friend of mine tells of watching American soldiers running German POWs on the beaches of Normandy following the invasion and clubbing them on the side of the head until they dropped if they didn't run fast enough. Another tells of the World War II soldier who collected Japanese ears as a necklace.

Yet the Vietnam veteran experienced a particularly dehumanizing war— both in its lack of justification, for some, and, for most, in its style of warfare —and returned to what was the second major contribution to their delayed stress problems: a country indifferent to them. They were immigrants from something so repugnant to their own people that it had to remain locked in their own hearts and minds.

Tom Hagel was blind drunk when he returned to the United States, propelled, as were many veterans, by two drives. The first was to repress and forget all that he had experienced in Vietnam. The second was to make up for lost time. His is a universal comment among veterans who returned driven to succeed: "I had a strong sense of being far behind. I felt I *had* to catch up."

And so Tom, who barely scraped through high school, finished college at the University of Nebraska in three years, got his master's, started law school in 1973, and graduated in 1976. He became a well-known public defender in Lincoln, Nebraska. In 1982, following a two-year law and humanities fellowship at Temple University, Tom landed a professorship, teaching law at the University of Dayton.

On the surface, his story points to success—a young man who, seemingly, put the shattering aspects of Vietnam far behind him. Yet there were years of immobilizing depression. Suicidal depression, at times. Unlike many veterans without the skills to move forward educationally or like many of the bright who were trapped in their depressions, Tom Hagel was able to cope by living two lives.

"My *modus operandi* was to sit by myself in a bar, get drunk, and if anyone said anything to me, I'd just go crazy. I was functioning only in school and then, later, at work. It was my way to escape."

Tom threw himself into helping other veterans obtain benefits. "When we first got out, we got $75 a month for full-time students and twenty-four months' eligibility. Then it went to $135 for full time—but by then, if you got out in 1969, you'd used your twenty-four months. After World War II, our family doctor went all through med school and his GI Bill paid for most of it. In 1972 I applied to three law schools and got accepted at all three. The only one I could afford was University of Nebraska, as a Nebraska resident."

Obsessed with the need to do for others, Tom became a live-in counselor for mentally retarded adults, even though he was having trouble coping with his own problems. He drifted through life and loves, marriage and divorce, depression and more depression—silent about Vietnam throughout. But the vivid dreams, the smells, the dead eyes followed Tom.

Above all, Tom was aware of being a stranger among the nongoers, first in his academic world and then as a lawyer. Although violently against the war, Tom despised the "paper radicals" he met on campus. "I was disgusted at how little they put into it. The attitude about the war seemed to be: 'I'm white, middle-class, and too good for this shit.' In law school I was the only one who had been in Vietnam." Tom found then—and now—total silence surrounding their disparate experiences of the sixties. No one ever mentions that wrenching time of their youth, even his closest friends, many of whom did not go. "I cannot recall anyone *ever* talking about it."

In law school it came out only once that Tom was a combat veteran. "An older faculty member knew I had been in Vietnam and asked me about it at a party. As soon as we started talking, there was just, simply, *silence*. Everyone got *real* uncomfortable. I purposely tried to make eye contact, but everyone looked away. Some tried to change the subject." The man with three Purple Hearts realized, "People don't want to believe it ever happened. You carried it all inside."

As much as Vietnam veterans derided VFW and American Legionnaires on their return, they feel a certain wistfulness for such unknown postwar camaraderie. "Men from other wars, in their hometowns, built lifelong relationships based solely on that," says Tom. World War II and Korean veterans often scoff at the notion of belonging to service clubs and attending war reunions, but Vietnam veterans see a major difference. Veterans of earlier wars were *free* to reject such camaraderie; Vietnam veterans never had that option. The few who went to local service clubs felt like outsiders and, with such an unpopular war, there was no climate for banding together and *identifying* as Vietnam veterans.

This postwar loneliness was especially shattering after the closeness they felt in Vietnam. "I never saw the buddy system so strong as in Vietnam," said General Eugene Lynch, veteran of three wars. Survival is always a major catalyst in battle, but in a war of little meaning, surviving and helping friends survive was paramount. "There was such a constant turnover," recalls Tom. "The wounded went off in pain and screams and blood and you never saw them again. We who survived promised to keep in touch. I did not. A few did write, but it was always so goddamn depressing. One buddy, when he stepped off the plane in San Diego, was served right there with divorce papers." Tom shakes his head. "Now that is *cold.*"

He pauses, remembering the wrenching partings in Vietnam and what that did to him. "Now I sometimes think I don't have certain levels of emotion others have. I'm great in an emergency. But something I had before, some deep level of emotion, just isn't there."

As with all veterans, there are certain songs Tom cannot hear without a swift, stabbing, bittersweet nostalgia for Vietnam. Otis Redding's "(Sittin' on) The Dock of the Bay" was playing when he stepped off the plane and into Vietnam. To this day, it is "pure Vietnam" to him.

Tall and attractive, Tom Hagel exudes a quiet, professorial charm. He never had much problem finding women, but his life has been a series of non-lasting relationships. He experimented in high school, but never had sex in Vietnam. "I saw some guys with bizarre forms of clap and I just said, 'No thanks.' In a whole year, my only sex was with a prostitute in Hong Kong."

When Tom returned to the States, "I never had any problem with a lack of desire or ability to perform, but as soon as a relationship got close, I immediately ran or would set up situations where things would fail. It was explained later that I was afraid of losing someone close. For a long time, I was convinced I really didn't deserve to be loved. Partly it was the experience of Vietnam and partly childhood inadequacies. I would push women so far that they would say, 'Get lost'—so I wouldn't feel guilty."

In close, one-on-one relationships with women—even after he would cry out in his nightmares—the subject of Vietnam never came up. Tom lived with a woman in college for a year and a half and got married after the first semester in law school. In months, it was over.

One incident propelled Tom to seek help. A six-foot-five truck driver made advances toward Tom's date one night in a bar. "I talked to him for twenty minutes as to why he shouldn't fight me." Tom laughs. "The basic reason was that I knew he'd kill me." Tom looked like a perfect Clark Kent-type target. Horn-rimmed glasses, tweed jacket, tie. The trucker reached for Tom's glasses, smashed them against a wall, and hit him. "Well, I just went nuts. Demolished him. Dislocated his nose. Smashed a beer bottle on his head."

Tom says it all with some disbelief today. "I was out for *death*. He was so tall I had to jump on a bench to hit him with the beer bottle.

"That violence just scared the hell out of me. It's so contrary to my beliefs. I've been told it was just a reflexive response to a threat to someone who had been in combat."

Worse than his feelings about losing control were his depressions. He was constantly thinking of ways to commit suicide, to make it look like an accident so that family could collect his insurance. A foolproof plan, Tom thought, was to make it seem as though he were cleaning the car carburetor. He would run a hose for the pipe so that the exhaust would go outside the garage. Only it would "accidentally" slide off and there would be Tom, working on the carburetor, getting sleepy—and "simply" falling asleep. "I wouldn't be sitting in the seat, but out there, at the front of the car. I even thought it all down to where I would have my hands dirty."

He searched his life for patterns of depression, but found none. "The last thing I ever was as a kid was depressed. When I went into therapy, all the pieces just fell apart." The tight control and workaholic successes disintegrated into gulps of tears as Tom confronted his feelings. Unlike many veterans, he found a sympathetic VA psychiatrist. "This guy saved my life. I was just so frustrated. I tried to talk to the family and got nothing but resistance. 'Oh, you don't have to see a psychiatrist.' I was on antidepressants and antipsychotics. All that does is slow you down. I didn't understand what was happening, except that something was deeply wrong.

"I don't want to use Vietnam as an excuse. There were many more problems that were contributing—my relationship with my father, all that stuff. I don't blame all this on Vietnam, but amazingly, as I started working on the guilt things of Vietnam, everything else became a lot easier."

In the end, the psychological answer is nearly always the same: learning to accept what happened. A simple thought, expressed in various ways by psychiatrists for much of the stress and problems anyone faces. A simple thought —difficult to achieve. Thousands of Vietnam veterans have not yet learned to find their way through to that acceptance.

"I had to learn to say, 'This happened to me. I have no control of the past.' I could either do something constructive—or piss and moan my life away. For a while I had a really wrecked personal life. Vietnam had a direct adverse effect on it. I *know* that was Vietnam."

By 1980 Hagel was "beginning to get some balance in my life. If I see someone still having the same kind of problem, I'd be sympathetic. Would I ever! But I would also say, 'Look, the final solution will *not* come from the VA, Congress, the service, or some veterans' group. *You're* going to have to make the decision that you *learned* from it, from *all* of it—or sit on your ass and vegetate.' "

By 1981, as time blurred the strongest emotions about the Vietnam War, an avalanche of media reports on Vietnam veterans brought them into public conscience. Veterans peered from the covers of *Time* and *Newsweek* and from television documentaries. Men telling tales of the past that haunt them still. Their wives and girlfriends, stoic or in tears, added to the picture.

As a national awareness and acceptance of veterans and their problems grew, a backlash emerged. It came, understandably, from some veterans who felt that all were being tarred as unemployed or unemployable, drug addicts or losers, or haunted by that new psychological phrase of the eighties, "post-traumatic stress disorder." Still, those denials often had an emotional ferocity bordering on the irrational. Leaders of Vietnam veteran counseling centers were heckled when they appeared on local television—sometimes by older veterans or Vietnam veterans who had seen little combat.

Families are often particularly resistant. Over and over, wives and girl-friends tell of unsympathetic parents: "Lookit old Charlie, he went to Vietnam and *he's* fine. So how come your husband is acting so strange?" Wives and girlfriends try in vain to explain, then grow silent.

Dr. Arthur Arnold, one of the few sympathetic VA psychiatrists I met, says, "Most of the guys we see are so *decent* from their early upbringings. It just breaks your heart to hear how they feel now. In Vietnam they were just a bunch of kids with this intense feeling of protection for each other. So if others are wiped out it's 'I should have been the one to die.' " Dr. Arnold's patients, who have problems severe enough to be hospitalized, live with the knowledge that they are alive and that intimate friends—whose friendships were forged in battle—are not. This knowledge follows them—while they are shaving or driving a car or listening to music or making love. "The poignancy," says Dr. Arnold, "is that they continually seek death *now,* motivated by survival guilt."

Unfortunately, the very community that should understand most often does not. "The reaction of my colleagues to delayed stress was negative," says Arnold. "We have a bunch of psychiatrists who are old-fashioned and rigid. They only can handle the standard psychoses. They do not want to believe that something that happened in Vietnam ten or twelve years ago is causing problems today." He smiles ruefully. "And yet, these are the same people who believe deeply that you can be adversely affected by the way your mother talked to you when you were two.

"I imagine plenty of World War II and Korean veterans were misdiagnosed," says Arnold, noting the numbers of aged alcoholics who populate VA hospitals. "A World War II medic was on an island in the Pacific where they were pinned down by the Japs for seventy-two hours. Nearly everybody was killed. He diligently sat there, trying to put little pieces of bodies together to be evacuated. He spent the next forty years drinking his life away, obsessed by this, and being treated as merely an alcoholic. He stayed drunk in order to survive."

Breaking the myth that "real men" endured the unendurable was a heavy price to pay for Vietnam veterans who spoke up after years of silence. Just as

Vietnam was modern technology's most reported and recorded war, so, finally, were its human aftereffects being meticulously catalogued as large numbers of men, by 1981, began to tell their tales. Some were the accumulations of emotional problems that killing and death have engendered for as long as there have been wars. Some were germane to the special differences of Vietnam. Some were, no doubt, fabricated for the benefit of the media, overly willing to portray them as lost souls.

The response of the public was fascinatingly and brutally insensitive. Mention the concept of post-traumatic delayed stress and many are immediately skeptical: "Losers, every one of 'em, blaming Vietnam for their troubles."

Then mention that it is a recognized disorder. People who have been held hostage or were flood victims or raped or have escaped gruesome car accidents in which family or friends died are now being diagnosed as having post-traumatic delayed stress. They can be troubled by "intrusive" thoughts that creep into the most pleasant of days. Mention such examples and there often comes a dawning of accepting recognition. It is easier to understand somehow. Tell them about the policemen who have helped clean up the carnage of plane wrecks, with human limbs hanging from trees like gruesome maypole ribbons. Years later they were still troubled by scenes that would not leave their minds. Or ask them to think of the 1982 Air Florida crash into Washington's 14th Street Bridge; films of struggling survivors being pulled from the icy Potomac were watched repeatedly on television. Collective depression lingered for days among Washington viewers.

Tell them to think of those animals we have all seen squashed and eviscerated on our highways, bloodied testimonials to our automotive deadly prowess. *And then to imagine that they were human beings.* Some soldiers in Vietnam saw them by the hundreds. Humans as casually dead as animals on our highways—bloodied and bloated, staring and silent, blown limb from limb. Sometimes they were former buddies, sometimes former enemies, sometimes former women. Sometimes former children.

Over and over, images that linger with many veterans are those of civilians. The old man who stares from a rice paddy at a starving, downed helicopter pilot, reaches for the AK-47, and then the pilot shoots him. And takes his rice. The Green Beret who killed a young Vietnamese woman considered to be a VC village organizer. He can still see her eyes. The soldiers who come upon the dead after they sprayed a village with their M-16s.

One black ex-marine captain: "It's hard to explain what happens once you start seeing people die. We might see it on TV or see it in the movies, but that's all. We very seldom hold a guy and watch him die like soldiers do in Vietnam. You think, Oh my God look at 'em, what is this, I could be next."

The trauma of seeing buddies die was intensified by witnessing the destruction of the Vietnamese people. Another marine remembered his buddies who were sent to check a village that had been accidentally bombed by the U.S. Air Force. "Most of them came back sick, sick, just sick, white and completely torn apart because they had never seen such a gross destruction of man, woman, and child."[3]

These are memories not pleasant to share. And Americans, who do not want to have their war mythology shattered, often do not want to listen. Those on the right paint troubled veterans as a minuscule group, the distorted province of the "bleeding heart left"—who need "veterans as victims" to shore up their negatives about that war. Those on the left—the old Vietnam Veterans Against the War, for example—are among those who champion the cause of troubled veterans. Some no doubt embrace them for residual proof of an "immoral" war, but the majority respond because they understand genuine human suffering, not because they seek victims to pity.

To be sure, in every television interview, in every Vet Center across the country there will be the histrionic and, frankly, tiresome veteran, playing out some psychodrama. Some, indeed, *were* losers before Vietnam. Some never saw combat. Most counselors who work with them are quick to sort out the genuine from the fake.

Dan was an unattractive man; soft, pudgy white hands trembled as he showed me an insignia he insisted he had taken from a dead VC officer after he had decapitated him. The counselor of the Vet Center said it was all fake. In a way, Dan is part of the Vietnam story—the disturbed loser who had found his way to a Vet Center out of a sick need for fake bravura.

For the most part, the real stories come with far less drama. Flat statements. Tears sometimes. The staggering emotion that lingers with anyone who has talked with veterans is the *gratitude* shown by these men all these years later that someone would listen. After an interview, I would often leave a room and cry, feeling inadequate and lost. No matter the empathy; how can anyone who has not experienced it truly understand the death and destruction of war? It sounds so trite, so unbelievably flat, when written: "I have never talked to anyone about Vietnam before. Thank you for listening." I was to hear it with heartfelt sincerity over and over and over.

Those years of silence were corrosive to many. The evacuation of Saigon "closes a chapter in the American experience," President Ford said in 1975. For many Americans, by inference, this meant "Forget the veteran." That attitude reinforced silence. Thousands of alienated and aggravated Vietnam veterans have *never* divulged to their families and friends the character of their Vietnam experience.

One veteran who spoke to no one was Steven L. Anderson, found dead of a bullet wound in June of 1978 in his parents' home. A note was found:

"When I was in Vietnam, we came across a North Vietnamese soldier with a man, a woman, and a three- or four-year-old girl. We had to shoot them all. I can't get the little girl's face out of my mind. I hope that God will forgive me. I hope the people in this country who made millions of dollars off of the men, women, and children that died in that war can sleep at night. I can't— and I didn't make a cent. . . ."

His mother said that Steve had never mentioned the incident to anyone in the family, had never indicated any disturbance.[4]

The pressures to remain silent, "to put the experience 'behind us' " hampered that very goal of laying Vietnam to rest. It defeated many from speaking out in therapeutic situations. "It complicates tremendously the problems veterans face in resolving personal conflicts rooted in their experience in the war," said Dr. Clark Smith.[5]

For the most part, the public hears only of the "crazed veteran" stereotype, reinforced every time a headline points out the ex-marine who holds up a liquor store or holds a wife hostage.

Reality is vastly different. For many more, who are still troubled, their desperations are quiet whirlpools. These men were *not* losers before Vietnam, nor are they now. Just men lost by an experience and a homecoming that no one cared to understand.

It was February 26, 1972, 8 A.M. in Buffalo Creek Valley, West Virginia. Mothers were drying breakfast dishes, children were on their way to school, husbands were going to work. Suddenly, without warning, 150 million tons of water and 50 million tons of mine waste came hurtling down—a massive wall of rampaging water thirty feet high and thirty feet wide—that devastated the narrow West Virginia valley. Within minutes, it completely wiped out sixteen towns; killed 125 men, women, and children; and left 5,000 homeless. After three days of lashing, heavy rain, the Pittston Company's giant slag dam had collapsed.

A decade later, a Vietnam combat veteran and psychologist, John Russell Smith, who has devoted years to the study of delayed stress, was driving through Buffalo Creek Valley to talk with flood survivors. It was raining and, instead of the customary twenty minutes, Smith had to inch along for an hour and a half in bumper-to-bumper traffic through the sixteen-mile hollow. It was an eerie sight; pounding rains slashed at a highway clogged with cars filled with families.

"That incident refuted the initial assumption of psychiatrists that when the 'stress' is removed, the symptoms disappear," said Smith. *"Ten years later, whenever there is hard rain in Buffalo Creek,* survivors pick up their belongings, pack up the car, and drive *up and down* the double-lane road—*waiting* for the flood to come again. Ten years later! 'We're not going to get caught this time,' they say." A caustic hardness came into Smith's voice, as he spoke at a conference on delayed stress. "And there are 'no long-lasting symptoms' to traumatic stress?"

Flood survivors had continuous nightmares. Anxiety turned to panic when it rained heavily. They found it hard to be close to people. Families broke up. Men went into explosive rages. There was an abusive use of alcohol. These are the same set of symptoms that psychiatrists and psychologists noted when they studied survivors of other natural disasters and of such man-made horrors as Hiroshima and concentration camps or victims of rape and airplane wrecks. *And* among Vietnam veterans.

Survivors sued the coal company for negligence and for improperly building the dam. An argument used to deflect and belittle the concept of delayed stress—one used often about Vietnam veterans—was the main defense of coal company executives.

"They claimed these people had to have been emotionally upset or have a predisposition toward mental illness—and that the problems they were experiencing *couldn't* be due to the dam break," said John Wilson, another expert on post-traumatic stress. Psychiatrists and physicians for both sides examined several hundred litigants as well as nonlitigants. They concluded that the problems were not *in any way* due to childhood experiences, *not* due to preexisting mental illness. Although less than 3 percent of the entire community had ever seen a psychiatrist or social worker, *80* percent of the litigants were viewed as psychiatrically impaired *following* the flood. "The conclusion was that this was produced by the disaster."

Tragedies were unending. In one mother's nightmares, her two little girls looked at her intently as black mud covered her body. Her two girls no longer lived—except in her nightmares. Both had been swept from her arms and drowned. Another survivor lost thirty pounds; vomited when he tried to eat, especially in the morning. When the flood hit and took his son and wife, he was having breakfast.

Many denied any disorientation, until—much as Vietnam Vet Center counselors function today—mental health aides urged Buffalo Creek survivors to "ventilate" their pent-up emotions and relive their traumatic experiences.[6]

Such enlightened measures helped many, but countless others still bear the emotional scars of their ordeal.

"One third [of the survivors] are as fully symptomatic as they were ten years ago," said Dr. Wilson. "And that was a flood that happened in one day. Imagine what happens to someone who lives through some horror that lasts for months."

In 1980 the American Psychiatric Association recognized the condition the Buffalo Creek survivors—and an estimated half a million Vietnam veterans— are suffering from as a bona fide psychological malady, post-traumatic stress disorder. This new category is largely due to the clinical research and evidence compiled by those who studied Vietnam veterans.

PTSD (Post-Traumatic Stress Disorder) seems a fittingly obscure phrase to come out of a war that gave us "harassment and interdiction" and "protective reaction air strike" and other code words for killing. It does not have that stark ring of World War I's "shell shock" or World War II's "combat fatigue."

It is important to emphasize that someone with post-traumatic stress is not deranged or mentally ill in the clinical sense. Most Vet Center leaders and experts, in fact, smart at the word "disorder" and feel it applies to only a small percentage of the most deeply troubled. John Wilson explains, "We have a situation where the person was 'normal' before the psychologically traumatic event and the symptoms characteristic of PTSD developed after, as a result of the trauma." Jack Smith emphasizes, "The stress recovery *process* is a *normal,* adaptive process of integrating catastrophic experiences. Every person with symptoms does *not* have post-traumatic stress *disorder.* The disorder is the impeded blockage of that normal sorting out, recovery process."

The psychiatric association's *Diagnosis and Statistical Manual*—called *DSM* and known as the "bible" of the profession—describes "traumatic stress" as that which is generally outside the range of usual human experience —that would evoke significant symptoms of distress in almost everyone. It is a grim litany that includes floods, earthquakes, car or airplane crashes, large fires, bombings, torture, death camps, rape, assault, military combat. The unexpected nightmare incident that can alter the average person beyond measure. The survivors, for example, in the Kansas City Hyatt Regency in 1981, who watched in horror as, within seconds, hundreds of dancers were suddenly squashed to death under tons of concrete when the skywalk collapsed. These are the kind of stressors being discussed in post-traumatic stress.

Characteristic symptoms involve *reexperiencing* the traumatic event. Commonly the person has recurrent painful, intrusive recollections of the event or recurrent dreams or nightmares. In rare instances there are dissociative-like states, lasting from a few minutes to several hours or even days. The individual behaves as though experiencing the event at that moment. Other major signs of PTSD are prolonged spells of anxiety or depression; outbursts of apparently senseless rage; chronic insomnia; nightmares; emotional distancing from loved ones; intrusive, obsessive memories and flashbacks; painful survivor guilt or impaired memory; chronic irritability.

DSM III emphasizes that PTSD symptoms are often intensified when the individual is exposed to situations or activities that resemble or symbolize the original trauma ("e.g., cold, snowy weather or uniformed guards for death camp survivors, hot humid weather for veterans of the South Pacific"). Vietnam veterans are often suddenly transported back fifteen years when they hear the *whup-whup-whup* of helicopters on a steamy summer's day. *DSM III* also notes that "Sporadic and unpredictable explosions of aggressive behavior are *particularly characteristic of war veterans* with this disorder."

Still, it should be noted, violence is far from the hallmark of post-traumatic stress disorder. Suicidal attempts are far more frequent among veterans than attempts to harm others, note PTSD experts.

These handful of experts were a lonely chorus for years. Now—although PTSD has plenty of detractors—lawyers, doctors, psychiatrists, social workers, politicians, and interested citizens are listening.

In an eloquent testimony before the U.S. Senate Committee on Veteran Affairs in 1980, John F. Wilson tried to further the understanding of post-traumatic stress disorder:

"If you were demonic and powerful enough to want to make someone 'crazy' following a war like Vietnam, what would be the worst set of social, economic, political, and psychological conditions you could create for the returnee?

"First, you would send a young man fresh out of high school to an unpopular, controversial guerrilla war far away from home. Expose him to intensely stressful events, some so horrible that it would be impossible to really talk about them later to anyone else except fellow 'survivors.' To ensure maximal stress, you would create a one-year tour of duty during which the combatant flies to and from the war zone singly, *without* a cohesive, intact, and emotionally supportive unit with high morale. You would also create the one-year rotation to instill a 'survivor mentality' which would undercut the process of ideological commitment to winning the war and seeing it as a noble cause. Then at DEROS [Date of Expected Return from Overseas Service] you would rapidly remove the combatant and *singly* return him to his front porch *without* an opportunity to sort out the meaning of the experiences with the men in his unit. No homecoming welcome or victory parades. Ah, but yet, since you are demonic enough, you make sure that the veteran is stigmatized and portrayed to the public as a 'drug-crazed psychopathic killer.' By virtue of clever selection by the Selective Service system, the veteran would be unable to easily reenter the mainstream of society because he is undereducated and lacks marketable job skills.

"Further, since the war itself was so difficult, you would want to make sure that there were no supportive systems in society for him, especially among health professionals at VA hospitals who would find his nightmares and residual war-related anxieties unintelligible. Finally you would want to establish a GI Bill with inadequate benefits to pay for education and job training, coupled with an economy of high inflation and unemployment.

"Last, but not least, you would want him to *feel* isolated, stigmatized, unappreciated, and exploited for volunteering to serve his country.

"Tragically, of course, this scenario is not fictitious; it was the homecoming for most Vietnam veterans."

Wilson interviewed close to a thousand veterans and has catalogued his findings in the DAV-commissioned "Forgotten Warrior" project. Wilson is not a veteran.

A child of Columbus, Ohio, "an All-American, Republican, John Wayne kind of town," Wilson, in fact, went to great lengths to avoid that war. It was clear that Wilson was "supposed to go." A turning point came when he saw some of his friends who went and came back "different."

"They drank a lot, didn't tell anybody anything about what had happened. Had a hard time picking up goals again. They'd say, 'I can't concentrate so well.' "

Wilson's fascination with veterans—and his conclusions about their problems—are not motivated by guilt. His moral decision, to become a conscientious objector, "was one of the hardest I had to make. My mother called me a coward. She wouldn't tell her friends I was a C.O." Wilson worked three years without pay, doing alternate service in crisis and suicide intervention. Unlike some nongoers, who turn their backs on veterans, Wilson says, "What I'm doing now is consistent with that [antiwar] commitment." He never encountered any resistance from Vietnam veterans for not going. "They felt I had made a clear-cut moral choice."

Wilson, young-looking behind his beard and glasses, laughs. "Someone once asked, 'Did you ever wish you were a vet?' After interviewing hundreds, I feel like one now.

"Intellectually, I'm glad I didn't go—but one side of me has an intense *curiosity* about war. I didn't want to experience that trauma and killing. But that quality of caring, of humanitarian concerns I see in some Vietnam veterans, that sensitivity and courage are attributes I admire greatly."

Wilson—the psychologist who works with others trained to understand the mind—smiled. "In terms of real crisis, involving family, children, etc., I've turned to Vietnam veterans. I don't turn to my peers. Veterans don't give you bullshit; they aren't phony; they won't fall apart."

The concept left me with a disturbing thought. Do men have to go to war to become sensitive to human everyday suffering?

Post-traumatic stress disorder has been around ever since man has been on earth. "The *name* is new," says Wilson. "The experience is not."

Still, an academic battle rages as many in the field resist the concept of PTSD. "Some psychologists who do social science research and diagnostic epidemiological studies reject PTSD," says one believer, Robert Laufer. Some argue that PTSD Vietnam anecdotal data is ideologically skewed or unreliable. There is, of course, another element. Like the rest of society, psychiatrists have buried the war. "Clinicians are so resistant to Vietnam veterans," says Laufer. "Who wants to talk about it?"

Although a proponent of PTSD, Laufer agrees with critics who see flaws in the diagnosis as characterized in *DSM III.* "There was not a lot of data. They did the best with what they had. Whether you're talking about the Buffalo Creek flood or the Vietnam War, the trauma can have a lot of different effects —such as depression—as well as PTSD. The main problem is describing the diagnosis. There is still a lot of work to do." (Some recent studies of a small number of institutionalized veterans have found other problems, such as alcohol and personality disorders, among patients who are also correctly diagnosed as having PTSD.)

The intriguing fundamental question, of course, is why some people who experienced similar traumas cope, while others do not. Wilson, Smith, and others have begun to examine combat veterans who have readjusted to ascertain differences. Preliminary theories point to the degree and nature of the trauma, the degree of the person's involvement in that trauma, and variance in an individual's coping mechanisms.

"There *are* predispositional factors. Those with a higher level of sophistication can be awfully screwed up by the experiences but can learn to handle. I suspect that people from high resource backgrounds and stabler families will as a group cope better, but who the hell *knows* who copes?" asked Laufer. "When we talk of 'predictors,' we are dealing with probability statements."

It is not uncommon to find indications of both stress reactions *and* healthy adjustment in the same person, which can explain seeming contradictions in veterans. "Social supports, societal reactions, and personality variables play a role in the pattern and course of stress reactions, but a broad process of stress recovery is apparent in nearly *all* survivors," says Jack Smith.

Art Blank, a psychiatrist who served in Vietnam and joined the VA in 1982 to direct the national Vet Center program, says, "Long-term presence of stress reactions to trauma is not unique. They isolated that with World War II veterans." (Some World War II veterans experienced delayed stress reactions as long as fifteen to twenty years after the stressful event, for example.)[7]

"What is unique, however, about Vietnam veterans and stress is the long-term persistence in *large* numbers."

Estimates vary regarding the number of Vietnam veterans suffering from delayed stress—either the severe form of disorder or still trying to integrate the trauma of Vietnam into their lives. They agree, however, that the numbers are high—anywhere from half a million to 700,000, approximately one fourth of those who served in Vietnam. Of those who saw heavy combat, the numbers are extremely high—more than half, according to some studies. If you add those who are busily *denying* problems—but who have not really integrated the Vietnam experience into their lives—the numbers are staggering. Jack Smith estimates as much as 80 percent of combat veterans have not yet worked through the experience, with about 15 percent of them "disordered."

Psychologist Arthur Egendorf, another author of the *Legacies of Vietnam* study, divides the troubled veterans into three groups. He feels that 10 to 15 percent fall into the disordered category that includes psychotics, drug addicts, incurable alcoholics. Another one fourth are in serious trouble, but salvageable. Far more common, however, are the men who feel they have put Vietnam behind them, gone on to careers and marriages, only to have something erupt years later.

Smith worked with veterans in Winston-Salem, North Carolina, highly motivated and successful veterans who fell apart when the Iranian hostages returned.

"They were Ph.D.'s working in educational psychology. They'd been fine. Suddenly one of them went down the halls at the hospital *raving* at the hostages. They were stunned at their own reactions. 'This isn't me.' '*I* don't have any problems with Vietnam—but *goddamn it!*' " Smith raised his voice in explosive imitation. "There was an overintensity in their reaction, that they recognized in themselves."

In 1982 Phil Caputo interviewed a former Marine lieutenant, David Novak, who had it all. A Ph.D. in mathematics, coming up for tenure at Simmons College, Novak had a contract to write three textbooks; there were four bright daughters, an attractive wife, a handsome Victorian home. Then the crumbling began; the perfect record of sobriety and dependability shattered. He came home drunk at 2 A.M. He'd been out looking for a marine to talk to. He *had* to talk about Vietnam with someone who understood. There were more evenings; being picked up for drunken driving, being found by police passed out in his car in a dangerous neighborhood. Finally he left home and moved into a $5-a-night flophouse full of destitute pensioners.

Novak's troubles were familiar to many veterans returning to college, where the pressure was insidious and palpable. "Though proud of his service, he never let on that he'd been to Vietnam," wrote Caputo.

When Novak first applied for a teaching job at Simmons College, the chairwoman of the mathematics department phoned his former employer and said, "But this person was a *marine!*" The reassuring answer came from his boss: "You can't tell. He doesn't *look* like one."

The greatest strain was not being a closet veteran, however, but in building up the elaborate pretense that he was the same man he'd been before Vietnam. Caputo, who had seen the worst himself, wrote, "But when you have been shot through the arm by a sniper and gone rolling down an embankment thinking you were dying, when three of your four closest buddies have been killed in action, when you've been in Hue during the Tet Offensive and put in charge of a burial detail for enemy dead and seen hundreds of corpses unceremoniously bulldozed into a mass grave; when, also in Hue, you've seen POWs shot to death because they were trapped inside a flaming hut and had to be spared burning to death; when, after Hue, you're sent up to Khe Sanh and spend every night cowering under the screech and crash of artillery, you can never again be the same man."[8]

Heavy combat is the one recurring element in many psychological studies. The most hellish moments of war left even those with the strongest coping skills—the best-ordered minds—defenseless and unprotected from the psychological wounds for which there are no Purple Hearts.

The idea that a soldier is prone to crack in war due to personal weaknesses —for generations a dominant theory—is still heard as a flip explanation for Vietnam veterans with problems.

However, the most startling finding in *Legacies of Vietnam* may finally lay to rest this "predisposition" theory as a major cause. The massive five-volume study, based on 1,380 interviews across the nation with Vietnam veterans and their nongoing peers, shows that post-traumatic stress is more prevalent than previously believed. A crucial finding is that the *persistence* of stress depends much more on the veteran's exposure to combat than on the emotional stability of his childhood. In light combat, soldiers from disadvantaged backgrounds *did* develop more psychological problems than those from more stable homes. But in heavy combat, all such differences disappeared. In fact, the study reports, "Under heavy combat, this finding is reversed. *Surprisingly, more men from the most stable families who were in heavy combat developed stress reactions than men from less stable families."*

The $2 million government study, the most comprehensive to date, is the first to use control studies to factor in probable or possible societal causes of stress, as well as combat.

Not surprisingly, veterans who stayed out of combat appear to be the least stressed, no matter the degree of family stability, with one exception. Those from the *least* stable background seemed to be as stressed by merely being in Vietnam whether they saw heavy combat or not.

On the other hand, while it takes much more to create stress reactions in men from stable families, the traumatic trigger can be devastating. "Men from the *most* stable families who were in heavy combat *continue* to be as seriously stressed as men from less stable families."[9]

The *Legacies* study at first theorized that combat itself caused delayed stress. After reexamining their data and interviews, a new analysis placed greater emphasis on witnessing or participating in acts of unnecessary violence as a primary cause.

"To label combatants as only those going out on patrols in a war like Vietnam—fought all *around people*—is a joke," says Laufer. "A guy in a truck just driving through could see a lot of shit. A *cook* we interviewed happened to see a whole batch of civilian bodies stashed in a cave by VC. Do you really think the people in Beirut being shelled are 'not in combat'? We're interested in the effect of that war experience, not some abstract of 'who saw combat.' "

Laufer interviewed 350 veterans in detail and feels that previous stories understated the incidents of what he terms "abusive violence done to civilians or POWs." Some 30 percent of their sample witnessed such acts. Extrapolating that to the population of those who served, Laufer says, "The rate is high. It goes much deeper than originally suspected." A major question was "did you *see* something" categorized as abusive violence. "Some saw atrocities committed by VC, some had graphic descriptions of torture done by somebody else, usually ARVN with the troop. So the question is what is the effect of seeing joints chopped off, or coming upon VC nurses killed, or watching someone taking target practices at civilians in rice paddies?"

In his sample, 9 percent reported committing some atrocity or abusive violent acts. "So you have 91 percent who did *not* do anything." But a large number, 30 percent—nearly one third—were silent witnesses. Whites and blacks were equally troubled by such events that they *witnessed*. Blacks were even more greatly troubled if they participated, feeling in retrospect that they had committed crimes against another racial group. The startling conclusion was that whites who committed—rather than witnessed—such acts remained surprisingly *untroubled*. After analyzing their interviews, *Legacies* authors surmised that those who were untroubled not only thought the war was right, but were revenge-filled over the death of close buddies and had an abiding hatred for all Vietnamese. They indeed subscribed to the "mere gook syndrome."[10]

Vietnam veterans—who have never been a united community—remain at war over post-traumatic stress. The Vietnam Veterans Leadership Program of Reagan's Action program points to earlier studies that "show little basis for the perception of Vietnam vets as troubled individuals." Other veterans fear this "Everything's okay" approach glosses over a sizable minority—one fourth—who still experience trouble to varying degrees. Both sides use different statistics to try to prove their point. Various studies have produced a welter of confusing findings to fit anyone's thesis.

In the *Legacies* study, a huge number of blacks remain troubled (40 percent, as compared with 20 percent of whites), which will be discussed in a later chapter.

Art Blank pointed to yet another study by a Fort Benning officer who served in Vietnam and surveyed the members of his class who had been officers in Vietnam. Almost all were businessmen and professionals, married, doing well. "And guess what?" says Blank. "Guess how many of that same number were experiencing stress symptoms? One fourth."

Today, according to the *Legacies* study, more than one third of Vietnam veterans who were in heavy combat are stressed, compared with less than 20 percent of nonveterans and Vietnam-era veterans.

Nearly one fourth of the men who saw heavy combat have since been arrested on criminal charges (compared to 10 percent arrest rate among veterans of light combat and 14 percent among nonveterans).

Positive social support counts greatly. Married Vietnam veterans are better off than unmarried. Being married and having spouse support is of more help to blacks and to combat veterans than to others. For veterans in large cities, having many Vietnam veteran friends helps to reduce current levels of stress reaction. For veterans in smaller cities and towns, strong "community" friendships help reduce current levels of stress.

Not surprisingly, lower income, irregular or unsatisfying employment, and lower current educational attainment are all associated with higher levels of stress among Vietnam veterans—especially among combat veterans.

Stories of combat veterans, far more starkly than any graphs or statistics, bring to life that netherworld of Vietnam. Phil Caputo chills you as he quotes Wayne Felde, a veteran convicted of murder: "The woods were on fire from napalm. You could smell the burned bodies. The point man was out in the woods. He was cut off from the rest of the company. He was screaming because he was burned by the napalm. Some guys said he was being tortured by the NVA. We couldn't get to him because of the NVA and because the woods were on fire, so some other guys in the company opened up on him and shot him to put him out of his misery. Come daylight, the fighting was over. We had to pick up pieces of our guys to send home. Arms and legs and three quarters of a whole person. Me and some guys got to the point man and when we went to pick him up, his arms came off because he was burned so bad. The smell was bad and we got sick again. We sent him and the other pieces back. I thought about their moms and I thought about my mom."

Felde describes a massacre in his interview with Caputo. "We were crossing a rice paddy when VC mortar fire came in. The shrapnel cut one guy across the middle. His guts spilled out. I grabbed his insides and tried to shove them back. It looked like afterbirth, and it just slid through my hands, and the guy died. Then we took some small-arms fire from a village. I don't remember if it was much, but we charged the village and started shooting. . . . There was total panic. . . . When something like that gets started, you can't stop it. There was nobody in charge and everyone was shouting and shooting, shouting, 'Shoot this! Shoot that!' and I went into a hut that was filled with people and sprayed it. We wasted everyone and everything in that village. We wasted the women and the kids and the old men and the dogs. . . . Then we burned the village to the ground. It was the most awful thing and I still dream about it. Listen, man, I dream this shit every night. . . ."

Caputo recalls his own stories: "A communications specialist in my battalion forgot to be paranoid. He was alone, stringing communications wire between two outposts in an area officially classified as secure. Nothing but friendly paddy farmers. Seeing he was by himself, a few of the friendly paddy farmers wounded him with carbine fire, took his rifle and equipment, and captured him. One of the farmers was later captured and under, shall we say, persuasive questioning, told what happened next: the marine was dragged into a village, where he was beaten with rifle butts and clubs, then executed with a shot to the back of the head. The usual surgery was performed on his genitals, which were then stuffed into his mouth. The body was tossed into a river. Apparently it wasn't weighted properly; it floated to the surface a few days later and was discovered by one of our patrols."

The burn that remains inside Caputo for those who vilified the soldiers is uncontained. "I would ask those who—from their safe editorial offices, their college campuses, and suburban living rooms—condemned the American soldier in Vietnam these questions: How would you have behaved in such an environment? What kind of person would *you* have become?"[11]

All these years later, it is time for the rest of America to stop wrangling over what can cause delayed stress, over whether there is a problem—because there *is* a problem. It may be comforting to dismiss the troubled veterans as a handful of crybabies and losers, but that just won't wash. One half a million or more people cannot be swept away that easily.

The government—all too slowly and too little—spends its pennies on veteran stress recovery and readjustment—and its billions on armament. The public—all too slowly and too little—has begun to understand. Both money and understanding are urgently needed if those veterans who are still hurting are ever going to be helped.

For purely selfish reasons, the country can gain much from an understanding of delayed stress. Some family counselors have learned that a knowledge of the stress recovery process can alleviate much of the tension and misunderstanding that occurs in such situations; the family member, for example, who cannot understand why another doesn't "snap out of" depressions following traumatic incidents in their lives.

On a larger moral note, the experience of Vietnam veterans should not be forgotten in a country where its leaders seem bent on repeating such third world interventions. "What may be most disturbing about the plight of the veteran over the past decade is that it suggests a future in which comparable subgroups within society may be more vulnerable to abuse than ever before," wrote Doctor Jeffrey Jay and David Harrington, who work with veterans. "The veteran's experience encapsulates a societal process yet to be widely acknowledged or understood in which individuals involved in morally troublesome actions are *disowned* by society; in which the media controls the image of a minority and slowly alters it over time; in which psychic numbing and isolation become acceptable mechanisms for survival in complex emotional and moral conflicts; and, most importantly, in which subgroups are assigned *blame* for problems the larger society refuses to face."[12]

2 The Afflicted

THROUGHOUT HISTORY THE NOTION PERSISTED THAT PSYCHOLOGICAL reactions to combat were the result of predisposition; an inclination toward mental or emotional disorders. Leading proponents, of course, were military doctors. How else could the military justify such reactions to war, if, indeed, wars had to be fought? A moral judgment—that the person was "unsound"— had to be made. "Treatment" included everything from contemptible scorn to downright torture.

For years the excuse was that it was the scum who went to battle and, therefore, the character of an entire Army was called into question. "The worst lot of men that we ever sent out to war were the reinforcements that went to Flanders in the middle of 1794 and to the West Indies in 1795–96. Both behaved infamously, as was to be expected from the scum of England. . . . I have no doubt that there was a good deal of 'emotional shock' among them," noted British military historian John Fortescue. The only problem with such withering comments is that Fortescue also observed that even the bravest shared similar "cowardly" reactions to combat and "went out of their minds in the old campaigns as they still do."[1]

By the time of the Civil War, character deficiency alone could no longer explain breakdown in combat or desertion. Men, including the most courageous of soldiers, were leaving the field of battle in droves.

The Union and Confederate armies stationed hospital ships near the Atlantic Coast, in order to evacuate their wounded. Both had to abandon the use of the ships. As doctors stared out from the deck, they saw waves of men clogging the gangplank, shoving on board, making it impossible to care for the wounded. They were suffering from what was then called "nostalgia"—a "temporary feeling of depression" that frequently pervaded the Army camps, when men, after continued exposure to battle, began to pine to a severe degree for home and an end to bloodshed. Tens of thousands tried to leave—on hospital ships, on foot. In 1918 Pearce W. Bailey, studying war neuroses, wrote that of the 600,000 deserters in the Civil War Union Army alone, there might have been a "numerous representation of modern-day shell shock."[2]

The Civil War produced a profound shift in military reports. "Now the distinction between normality and abnormality becomes not whether they [emotional reactions] *occur,* but rather whether they *persist,"* noted psychologist Jack Smith. In other words, even the bravest could have momentary emotional lapses. Returning to battle was the key test of the "normal" real man.

Still, the long history of blaming psychological reactions to combat on "predisposition" continued through the horrendous fighting of World War I, when human waves were mowed down in futile campaigns. World War I's mode of warfare, artillery fire, produced widespread fear—so much so that military doctors had to quickly make a distinction between "fear" and "cowardice." Fear itself was considered a normal outgrowth of war and carried no stigma. Cowardice became defined as lack of self-control, while the courageous faced fear "like a man."

"Shell shock" was also introduced—a term apparently coined by soldiers to denote dazed reactions, bordering on concussions, which often followed the explosion of artillery shells. Psychiatric observers then applied this term to describe the physiological reactions which caught their attention. They tried to distinguish between two kinds of shell shock—that which resulted from such understandable circumstances as concussions (commotional) and that which had a purely psychological basis (emotional). Only "commotional" became the "good" term—deserving the rights and privileges of being called a disease. *Emotional* shell shock was treated as a "disciplinary" matter. It was seen as resulting from a failure of self-control and, therefore, from a defect in character.[3]

Military psychiatrists were in a dilemma. The battle raged, with "predisposition" winning out over "occasion" as the cause of combat stress. Some World War I studies showed that a fair percentage *could* be considered "predisposed" to psychological problems; however, little attempt was made to compare the backgrounds of men evacuated for war stress to those of the overall soldier population exposed to the same stress. Whenever such attempts were made, results were equivocal. In all wars, there have been countless numbers from strife-torn, unstable families—some who have grown up in the most depraved circumstances—who have, indeed, fought, not only without breaking down, but heroically.

Predisposing factors did not predict breakdown, later studies would prove. For example, *half* the sample of 150 successful combat flyers studied in 1944 had a family history of emotional instability. Furthermore, psychoneurotic tendencies were found in one third of this crack combat flyer group.[4]

The doctors and psychiatric observers of World War I soldiers, however, persisted with the notion that psychiatric combat reactions resulted from a pathological failure in the self-control of fear. Predisposition served them well because it put the responsibility on the individual and was a compatible explanation for malingering and cowardice.

Treatment for such "malingerers" varied, from hypnosis to torture. One method, employed at certain French centers, consisted of "the brusque application of galvanic currents strong enough to be extremely painful." An overhead trolley carried long connecting wires the whole length of the room, "thus making the patient unable to run away from the current which is destined to cure him."[5]

For "hysterical deafness," the patient was taken to a dugout near the front lines that was frequently shelled and given an injection of ether. Supposedly the surroundings and the injection—"not dangerous but extremely painful" —cured the deafness.

Critics of the electric shock used by the French, British, and Germans pointed out the frequency of relapse, the number of patients who committed suicide upon "cure," and the death of two patients in therapy, but the process continued.

Lewis Yealland, the most outspoken of the British practitioners of disciplinary therapies, was fond of torturing into "normalcy."

A twenty-four-year-old private, totally mute for nine months, had witnessed some of the most incredible battles of World War I: the retreat from Mons, the Battle of the Marne, Aisne, and the First and Second Battles of Ypres. Sent to Salonica to take part in the Gallipoli expedition, he collapsed and woke up mute. He was strapped down in a chair while strong electricity was applied to his neck and throat; lighted cigarette ends had been applied to tongue and hot plates placed at the back of his mouth.[6]

Yealland argued that these techniques failed because they had not been thoroughly applied.

He took the private into the darkened electrical room and locked the doors. Electricity was applied for one hour, at the end of which the patient could say "Ah." After two hours, the patient tried to get out of the room. Yealland said: "When the time comes for more electricity, you will be given it whether you want it or not!" He raised the voltage to very strong shocks and continued for a half hour until the spasms of the neck had disappeared and the patient could speak in a whisper with no spasms or stammer. Yealland often had time left over for his little frills. To one patient, he said: "Your laugh is most offensive to me; I dislike it very much indeed . . . you must be more rational." And turned up the voltage.[7]

Such bestial disciplinary treatment was reserved for those arbitrarily judged to have character defect because they cracked. Those deemed sufficiently brave (and willing to return to the front) were mostly subjected to analysis. Elaborate tests were set up to detect the true malingerer, the partial, and the quasimalingerer. However, such distinctions defied observers. Concluded one authority, the "signs of genuine [war] neuroses and simulation [malingering] are identical. . . ."[8]

Astoundingly, one study—not examined by the present-day VA apparently—presaged delayed stress by about fifty years. A great many men while in the thick of battle in World War I showed no evidence of strain—but developed a "severe neurosis" after the fact, following demobilization.

Such revelations left military psychiatrists in a quandary; they continued to cling to predisposition—the "good" versus "bad" soldier.

The emphasis on predisposition was rooted in other reasons besides macho revulsion to not "acting like a man." Rates of shell shock casualties reflected on the level of morale and discipline; no military doctor wanted to blame the military. If shell shock could be described as a legitimate problem, authorities were worried about escalating demands for compensation.

When World War II began, predisposition was still viewed as the primary cause of breakdown. Emotional problems of soldiers "were invariably dismissed as ploys for compensation and illegitimate claims" wrote Emanuel Miller in *The Neuroses of War* in 1942. Miller pointed out *forty years ago* what Vietnam veterans, bitter at the VA policy, would echo in the eighties: "This attitude toward compensation persists today and has come to stigmatize discussions of long-term or delayed combat reactions."

Elaborate screening systems were designed to weed out "predisposed" men likely to break under combat stress. Large numbers were rejected as psychiatrists looked for personality deviations such as instability, seclusiveness, sulkiness, sluggishness, lonesomeness, depression, shyness, suspicion, overboisterousness, timidity, sleeplessness, lack of initiative and ambition, uncleanliness, stupidity, dullness, resentfulness to discipline, nocturnal incontinence, sleepwalking, recognized queerness, suicidal tendencies, mental defects and deficiencies, psychopathic personality disorders, and chronic inebriety.

Some of those symptoms sound like the province of any average adolescent male. It is not surprising that screening produced a rejection rate of three to four times that of World War I. Some 2 million were rejected for the draft in World War II on psychological grounds. The screening was abandoned after it proved a *resounding failure.* For example, large numbers of men were designated as psychoneurotics in the North African campaign. At first they were simply viewed as failures of the screening system. However, the British evacuation at Dunkirk caused a reevaluation.

Panic and hysteria on the beaches of Dunkirk were widespread among soldiers exposed mercilessly to dive bombers while waiting evacuation. Observers were forced to conclude that, under such conditions, even normal men would break.

Combat exhaustion, an "Every-man-has-his-breaking-point" theme was introduced to explain the heroes who broke. It was noted that "casualties began to appear when morale which had been fanatically high, had been undermined by the *hopelessness* of the situation, the cumulative trauma, doubts concerning leadership, the mounting resentments."[9] (A generation later, such hopelessness, distrust of leadership, low morale, and resentments would trigger much of the stress in Vietnam soldiers.)

Still, the military mind bought little of such findings. Major General Paul Hawley, Chief Surgeon, U.S. Army, 1944, sounds as though he would have been at home with Britain's sadistic disciplinarian Lewis Yealland in World War I:

> . . . If every soldier knew that he would be executed for cowardice, for malingering, or for a self-inflicted wound, the vast majority of the weaklings would choose the more favorable odds offered in facing the enemy. . . .[10]

However, there were improvements in treatment. During World War II, soldiers suffering combat exhaustion received brief rest and recuperation. Hypnosis or sodium-pentothal-induced sleep enabled many to speak freely of experiences previously repressed. When rest and catharsis didn't work, group therapy pressure was used to implant the *will to fight*.

Another form of therapy consisted of trying to shame them back into fighting and, once again, electrical shock was used.[11]

A famous World War II incident revealed the depth of contempt for soldiers suffering psychological symptoms. On August 10, 1943, General George S. Patton, striding through a hospital, slapped a soldier. As Seventh U.S. Army commander in Sicily, he had five days before issued a memorandum branding as "cowards" men claiming to be nervously incapable of combat. After the slapping scene, Patton made a public apology but the thought lingered; psychiatric casualties represented cowardice, poor motivation, or weakness of character.

During the early months of Korea, exhaustion after prolonged battle was acceptable since it reflected an *inability* rather than an *unwillingness* to continue fighting. After the first year of the Korean campaign, however, warfare became more static, with intermittent episodes of intense combat. The problem could not be blamed therefore on prolonged periods of fighting.

Extended long-term psychiatric reactions to warfare were mentioned in the literature of war neuroses. Unfortunately, they were seldom studied. Effort was spent on a quick fix rehabilitation of men so that they could return to combat. A study of any significance on long-range problems of World War II veterans did not surface until 1965, twenty years later.

The combat fatigue syndrome, *which was expected to vanish with the passage of time,* has proved to be chronic, if not irreversible, in certain of its victims. Many are only now appearing for treatment as aging exacerbates their symptoms.[12]

Still, in the VA bureaucracy, it was extremely difficult to qualify for a diagnosis—and thus compensation—of combat stress reactions. A veteran had to *prove* a past history of comparatively healthy emotional and social adjustment as well as severe, prolonged exposure to traumatic combat.

Vietnam was the first war in which the military lavished concern on reducing physical exhaustion and, thus, combat fatigue. One-year tours of duty, R and R (Rest and Relaxation), psychiatrists at-the-ready seemed to be working. Psychiatric casualties reached an all-time low. Vietnam psychiatric casualty rates were less than one third of those reported during stressful periods in Korea and one tenth of the highest rate ever reported in World War II—101 per 1,000. Patients hospitalized or excused from duty for psychiatric reasons in 1967 were approximately 10 per 1,000 troops.[13]

However, distinctions were made between those who had real combat fatigue and *"pseudocombat* fatigue." The latter were individuals who broke down under what was judged to be lesser stress.

This so-called pseudocombat fatigue group did not respond well to treatment and willingness to return to the war zone remained the key between the "good"—and truly traumatized—and the "bad" malingerer.

During the war, military psychiatrists were effusive over changed conditions of warfare. The twelve-month tour was seen as a great ameliorator—it was not until years later that veterans spoke of survival guilt they felt on leaving buddies, the sense of immobilizing self-preservation that took over when they were "short," the lack of unity and *esprit de corps* of constantly turned over units. Another misinterpretation was to assume that conventional warfare brought *more* emotional problems than the now recognized psychological horrors of guerrilla warfare. "Soldiers [in Vietnam] do not have to spend lengthy periods of time in trenches or foxholes and are rarely subjected to continuous artillery bombardment."[14]

Art Blank, a psychiatrist in Vietnam, was stationed at the 93rd evacuation hospital, Long Binh, and the Third Field hospital in 1965–66. "I was one of those Army psychiatrists who said Vietnam wasn't creating any psychiatric difficulties." He laughs ruefully; his job for the past several years has been nothing but working with troubled Vietnam veterans. "The psychiatric problems were always *there*—but they weren't coming to see us psychiatrists in Vietnam. They were closing it off by smoking dope."

Dealing with emotions through drugs was not the only reason given for low combat psychological casualties. Many simply denied any problems—and turned up with physiological symptoms. Patients hospitalized for evaluation of suspected ulcers, diabetes, weight loss, and migratory arthritis were later found to be reporting psychosomatic symptoms and were actually suffering from acute emotional turmoil, instability, and insecurity. These unrecognized psychosomatic symptoms accounted in part for the so-called low incidence of psychiatric disorders.[15]

Moreover, one in twelve veterans became "administrative problems"—and rather than risk court-martial accepted less than honorable discharges. Years later, many were regarded as acting out stress reactions at the time.

Rather than the "predisposition" attitude that anyone in his right mind would get over war, perhaps the more accurate view is that anyone in his right mind would *not* entirely ever get over war.

As William Mahedy, former chaplain and former director of a San Diego Vet Center put it, "There may have been some psychopaths over there who got off on killing. But *we* don't see them. We see the sensitive, troubled guys."

One fact is central to their problems: profoundly conflicting moral judgments are at work in war. The task of the military is to "detrain" all the "Thou shalt not kill" beliefs of childhood; to make the men, as the Marines so dehumanizingly term it, "fighting machines."

Or, as one World War I major general put it, discipline meant "giving your men such a hell of a time when they are behind the lines that when they face the enemy they are *glad* to go over the top and get shot."[16]

Not all went so willingly to kill. Historian S. L. A. Marshall, in 1947, noted that the most difficult challenge in warfare was not fear for one's own safety, as commonly supposed, but rather the *reluctance to kill*. Psychiatrists studying World War II soldiers found that "Fear of killing rather than fear of being killed was the most common cause of battle failure."

> The fear of aggression has been absorbed by him so deeply and pervadingly —practically with his mother's milk—that it is part of the normal man's emotional makeup. *This is his great handicap when he enters combat.*[17]

While many men can effectively function during war, their thoughts afterward are often another matter. A terrible irony is unavoidable: one study of Vietnam combat veterans revealed that men with "good adjustment" felt no compunction about killing in Vietnam—while those men "sensitive to conflicts over killing seemed to be most negatively affected after the war."

It appears that individuals who were high in authoritarianism were relatively able to cope with the most brutal acts of the Vietnam War and to compartmentalize these experiences. They express less bitterness toward the military, are more hawklike in attitudes and less introspective of their own behavior and experiences. [On the other hand], Low authoritarians are likely to be more conflicted and sensitive to the paradoxes of the Vietnam conflict.[18]

One doctor today finds that his severely depressed Vietnam veteran patients often come from rigid religious backgrounds of "right" and "wrong." They "cannot resolve what they did in the war with their lives today."

The unresolved nature of Vietnam is vital to understanding why some veterans are troubled. After all, coming home from war has always meant readjustment—nor is there anything new in civilians becoming wary of a returned killer in their midst.

"After cannon and bayonet charge, a man might come home and seem queer for a while. For the common soldier, the first five years of peace are the hardest. . . . If, five years later, the ex-soldier is still looking for a job or nursing injuries of body or mind, he may fairly be thought unemployable or permanently scarred," wrote historian Dixon Wecter about Civil War and World War I veterans. Many in the civilian population expected a soldier to "come back a rake, a thief, and probably a killer." Writing of the World War I veteran, Wecter noted "He imagined slights, took civilian neglect or teasing too seriously. He returned with a chip on his shoulder."[19]

The soldier has long felt aggrieved by the profits civilians gained from his war, which compounded their adjustment problems. In 1868 Major John C. Cremorny of California lamented that of all applicants for work or office "the soldier is the most spurned and ignored." One Civil War veteran who couldn't get a job complained, "Yesterday I was a hero. Today I'm just another one-legged boy." After World War I, inflation, lean times, and a ruling class of new rich who had profited during the war culminated in the famous "Bonus March." Veterans smoldered as "old classmates in high school who had convinced draft boards of the flatness of their feet were now married, living in comfortable houses, driving snappy cars. Some in government jobs had weathered the war in swivel chairs. . . ."[20]

Many World War II veterans still remember with bitter clarity men who advanced their careers because they remained home in jobs classified as vital to the war effort.

Vietnam, once again, created a more intense intragenerational confrontation of postwar competitiveness. And, of course, their pariah role in society during raging antiwar days and subsequent defeat created an altogether new dimension to the problems of returning soldiers.

All these years later, "blame" and "responsibility" permeate discussions about Vietnam. "Blaming the war on someone else is a continued form of denying," says Smith. "Military men blame policy makers, right-wingers blame the pinkos and media and protesters, the left blame the right. The need is still there to blame someone else."

Smith tries to help veterans to work through such feelings as "I know *I* was responsible for such and so, but *I* didn't start this war."

"Veterans want Bob McNamara and Kissinger and Nixon and every government official who had anything to do with the war to own up to their part." It is a wishful, fruitless dream. No leader of that war has ever had the courage to admit *anything* to the veteran. Instead, they were the biggest transgressors in shoveling the veteran out of sight.

In 1972 Richard Nixon successfully vetoed the Veterans Health Care Expansion Act, for example. He said it was fiscally irresponsible and inflationary—even as the United States was still spending billions blowing Vietnam to smithereens.

"You have to help veterans get past that," says Smith. "McNamara *denies* any responsibility. Many are involved in undoing. It's a way of alleviating guilt and responsibility. What McNamara did at the World Bank, I believe, was expiation for Vietnam: 'If I do something good here, I don't have to worry about the past.'"

Smith contains himself until he starts to list America's policy makers. "Kissinger, that SOB! He can burn in hell, as far as I'm concerned. He *knew* the consequences of his actions, could reflect on them, and *still* said, 'To hell with the human issues.'"

Jack Smith is a tall, blond ex-marine with intensely emotional feelings. "I have come to realize that Vietnam will never be behind me."

Going to war was a rite of passage. "I needed to find out for myself if I was a man." He was a gung ho marine whose tour began in January of 1969 as a staff sergeant in charge of counter-mortar radar surveillance teams on the DMZ. He returned outraged by the war and joined Vietnam Veterans Against the War. This act was not paradoxical to the soldier that remained within Smith.

"I saw that as *continuing* my responsibility as a marine. If we were there to 'win hearts and minds' and I saw that mission distorted, I had an *obligation* to come back and tell the people it was being thwarted." Committed to working veterans through delayed stress for ten years, Smith says, "I probably will be at it for another ten. What we're doing is questioning that fundamental assumption that war is just okay and noble. Men like Jim Webb have not found any way of abandoning that warrior myth; others of us have."

Nine members of Smith's family—brothers and cousins—went to Vietnam. "Our ideas of patriotism were profoundly altered. But if you *haven't* been to war, like many in our generation, those concepts are *never* in quite the same way undermined or tested. I don't care if the guy is a right-winger, his ideals were *threatened* in Vietnam—and either undermined or strengthened. For the West Pointers, the fact that civilians didn't back them up left them with a great deal of sorting out to do about patriotism, too.

"The guys who didn't go didn't have an experience that profoundly changed or, perhaps in some cases, strengthened that concept."

Smith's reactions to the war led to bizarre acting out. While protesting with VVAW, he was a consultant to the Army when the seventies' drug scandal broke. Smith joined the colonels and other military men—wearing a full beard, flowing hair, a white star on a blue field sewed to the crotch of his jeans. The response was predictable. "If they had had a gun, they would have shot me."

Smith realizes now that his dress was "a way of distancing myself from what I had been as a marine—while I renegotiated with myself as to where I stood. I was afraid of being sucked back into it." Strangely, Smith found an affinity with some of the military high-ranking officers. "We had the same commitment about protecting the troops. The best would say, 'You're absolutely right. I would not sacrifice the troops for some insane action of some colonel [who would] send my guys to a slaughter.' They felt, in their own way, like I did—that we as a country were not being honorable in our mission."

Combat is the best predictor of psychological aftereffects, but combat alone is not the cause of stress. "All individuals go into war with a set of moral values," says Smith. "What may trigger conflict over these values are as myriad and as varied as the people." Smith sees three factors that contribute to stress: 1. the degree of horror or intensity of the traumatic situation; 2. the degree of conflict over moral values; and 3. the degree of personal culpability and responsibility or what one *perceives* to be personal culpability and responsibility.

Deep conflicts can occur when personal moral standards clash with the tenets of fighting. "We antiwar vets broke with our military because *they* were not consistent with what we felt and were. We were forced to fall back on our personal standards. And even there we had differing standards! I had fierce battles with some of those in VVAW who supported the NLF."

"Blame" is the cornerstone of Smith's thinking and he is still sorting out his own memories of personal blame. "There is *always* a certain factor of guilt in tragic situations—but not nearly so great if you didn't feel that you somehow contributed."

In Smith's case, he is haunted by his failure to act in a couple of instances. "I became alienated from the Marine Corps because I was considered a 'gook lover' and 'nigger lover.'

"One time we discovered tunnels headed toward our bunker and equipment. We blew up all the tunnels. The villagers who had been taken to refugee camps used to forage through our garbage dumps. We figured that either they were sympathetic to the NVA or had been forced by the NVA to carry away in their baskets dirt from the tunnels they were digging. So we decided to punish them. They were mostly women, children, and old men. They went to the garbage dump one day and the marines let fly with CS gas canisters. I went in with my usual liberal horseshit about winning hearts and minds and that these people were just victims, caught between the NVA and us. Because of the gas, they started vomiting. There were a squad of grunts lined up, lobbing gas canisters. When the Vietnamese all clustered together, they opened fire, shooting at the dirt at their feet, making them dance like in the cowboy movies."

Smith pauses, as intense in telling this story as if it were yesterday. "I realized it was fruitless for me to say anything. I walked back into my bunker —and for years after I came home I still was never able to forgive myself for not stopping it."

Could you have?

"No—but I still can't forgive myself, even though I *know* that's not a rational answer."

Veterans Smith has helped were profoundly affected by their individual internal moral compass. Smith relates one case as if it were happening to the listener.

"A squadron is in a firefight, getting ambushed, and the enemy is on the other side of a swollen stream. You and your best buddy start to wade across. He gets to the other side, but you are swept away. In desperation, you reach out the butt of your M-16. He grabs it and pulls you out of the river. You're halfway out. Your hand slips—and accidentally fires a bullet into his chest.

"Now the guy who did *that*," continues Smith, "had a stress disorder for fourteen years. He came into therapy because his wife told him he was crazy. For fourteen years he's been driving forty-two miles out of his way around the town to work. He refuses to drive through it. After he comes into therapy, he suddenly remembers. The guy he killed was *buried* in that town. He felt so guilty he had totally blocked that from his mind." Smith worked with the man until he was finally able to one day sit at the graveside, sobbing, and hold a conversation with his dead friend. The man is still in therapy but getting better.

"A veteran worked with the ARVN. One day they captured an NVA nurse. The ARVNs began molesting her, stripping her, urinating on her, and raping her. He did not participate—but stood by while this was going on. Years later, in the clinic, he revealed he has a sex problem and was involved in sadomasochistic sex acts, with himself being punished. It took several sessions before he remembered the rape incident.

"A technician in Vietnam watched one day as the women who worked around the camp were taunted with sexually suggestive catcalls by soldiers driving by in a truck. One of the Vietnamese women gave them the finger. The soldiers in the truck took C rations and started throwing them at the Vietnamese, hitting them in the head, hurting many. Seven years later the veteran started having nightmares and all the symptoms of stress recovery, even though he'd never been in combat. He blames himself for not having stopped them."

There are, of course, positive experiences to service and combat in Vietnam. No expert in delayed stress attempts to paint a picture of total grimness. In fact, some are trying to find out one of the real mysteries—why some people, seemingly from similar backgrounds and in similar circumstances—respond more positively and have fewer or no problems.

Those who have made it psychologically out of Vietnam are by no means all papering over their problems with denial.

Experts do not dismiss the concept of "predisposition" or individual factors that help shape one's responses. They only say that background is no *predictor* in judging who will have problems. Nor do they wish to get into chest-thumping arguments about which war was more traumatic, what incidents were more traumatizing than others, or reopening the insoluble debate between right and left on Vietnam. They simply want to help the veteran.

"If America wants its Vietnam veterans to be cleansed," wrote Phil Caputo, "it must give them genuine compassion, dignity, and respect: compassion for having been misused, dignity for having answered the call to arms and doing their duty as they saw it, respect for having had the courage and tenacity to survive."[21]

For many veterans, whose festering and silenced troubles went unrecognized for years, such compassion, dignity, and respect will come too late.

3 The Criminals

PETER KRUTSCHEWSKI, ONE OF VIETNAM'S MOST HIGHLY DECORATED combat veterans, became a self-made oil millionaire—and then spent months in prison, sentenced to ten years for smuggling marijuana. Another decorated combat veteran, Charles Heads, shot and killed his brother-in-law. A third, Lewis Lowe III, robbed two fast-food restaurants and pleaded guilty to seven previous robberies.[1]

The three had more than Vietnam in common. Their defense attorneys argued that their combat experience led to severe mental and emotional problems and that they were extreme cases of post-traumatic stress disorder (PTSD).

All had seen horrendous amounts of combat. Krutschewski's friend went in his place on one helicopter assault mission and was killed. Heads watched as a massive booby trap blew his sergeant "into a million pieces." Lowe, a demolitions expert, had to reach inside the wounds of dead comrades to defuse booby traps rigged by the VC.

The most controversial aspect of delayed stress is the use of PTSD as an insanity defense in criminal proceedings. Many cannot comprehend or sympathize with a Vietnam veteran who holds up a 7-Eleven store or does battle with the police or holds hostages in a bank, for example. However, delayed stress experts often feel that they are acting out of two impulses. One is a risk junkie's search to recapture the thrill of combat; another is guilt. Many show little resistance or intent to pull a trigger. The theory is that they *want* to get caught; they are seeking a form of self-destruction, a symbolic suicide.

As lawyers began using PTSD with increasing frequency in the early eighties, the reaction, even among those who understood delayed stress, was frequently unsympathetic; traumas may *explain* a person's action but don't excuse it. In fact, PTSD experts often emphasize that they refuse to testify unless they are certain the delayed stress factor is relevant to the case. Their arguments have been moving and plausible for any number of juries; acquittals have been granted from California to Alabama, Pennsylvania to Louisiana.

The following landmark cases sketch the circumstances and outcomes for three Vietnam veterans whose war echoed in the courtrooms a decade later.

In Folly Cove, on Cape Cod, a mansion with walls of glass sits forty feet above the sea. On July 23, 1975, Jamiel ("Jimmy") Chagra, a former Texas carpet salesman, stood in the living room, speaking into a walkie-talkie to two men pretending to fish from the bow of a pleasure craft far below. Peter Krutschewski—"The Audie Murphy of Vietnam," his lawyer called him— trained his binoculars on a vessel anchored on the horizon. In its hold were 57,000 pounds of prime Colombian marijuana—912,000 one-ounce lids.

For months, Krutschewski had fed his thrill-seeking needs and his wallet in daredevil smuggling escapades from St. Thomas to Morocco. Now he was feverishly waiting to score big. A successful unloading would gross almost $14 million. For three nights, in darkness, Krutschewski supervised the off-load. The same adrenaline-charged thrill that he had felt as a Cobra gunship pilot took over. An ingenious pulley system hauled nets loaded with mari-juana up the cliff; bales upon bales were piled in the glass house, then smug-gled behind second-hand furniture in trucks. A week later, the marijuana was trucked out of state to wholesalers.

For five years, the Folly Cove smuggle went unsolved. Krutschewski took his earnings to Las Vegas, rolling for thousands. He hit town with $300,000, lost all but $10,000 playing blackjack, then wound up winning nearly $300,000 more. He reported the winnings as income and paid the IRS more than $85,000. Still, the lucrative Folly Cove venture was a "turning point. . . . I didn't want to become a criminal."

Krutschewski borrowed $10,000 to start an oil exploration and drilling company in Lansing, Michigan. Michigan became one of the top ten oil-producing states following major finds of oil and natural gas during the seven-ties. Krutschewski's luck was with him. He hit thirty producing wells in a row, was making $100,000 a year, and estimated his net worth at $2 million. The picture of a prosperous young businessman, Krutschewski played coun-try club golf, served on a township economic development council, and voted Republican. The beauty of it all was that his thrills were legal this time. "Being in oil is like smuggling or gambling," he later said. "Sweating out a well—that's really being on the edge." He never once returned to criminal activity.

Then, early one morning in 1979, driving to work with his bride of one month, Krutschewski was pulled over by the police. Squad cars converged, screeching to abrupt stops, just as in the movies. The statute of limitations had nearly—but not quite—run out on his Folly Cove smuggling caper. In just weeks he would have been free. "I worried constantly the entire five years about being apprehended. . . . I was always the happy-go-lucky guy, but tragedy is part of my life now."

A book could be written on members of the sixties generation and marijuana and cocaine smuggling. Krutschewski's smuggling cohorts were on both sides of Vietnam—flying buddies and Michigan State University friends he met on return. One is the son of a former small town mayor, another the son of a business executive. One smuggler was a former semipro football player.

One of his former classmates, Robert Rankin—handsome, articulate, richly enjoying the exotic beaches that his marijuana smuggling bought—was caught, turned informer, and fingered Krutschewski as the college buddy who gave him his start in 1973.

Krutschewski was acquitted of a federal charge that he masterminded the Folly Cove caper, but was found guilty on four counts of importation and possession of marijuana. Krutschewski pleaded guilty by reason of temporary insanity caused by PTSD. His criminal activity grew out of the traumas of his extraordinary number of missions and his thrill-seeking need to recapture the intensity of combat, lawyers argued. The jury rejected the plea.

The caprice at play in such cases was illustrated in the case of Michael Tindall, another of the Folly Cove smugglers who used PTSD as his argument before a different judge and jury. They bought the thrill- and risk-seeking temporary insanity PTSD argument and acquitted Tindall. Tindall and Krutschewski were the first to test PTSD in a nonviolent *premeditated* crime. Krutschewski's sentence of ten years and the maximum fine of $60,000 seemed unduly harsh, considering the fate of the other eighteen smugglers convicted with him. Nine received suspended sentences, seven were sentenced to between four and six months, one received a fifteen-month sentence, and another received five years.

Judge Skinner—an avid sailor—wanted to "send a message. I know that people who work around the docks are constantly being offered huge amounts of money to deliver marijuana. Some of them take it, figuring the judge won't do anything about it."

Making Krutschewski a symbol of the follies of drug smuggling seemed a fruitless attempt at deterrence, given the astronomical profits in pot and cocaine smuggling.

The U.S. Drug Enforcement Agency (DEA) estimated that more than *$1 billion* worth of marijuana, at wholesale prices, is smuggled into or through Massachusetts alone every year. The DEA guess is that only 10 to 20 percent is intercepted. Most of the marijuana enters from Florida. Fishermen have been offered as much as $10,000 for a day's use of their boats to off-load. While organized crime has moved into marijuana smuggling, another kind of "white collar" organizer is big in marijuana smuggling, as opposed to the element who traffic in hard drugs. They are the sixties generation grown up.

"The new organizations are run largely by middle-class college graduates in their early to mid-thirties who started smoking grass in high school or college in the sixties," wrote the Boston *Phoenix*.

Like many of his generation, Krutschewski feels marijuana—the drug of choice of their adolescence—should be legalized and saw nothing wrong with smuggling grass or hash. He recoiled, however, at the deadlier elements of the narcotics trade: smuggling harder drugs, using guns, the mob that inevitably moves in. After Krutschewski cashed in his smuggling chips, one of his acquaintances was among five men murdered in unsolved killings believed to be drug-related.

Risk taking is hardly the major motive in an illegal business that offers enormous financial rewards. Many of the sixties generation continue to demand marijuana—and, more recently, cocaine—in large quantities. (More than 15 million Americans have tried cocaine at least once, with a major rise among a younger generation, according to the National Institute on Drug Abuse.) As long as these drugs remain illegal, smugglers will be in business.

Krutschewski was just days away from jail when we met in Washington in December 1981. He was propelled by understandable urgency; still, his nervous energy, staccato starts and stops, seemed endemic to his nature. Judge Skinner had turned down a plea for alternate service; Krutschewski's appeals were exhausted; his business was suffering from the publicity. His young, blond wife Jan, her wide brown eyes open in perpetual questioning, seemed stunned that this windfall of a husband had been caught for dope smuggling, shattering their idyllic one-month marriage. She listened without expression.

The high-living aspects of his lifestyle still remained. In his posh Madison Hotel suite, wine cooled in a bucket. Slim, Krutschewski nonetheless had an incipient paunch that stretched the buttons of his brown vest; nervous eating was adding its pounds.

His reddish-brown hair fell forward as Krutschewski, affable and earnest, poured out his story.

By the time he was discharged in 1970, after two tours, Krutschewski had flown more than 1,000 missions, logging over 1,500 hours of "trigger time" (combat hours, when he was firing or taking fire). Without question one of the most highly decorated combat heroes, he won fifty-five medals, including forty-four Air Medals, two Bronze Stars, and two Distinguished Flying Crosses.

One Distinguished Flying Cross was for saving six companions: "Operating in conditions of extremely low visibility, he continually made low-level attacks on the enemy positions. His sound judgment and courageous actions [made possible] the safe extraction of the six men." Another award citation attested that "Through his courage and determination, Warrant Officer Krutschewski contributed greatly to the successful combat assault of the A Shau Valley"—one of the most ferocious large-scale battles of the Vietnam War.

In a short time, Krutschewski was addicted to the awesome power other former gunship pilots repeatedly recall, but at first he was so scared that he couldn't eat and lost thirty-four pounds. A friend lied for Krutschewski and took his place in one mission. "They assaulted the A Shau Valley. Everybody aboard the craft was killed." The death of that friend brought heavy guilt and a fearless resolve to make up for it.

The Cobra gunship is one of the most terrifying killing machines known to man. Phil McCombs, a former Army sergeant in Vietnam and a Washington *Post* reporter, described the feel of it for all the Krutschewskis, for all the American teenagers whose deadly, exhilarating Atari-style fantasies became reality.

A single Cobra helicopter has the capability "in the almost caressing phrase of military tacticians—to 'vertically envelop' the enemy with the fire-power of a battalion. Its weapons include the minigun or machine gun firing 4,000 rounds a minute, the 40-mm. cannon firing grenades at machine gun speed, and seventeen-round rockets—each of which can devastate a hamlet." Over Vietnam they swooped and raced, spewing death with a terrible roar.

"The gunship pilot was the glamour pilot. Great ego feeding," recalled Krutschewski, remembering the GIs on the ground who would cheer as he came in "blasting away." "I flew over half my time three feet off the ground." His eyes shine with excitement. "The sensation of doing two hundred miles an hour at three feet off the ground is like doing a thousand."

In any other war, the warrant officers who flew those Cobra gunships would have been dashing, daredevil, flyboy inspirations for numerous gung ho films. They would have been like the legendary Lafayette Escadrille of World War I—that most glamorous flying unit that became the beau ideal of American heroism and glory. They would have been like the World War II bomber squadron leaders who took off in their goggles and white scarves, always in the mist of England it seemed, at least in the movies.

Warrant officers were "in between real-live officers and enlisted men" recalled Krutschewski. "They became the backbone of the helicopter force."

They were mostly just kids; teenagers, often with a little college education, and they were ballsy and they wore bandannas and other signatures and met death with their morning coffee. "Because of their youth, there was nothing they wouldn't attempt." The American public thought little of their deeds, but in Vietnam they earned glamour and respect and that sense of awe that came with the belief that they were crazed, gutsy adventurers.

Life expectancy in a Cobra wasn't much. Krutschewski lost 66 out of 101 in his class the first year. Enemy bullets ripped through the metal skins of their choppers with distinct and sickening thuds. Although Krutschewski was shot down twice, he was miraculously not wounded.

Delayed stress expert John Wilson was asked to examine Krutschewski and contended that smuggling was a "panic search to find something to give legitimate meaning to his life and at the same time give the 'fix' that he got flying the chopper." The prosecutor, on the other hand, argued that there was no PTSD temporary insanity to his action; Krutschewski simply enjoyed extremes, excitement, and challenge. His smuggling acts "were calculated decisions."

Little was said in either courtroom arguments or major newspaper articles about Krutschewski's moral conflicts during the war. Therefore, it comes as some surprise when Krutschewski frequently volunteers to vent troublesome incidents of Vietnam.

Pride in service and paradoxical anguish over the nature of the war seem to rest in equal measure in Krutschewski. Patriotism was a "top priority" to this son of a Troy, Michigan, carpenter. He dropped out of Michigan State in 1967 for one semester, was reclassified and drafted, learned about the warrant officer program, and became an honor graduate in his flight class.

One minute Krutschewski says, "I have the highest esteem for what I did in Vietnam. I didn't like many of the things I saw in Vietnam, but the bottom line is we were there because our government sent us. A soldier does not pass judgment on his country's decisions." The next minute he speaks scathingly of being in Laos and Cambodia "when the public was told we weren't."

There are stories that "still eat on me. Once there were about thirty or forty Viet Cong firing and they were mixed in with water buffalo and more than a hundred villagers and this colonel ordered us to roll in and kill 'em all. And I *actually* gave my commands!" he recalls almost in wonderment. "It was a nasty thing. One captain in the scout ship refused. The next day he was gone. They just removed him. A very nice guy. . . ."

Krutschewski leaps up from the chair and paces in the suite. "I mean, what *do* you do? Half of them are baddie guys. The other half are goodies. But if you have *any* smarts, you know that they're not *all* bad people there. And you're watching them die. . . . Oh, I can remember seeing a rocket go right between one of those people's legs. I killed lots. *Really* lots. A lot of innocents, too.

"The atrocities of war are caused when there is no recourse. When there is no recourse, Americans are just as brutal as any person. In free-fire zones, if anything walked—I don't care if it was *babies*—you could kill 'em and there's no recourse. One pilot used to drink a lot and he'd throw up in his helmet every morning. If he felt bad, he'd just kill anyone he saw. I cry to this day when I read or see something about Vietnam. To this day."

The stories are many: an officer who saw 200 civilians scavenging at a dump outside a camp, kicked out a box of C-ration candy from a helicopter, watched them converge, and dropped three willie peters [deadly white phosphorus grenades] on them. A colonel who told Krutschewski to "hover over there," took out a .45, and killed an old Vietnamese farmer hoeing his rice paddy. A soldier in a truck who picked up a fifty-pound sandbag and hit a Vietnamese coming toward them on a bicycle right in the chest, killing him.

Krutschewski seems disturbed by the fact that he stopped nothing he witnessed, even though he has elaborate defenses; the rules of free-fire zones, the "That's the way it is" pervasive attitude around him at the time. Today he says, "I was sad all the way through. For everybody. I think that's what Vietnam left me with most—a great sadness: for the pain, the grieving tragedies. But I'll always be glad for one thing Vietnam taught me. You know what

really permanent harm and hurt is. It makes you feel lucky for what you have
—versus people who are always bitching about trivial things."

Laden down with medals, Krutschewski returned from Vietnam in 1970.
"Ten days later I was back at Michigan State as a senior, like it never happened. Just like it *never happened.*"

Krutschewski disliked antiwar groups on campus. He thought they were
too self-righteous to really understand the war—but he also avoided Vietnam
veterans because he thought most were "too narrow-minded."

"The whole time I was in school I was replaying the war without ever
telling anyone about it. I was tense and edgy and serious all the time." Rage
at the way Vietnam veterans were treated was buried deep. "Not only could
you not talk about it to anyone, you had this righteous feeling that you had
done a job well! And you couldn't say that."

Krutschewski got a B.A. in business administration, but his dream was to
continue to fly. He went to airline flight school training in Benton Harbor,
Michigan. Workaholism ruled his life. In six months of school, Krutschewski
worked around the clock on three jobs and got his airline pilot's license. "The
VA paid 90 percent of my flight licenses. But there were no jobs, the market
was so flooded."

In 1971 Krutschewski drifted to Aspen, Colorado, worked as a bartender,
hit the slopes for exhilaration, and sent out résumés. One night Jimmy
Chagra found him in a bar. Chagra claimed he could get large amounts of
marijuana in from Mexico and was looking for a pilot. Krutschewski was also
looking—"just looking for something that would let me use the skills I had
learned in Vietnam." It was a perfect union.

A few months after Krutschewski began his prison term, Judge Walter
Skinner, who handed down the tough sentence, surprisingly had a change of
heart.

Washington attorney Joseph C. Zengerle—counsel to the Vietnam Veterans
of America, a Vietnam veteran, and Assistant Air Force Secretary to the
Carter administration—had carefully prepared a forty-page *amicus curiae*
brief requesting a reduction in Krutschewski's sentence. After considering the
brief, Judge Skinner changed the conditions of Krutschewski's imprisonment,
making him eligible immediately for parole. He also asked the Parole Commission to "decide on a national basis on a policy toward such veterans."
This was the first time a judge had ever indicated that there should be such a
policy.

Krutschewski pleaded unsuccessfully for alternative sentencing; he would
donate $1.75 million to convict rehabilitation programs and would work with
mental patients thirty hours a week during four years of probation. His proposal was caustically denounced by the U.S. Attorney's Strike Force Against
Organized Crime and a Boston *Globe* readers' poll favored Krutschewski
going to jail by three to one.

Skinner's ruling for leniency in the case of Vietnam veterans who were considered PTSD victims came at an interesting time. The age-old cries of crowded prisons and inadequate rehabilitation could have favored the veteran. As William Brennan, an official of the American Correctional Association who headed a Justice Department outreach program for incarcerated veterans, said of Krutschewski, "He could really help in some youth program. Wouldn't that be better than paying the $20,000 annual cost to keep him in jail? It's not going to serve any purpose putting that gentleman behind bars." But it was also a time when the country was enraged by the John Hinckley innocent-by-reason-of-insanity verdict in the shooting of President Reagan and suspicious of all insanity defenses.

Krutschewski was sent to a Minnesota prison. A preliminary assessment set incarceration at forty-six to fifty-two months before he would be eligible for parole. However, a hearing panel, after listening to oral testimony by Krutschewski's lawyer, Zengerle, later recommended he be incarcerated no more than eighteen months because of the psychological wounds he suffered during the Vietnam War. *This marked the first time in either the federal or state parole system that an individual prisoner was explicitly given more lenient treatment for PTSD.*

The panel was greatly influenced by the fact that Krutschewski's thrill-seeking days ended when he apparently put the stress of Vietnam behind. Of his own volition, Krutschewski left the lucrative world of drug smuggling in the mid-seventies and never returned to it.

In the summer of 1983, he was released from prison.

Lewis Lowe III entered the Marine Corps with a "John Wayne complex," getting his parents to sign for him when he was seventeen. A black teenager from the Deep South of Alabama, Lowe saw an astounding amount of combat—eleven consecutive major battles, including the murderous 1968 Tet Offensive. Moreover, he was in combat for all but five or six *days* during the thirteen months he was in Vietnam.[2]

In 1982 Lowe was charged with robbing two fast-food restaurants. He had pleaded guilty previously to seven robberies in another state and had served prison terms for them. His defense attorneys set about proving that Lowe was so mentally and emotionally scarred by his experiences in Vietnam that he subconsciously hoped to be killed by putting himself in dangerous situations. Survival guilt and relived traumas made Lowe feel that life had no value, testified Dr. Joseph Gelsomino, director of a Florida Vet Center.

It was no easy task to convince twelve jurors in a law-and-order, Bible Belt state like Alabama of such a suicidal "death wish" defense. The insanity plea, in any shape or form, historically had met with little sympathy. The courtroom was pin-drop quiet as experts, his parents, and Lowe testified. Mrs. Louis Lowe stared ahead, in her Sunday best dress, small gold loop earrings and glasses, and spoke of praying for years that her son, drastically altered by Vietnam, would get help. "We couldn't get him to sleep in a bed." He insisted on having his shoes beside the lounge chair where he tried to sleep. Combat paranoia lasted for years. Whenever there was a loud noise, he would jump up, grab his shoes, and think he had to get out of the room. He paced for hours and couldn't sit down long enough to even eat a meal. His mother sought help from the VA hospital; his father had taken him there in an emergency and Lowe had been turned off by their indifference. He refused to try again. His mother persuaded him to go to Philadelphia, stay with her brother, and be treated there. Instead, Lowe began a series of robberies that landed him in prison.

Lowe had told his parents only one brief, tragic story of Vietnam. A friend took his place as point man on a search and destroy mission and was killed. That terse sentence masked an incredible amount of gore and carnage. Lowe's painful recitation of his war experience convinced the jurors that he needed help rather than incarceration.

Demolitions experts like Lowe knew constant terror in a land as booby-trapped as Vietnam. Some mines weren't detected by a mine sweeper. Lowe would get on his hands and knees and look for the mines, praying that he would find them before they found him. The stress was suffocating. One day, pinned down by enemy shots smashing all over the place, Lowe tried to defuse a fifty-pound bomb. The heat and anxiety and tension, pulsing blood pressure, hands that simply could *not* shake, the concentration that was needed all came together in a sweat-sodden instant. Lowe suffered a heat stroke.

Something more horrible than defusing bombs always waited. He could not just pass the dead. The VC were experts at rigging grisly human booby traps of men who no longer breathed; men who had been marines just like Lowe a few hours before. He had to fish, gingerly, literally having to reach inside wounds, inside intestines, and feel around with his bloodied hands—or poke the bodies with bayonets—so they could defuse the trap to send the bodies home.

Twisting his hands in his lap, Lowe had difficulty speaking as his lawyer questioned him at the trial. He started using drugs in Vietnam to calm himself. His job "didn't call for no shaking hands. You can't be trembling." Lowe saw more than thirty of his Marine platoon members cut down in less than thirty minutes, trying to run in a river. When the lawyer asked if Lowe felt he had won the war, he said, "Each individual won their own war." Lowe won six medals, came home feeling betrayed by his country; "It abandoned the job it was doing." What was that? "To win the war."

In that Alabama courtroom, the defense tried to recreate in the minds of the jurors the worst of war. A close friend of Lowe's "was hit by machine gun fire and fell on a land mine" less than two weeks before he was to leave.

Attorney Mark White asked, "Did you help recover his body?"

Lowe's voice was so low that everyone strained in the courtroom: "What was left of it."

Then the attorney turned to the jurors and asked them a direct question. "What effect do you think it would have on you if you had to pick up everybody in this room that had been blown into seven pieces and put them in bodybags?"

It was the fall of 1980. Birmingham, Alabama, Burger King cashier Letitia Adams hardly noticed the man who ordered a double cheeseburger. Then he pulled a gun, told her to give him the money, and ordered her not to touch the alarm. The Burger King was ingeniously rigged for robberies; Adams pulled out "bait money" that set off a silent police alarm and triggered a camera that would catch the robbery on film. Lowe got away before the police arrived.

Six weeks later Lowe came up to the drive-in window of Mrs. Winner's Fried Chicken establishment, pointed a gun, and demanded money. The manager, Frank Cook, testified that Lowe said, "I'm serious. I'll blow your brains out." A patrol car just happened to turn into the drive at that time and Lowe ran. The suspicious patrolmen gave chase and caught him.

Lowe's trial became the first in Alabama to seek an innocent verdict on the grounds that the defendant was mentally scarred by his war experience. Joe Gelsomino, a former Vietnam veteran and psychologist, testified that Lowe's was one of the most severe PTSD cases he had encountered. So did Dr. Harold Jordan, chairman of Nashville's Meharry Medical College. His severe form of PTSD led to preoccupation with death and suicide, Gelsomino testified. However, Lowe wanted someone else to kill him, rather than take his own life, because he felt that would be less traumatic for the family. Lowe's extraordinary combat time, surrounded constantly by the death of others, filled him with shattering survival guilt, Gelsomino said. Lowe needed extended hospitalization and then prolonged supervised outpatient treatment. Confinement in prison would only exacerbate the disorder, the psychologist said. He argued that although Lowe carried a gun, he was more a danger to himself than anyone, pointing out that Lowe sometimes waited in the neighborhood for thirty minutes after he committed his robberies for the police to come. These were the acts, said Gelsomino, of a man asking to get caught, crying for help.

The prosecution attacked the post-traumatic stress disorder argument. "This is not the trial of the Vietnam War," said Prosecutor Mike Whisonant, who argued that, even if Lowe had "Vietnam syndrome," the main problem was a robbery-supported drug habit. Yet his argument was damaged by the fact that even the state's witness, Dr. John Callahan, said Lowe was sick—a point stressed by Lowe's attorneys in closing arguments. Callahan said Lowe's flashbacks, poor sleep, and drug addiction would be symptoms of PTSD—even though he said this would not excuse the ex-marine for committing armed robbery. Whisonant argued that an innocent verdict would give drug addicts from Vietnam an excuse to rob and assault. Whisonant drilled away on Lowe's drug habit. "I took things I didn't even know the name of," said Lowe—a daily user for twelve years, supporting his habit with military benefits and odd jobs. "Isn't it a fact you robbed to finance your drug habit?" asked the prosecutor. "No," said Lowe. "I was full of them when I robbed."

Lowe's apparent pain and desire for help touched the jurors. "I don't prefer this kind of life," he said. His attorneys stressed another important point; Lowe would not be returned to the streets but institutionalized where he could get help.

In an historic Alabama verdict, jurors found Lowe not guilty "by reason of mental defect." It became the banner story in Birmingham, an item in national news magazines, and touched off letters of both outrage and support.

Lowe's mother sighed, "At last he's going to get helped. We've prayed and prayed for this. It's been so long."

Long ago, in another world, Charles Heads was on his first patrol in a reconnaissance unit when he saw his platoon commander blown to bits by a booby trap. "Sergeant Barnes stepped next to a rock. I heard an explosion—I've never heard an explosion like that in my life. In a minute, pieces of shirt and flesh were falling. The guy literally disappeared. We couldn't find his head."[3]

Heads recounted that story, testifying in 1981 in his own defense at his murder trial. Wellborn Jack, Jr., his lawyer, turned to the jurors and graphically described what happened to Heads. "A piece of the chest cavity fell on his back and he ran off down the hill screaming. . . . We want you to know what happened in Vietnam and it wasn't a John Wayne movie."

On the stand Heads recounted his first kill. "I opened up and hit him and it spun him completely around toward me. The bullet tore his skull wide open."

It was, said Heads, "hard to kill the first time." Then the necessary numbing took over. "The third, fourth, fifth time, it became like a job."

The ex-marine from Houston, Texas, was glory dreaming when he joined the Corps at eighteen; he wanted to get out of the ghetto and wanted "to be with the best." There were all those simplistic teenage reasons; he liked the way the uniform looked and he liked the "Marine Hymn." During basic training you were "taught not to think. They train you to kill." Heads volunteered for the 1st Reconnaissance Battalion and became a "Reconner." His unit's motto was "swift, silent, deadly." Its emblem, a cracked yellow skull. Their mission was to collect intelligence deep in hostile country, staying out in small patrols for weeks. He went on thirty-eight recon missions and had seven confirmed kills, including a woman and an old man.

Heads filled three photo albums with pictures of friends, many of whom never came back. "They were a family I could trust—even with my life." After some were killed, Heads scrawled across a photo of himself, in fatigues and helmet, "Kill all of the bastards." Heads took pictures of mutilated bodies, but, he said, the photo developing company wouldn't develop them.

After nine months in country, his reconner days came to an abrupt end deep in nowhere land, a place called Ben Giang or Atenna Valley. His sixteen-man patrol was shot to pieces one misty morning in an L-shaped ambush by a battalion-sized VC regular unit. Heads was point man and was hit first, twice in the gut. The patrol held out long enough until close air strikes arrived. Helpless, Heads was lifted up through thick jungle canopy in a horsecollar, a stiffened stick figure of a man, pulled by cable hoist to a hovering chopper. All the while, they were under fire. A friend, Johnny Porter, struggled and strained to get the wounded Heads into the horsecollar. In the Da Nang hospital ward, Heads could not move as he lay in bed. He asked anxiously about his friend Johnny Porter. They told him he was in the next bed. Porter, shot through the neck, was paralyzed from saving Heads's life. The memory haunted Heads for years.

Heads would not see him again, not for more than a decade. Not until Porter came in his wheelchair to testify at Heads's trial.

Ground fog rolled in the field across the street from Roy Lejay's Louisiana home like the mists sometimes in Vietnam. It was quiet and still, shortly after midnight. Nearly two inches of rain had fallen that day. Seven Vietnam veterans—a psychiatrist, psychologist, and five former reconners—who saw the field or videotape of it would say later that it symbolized or resembled Vietnam.

Heads watched the tree line silhouetted against the sky. He had come in search of his wife, who had left their Houston home after a fight. Four times he approached his brother-in-law's house, rang the bell, shouted to speak with his wife. Three adults and eight children made no sounds from within. Finally Heads started to walk in defeat to his car. Suddenly, something "hit" him with a boom. Propelled with "phenomenal strength—I was on automatic," Heads banged the locked door open with his foot, gun in hand. His brother-in-law stood in the hallway, a gun in his hand, too. Heads opened fire, killing Lejay with a shot through the eyes—then stalked the ranch house like he had the straw hooches of Vietnam, but killed no one else.

When the police arrived minutes later, they found Heads wandering in a daze inside the house in the midst of frantically scurrying children. His arms hung at his sides. In one hand was his own weapon, in the other was the gun he had "secured" from his brother-in-law's body. Heads was led quietly away.

As he told his story in 1981, Heads had already been convicted once of first-degree murder in the 1977 gun slaying of his brother-in-law. That 1978 conviction was later overturned. A new trial was granted because the jury had been erroneously instructed that "A man is presumed to intend the natural and probable consequences of his act."

As Heads spent four years in prison, lawyer Wellborn Jack, Jr., could not get the case out of his mind.

"I kicked myself in the ass. I represented Heads the first time when they found him guilty. I was unable to prove that he was suffering from any insanity; psychiatrists never found any evidence of any *recognized* mental disorder. In 1980, after the American Psychiatric Association recognized PTSD, I knew that's what it was—and I had what I needed."

Jack, a lanky Southerner in his mid-forties, remains fascinated by Vietnam —an honorable venture when he was in law school in the early sixties. Jack drawls that he was "getting a taste of adventure as a 'weekend warrior' in the National Guard Special Forces Unit." President Kennedy impulsively authorized the wearing of the green beret. "You can't believe how *thrilled* these highly educated, sophisticated, and highly trained members of our unit were when we could wear our little green berets. . . .

"For me, the era closed in 1975 with the televised helicopter extraction of the last Americans from the embassy roof in Saigon." That image is embalmed in TV footage—chopper blades whipping hair back from faces of stricken Vietnamese clinging to helicopter skids in desperate panic.

"I had the same reaction to that event as many Vietnam vets, my client included: 'All of that [the pain of the last fifteen years] for this—for nothing.' That image is more troublesome and difficult to put behind me than the images of Kent State, the Kennedy and King assassinations, the burning of Watts, the peace and freedom demonstrations, or the nightly TV Vietnam combat footage. That fall of Saigon marked and continues to mark a turning point—end of an era, profound sadness, and a new beginning without a great deal of hope."

Those Vietnam memories helped Jack understand his client. "It wasn't like Charles to kill his brother-in-law. I had come to believe what his cousin told me, 'If you really know him, you can't convict him.' "

Delayed stress in veterans had intrigued Jack before there was such a name; when he defended a World War II vet in a murder charge earlier in the seventies. "I argued he was not guilty by reason of insanity. He had reenacted in Shreveport, Louisiana, exactly what he had done in France. In World War II he had filled a bottle with gasoline, lit it with a rag, and heaved it through a slit in a pillbox. The proud unit gave him a Zippo lighter. In the seventies, he's having wife trouble. He took the old Zippo, crawled up to the house, lit a bottle of gasoline, and heaved it through the window. He had a liter for the Germans, a whole gallon for his wife. He had never had any difficulty with the law before or after. He disassociated under stress." Because the case was so bizarre, the World War II vet was judged not guilty by reason of insanity well before PTSD was known.

The second trial of Charles Heads, an indigent client, became a personal, obsessive mission. For over a year Jack analyzed what kind of jury would be sympathetic. "The single most salient factor in determining present attitudes on Vietnam vets was age. Those thirty to forty-five had the most favorable attitude toward Vietnam veterans and those who might have problems. The least favorable came from the Moral Majority and dyed-in-the-wool Republican types. You want people who were not old enough to have been in Korea but whose lives were likely to be affected by Vietnam one way or another."

This included those who had avoided the war and were the same age as veterans. "Maybe it is still true in some ultimate sense that—as Vietnam veterans have repeatedly told all of us who will listen—'No one who wasn't there will ever understand.' But this jury came about as close as any group of nonvets is likely to. They perceived the existence of some dark and hidden reality."

The moving testimony of men in Heads's company—who flew in from all parts of the country at their own expense for the trial—brought a unique perspective to the concept that Vietnam could have so affected Heads. Jack was lucky in being able to introduce usually inadmissible background. To argue the effects of PTSD, he was allowed to saturate the courtroom with vivid accounts of Vietnam.

In Vietnam, as a combat psychiatrist, John Yost's job was to decide when servicemen had had enough and needed to be shipped home. "Ten or twelve patrols was significant stress in a Green Beret. Charles's thirty-eight patrols was extraordinarily high, the most he had ever seen," said Wellborn Jack. *"Every man he talked to from Charles's unit had suffered severe symptoms."*

Dr. Yost, a Colorado psychiatrist, sought to assure the jury that he did not automatically buy the PTSD argument. After examining six other Vietnam veterans on trial for murder—and finding four who had PTSD—he did *not* testify for any because he felt the killings were unrelated to the disorder. In his opinion, Heads was in a disassociative state when he killed his brother-in-law.

Dr. Tom Williams, psychologist and former Vietnam Marine Corps infantry company commander, had treated more than 250 veterans by the time of Heads's trial. Heads had coped with his delayed stress by denying it—until new stress brought it back, Williams felt. Then Heads used the survival tactics that served him well during the original catastrophic stress.

Heads described the shooting in a broken, fragmented narrative that indicated disassociation with the action, according to Williams. Heads said, "It was just like the time I got ambushed [in Vietnam]. I was running to the house and hit the door. I went right back [to Vietnam] and didn't fear nothing." Heads said that, inside the Lejay residence, he felt "Woo, just like in a firefight." More combat lingo came when Heads was asked if he looked at Lejay after the shooting. "No, I didn't *check him out.* I kept moving."

In cross-examination, Williams himself became agitated when questioned about the morality of killing, even the enemy in Vietnam. Williams responded with memories of body count favors. "Are you kidding? They gave us ice cream for that."

Heads was no stranger to violent death when he got to Vietnam eight months after graduation in Houston's Fifth Ward, a black ghetto once called "The Murder Capital of the World."

Heads was nine years old, standing on the lawn not more than twenty feet away, when he saw his father raise his arm. A shot shattered the day and Heads saw his mother fall, blood bursting. "Charles tried to get to her," his sister testified. "But there were just so many people holding us back that we couldn't." His father was sentenced to life in prison.

Delayed stress experts testified that the trauma of witnessing his mother's murder made Heads more susceptible to PTSD. That murder was buried away, just as Vietnam stayed buried for years after his return from the war. When Wellborn Jack first asked Heads about Vietnam, the ex-marine sketchily remembered few details—only that he had seen a sergeant blown away by a booby trap, that he got shot, and had seen others killed. "He avoided the question of how many, by whom, and how. The only names of reconners he remembered were 'Jersey,' 'Chief' and 'Leaks.' It was difficult to understand how Charles could remember so little about the men he had been closer to than anyone in his life. But experts explained that memory impairment was characteristic of PTSD."

This was how Heads could cope and achieve much in life without manifesting gross symptoms of disorder after the murder of his mother, after Vietnam. There was no history or even a suggestion of psychiatric diagnosis, treatment, or need in Heads's military record. Although he complained to VA doctors of residual pain from his wounds as late as 1976, there was no hint of either psychiatric diagnosis or disorder. Psychic wounds were denied all around. "But that defense mechanism of denial," Williams testified, left Heads functioning "on the extreme edge of vulnerability."

There was little evidence of this during the seven years after Vietnam before Heads killed his brother-in-law. Heads had been steadily employed as a letter carrier, living with his wife and three children in a quiet Houston suburb. His wife was also a postal employee and their joint incomes exceeded $30,000 a year. It was a perfect suburban snapshot: manicured St. Augustine grass, Lincoln Continental, customized van, Yamaha motorcycle, good guitar, nice family. Heads was admired by friends, neighbors, coworkers. Only his wife knew of the nightmares that could not be snuffed out or his trigger-charged nervousness. One time, half-asleep, he leaped up to attack his grandmother when her soft walking reminded him of someone crawling toward him. There were no Vet Centers of rap groups, no one to listen. "For society back home, Vietnam just didn't fit."

Trying to "make Vietnam fit" for the jury was a continual concern of attorney Wellborn Jack. As he questioned prospective jurors, Jack was surprised; many told him point-blank that keeping up with the war "got too much to bear." They stopped watching it on TV and "tried to forget it." Rather than a negative, Jack saw a positive in this reaction. "They were demonstrating their *own* use of the mechanism of *denial.*"

A number of jurors had seen the major Vietnam films; *Apocalypse Now, Coming Home, The Deer Hunter,* and *Friendly Fire.* Most had weapons in their homes. Two jurors had cousins who had been in the Vietnam War. A Vietnam-era veteran became the foreman. He was glad to have not gone to Vietnam after knowing those who had. One of his neighbors had lost both legs in the war. Most of the jurors believed that prior experience affected later behavior, particularly childhood experiences.

What they heard from the men who fought with Heads was crucial. The five former members of Delta Company spoke emotionally and sometimes tearfully of their life together.

They had not seen each other in fourteen years. Rather than shy away from delayed stress, they wanted to publicize the plight of veterans suffering from PTSD. All five, businessmen with families, suffered severe depression, marital problems, flashbacks, nightmares, uncontrollable emotions, and anger. The strongest, most experienced, and highly trained among them had been in regular psychotherapy since returning from Vietnam. Another, a successful businessman, was actively participating in a rap group.

"They were not asking for pity," recalled Jack, "but giving these accounts for the first time ever to help a fellow recon team member whom they called 'Farmer.' They asked only for understanding." The trial, in the end, became therapy for them.

"It opened a lot of sores," said Robert Stomp, who owns a Kansas City construction business. Robert Sylvia added, "We were trained not to open up. That served a purpose—but we can't continue to live our lives under Marine training." Sylvia, who owns a truck repair business in Massachusetts, choked up when he testified that "Charles was a darn good bushman. Our lives depended on that man. He kept us alive a lot of times. That's why it hurts so much to see . . ." He could only shake his head and blink back tears.

The two most emotional moments came when the paralyzed Johnny Porter and Heads's fifty-one-year-old former platoon commander, Ronald Benoit, testified.

Johnny Porter, paralyzed from mid-chest down, spoke from his wheelchair of the day that changed his life from a lively adolescent to a man who would never walk again. It was when he saved Heads's life by helping to lift him by horsecollar out of the jungle. "I caught a bullet in the right side of the neck," he said, with a slight Oklahoma twang. "I couldn't move, couldn't hear. I was speechless, but I knew what was going on."

Porter spent the next five or six years lying around, drinking twenty to thirty cases of beer a month. The nightmares came and there were suicide attempts. Porter spent days at a time holed up in his locked room, refusing to see his family.

As he spoke of his post-Vietnam life, Porter hunched down in his chair, sobbed, and had to be taken from the courtroom. Other squad members crushed around him in the hallway, patting his arm, muttering awkward words meant to reassure.

Benoit, the most decorated soldier in the state of Vermont, took the stand for three hours. He served in Korea, as well as Vietnam, and told the jurors there were many major differences. Like many military men, he anguished over the way the war was fought in Vietnam. "In Korea you knew you had support and we fought to take ground and *hold* it. That wasn't the case in

Vietnam." He was a recon man in Korea as well. In Korea most reconnaissance patrols lasted several hours, "never longer than eight." In Vietnam
recon patrols sometimes lasted nearly two weeks. "It could take your support
hours to locate you because you were so far in the jungle."

Benoit, who holds the Navy Cross and two Purple Hearts, had one word
for his return from Vietnam, "Bitter. My personality changed completely."
Benoit said that he too suffers from flashbacks, recurring nightmares, and
memories of the horrors of Vietnam. At the time of the trial, he was under
psychiatric treatment for severe depression and delayed stress.

Now a balding businessman, Benoit has sad eyes that stare from behind
steel-rimmed glasses. Survival guilt and the sense of responsibility that he
carried for other men's lives seem a heavy burden. Several times, tears would
stream down his face and he was unable to continue. Heads, watching him,
bowed his head and quietly wiped tears. Benoit told of the deaths of several
platoon members. He, like the others, cannot forget the massive blast from
the booby trap that blew Sergeant Barnes "into a million pieces." Benoit had
moved his men to an area among some rocks. The rocks were rigged with
bombs that the Viet Cong set off by remote control. A Marine motto is to
never leave a man. Benoit called for an emergency evacuation of the many
men wounded in the bomb blast, but would not leave without his platoon
sergeant. He sent some men to look for the sergeant, "All they had left was a
piece of his leg, a dog tag, and a shirt. When I knew there wasn't anything I
could do for him, we left."

There were other stories. On a search and pickup mission, Benoit found the
bodies of American soldiers beheaded and dismembered. A rookie nineteen-
year-old—who had been in Vietnam only three days—had both legs blown off
after tripping a trap. Another time, American "friendly fire" shot Benoit's
men by accident.

"There would have been more deaths and maiming had it not been for
Heads," said Benoit. "He was one of the most dependable point men. The
point man almost has to have second vision. If he gets hit, we all get hit."

The jury's dilemma was to decide whether Heads shot with a specific intent
to kill his brother-in-law or was reliving flashbacks and "could not distinguish right from wrong." One delayed stress expert characterized Heads as
being "a combatant on automatic." Heads was reverting to that survival
mode because of the extreme stress he was experiencing at losing his wife.

On the other hand, the prosecutor, Jim McMichael, depicted Heads as an
angered husband who told his wife he was "mad and was going to whip her
butt. He came with the intention to bring his wife back and the force to do it
with. Why didn't he shoot the children if he were having a flashback? Why
didn't he shoot the police?" "Fighting for freedom" in Vietnam was not
something the jury should put aside, said McMichael, but added, "I want you
to tell him that freedom doesn't mean he can do whatever he wants."

The jury however, felt that Heads needed psychiatric help, not more prison. One juror, Carol Whittington, expressed a common view, "I'm more aware of feelings they had when they came back from Vietnam and what went on over there."

Four experts testified that if there had been treatment for PTSD available for Heads at the time of the killing, his brother-in-law would probably be alive.

In October 1981, the bailiff read aloud the verdict: "Not guilty by reason of insanity." Heads embraced his attorneys, then sat shaking his head and rocking back and forth. His attorneys presented the judge, Gayle Hamilton, with a copy of Dr. Tom Williams's book on Vietnam veterans and PTSD. The judge, an ex-marine, said, "You all didn't know it, but I was a combat veteran and there were times when *I* sat here and hurt and ached."

Heads's case set a national precedent. It came in the rural Deep South, where tolerance for such suspicious things as psychiatry and insanity pleas is low. Two Louisiana veterans had previously tried the PTSD route and had been convicted. In eighteen years of practice in Shreveport, Wellborn Jack had heard of only two cases of jurors buying a general insanity argument. Letters to the editor brought livid reactions, but Jack stressed that Heads would "remain in custody until cured." Neither Jack nor Heads—grateful that he would finally be getting help—were prepared for the next blow. Several months after his trial, Heads was still existing in a seven-by-nine-foot prison cell, waiting for an appropriate mental institution to be found. Few VA facilities had the expertise for specialized in-patient treatment for PTSD.

The best, at Bay Pines, Florida, was off-limits because the VA refused to comply with the custody requirement that the court would decide when and if Heads should be released. "We have to have the authority to release someone when we think they're ready," said K. K. Westmoreland of the Louisiana VA.

For months, Heads waited for in-patient treatment. Finally he began his treatment and by the fall of 1983 had moved to out-patient care. His lawyer reported that he was "doing fine" and was soon to get a job back with the postal service.

The argument that anyone will use Vietnam as an excuse remains strong. While true in some instances, many who resort to criminal acts are often desperately and deeply traumatized by Vietnam and in need of help.

"Even with the most *severe* cases of PTSD, violence is the exception rather than the rule," said Wellborn Jack. "It's mostly depression, sometimes suicidal. These men should not be feared. We never gave them a homecoming. The least we can do now is whatever we can to heal the wounds which have not healed."

4 The Vet Centers

BRUCE REACHES UP WITH HIS LONG, SLENDER HAND, THE FINGERNAILS AS long as a woman's, using a handkerchief to wipe the spittle he cannot control despite his constant wind-sucking intake of breath. His mouth is wired together. There are strange grimaces for smiles. It is wired together because Bruce was one Vietnam veteran who couldn't kill himself—although he tried. One night Bruce carefully picked up a gun, sat on the john, and tried to blow his brains out. The bullet went through his neck and twisted and came out, shattering his jaw.

Five weeks later, Bruce drove up the winding ghetto streets of East Los Angeles, with its graffiti in Spanish and its out-of-work Chicano gangs, and up a steep hill to a shack high above the city. A curtain separated the living room from the bed; the red Victorian couch sagged.

Bruce was only thirty-three but looked ancient. Deep circles formed under his eyes, the color of faded jeans. There was an air of cowed loss of self-esteem. After Vietnam, Bruce went from the three-martini-lunch world of a top advertising artist to Skid Row—from paychecks to welfare. "Financially, I just assassinated myself." He became a coast-to-coast drunk, tried to commit suicide three times.

Bruce came from a broken home. His one interest was art; in the third grade, Bruce would fold his arithmetic very neatly, all squares, decorate the paper, put his name on it—and turn it in blank. He took the entrance exams to art school, but it was 1966 and he decided to go into the service. "It was just something you had to do."

Bruce's views on Vietnam and the government came in bursts of bitterness: "One night I was on duty and drinking a beer. It was right after Robert Kennedy got shot. We were all just sitting, talking about the whole thing. I was off my post by a few feet in a hut so I got court-martialed, but the first sergeant of the squad was my character reference. All that happened was they busted me down to airman basic."

Bruce, one of his generation who rebelled at the "ridiculous bullshit authoritarianism" of service, stayed drunk or stoned as much as he could in

Vietnam. "It wasn't the danger, more just the tenseness, waiting. To me the whole thing was just bullshit. I was in country exactly three days and I see these little kids on the road saying, 'Fuck you, GI.' " That shattered World War II images of urchins smilingly receiving bubblegum from GI Joe. "I said right then, 'What the fuck am *I* doing here? These people don't even *want* me here.' "

When Bruce returned, he resisted using Vietnam as a scapegoat. "I felt it would be a cop-out. I was into my thing, going to art school, getting into advertising pretty heavily, got married. I didn't relate to veterans talking about their problems. 'Hey, man, you know, that's over and done with.' I told them, 'I can't keep that hangover going. Nobody's going to do anything for you. You gotta do it yourself.' " He stops. "I guess I was pretty insensitive."

Meanwhile, terrible depressions began. "I was surprised. I was not used to feeling depressed. I was trying to eliminate it or hide it with booze."

Two years after Bruce got out of the service, he woke up one morning and noticed a lump on his neck. Doctors removed a gland on the right side of his neck. "Then they removed my spleen. And, uh, there was massive radiation." The look of fear lurked around his eyes. Bruce was only twenty-two at the time and he had Hodgkin's disease. The cancer has been in remission a long time now, but he wonders a great deal about Agent Orange. "Hill 327 was stripped while I was there. I watched them spray it every morning."

Bruce went to the VA and filed a compensation claim. "I felt it *was* there at the time I was discharged; they just wanted to get rid of me. After two years of fucking around with that, I wrote Senator Cranston several times. It took about a year—and then they denied it. I appealed. They took about another year and I just said, 'Okay, fuck it.' Just dealing with the VA is a hassle."

Bruce felt he didn't have time to be sick. "I had a wife to support."

He had known her in high school but broke up before going to Vietnam. "I felt it was infinitely better than wondering what my old lady was doing. I developed the attitude that if something does happen to me, it doesn't matter anyway. It really fucked up a lot of guys' heads. The infamous 'Dear John' letter. In someone that young, it really instills an attitude of distrust. That nothing matters anyway."

Their marriage began to founder after the cancer and heavy drinking. She wanted children; Bruce was scared both of the cancer and his inability to feel close enough for family commitments. It was the only thing he cried about in a five-hour interview. As he spoke of children, the tears came suddenly and washed down his face as he held his hand to his mangled mouth.

The drifting began; Los Angeles to New York and back again. Fewer and fewer jobs. Newer and newer women . . .

The gunburst exploded in blood-gushing, terrifying noise in the bathroom. A girlfriend, eyes glazed with horror, called the police. They saved Bruce. Eight months later, Bruce had moved into a steady Thursday-night rap group at a Vet Center in Los Angeles. Doctors were reshaping his jaw.

One night, speaking through the bizarre-looking face guard doctors fashioned for his jaw, Bruce told a group of wide-eyed college students about a war that was ancient history to them.

Bruce's tone had changed; there seemed an element of hope. He had accepted the idea, finally, that he had to talk out his past so that he could get on with the future. Bruce, the loner, was being saved by the camaraderie of a California Vet Center.

In Birmingham, Alabama, six-foot-five-inch Charles Richardson eased himself off the Vet Center couch and demonstrated the "Thorazine shuffle." The phrase brings knowing looks to many veterans who were given large doses of the tranquilizer by the VA. It was standard operating procedure for years, before the Vet Centers. Being drugged into docility was the "enlightened" approach to Vietnam veterans' problems of rages, violence, depression, anger.

A black from Selma, Richardson was just a child when all those famous black and white men and women came to his town to march. His mother wouldn't let him out of the house to watch; it may have been history, but, she said, it wasn't a good time for colored boys to be on the street.

"I went to Vietnam to escape Selma," Richardson said, a sardonic look that clearly said "Sheeeiiit" playing on his face. Richardson dropped one arm and dragged his foot, like a huge wounded bird, in imitation of the muscle-bound paralysis that too much Thorazine induces.

A 1977 National Academy of Sciences report on VA hospital care criticized the VA for depending too heavily on the use of antipsychotic drugs. Three quarters of all psychotic patients were receiving at least one such drug on a given day and 20 percent were receiving two or *more* such drugs—in violation of VA procedures. Of 26,000 prescriptions for antipsychotic drugs surveyed, 16 percent were above the recommended dosage. The report led to a review of drug practices in VA hospitals. Although the use has purportedly lessened, many veterans using VA out-patient clinics complain that all they get is drugs, not treatment.[1]

That is the way the VA dealt with Richardson's explosive "craziness" when he came back. The Vet Center was helping Richardson cope with his life—without drugs.

In Brooklyn, Steven Cytryszewski still fights nightmares and bouts of panic. "Sometimes I wake up screaming, 'Incoming rounds!' When I drive along a road with trees on both sides, I don't look at the road, I look at the trees. I'm looking for snipers."

Cytryszewski, like many veterans, is highly critical of the regular VA programs. The Vet Centers opened their doors with a reassuring motto: "Help Without Hassles." Cytryszewski said of the centers, "Nobody *laughs* at me. If I tell them I hit the ground when I hear sudden noises, they say they do, too."

They come into the Vet Centers across the country these days—businessmen, lawyers, actors, truck drivers, carpenters, the steadily employed and the down-and-out jobless. Big, beefy ex-marines in T-shirts that reveal their DEATH BEFORE DISHONOR tattoos sit next to men wearing coats and ties. They are there to talk through and exorcise the past so that they can get on with the present.

For years there was no such haven. The VA—with its hassles and red tape and papers and long waits and doctors who couldn't understand them—was just one more place to resent. Veterans pleaded in vain for readjustment counseling. After a decade of refusing to appropriate money for such centers, Congress finally coughed up a mere pittance—$12 million for 90 centers in 1979. By 1983, the need for the centers had not abated. There were by then 135 centers, funded at a cost of $21 million, an astounding 5,500 new Vietnam-era veterans were coming in across the country each month, some 4,000 of them having served in Vietnam. In just three and a half years, by August of 1983, 200,000 veterans had sought help in the centers. Although administered by the VA, the centers are on the streets, far removed from VA facilities.

They are run by a mix of maverick counselors and, increasingly, mental health professionals with traditional training. Some of the combat veteran counselors do not fit easily into clinicians' white coats or bureaucratic pigeonholes. This is both their strength and their weakness. They have a vital rapport with veterans, but some lack the ability to administer in a way that pleases VA bureaucrats. Most have some psychological training and all centers have at least one veteran—many of whom freely admit that they have been plagued by their own stressful memories of Vietnam.

Overworked and underpaid—the doors are open from 9 A.M. until 9 P.M., unheard of at most medical centers—Vet Center counselors are prime burnout targets as they relive the pain of their clients, handle psychological emergencies, and reach out to find the deeply alienated who do not seek help.

The centers' simple premise seems so obvious that it is unfathomable why regular VA doctors remain so destructively obtuse. Talk is the first step to exorcising the past and that is what the counselors let veterans do—in a group where they can find trust. Many veterans who go to Vet Centers had tried regular VA doctors. *Most report that doctors never even asked them about their Vietnam experiences.*

The financially strapped, understaffed program is not without its flaws. Some of the centers are poorly run. Some counselors are on such ego trips that they do little for the men who seek help. Some wives complain that their husbands were worse off after visiting centers where they reopened emotional wounds and inexpert counselors were unable to guide them forward.

"I stopped going to the center—all there were were a bunch of guys strung out on pot and alcohol and I didn't need that," is a complaint of some disillusioned veterans.

David Harrington, a former combat marine, and psychiatrist Jeffrey Jay, who runs a "Back-in-the-World" program for veterans in Washington, D.C., stress that their program, for example, reaches out to address the present and future more than do the Vet Centers.

"Many Vietnam veteran rap groups, based on a belief in the post-traumatic diagnosis, emphasize the opportunity for catharsis," said Harrington. "Our goal is to help veterans move from an understanding of *past* responsibility in the war to *present* responsibilities to themselves and their families."

The majority of the Vet Centers, however, function well in a very crucial neglected area. It is that amorphous ability to make contact—to reach people others cannot. It is the same mysterious bonding that Alcoholics Anonymous has for people who went through years of psychiatry to no avail and then become faithful AA converts.

By the summer of 1983, veterans were pouring into centers, in part because public attitudes had changed. "They now feel it's okay to talk about the war in certain places and they won't be criticized," said one counselor.

Many counselors reported that a sizable number had growing concerns over Central America. "It would be wrong to call all Vietnam veterans anti-war," said Ray Scurfield, assistant director of counseling for the Readjustment Counseling (Vet Center) program, "but a substantial number are. They are worried that younger relatives may have to go through what they went through. And then you have the others who say that, if called, they'd go again. We see both types having problems. A high proportion of clients are working through guilts about war incidents that involved attacks on women and children."

Although the erecting of the Vietnam Veterans Memorial and increasing favorable outpouring from the press and public about veterans eased stress for some, others remained bitter and felt this response was "too little, too late." Indeed, many veterans could have been far more productive years earlier with minimal help. An enveloping fear of mental illness haunted many. "Just to find out that it's *normal* to have flashbacks or continued nightmares went a long way to relieving their problems," said Scurfield. In fact, many are able to leave behind the worst of their bitterness, fears, and memories after weekly visits of only a few months.

The crucial ability to listen to veterans' dark dreams and secrets without passing judgments, to help them lift the burden, is a quality lost on Reagan's administration. In the spring of 1981, Ronald Reagan was recommending that the centers, barely one year in operation, be gutted. This was particularly galling to veterans as the President was simultaneously pulling off a P.R. stunt, pinning medals on Vietnam veterans—an act many viewed as a flag-waving attempt to prime a new generation for massively funded military ventures. Alexander Haig, the Secretary of State who would be ousted a year later, was futilely attempting to drum up support for El Salvador and trying to put a new face on Vietnam; it was time we dropped the "sackcloth and ashes" image about that war, he said.

Scoffed one former Vet Center leader, Don Reed, listening to the might-is-right rhetoric, "The way to forget *old* veterans is to create *new* ones."

A California veteran, Shad Meshad, pioneered the Vet Center concept a decade ago. For years he worked with veterans on his own. When the Vet Centers were established, he turned down the directorship because he wanted to continue working directly with veterans. He runs the West Coast region.

A medical service officer in Vietnam, Meshad was shot down in a helicopter. "I split my head. I was scalped." Meshad pulls back the bangs he wears to hide the scars. "I could feel my whole face slipping. Like an old basset hound, my face just kind of fell down. I tied a bandanna around it to hold it up."

Years of painful operations on his head and back, six months of "terrible readjustment problems" turned Meshad into a zealot for veterans. At the time that Reagan was considering gutting the Vet Centers, Meshad was interviewed on Atlanta TV. The TV program spliced in a videotape of David Stockman, Reagan's OMB program-cutting wunderkind who had put the centers on the hit list.

Stockman had spent some of the war at Harvard Divinity School, which conveniently carried a student deferment. When he left, Stockman entered the government, not the ministry. When he moved to cut the Vet Centers, Stockman became the point man for all the veterans' frustrations. "We're being slapped in the face by a guy who was hiding out in divinity school," said John Terzano of the Vietnam Veterans of America. And Jim Webb sputtered, "Maybe if he'd had the balls to go, he'd have the compassion to understand some of the problems of veterans."

Meshad looked darkly at the screen. Stockman has an unfortunately prissy way of smiling. "Obviously," he said on the screen, "Vietnam veterans have special problems, but I don't know that we can spend money running programs to provide centers"—and here he curled his prissy smile—"and 'rap sessions' and so forth. I just think that's a *dispensable expenditure.*" The moderator asked Meshad for his reaction. *"Totally* the man really doesn't understand the Vietnam vet," exploded Meshad. "He does not know what a Vietnam vet *is,* does not understand what a rap group *is.* It is probably the best mental health delivery program in the United States today. It's okay to say 'Vietnam' there. It's like in sex therapy, 'It's all right to talk about sex in here.' So it's all right to talk about Vietnam in the center."

The outcry in the media from constituents surprised Congress and forced them to champion the centers. No matter; a full year after Stockman suggested cutting the centers, he still showed indifference. Did he feel it wise to recommend the centers be cut?

"It sure didn't do any good in terms of my situation, or P.R.-wise. But it was just another case of a *'noisy interest group'* that led the general press and public to believe things that just weren't so." In what sense? Stockman waved his hand impatiently, "They implied that without the centers the Vietnam veteran had no chance to get counseling or psychiatric service. He can get *all* of that in the VA."

I protested that the VA's inability to handle veterans' problems had created the need for the centers in the first place. Stockman shrugged. "I wanted the function performed within the VA system and if the VA system had to bend or change or sensitize their staffs, that was fine with me. It was a 'policy management' point of view."

It is, of course, laughable to assume the VA would provide such a service in its regular facilities when they had not seen the need to do so years earlier. Most VA doctors are resistant and not motivated to understand the difference between the Vietnam veterans' stress and standard psychoses like schizophrenia and manic depression.

Reagan's OMB czar was hardly his only appointee indifferent to Vietnam veterans. It took nine months to appoint a director of the lumbering VA and when he did the choice could not have been worse for Vietnam veterans.

Robert Nimmo's "qualification" was that of California crony to White House counselor Edwin Meese III; his expertise seemed to be in golfing. The day of the Vietnam Veterans Memorial groundbreaking, Nimmo was nowhere in sight. He was out golfing. He felt the agency was "coddling Vietnam vets."

In 1982 Nimmo came under attack for damaging the effectiveness of the Vet Centers by imposing strict travel ceilings that limited psychiatrists' and trained specialists' visits to counseling centers. For months he stonewalled a congressional request to investigate whether Agent Orange had harmed American GIs. Nimmo's VA did not even decide what scientific protocols the study would use, let alone launch the study. In 1983, three years after the study was mandated, Congress finally took it from the VA and put it into the hands of the Centers for Disease Control in Atlanta. Former VA officials who had quit in protest of Nimmo claimed that the agency stalled the Agent Orange study because of Nimmo's concern that it could result in untold millions in compensation if a direct link between the military's use of toxic chemicals and veterans' health problems could be shown.

The budget-conscious Nimmo, however, observed no such austerity when it came to himself. He used an Air Force plane to fly from Reno to Washington at a cost of $5,600. In violation of a presidential directive, Nimmo spent more than $54,000 to refurbish his Washington office. He sent his old furniture to his daughter's office. He also spent $6,441 of taxpayers' money for a chauffeur to drive him to and from work—a privilege his position did not entitle him to under the law. (He repaid the money out of his own pocket after there was public outcry.)

Meanwhile Chuck Hagel, who had gone to the VA with patriotic fervor and a desire to help the Vietnam veteran, became increasingly disillusioned. Nimmo was tying Hagel's hands on everything from Agent Orange to Vet Centers. In frustration he handed in his resignation to Reagan, hoping to smoke out the problem.

A former Green Beret and double amputee had already left in protest and others would follow. Hagel was a rare find for the VA—liked by both the traditional service organizations and alienated Vietnam veterans. Protests from both Republicans and Democrats on the Hill grew louder. Veterans' service organizations demanded Nimmo's ouster. Flying to his ranch retreat, Reagan was treated to a blistering editorial in the Los Angeles *Times* entitled: "The Wrong Man Is Leaving." But the California connection was thick. Chuck Hagel was out, Nimmo in. Finally, months later, in the fall of 1982, Nimmo resigned.

Art Blank, appointed by Hagel and the VA's chief medical officials, stayed on to direct the Vet Centers. As public awareness grew, Congress—so long indifferent to the concept of readjustment counseling centers—voted to extend the program for four years in November 1983.

While the centers function for the most part with little problem, some Vet Center leaders report that animosity still exists in some communities. A 1982 incident in an Alabama Vet Center points up several societal attitudes that remain about Vietnam veterans. One is a deep-set prejudice against those who seem to fit the pejorative image of "drug-using hippie veteran." The second is a prevalent suspicion by conservative law enforcement and political forces, including some within the VA, of the unorthodox centers. The Alabama justice system placated such prejudice.

The Birmingham Vet Center, one of the first in the nation, opened with national fanfare in 1980 and for two years was consistently honored by civic groups. Its director, Don Reed, was a flamboyant orange-haired former captain and Vietnam combat helicopter pilot. Tom Ashby was his lean and lanky counselor. Neither one concealed his long-standing antiwar views, for which they were sometimes attacked on local talk shows. When Jeremiah Denton, the former POW and Alabama senator who sees Communists around every corner, opposed refunding of the Vet Centers, Reed and Ashby were vocal opponents.

In the summer of 1981, Grady Gibson walked into their Vet Center and presented himself as one of Vietnam's emotional casualties. In a good-ole-boy twang, he talked of marital difficulties, drinking problems, periods of confusion, and severe headaches alleviated by "that white powder that is real good." Cocaine, of course. He told Reed and Ashby that his wife had money, that he dabbled in investments, and hinted that he would lavish large sums on a veteran community-based program.

"I thought, God *damn!* Our ship has come in," recalled Reed. "For weeks he offered us *his* dope. I've never made any bones about smoking marijuana. (None of us can *afford* cocaine.) Well, after some time he claimed to have run out." Reed, a "professional veteran" who has never gotten past the war himself, places a special value on veteran camaraderie; sharing his dope with a "brother" seemed natural. "Besides, this guy was going to help get a veterans' program off the ground."

One day, when Birmingham center members were at the opening of a new center in Mobile, members of U.S. Federal Attorney's Office, VA Inspector General, the Drug Enforcement Agency, and the Alabama Bureau of Investigation swooped down on the Birmingham Vet Center. Grady Gibson was not a good-old-boy troubled veteran but an undercover agent sent to get something on the center. The case was quickly labeled "Vetscam."

Reed and Ashby were suspended without pay. Other Vet Center counselors were warned by the VA not to help them with their considerable emotional and financial worries. They were finally charged with conspiracy to sell drugs and unlawful possession of drugs. The amounts were minuscule—possession of 23.1 *grams* of marijuana and distributing or intending to distribute 5.2 grams of cocaine, distributing and selling 7.5 grams of marijuana.

Even before the indictment, however, the basic concept of the Vet Centers was being tried in the Southern conservative press. The Mobile *Press Register* editorialized, "Our suspicions that the most costly counseling program for Vietnam veterans was just another nonessential drain on the federal treasury were pretty much confirmed recently when authorities started looking into the Alabama operation of Vietnam Veterans Outreach Centers."

The idea that the congressional expenditure for Vet Centers is a "costly, nonessential drain" is, of course, ludicrous; $21 million would barely buy spare parts on a B-1 bomber. "About an hour's worth of firepower during the bombing of Vietnam," said Meshad caustically.

However, the climate seemed right for such negative thinking. Few in Alabama questioned the incredible government expense for an investigative operation that netted so little.

Two witnesses testified that on one occasion Gibson snorted roughly two dozen lines of cocaine. Gibson testified that he had simulated smoking grass by pinching on the end of a joint. He told the jury he had always been "fortunate enough" to find a sink on the sly into which he would pour cocaine.

During the trial it was pointed out that no profit was ever made on the transactions. "I've been working fourteen to sixteen hours every goddamn day in that Vet Center," said Reed. "We work with some heavy drug users, but that is one group the outreach is *for.* We're not there to be moral with them—we're there to help them."

Reed's freewheeling style of helping them, however, was criticized by many Vet Center leaders and delayed stress experts who have tried so hard to change the image of "doper" veterans and Vet Centers. At an administrative hearing to determine if Reed and Ashby could return to their jobs, Joe Gelsomino, leader of the Tampa, Florida, center, testified that there was "absolutely no reason" whatever to smoke pot with clients. Later he told me, "That's like an alcoholic being given a drink by a counselor." Reed argued that he was dealing with reality. He allowed clients to smoke pot in the center and sometimes smoked with them because "Sometimes these guys have kept things pent up for *years;* sometimes they have a lot of guilt about what they did or saw over there. I'm not going to appear like I'm sitting in judgment by telling them they can't smoke." Gelsomino argued that any good done in therapy with a stoned veteran would not truly help him face his problems.

Art Blank was even more vehement: "99 and 44/100 percent of the Vet

Center leaders around the country would think that smoking pot with clients was an *outrageous* thing to do. All of us in the program realize that whole thing resulted from entrapment, but we feel they acted very irresponsibly and brought discredit to the program. That is why they weren't supported."

In the end, federal prosecutors dropped all drug-trafficking charges against Reed, who pleaded guilty to the misdemeanor charges of possession of small amounts of marijuana and cocaine. Reed was given a stiff three-year probation that included weekly urine checks.

It all might have seemed like a thwarted case of government hounding, except for the postscript. In the wake of a heavy-handed investigation which turned up little and undeniably smacks of entrapment, several careers were ruined. The defense cost for Ashby and Reed, who made little in their years of helping veterans, is enormous. After the conspiracy charges were dropped, Ashby was charged with one possession count and another vet counselor and university sociology professor, David Curry, was indicted on three counts of possession of cocaine with intent to distribute. The amount of cocaine totaled less than one ounce.

The jury bought their entrapment defense on two occasions for Curry, but not on the other. Ashby was found guilty on the one possession count. The judge ordered both men to a ninety-day psychiatric evaluation at a federal correctional institution. As required by law in cases involving an evaluation, both men received maximum sentences: Curry was handed a thirty-four-year prison term and fined $80,000; Ashby got thirty years and $59,000.

They are free pending appeal, but if appeals fail the psychiatric evaluations will be the basis for determining reductions in their sentences. That the government would spend ungodly sums to investigate and to prosecute for possession of such small amounts of drugs begs many questions; not the least is how politically motivated this was. The U.S. Attorney, in his closing plea, asked the jury to "do something about the cocaine problem in Mobile," but Gibson's months of taping conversations with Vet Center members and their clients turned up no dope ring. "I never have been a drug dealer and that was the gist of their charges," said Ashby. Ashby, Reed, and Curry all were active in VVAW (Vietnam Veterans Against War) as were some of the original Vet Center leaders. (Blank estimates that some 10 percent of the 567 Vet Center leaders were VVAW.) Their political posture was anathema for many who viewed the military as inviolate—despite Vietnam.

"Listen to Grady's tapes and you hear over and over again Grady asking for dope. And then this other 'Vietnam veteran' mysteriously walks into my life and *he* has some coke. I bought four grams and thought it was going to be $400. He let me have it for $90 a gram so I meet Gibson in Mobile and give him the grams—and $40 *back*. I got fifteen years for that," said Ashby.

"We were stupid and indiscreet, but I was lulled into a false sense of security. Major VA officials from Washington had smoked marijuana in the center after hours on visits," he contends. Ashby is probably right when he says, "This could not have happened in any center outside the Deep South. The case was tried in Mobile—not Birmingham, where it belonged—and the jury was from places like Eight Mile, Alabama. They didn't understand the difference between a *gram* of cocaine and an *ounce.*"

Without a job and broke ("It cost $4,200 for the transcript alone, which you have to pay for if you want to appeal"), Ashby says, "The only thing that keeps me from being depressed is my anger. I've borrowed on my insurance to pay the lawyer." He laughs. "To some extent, I'm enjoying the luxury of being a 'big-time criminal.' I don't plan ever to do anything for society again. I should have known better than to try in Alabama. I just don't fit."

The presiding judge, W. Brevard Hand, was the Alabama judge who ruled in favor of prayer in the schools—which was overturned by the 11th Circuit. Clearly taking a dim view of the defendants, he told the rural jury that Ashby was "highborn"—a phrase guaranteed not to set well.

In the days when Ashby was unknowingly under surveillance by Gibson, he sat in his mother's antique-filled home in Tuscaloosa and recounted many years of bucking the tide in Alabama. Both his parents had been professors at the nearby University of Alabama. Ashby returned to the University after Vietnam, determined to work for peace. One night after the Cambodia invasion, Ashby and a small group held a candlelight vigil. Some of Bear Bryant's football team crashed down to stomp out all the candles. "I had hot wax on my fatigues for days," drawls Ashby.

Before Ashby became a source of embarrassment with his "weird" antiwar activities, even before Vietnam, there had always been that streak.

As a high school sophomore, Ashby had become an agnostic when blacks tried to enter the First Methodist Church and he saw them barred entrance. "Either we were all God's children or we weren't. The pastor agreed, but said, 'The time is not here.' "

Ashby breezed through high school, partied through college, flunked out, and was drafted. In basic training, his antiwar sentiments were already forming. "We were being taught to hate a whole race of people and inherently I *knew* that was wrong. I'm not a pacifist. I can see where you have to protect yourself. But I recognized we were the aggressors even before I *went*—that's what I feel most guilty about.

"I was with the 1st Cavalry in the fire direction control unit of the 105th Artillery. When the infantry made contact, they'd call back the coordinates and ask for a certain kind of round and we'd fire it in. Only once did I ever see the enemy. I was on the second lift going into the A Shau Valley and after I landed, I saw fifteen helicopters shot down in three hours. One Chinook pilot hit a tree; the Chinook was full of rounds for the infantry and it caught on fire. Those rounds clipped off, flying all over the place for hours. I saw seventy-five to a hundred people just zapped in those helicopters. I think of myself as a damn good American because it wasn't easy being a spokesman for the antiwar movement in the South. I mean, I *got* hate mail." Ashby studied counseling at the University of Alabama, then worked for legal services, helping the poor. Every move he made for several years was guilt-motivated. "I had to do something that would offset some of the things I had done in Vietnam. We just had no respect for the lives of Vietnamese. And I participated."

Ashby's antiwar sentiments were not voiced while counseling veterans. "If a guy is secure in the belief that 'I'm proud of what I did: our leadership didn't let us win, but it was the right thing,' I'm not about to tear that from him. It took a long time for me to relieve the guilt, to understand *myself.* A lot of guys, all these years later, now coming into the center, tried to deny that Vietnam had any effect on them."

As the image of veterans began to turn around in the early eighties, some Vet Center leaders reported a new problem—a far cry from the days when veterans were reviled. Some men were fixated on the idea of the Vietnam veteran as cultural hero. "Our intuition is that this transformation is reflected in the role-taking of certain seriously disturbed individuals," stated Joseph Law, Jr., and Thomas Johnson of the Mobile Vet Center in 1983.

They encountered at least three men who told dramatic stories of Vietnam that were fake and they warned other Vet Center personnel to check clients carefully. "If our thesis is correct, many individuals who are downtrodden in society may be attempting to take on the role or emulate what they consider to be a high-status individual—the Vietnam veteran."

One man came to their center highly agitated and stated he was a Marine veteran now a police officer. He complained of anxiety, insomnia, startle responses, and periods of amnesia. While learning a relaxation technique from the counselor, the "veteran" slipped into a deep trance and began to relive events from Vietnam. He talked excitedly about being ordered to kill civilians, then began to cry and sob for several minutes before he was brought out of the trance. He professed considerable relief and left in high spirits. Finally he was hospitalized at a VA facility. Routine checks revealed that he had never served on active duty in the military.[2]

Trust on both sides—what most Vet Centers strive for—means hours of confidence-building, taking the midnight phone call when someone is troubled or threatening suicide. San Diego Vet Center Director William Mahedy interrupted an interview to take a phone call. He listened to the distraught wife, then asked, "Has he passed out? *Where is the gun now?* You have it? Okay. Now don't panic. I'll be right over," and raced out the door.

It is especially tragic to see a veteran go under who looked as if he was being helped by the Vet Center. Early one morning in Columbus, Ohio, Gerald W. Highman called his father.

"Dad, did you get a good night's sleep?"

"Yes."

"I just killed Joann." Gerald Highman's voice was ominously calm. He said he was going to kill himself next.

"Oh my God, no. Jerry. Please don't do it. I'll come right over."

Merrill Highman raced with the police to his son's home. The couple was lying in pools of blood in the bedroom. Gerald's wife was dead; he died a few hours later in a hospital.

The twice-wounded former marine was "pretty mixed-up" when he came home, said his father. "He'd do good and then no good." After ten years of depression and combat flashbacks, Highman seemed to be doing better. He had a steady job and married his childhood sweetheart just six months before the murder-suicide.

A year before he shot himself, Highman started going to the Columbus Vet Center. "Lately," said his father, "Gerald was like his happy old self."[3]

For every one the Vet Centers lose, thousands are helped. Despite years of resistance to the counseling concept, the government simply could no longer ignore the frightening statistics. Paul Starr, a sociologist who wrote a study of Vietnam veterans for Ralph Nader's Center for the Study of Responsive Law, said, "Suicide appears to be one of the leading causes of death among Vietnam veterans in general and disabled veterans in particular."[4]

One such veteran was Eddy Erikson. One day his wife Joan returned home from work and became apprehensive when her husband was not in sight. They had moved to Largo, Florida, from New York a month earlier to get away from the scene of Eddy's four suicide attempts.

Joan Erikson found her husband's cold body in their bedroom closet. He was kneeling, hanging from a rope tied to a five-foot-high clothes pole. Erikson was collecting 100 percent disability payments for neuropsychological disorders. He left behind a lavender plastic medical ID from the VA.

Erikson was an eighteen-year-old door gunner in a helicopter gunship with the 101st Airborne Division at Phu Bai. As the months went by, he saw four close friends killed in combat. The final death changed him irrevocably. Michael Murphy was his last and closest friend. Hit by enemy fire but still alive, Murphy fell out of the gunship before Erikson could catch him, just as the helicopter was taking off. The others in the gunship had to hold Eddy back. He tried to fling himself out to save his friend. Later that day, they brought Michael Murphy's body back to the base camp. Erikson was given his friend's unopened mail. With trembling fingers and sobbing, Erikson opened the letter from Murphy's wife. She was ecstatic and she had written her husband the good news. Michael Murphy had just become the father of a boy.[5]

No one knows for sure if the Vet Center program could have saved Erikson, but the programs have saved many others.

"We scrupulously avoid letting political factors influence us in hiring. I'd say we are a mirror distribution of the attitudes of the 3.4 million Vietnam veterans—47 percent of whom feel we should have never gotten involved in Vietnam," says Blank.

Some who seek help have only vague, minor difficulties over Vietnam. One such veteran is Tim Noyes. He has never thought of suicide, of taking someone hostage, hitting someone, or even expressing any defined rage. William Mahedy, the former Vietnam chaplain who has worked with so many veterans that he has lost count, cautioned, "We don't see those three or four out of five who do *not* have significant problems of adjustment, so I cannot say what the character traits of *all* Vietnam veterans are. But in the ones we see, a sense of being *out of phase with life* is the most common feeling, that somehow the Vietnamese experience has 'set me apart.' Some vague malaise, that 'the country never appreciated us.' "

Noyes remained tentative and skeptical of the centers long after he first sought help. He did not identify with those who seemed possessed by Vietnam, nor with many of the down-and-out.

Handsome and star-struck, Tim Noyes graduated from high school in 1966, headed for Broadway and auditioned for *Hair,* the antiwar, antiestablishment musical that spoke to the young and outraged the old. Noyes was "totally oblivious" to the real war in Vietnam. He didn't get the part, ran out of money, and, as happened so easily in those days, a girl he had known briefly "showed up on my doorstep with a U-Haul trailer of belongings. So we lived together for a while."

Noyes laughs as he recalls his fate at age nineteen; a sixties American tragedy out of Theodore Dreiser. "She got pregnant—and I got drafted." They got married on a weekend pass. Being drafted brought reality into focus. "I was scared shitless," says Noyes, his voice a strong whisper for emphasis. "I hadn't formed any opinions—about the morality of the war or even whether I was going to be in it." Infantry was not Noyes's idea of fun, so he went to flight school afterward. "I came out of the infantry with these uneducated, backwards people to be with a pretty intelligent bunch. And we still were all scared shitless."

Noyes, the new warrant officer, arrived in Vietnam a day late. "Got drunk on the plane going over. I was one of three guys on the whole airplane that was sitting with a woman. A nurse who was a captain. I had smuggled a fifth of Canadian Club on and we just got bruised. I got off the airplane in Honolulu and there was this fishpond with gigantic goldfish. The last thing I remembered, I was paddling around in this pool, tickling the fish." Noyes woke up on an airport bench the next morning with a hangover, hitched another plane to Saigon, and found his unit.

Noyes was scared for about a month, "when I was thinking of surviving. This sounds weird, but one day it dawned on me I *was* going to get killed. I was just crazy and reckless enough that I was *not* going to live through that year. And so, once I knew that, I relaxed. Not only did you get used to people shooting at you, it was fun. 'Cause when they were shooting at me, I knew where they *were*—and I had rockets. That's the only way I could kill them. Shoot at me—then I'd know where they were. I was a good hunter."

The skills did not help him afterward. "I'm having a lot of trouble with life right now," explaining his first visit to the Los Angeles Vet Center. He quickly brushes off the present to return to Vietnam.

"I didn't make any friends. I was told not to by everybody who had ever been there before me." He is extremely proud of the fact that no one who flew with him ever got hurt. "We had a black scarf with our platoon patch, which you earned by killing your first man. I guess . . . it took the edge off killing your first human being. Something was worthwhile for it." Noyes bursts into a mocking chuckle. "A *scarf!*"

At first he bristles at the idea that warfare might have been traumatizing. "It was *exciting!* The most power I ever had and probably ever will again. I got to play God for a year. I had the ultimate power. I could look down on the ground and see a man and could say, 'I'm gonna kill him or I might let him live.' "

How did you decide?

"You learned to distinguish between the eligible and ineligible. Like the real old guys, the ones that didn't look scared. Helicopters were universally feared by the bad guys. You could see their reactions. They'd run and hide in rice paddies or reeds."

Wouldn't a civilian do that?

"They were told, 'If you're not doing anything wrong, *stand* there.' "

Were they killed anyway?

"Not by me. I knew one guy who killed everything he saw—and ended up in jail for it. They couldn't prove he was actually the one who killed all those people, so they just sent him home. I ran into him a couple of years later, in a bar in Lowell, Massachusetts. I'll never forget. R—— was still wearing his flight suit shirt with his patch. He couldn't get over Vietnam.

"I was very detached," recalls Noyes. "It was like target shooting. I was one of the best. You had on earphones to radio other helicopters and you could tune into radio stations." Death could be set to music. "It was trippy."

The voice is slowing down a little. "I only once killed . . . some . . . that I didn't, uh, feel too good about killing.

"We were flying in a really nasty area." Noyes looked down and saw some saffron-robed Buddhist monks threading their way through a valley. "It was a Sunday morning and we were listening to church music on the radio. I called back to the commander in control and said, 'You know these guys aren't eligible. They're wearing monks' robes.' He checked with the Vietnamese commander of that area and the answer was 'You can kill 'em. If you want to, kill 'em.' So we shot at them and finally I said, 'Let's kill 'em and be done with it. To hell with it.' I shot some rockets at them. One of them . . . I, uh, watched the guy crawl away from his leg. And I said, 'No, I can't shoot 'em anymore.' I felt really strange about it. I said, 'I don't think they're bad guys. I think I've done enough, so I'm not going to shoot them anymore.' I called control ship and"—Noyes repeats the line almost in the cadence of a firm, stubborn child—"told them, 'I'm not going to shoot them anymore.' "

Finally Noyes's face falls. "You know, I've told that story before with a sort of devil-may-care attitude. It's not really devil-may-care. Told it mostly to guys who were in Vietnam." He half smiles. "You don't tell it on the first date. I told it cavalierly, more than macho. I think that's a defense. If I told the story with the kind of impact it had on *me*, I probably wouldn't tell it."

That was the only incident that troubled Noyes. "Being in the air gave you distance. I was not down there getting it in my face."

Noyes got forty-seven Air Medals and a Bronze Star. "I was a war hero. I *felt* like a war hero when I was finished. In any other war, I would have been. I had done a good job." He speeds up the words as if it were a litany he has repeated often to himself, "I killed people I was supposed to kill and I hadn't killed the people I wasn't supposed to kill, except maybe that once. I put myself in some hairy situations and I got through it and the guys with me were better off for having *me* there." Finally the crux of his anger is revealed. "That's my big bitch with the country. *I have not been allowed to be a war hero!* Not that I want to be—but I'd like to get it out of the way, so I can go on living my life."

It took Noyes about fifty hours to get from Vietnam to home. People blown apart by his rockets were fresh in his mind as he took his wife to bed. "We stopped living together shortly after I got back. It would really be convenient to say 'Yeah, the war fucked us up,' but I can't say that. I had no business getting married in the first place."

Noyes went to design school, worked as a draftsman for a Boston architect, then started his own small draftsman design group. "One morning I said, 'This isn't what I want. I want to act and if I don't do it now I'll never do it.' "

California sunshine creeps through the smog, surfers down below zigzag their way to shore as Noyes drives along the Santa Monica Freeway. Los Angeles: "What's your sign?" city, beach bums and karma, Hollywood dreams while busing tables. Noyes is like thousands who come here, the hopeful Robert Redfords of tomorrow. He acts with a serious company and has done well with TV commercials. In one, shown nationally in 1983, Noyes is at the wheel of a Datsun, saying, "We just stole this car." Said Noyes, "This is a long apprenticeship, but I'm going to stick it out."

A year had passed since our first talk. A gradual acceptance of himself had grown. "I've been able to deal with a couple of things." Noyes brought up the monk-shooting episode again. It was the first time he had spoken directly about Vietnam and his feelings. "I thought that since I fought in a *bad* war, therefore I was a *bad* person. It was never any conscious thing. I remember I would use that as an excuse. I would do something just totally buffoonish and I'd say, 'Heyyyyy, forgive me. I was in the war.' All as a joke. And it just dawned on me recently the truth behind that. I did *exactly* what my government told me to do. And I did it as well as anyone could possibly do."

Noyes had stopped blaming himself. We last saw each other in the winter of 1983. Noyes was long removed from the Vet Center. It was hard times for the building industry and hard times for Hollywood. No one was taking any chances. "My two careers—I sure know how to pick them," he said with a laugh. With an ease that was totally lacking months before, Noyes said, "You know, there are a lot of things about that war I'm not proud of." There was, after the earlier stages of denial, a feeling of real acceptance. "But I can *say* that—and go on to other things."

He was still determined to stick it out, waiting for his break.

"What the hell," said Tim Noyes, thirty-four and holding. "Life goes on. Life goes on."

That summer we talked on the phone and he seemed happier than ever— except that he was concerned about the buildup of troopships in Central America. "When are they ever going to learn? Fighting for peace is like fucking for virginity."

Ambivalence about Vietnam such as Noyes expressed is common and sometimes produces baffling contradictions. "The Vietnam veteran participated in *the* historical experience that broke down the mythology of America's 'right and might,' " said counselor Mahedy. "Yet he had previously *committed* himself to that and still wants to believe in it, even though his own experiences may cause him to reject that or feel alienated. So the ambivalence is there, burned into his soul.

"That's why clinicians often can't treat these men. There are a lot of misdiagnoses. Like a guy who was absolutely eaten alive by guilt. He was suicidal but not in the clinical sense. The VA doctor said, 'There's nothing *clinically* wrong.' And there isn't. But someday he'll probably kill himself."

He spoke of Larry, the veteran who had seen his friends slaughtered at Khe Sanh, only to have the government abandon it. "His stress has *nothing* to do with clinical symptoms. He has a profound loss of meaning because of Vietnam."

After hours of verbal sparring, Larry fumbles for his feelings. "To me, in life there is no joy. After Vietnam, it all stopped. My theory is I'll never climb out of this. I'm not suicidal and there ain't nothing I'm afraid of—which is another one of my problems. Every normal human being *would* be afraid of something. My wife talks about the future. There *is* no future. Only the past. Happening over and over again. It's in my ears and my nose and underneath my fingernails. My wife says"—and Larry mimics a falsetto—"'Gee, Larry, when you're feeling bad, just think of something happy!' That takes care of it for her," says Larry in disgust and despair. "She can't understand that I can't *think* of anything happy."

And then there are men with all the trappings of success who seek help from the centers. Dr. Dennis Hoban, director of education services and research at Wake Forest University School of Medicine, was a Marine first lieutenant in Vietnam. A blond, grim man, he seemed the epitome of Mahedy's alienated stranger at home. "I have found it *impossible* to put Vietnam behind me," said Dr. Hoban. "Memories still inundate me *daily.*" His homecoming is etched in angry memory. The woman next to him on the plane who refused to speak to him when she found out he was returning from Vietnam, the antiwar professor who singled him out for ridicule and contempt, the coed who followed up the professor's theme and verbally attacked him. "I backed off. I just wanted to kill her, basically, and I still do. I *wouldn't*—but I feel that way." He is only comfortable speaking of Vietnam with those who have been there. Dr. Hoban has a continuing dream: "I keep missing my plane out of Vietnam. Is it over—or not over? I don't think I have control over that. I wish I did."

William R. Loftin, Jr., a corporate executive, has a personal income "well into the six figures." He is a former POW who spent one year and nine months in a bamboo cage from which he subsequently escaped. He holds a master's degree in philosophy from Heidelberg. In 1980 he attempted suicide.

After four months at the Little Rock, Arkansas, Vet Center, Loftin wrote in support of the program: "I was a captain, U.S. Army, stationed at Camp Red Devil near Dong Ha [near the DMZ between North and South Vietnam]. I was involved in intense and frequent combat. Before my capture and escape, I was decorated several times for merit and valor." Loftin spent ten years in the Army. "Until my experiences in Vietnam, I had every intention of making it a career." He returned to the "typical vet's treatment by the American citizens. I withdrew and tried to shut away the shock, fears, horrors, and utter confusion. It was a mistake because I desperately needed help."

The past churned inside. Loftin became "very antisocial [he joined an outlaw motorcycle gang] and began to drink heavily and got involved with drugs. I refused to discuss my problem with *anyone* [family, friends, doctors]. I remarried and it also ended up in the courts. I finally attempted suicide."

At that point, Thomas D. Raney, chief executive officer of T. J. Raney and Sons, where Loftin was a vice-president, contacted Luther Johnson of the Little Rock Vet Center.

"It took a lot to first even begin to talk about my experiences and to realize how badly holding all this inside was harming me and those close to me. The Vet Centers and continued study of post-traumatic stress are *vital*. I didn't know what post-traumatic stress was. I know now that, over a decade after combat, it almost killed me and created years of unhappiness."

And last, some of the men who come to Vet Centers are pure losers. Still, their numbers are small, considering the open-ended cast to this outreach program. They accurately reflect a certain percentage of men who went to Vietnam. "The Army takes your average Joe Citizen, so you're going to get a mix—a certain number of potential paranoid schizophrenics, potential sociopaths, some very sensitive people, a few geniuses, a lot who aren't too bright, and a lot of average nice guys down the block," says Mahedy.

The losers are seldom looked on as good candidates for help. "They just want to piss and moan about life and use Vietnam as a goddamn excuse," said one center leader. "I wouldn't say there's more than 10 percent—and we get rid of 'em fast."

Jack, cocky, skinny, tattooed, brushes his long blond hair back from his face as he sits in a Vet Center in the South. Jack has walked with trouble through life.

"My parents are many times married and many times divorced. The only time I saw Dad was when he was drunk. He was a bartender. He'd be home drunk on Sunday when the bar closed." As a teenager, he lived with his mother and a stepfather who was in the service in Okinawa. Jack got thrown out of school for skipping so much and joined the Army at seventeen. He figured he was smart enough to avoid Vietnam by laying back through basic, refusing to cooperate, "but they put me through anyway." As a medic, "You'd have friends who were alive and run into 'em dead later that day. I don't like remembering it. I mean they had beautiful women, nice beaches, and good dope. But it wasn't worth fighting for. They had little kids passing out a Japanese imitation of the Zippo lighter—and some had plastic explosives in them. They could take a piece of bamboo and make a thousand weapons out of it. If you went downtown to solicit a young lady, you're not sure she was going to take you down a couple of dark alleys and you'd never make it back. It told on you after awhile. You just got such an intense hatred for either side. They were just short little Vietnamese people, you know."

Jack, buying into the scams that were everywhere in Saigon, sold dope to other GIs. He was disciplined several times; "I told them to shove the Army up edgewise."

Back in the States, Jack was busted for drugs, went to prison, served seven months, and got probation. "I found dealing tremendously profitable. Had thousands of dollars in my pocket, a Harley [Davidson], all kinds of girls. I could throw one out and two or three more would be waiting in line to get in." He bummed around, "dealing, living on the strip, living with a motorcycle club, and fighting with other gangs." Finally he studied computer programming, went to work for Blue Cross and Blue Shield. "One day, out of the blue, they told me, 'Well, we can't get you bonded with that drug record.' "

Jack drifted into the Vet Center after another altercation with the law. "The cops caught me sleepin' in a church and charged me with third-degree burglary," he claimed. The case was pending, Jack was out of a job with no place to live, no food. "The center helped me get a job as a janitor with a realty company." Jack seems uncertain about his future. He spoke of a new law that might give him a chance to seal his past record so that he could get jobs, "be bonded, and start all over again."

Still, the straight life seems unlikely. Decidedly unrepentant, Jack ponders the influence of Vietnam on him. "The ease of making money dealing there got me into dealing here."

If you *could* erase your record, what would you want to be doing?

"I'd do exactly what I done before." He shrugs. "It's just my way of life."

For the first time in his fast-paced narrative, Jack reflects.
"I think Vietnam was just there to go along with what I was."
He drags on a cigarette and grins nonchalantly.
"It just followed the flow."

5 The Disordered

A DECADE AFTER THE LAST AMERICAN TROOPS LEFT VIETNAM, ONLY A few fledgling hospital programs dealt with severely disordered cases of delayed stress. Frustration is high for the few dedicated doctors and nurses who work with these men; they know that if the beds were emptied tomorrow, they could instantly be filled with troubled veterans.

The Bay Pines VA Hospital in Tampa, Florida—a cluster of low-slung whitewashed buildings surrounded by palm trees—warehouses mostly the elderly from past conflicts. It is their turf, their music. Walking near the cafeteria—labeled CANTEEN—is like being in a time warp. Glenn Miller and Tommy Dorsey blare from the compound loudspeaker. The men listening are mostly silver-haired.

Dr. Arthur Arnold, chief of psychiatry in 1982, fought hard to get twenty beds on the psychiatric ward just for Vietnam veterans with severe post-traumatic stress disorder. They are mixed with psychotics, manic-depressives, schizophrenics who are hallucinating and mumbling. "My mother really did a number on me in the press," mutters one, shuffling by in slippers. The Vietnam veterans gingerly coexist with these older veterans, whose actions are unmistakably different. The Vietnam veterans on the ward are not diagnosed psychotics and bitterly resent being housed with them.

The psychotic deals in the world of hallucinations, delusions, and fantasy, whereas the Vietnam veteran nightmare is based on reality. "A paranoid patient may say, 'There is an FBI plot to get me'—but a Vietnam veteran who feels betrayed by his government for abandoning him in the war is dealing with a real suspicion. They have a psychological disorder, but they are not psychotic," says Dr. Arnold. "Adolescent history is crucial. The presence of a psychotic disorder, by definition, begins at twelve or thirteen. The typical psychotic adolescent manipulates, lies, cheats, steals other kids' bikes, and so forth. There were some in Vietnam, I'm sure, but I tell you I think they were immune. They knew guerrilla warfare all their teenage life. These fellows we see had jobs after school, belonged to the Scouts, didn't steal, played sports, got okay grades. We commonly get a history of a really decent kid, some from the most appalling life situations—mothers drunk all the time, you name it."

Is it inevitable that a person from such a childhood, given enough pressure, would eventually snap?

"No way. Some of the most outstanding, creative people come from troubled homes." The touching irony, Dr. Arnold said, "is that veterans who seem to be the most vulnerable are idealistic, naïve, hardworking, patriotic, dedicated to a course. These predisposing factors created tremendous disillusionment. Some of the most troubled are those with punitive fathers who had unrealistic expectations of doing *everything* right."

Only one Vietnam veteran Dr. Arnold examined had a combination of schizophrenia and delayed stress disorder. A Catholic from a rigidly disciplined family, he had a psychotic episode—saw the Virgin Mary and also had "newsreels" in his head about combat. "His job was to call out coordinates for mortar fire. Once he found out the call had been *wrong*. Here were all these other teenage soldiers, mutilated and killed by 'friendly fire.' He realized he was directly responsible. He *really* has some very schizoid features, based on his childhood; he is obsessional about good and bad and religiosity."

While genetic and personality factors are sometimes involved, Dr. Arnold says of his patients, "If it hadn't been for the Vietnam experience, the problems never would have surfaced. They were adaptive and functioning *before* Vietnam and they no longer are in the aftermath."

Veterans with severe delayed stress often react with a rage and uncooperative "bad attitude" that mirrors some of the symptoms of schizophrenia. Thorazine, often effective in treating the florid hallucinations of a schizophrenic, had an extremely deleterious effect on veterans with delayed stress, numbing them, closing off their muscles, and making it impossible to function.

In the seventies Dr. Arnold, then chief of psychiatry in the Tacoma, Washington, VA hospital, was as unknowing as his colleagues and treated Vietnam veterans no differently from other patients. "One fellow was under his bed shouting for medics, hollering about enemy fire. I figured he was having a nightmare but was struck at the time that he seemed to be *reliving* it. I didn't know about flashbacks." The veteran was drugged with Thorazine and Dr. Arnold is haunted by that man. "If I'd only known about post-traumatic stress disorder. It's terrible when you miss one like that. After *DSM III,* I suddenly knew *we* have people with this condition!"

The next time a Vietnam veteran stormed in, shouting about being drugged and ready to kill the next doctor who "laughs at me, calls me a junkie," Dr. Arnold listened. The veterans at Bay Pines Hospital in Tampa wanted a doctor to work with their special depression, more physical therapy and exercise, group therapy with each other. Weeks of feverish planning resulted in the nation's first program to deal with Vietnam veterans hospitalized with PTSD. It was met with resistance and ridicule every step of the way. There was no money for additional staffing, and one Vietnam veteran psychologist had to leave because reliving the war was too painful for him.

The vital trait needed by the doctor is understanding. "My colleagues think I'm a bleeding heart, kinda goofy," said Dr. Arnold with a soft smile. He once broke into sobs at a seminar while talking about his veterans. That lack of professional distance is the precise element that reaches his patients. In addition to structured group sessions, there are daily exercises and weekly ball games with patients and staff. "Some don't know how to laugh anymore. In the ball games they root for each other. It is an absolutely critical factor in breaking down the artificial doctor-patient relationship." They are reliving the interdependence they knew as buddies in the field, learning to trust again.

Always, the ultimate goal is acceptance. One of Dr. Arnold's toughest cases was an enraged veteran who pounded on the doctor's desk with a motorcycle helmet until he broke the glass. He stomped out of the program, but came back and is now doing "exceedingly well." The veteran said he had been involved in a mini-My Lai. After a friend was blown up, he participated in machine-gunning several villagers. "He had terrible feelings of being a murderer."

How do you deal with that?

"We're not dealing with fantasy, we're dealing with real-life experiences. You have to say, 'Yes, you killed.' Sometimes you have to say, 'Yes, you were a *murderer.*' But you say it in such a way that it will strike some chord so that they can accept it and deal with it."

How about the rationale that the country sent them to do this job?

"We're dealing with a subgroup who can't put the responsibility on someone else. It's really a million-dollar question how some can deal with that and others can't. Some are able to pull out of it by sheer will. The ultimate road to recovery comes when they can say, 'I will not let this wipe out the rest of my life.' If they can't lay any of the responsibility on anyone else, they have to accept themselves. It sounds easy. It's probably the hardest thing to do."

One crucial goal is to get the men to capitalize on the more positive experiences of Vietnam. "A lot never felt as useful and productive as when in the military," said Dr. Johnson. "There was a bonding and pairing in that climate of extreme danger and fear second to none. It's literally like losing a part of yourself—psychologically—when friends are killed. That's one reason therapy has to be like it is. Unless you can create an environment where you can create feelings of intimacy, they build shells around themselves."

Among other things, the veterans have to deal with three tough barriers. "The rest of the staff feel that schizophrenics and manic-depressives have a legitimate *right* to expect treatment," said Dr. Arnold. "But when we say these veterans are not psychotic that means to them, 'Then what business have they being here?' On the one hand they're not crazy, but on the other their problem can take longer to treat."

Getting compensation for delayed stress is a second problem. The adjudication board looks at the matter uncomprehendingly and seldom sees the disorder as war-related, no matter what the psychiatrist says. And so those who are barely holding on to jobs have the added frustration of taking time out for treatment. They are, in effect, going broke while trying to get well.

The vocational rehabilitation offered by VA is also considered "make work" and useless. Sometimes the patients get jobs within the VA, but these can only last for six months. "Often they are right back where they started, not actually trained for anything. We wanted to give them real-life employment possibility, not just empty talk."

In one year, fifty-six men were discharged from the program. Dr. Arnold estimates about half are doing well, either on an out-patient basis or treatment-free. "Some have mixed feelings; they're not sure they want to go through what you have to do to get well. I've seen World War II and Korean veterans tell stories. It's to establish camaraderie. For these men, it is like lancing a boil. Letting a little ooze out a time." Dr. Arnold and other PTSD pioneers desperately hope others in the country will follow, not just to aid veterans but the public-at-large. "Delayed stress is one of the major public health problems existing today and it goes relatively unnoticed," said Dr. Arnold. The medical profession is missing a unique opportunity to examine the veterans. "Here in the VA we have a tremendous number of cases that can be recorded and studied. One factor in the disorder is profound sleep disturbance. That has never been studied."

Studying the Vietnam veteran and his adaptive process could lead the way toward treatment and understanding of others with similar reactions of anxiety and impacted grief, such as a father Dr. Arnold knows. Filled with anxiety and impacted grief, he had flashbacks when he got in a car after his family had been wiped out in an auto wreck. He thought he was going crazy.

It has become more common in recent years to isolate the four stages of mourning any deep loss—denial, anger, deep depression, and finally acceptance. If the process is blocked, as it was for many closet veterans, it can cause deep disturbances. Recognizing this could alter treatment of any person so traumatized.

For example, no television network missed the anniversary of the Kansas City Hyatt Regency skywalk tragedy. Survivors were interviewed, but no one picked up on the strong presence of delayed stress. Their quotes sounded interchangeable with combat veterans. *A year later some were just beginning to be able to talk about it.* Most had tried to bury and deny the horror. One woman said, "But it is with us all the time. We have not slept a night through since." And a Vietnam veteran who helped with the rescue operation said he had not seen anything like the horror of that incident in Vietnam. At least the soldiers were somewhat prepared for combat, he said. The skywalk fell without a second's warning.

Dr. Arnold sighs as he thinks about delayed stress treatment.

"The potential for the *rest* of the country hasn't begun."

The three men sit in the sparse conference room, drinking coffee. Al Wilder is tan, dark, thirty-eight, a former platoon leader, an ex-Army officer, a businessman who has made and lost small fortunes. He tried to kill himself twice.

Stephen Wenzel, an engineer in Vietnam, talks in nervous fits and starts, has bitten his nails to the quick, and is filled with anger that his post-Vietnam nervous condition cost him his career as a circus perfomer on the low wire.

Ralph Hansen is scrawny-thin, eats little, has hollow cheekbones and lifeless eyes. A former special forces soldier who says he participated in Operation Phoenix, a program for routing the VC that included torture and selective assassination, Hansen cannot forget his role as an assassin. He, too, tried to kill himself.

At one point, Hansen and the others talk as casually of trying to kill themselves as others talk about going to work.

"I was going to start my own little war," said Hansen. "Came as close as I could possibly get to pulling the trigger."

Why did you want to die?

"A lot of reasons. I was going to school full-time and working twelve hours a day and I guess that got to me." Then he quietly says, *"Assassination team.* That label. A lot of people just can't cope with that. I opened up to my girl once. She doesn't know if I can be that kind of person again. It frightens *me,* knowing I can kill that way. I felt myself reverting back to some of the training and that's when I sought help. I was in a flashback and when I came to I found myself dressed in camouflage fatigues, my face painted black, in a yard at night. I had just," he volunteers, "slit this dog's throat. That really frightened me."

Al Wilder interjects, "We're victims of our beliefs, in believing in the American ideals, not reality. They asked for our help and we gave it. I felt so much rage and frustration to come back and find the American ideal no longer there. I tried to kill myself with drugs. I've seen so many mutilated bodies, that's the reason I chose that way. I wanted to spare my family from going through that mutilation."

Wenzel says, "That's logical."

Hansen interjects, "There was a test once. 'Would you commit suicide with yourself or with others?' If with others, you were an exhibitionist. If by yourself, you were manic-depressive." He shrugs.

Why did they physically want out?

"You're looking for relief. You can't cope with the way you are, causing more pain with other people," says Wilder. "It's a way of going to sleep—and ending it all. You do it to take yourself out of that *forever."*

Wenzel nods. "This is a rough way to live. We don't *want* to feel this way."

Hansen adds, "We don't have any close friends. . . . In most cases, they're no longer around."

Statistics on Vietnam veteran suicides are sketchy but those that surface are disturbing. For years, one statistic has been widely and *incorrectly* used—

that there are 23 percent more suicides among Vietnam veterans than among their peers. This stems from a White House task force on veterans showing that suicides among *institutionalized* Vietnam veterans were 23 percent higher than among other institutionalized patients in the same age group. Some veteran studies extrapolated that institutionalized percentage and incorrectly applied it to *all* Vietnam veterans. There simply is no way of measuring suicides among the Vietnam veteran population at large; records are not kept according to military status.

"We know there are a lot of suicides among veterans on the outside that never get reported to us," said Dr. Jack Ewalt, the psychiatrist who heads the VA's mental health division.

Anecdotal evidence suggests that suicide is, however, a serious problem. "It's not only suicides you have to look at," said Dr. Victor De Facio, a clinical psychologist who has counseled hundreds of veterans. "Single-car accidents are often suicides. Or those covered up by the family—or drug overdoses. Alcoholism is another way to kill yourself. Another way is to simply rot. These are the veterans who have given up—the 'living dead.' The more time passes without giving assistance to veterans who need it, the more we lose."

Sadly, many are already lost. In 1972, while the war was continuing and veterans were shunned, a study of psychiatric patients at the Minneapolis VA hospital showed that more than half (54.1 percent) of Vietnam-era veterans showed suicidal tendencies compared to about one third (35.4 percent) of World War II veterans. Some 9,000 Vietnam veterans were hospitalized in 1979—only 28 percent of the total population at VA hospitals. However, an astounding 64 percent were hospitalized in psychiatric programs. (Generally, the proportion of veterans from other wars in psychiatric wards is the same as their percentage in the general hospital population.) In 1977 Vietnam veterans accounted for 40 percent of all hospitalized patients discharged from the VA hospital system with psychotic diagnoses.[1]

Most seem not to have been helped nor understood. Many squirreled away their sleeping pill allotments to attempt suicide later. Labeled "psychotic," the true but then unknown diagnosis was, more frequently, delayed stress.

Many of the disabled who are alive today feel that the camaraderie and gallows humor of their encapsuled hospital experience helped them to cope better than the physically well who were immediately thrust back into society. But these are the "survivors." Bobby Muller, the paralyzed director of Vietnam Veterans of America, shared a ward with eight other disabled veterans in 1970 at the height of the Vietnam controversy. *Life* magazine shocked the nation with an exposé of the neglect, filth, understaffing, and overcrowding of that ward at the Kingsbridge VA hospital in the Bronx; photos of gaunt paraplegics left untended, urine bags filled to overflowing, looked as if they could have been taken in a prison. Of the nine, Muller is the only one alive. Five died of overt suicide attempts. The others were suspected suicides. "Suicides among disabled combat veterans is disproportionately high," said Muller. "The waste of lives is incredible."

Ralph Hansen and Al Wilder enlisted, profoundly patriotic. Wenzel was drafted. All three feel cheated in some way by their Vietnam experience. They can explain some of their feelings, some of their actions, but are not sure why they are the way they are, nor how to cope. If they knew the answers, they wouldn't be here.

"I was married before Vietnam," said Wenzel. "When I got back, I had a lot of problems but didn't relate them to Vietnam." He jiggles his leg up and down, folds his arms tightly across his chest as if trying to contain himself. "All my life I was performing an act on the low wire. I came back and it was too much of a physical and mental strain. I lost my career, my wife, everything. I was physically violent. Beat her up. I told myself I needed to see a psychiatrist. I came in in 1971 for five months. *It was absolutely no help whatsoever.* The doctor kept trying to relate it back to my childhood—and I was trying to pour my heart out about the way I felt. I was twenty-three and they were in their sixties. I came back in 1975 and it was basically the same thing. Kept asking me if I had a problem in childhood." Wenzel caustically replied to them, "I guess the biggest problem was I couldn't get the keys to the car when I was sixteen.

"This time I've received more help in three weeks than in all the programs combined in ten years. But it has a long way to go. The worst is that you're on a floor with weird, crazy, old people. Our problems don't relate. And I don't want to be an auto or air-conditioning mechanic. That's what they train you for! I'm desperately trying. I'm not *here* for a handout. There's a guy in this program who is a fantastic artist. No way they're helping him with a career in art."

Wilder speaks up. "The reason there are 24 percent incarcerated combat vets is, the way we learned to cope wasn't acceptable to society. If the strain got too much for me, I used to leave my family—thirty or forty days. Things would build up and I would get drunk and after six months, nine months, a year, maybe it'd happen again. What I was doing was coping by taking a walk, rather than by physical violence."

Ralph Hansen nods. "There's a wall. I'm not allowing myself to get close to anybody. Eventually Vietnam is going to catch up to you. I don't care if you're a cook or a grunt, from day one you didn't know who was friend or foe. Each one has a different tolerance point. You talking about these people who are successfully working. I wonder what they're like, if you could see 'em on a night when it's thundering and lightning. . . ."

Wenzel, who was in Vietnam in 1968, wants to prove you didn't have to be in combat to be under stress. "Guys came out basket cases from rocket attacks at base camps. I was a trained combat engineer, wasn't grunting around the countryside. We'd usually set up right by the bridges. Of course, the first thing the Viet Cong tried to take were those bridges. Every night there'd be snipers, rockets."

They all start talking at once. "It wasn't a war to start with," Wenzel says. "If they'da let us win the damn thing . . ." Wilder steps in. "It makes me feel I gave up a lot of me."

Hansen says, "In '67 when I came back, we didn't even get halfway to Grand Central Station from Port Authority and there was an incident where they called us 'baby killers.' It just stuck with me. I was nineteen and there was no denying the fact that it was done by *us.*" His face is without animation. He never smiles, never frowns. Only his eyes look pained, like a dog that has been punished. "And there were *murders,* special missions . . ."

Wilder: "I was a platoon leader. My first concern was my men. I ran search and destroy missions. Stayed out twenty-five days, came in three or four, and then went back out. Night patrols . . . ambushes . . ."

Wilder makes a point that many veterans have made. After warfare, many returned home unable to feel that they were "governed by the consequences of their actions. I used to get drunk and shoot at streetlights. I wasn't looking to get caught or shot at."

Wenzel smiles for the first time. "I used to do stop signs."

Hansen says, "Death doesn't mean what it did, after coming out of Vietnam. We became partners with it."

We talk about other men who came so close to death but react differently and feel that life is precious to them. Hansen looks wistful. "I'd like to be there."

Wenzel feels the same way and doesn't deny others that right. "I definitely believe in a God. I, too, thank him each day for being alive. I *really* wish I could just be a normal person like I was before. I'd love to be performing like I was, but I'm so hyper. I tried a couple of performances in New England and I just couldn't handle it."

His nervousness seems endless. He has had some glands removed and worries about Agent Orange. He was in a heavily sprayed area. "My wife was the first person to tell me I had a problem. We *really* had a happy marriage before. Ambitions, goals. Had the world in our hands. She was a dancer in the circus." His face falls. "It really just scares me to death to know how violent I was when I came back, especially with a tender little woman like her. I talked to her a few weeks ago and was able to tell her how I'm coming in treatment. It was all just kind of sad. She's remarried to a lawyer."

He was not getting out on a weekend pass. "I don't have anyplace to go."

Hansen seems obsessed with his girlfriend's reaction to his confessional. "You finally let down the barrier, after all these years. *The first person you tell backs off.* On the fifth date, I just broke down and told her. Project Phoenix. They've got things in there that are *still* classified," he says in a torrent. "You had to kill on a *personal* basis and yet you had to be impersonal to the fact you're doing something against your moral upbringing and you justify and rationalize."

Initiated by the CIA in 1967 and administered by the U.S. military command, Operation Phoenix was designed to demolish the Viet Cong's capacity for espionage, subversion, and terrorism. Communist chiefs in several provinces, wise to the antisubversive program, obtained government identification cards and jobs for Viet Cong cadremen. Many of the South Vietnamese used in the program to rout the enemy could not be trusted; VC often were tipped off about ambushes. By December of 1970, some 17,000 Viet Cong had been taken out of circulation, through killing or capture—some 63,000 more were still at large, not counting the estimated 6,000 Red agents who infiltrated the South Vietnamese Army and government.[2]

Americans such as Hansen worked with a band of South Vietnamese—many of them hoodlums, soldiers of fortune, draft dodgers, defectors—who were paid well by South Vietnamese standards to hunt down VC. Extortion, terror, and torture were common. Although the U.S. Government officially protested that Phoenix was not an assassination program, the highly secret and unconventional operation nonetheless was marked by indiscriminate anti-VC terror.

Some of this came to light when Francis T. Reitemeyer and Michael J. Cohn, two Army lieutenants assigned to the Phoenix program, received honorable discharges after convincing a federal judge they were legitimate conscientious objectors although in the service. Their antiwar feeling crystallized during their training. They reported that their instructors informed them they might be required to maintain a "kill quota" of fifty Viet Cong a month. The Army unsuccessfully fought their honorable discharge and denied such nefarious activities. However, by late 1969 there were public reports of U.S.-led teams ranging stealthily through enemy-held territory, raiding hamlets, torturing suspects to gain information, taking or killing prisoners. At one time, the swift decapitation of identified VC leaders was a common practice of the South Vietnamese team members. "These were the ears-and-head guys," remarked one former U.S. adviser in 1970. "They were paid so much for the ear of a VC cadre and so much for the head of a VC leader."[3]

In congressional testimony, two former U.S. military intelligence agents testified that Vietnamese "were indiscriminately rounded up, tortured, and murdered by Americans in the effort to eliminate Viet Cong cadres." Another former agent, K. Barton Osborn, testified that in a year and a half he "never knew an individual to be detained as a VC suspect who ever lived through an interrogation—and that included quite a number of individuals."[4]

The memories pound away in Hansen's mind. "At the time, I didn't question. I thought I was doing something right. We actually thought it was something to help the war effort—but you can't help but blame yourself now. . . ."

Still, he points out something that the radical left refused to acknowledge about Vietnam and that was the murder and terror tactics of the other side. The Viet Cong countered with the death and torture of Vietnamese civilians suspected of cooperating with Operation Phoenix.[5]

"In many instances," continues Hansen, "myself and my team would go to a village and we would give them fatigues, boots, belts, food, take care of the children. We had a medic with us. Sometimes we had a chance to walk back through a village that was helpful to us and see some of the cruelty inflicted on them just because they *accepted* our help. They were not *collaborating*. In this one village there were two old ladies left, sitting crying. We searched the hooches." His eyes welled up. "There was nothing but legs, arms in some. We found where they had taken the men and boys and we went on a vengeance trip and leveled it. You wanted to be crueler to them than they were to those people."

Wilder interjects, "It got to the point where, if I lost a guy, twenty had to go on the other side. Where I was, anything that moved at night was killed. Soldiers are trained to fight and kill. If you put them in a war, they're *going* to fight and kill—and when they come home you can't tell them it was *wrong*. That's where the problem comes in. I still feel for those Vietnamese people stuck in that country who can't get out. . . ."

"When we got back from that time, we went in for debriefing," continues Hansen. "My CO said, 'I hope you got it out of your system. It's not going to be done like that anymore.' We risked our lives for revenge or payback." Such incidents created terrible conflict in Hansen. "The next time you saw a kid, you were still sensitive. You wanted to do something for him, give him something. But now a lot of guys were afraid to show affection. If you helped them, they might get hurt."

Wenzel interjects, "How do you set a child on your knee if you've ever blown one away?"

Al says, "With my kids, I'm so overprotective . . ."

Hansen: "You spend a lot of time trying to make up. I *gave* away a living room suite to a friend. Couldn't believe I did that. Or that I lent a car to a guy for three months. I wasn't atoning, by no means, still . . ."

We talked about this paradoxical combination of generosity and distance among many veterans. "You would give your family everything and anything, but you're still detached and they sense that." Hansen has been married three times and has two young children. "I would give them anything—but if anything happened to them, there would be a hardness that's embedded in me." All the men see a deep pain in reopening the wounds, in becoming vulnerable. "It's like opening up an appendectomy scar," Hansen said.

He starts talking about his childhood. "A lot of psychiatrists want to say that the way you were brought up before Vietnam molded your life and that's why you can't adjust. To a certain extent there's some truth there, but you can't blame it all on that.

"I wasn't happy as a child. My father and I never got along. He was in the Korean War, decorated, and he couldn't adjust either. He was authoritarian and drinking all the time. My mother and him would get into fights. One day I thought he was going to strike my mother. I took a fork and stabbed him in the shoulder and ran out of the house. I was six and a half. Next day they shipped me off to a Catholic boarding school."

That was the only violent act of his childhood, Hansen says. He was not aggressive. "Quite the contrary. I was pretty much a quiet kid.

"I think my childhood only made me a little bit more controlled in Vietnam," he goes on, pouring out his story in a disquieting monotone. "When we went through screening, they wanted to make sure we were psychologically capable of killing people on a more personal basis, without creating a machine—a human doomsday device. There were three psychologists and two shrinks who wanted to see if we could kill, day in and day out. Personal yet impersonal. We had the inkblot tests, word-association tests. Like, they would say, 'What would you associate with the color red?' I said, 'A crayon.' They said why? 'Because it's a color.'"

Do you think they were expecting you to say you associated it with blood?

"I don't *know* what they would have thought. After we got home, we had all kinds of tests again, to see that they weren't letting an incorrigible out in the streets. All of us were *very* self-controlled. That's what it was like during my childhood. If I firmly *believed* a rule was right, I obeyed it. In Vietnam I accepted what I did. I don't have any problems with it now, really." Hansen is clearly awash with conflicting emotions. Later Hansen contradicts himself. "It does bother me. I have nightmares about a lot of things. I'm not blaming myself or the military. If I did wrong, I'll suffer the consequences." He looks around the ward. "Maybe this is the consequence."

"I'm scared of myself," Hansen adds later, "because of the destructiveness I'm capable of. And I wasn't that way before Vietnam."

The men are anxious about what will happen to them when they leave the program. "There's these old guys here, drawing $1,140 a month compensation and never even saw a war. They're nuts and they've been here since this place opened twenty years ago," says Wenzel. "But Vietnam veterans in here have to fight to get benefits. We can't stay indefinitely. In three months I'm supposed to find a place to stay."

Wilder explains, "It takes some six months to process a claim for delayed stress. I got service connected in March and I put in the claim last July. It's 100 percent disability—$1,322 a month—as long as I'm in the hospital. When I leave, there will be a final adjudication to determine whether it should be 10 percent, 30 percent, or whatever."

For Wenzel, the luck of the draw was different. "Adjudication turned me down. I was sent to a guy who wasn't familiar with delayed stress. Most doctors even tell you flat out they don't believe in it. We don't get to see the adjudication board." Wenzel adds in angry jest, "That's the only reason they stay alive."

He burns at the way the government money is being spent for defense. "One tank would pay for this program across the country."

They worry about life outside. "We don't know yet what kind of stigma there will be from being in here," says Wenzel. "The doctors say that on a job application to leave that part out. How do you leave out five or seven months of your life? How many people have any understanding of this? How many are going to run when you say, 'This man has been in a psychiatric ward'?"

"It's bad enough being a Vietnam veteran," says Wilder.

Hansen has read with a fine eye newspaper accounts of Vietnam veterans. He reiterates an anger felt by many. "Four days straight, they ran a story of a Vietnam veteran who killed his family and himself. And then a story about another who ran a car into a wall. Next day my girlfriend said, 'Did you read the paper? What did you think they did *that* for?' " For outsiders, there is always the lingering, negative Vietnam connection, Hansen feels.

"That's why most don't tell they are vets. Your neighbors don't know. I'm flat serious about that." Wenzel agrees. "People shy away from you."

It is time to go. In Hansen's sparse and neat cubbyhole, there is a picture of a girl, a paint-by-numbers picture, a cup with LOVE on it, and a poster. The poster shows a line of rock-climbing soldiers silhouetted on the face of a hill. He insists on taking it from the wall and offering it as a present. I reach to touch his arm, some gesture of thanks and hope for his future. He immediately stiffens.

As the elevator door closes, I see Wenzel and Hansen, staring goodbye.

In the car, the poster is unfolded. Thinking of Hansen, the words to the Army recruitment song—bald appeal to uncertain youth—have a special, bitter poignance.

> *You're somebody special*
> *So much you're gonna do*
> *So you're gonna reach out and take it*
> *'Cause it's all there waiting for you.*
>
> *Be all you can be,*
> *Keep on reachin'*
> *Keep on growin'*
> *Be all that you can be*
> *'Cause we need you in the Army.*

6 The Significant Others

AL WILDER WHEELED HIS CAR OUT OF THE BAY PINES LOT. ON RELEASE for the weekend, he was going home to his family a short distance away, near St. Petersburg Beach.

"You *have* to talk to Phyllis," he said. "I don't know how she puts up with me."

On the way, Wilder filled in the past. At thirty-eight, his dark hair was beginning to thin, yet a surface vestige of a boyish, easygoing personality remains. He joined the Army at seventeen, anxious to leave his small Georgia town. "I didn't like the ignorance you sometimes have in a Southern community." He loved the military: Europe, OCS, then Vietnam in 1966 as a second lieutenant. He had been in country only four months when his platoon was ambushed in a firefight. "It lasted forty-five minutes to an hour. I got shot through the left front thigh. I was due for promotion to captain; they wanted to send me to psychological warfare. I couldn't walk without the aid of a cane. I got up and broke the darn cane—and never used it again."

Out of the service, Wilder was "bitter, unhappy. It's hard to explain. The craziness of shooting up the streetlights. As a teenager I'd never been in trouble. Loved water skiing, had *lots* of friends. Vietnam altered my thinking. I have no fears—but instead of freeing you up, that causes problems. If you're doing something against the law, like writing bad checks, you don't fear reprisal. I just lost respect for everything after Vietnam. Now I feel politicians are as crooked as the day is long. Everything I learned as a kid turned out to be a damn lie."

The first time Wilder overdosed, he took every pill he could find in the medicine chest. The second time, he planned it for three weeks. "I took enough—100 tablets of 50 mg. of Elavil—to kill four of us. I got them from out-patient care. Their philosophy was just, load you up. I saved them.

"The depression is constant. I guess it's just failure. Everything seems to turn out bad. There were seventeen different businesses. When I didn't fail, I walked away. I was doing real well, had some interest in a firm manufacturing refuse containers, grossing $100,000 a month. I walked away from it."

Wilder outlined a spiral of anxiety and guilt. "You hate yourself for what you put your family through, like disappearing and the fights that's caused, because they don't understand. Whenever I felt anxiety I would just leave, rather than inflict that on them."

Do you feel Vietnam contributed to this?

"It's a combination of that and the fact I gave my youth to the military. [It would later be revealed that he has guilt over the death of men in his platoon.] The military fulfills all your needs. You have their moral standards; no need to formulate your own." Once Wilder left Vietnam and the military—which he had hoped to make his career—he seemed incapable of making and sticking to decisions.

At the moment, he seemed upset about leaving Steve Hansen, the most lost and depressed of the hospitalized trio, for the weekend. "He defends Phoenix and all that because that's still part of the denial. He wants to believe that he isn't that bad off—or if he is, that it had nothing to do with Vietnam."

None of this defense squares with the haunted man Wilder sees. "I finally just got him to eat last night. We barbecued hamburgers on the grill at the beach."

Such intense companionship for one another among the veterans often leaves families feeling resentful, bitter, and outside the problem and the treatment. "I don't know any vets who are happy," says Wilder, "but until last year I was never involved with any. I always thought this was just the way I was. I didn't know anyone else felt the same."

As we turn up a quiet residential street, Wilder says, "I'm probably one of the very few combat veterans who has been married nineteen years—and to the same wife." Some statistics bear him out. The DAV (Disabled American Veterans), in its readjustment outreach program presentation, used this statistic: Of the married veterans, 38 percent were divorced within six months of their return from Vietnam. However, there are no definitive studies on veterans' divorce or how they compare with their nongoing peers.

It could be the scene of any father returning from work: a world of tricycles and bicycles, cats and dogs, skateboards and boats anchored in backyards. Michelle, twelve, Lisa, ten, and Joey, fifteen, turn from the television with just the same amount of interest that many a working parent has heard. "Hi, Dad."

Phyllis and Al say their hellos in the offhand gestures of any long-wed couple, yet something else is present. An undercurrent of angry futility seems to permeate Phyllis. She sits on an enclosed porch in the Florida heat, drinking iced tea. Five years older than her husband, she has gained weight and her face, under short-cropped bleached blond hair, is without makeup or artifice. There are no attempts to smile or put on an act for an unexpected visitor.

Blunt and honest from the beginning, Phyllis says flatly, "Vietnam ruined our lives. Totally tore our lives apart." She shouts to Al, fiddling with the lawn mower in the backyard. "Al, how honest you want me to be?" He says to tell the truth.

They met in Germany in the early sixties—a romantic, exciting time. Phyllis was in the Army Intelligence Corps, interrogating defectors from Berlin. Three years later, as Wilder was on his way to Vietnam, Phyllis found out she was pregnant. "It seemed a miracle—our first child after three years of trying."

There were eager letters of love and concern, a time she clings to now. "I keep remembering the Alan of before. After all, we had been married three years. He was affectionate, considerate, kind. It sounds like a storybook, but it's true. When he returned he had a quick temper, no patience, could not concentrate. I can't say all the problems are Vietnam but, like I say, I keep remembering him before.

"Alan does not physically abuse me—but he's been so unfaithful so many times I've lost count. He was *never* before. Not a mean bone in his body. There was never anything in his character that would make you think he could be this way. He was loved by everyone who knew him."

Wilder returned to the United States when Phyllis was in the final stages of her pregnancy. They were living in Chicago. "Alan took me for a checkup. He was in uniform, using a cane, and this lady, as she walked by, spit on him. I'll never forget it."

The antiwar climate at home left many families feeling as isolated and disturbed as their men. "When Alan was in Vietnam, my stomach would turn when I would see them burning draft cards, not knowing if he would ever see the baby. I was always proud that Alan accomplished what he did. He went from enlisted to officer. There's nothing that man couldn't do.

"Since then it's been a nightmare. What happened in Vietnam, I don't know. Alan does not talk to me about it. He got the Bronze Star. He fought to stay conscious and called in the artillery after he was wounded in that ambush." There are certain nightmares, a nervousness in the tropical rainstorms of Florida, but little talk. Mostly, there is just the unpredictable and maddening disappearing from their lives.

I told Phyllis that Alan seemed grateful for her, that he had remarked, "I don't know how she puts up with me." She replies, both angrily and wistfully, "That's the first *I've* heard of it."

There seems a Walter Mitty quality to Alan's disappearances. "His affairs never lasted long. He wined and dined them like he was living in another world. He was pretending to be something he wasn't. Like, he'd say he was an airplane pilot. They didn't know the difference."

She sighs. "See, Alan is very sure of me."

That you won't leave him?

"I won't say that. Right now, I'm torn inside. Probably the biggest reason he is sure of me is that he knows I love him." Her voice goes firm. "But right now, I do not *like* him. What he's done to us.

"Both times he O.D.'d it was a shock. First time, the kids and I walked in and he was sitting on the floor, crying and rocking back and forth. The second time was on Rosh Hoshanah. We got back from my parents'. Something made me wake up that night. I found him unconscious on the floor in the living room. I called the paramedics. He was unconscious three days in intensive care." The voice turns bitter. "When I saw my son crying, 'Dad, we love you, we need you, don't leave us . . .', one part of me wanted to *kill* Alan for doing this and one part felt so sorry for him that he had to do that."

Suicidal patterns of Vietnam veterans have taken terrible toll on many families. "Joey's been in the hospital for *ulcers,* at *fifteen.* He is a boy with twenty certificates of scholastic achievement, bar mitzvahed. He won an art scholastic award, competed in the whole state of Florida. When his father O.D.'d, Joey got into trouble for the first time in his life. The school door was open and he went in and smashed some things up. The kids and I go to a mental health clinic to try to deal with this. What more can I do to understand this? Sometimes he's made me feel less than a woman. Why do I stay? First, I believe in the family unit. The kids idolize him. On the whole he's gentle with them. He doesn't discipline and comes off as a good guy. I come off as the nag. Still, they can't help but feel edgy about him."

Phyllis is more than a little disgruntled at the treatment the men get in Vet Centers and at Bay Pines. "They build this world for them there and work on *their* problems. *Well, what about ours?* I am tired of hearing about what these guys are going through. I went to a wives' group and I walked away worse than when I went in.

"One of the women was concerned about her sex life and the attitude was: 'Well, you shouldn't be talking about that right now.' That somehow we're selfish when we talk about *our* needs, our *children's* needs. Don't they think we've suffered any?"

It is a continuing theme of feeling left out, a cry for someone to listen to her. "It's 'They count and *only* them. Like the ball games. Joe would like to join, but they say, 'No, it's only for them.' I feel the family should be brought in more. I go to the women's groups, but I don't need six women saying, 'My husband did this' or 'My husband did that.' I want *answers.*

"I did not know of delayed stress. I just thought he was a son of a bitch, to be honest. First I heard of it was when he O.D.'d." Phyllis is in a new group of wives. "Now I talk with some wives and it's uncanny. A new woman came in, doesn't know me from Adam. It is the same story of my life. I wonder, How could you have all the symptoms the same if there wasn't some common cause? Stress is one thing, but this is so similar: unfaithfulness, antiauthoritarian, not caring about anything, not being able to hold jobs. From all over, I hear the same story."

Cynics could argue that such symptoms are not known to Vietnam veterans alone. After all, divorce courts are filled with women detailing the same complaints. However, those who work with veterans say they manifest such traits to a heightened degree. And where they are able to obtain family history, as in the case of the Wilders, the difference before and after Vietnam is often striking.

Some wives have complained that the female Vet Centers are filled with girlfriends and wives who are "whiners and complainers." Still they, like their men, often benefit from the camaraderie. The hardest part, for many, has been the pressure of going it alone and receiving no sympathy. "My mother is very domineering. Typical Jewish mother. 'What kind of hospital *is* this'—she asks—'that Alan can come and go? This delayed stress is a cop-out—so now he doesn't have to take care of his family!' "

Like many couples, Alan and Phyllis seemed to have married each other to fulfill missing traits in themselves. She has a Northerner's bluntness; Alan was not used to confronting feelings.

"Alan's family is extremely cold. His dad died when he was thirteen. I was from a family that celebrated birthdays, everything. We are a kissing family. I could see Alan reaching out, before Vietnam, for affection and love—and he *gave* it. When he came back, he was very cold. He had a good friend, another lieutenant, who had his arm blown off." She reveals a significant guilt. "A lot of men were lost and he blames himself, although he doesn't say much about it."

Phyllis remained skeptical of the Bay Pines treatment. Alan has been four months in the combat unit delayed-stress group.

She sighs, "Now they're talking about sending him to school. A 'no-stress situation.' Well, damn it, that's life out here! They're being too coddled. The only positive is, I know he's *there* and can talk to someone. I know he's not home—or running around. But is this the way we're going to be for the rest of our lives? When the guys come out, the wives, all this time, have such bitterness and hostility that *they're* ready to explode. It's for *me* to say these things to Alan. Not for me to go and bitch to another woman. You know, I think if he said, 'I'm sorry for all the BS I've put you through' and really meant it, it would wipe out all the bitterness."

There have been hard times. "Alan has no value of anything." Right now, the garage is filled with ceramics and molds. The two of them make ceramic knickknacks—Florida ashtrays with birds, fish, palm trees—and sell them to gift shops.

"We're hanging on," says Phyllis.

What would it have been like if he had not gone to Vietnam? She sighs. "At this stage of the game, he would be settled in his own business or in some line of work. We'd have money in the bank. We'd be doing a little more."

How does she see the future?

"Scary."

Why does she stick it out?

"I don't know. We're used to each other. Basically, we care for each other."

But for now, it is sometimes easier when Alan is at the hospital. "It's great when he's gone. On weekends, it's like walking on thin ice."

Joey jumps up nervously when his father says he is leaving the house to drive me home. "Can I go with you, Dad?" Alan Wilder nods yes. In the car there is idle chatter about school.

Joey has a boat, a gift from his grandfather. There is just of hint of pleading, a longing for a normal Sunday afternoon, an edge to the question, a need for security in Joey's voice.

"Dad, can we go out tomorrow on the boat? Can we, huh?" "Sure, Joey," said Wilder, a nearly imperceptible sadness to his voice. "Sure, son."

They are called "significant others" in the jargon of psychologists and sociologists attempting neatly to package all the mothers, wives, girlfriends, children, fathers, cousins, aunts, uncles of Vietnam veterans. They are a civilian "army" of millions who were deeply affected by the tragedies of Vietnam.

Of those most "significant others"—the wives or girlfriends—little is known about those married to or living with veterans who have not surfaced with problems; the men who are either coping or suffering silently, the men who are either genuinely successful in putting Vietnam behind them or are steeped in workaholic denial. Only recently, in fact, have the Phyllis Wilders —living with or married to veterans with delayed stress—been considered vital components in the therapeutic process. Their own problems, needs, anxieties, strengths, and weaknesses are now being examined in several Vet Centers, run by both the VA and Disabled American Veterans (DAV).

To date, there is no national study of the special implications or repercussions of Vietnam veteran delayed stress among their wives and girlfriends. Studies have shown that married men in general are consistently better off, mentally and physically, than unmarried men. Unmarried men and women have higher mortality rates due to suicide, murder, accidents, cirrhosis of the liver, lung cancer, TB, and diabetes than married men and women—and this effect is consistently stronger for men compared with women.[1] However, the *degree* of spouse support in a union has important consequences for both mental and physical health.

When comparing Vietnam combat veterans with noncombat or era veterans and a third group of nongoing peers, there are devastating differences. In one major study of the Vietnam Generation, married men in all three groups are consistently better off, in terms of psychological adjustment, than men who are not married. However, this effect is heightened for Vietnam veterans. Those with low spouse support were extremely demoralized and stressed. In many instances, a terrible relationship was far worse than being single. While combat exposure alone tends to increase the probability of psychological problems, unmarried men and married men with little spouse support were drastically more troubled. *A full half of these men are demoralized and experiencing stress reactions.* Conversely—and this may be a major factor in differentiating between combat veterans who have made successful readjustments and those who have not—men who had *high* spouse support were as well off psychologically as men who experienced no combat.[2]

The study concludes that being married—and happily so—does reduce the deleterious psychological effects of combat exposure. Not only that, being unmarried tends to have an effect in preserving stress reactions. Some 51 percent of the married who had a stress condition at the time they left the service still experience stress reaction. However, 71 percent—a full 20 percent *more*—of the unmarried men with past stress conditions also report having them now.[3]

Leaving aside the probability that some selection process is at work (i.e., those with troubled personalities may have difficulty finding or keeping a mate) or that social factors play a part in the unmarried's sense of self-worth, the study strongly shows that wives and girlfriends play a vital part in the well-being of combat veterans in particular.

Veterans themselves support this view. The maimed and mutilated men left by wives and girlfriends to linger through long rehabilitation struggles were among the earliest Vietnam drug and suicide casualties. While college girls were making love with their nongoing colleagues to the Beatles or the Rolling Stones, country bars were playing a different ballad. It was the mournful dirge of a veteran wounded in "that there Asian war," begging his wandering girlfriend, "Ruby, Don't Take Your Love to Town."

Veterans often have said they could not have made it through this past decade without wives or girlfriends. Few of the men and women can articulate the intangible and deeply personal emotional benefits of such relationships. Mostly it is a sense of being there, of not giving up hope, of standing by. In Muncie, Indiana, Lonnie Sparks's wife watches as he sits in their backyard, hoisting his two daughters over his shoulders as they giggle with delight. Lonnie's arms have a strength far beyond the average man's. Both his legs were sheared off at the hips by a land mine.

Becky was working in the beauty parlor, setting a customer's hair for the bouffants that were teased to astonishing heights in those days, when her father walked in with their minister. She knew instantly that something terrible had happened to Lonnie. At home, the Western Union telegram, the kind that came to families all over America in 1967, waited on the TV set.

A decade later, she held out a fistful of the weathered telegrams. "I couldn't take my eyes off this one line, 'traumatic amputation of the leg.' " By the time she saw her husband in the Denver hospital, he had gone through his "mental sorting out and depression." A man of few words, Lonnie Sparks says today that he never worried about his wife leaving him; "That was up to her."

As she watched Lonnie Sparks playing with her children, both of them born after he returned from Vietnam, Becky seemed truly puzzled why other wives would be so repulsed by a husband's war wounds as to leave. She offers no explanation of her acceptance.

As Sparks agilely pushed himself up with his arms and into his wheelchair, Becky recalled the curious stares. "Adults would follow us up the aisles in stores, acting like children." A hint of irritation crossed her pretty face. "I was always 'the gal that was married to the guy with no legs.' I wasn't 'Lonnie's wife' like I was before."

Another woman in the Midwest, attractive with deep brown eyes and shoulder-length brunette hair, looks over at her husband casually sticking the stump of one leg into his prosthesis and loafer. She does not want her name used as she speaks of her initial revulsion. She had remembered him the way he was: running on the beach, playing tennis, making love. At first, her husband deliberately left the stump barren of his stocking, forcing her to face the worst. "I wanted her to confront this ugly-looking thing from the start. If it was a problem, I didn't want her to feel she had to stay." A feisty, humorous man, he went back to school and is now a successful lawyer.

"It didn't take me long," his wife said, "to realize it wasn't his *leg* that mattered, it was him."

Delayed stress was a mysterious crippler of another sort, that left no visible scars. In many ways, wives and girlfriends were faced with a struggle that was, if not harder, more demolishing to *their* self-esteem. Living with men who seldom spoke of their troubles, flew into rages, drank too much, were verbally abusive or couldn't keep their jobs, the uncomprehending women often turned bitter, defensive, hostile.

By the time they sought help, many were as troubled in their own way as their husbands. Candis M. Williams, married to Tom Williams, a clinical psychologist and Vietnam veteran, is herself a clinical psychologist. While she was studying for her degree, Candis began one of the first women's groups at the DAV Outreach Center in Denver. In 1980 she corroborated some of Phyllis's anger. "It has been a frequent bias in psychology to focus on the individual who has problems, which essentially ignores the effects felt by those who are close." This is compounded by the fact that the veterans and therapists are men, talking about a male-dominated war-related phenomenon. Their wives—bystanders to disaster—are still trying to comprehend a war that happened 13,000 miles away. The partner is not considered to have special problems herself, nor problems related to her husband's poor adjustment. In addition, women are products of a culture that views them as the supportive care-givers; they can often be conflicted about seeking help.

Williams found that most of the women in the group felt they had failed to get results with their nurturing, caring, and supportive roles.

They had little self-esteem and identity and, like the men, felt helpless and demoralized. Of course, they brought individual characteristics and problems, different needs and expectations, with them. One dilemma is that there is no common denominator among these women other than the war experiences of their men. Counselors like Williams, trying to foster more self-esteem and independence, increased marital adjustment, and decreased helplessness, worried that women's support groups would be just another women's auxiliary. Williams found that some women benefited greatly and others did not improve. "Letting off steam" and sharing with others seemed to be a crucial benefit, however, for most.

Many of the women did not come to the relationship untroubled. "I suspect that many of the women partners—and most of those who met their partners following the war—had deficient life-coping skills to begin with and brought these into the relationship. Hence, we have not one but *two* persons coming together who have equally poor self-concepts and minimal experience in maintaining healthy relationships," Williams theorized. The inference is that men with problems were attracted to women with problems and vice versa. "This is a broad assumption, but, to the extent that it is applicable, there is all the more reason to include women partners in treatment. Many of these women would not be in such dysfunctional states were it not for their partners."[4]

This is an important point. In interviews with wives and girlfriends across the country, I have witnessed many similar women. Some of them were given to high drama and bombast; others were shy to the point of being monosyllabic. Many had personality problems. Many, frankly, seemed to be whining their lives away with minimal education, skills, or desire to do anything more. Some had married confused men out of a deep need to find someone less whole than they. Others could be sardonically humorous about their plight.

The problems with their men, however, do follow the already enumerated pattern. Phyllis Wilder might take small comfort in one item in a list of wives' classic reactions cited by Williams: "She is anguished by the man's frequent extramarital affairs."

Women frequently describe their husband thus: irresponsible, exhibiting erratic behavior without reason, such as rage alternating with remorse (termed a Jekyll-Hyde Syndrome), extremely demanding and considers only his needs, isolates himself with a leave-me-alone attitude, unable to express or share feelings, to handle frustrations or even the good things that come along —a feeling that he is unworthy. He lacks self-esteem, suffers great insecurity, and feels worthless and helpless. As with the Wilders, a common pattern is that both partners build defensive barriers and are unable to be supportive of each other.

Although some of the veterans can become quite violent, wife beating does not fit the usual battering pattern, which is characterized by two or three abusive incidents which are then continued in a cycle that is almost impossible to break. With veteran couples, there seem to have been one or two incidents which are extremely frightening—often for both partners—and are *not* repeated. In fact, it is common for one if not both partners to seek outside help.

On the other hand, veterans can often display a deceptive and ominous meekness that masks seething, near-lethal anger. It can be terrifying for those close enough to recognize that a volcanic eruption is being suppressed. "My husband will take a seat by the kitchen in a restaurant, ask for a steak rare and get it well done, and *never* complain," one wife said. He scared her with his quiet explanation. "I am so afraid to let go—because I think I would go completely out of control." Many wives mention this behavior pattern.

As one veteran explained it to me, "If some guy cut you off the road, you might give him the finger, honk the horn, or shout through the window. *I* would chase him, force him off the road, drag him out of the car, and beat him to a pulp. I did it once and, believe me, it scares me to live with that kind of rage."

And then, with their seductive charms, there are the others who can be gentle and sensitive-appearing—but never, ever, let anyone get close.

He poured out the lotion and in quick, even strokes began to massage her back. They had been out together a few times, but there had always been a certain restraint. He was different from the other men she had met in law school. He was older, for one thing, but there was a cutting edge to his maturity that she could not grasp.

Now they were at a friend's house for the weekend. They had been in the hot tub and had smoked a joint. She was moving into a state of complete relaxation, concentrating on nothing more than the tactile pleasures of his hands.

Slowly, slowly he started to trace the stiffened muscles, using the heels of his hands to ease out the small aches and pains. Down the neck, the shoulders, through the small of her back, then back up to her shoulders. She put her hand up, over her shoulder, and their fingers touched. Suddenly she rolled over and they began to kiss, deep, long, passionate kisses. His mouth traced down from her mouth to her neck as he undid her robe, then moved slowly and gently over her breasts and down her body. He parted her thighs and the only sound in the room was the rock music he insisted on playing constantly, a backdrop to his life, and her soft moans as he kissed her over and over until she came. They made love easily, tenderly, and passionately. She was astonished by his tenderness as they made love and then, later, as they lay cuddled close, his arms locked around her for hours. His body was beautiful, with long, slender legs.

He had killed—and often—in Vietnam, from a helicopter that raced across the earth. Once he felt comfortable with her, he talked about Vietnam in a surface way, particularly about the death of a friend. After a while she would try to mask the boredom, wishing he would get on to other things. Still, there was always this sweet tenderness.

It had not always been that way. When he first came back, he could not make love to anyone. He had been nineteen when he went over, a high school athlete and class president who, one afternoon, took his cheerleader girlfriend to his parents' home when they were out of town. They fumbled through a quick and unsatisfactory grope that led to her loss of virginity and to his fear that she would write him a letter at boot camp that she was pregnant. That letter, fortunately, never came.

In Vietnam it had been put your money down and take your chances. He could still remember the crassness in the transaction. "Fuckee fuckee, suckee suckee," the almond-eyed whores, who were really just girls, would say to the men, who were really just boys. Occasionally there was a nurse, but her feelings, too, had been so cauterized by the war that it was a desperate mutual need to break the tension, not much else.

Being with women who expected more was something he could not handle for months.

They saw each other for three years, living together the last year. He smoked pot the first thing in the morning, drank beer for breakfast, scotch at night. It astounded her that he could study and keep his grades up and carry on lucid conversations. His IQ was exceptional; he grasped things quicker than most and so he was able to compete in school. Still, his incessant pot-smoking isolated him from others. A postwar marriage had ended in divorce. He was devoted to his son when he saw him, but quickly admitted that the boy's normal seven-year-old rambunctiousness made him nervous. He willingly relinquished the child to his mother. He blamed himself for a terminal selfishness, then would cry out of desperation, knowing that his unexpressed emotions were deeper than that.

One day his girlfriend came home from classes and realized that her lover had spent the entire day in bed, stoned. The rock station, as always, blared too loud to talk. She shouted that he was being selfish, thinking only of himself, that he had to face the future. He didn't get angry. Didn't even react. She knew then that nothing she said or did would make much difference.

They drifted apart. Occasionally she wonders what happened to him. For a long time her heart grieved for something that could have been. The bad times were not remembered—only that special sensitivity and tenderness that would slip through.

Many of the men went to Vietnam too young to have formed close sexual relationships. And in Vietnam they missed a vital phase of adolescence—establishing intimacy with females. "It was difficult to try to establish real relationships with women when you came home—after you've bounced in and out of claptrap houses in Vietnam," says one counselor. "What's acceptable in war is not acceptable by American standards. Warriors *fuck* women, you don't *make love.* And there is another point. The most severe problems we see concerning sex come from combat veterans who were involved in killing women and children."

I mentioned a captain, Thomas Carhart, who had spoken of the hard-on he got in battle. While most other combat veterans appear dubious at such a physical response, some do not. "There *is* something psychologically very close about sex and violence. A lot of guys experience an involuntary erection, that's been documented through wars," says the counselor. "Now an eighteen- or nineteen-year-old gets this erection during a firefight and he says, 'There's something going on here I don't understand, but I *do* understand that it happened when I was killing people.' He can make a simplistic, frightening connection, 'Was I *enjoying* doing this?' "

Some of the men's feelings about sex and battle are tied together in murky ways that their women cannot possibly understand. "A lot of women and children and old people who were just civilians were killed. We weren't prepared to do that. Damn it, we were brought up to kill *men* in warfare," said one veteran. Some could not have sex on their return; others could, but could not establish close relationships. It was as if their compassion valve was shut off. Others denied there was any problem, but were cold to their women. A common feeling of many veterans, especially those who had close friends killed in Vietnam, is a fear of getting intimate. On the other hand, they can still manifest a near-aching sensitivity that can be very appealing to a woman bent on nurturing a man.

William Mahedy, who counseled soldiers in Vietnam and for a decade after the war, said feelings of intimacy were frozen to survive in Vietnam. "Obviously, all through life tremendously crucial things occur, but the older you are, the less chance there is that they are going to alter your basic path. When you're nineteen, you're still pliable. A lot of veterans say, 'I would *like* to care. I would *like* to love my wife, but I can't emotionally.' The maturity has been arrested. You have some that say, 'That's no problem, crying, caring, being gentle'—that's the problem in the abstract because they *are* all different people and they had different experiences. Still, the Vietnam veteran has a very peculiar combination of machismo and sensitivity. As much as the John Wayne culture is rejected—and these guys will tell you that the John Wayne stuff is just horseshit—there's still a lot of machismo out there. Because Vietnam was the most macho game in town. John Wayne was a terrible actor, but he epitomized something that has been there since our Colonial roots.

"You see a lot who don't want to have kids—maybe they killed children in Vietnam," says Mahedy. "Maybe they just don't think the world is any place to bring in children. Maybe the life and spontaneity of a child make them uncomfortable because they can no longer feel that way. There are just all kinds of possibilities. And then you see men whose prime love is their three-year-old child. Sometimes this is *more* precious because they've seen death or because they might not be able to have an intimate relationship with the wife, so they concentrate on the child. On the other hand, you have a lot of veterans who are afraid they might throw the kid across the room.

"There often coexists what appears to be opposite emotions in the same person. I just find I learn something new every day."

Mahedy returns often to the arrested adolescent theme. "If they could stay seventeen forever, there'd be no problem, but they are adults now. Most women *know* by the age of nineteen that sex should involve tenderness and sensitivity and fondling. Most men don't. The average eighteen-year-old American male has his mind firmly on his genitals. The time of learning is in late adolescence, when he finds out what the woman really needs. Now, if that was arrested by war and you come back with that experience sitting in your system, it could be very difficult to sort out.

"Remember, three out of four vets overcome such problems—if you believe the statistics. Life itself is able to break through some of these things. The realization dawns, 'I'll take the risk and love again.' Vietnam is there, but integrated."

For years immediately after the war, wives would drag their husbands in, insisting they were crazy. William Mahedy used to stop them cold with his appraisal. He would look at the two of them, never having discussed anything with them, and say to the husband, "I bet you won't sit with your back to a door in a restaurant." And the wife would blurt out, "Why, no, he won't." Then Mahedy would say, "I bet he won't kick a can or walk on a piece of paper." The woman, her eyes widening, would nod that he was again correct. "I bet you he will always take a different route to and from work." The woman by then demanded, "How do you know all this?" Mahedy recalls, after seeing the latent responses of nervous combat veterans, "I can just click them right off. She thinks he's bonkers and *he* thinks he's bonkers. And when he walks in some center and someone says, 'Welcome to the club, you're one of several thousand'—what relief!"

In listening to wives of veterans, it is important to keep in mind personal dynamics. In all close relationships there are patterns to rage and anger, inability to express emotions or to understand one another—but in dysfunctional families they tend to *rigidify*. When the counselor helps the veteran to improve or change, he is also altering the rules and roles of his family. Sometimes wives undercut the treatment for no other reason than that they are frightened of any kind of change, no matter how "beneficial."

A great fear of veterans is that wives will be shocked at their war experiences and respect them less. Once acceptance is gained, the fear of openness may dissipate, along with many of his problems. Often the marriage is being stressed by problems other than the Vietnam experience. These events put pressure on the veteran, perhaps because they place him in a position of impotence, anger, or guilt similar to what he felt in Vietnam. His actions also may serve to keep the marriage together, as his wife might leave him if he were 'well.' Or he may feel trapped and be using his combat-related problem as a threat or weapon which she is unable to counter.[5]

Wives tend to personalize and blame themselves when things go wrong, even though the men are more likely troubled by unresolved conflicts about Vietnam.

David Harrington and Dr. Jeffrey Jay, who treat veterans and their wives in Washington, D.C., recounted the story of Tony. He saw his friend, a medic, stabbed to death by a Vietnamese mother while he was treating the rest of her family—father, grandmother, and infant—that had been detained for questioning. In the instant it took the woman to stab his friend, Tony shot with lightning automatic fire the entire family, including the infant. A decade later, Tony's wife said in group therapy that she thought his bitterness and indifference were reflections of her inadequacies. However, Tony admitted that he would not have children because he felt that a man who could react so quickly and violently was not fit to become a father.

Roger, who killed three Viet Cong and continued to fire at their inert bodies, felt years later that his actions were morally wrong. After many visits, sweating profusely, he finally told his story. When the group offered acceptance and understanding, he was able, for the first time, to describe to his wife his tangled reactions to Vietnam. She had assumed Roger was angry and hurt about something within their marriage, never guessing his behavior was related to his Vietnam experience.

A numbing emotional isolation has become an accepted part of everyday life among the families that Harrington and Jay see. Their objective is to get the veteran to fit the pieces of his war experience together, to understand without guilt or recrimination. He can then shed some of the psychological armor that has separated him from those close to him.

Obviously, there are myriad reasons for the turmoil these families are in. Treatment is complex and, for many, answers are uncertain. It is impossible to detail in one chapter a cure-all or even adequately to examine the techniques for family therapy and veterans. However, listening to the following women in one Florida group session may provide a glimmer of understanding.

The eight women had been together for several sessions in the Tampa Vet Center. When asked why they came and what they were getting out of the experiences, the answers were similar. They came out of a desperate need for companionship and support and to share their problems with someone else who understood.

Lana, blond with blue eyeshadow, tall, good-looking, quick-minded, said, "I came after talking to an 'outsider' friend not married to a veteran. I envied the way she and her husband could argue. They argue, it's a 'spat.' *We* argue and it's World War III. He leaves and comes home the next morning. He's been coming to group, so he's not that bad anymore."

Sandy came to the Vet Center when she was separated from her husband. "It helped me a great deal. We're back together." She shrugged and said sardonically, *"He's* one of those who 'does not have a problem.' " All the women laugh. "The support here for me is just fantastic."

Would that not happen if it were just any group of women, like the consciousness-raising sessions of the seventies, or Alanon? The women vigorously say no. "We're all in the same situation. Married to or living with vets." Is that enough commonality? They quickly chorus yes.

Lana takes over. "Even if we have different experiences, there are basics. The anger, depressions, inability to get along with others, low self-esteem, desire to die, not giving a shit. They figure they've already lived through Vietnam; what more can hurt them?"

The wives chime in. All their husbands had been in combat, some were alcoholics or on drugs. "He's into the hard stuff," said one. "It's hard to understand how he can take food out of our mouths and put it in his arm. He's talked to me more than anyone about what went on, but a lot of things he won't even touch on. He was in special forces and they blew up villages. When he did talk, he cried. You could see how hard it was for him. He got hooked over there. He's been in the hospital a couple of times, but it never worked out."

Sally, a slim, pretty, quiet girl, is younger than the rest. "I first came when I realized my boyfriend was an alcoholic. He had a seizure one night—screamed in pain. All he did was talk about dead bodies and the way the American soldiers used to put dead bodies together, arrange them in position like they were dancing. Just off-the-wall stuff. He could not remember a single thing the next day."

As her story unfolds, the girl appears to be one of those who had as many problems as her boyfriend; he found solace in someone as bad off as he was. "I had a couple of nervous breakdowns and he really grounded me a lot. He was very afraid of coming to the Vet Center. A lot are. They're afraid something's wrong with them and they don't want to admit it. He went through a rehabilitation program, but he's using alcohol again."

She was the only one in the group not living with her mate. "I couldn't stand the stress any longer. I've learned through coming here that I have to take care of myself. I'm going to school. I've decided to be healthily selfish, even though I still love him."

Many of the men opposed their wives' coming to the program. "I'm turning into a 'lesbian' or whatever for coming here," cracks a petite blonde. They all laugh. "There's that macho thing. They're afraid of us talking together. We've all changed since we started three months ago. We feel stronger—and they don't know how to take that. Before, when arguments would start, you'd argue back and tears would flow," starts one. They talk at once: "now you rise above it" . . . "get out of the emotional and into the intellectual."

Dee, with a heavy Southern accent dripping with good-humored sarcasm, said, "When I first started coming here, he told me it was a damn good idea. *I* had a helluva lot of problems." The women laugh knowingly. "Well, he wanted to know what 'the girls' said about *him* and I told him, 'I'm not going for *you*. I'm going for me. Your name wasn't even mentioned.' That just broke his heart. He's got a humongous ego."

Joe Gelsomino, the center director, brings up an important point that continually surfaces in his therapy: "The husband has a Vietnam-related problem and the wife or woman in his life tends to be the dumping ground for that. But she doesn't see Vietnam or himself as the problem—she sees herself as the problem. That cuts across all the groups."

"Just that knowledge alone has helped me quite a bit," says Sally. "Before this group, we all felt *we* caused these outbursts," said Lana. "They had a way of making us feel we were wrong." The women are not helped by other relatives or friends, who do not understand. They all speak of fathers and mothers who impatiently ask why their husbands just don't shape up.

"Even the Alanon people don't understand," chimes in a wife. "The normal alcoholic is different than the combat veteran alcoholic. He doesn't have half the struggle the Vietnam veteran has," says Penny, a nurse, married to a heroin addict. (This view is corroborated by experts on delayed stress who feel that a lot of the alcoholism among veterans is untreatable without association with veteran groups to help them understand their particular stresses.) "Alcoholics are going to drink, no matter *what*. But I know my husband takes heroin and drinks to deaden the pain he feels."

"I work in the field of psychiatry," Penny says and laughs before the rest do. Lana interjects. "We're all curious. We want to know why you got involved, with your background. I mean, we went in *blind*. She *worked* with Vietnam veterans with stress. So why did she marry one?"

"Glutton for punishment," said one wife. "Yeah," replied Penny, no longer laughing. We talked about the nurturing instinct. "I've thought about that," said Penny. "It could be. I don't know."

The talk turned to a central theme, that many of the men often manifested a depth of caring and compassion at odds with their stress behavior.

"There is caring for *other* people. You others don't live with them, see their weaknesses, vulnerabilities, bad points. You're an outsider and they're on stage with you. And I am *quoting* my husband," says Lana. "He is *exhausted* at the end of the day because he spends it 'on stage.' He's impressing everybody, helping everybody, breaking his butt to do everything that is not in his job description."

Do the men, aware of unfair negative stereotypes of veterans, have to prove to the outside world that they're good guys?

"Mine would do anything for anyone else. . . ." "Mine *is* a good guy." "He's kind, he's just screwed up. . . ." "Mine can be fantastic. . . ."

Penny, the nurse, says, "It's a need for acceptance, I think." The others nod.

"I think a lot of things that happened to Vietnam veterans are not more abnormal than with anyone else. It is just magnified," says Sally.

Why?

"Because of their level of frustration. Jim has a conflict about who he is that is constantly uppermost in his mind. So everything else that happens during the day gets blown out of proportion. Jim is *obsessed* by the change that came over him in Vietnam. What he had to become in order to survive. He is really very peace loving. Loves nature, meditative things. He's fascinated by werewolf movies. He identifies with the Dr. Jekyll and Mr. Hyde concept. A lot of times that's what he feels like. A mechanic worked on his car and he felt the mechanic did him in, but he avoided the confrontation because he was afraid of unleashing his anger. He's afraid of hurting me, like when we're making love. He's constantly absorbed with this conflict and so everything in his daily activity becomes an extremely arduous task."

Jim had one year of college, had demonstrated against the war and remained in conflict while in Vietnam. "His father said, 'All you have to do is this, Jim. That's all I'll ever ask of you.' He felt he had to go. Now he feels really, *really* bad. He thought about going to Canada, but he went to Vietnam against his conscience. When he got over there, it just reaffirmed everything he already believed. He quit the war. He was a gunner in a helicopter and after nine months he wouldn't go out anymore. And they didn't do anything to him. He stayed on the base, smoked pot, till they let him come home."

Other men of the wives in this group were apolitical or hawks or "military men," but they too came back troubled. Three of the wives had been married before Vietnam. They noted marked differences.

"We had been married exactly a year when mine got drafted," said Sandy. "He had been drinking before, but after coming home, his whole personality is different. Much more aggressive, goes into very, very deep depressions. Has contemplated suicide. Very unhappy in any job he's had. He tells me only bits and pieces but it was horrendous. He was in artillery. On Hill 54."

Dee said, "Mine was a very good kid, brought up strict, under his daddy's Navy thumb. He joined the Air Force. When he went over he was gentle, kind. When he came back he was abusive—and he would *never* have been that way before."

Emma said, "I watched my husband go from a nice, gentle man to a cruel and vicious man after Vietnam. He was in a truck that blew up. And they say, 'Throw him over 'cause he's dead.' Only he was alive and concussed. The way they found out he was alive, they was flying them back and he started moanin'. He had a head injury, eye injury, now he gets seizures, has high blood pressure. You name it, he got it."

All the women say their men were deeply aware of being in an unpopular war. Penny said, *"They* didn't want to be there either. They were ordered to do a lot of those things. They [the military] didn't care if it was women or children, everyone was the enemy and they were told to shoot." Emma adds, "My husband, when he's drinking, he say, 'I got a lot to give an account for. I have went into people's houses and killed children and women.' "

Karen says, "One thing that most characterizes the Vietnam vet—he can't leave what he did in perspective of where he was and under what conditions. He looks at it sitting in America with no guns around and no threats and says, 'Oh my God, what did I *do?*' He cannot say, 'But that was because I was in combat and I wouldn't do that here.' "

That led them to the rages that so frighten them and that are often so controlled in public. Gelsomino reiterates that with combat veterans there is a "fear of what can happen should they lose control. Part of their identity is being seen as someone who *can* kill and one of their fears comes from the unleashing of that."

"I lost a TV set over the guys who went to Canada," said Dee. "They said something about how they were gonna get the same benefits as veterans and my husband just tore the TV apart. He just went off."

Another wife said, "I keep telling my husband, 'You gotta get a handle on yourself.' " One night she and the children had started a barbecue. Her husband came home from work and flew into a rage because someone had forgotten to set the fork and spoon at his place. "He thought we did that on purpose, that we didn't want him there!" She throws up her hands. "Ridiculous!"

Lana adds, "It starts from the ridiculous—and then goes on for four hours."

But isn't that true in marriages or living with someone? You look back and can't even figure out what started the fight?

"You're right," says Gelsomino. "The pattern of allowing the stresses of daily living to build up exists in people who never went to Vietnam, never saw combat. And they come home and take it out there. However, *what's compounded with the Vietnam veteran is that he is already partially or totally saturated with stress that he never dealt with from way back then.* He's at the igniting point and doesn't have any means of communicating and letting it out in healthy ways. As they feel the problems of daily life there is an overflow, which is dumped on the people he's closest to. So he literally makes up his anger about the fork and spoon, for example. That has a very battering effect on their women. Afraid of their possible violence, the men go out of their way not to express anger at the people they probably *should*—like the boss or the mechanic who doesn't do a good job on the car."

Equally so, there is a paradox in how they treat their women. Their women often get the worst of their anger, but are also put on a pedestal. They often, indeed, have good sex lives. "It's not *all* bad," said one wife archly, as everyone laughed. Another adds, "Sometimes nothing happens for months and months and then all of a sudden hell breaks loose. Things *can* be good because they have depth of feeling and warmth. It's been my experience that a Vietnam veteran prizes his woman above everything else." Many of them nod.

Yet their husbands' own lack of self-esteem hampers them. While some had trouble holding jobs, many of the men work—Dee's husband in a steel factory, Lana's with the phone company and "hates it." Sandy's husband was in the military for ten years, then was a real estate salesman but "couldn't handle all that bullshit, as he calls it. Then he tried shrimping." Sally, the one with the alcoholic boyfriend, said work was never a problem. Still, in some form or another, most felt that the men give up on themselves. "There's a sense of not being able to click anymore, to have close friends."

Can the women listen to some horror story of Vietnam and not be horrified?

"No," says one decisively; others nod. "How can you *not* be bothered? It is hard to say, 'I understand.' "

One wife tried to get across that gulf. "When he talks about anything he's done, I just say, 'You're here because you did things you had to do in order to stay alive and that's all that matters to me.' Still, I don't think he can look to me for that kind of relief. It has to come from other veterans."

Finally we discuss the future. All of them felt that their husbands desperately needed them. Only Sally, on her way out of her relationship with Jim, demurs. "I feel I was too much of a crutch—and I was also stifled in my own growth."

The other women express traditional role values. "I stayed because I felt I've got to go that extra mile. That's being a woman," said one. Another insists, "It's not all bad. We lost a child seven years ago and my husband, who was a medic, pulled me through. I would have killed myself without him."

Gelsomino says, "There are positives about the war experiences we haven't been able to get to with these men." Penny, the nurse, agrees. "Most of them deny there was any positive. My husband does, even though he brought men back, *saved* lives."

We talk of the men who, unlike theirs, do accept the positives and are not haunted. "They have been able to use their experiences *for* themselves instead of against themselves," says Gelsomino. "If there is a goal through this whole process, that is *it.*"

Unlocking those steps is not only difficult; it can be risky.

"Steve's frightened. He doesn't feel he has a grip on anything," says Lana. Suddenly her flipness is gone. She holds back tears, brimming in her eyes. "He doesn't feel he has a helluva lot of chance . . . that he's not making progress fast enough. He's scared—and has been for several years—that he is crazy. I don't think he's going to survive it." The tears fall as she looks pleadingly at Gelsomino.

"Survive what?" he asks.

"Any of it," she says grimly. "Last night he wanted someone to lock him in a closet so he could just drink."

"You begin to lance a boil that's been there for a long time and there is a sense that things are getting worse and more painful because you're coming in contact with these feelings," Gelsomino says quietly.

"He'd been on his best behavior," continues Lana. "Then he watched 'Medal of Honor Rag' [a TV drama about a suicidal veteran who gets himself killed in a holdup]. He got real quiet and played the organ. That's not his pattern. He said, 'I know it's only a show, but it makes me feel sick . . .' "

"He is beginning to feel. When you do that, you risk feeling the shit along with the good," says Gelsomino.

Karen interjects, "I have the same fears [about her husband]. He's made so many starts. I don't want him to fall on his face again now that he's confronting everything in group."

Gelsomino refuses to sugar-coat. "He probably will. Two steps forward and one back. But if you keep going . . ."

The nurse says her husband has no motivation. "I feel I'm pulling the load." "You *are,*" says Gelsomino. "Your husband was into heavy-duty numbing."

At last there is a real breakthrough in how they see their roles. Sally keeps looking to the group for assurance because she is going to leave her boyfriend. She feels the others are taking on too much—while they seem fiercely determined to combat her view.

"Steve is sick and needs help," Lana says. "If he gets his stuff together, I sure don't want another woman to have carried the load." Sally protests, "I just don't see why a woman has to live continuously with stuff she doesn't like."

Another argues back, "There *is* something there. It's not necessarily a sick kind of love, but seeing your man right at the threshold of being able to improve." Another says, "I've experienced the highest highs and lowest lows. Out of the blue he can be witty, fun, optimistic. He put me through hell, but I stood my ground."

Gelsomino interprets: "That's a way of pushing you away, 'How could you possibly love me?' "

Sally is determined to be independent. "Even making love, I keep my own space, to not be an extension of him."

Another wife answers, most revealingly, "I *like* being an extension. I don't want him to get so independent that he won't *need* me."

Isn't there some masochism in these roles? Doesn't Sally have a point?

"There *is,* " says Penny. "But what are our chances?"

Lana nods. "If we get a divorce, what are our chances of marrying another veteran?" Unlike the women on campuses in the sixties, most of these women come from working-class or military backgrounds and come in contact daily with veterans. "Or what if we married a *normal* person? How do you live with them?" Another cracks, "You mean one that cuts the grass, actually goes to the store?"

An awareness of their own behavior patterns finally emerges.

"We came up with the big revelation at group last month," says Lana. "We *thrive* on this. This keeps us going."

Because you need to feel needed?

She ignores the question. "I love him. Inside, there is a very deep, loving, tender, creative, intelligent man."

Another wife interrupts. "I think we're working for that man who was there *before* the war. To get him back. Will we ever get there?"

She shoots a pleading, questioning look at Joe Gelsomino.

Then she says, "He will not answer that question." She sighs. "We've asked him before."

Part IV
Making It

"When Johnny Comes Marching Home"

BY PATRICK S. GILMORE

When Johnny comes marching home again,
Hurrah, hurrah!
We'll give him a hearty welcome then,
Hurrah, hurrah!
The men will cheer and the boys will shout
And the ladies they will all turn out
And we'll all feel gay
When Johnny comes marching home!

1 Successful Veterans

WHO ARE THE VETERANS THAT ARE "MAKING IT"? WHY HAVE THEY moved beyond Vietnam while others have not? Why are they the majority of veterans—albeit a smaller majority of those who saw heavy combat?[1]

Why do some men return from the horrors of battle emotionally wounded for years, some to a debilitating degree, while others do not? In this most inexact of endeavors—attempting to quantify human reactions to stress—suppositions and theories abound. One view holds that those from the least stable backgrounds—without well-developed coping skills—would be more stressed. Others theorize that those from more sensitive, stable backgrounds would be more traumatized by war and death. Both arguments are in part correct. *Legacies of Vietnam,* the major study on Vietnam veterans by the Center for Policy Research, found that, as pointed out in the delayed stress section, soldiers from the least stable backgrounds were troubled by the whole Vietnam experience—period. Those from the most stable, however, were *more* likely to develop stress as a result of being in heavy combat.[2]

There are, obviously, myriad factors involved in successful readjustment after Vietnam. They include: the degree of combat and extent of military preparedness, age at the time of combat, whether the veteran enlisted or was drafted, sense of justification in the cause, degree of support from family and friends, personality characteristics, coping skills, antiwar sentiment in their return environment. Even where they came from in the United States and period of service play a part. Veterans from the earlier days of the war were 20 percent less stressed than those who returned in the demoralizing dog days of "Vietnamization." Some obvious reasons come to mind. The earlier veterans were often enlistees, filled with patriotic duty. While the way the war was fought disillusioned many of them, they still retained a high degree of personal pride in their service and/or felt the cause was justified. Many veterans who went later formed a nihilistic subgroup. Often reluctant draftees surrounded by antiwar peers, by 1970 they were fighting in a war largely perceived as a failure. In fact, some of these veterans had participated in peace demonstrations before they went to Vietnam.

The subject is extremely complex; the answers amorphous. To say that some stress remains does not mean in any way to imply that all Vietnam veterans had to overcome some psychological *disability* before being able to pursue successful careers or lives. Numerous successful veterans speak out throughout this book, but the subject calls for special amplification. There has been no comprehensive study of the majority of veterans who have not sought help and have gone on with their lives successfully. No one veteran is either "this" or "that." Many of those now making it endured enormous pain and suffering and retain vestigial regrets and sorrows.

People tend to react to all sorts of traumatic experiences—such as a death in the family or a divorce—initially by punishing, pitying, isolating themselves, or denying.

Their problems can become permanent when they do not work through these reactions to alleviate conflict. One way is by laying responsibility elsewhere. Thus hawkish and dovish veterans can equally blame the same government: "If people are going to die, we should have fought to win" versus "We should never have been there; we should have left it to the Vietnamese." There is a danger in trying to resolve war experiences that way. By denying or ignoring *any* personal responsibility, these people can feel both impotent in handling today's troubling situations and baffled as to why change is so hard for them to achieve.[3]

Among the complexities of sorting it all out, two strong patterns emerge and help to explain those who are making it. First, it is essential to put away unresolved feelings about the war. Unresolved war experiences are better predictors of whether Vietnam veterans will say "something is wrong" today than the mere fact of having been in heavy combat. The second pervasive attitude among veterans who have overcome readjustment problems is the crux of their difference from those who have not. *An overwhelming number feel profoundly lucky for having survived.* They have overcome survival guilt and are consumed with gratitude for being alive. That reaction takes various positive forms, from helping others (many report a strong sense of compassion for others) to a passion not to waste one second of their lives. Sometimes this breeds driven workaholics.

Still, the Vietnam experience exacts its paradox. Despite their appreciation for life, many remain saddened and troubled by an inability to feel strong emotions anymore. It is as if deep feelings had been drained from them during their youth, never to return.

The only study to date that attempts to analyze different categories of "stable" and "unstable" veterans is the five-part *Legacies* study. A random subgroup of 440 veterans was selected out of 1,440 respondents for analysis of individual lives. The authors of the study are cautious about ascribing reasons for various behavior. However, they point out that even among those described as "stable," the men differed markedly in the extent to which they have "worked through" Vietnam. "The vast majority present a 'mixed picture' of negative and positive long-term effects."[4]

In this "stable" group, approximately one fifth have forestalled inner conflict through emotional avoidance, about half remain troubled by unresolved war experiences, and most deal with the war by avoiding troubling issues. "Those who assume responsibility for the implications of their experiences are a minority." The study cited men who remember a war incident but no emotional response. One example was a man who remained obsessed with killing—all the while describing himself as "well-adjusted, no hang-ups, the same old happy bum." The authors concluded that "few clinicians would fail to note his defensiveness and *compensatory* bravado."[5]

Much of the avoidance is more subtle and hard to detect in men whose lives seem stable. As many as 20 percent of the Vietnam veterans in this study meet major work and family challenges fairly adequately but remain "stuck" in their war experiences. Moreover, "about half in our sample say, 'Things are going well,' yet register circumscribed complaints" (job or marital problems, psychological vestiges of the war, or excessive drinking). These men are capable of functioning. Since they "usually do not think of themselves as needing help," said the *Legacies* authors, the needs of "this much larger group have been virtually ignored."

Among their stable category are a smaller number of men labeled "exemplary." All of them, including those from blue-collar homes, had some college, many come from intact families, and many had enlisted. They are skilled problem solvers, do not block out negative aspects, and are self-disciplined. Having faced death, they now take charge in life and often feel emotionally stronger than their nongoing peers. They often were very close to buddies in Vietnam. They participate in religious, community, and professional organizations. Above all, they have reflected on their Vietnam experiences and worked through them. Many were deeply disturbed by a "no win" military strategy and view the numbers of men killed and wounded as one of the biggest atrocities of the war.

It has been my experience that men of this sort have often seen the worst of battle. They have successfully examined Vietnam. There is no avoidance or denial; seldom do they gloss over whatever remains uncomfortable about Vietnam or their homecoming. What seems to set them apart from others who feel that they have no problem is, in fact, their attitude toward those veterans who *do* have problems. Consistently tolerant of troubled veterans, they do not defensively label them as a handful of losers, as do some of the other so-called successful veterans. They often point to crucial moments in their own lives—talks with friends, support from loved ones, a turning point in their careers—that kept them from going off the deep end. They, in fact, will use words like "insane" or "crazy" to describe some of their feelings on first coming home. There is a characteristic sense of deriving some benefit from their ordeal, as well as that oft-mentioned gratefulness for being alive. Why they have turned out this way often remains a mystery to them as well as others. It seems easier to define the troubled veterans and their feeling of groping with problems than it is to define successful veterans and why read-justment occurs. "Maybe it is okay that there is no explanation," says David Harrington, a veteran and social worker. "A lot of factors you can point to, but there is no standard method or reason why people cope."

For example, it has long been presumed that the most educated, from stable homes, who were older at time of combat, would have fewer problems.

However, a study of a 1968–69 Fort Benning Officer Candidate School class revealed some surprising information. Out of 129 men, 106 returned completed questionnaires. It was an extremely well-educated and financially secure sampling compared with the overall population of Vietnam veterans. Some 95 percent were in professional white-collar positions and 91 percent were college graduates. Before entering the service, 72 percent had already graduated from college and an additional 23 percent reported some college. Their mean age during Vietnam service was 23.7 years, far higher than the nineteen-year-old overall average. "One could infer that they, compared with the total Vietnam veteran population, were more mature and developmen-tally secure during their combat experience." However, the study found that 43.2 percent were experiencing moderate to strong symptoms of post-trau-matic stress disorder a decade later, "somewhat surprising in light of the unique characteristics of the sample. By most societal standards the subjects in this study are functioning quite well." Those with no post-traumatic stress were asked what was critical to post-combat transition. The perceived help-fulness of the veteran's family on his return home was paramount. Those with PTSD perceived their families as unhelpful. Those experiencing the disorder also were in heavy combat and reported a more immediate release back into society following combat.[6]

The *Legacies* authors attempt to ascribe regional variations to the personal-ity trends among veterans—at the risk of incurring the wrath of America's regional chauvinists. They warn that their views are "impressionistic."

Their northeast sampling includes Brooklyn, Westchester County in New York, and Bridgeport, Connecticut. The Midwest: Chicago and urban and rural areas of South Bend, Indiana. The South: urban and rural areas near Columbus, Georgia. The West: in and around Los Angeles.

Northeast: Veterans revealed an emotional complexity matched, in some ways, among men on the West Coast. Northeasterners, however, seemed "more serious and less quixotic." The Northeast veterans came out ahead in emotional sensitivity and dynamism.

South: The majority led stable lives—as married, working men. However, almost all had complaints of varying severity and even the so-called stable group were not free from problems. Among those considered successful (most likely to be white), there was still a lack of compassion for others and a repressive coping style. The study concluded that the majority of Southerners, including many who viewed the military and Vietnam as the high point in their lives, had not dealt with their war experiences to an appreciable extent. Avoidance was the most common pattern and few expressed guilt over their actions in war.

Midwest: Mostly classified as stable, with a very small number registering major complaints. Modest self-effacement ran through their personal comments. It was as if the war simply came and went, for most. Almost half said the war had no effect on their lives, including those who were in heavy combat, witnessed atrocities, or were wounded. There was little introspection. Most basically approved of the United States presence in Vietnam. Many remained oblivious to the controversy of the sixties. There was a stolid heartland-of-America-no-nonsense approach to "getting on with your life." They were not avoiding, so much as sealing off with an "unshakable resolve."

West Coast: Characteristically, a much more "let it all hang out" reaction. Much introspective self-examination. Among the most stable, this produced an honest and sensitive self-awareness, compassion, and empathy for others. Those regarded as being stable but having problems were, in contrast to their counterparts in the South and Midwest, quite verbal and sensitive but had problems with drinking, drugs, or emotional concerns. Unlike those in the Midwest and South, they readily acknowledged the positive and negative impact of the war on their lives. Rather than avoidance, many more experienced trauma and guilt.

The study concluded that problems and conflicts were most prominent in the Northeast, where many more men acknowledged that Vietnam changed their lives. Combat seemed to have taken an especially heavy toll.

Midwest veterans appeared the most "psychologically robust," least conflicted and least concerned with the heavier questions raised by Vietnam in their lives.

Overall, heavy combat contributed to more stress—except in one category. For veterans from small cities, there were apparently beneficial effects of combat exposure. No conclusive explanation was given. A general guess is that pro-war sentiment was more prevalent in small towns; there was a closer bonding of community and a hero's welcome for the combat soldier. However, the study cautioned that even among small town returnees, combat veterans drank more, were arrested more often, and had more medical problems than their peers in this study.[7]

More and more Vietnam veterans are surfacing in prominent positions. They are officers of banks, successful entrepreneurs, and politicians. Fred Smith, the president of Federal Express, returned from Vietnam and began making millions. Bob Kerrey, Governor of Nebraska, is a Medal of Honor winner who lost part of his right leg in Vietnam, joined antiwar protests, built a small business empire of restaurants, bowling alleys and racquetball clubs before running for office.

On Capitol Hill, in the 535-member Congress, 14 members served in Vietnam. Some 29 served on active duty and 16 others served in the National Guard or reserves, often a way of ducking active duty in the sixties. As military service once again is honored, however, politicians are acknowledging their Vietnam-era reserves or stateside military status. Of the several members of the freshman class of 1982 who joined the Vietnam Veterans in Congress caucus, not one of the Vietnam Generation age group served in combat. (Two new members, combat veterans of the Vietnam Generation—Thomas Carper (D., Delaware) and Thomas Ridge (R., Pennsylvania)—did not join the caucus. And John McCain (R., Arizona), a former POW, is older, in his late forties.)

The divisions are still strong. In 1983 an informal counter-caucus was begun by Vietnam combat veterans in Congress, many of them conservative, who disliked being lumped in with those in the National Guard or reserves.

In 1981 the Vietnam Veterans Leadership Program (VVLP) was begun by veteran Tom Pauken, director of Reagan's Action agency. Carter's Action director was antiwar activist Sam Brown. Pauken is staunchly right-wing. Just as Brown's appointment was attacked by conservatives, Pauken's was attacked by liberals. The VVLP project had its immediate critics on the Hill and among some Vietnam veteran activists who felt Pauken would impose his political agenda on the agency. In addition, the General Accounting Office (GAO), in preliminary investigation, was critical of the $2 million annual expense for a program that in two and a half years counted a little over 1,000 job placements. Critics charged that even that number was exaggerated. VVLP directors countered that one primary goal of the project was to raise the image of Vietnam veterans—as successful veterans "networked" with those less fortunate. Democratic congressional members decried Pauken's justification for VVLP at the same time he was attempting to gut the Vista program, the domestic equivalent of the Peace Corps, to help the poor and disadvantaged. "Developing a good image for veterans may be fine," said one congressional aide and a Vietnam veteran, "but how much are you going to spend for P.R.? It may be well-intentioned, but this program is using funds that previously were used for important projects for the poor, like storefront centers." Critics claimed that the VVLP "amounted to little more than a superficial display of conservative style."[8]

There are justifiable concerns on Capitol Hill about the expense and effectiveness of the program, as well as Pauken's ideological agenda. Critics point to his choice of regional directors—a right-to-life activist in Texas and a former director of the Conservative Union and antibusing activist in Colorado. Pauken has campaigned for conservative political candidates. Pauken's reputation for right-wing zealotry trailed him throughout the implementation of the VVLP. Some Democrats charge that he is building a veterans' network for the purpose of electing such politicians. However, directors Bill Jayne and Ed Timperlake and the men they found throughout the country were sincerely motivated to help other veterans.

These VVLP veterans—successful businessmen, bankers, and lawyers who volunteered their time and expertise for no pay—have certain characteristics in common. All point to close support from family and friends as vital in their own readjustment. Most were from patriotic homes, were better-educated than many veterans, enlisted, felt the cause was right. Timperlake insisted, however, "This program does not refight the war. Anyone who served in Vietnam has his right to think or say whatever he wants to about it."

By 1983, some VVLP organizers across the country were working closely with their area Vet Centers, thus smoothing potential friction. While many of the Vet Center personnel tend to feel the war was wrong and many VVLP firmly believe it was a well-intentioned cause, any ideological arguments were overshadowed by the sense of camaraderie, of "having been there."

Paul W. Bucha, thirty-nine, owns an international marketing firm in New York and is a graduate of West Point and Stanford Business School. He was a company commander with the 101st from 1967 through 1968. "Networking is the key. Most guys from previous wars had that network automatically. The guy who wanted to start an ice-cream parlor knew the guy at the bank from serving together in Germany. We went alone, came back alone, and stayed alone." VVLP leaders reach out by word of mouth, advertising, promotional events to find other veterans, to help the unemployed and underemployed.

"One well-educated black veteran, with the Justice Department in Jersey City, four businessmen, a state senatorial leader, and I got together," said Bucha. "We didn't even know each other before this program or that we were veterans. Some one of us knows of a veteran who needs help, say, and it's 'Will you sponsor him?' and another says yes and all of a sudden a guy has a job. Across the country we are growing, with a common linkage. We're all members [as Vietnam veterans], whether we like it or not. Because we're people of the sixties, we're a lot different from a World War II group. We were bombarded by JFK's concept of serving your country and helping your fellow man. Whether you went to Harvard or dropped out, you shared that perspective. While I was teaching at West Point, for example, I was involved in programs with drug addicts. I found out the ratio of drug users and abusers was the same in that generation whether you were a veteran or not.

"One guy I know has a master's in English—and fifteen jobs since Vietnam. He's obviously having some problems. We got to know each other through VVLP. He heard of a guy in a Vet Center who was divorced, an alcoholic, and had problems, emotional and legal. We found him a lawyer. He told me what he wanted was to drive an oil truck. One of my contacts was a guy who owns an oil company. I put him in touch. He's driving a truck for him and we're friends. A Vietnam veteran has an amazingly high regard for human life and compassion. We're tapping that."

Bill Ryan, thirty-seven, a lawyer and chairman of the New Orleans VVLP, also serves on a Veterans Affairs Commission ("I was the only one under seventy years of age"). Severely wounded in 1969 as a Marine Corps platoon commander, Ryan is blind in one eye and has impaired vision in the other. He returned, graduated from both business and law school, and is a successful developer and buyer of business real estate.

One of twelve children from a "good Irish family in Buffalo, New York," Ryan credits his family and upbringing for his positive outlook after Vietnam. In fact, three Ryan brothers were in Vietnam, all at the same time. Ryan went to school on a football scholarship and feels that his competitive nature enabled him to overcome his war wounds. He is "disappointed" at the "terrible way the U.S. Presidents and political system manipulated the situation, not being honest about 'containing communism,' and that they never intended to win. They never told us!" The nightmares of anyone who has been in heavy combat "are always going to be there, but it also makes you tougher, self-reliant."

Ryan also knows that a job goes a long way to bolster self-esteem and alleviate problems. "In the past six months we have placed 137 guys—and that's no BS statistic. They are the disabled, the unemployed, the underemployed, and some structurally unemployed who haven't worked for eight years. Some are $6 security guards, one is an assistant management trainee with a fast-food franchise, a couple are in hotels, a couple in offshore oil drilling. Petroleum Helicopters, Inc., which services the offshore oil and gas industry, is filled with Vietnam veterans; the senior vice-president is a former combat pilot. Out of 2,000 workers, 1,300 are Vietnam veterans. We do a great deal of work with SBA [Small Business Administration] and conduct seminars on how to get jobs. Sunbeam Bakery just got our leadership award: out of 280 employees, 160 are Vietnam veterans.

"We're even working with the American Legion, DAV, VFW. Those service organizations now agree they dumped on us. They need the membership, sure, but there is a guilt. We're setting up two panels of five each and offer to go to universities and colleges and select high schools to explain Vietnam by those who fought it. We have every perspective—from colonel and line officer down to a grunt.

"Mostly we're out there trying to help guys who are a little down, who never got that break when they came back and were really sunk by the fact that nobody cared. The VA should have set up a transitional reentry program. Given the climate in the States when we got back, we all could have used it."

Rick Barnes is a lieutenant on the Dyer, Indiana, police force. He enlisted at seventeen, served around the DMZ in 1966 and 1967, and was twice wounded. He received the Silver Star when wounded during Operation Union. "I was the highest rank that made it out of that operation alive." Although a corporal, Barnes was a platoon leader because so many officers had been killed. He could have returned in a very negative frame of mind. Barnes still smarts at "the imaginary lines we couldn't cross. The VC could shoot at you, but you couldn't go across.

"I'll never forget, we were clearing out a VC village stronghold and we lost more than five guys. As we cleaned out the ville, we found medical supplies stamped 'Berkeley, Calif.' in this VC stronghold! That enraged us. Here our guys were being killed and wounded and our own people are sending them medical supplies."

Lying on a stretcher, in bandages, Barnes thought as his plane touched down in the United States, "This country *owes* me something. What saved me from continuing that way was being in an amputee ward. On all sides were guys with no legs, no arms, no eyes—and I had two of everything. I quickly changed my attitude."

In an ironic twist, Barnes was just starting a VVLP project with incarcerated veterans in the summer of 1983. "As a policeman, I put them there and now I'm going to help them. If they can get their heads straight, get jobs, they may turn out okay."

This book is filled with men who are making it, many of them having taken far different paths to reach their readjustment. The Hagel brothers are a case in point. Chuck Hagel returned convinced the cause was right and had minimal surface readjustment problems—although his brother, Tom, thinks he is denying and avoiding a great deal.

Within a year after leaving the number-two job in the Veterans Administration, Chuck Hagel was a successful entrepreneur. His company, Collins, Hagel & Clarke, Inc., owns the majority interest in five wireless, cordless telecommunications companies aimed at an international market. Hagel started with five people in 1982 and by the end of 1983 had 100 employees. He plans to run for the Senate, "but that's two or three years off."

After severe readjustment problems, Tom Hagel was ebullient in the summer of 1983. He was teaching law at the University of Dayton, had just been admitted to the bar, and was "in better shape than I have ever been since Vietnam. It is a combination of time, working through Vietnam. I still have a lot of strong feelings. In fact, at a picnic recently, a house across from the field just happened to explode into flames. Seeing that triggered a lot of memories and I had depressions for a few days. I know I'm going to live Vietnam the rest of my life, but it is not going to stop me. It's time to close that chapter and move on." Characteristically, Tom Hagel was still helping others, on the board of the Dayton Head Start Policy Council, and had become an officer in one of his brother's companies.

For those at the top—in business, law, journalism, or politics—there is a knowledge that they are vastly outnumbered by those who did not go. Still, as more veterans move into prominent positions, they are forming an invisible network. William Broyles, Jr., one of the few Vietnam veterans who became a national media leader as editor-in-chief of *Newsweek* until he resigned in 1984, says, "I'm finding more and more veterans, such as some executives in major corporations. It's an amazing discovery to find men putting their hands on the levers of American business, politics, and media who were there [in Vietnam]."

Perhaps there is no more startling contrast than to look at the cross-section of those who went to previous wars. For men now in their sixties of all stratas, going to World War II was the norm. Although Korea began the student deferment, many men went as officers straight out of college. Since there were far fewer men in that generation, the likelihood of going to Korea was expanded, as well as the possibility of serving stateside. Not so with Vietnam.

"One of the main reasons for My Lai is that the people who should have been officers just weren't there," said Broyles. "Calley should never have been an officer."

Broyles adds, "The choices truly had a moral resonance. No one I knew in college was going; a lot went from my Texas high school. I want to make it clear that I tried every deferment to get out. In college it was automatically assumed you had that right. When I finally decided I couldn't be a C.O. and was drafted, I joined the Marines. I was with the First Marine Division in I Corps, west of Da Nang."

Broyles draws no conclusions on foreign policy attitudes among those who went or did not go. "I don't see a higher sense of cautiousness and morality on the part of those who *did* go. Some feel that way; others from combat feel we have to 'get tough.' "

What is different for Broyles, surrounded by other journalists who were not in combat, is the personal pain he feels over such tragedies as the 241 marines in the multinational peace-keeping force who died in the Beirut terrorist attack last fall.

"It is not *abstract* with me. They are not numbers. The tragedy of Vietnam and Beirut is that we shouldn't send troops unless it is clearly in our interest. Beirut was an outrage. It never should have happened. Those men who were killed were real people, patriotic young men, not some two-dimensional warmongers. It breaks my heart."

Tony Pirrone, an executive with Mobil Oil, was a helicopter pilot and captain in Vietnam in 1969 and 1970. He went to Ohio State on an ROTC scholarship. "I needed the money. I took the advanced course and, before I know it, I'm in. I was scared, but coming from a blue-collar family, it was my duty to go in. Just as I was ready to leave, my mother, a little Siciliano, wanted to give me the money to go to Canada!" he says with a soft laugh. "I survived in Vietnam by looking at it as a job."

He is very cynical about Nixon's Vietnamization policy. "Withdrawal and Vietnamization were very tough on those of us left behind. Kissinger ought to be hung instead of giving speeches. We were at 60 percent strength. We couldn't get spare parts. The whole thing just fell apart." After he returned, Pirrone stayed in the service, teaching others how to fly helicopters.

How did you get your job with Mobil Oil?

"It wasn't easy." Pirrone decided he wanted to go with a Fortune 500 company and was very determined to succeed. He remembers an interview with Procter and Gamble. "To this day we don't use Crest toothpaste," he says caustically. "The damn guy wanted to see the needle tracks on my arm!" He tells the story with controlled anger still. "It was about the time the drug issue was really starting to come out. This guy first said it was warm and why didn't I take my coat off. I said I didn't want to. One thing led to another and we got into an argument and finally he said right out, 'Take off your coat. I want to see your arms,' " recalls Pirrone, pointing to the inside of his arms at the veins. "I almost decked him."

Like many veterans Pirrone, "got caught up in being very competitive. I was four years behind everybody. No company enforces veterans preference. I turned my frustration and anger into my job and caught up and surpassed many of the others."

There are the "superveterans" who became well-known *because* of their Vietnam experience, authors like Phil Caputo and Jim Webb, men like Max Cleland, a triple amputee and former VA administrator who is now Secretary of State of Georgia; Bobby Muller and Jan Skruggs, who have spent a decade working on veterans issues. Muller, a paraplegic, worked tirelessly from his wheelchair to get recognition for Vietnam Veterans of America (VVA). Skruggs, wounded in Vietnam, had a lofty dream that there would be a memorial for veterans. After years of seeking money and support, he dedicated the Vietnam Veterans Memorial in 1982 as some 250,000 looked on.

A large number of successful veterans, however, fit an unspectacular middle-American classic mold. They returned to become IBM salesmen and branch managers and farmers and middle-level business executives and postmen and mechanics.

For example, says Tom Ashby, a former Vet Center counselor, "On the surface, I know guys who look very successful but are really having problems. I also know some who don't look so successful, but I consider them successful in that they have *accepted* what they did, learned from it, and have gone about their lives. However, they may not have been very adept at doing anything in the first place, so they may not have risen in any way that society measures them."

Many veterans found positive forms of catharsis. One New York postal clerk, wounded in Vietnam, Raymond J. Barkley, Jr., turned his anger into art. At first he twisted wire sculptures into horrible reminders of war. It took thousands of coat hangers and three years to construct a six-foot body torn apart by a bomb. "You can't get a better anatomy lesson than in Vietnam," he said dryly. As the years went by, Barkley was able to turn to lighter subjects. When he found himself sculpting a butterfly, he felt that was a metaphor for the freedom from his nightmares of friends who died. George L. Skypeck, wounded in the 1968 Tet Offensive, is an artist and poet. "Without my art, I would have serious problems." His angry, sad poetry was in memory of his friends; ". . . where the cold fingers of Death's bony hand silently rapped the cadence of persistent loneliness on once gentle hearts . . ."

John Schaefer, a physical therapist, epitomizes many of the men who went. A former marine, Schaefer described himself as a "late bloomer" who dropped out of college and went to Vietnam out of a sense of duty as well as vagueness about the direction of his life. Once there, he saw little purpose to the war, and was wounded slightly when an American misguided mortar round fell short and left six wounded. Schaefer decided that his only goal was to survive. "It sounds selfish but it really was 'save yourself' as far as I was concerned." It took a year to readjust—not just to the war but to the changes in the culture. "Guys with crew cuts when I left had become long-haired dope freaks."

He may have gone into physical therapy out of some undefined need to help others after Vietnam, but Schaefer returned with few ideological responses. "I could not give a damn about the Vietnamese—any of them." Schaefer admires men his age with true convictions against the war, but those who "just ducked it" earn some contempt. However, there is no outrage. On the whole, Schaefer was glad to grow up in the sixties—"an exciting time that forced you to think out your positions"—and was ultimately strengthened by Vietnam, although there was some regret for the lost years and innocence lost. "I was really idealistic, naïve."

Distrust of the government is, typically, pervasive. All in all, however, he sees Vietnam as a vital part of his life, safely put to rest. For him and many others, it was not just another time. "That," he says, "was in another *life.*"

James Lawrence, a former professor and businessman from Alabama, epitomizes the successful veteran who remains filled with positive and negative responses to Vietnam; all the negatives are unacknowledged and submerged and come out in offhand remarks. For example, Lawrence says, "The minute I got on the airplane and left that country, the war was over. When I knew we were past the end of the runway where the machine guns might be, a hundred pounds were simply removed from my shoulders. I put it behind me. The veterans who can't cope see themselves as losers." Yet, later, Lawrence blurts out defensively, "Nobody cared about us. But so what? It doesn't bother me. *To hell with them.* I'm proud of having gone over there."

Lawrence went to the Citadel, went to Vietnam in 1965 as a second lieutenant, and saw a horrendous amount of fighting against two large divisions of regular NVA forces at Landing Zone X-ray "basically at the foot of the Ho Chi Minh Trail as it comes into South Vietnam. These troops had big silver belt buckles with red stars, helmets, and were armed with AK-47 automatic weapons. For four days they came pouring off that mountain; we kept wiping them out. The battle was brutal. I think they had to be on something, the way they charged. One charged with a *bugle*—that's all he was armed with."

They were given orders to move on to Landing Zone Albany, where they were caught in an ambush and slaughtered. Lawrence, concussed and paralyzed, lay in a section with the wounded for hours before they could be evacuated. Unable to move, Lawrence listened to the sounds of death. Later, he would count fifty-eight names of the dead he knew.

Today Lawrence looks predominantly at the positive values of his war. "I came out of the war without the scars of war. I can't therefore jump into the mind of someone who's been really altered by it and understand his problems. But where would a lot be, say, if the war hadn't existed? Would they still be losers? I contend they would be.

"The war gave me a tremendous amount of strength to handle stress." Lawrence mentioned an attitude common to many successful veterans. "I watch people crack up in the world of business and I think, 'What's wrong with you guys? This is trival, just little daily stress.' And I think I must be something special. The other thing, the war made me appreciate what I've got. I'm talking about everything from milk shakes to the American flag. Literally, that was my first request, lying paralyzed in the hospital—a chocolate milk shake."

Lawrence returned to teach American literature at the University of Alabama, then took a gamble on real estate. As a branch manager of the largest real estate company in Alabama, Lawrence is doing very well financially.

"I made the transition from academic to business in just two and a half years. I think Vietnam had a lot to do with that. It left me with a combination of determination, appreciation, and sensitivity. Without the Citadel and Vietnam, I might be a ne'er-do-well in southern Alabama."

Lawrence admits that if he had returned a double amputee or paralyzed, unmarried, not having known a family, "I'd be pretty bitter and sour. You'd have a hell of a hard time getting me to do your 'Rah-rah, America' number."

Lawrence married a woman from his hometown, Troy, Alabama, now an English teacher. "I just don't have those negatives. This is my first and last wife, hopefully. This is my first night of two drinks in a month. I've never used drugs."

Finally the rosy picture is marred by two deep-seated emotional responses to the war. After hours of extolling the virtues of having gone to war, Lawrence gets very emotional about the thought of his own son, now six, going to "another Vietnam" and says he would do what he could to stop it. Secondly, he is carrying quite a degree of survival guilt. Lawrence frequently mentions one of his closest friends, Don, who was killed, referring to him in a terse, too tautly controlled manner. "He was my roommate in paratroop school and on the boat coming over for thirty-one days and he was married and I wasn't and I got all the home-cooked meals at his home in Fort Benning. He was killed and mutilated not far from where I lay paralyzed."

Later, Lawrence chokes up. "I didn't understand why Don died and I lived. *I* was the goof-off. He was president of the student body, good-looking, smart. I was not near the student leader he was."

And finally Lawrence explains what has carried him through these years. "Vietnam started me on a trip that convinced me of a higher being. When I realized all this was an awful dirty joke—" He starts again. "Had I gone through all this—losing friends, watching their bodies rotting on the ground —I could never have accepted it without something to cling to. The experience guided me toward a trip to find out what that was. What I came to was Christianity. As I say, life would have been a dirty joke without it. Don couldn't have just *died* when they put his body in the ground. I had to think there was the essence of Christ and the idea that there's a better life after this one." There is a long pause. "I've *got* to believe that—or else I'm your *next* suicide candidate."

2 From Losers to Winners

A REMARKABLE NUMBER OF EXEMPLARY VETERANS I HAVE MET WERE teenage "incorrigibles"—high school truants and dropouts, youths from broken homes with alcoholic parents, small-time troublemakers with little ambition and seemingly little future. They sound like case histories of those destined to fail. Predilection theorists, who insist that background controls psychological responses to war, would have been baffled in the extreme by their adolescent records.

One ex-marine, a high school dropout who had a D-plus average, a father who died an institutionalized alcoholic, and a mother who married numerous times, is now a successful San Diego architect. Another, a self-described punk from Boston, a constant truant who stole food from boxcars to help his mother feed their family, wound up in Ivy League universities after Vietnam and is now a successful Washington, D.C., lawyer. A Catholic youth, another constant high school truant, returned from Vietnam to ace his college courses and is now a successful businessman. Another high school dropout became a marine and was blinded by a booby trap. After learning Braille he completed high school, earned two undergraduate degrees and a law degree.

Their stories are the stuff of Hollywood melodramas, the bum who becomes "an officer and a gentleman," the kind of man the military claims to "shape up" in large numbers. For them, the military became a support system they never had at home. They found opportunities and a way out of a dead-end life. Vietnam was a hard way to grow up, but they derived something of value out of the experience.

The red Ferrari is parked outside of Michael Jones's spacious office. The San Diego architect, in his mid-thirties, makes over $150,000 a year and is happily married to his second wife. His eyes crinkle into a ready smile. He stretches back in his chair, a picture of a man at ease with himself.

Were you always this way?

"Shiiiiit no! I came out a basket case. Civilization has all kinds of barriers to keep people from being animals. Over there, resolving the situation with

violence was the accepted point of view. The only thing that saved your ass
sometimes."

Jones stops for a second, twiddling a pencil. "That was the hardest thing
for me to deal with. I had literally killed thirteen people—that I had actually
witnessed. Bullets going from *my* rifle, seeing the body fall, and going up and
looking at them. I don't know how many others I killed, shooting at flashes in
the night and all that crap. The military is a reward system for violence. They
reward you for that—with promotions, medals, prestige, peer admiration—
and that's what keeps the military together. So we're instilled with the knowledge to kill—instantly, reflexively, that it's right—and put in an environment
and told, 'Okay, do it.' Then, snap, you're home. Literally shooting someone's head full of holes and in hours you're walking the streets of San Francisco. The military really fucked up in not decompressing and recognizing the
need to say, 'Hey, let's identify some problems.' "

Jones, the reconnaissance jungle fighter in 1965–66 in Quang Tri province
who three times was the only one left alive in his team—went directly from
Vietnam to UCLA. "I was extremely lucky to be accepted with a zip-shit zero
intellectual background. The chairman of the UCLA Architectural Department was an ex-marine who let me in under probation. 'If you don't get a C
average, your ass is in night school at Santa Monica,' " he said.

Jones quickly acquired a girlfriend, who took on extreme importance. "I
desperately needed someone at that point and she was there. But I didn't
mean the same thing to her. When she had the *audacity* to cheat on me,"
Jones says archly, grinning at how injured he had been, "that was a capital
offense."

Jones loaded his high-powered rifle, drove to the house where the woman
was staying with a boyfriend. Jones sat there for several hours. "Had she
come out with him, they'd both be dead—and I'd be in jail right now. I had a
thirty-five-caliber rifle with a scope about that big," he says, making a circle
with his fingers. "I coulda shot the guy's cuff links off. There's no question in
my mind that I could have killed them instantly, *without* hesitation. Lucky
for me, no one came out. Finally I said, 'What the fuck am I doing to
myself?' I went home, threw the rifle on the garage workbench, and went
straight to the UCLA counseling center."

Jones refused to budge when the indifferent receptionist said the counselor
could not see him for two weeks. The counselor noted his insistence and, after
a forty-five-minute conversation, called his wife and told her not to wait
dinner. They talked from three-thirty until midnight and the next morning
Jones was back in the office at nine A.M. "I just freaked the guy out—some of
the gory details about Vietnam. I was a young kid who didn't know what the
hell I was. I had been through the most radical changes, bouncing off of
people and concepts and emotional and traumatic events. There I was, a high
school dropout with a D-plus average and a Vietnam veteran. *That's all I
had.*" He is still somewhat awed at the way his life has turned out. "I was

different than a lot of veterans because I faced it and was willing to talk about Vietnam. My attitude and that doctor probably saved me.

"The counseling sessions instilled confidence in my own abilities. I was really down on myself because that girl had rejected me and because I didn't have the credentials the other kids had. They had their clique. I had none of that."

Jones's father was in the Navy in World War II, an upholsterer and an alcoholic who was committed about the time Jones enlisted, at seventeen. A lasting remembrance is a final "knock-down-drag-out fight. I was really crying. It was no competition physically. I was an athlete and he was in the advanced stages of alcoholism. My mother—uh . . ." The story is painful. Jones turns his head away. "It was a motherless home. My mother's been married about six times," he says, quickly brushing it off. Jones lived with a friend's aunt and uncle, then drifted. A poor student for years, he flunked second grade, did well in only one course, an experimental class in drafting. College was viewed neither as a haven from Vietnam nor as a requisite for life. "Nobody in my family ever graduated from college. I wasn't motivated to try to excel." The Marine Corps became home. *I literally had no place else to go.* Without it, I probably would have wound up pumping gas or in prison. Guys there were just like me; in the military either because of escape or they were pursuing something and weren't quite sure what that something was."

Jones's training for Vietnam in 1965 was "night and day difference from later, when they were just throwing bodies in there. I was in the UDT school, Ranger School, went to general guerrilla warfare training and survival school in Panama. In Vietnam I was in a reconnaissance unit and operated with the CIA and intelligence groups. Basically we traveled in four-man teams and were put out on listening posts, watching enemy traffic, air strikes, and staged ambushes from a distance, trying to monitor the damage that was done and monitor the movement on the Ho Chi Minh Trail. There were only about 150,000 troops totally in Vietnam then." He laughs. "Even though I was in intelligence and all that, I really didn't know what was going on five to ten miles away unless it had something to do with the operation we were involved in. When I would meet for about five days at a stretch with the CIA people— basically bag men who paid off the mercenaries, montagnards, and people like that—we would get a lot of information.

"We were brainwashed and pumped up with propaganda—saving the world from communism, the domino theory. I swallowed it hook, line, and sinker. I was just the type the military needed. A classic robot." Later he felt deceived and developed a deep distrust of politicians and the military who "allowed something like Vietnam when they knew the futility of the strategy."

Jones was in "three different situations where I was the only person left alive." He handled it by "going numb, disassociating myself." One he recalled was "such a crazy mission. It was 1965 and the North Vietnamese were

claiming they did not have units in the south sector. Our intelligence gathering said there was a North Vietnamese ranger unit. We were sent out with
two Navy duck teams and two Marine reconnaissance teams. Our mission
was to go through the river delta, where we thought the North Vietnamese
unit was, and to grab a perimeter guard. Just to knock him out, coldcock
him, and take him back for questioning." He looks rueful. "That was the
whole mission.

"We were let out of a submarine about 2 A.M. at the mouth of the delta.
Four people in each raft. I was in the last raft. We got two, two and a half
miles upriver. We had little grease guns which were little automatic rifles.
They were in plastic bags because we were ready to go in the water, come up,
and maybe grab somebody who was right alongside the river. All of a sudden
flares went off."

Jones keeps sighing, the way people do when remembering something intense, even as he speaks almost in a monotone. "The intensity of the fire was
incredible. I mean, the water was literally *churning* with bullets. The kids in
the first three rafts were killed instantly—in the head, face, shoulders, everything. The kids in the front of my raft were all shot in the head and chest.
And a burst of automatic rifle fire came right across my lap. The guy next to
me was rather tall and his knees were up about maybe six, seven inches
higher than mine. He got hit in the kneecaps and fell forward." Jones demonstrates, leaning forward over his architect's desk. "And he got shot in the
neck and the head. The kid in the front fell over in the water. There are five
parts to the raft that inflate. Maybe it was just the angle of the direction, but
our raft didn't sink. It still had part of the bottom plate, which is inflatable,
and part of the piece of the side is inflatable, so it was still floating. I wasn't
hit at all." Jones repeats it, still in awe. *"Wasn't hit at all.* The flares hit the
water and then it was dark again."

And Jones was the only one alive. "My heart was like that," he recalls,
tapping steadily on the desk. "I mean, I could *hear* it banging! I'm waiting
spread-eagled for the next barrage of flares. A thousand things went through
my mind. Shit, there was nothing I could do. I thought, This is it. I unbagged
the guns, loaded them, and all I could do was wait and if they came at me it
was just a suicide John Wayne number. After some of the atrocities I had
seen, there was no way I wanted to be captured alive. So I laid there . . .
and laid there . . . and laid there. Nothing happened! There were no other
flares, no more shooting."

Jones drifted. "Luckily we had what was called an abortive rendezvous
signal. All we had to do was put a couple of prearranged beeps on this little
radio signaling that something had happened and to maintain the rendezvous
point. It took me until—aw shit, four o'clock in the afternoon before I got
back in the ocean." He was on the half-inflated raft with two dead marines for
the first four or five hours. "I was trying to get back with the bodies on the
raft. The raft was only partly inflated and the gunnel [gunwale] tube, which is
a big round thing that goes around, was so full of holes there was no way it

could be repaired. We did have some repair kits, but it was just too badly gone." Jones, fearful that the raft would sink, put the bodies overboard.

"I was hardened a bit by then. I'd seen a lot of people blown up. Today I see these MIA lists and I know a lot of those were kids who were just killed and never recovered. The military bullshitted people, too. They would send back an aluminum coffin with nothing in it. I am sure that was the case with some of these kids that were never recovered."

Another time, Jones's jeep was hit by enemy fire, the engine exploded, and they crashed into a tree. "That blew one kid away and the other was hit by these guys about twenty times. The impact threw me rear end over appetite onto the ground. I managed to hold on to the machine gun and I fell into a gulley. Bullets were bouncing off the jeep and going over my head. I looked under the undercarriage of the jeep and saw three guys coming up the trail, carrying grenades. They were kids, about sixteen years old. When they got close enough to throw the grenades, a couple didn't go off and the ones that did just kind of shot over. I shot those three. When the jeep hit, all the cans [of ammunition] fell on the ground so I had all this ammunition. I was scared shitless, shooting bushes, trees, spraying everything in front of me. I was shot and didn't know it. You get in a hyperstate of shock. I didn't hear any noise and decided, 'Well, shit, they're sneaking up on me. Now what am I gonna do?' I looked down and saw my foot was all bloody. All of a sudden the pain shot to my head when I saw that. I lay there for what seemed an hour but was maybe just minutes and started crawling like a snake in the grass to our portable radio, which was thrown from the jeep. I got the nerve to whisper a call on the radio. I don't remember to this day how I knew the coordinates, but I gave the coordinate location. It seemed like hours and finally I heard the *whup, whup, whup* of the helicopter."

In retelling his Vietnam days, Jones cannot get over how lucky he was. His foot was operated on and today is "amazingly strong. Needless to say, I feel like I'm living a charmed life, believe me."

The stories are told as distant emotions. Only one, a lone killing, haunts him. "It was hotter than a son of a bitch. I was by myself, just relaxed. All of a sudden, from about here to the end of the block, I see another guy standing there. Just a kid with an AK-47. We stared at each other. He froze and I froze. The average Vietnamese wouldn't know the definition of democracy, communism, or socialism; wouldn't know who Thieu was; wouldn't know who Johnson was. These guys were just trying to exist and their life is being threatened by the Viet Cong and North Vietnamese. They tell them, 'These Americans will kill you and we will protect you, but you have to help us kill them. And just to show you we mean business, we'll rape your sister and cut the head off your mother.' That terrorism makes a believer out of you.

"You're not dealing with the rest of the crap you read or what the intellectuals argue over in Washington. I didn't want to shoot him and he didn't want to shoot me. The question was, was he going to walk away or was I going to walk away? If he'd walked away, so would I. But he didn't. He went for his rifle." Jones pauses as he remembers aiming and shooting him. "I probably thought about that incident more than any of the others. It's just a different dimension. To have the time to *think* what you're going to do, that you're going to kill someone, that was just incredible."

Today Michael Jones looks at his high school and Marine days as if they belong to another person. "College was a renaissance for me, a total rebirth. Just a complete mental change from the attitudes and values I had before. Almost like looking at life for the first time. I completely challenged everything I'd ever heard up to that point. The Marine Corps and Vietnam happened a long time ago and I've changed a lot."

And yet, it was a major "learning experience" that gave direction to his life. The gratefulness is inescapable.

"I went through a lot of crap over there and God had the opportunity to take me off this earth, but he left me here for me to go in some direction. Not that I'm a religious person, but I have the feeling that I'm unconcerned about death. If I died now, I would not be *afraid* of it."

Nor was Jones afraid to push past what would have seemed like wild expectations before Vietnam. "As bad as all the experiences of being in the military—just in terms of the people and the structure, a collection of incompetent assholes who rise up through the organization by merely being there, not for what they do—it gave me time to mature and think." He laughs. "When you check out, one of the final points is your 'career advisory.' This guy looks at my record." Jones does his imitation of his reenlist pep talk: " 'Jesus Christ, you dropped out of high school with a D-plus average! Listen, the stuff you did in Vietnam, if you go and reenlist now we'll give you a bonus of about $1,500, promotion to sergeant, and, man, you're on your way up. There's no question you'll make gunnery sergeant in five years. Christ, you might be able to earn maybe as much as *$10,000 a year* and you won't have a problem in the world! What's this business of you getting out of the Marine Corps? If you get out, you'll be back *begging* to enlist. And we're not going to be giving you the same choices then.' "

Jones recalls, "I thought, Son of a bitch. I will *not* enlist. That guy just pissed me off. Vietnam and all that bullshit, *that* legitimized my whole existence and 'set the stage for success.' " He laughs sardonically. "All the way up to $10,000 a year."

Jones moved onto a campus surging with antiwar activity. "I couldn't wait to let my hair grow. To blend in. But I was appalled at my own peer group supporting the other side. In retrospect, I don't think anybody thought Thieu had that much control, so buttressing that was a waste." Like the majority of combat soldiers, Jones feels we could have "done the classic sweep through, like we did in World War II. The way they tried to pull it off was just the biggest bullshit. Who the hell wanted to be the last guy blown away trying to get the hell outta there?

"But I was trying to remove myself from that when I came home. I felt helpless about the political aspects." Still, Jones, like many veterans, lived with the war daily until it ended. "I kept thinking of the people over there, wondering, thinking. My confidence that this country could deal with an international crisis was totally eroding."

The worst aspect was being a survivor among the untouched. "The hardest thing was watching the nightly news with them. First thing, 'Well, today in Vietnam 76 people were killed and 120 wounded and here's Garrick Utley, flying over the Mekong Delta. . . .' And you see the helicopter and you're at some friend's house and the kid says, 'Can I turn on "The Flintstones," Daddy?' and he says, 'Yeah, what the hell.' Or, 'It's time for "Ironside"' or whatever. *That* was hard. To see a camera sweeping over a country where I'd been and all that had gone on and people not giving a damn."

Jones, however, had some understanding of the way the war looked, back home. "Watching TV about a month after I came back, I saw a bunch of marines guarding a compound which held mostly women and children. All these marines about twenty feet apart with machine guns, watching all these people. For somebody who didn't know about Vietnam, watching that in their living room in Los Angeles or Phoenix or wherever, it looked *shitty*. It looked like, 'My God, what are you going to do? Shoot this old lady if she comes up to you and screams?' But as a guard, you didn't know *who* they were. Infiltrators and VC were all over."

Jones became a professional student—UCLA, California Polytechnic Institute (Cal Poly), San Diego State—for about seven years. At Cal Poly he was student body president and president of a veterans' group. "While I was working on my campaign, the committee was discussing whether they ought to play up the fact that I was a Vietnam veteran decorated by President Johnson and all that kind of stuff. *Everyone* said, 'Hey, let's forget *that*. Let's not even bring it up.' I felt that was right. By then [1971], I was already ashamed of the entire experience. I had gravitated into a totally different intellectual level. Sometimes it seems like that was a different person all that happened to. Certain friends are still carrying around the scars of the war; guys who don't have arms or legs and have to live with that every day. The psychological scars are there—and deeper in certain instances—but not with me. I felt *lucky*—to be back. And *lucky*—to be given the opportunity to go through school and to change the course of my life."

Jones was making up for lost time, having an active "social life." "In Vietnam I wasn't into the prostitution scene like a lot were. But I did get to be friends with a woman who was kind of a Mamasan. I gave her some money and she brought a young girl and her family over from some village fifty, sixty miles away." Jones kept her and her family for a while. "It wasn't much money, the way those people live."

Jones was married for a short time after he returned to the States. Now he speaks enthusiastically of his present, second marriage. His second wife, Jones keeps repeating, is a feminist who "does her own thing. She's a CPA, an accountant. Appointed to a board by Governor Brown. She keeps her own name, own money, own account." Jones has gotten involved in the feminist movement himself. "I don't consider myself macho at all. I think any asshole can pick up a gun and shoot somebody—and that's exactly where I was—and that's where the machoness comes from."

They have no children. "We don't believe in that. Maybe we're too selfish," says Jones, who likes their European and Hawaiian vacations, their friends, their dual careers. "Maybe we're too materialistic, but we don't want to change our lifestyle."

Did Jones think he would have had the same commitment to achieve had he not been in the military or Vietnam?

"No," he answers quickly and emphatically. Jones knows only a few veterans now and they have all become fairly successful. "There was a time, when we banded together on campus, that all were dealing with problems, but I don't know any like that now."

How does he see himself in ten years?

The smile comes. "Either very rich and very happy—or very poor and unhappy. I take it one day at a time. One thing Vietnam did for me, I live a lot better for the 'now' and enjoy life on a day-to-day basis more than anyone I know. When you live with death for so long and some of those bullets hit you, you say, 'Welllll, shiiiiit.' After that, I figured that a lot of things in life are just luck, happenstance, and chance."

At thirty-six, the face is unlined. The round, pink cheeks, the blue eyes and blond hair are that of a slightly aged altar boy. Hubert Brucker's youthful face make his stories of death and destruction seem even more ghastly; he must have looked ten in Vietnam.

A twenty-year-old Army lieutenant with the 4th Infantry Division, Brucker saw heavy fighting in 1967 and 1968, then, after being wounded, became a military adviser to the Montagnards. He remembers the especially heavy slaughters among the first units moving into Dak To in 1967. Unlike many Vietnam combat soldiers, Brucker fought in large-scale operations against the North Vietnamese Army. "I rarely ran across VC. It was all regular NVAs—heavy equipment, uniform against uniform. They were *very, very* strong and well-equipped."

Brucker recalls how they had been chosen as lead platoon, how they were marked for wounding and death on the huge map the commanders unrolled. "All arrows pointed at this one hill—and that's where we were going in. We were being used as bait to draw out these guys."

Three or four horrible battles come back to Brucker all the time. They had used C-4 explosives to topple huge trees ("blowing an LZ"—Landing Zone) to set up a small perimeter. "We were waiting for the helicopters to medevac out the wounded. It was getting towards dark. We could hear the helicopters coming in. Maybe it was the muffling of the helicopters, but we didn't hear the *thunk* of incoming mortar. All of a sudden, the fellow I was talking with wasn't there. It just took the whole half of his head off. I don't know how he lived another night, but he lived for two days. His body was quivering all the time."

That was the start of an assault that was brutal. "Tremendous amount of fighting. Mortars never stopped coming for three hours. We had the steepest part of the hill and those guys were coming right down a chute at us.

"Three hours later, I get a call from the company commander. He wanted me to go around the other side. He'd been trying to raise the A platoon on the radio and wasn't getting anything.

"I told him, 'You've got to be out of your fucking mind. I am not getting out of here.' He told me, 'You can't say that—this is a direct order.' I said, 'I don't give a damn about orders. They're probably dead and you want to send me?' " After arguing back and forth on the phone, Brucker and a sergeant crawled around to the other side, in the dark. "The first bunker I jumped into, a couple of guys were dead. A guy's head was wrapped from his nose all the way up. He got hit and couldn't see. He was just there alone, moaning. I went from bunker to bunker. People were in terrible shape, a lot of dead. We had few injuries compared to them and I couldn't figure out why. Then I dropped a flare and in the light I could see the NVA drop down. They couldn't have been more than thirty-five yards away and there were masses of them. With that, my radio operator was very badly hit. I wanted to find the command bunker. I found dead NVA in the bunkers; they'd overrun them. Must have been fifty-seven, fifty-eight NVA bodies around. I could hear them all through the night, dragging away their dead. They used to use these crude homemade 'body hooks' to rescue their dead.

"The captain was still alive, but I could tell he was in terrible shape." Brucker pushed the man's intestines in, holding them, trying to save him. Brucker was hit in the knee and groin area by shrapnel, but although it bled a lot, he was not seriously wounded. He would get the Silver Star for his actions that night. He speaks of it calmly now. "Five years ago, I would have been sweating, telling that story."

There is much more he is not telling. "I don't want to remember it again."

Yet Brucker cannot forget one scene. "We were there three days, couldn't get helicopters inside. Inside the perimeter, we stared at the bodies. They were rotting in the sun, loaded with just hundreds of flies." The smell of decaying human flesh is unforgettable to veterans.

"The helicopters couldn't land, so they got this cargo net." Like rotting fish, the men were put into the net. "There must have been thirty bodies." When the bodies were jostled—as the cargo net swung back and forth in a wide arc—fluid and blood sprayed down through the sky. "Arms and legs were falling out. . . ."

Brucker presses his lips together, and reaches for yet another of his chain-smoked cigarettes. "People talk about My Lai and how they don't understand it. *I* understand it. That day I could have gone down the road and shot *anybody* who was Vietnamese. The feeling of loss and frustration is just so deep. In Vietnam you learned to love each other, intimately; I was closer to men over there than I ever was to my family. I've seen soldiers just riddle Vietnamese bodies already dead—just shoot them and shoot them, to get something out of themselves."

The frustration was built into the military strategy. "One time we were going after NVAs and I ran right off my map. They had headed right into Cambodia. I said, 'We need a new map.' " The answer was that that was all the map they were going to get. They were not to go into Cambodia. "Our orders were to come back."

And there were other frustrations, when human error ends in profound human waste. "The company commander called for artillery barrage. The rounds fell short—right in the middle of my platoon. I was sitting in front of my radio operator, with my pack on. Snipers always try to get the radio operators and I was paranoid about that. He was sitting up against a tree and I was leaning back, my hands on top of my pack and laying back on his legs. That way, no one could see the wire from his headset. All of a sudden this *fantastic* sound comes. The shell landed to my right about thirty-five feet. Deafening sound, then popping shrapnel, little cuts on the skin and some on my face. I reached back and felt nothing but blood and pieces of flesh. I thought, God, I must have a terrible wound in back and just can't feel it. Then the radio operator yelled, 'Don't move. Stay where you are. My fuckin' foot is killing me. Don't get up!' I got my pack off, turned around. His right foot was all gone, hanging, and blood was gushing. He lay back and, finally, went like that," says Brucker, imitating a man relaxing into death. "Major arteries had been hit. In two days' time, he was going on R and R."

The carnage was everywhere. "Just unbelievable amounts of screaming. A black guy lost his penis, another guy got his arm blown off, another a leg. Everybody yelling, 'Medic! Medic!' The poor medic was going crazy. They had an investigation," says Brucker with a sigh. "Who knows what it was? After all those opportunities to get killed—we had to get it from ourselves."

More than anything, Brucker seems torn by his memories of his men. "There were a lot of individual heroics. We had a medic, Marvin, a short, thin little guy, very pale no matter how long he stayed in the sun, rotten teeth, chewed tobacco, from West Virginia. He had long since given up carrying a gun, which really blew my mind. He'd just say, 'Lieutenant, when the shooting starts I'm too *busy.*' He was fearless. Someone would yell, 'Medic!' and he'd jump up, caring for people in the most awful circumstances. Totally unassuming. He'd just say, 'That's my job.'

"And then there were guys who took out machine guns. Not doing a John Wayne, just going at them out of personal courage, to stop them and save others. And there was all this courage of turning to help your buddy."

Brucker grinds out the cigarette.

"It was," he said, "a real personal war."

Brucker knew Nancy Mariani, a striking brunette, from the time he was thirteen. "I was always knocked out by Nancy. She was my princess, but she wouldn't go out with me." Brucker ran with a wilder crowd, was a truant and fun-seeker. "He was a great friend," recalls Nancy, "but I never saw any ambition in Hubie. I had no interest in living my life with a man of no ambition. I had come from a family of successful men—my father was the clothing designer for the Marine Corps, my grandfather came from Italy and started his own construction company." Brucker hung around the Mariani household on Sundays, drinking up the warmth and conviviality of the Italian family after the loneliness of his own home.

Hyperactive, Brucker was in continuous trouble at the Catholic school where he'd been consigned to the lowest track with the worst teachers. "I started to believe I was not too smart, as far as being able to compete with my peers," says Brucker, laughing, "and a lot of them were *gorillas.*" Brucker got arrested half a dozen times for pranks, although he was never booked. "I'd say, 'I was hitchhiking and these guys just picked me up' and the cops believed me." School was a spiral of lousy grades and behavioral problems. By the time he was in high school, Brucker had achieved the distinction of being on permanent detention. "I punched out a nun in the seventh grade—to the undying envy of many people ever since. I was studying to be an altar boy and they caught me smoking."

Brucker's father, a traveling salesman who had played semi-pro baseball and was an amateur singer, was fifty-four years old when his son was born. Brucker thinks his father was frustrated by his half-talents. He was home six weeks out of the year. His mother was a "strict disciplinarian," Brucker first recalls. Later he tells it more accurately. At times he would be locked in the bathroom with her while she wielded a cat-o'-nine-tails. "She had all the discipline and it was rough on her," Brucker tries to explain. There were times when she would "get sick. She wasn't an alcoholic, but she'd just get a bottle of gin for a couple of days and get away from it all." He developed a distaste for religion from those days, saying the rosary every night on his knees in the living room with its plastic Madonna and plastic roses.

In his senior year, Brucker worked full-time for a restaurant and astounded everyone by scoring in the 1100's on his SATs. Brucker went to St. Vincent College in Latrobe, Pennsylvania. "The school owned a brewery. Leased it to Rolling Rock. I was in absolute heaven. Out drinking every night. I lasted till Christmas." Brucker left with a startling achievement—scoring an 0.6 on a 4-point system.

When drafted, Brucker hoped his heel bones, shattered in a jump at the age of twelve from an icehouse door, would disqualify him. They didn't. Brucker's father told him to "Take it like a man."

Pudgy and five feet nine inches tall, it took Brucker as long to run the mile as others in boot camp could walk it, ten and a half minutes. By the end of training, he ran the mile under six minutes. For the first time, a hidden desire for achievement emerged. He made OCS and thrived on tactical training. Out of a class of 102, less than half—48—made it. Once in Vietnam, in 1967, he saw young officers diminish one by one. "I'll never forget when we first landed—we were forty-five kilometers from the Cambodian border. I saw these haggard, gaunt men in dirty clothes. In the field, you just wore them until they fell off. They never washed. They looked like prisoners in Dachau. Once you got involved and became like them, you didn't even notice."

Brucker finds comfort in having been a good officer. "I did a terrific job of keeping some people alive. If I'd been a grunt, without much purpose, I would have felt totally different about the experience." As it was, the war soon lost a "lot of glory because of the deaths and carnage and because there seemed no purpose to it. I was able to cope so well over there because I was responsible for so many. That kept me from going over the edge."

On any résumé, Brucker would appear to have returned from Vietnam filled with an almost robotlike resolve to succeed. He finished college in three years at La Salle College in Philadelphia, then became president of a veterans' club. He became proficient at labor relations, survived a firing by a boss who happened to be related through marriage, and by 1982 was making $50,000 as director of marketing for a construction company. There is another side, however, that doesn't surface easily.

"Talk about cultural shock," he said, remembering his trip home. "The day before I am with the Montagnards in some remote village and then I am on a commercial jet with these beautiful, round-eyed American stewardesses." In San Francisco airport, "I felt naked without a gun."

On campus, he was "appalled by the attitudes toward the guys who went. And La Salle wasn't the University of Pennsylvania or Penn State. There was no SDS. We veterans went to other colleges, speaking. The message was, we didn't really care much about the war, that we had done either what we felt we should have at the time or didn't perceive that we had a choice. We tried to tell them that we were ordinary people. We didn't kill babies, didn't whole-sale try to kill people. 'We are like *you* and we all have feelings and we'd like to tell you about them.' " His association with the 21-member veterans' club —on a campus of 1,170—was vital to his readjustment.

He muses about his reasons for going. "I was taught we were saving a country and I believed it." Brucker feels that those who went later had reason to be more psychologically troubled. "They were exposed to all the unrest, bitterness, peer pressure, and pettiness of the way the war was fought. I now feel we made some drastic mistakes. I blame a lot on Johnson for escalating it."

He remains bitter about his reception from peers. "I don't have one contemporary of mine who went. They took it easy and then told *me* I was the asshole. The paper wrote up my Silver Star. I was the only kid on the block who went—but no one would talk to me about it." The pain is finally beginning to show. "Those were really, really difficult days." In Vietnam Brucker built a wall around his emotions in order to survive. When he returned, the only person he allowed inside was Nancy Mariani. This time, there was a difference to Brucker. Two years after he returned, they were married.

"Nancy saved my sanity," says Brucker. "I can't even contemplate what I would have done without her. I don't think I could have opened up to any woman I had not known before Vietnam. In the last six months, I've been much more open. But I can truly say that Nancy and our children are the only people I really care deeply about in life. I lost so many men that I had opened up to and shared life with. They had all been taken away from me . . ."

For the first five years, Brucker never slept through the night. His nightmares—or rather, his mental videotapes of the past—intrude still.

Helicopters are a grim reminder, as they are for many combat veterans. "I wake up in abject terror. I can't move my arms. I'm petrified. Nancy'll hold me and I'll get over it. Once in Vietnam, I was in a portable outdoor shower in this little compound. A sapper attack, three or four guys, ran in with bandoliers. I was hit lightly in the chest. . . . Every day since then when I'm in the shower, I am *totally* afraid. I know it's irrational. It's gotten so that if the kids walk into the bathroom, they say, 'It's me, Daddy.' They know that Daddy's afraid of the shower."

Although Brucker went through a period of trying not to relive the war, he had the need to tell Nancy. "I've poured it out for hours. I could see the emotion on her face and know it was tearing her up, but I had to get it out."

Nancy's brown eyes grow round. "To have seen the things happen to your friends that Hubie did! I wouldn't have survived. I would have vomited to death!"

"Now I feel good about myself—but I haven't figured it all out *yet*. Where's my catharsis? Who washes my brain out? A lot of us are willing to take the responsibility of the war, but who [among those who didn't go] wants to talk about something that is a bummer? If I get in conversations with a contemporary, I *never* talk about Vietnam. Anyone over fifty, I can easily talk about it and they can understand."

Nancy Brucker is the manager of newsroom assistants for a major newspaper. "Nancy has all these kids in their early twenties—too young to be involved in either part of the war. It's history to them and they say, 'Wow, what was it like?' Not, 'Oh, you asshole for going.' They are uncritical of me and that has been extremely good for me. It's a way to get it out of my system.

"I feel I am pretty much together, but I have a tremendously hard time trying to figure out *why*. I still feel guilt. Some of my buddies are physically handicapped and they carry that forever. One artillery officer was very seriously wounded. I kept him alive. He lost an eye, part of an arm, and there was a terrible hole in his chest. I never thought he would live. Now he's very solicitous of *me*. All he could talk about was how great I was because I had saved him. His whole life is that experience. Every time he looks in the mirror, he sees it."

As his own pain began to lessen with time, Brucker was able to concentrate on the positives. Had Vietnam not happened, Brucker feels he would have remained working—unhappily—in the restaurant business without an education. Both he and Nancy feel they would never have married. The woman who once dismissed him for lack of ambition now has to tell him to slow down.

One positive legacy is Brucker's approach to stress. "No matter how intense business gets, I always walk away from it. Labor negotiation was always a game to me and in my new job it's the same. I remember sitting under a tree in Vietnam and recalling everything I took for granted before—walking down the street, getting a soda, smelling flowers, being able to *change clothes.* I now take lots of time to smell the flowers." Like Jim Lawrence and others, he is sometimes contemptuous of the concerns and self-absorption of those who didn't go. "In meetings they work themselves up about something that to me seems meaningless. I want to slam my fist on the table and say, 'You assholes, bullshitting about these minuscule things.' Or some guy is having a difficult time dating this girl and it's destroying his life and he's going to an analyst. I want to say, 'Listen, you little idiot, let me tell you what can *really* hurt . . .'"

Nancy, like her college colleagues, opposed the war, but dwells more on the way it was fought than whether we should have been there. "I'm *very* displeased, angry, and annoyed at that war. It makes my toes curl. A war of attrition. Is that any way to fight? When Hubie tells of the horrors, evils, pain, suffering, and dying in an *ugly, ugly* manner for something being controlled by politics!

"But I am proud of what Hubie did." She pauses. "It's horrible to say—I hate to even mention it—but the military and Vietnam made Hubie one of the most capable men, with a broader perspective than anyone I know. He turned into a mature, sympathetic, serious, capable, sensitive man with a perspective beyond his years. A lot of those qualities were gained through great pain and suffering."

Negatives and positives coexist. Her husband grieves for a youth cut short. "A whole side of me is gone forever. I really *liked* myself before Vietnam. I came back with an old man's view of everything. I'm rarely moved by anything. Nancy gives me a gift and I say, 'It's beautiful. Thank you.' But there's no excitement about it. There's a part of me that's cut out. It's lost. It's dead."

The paradox remains. On the one hand, Brucker has an envious appreciation for life and living. On the other, he remains untouched by much.

"I see so much of life," he says wistfully, "like a bystander."

Darkness came for David L. Huffman when he was blinded by a booby trap. With little formal education, the Marine rifleman found life especially hard after Vietnam.

"When I came back I was kinda wild," recalls Huffman, who spent eight years of his youth in an orphanage. "In 1970 I was in a car accident and broke both shoulders and my spine. I was two months flat on my back and another two months in a brace. I floundered for a couple of years, looking for unskilled employment, but I couldn't nail things down."

Huffman was saved by the one thing that had caused him so much misery before Vietnam—school. After learning Braille, he completed high school, then earned two undergraduate degrees and a law degree from the Delaware Law School. In 1982 he was preparing for the bar examinations. Whatever he does in law, Huffman intends to devote his spare time to helping other disabled vets. He has participated in the Vietnam Veterans Leadership Program (VVLP), stressing a positive image for veterans.[1]

The two mid-thirties trial lawyers have a cocky assurance and a gutsy, no-holds-barred approach to the law. They walk into courtrooms and size up the opposing attorneys. If they are the same age, a subtle but withering contempt shades their attitude. "I want to whip their ass," says Paul Regan. "So many are 'perfect little men.' Not a bruise on their lives. They were too busy ducking the war to have any. Their concerns are *minor* concerns. They're not tough in here," says Regan, touching his chest. "I know other lawyers who are Vietnam veterans and you can almost spot them. They are very powerful trial lawyers, very sure of themselves, and they're not kissing the judges' asses."

Norman Townsend, a Vietnam veteran lawyer with a hearing loss disability from the war, agrees. One day in a courtroom, after winning a civil disobedience case for a group of nuclear protesters, Townsend spun around to a woman who was not so successful in her case. She stood with her two high-powered corporate lawyers, both of whom had ducked the draft. Townsend said with a grin, "The next time you want help, don't count on your 'uptown lawyers.' "

Vietnam veteran lawyers I have met like the excitement and give-and-take of trial work rather than corporate law. Like other successful veterans in professions dominated by their nongoing peers (such as teaching, journalism or business), Townsend and Regan feel they can best any of them in tense, competitive situations.

Both were high school dropouts. Both were combat veterans who saw relatively few traumatizing moments and only Townsend was slightly injured. They returned with different feelings about the war, but strengthened by it.

Regan pours wine into long-stemmed glasses in his duplex townhouse with its tasteful blue-and-white-dotted velvet sofa, butcher block table, oriental rugs, and lots of ferns. Fetuccini Alfredo and Bibb lettuce for dinner; candles on the table and old Bessie Smith records in the background.

No one meeting him today would believe that Regan as a kid systematically stole food from freight cars and mugged drunks reeling out of pubs to get food for his seven younger brothers and sisters. With him was his pretty red-haired slim girlfriend, a lawyer also, from a middle-class background. She started college in 1970. No one *she* knew would have dreamed of going to Vietnam.

"There was *one* veteran on our small campus and everyone sort of stood back from him. He was different because he got the VA monthly benefits. I felt they should not have gone to the war. They should have done anything except to go. Canada, whatever."

Did you stop to think that a lot of those who went could not afford college or came from homes where higher education was not considered necessary to their lives? Or that a lot of your friends were able to avoid the same decisions about war because they were in college?

"Coming from my neighborhood, you didn't think like that." Regan had been eyeing Judy impassively. He interjects caustically, "I find it interesting that the poor fuckin' vet was ostracized on your campus." She nods. "They were ostracized *everywhere,*" continues Regan, "although I wouldn't tolerate it for our people at Brandeis." Regan, who got into Brandeis University on a Great Society program, encouraged other veterans to enter through the program. "The first year, I didn't want to waste my time with the regular students. My veterans were my emotional tie and I had no time for social life. I had a ninth-grade education and had to study my ass off. I was thrown in with kids from Scarsdale with 780 SATs in math."

A strong hostility remains for what he consistently terms the "draft dodgers." However, a condescending soft spot coexists for most of the Brandeis students he knew. "All these intellectuals. They were *sooooooo* removed from life as I knew it." There were, however, a vociferous collection of SDS members who infuriated many of the veterans. "Those assholes walkin' around with the VC flags," says Regan, "while our guys are sittin' in class without limbs."

Brandeis was as much a culture shock as Vietnam had been three years earlier for Regan, who grew up roughing it in the insular world of South Boston. There were strata of poverty, as well as degrees of criminal activity, within Southie. There was a fierce pride and curious ethos that sanctioned stealing food more than going on welfare. "You *knew* who was on welfare and everybody made a point of it. Those on welfare had dental care. Christ, my teeth were gone by the time I got to the Marines. People on welfare got tetracycline tablets for their *acne!* It was unbelievable. Which is why Southie as a community is so *very* hostile to the welfare society."

Regan was "filled with rage," much of it directed toward his father. "His clan were notorious brawlers. My father ran three or four crap games and my mother wouldn't marry him unless he gave up gambling. So he gave up gambling and took up drinking. He was a longshoreman. That waterfront is a very tough place, bookmaking, loan sharking . . ."

Regan had terrible fights with his father, punching him in the face, refusing to sit in the same room. They watched television and ate dinner in shifts from the time he was thirteen years old. Regan delivered papers at the age of ten, shined shoes at twelve, quit school in the tenth grade, and joined the Marines. "I knew that if I didn't I would probably kill someone. I was a little punk with a lot of rage in me, like a lot of kids. Why? Because things were bad. A lot of hunger, frustration, that feeling of not going anywhere. There were a lot of bright guys, but an anti-intellectualism prevailed in South Boston." Not only was it difficult to scrape up the money for even a state university, the idea of pursuing an education was not natural.

When he could not legally provide enough for his mother and the eight children, Regan broke into freight trains. "It was very much a community thing. You'd get the first load and then you'd tell everybody in the neighborhood, 'I found a carload of canned Chinese food,' and then you'd lead 'em to it. At the waterfront there were miles of freight yards filled with food, canned goods, meat. The local judge generally would slap us on the wrists. He was a good guy. The longshoremen were on strike and he knew it was longshoremen's kids."

His mother stopped asking questions. "She had hungry children. She cried, then took the food. And I cried," Regan paused, remembering, "but it was even sadder when my younger brothers and sisters would cry and say 'Mommy, I want a sandwich.' My mother would go for three days pretending there was food coming. 'Your fathah's comin' home soon and everything will be fine,' and that son of a bitch would be out drinking. After a while of watching that, I'd go out—and then *beware,* whoever you might be.

"If I've achieved any success in life, it's completely due to my mother. She was a saint. As long as I can remember, she would put all the kids to bed at night, leaving me to watch them, and at ten-thirty P.M. she would step out into the cold, walk several miles to save carfare, and punch in at Bay State Bindery Company, where she worked on cutting machines, binding books. After working the graveyard shift for eight hours, she would come home, wake eight kids up, and cook all of them breakfast and send them all to school. She'd nap a few hours and then begin all over again."

As Regan got older, he was able to get better-paying jobs and assumed the man-in-the-house mantle. "The girls always had to feed me first. There's a strict hierarchy prominent in old Boston Irish homes and I think there's a meanness in that. The expectations of the men are increased and those of the women decreased." Regan laughs. "I remember Brandeis being very unusual because the women had a point of view. I couldn't believe they would not only speak up, but give me shit! And they were strangers!"

Regan is lean and lanky, with an easy, loping gait; a young Lee Marvin with a drooping mustache, blue eyes, a manic grin that stretches across his long face. He is typecast by some, he feels, because of his "cabdriver accent." He is a quick and accurate mimic, slipping from Irish lilt to ghetto "mo-fo's" with ease. In Marine boot camp he formed a quick affinity with blacks, even though he came from an area that would erupt in deep racial clashes during the seventies school busing. "They were, like me, used to juvenile gang warfare and wouldn't run on me. They knew the same kind of violence. I didn't trust suburban kids at all."

Regan hated boot camp. "It was harder than the goddamn *war*. They'd get up real close, those goddamn Southern Scotch-Irish drill instructor bastards, and they'd say, 'You pimple-faced, piss-complected, pus-filled puddle of puke. Yew got a girlfriend?' 'No, *sir!*' " Regan is in full Southern imitation. "Then they'd drawl, 'Ah didn't think so.' " He laughs. "Even that kind of abuse is pretty serious when you're seventeen and every pimple is a major crisis. My drill instructor, Staff Sergeant James A. Stafford, what a bastard. A very good drill instructor. Crazy as hell and interested in teaching you the best way to 'kill the gooks.' "

By the time he got to Vietnam, Regan was prepared. He insists, "I never had a nightmare over it and I killed a whole lot of people probably."

He stops in astonishment. "I couldn't kill anybody *today*. God! Well, if somebody came here and gave me shit, it would be all over. But you could *never* get me to go somewhere and kill somebody. That's over."

Did you believe in what you were doing?

"Yes. Goddamn yes! That is *very important*. I believed all of that. When I was there—and even now—I believe that what I did provided a vehicle for the people of South Vietnam to have a little leverage in their own lives. I am *certain* the North Vietnamese wouldn't give them that.

"All that stuff about thinking that China would come in is bullshit. All we had to do was flood the dikes, mine the harbors, fuck the place up a whole lot, and pull out. We didn't have to stay there. But we played rinky-dink.

"I was pro-war until I read *The Best and the Brightest*. The whole point seemed the complete bullshit of it. We weren't doing anything right. Why did we waste thousands of people?"

Regan was with an artillery battalion North of Chu Lai on Hill 54 during his first tour; "I went home just before Tet, then extended my tour. I joined an armored landing vehicle tank [Amtrac] battalion. Why? Because I hated the Marines and the rinky-dink boot-shining regimentation back home and you were subject to it for the rest of your time 'in the crotch,' as we said. Besides, if you extended, you got an early out. Also, I felt I was doing something worthwhile.

But, I interject, we were burning homes, destroying crops, bombing and napalming and defoliating . . .

"We were trashing the country. No question. Did I say it wasn't stupid? I'm only saying I *felt* we were taking care of these kids. I was in a secure area. And kids went to school, etc. We had secured an area and they were generally free from the violence that was endemic in other areas. Since I wasn't risking my neck, except during an occasional mortar or ambush attack, I felt it was a thrill, so I came back. I was immediately transferred into the DMZ during Tet and the shit hit the fan. Day and night. Lived in bunkers and were shelled all the time. I saw hundreds and hundreds of NVA movin' south all the time." The disgust and frustration remain in his voice. "And we'd have a 'cease fire' and you couldn't open up on them and you would just count them and it was just all fucked up."

Regan returned without a scratch. He is careful to say that if he had been severely injured his outlook would be different. He came back, typically, jumpy and on edge, "wanting to get away from everyone" and burning with rage at the antiwar movement. He feels the veterans "got screwed" and champions programs that help them. Yet Regan does not buy the delayed stress argument.

"With exceptions, like my friend getting his leg blown off and living in buckets of ice for months after your skin is burned off—*that's* different. Had I been wounded I would have been a lot more screwed up emotionally, but I think it was basically the personality of the guy in the first place."

We talk about the view that Vietnam's specialness caused problems—hills taken and abandoned, enemies he counted but couldn't kill, friends killed in a losing war, the special terror of guerrilla warfare.

"What difference does it make what kind of war it is? That's all bullshit."

He stops to think. "Maybe if you grew up tough, you were better off. I remember being very close to the blacks, Puerto Ricans, and the Mexicans while in Vietnam. I *wanted* to be near them. We understood each other perfectly. I was very disappointed that when we came home, we separated again. I used to give the clenched fist, 'Ongawa, Black Powah,' all the time."

Regan picks up an article in *Psychology Today* and jabs a finger at the piece. "It's all about how 'guilty' we are. *I* never killed a kid in my life. Never killed, never raped any women. Never did any weird shit. And I didn't *see* much of that. Only one guy, who shot a water buffalo for no reason and a kid was sitting on it. He coulda killed the kid. Everybody knew he was nuts. The other marines were afraid of him. He was just a gutless punk. This shrink writes about how we are all guilty because of all the atrocities we committed. I don't know what he's talkin' about!" Regan reads contemptuously from the article: " 'There was a grief revealed by his gaze that he could not admit to me or, perhaps, even to himself, possibly because he had little hope of finding a useful way to deal with it.' *Perhaps, possibly,* " mimics Regan.

Regan had a point. The article was superciliously intellectual, the overall impression one of condescending compassion for the "troubled" veteran. Since the psychologists and sociologists who write such articles are often nongoing peers with antiwar backgrounds, most veterans are, understandably, quickly hostile if the tone is patronizing.

Rather than guilt, Regan felt that "the common denominator about veterans was that they would not take shit from anyone."

After a few months back home hanging around, Southie lost its appeal. There is a vital difference in repressively not talking about Vietnam and truly being able to let it go. "I got so *tired* hangin' out, smokin' dope, drinkin' booze in Southie and talkin' about all the killin' and dyin'. 'I'm so sick of the war stories,' I says to myself. 'What am I goin' to be doin' ten years from

now? Tellin' about the time I was pinned down in some fuckin' rice paddy?'
It's dumb."

The metamorphosis of Paul Regan had begun.

When he was kicked out of high school, which was often, Regan, bored
with the less than inspiring curriculum of Southie's public schools, would
read books in the library. "I loved Horatio Alger," he says, laughing.

He is grateful to both the Vietnam War and the Great Society programs.
The war made him want to do something with his life; the program got him
into Brandeis. "No way would I have gone to college. The war on poverty
was one of the most humane experiences and provided me with the vehicle to
change my life. In quantum leaps! At best I would have gone to Boston State
and my kids to B.C. [Boston College]. And I just jumped over all that to one
of the top schools in the country." Despite educational disadvantages and a
ninth-grade education, he held his own, not only at Brandeis but at highly
competitive Georgetown University Law School. "Brandeis gave me a scholarship. I could not have afforded Brandeis on the GI Bill—or Georgetown.
The benefits were nothing if you wanted a good education. I had to borrow
my brains out to go to Georgetown.

"I'm very hostile to the government for setting us up for that chickenshit
war, giving us bullshit benefits, and then bringing back the people who
ducked it in the so-called 'amnesty' program. I stuck my neck out for patriotic reasons. My friend, they blew his leg and half his skin off and it's not easy
to forget that. And he and others like him *have* been forgotten in a lot of
ways. It's important to know that the guys who risked their lives have given
more and are owed far more and are stronger than the people who copped out
in jail, even. I'm a criminal lawyer and doing time is not such a big deal.
When you do time for draft, you do it with John Dean at Lompoc. Your life
hasn't been risked."

Some of the men feared jail rape, I mention. Regan is unconcerned.

"Then they shoulda taken their chances with the NVA."

Regan burns as he remembers being turned down for a job once. "All the
interview had to do with was the war and did I kill anybody. Another time a
typical draft-dodgin' son of a bitch was giving me a hard time at this law firm.
Well, shortly after I got hired, *he* got fired."

There is an obvious intertwining of class in his anger at a type of draft
dodger whom Regan perceives to be sneering at veterans. "The 'morally
superior' upper middle class, opposed to all us 'working-class kids and punks
from the slums' who obviously went and *loved* it," he says caustically. He
refused to go with a "fancy" law firm. "I wouldn't know anybody there," he
says. "They would have been the same assholes who didn't go and I didn't
want to put up with that."

Regan's hostility has been a galvanizing, rather than debilitating force, he
says.

"It's very important to win, to whip their ass in trial. Some of 'em I *really* want. The prototypes of everything I resent—inherited money, pampered assholes with power, especially prosecutors who went right through school, didn't lose three years in the service."

Regan plays hard but is a consummate workaholic, still climbing out of Southie's slums, driven because "I lost three years of my career time in Vietnam." In a short period he became the managing lawyer of his twenty-lawyer firm.

For all his resentment of a certain type of nongoer, Regan has many friends who were deeply committed antiwar participants; their sincere commitment and lack of condescension toward him made the difference.

When first asked, his girlfriend sees little difference in Regan and the other lawyers his age with whom she works. Then she adds, "I see the ones who aren't veterans as maybe not as sure of themselves. They're a bit more lacking in compassion, a bit more self-centered."

Regan feels that feisty veterans, who challenge and fight the negative stereotypes of themselves, are the comers of tomorrow. "I couldn't watch movies about us for years." Regan delivers a quick scenario of the standardized plot: "The typical 'crazy veteran hiding in the hills, reliving it, shooting at kids or women or cops and finally coming down a blubbering idiot, crying into the arms of his mother and being put in the nuthouse *where he belongs.*' I *hated* that."

There is enough anger and denial within Regan to categorize him as one of the qualified "stable," as defined in one sociological study; while not free of residual negatives and angers, he is mostly unfettered by them.

"Sure, it was traumatic. That's why so many kids lost their earning potential at first, because when we first came home we were all a little nuts, unable to concentrate.

"I lost a lot of youth; I would have had a *girlfriend* for the three years I was in service." Then he laughs. "I was better off, because I probably would have ended up knockin' someone up and bein' married with fifteen kids."

Once again, the pattern of counting one's blessings emerged. "The war was a positive experience. I learned about the world outside of Southie. I learned all about life and death. I'm sure you've seen all this bullshit, 'You haven't really lived till you've almost really died'?" Regan drops the tough-guy stance for just a second. "Well, it's true."

In college Regan steadily dated Christie Hefner, now president of Playboy Enterprises and a Phi Beta Kappa and *summa cum laude.* It was no small item of awe for many of his *Playboy*-reading classmates. He saw life at her father's Chicago mansion and met Hollywood agents and saw riches unheard of in Southie.

But there was much more. "I learned about books and reading and caring and the theater. I learned about poetry, without laughing at somebody who was reciting it."

And there was a final lesson that seemed to be of extreme importance to Regan.

"I learned how *not* to be such a tough guy."

Norm Townsend was a California kid, from a more stable lifestyle than Regan, but the present-day feistiness is similar. His ideological metamorphosis was startling. In 1964 Townsend was a "Youth for Goldwater." "I got my picture in *Life* magazine—1964 election night coverage, a shot of Los Angeles campaign headquarters with everybody standing around crying." He became a Green Beret—and returned a dove active in the peace movement and in 1981 helped defend the Berrigan brothers.

"I really don't know the 'cognitive process' that caused me to change." The stilted phrase is out of sync with his vaguely hip Southern California look: cowboy boots, blue jeans, faded blue shirt, beard, gray-blond longish-but-sculpted hair that curled at the neck.

His was a prosperous but drifting childhood. Townsend's father was an engineer who worked for aircraft companies and was much in demand in those days. A stretch in Oklahoma is remembered with displeasure, but Townsend "fell right into the California lifestyle." So much so, he says with a laugh, "that I got kicked out my senior year." He was senior class vice-president, his mother was president of the PTA, and it was six weeks before graduation, but Townsend had skipped so much school and had done so poorly that they kicked him out anyway.

The next step on his road to Vietnam was a pregnant girlfriend. The pregnancy would end in a miscarriage, but they were already married by then. A wed teenager, Townsend set about being a family man, without a high school education. He tried working in a machine shop, but hated it. A friend went to OCS. "I felt, if *he* can be 'an officer and a gentleman,' so can I." Townsend enlisted, intending to make the military a career. "I was raised very authoritarian and, with that kind of background, I fit right in. Even so, boot camp was ridiculous.

"OCS was like a college fraternity hell week for six months. You'd run five miles holding rifles overhead. Arms started falling asleep, people would fall by the wayside, they'd scream at you if you tried to help them. They made you crawl two miles on your stomach, just basically to see if they could make you break. Those who said 'Fuck you' or had nervous breakdowns were ragged out."

What about the time-honored concept that there was a practical, worthwhile goal of fostering discipline in such methods?

"I would have bought the discipline, but not the unnecessary stuff. The most sadistic was when they put us in fake POW camps and tortured us. Put you in a hole, lay a fifty-five-gallon drum on top, and beat on it for four hours. Take a pole and make you sit with legs around it and lean you way back. I can't remember how it worked, but it hurt like hell. Made us catch rabbits, kill them, and eat them raw. Had to escape in the middle of the night in the

Okefenokee swamps with no flashlight. I don't really know how realistic it was if you were ever captured.

"I graduated seventy-fifth in a class of 141. After OCS they sent me to Airborne Jump School, military intelligence, and then Okinawa Jungle Training School." He was one of the young, baby-faced officers. "They called me 'Captain Kid.'

"I figured if I was going to make it a career, I might as well make it right. Intelligence school sounded glamorous—spies—it seemed safe. Nobody was going to shoot at me. I loved wearing the Green Beret. Talk about being cocky." Townsend laughed. "I volunteered to go to Vietnam. It was amazing, the amount of brainwashing that was accomplished. For everybody. The body count was the most gruesome aspect of brainwashing."

At first, Townsend was only peripherally aware of protest.

"*Stars and Stripes* and Armed Forces Radio mentioned a bit about the peace movement but it was always 'Communist-inspired,' so any thoughts I had were negative and remained so for a long time after I got back. I wrote my mom a bitter letter: 'I don't understand these people protesting the war. They ought to be over here and see my friends killed.' I finally came to the realization that the Vietnamese wanted to be left alone."

Life is not pleasant there now, I comment.

"I don't see how it could be worse than when we were there. By the time I started at UCLA, a philosophy professor helped me work through a lot of bitterness and anger. It came from all these friends being killed and I couldn't make any sense out of it. I finally came to the sense that we were just messing Vietnam up. I realized all our so-called aims didn't mean shit to them.

"I had it easy, compared to most of the guys I knew. Six months of my time I did intelligence briefings in Saigon and when I was out [on covert missions to Cambodia] we shot only at bushes. But a *lot* of good friends got killed—50 percent of my [infantry] OCS graduate class were dead within eighteen months. If I hadn't gone to military intelligence, I would have ended up in a combat unit."

After Saigon, Townsend went into Cambodia with MACV SOG (Special Operations Group). He speaks sarcastically. "Big secret. We had to say on threat of prosecution there were no Americans there. The whole purpose was intelligence gathering. Usually there'd be two Americans and several Montagnards. We were supposed to be monitoring traffic on the Ho Chi Minh Trail. If we ran into North Vietnamese, we were supposed to run—literally—because this was covert. Most of us obeyed that concept. There were some psychotic killers. They got their biggest thrill out of offing gook farmers. You put a uniform on some guys and they just get cocky. See who could outgross each other. Grossest thing I saw was a guy got drunk and ate out a bitch dog in Okinawa on a $50 bet. There was that elite caste to it that attracted some real macho types. Mostly though, there were a lot of good people."

Law had always fascinated Townsend and after Vietnam he decided "Why not?" "After all," he says caustically, "I had the GI Bill—even though it was *six months* coming. I got $170 a month; that was nothing for a college education and *nothing* for law school, but even to get that you had to know the system. I was stubborn and persisted, but some guys ran up against a barrier and quit. The VA didn't tell me how to file for a hearing loss, nobody counseled me on my benefits; they just shuffled me out the door. I wound up with benefits only because I had the gumption to go get them. Plus, I didn't have the disadvantages. I'm not black, not from the ghetto."

College was a serious time. While in Vietnam, he and his wife had divorced. Townsend was a commuter student and worked as a special-delivery messenger. There was Peirce Junior College, then San Fernando Valley for two years, UCLA for two years. Townsend scored in the high 90th percentile of his LSATs and went to George Washington University.

Today Townsend worries about some veteran friends. "A Mexican-American who had three quarters of his friends killed and saw a lot of action experienced real trauma and guilt. People died in his arms. I escaped that. I was also real fortunate in that I had that one professor who listened to me when I returned or I might have been a candidate for more help. My friend needed to live life on the edge, drinking, fast-car driving, wouldn't permit any attachments, couldn't talk to anybody. I know delayed post-traumatic stress is part of his behavior. I didn't realize it until I started researching it for legal purposes. He finally fell in love and last I heard is all right and working with Schlitz Brewery."

Townsend moved more and more in the direction of pacifism.

"We can't control what anyone else is doing as much as we would like to, but we can control what *we* do. I'm all for unilateral nuclear disarmament." The former Goldwaterite says, "Instead of destroying a village to save it, we now talk like people willing to destroy a world to 'save' it." (At the time, President Reagan had raised the specter of limited nuclear warfare in Europe.) "Nazi Germany killed 6 million and now we're talking about the destruction of perhaps 600 million human beings and we are learning to live with that!" Townsend cries out.

Townsend defended the Berrigans and other activists who broke into a Defense facility, beat in the head of a nuclear missile nose cone, and poured blood on it.

Isn't it naïve to try to stop the nuclear arms race with one gesture like that?

"If you're going to judge protest on what is accomplished overnight, most are failures. They *knew* there was no practical sense that beating in those two nose cones would stop everything now, but they wanted to dramatize that we've gotten horribly complacent, learning to *live* with the ever present threat of nuclear annihilation."

The Berrigans got three to ten years. "An incredibly high sentencing, but they could have gotten thirty years."

Although many of his clients are civil disobedience cases, Townsend is not blind to their faults. "They feel because they did it for a moral reason they have a right to better treatment in jail. I got a call two weeks ago from one, 'They won't let me have a vegetarian diet.' There is a certain elitism that bothers me."

Townsend is appalled at the nongoers of yesteryear who now champion the draft, often on the grounds that the all-volunteer Army is so disproportionately poor and black. "You can bet in any draft system devised, the chosen ones will get out of it, either through an office in the Pentagon or whatever. The ones with connections aren't going to get shot at. There's never been a draft that hasn't been used. With the bellicosity going on now, I feel it would be used.

"The social budget cuts are absurd. There's *nothing* more inflationary than building bombs and stockpiling them in a building and then throwing them away in four years," said the former Green Beret. "We've got to stop this madness."

3 The Wounded

MANY OF VIETNAM'S WOUNDED, WHO SURVIVED THEIR INITIAL years of recovery, seem driven to excel far beyond men who are physically whole. There are the blind who have become lawyers. The legless who have held political office and managed businesses. The one-legged who have become expert downhill skiers.

Many others do not fit the neat, stereotypical career "success" package but are successes in their day-to-day survival and acceptance of their drastically altered lives.

Some 6,655 veterans lost limbs in Vietnam and receive varying degrees of compensation. For example, (using 1983 figures) a single veteran who has lost both legs above the knees received $1,661 a month; one with both legs lost below the knees received $1,506. A veteran with one leg off above the knee received 60 percent disability and an additional monthly stipend for the loss of a leg, for a total of $506. One leg off below the knee is considered a 40 percent disability, and with the monthly stipend the check comes to $311. There is a marked decrease from 100 percent to 90 percent disabled—$1,213 a month versus $729.

Although some government agencies paint a rosy picture of veterans' employment, Ron Drach, a DAV (Disabled American Veterans) director, disputes that: "Every month since 1970, when the Bureau of Labor Statistics began collecting data, Vietnam veterans have always exceeded nonveterans in unemployment. There are now about 856,000 unemployed. It is hard to compare [unemployment numbers] with peers because their group is so much larger, but veteran unemployment is *proportionally* much higher.

"While there is no official unemployment data on disabled Vietnam veterans, the Carter administration estimated that 50 percent of the disabled Vietnam-era veterans are unemployed," says Drach, who lost a leg above the knee. "We know it is very high." He sighs. "We try to destroy that image that all veterans were whacked out, and some of us groups who do that are 'too successful.' Now people don't think there are any problems. 'Forget about the Vietnam veteran.' We overdid it."

Lonnie Sparks deserves to be remembered. He is one of those who does not work. His only dreams were to follow his father into the local auto plant. He is as Middle American as his hometown of Muncie, Indiana, where they grow national high-school basketball champions. Sparks was drafted and says, even today, "I really didn't know what we were doing. I just did what they told me. I was a foot soldier. *I just carried an M-16 and shot at them what shot at me."* The fear was there always. "We lived mostly in the dirt. Wrote letters by moonlight." One day Sparks stepped on a mine. "I was awake when they put me in the helicopter. I seen one of my legs layin' on the ground." He lost both legs. Now he talks quietly but flips the top of his cigarette lighter rapidly as he remembers.

The overall impression of Sparks is one of gentleness. When one of his daughters leans against his wheelchair, he holds her hand, strokes her hair. When she asks what happened to him, he says he stepped on a huge fire-cracker. Sparks takes pride in his agility. He hangs out with a gas-station owner, Phil Clark, who is like a father to him and beats him at double solitaire. Sometimes Sparks works on the cars. In the early evenings Sparks plays pool at his favorite bar and in the winter plays wheelchair basketball for the Indianapolis Mustangs. Lonnie ponders why he has adjusted so well. "I knew I was going to live," he recalls. "I just tried to make the best of it." There is a fleeting moment of sadness. "I'm still trying to make the best of it."

Then Sparks, who has no legs from the hips down, demonstrates an amazing ability to look beyond himself, to find others who are more afflicted. "Just layin' there in the hospital, watching the guys that was in worse shape . . . that stuck with me." He is almost apologetic when he talks of his financial needs. Sparks is 100 percent disabled, gets more than $1,600 a month from the government, partial payment for his home, and a clothing allowance.

"I don't mean to sound greedy, but we could use more. I wear out my clothes fast, crawlin' on the ground, lifting myself in and out of the chair. There's so many guys here that can't find work," says Sparks, who is loath to compete with them, despite his automobile mechanic's ability. "I can't see myself taking a job from one of them that really has to make a living."

Neither Sparks nor his wife show any bitterness about the way the war was run. Sparks says, "I just thought it was all these chiefs and all these Indians."

For many veterans a necessary emotional healing process is to consciously or unconsciously give meaning and justification to a war short on meaning and justification for many others.

"We *have* to keep thinking this was done for a good cause," says Becky quietly. "If he ever thought it wasn't, it would destroy Lonnie."

Dale Wilson, thirty-four, was one of Jim Webb's *Fields of Fire* men, serving in his platoon from April 1969 until February 1970, when a command-deto-nated mine ripped away both his legs and an arm. Wilson had only a short time to go.

Wilson lives on a farm near Troutman, North Carolina, "just a little stop with a red light," near Statesville. After months in hospitals Wilson got his bachelor of arts degree in sociology and modern archeology at Catawba College, then opened up a restaurant. "Sixteen hours a day, I had to put on them artificial legs. In college," he says with a smile, "it seems like all my classes was on the second floor."

Wilson returned to an accepting environment and little antiwar sentiment at his Southern college: "I respect only the ones that went to jail. Carter just destroyed everything when he pardoned the draft-dodgers. It would *still* take two or three guys to get my fingers off a guy's throat if he was talkin' that [antiwar] trash. Personally I'm glad that I went, rather than wonder what it was like. I think a lot who raised so much hell of not wanting to go maybe were trying to justify their *fear* of going, justifying a reason to get out of it. That's not the kind of person I want to teach my kids the history of the Vietnam War. This town's lost a lot. One street in Statesville, three boys were killed. Still because of no recognition, we don't stick together. I'm with the DAV and it's hard to get the younger men out."

After the war Wilson says he became "closer than ever to my dad. I remember the first time I walked on my little ole clumsy legs they made me at Naval Hospital. I staggered up the stairs. I still remember the tears in his eyes."

Wilson met his wife, "a super girl," while at junior college. They have been married twelve years and have two children. "She doesn't treat me any differently. The kids—I used to wonder before you have them what they're going to think. It's really amazing; it doesn't affect them at all. One day I was hurrying up my son to go someplace, and I said, 'Get your legs on and let's go.' I meant pants of course—it just cracked him up."

Delayed stress is something Wilson has not given a "whole lot of thought. A lot of 'em you just don't know, whether they're using it as an excuse. A friend called me from Wisconsin. Said he's gone through it. A lot of his trouble was accepting his amputation. Wouldn't admit it to himself. I don't want to put anyone down though."

Wilson has an abiding faith that the war was right: "Anytime you're stopping the spread of communism is always important. My dad went to his war, I went to mine. I don't feel bitter about the oriental people. I often wonder how they could side either way. We looked like giants. Between the NVA, the VC, and us, I feel real sorry for them. Seven of us got together a few weeks ago, and we all agreed it's just this type of thing: When your country says go, it is not up to us to decide whether it's right or wrong."

Over and over he tries to see his injuries in a positive light. "After eighteen years of freedom in this country, I feel like two legs and an arm wasn't a lot to sacrifice.

"A lot better guys than me died over there. I say don't sweat the small stuff. I've got to realize the limbs are gone and aren't coming back. You're just going to live till you die, so you might as well make the best of it."

Although he has nightmares and flashbacks, Wilson was so busy with real pain for months that he "let my nightmares go." They almost seemed trivial compared to the phantom pains that amputees experience. They "feel" leg pains even if the extremities are gone. "It hits you regularly for months."

Wilson emphasizes that a major readjustment process occurred when he was on a ward with twenty or so other amputees. "You helped each other out." Most amputees in fact feel that, despite their traumatic injuries, they gained through the sharing and readjustment time spent with other veterans. The gallows humor among hospitalized comrades was a stinging antidote to self-pity and carries over into their lives today. Many display an awesome, macabre toughness. Nat Ward, a San Diego lawyer, sticks his stump into his polished, hand-tooled cowboy boots and walks out to his car with a barely discernible limp. In his pocket he carries an embossed Old English–script calling card. At the restaurant Ward checks to see if the car next to him in the "Handicapped Only" spot had a special handicapped license. It did, but if it had not, Ward was ready with his card to slip under the windshield wiper: IF YOU'RE NOT HANDICAPPED, THEN GET THE FUCK OUT OF HERE.

And Mike McGarvey, who served under Jim Webb, had a dotted line tattooed where his arm was blown off, with these words inscribed above it: "Cut across the dotted line."

Men remember a crucial bonding of black humor, for survival—such as dedicating "You'll Never Walk Alone" to a double amputee while he was recuperating in a ward. One veteran who had lost only one leg became best buddies with a man who had lost both. He would tap his one good foot and say, "Remember when you could do that?" His friend recalls, "That lack of pity is the only thing that saved me."

Many of these wounded men share a common impatience with veterans who claim psychological wounds. Although they were toughened by their injuries, they were also cossetted in rehabilitation wards with one another at a time when they desperately needed it. Many feel that a moratorium from the outside world—a moratorium unavailable to the veteran who returned physically whole but emotionally troubled—fostered a healthy outlook. They have a hard time understanding the men who claim psychological problems.

"So many of them say it was so terrible, the way they went from the field of battle to home within hours. I agree," says Jeff Barber, who lost a leg in Vietnam and worked with veterans seeking jobs, "but I don't know anybody, including me, who was willing to come home by *troop ship* rather than by jet. The same guys who are now saying, a decade later, 'If only someone had talked to me,' are the same ones who just wanted to come home and get the hell out of service.

"I have some doubts about some of these guys, although there *are* some very honest ones. One guy I know has 50 percent psychiatric disability. He says his problems are Vietnam-related, but I have trouble with that. I've known so many people who've really been able to pull it together and go on.

A lot more have moved on than haven't." Barber seems ambivalent as he starts musing, almost to himself: "I've seen both sides. I've seen a lot of screwed-up guys too. One guy had a scar from his hairline down to his lip. Shrapnel ripped his face. He'd never put in for a disability claim. Just didn't want to have anything to do with the VA. He had sixteen jobs in the last years, had a lot of kids, didn't know which end was up. He was a truck driver who couldn't drive. Had four DUI's [Driving Under the Influence convictions]. He really had problems, besides being unemployed. I took him to the Vet Center and he was ready right *then and there* to talk about what was bugging him. They said 'Could you come in Saturday?' Well, I lost that guy right then and there. He thought it was the same old runaround.

"Still, I wonder if a lot of people just don't like to go around saying 'Hey, poor me.' "

Max Cleland, Georgia's secretary of state and former VA administrator, is a triple amputee who can never forget the therapeutic camaraderie of the men in The Pit, also known as Ward One of the Walter Reed Army Medical Center, where the most severely wounded Vietnam veterans were hospitalized. A few years ago 150 veterans were invited to a dinner. Among them were 7 men who had been in The Pit and who celebrated a "Max Cleland Alive Day" roast with jokes ranging from latrine to gallows humor.

The whole evening went like a script from "M*A*S*H." Major Jon Lawton talked about the night when eight of the patients had escaped from The Pit to a nearby go-go bar. "Every damn one of us had lost an arm or a leg or an eye or something—and here was this go-go dancer asking 'What happened to y'all?' One of us said, 'Lookie here, honey, we had a skiing accident . . .' " The 150 dinner guests drowned out the rest of Lawton's sentence with laughter. He continued, explaining how he sneaked the go-go dancer back to The Pit. She agreed on one condition—that there would be music to dance to. But the tape recorder was broken, and there was no music. Lawton continued, "So I told her, 'Don't worry, honey. We'll *sing!*' There we were, eight drunks, all singing eight different songs. So I shouted, 'We'll all sing "The Star-Spangled Banner." ' " They did, the go-go dancer undulating to "Oh, say can you see . . ."

Brigadier General G. L. Baker, commanding officer of Walter Reed, recalled the dressing-down he got from his commanding officer about the night of the go-go dancer incident. "He wanted to know just what kind of an operation I was running and what he could do to 'punish' those horrible individuals who pulled that stunt." They were men like Major Lawton, who had caught twenty-two bullets and had spent more than a year in a cast. Baker recalled, "I replied to that commanding officer, 'Well, sir, exactly what *else* would you like us to do to them?' " Baker was interrupted by loud, emotional applause.

Jim Mayer, Cleland's executive assistant in the VA and now employed by the Paralyzed Veterans of America, kept up a relentlessly nonmaudlin blitz in a style patterned after Steve Martin. As Mayer moved around at the mike in his highly polished loafers, it seemed impossible that he himself had lost both legs below the knee in Vietnam and was wearing artificial limbs. When Mayer introduced John H. ("Red") Leffler, who lost an eye in Vietnam and wears an eye patch, Mayer said that Leffler moonlighted as a "part-time salesman for Hathaway shirts." Bill Johnstone, who handled Cleland's unsuccessful 1974 campaign for lieutenant governor of Georgia, said that Cleland's post-Watergate morality slogan was "Support Max Cleland—he can only put one hand in the till."

Nonpitying jokes kept many amputees going during the depression days of rehabilitation. Cleland was just one of countless wounded veterans who resented being treated like embarrassing relics of an unwanted war. "The reason I'm alive and celebrating life ten years after is because of you people here —who would accept me as I was," said Cleland at his roast. "A special thanks goes to the guys in The Pit. You were the first to accept me as I was."[1]

For several months, Jeff Barber, an amputee, convalesced with other veterans in Denver, Colorado, living a cloistered life where no one was different. They learned to ski together, and Barber became a champion downhill skier in international races for the handicapped, winning medals in Europe. His challenges on the ski slopes and friendship with other amputees did a great deal to rebuild his confidence. "At one point, however, I realized I couldn't hang around these guys forever. Some of them are still hanging out together, skiiing, whatever." Barber felt the need to push himself into a harsher, more competitive world.

Crutches dig into his armpits as Jeff Barber navigates a hilly street in La Jolla, California. His brown corduroys, where the right leg should be, drag the ground. Rather than lug it up one flight of stairs, Barber leaves his backpack, filled with papers that other businessmen would normally carry in attaché cases, on the ground floor of the small hotel. In the liquor store, someone had to carry the six-pack from refrigerator to counter, and a friend had to a carry the beer to the apartment.

Watching Barber, it is impossible to ignore the extraordinary effort it takes simply to get around. Moves the nonhandicapped do by effortless rote take enormous energy. Yet Barber's fierce pride begs for no pity. After a short time others forget about his missing leg.

"I don't like the word 'disabled,' " Barber says. "I don't consider myself now disabled or handicapped. I can do pretty much what I want to, within certain limitations. I can go on my crutches as far as most people can walk. I can ski better than most people with two legs. My head's in a good place. I swim, sail, go to the beach quite regularly. I just can't get into this idea that there is something abnormal about me—because there's not.

"You know, it's funny. People feel that a person's handicap affects the mind in some way. I'm serious! If they see a guy rolling down the street in a wheelchair—it has an effect on his mind, they figure. They *shout* at you, as if losing a leg affects your hearing."

That awkwardness and distaste for the physically "different" creates barriers for many disabled Vietnam veterans. "People are just turned off by them, and don't take the time to get to know them," Barber continued. "People don't think that way of me because I present a different image; Take me as I am. I don't care. If you have any hang-ups, they're *yours.* Don't hassle me with them."

Barber was not always so at ease. "For a while I was uninterested in relationships with women. I think it took us disabled a lot longer to establish relationships when we came home. I just was not sure how a woman would react, you know . . ." Now Barber lives happily with a woman colleague whom he met at work. "We talked philosophy for hours. For weeks the leg never really came up. What's in a leg? There's nothing to it."

As with many disabled veterans, Barber's injuries cause never-ending complications and painful surgery all these years later. He has had more than thirty operations on his knee. During such periods it is too agonizing to wear his prosthesis; he is forced to use crutches, which cuts into his pride and mobility. "Years ago I would have hated to go on the street with crutches, but I just decided life's too short to worry about *that.*"

Barber speaks without bitterness or humor, in a flat, unemotional voice. Such control was hard-fought. Even his own parents were not able to cope with the altered young man whose leg was blown off by a mine. "My mother was raised with this idea that, um, people with missing limbs were less than perfect. This society places so much emphasis on whether you're skinny or fat, how you look, what your hair is like. I don't like society's values. I like my own values."

Blond and bearded, Jeff Barber looks like many West Coast men in their mid-thirties; he uses the California patois, the "where-I'm-coming-froms," like a first language.

His attitude today is in marked contrast to how the ex-marine felt in the late sixties. For the first six months, Barber was so doped up in the hospital, he didn't know whether it was day or night. "The first three months it was straight morphine, then Demerol. During my latest surgery, a few months ago, I was very pleased with myself. The surgery was on Friday—and I was back to work on Tuesday."

For a while Barber was gripped by debilitating anger at what he had experienced. When he returned from Vietnam, he was judged 100 percent permanently disabled: "Loss of one leg, arthritis, two protoplastic arteries in one leg, a combination of about ten different things. Well, I worked for two years and didn't hear a word from the VA. Then I got a letter saying: 'Your condition has *improved.* We're lowering your disability compensation to 80 percent.' They had no way of knowing if it had improved. They hadn't seen me in over three years! They had no idea if I was alive or dead. It's a matter of semantics. Because I had a job, they felt I shouldn't be earning 100 percent disability anymore."

Barber was furious. "I filed an appeal. I was having surgery three, four times a year. I felt the reduction from 100 percent was unwarranted." Like countless other veterans, Barber found a bureaucratic nightmare when he tried to appeal his disability cut. "The VA limits your legal means. You can only pay a lawyer ten dollars to file your appeal to represent you. What lawyer's going to represent you at that price? So that's one thing people are really turned off about. They can't fight the system." (Under federal law, veterans are not permitted to take the VA to court to challenge VA-benefit decisions.)

"Not only does all the hassle turn people off, what incentive is there to go to work if they're going to cut your disability?" asks Barber. Even after they get jobs, many wounded veterans worry. Vietnam's lasting signatures are not only there for all to see; those wounds often require painful ongoing surgical and medical care. The fear that they may not be able to hold down the job is compounded if they feel they may never regain 100 percent disability in the event that they should again be unemployed. Barber, for example, would make the same amount collecting 100 percent disability and social security as he does working full-time and collecting 80 percent disability. "I'd like to see a sliding scale. A veteran gets a job at, say, $12,000 a year. No cut. If he gets a raise, they should reduce the pension by a certain amount. But *only* to a certain degree. Say, if you have two legs off, it can never go below $1,500 a month."

There is a Catch-22 that haunts many disabled veterans. One veteran was getting 100 percent disability—for the loss of one leg, the use of one arm, and unemployment due to emotional problems stemming from his war wounds. To keep the total 100 percent, he had to periodically see a psychiatrist and convince the VA that he was still unemployable due to emotional problems— even though he would have liked to free himself of that stigma, once he began to cope with his life. To find a job that would give him the same dollar amount as his benefits—not only the stipend, but tuition for his children's schooling, tax abatement on his home, etc.—he would have to make no less than $35,000. This was hard to come by for someone who had only a high school education, let alone someone who was disabled. He moonlighted on one job but said, "I don't like having to sneak about it." He hates a loser image, "but I can't brag about a job even if I have one on the side. When people ask my occupation, I have to say nothing."

Today Jeff Barber seems a pragmatic, gentle man. There were years of "raising hell with the VA," calling in the TV stations to publicize the agency's ineffectiveness, fighting with lawyers. He was unsuccessful in his disability compensation battle. At some point Barber changed. He slowed down his drinking and stopped smoking pot. "It influenced my thinking quite a bit. I felt totally ripped off by everyone. One day I just realized that it took a lot of wasted energy to raise hell with these people." He decided to work from within and became a Labor Department specialist in the San Diego Disabled Veteran Outreach Program (DVOP), searching out jobs for veterans.

The work was both gratifying and frustrating—gratifying because Barber was able to help many veterans; frustrating because he realized, working from within, that veterans' complaints about hiring prejudice were all too true.

However, once he joined the bureaucracy there were rewards in his work. "In half a year I did more from the inside than I was ever able to do from the outside. In five months I've worked with some 150 people and probably placed 80 of them" (in jobs). Barber, remembering the way he was treated, took great care to provide support. If a man had a morning interview, Barber would follow up with an afternoon phone call. One machine shop took eight of his men. The owner was from England and had been helped by strangers when he first came to America. He was receptive to giving others a break.

Large companies, however, were unsympathetic to the point of hostility. "Some people I've worked with have masters' degrees, credentials all over the place—this, that, and the other. Big companies won't touch these people. All they've heard is that the Vietnam veteran is a crazy guy who uses drugs. They just don't want to take a chance. We've got to make people aware that these are real people—not all drug addicts, not all alcoholics, not all into delayed stress. I'm on this council, working with the National Alliance of Business, to make them aware.

"Any company that has $50,000 in federal contracts is *obligated* to give special consideration to handicapped and Vietnam veterans. They *don't*. It's all on paper. We send them Vietnam veterans for 'special consideration.' They give various reasons why this person just doesn't have the exact qualifications. They smile and say, 'Don't call us, we'll call you.' There was a personnel job, for example. Out of eight or twelve men I sent, at least *one* should have gotten it. Not one veteran heard back. It's a *big* problem, and guys get really depressed."

Sometimes, ironically, the difficulty comes from being a targeted group. Some programs give employers tax incentives for hiring entry-level personnel. "You give a veteran a slip of paper, and he takes it to the employer. The employer sees a Vietnam veteran—a thirty-three-year-old man—at a real *low income level,* and all of a sudden it shows that he hasn't got his shit together. It's got bad connotations. The tax credit is showing very blatantly that this guy is a disadvantaged Vietnam-era veteran. If we can just get the personnel director together with these men, without these slips, I think it would make both feel at ease."

Barber concentrated on a pragmatic approach to job counseling. "We don't talk about Vietnam. I deal with the here and now, with today. What the veteran's been doing, what I can do for him."

Barber is not a veteran who needs to justify the war in order to psychologically lessen the loss of his leg. He went to Vietnam as "just an ignorant kid who had had a very nice life." Although his parents were divorced when he was twelve, his childhood memories were generally pleasant. "I spent my summers with my dad and thoroughly enjoyed all the freedoms. He ran an athletic club and restaurant in Salt Lake City. Posh place, where all the

Mormons could go and drink on weekends." Barber's mother ran a blood bank for the University of Colorado Hospital. Barber made average grades and was uncertain and undirected about his future. He joined the Marines "to see the world," Barber says caustically. "I often regret going.

"There was *nothing* good about Vietnam in any way, shape, or form. There was no reason for people to die over that total waste. If this country gets into another war, I would try as hard as I could to get on a draft board and grant as many C.O.'s as possible. The country doesn't have a right to take people's lives—especially for economic reasons. There is so much talk of oil and the Middle East. Americans should be developing solar energy, other things. I can't see fighting and killing for economic reasons. That's what was so wrong about Vietnam. How rich did Dow Chemical get from making napalm? And all the others who made rockets and helicopters and bullets?"

A year after Ronald Reagan took office, Jeff Barber was out of a job. And many veterans across the country were without their job-hunting outreach programs and veteran helpmates like Barber. At first, the Labor Department's DVOP project was severely curtailed by budget cuts after Reagan took office, but activists kept the program afloat.

In 1983 Jeff Barber moved along the crowded avenues of Manhattan, dressed in a business suit. He worked in the personnel department of a major publishing firm.

He wore his prosthesis. The only thing that distinguished him from other junior executives was his slight limp. No one gave it a second thought. He could have gotten it jogging.

Part V
Resistance

"I Ain't Marchin' Any More"

BY PHIL OCHS AND BOB GIBSON

It's always the old to lead us to the war
Always the young to fall
Now look at all we won with a saber and a gun
Tell me, is it worth it all? . . .
Call it peace or call it treason
Call it love or call it reason
But I ain't marchin' any more.

1 The Deserters

THE VOICE IS WARY ON THE PHONE. HUGH HAS BEEN A FUGITIVE SO LONG now that being both hunted and cautious seems natural. Finally he agrees to talk.

The Burger Kings, shopping malls, and gas stations lead the way in endless monotony to his small tract apartment in a Maryland suburb of Washington. The brown living room drapes are closed and held together with a safety pin. The whole room is a shrine to babyhood. In the semigloom toy trucks and blocks and a Walt Disney wagon crowd a corner. Under the TV are diapers. The smell of Johnson's baby powder lingers.

A father, in his mid-thirties, barefoot, in jeans, settles on the sofa, cradling an angelic, red-haired son. The baby stares contentedly as his father tells a bitter tale of patriotism, duty, service in Vietnam, disillusionment, and finally desertion.

If Hugh had been an upper- or middle-class youth, he no doubt would have been a conscientious objector. But Hugh grew up as a Catholic in central New Jersey, the son of a plumber, one of five children. He knew nothing but parochial schools, with their mix of upwardly mobile college-bound and working-class youths just waiting to graduate. Hugh identified with the latter. "All we thought of was having a good time."

Hugh was indoctrinated into anticommunism along with the catechism. "The nuns used to beat it into us. We didn't know what communism *was*, but we knew it was *bad.*" Hugh's alienation and antiauthoritarianism, nurtured in Vietnam, extends to Catholic hierarchy doctrine. "The Pope goes around in countries like Africa, telling them that birth control is a crime and to have sixteen kids when they can't feed two of them." He doesn't hide his disgust. But in the sixties Hugh was buying everything the church and government said, especially the buildup of patriotic rhetoric after the Gulf of Tonkin. "They portrayed that as America being slapped in the face by the dirty Communists. Every night the six-o'clock news portrayed the American government as the savior of the Vietnam people."

One day in Hugh's senior year, a marine came to his school from Vietnam, a glamorous visage in his dress blues. Antiwar riots belonged to a different breed. "The cops used to beat them on the head, use tear gas, lock them up." No outrage gripped Hugh. "I thought, well, if the government says it's wrong, it must be wrong."

Hugh absentmindedly brushes his lips softly against his son's cheek. "One thing I'll regret all my life. I was coming home from Fort Dix and saw some protesters at the Port Authority. This was just after basic, where drill instructors were telling us we were 'killing machines' and how we were 'gonna kill Communists' and going on about those 'dirty protesters.' " Hugh, at eighteen, looked across a deep schism that separated him, a young man in uniform, from others his own age in jeans and pony-tailed hair, yelling "Hell no, we won't go." "I spit at them and walked away." Hugh's words are bitter, soft. "I was so stupid then."

The year was 1968, a soft afternoon in June. Six high school graduates were sitting on a park bench in Jersey City, drinking beer and wine. The pigeons barely lit before some loud guffaw or a slap on a shoulder set the birds flying again. Someone joked about going in the service. So they all walked the two miles to their friendly recruiter, laughing, talking about girls. Hugh had just one burning question.

"Will we get to go to Vietnam?"

"Oh, *yeah*," said the recruiter, trying to keep his face blank. "No problem."

Hugh was seventeen and had to get his parents' permission. That too was no problem.

His father had been in World War II and, like thousands of America's working-class fathers, it was inconceivable to him that his son should not continue the tradition. Your country called, and you went.

Hugh's older brother was already in the Navy, and his father talked proudly about Joe going here, Joe going there, Joe in California, Joe in Hawaii . . .

That summer Hugh joined the Army with an eagerness unmatched by anything he has done since. Never in his wildest thoughts did Hugh imagine he would be one of the 93,250 deserters of that war. One of 20,000 who served a *full* term in Vietnam, collected medals, and *then* deserted.[1]

"The young soldier just does things to irritate us," said one veteran sergeant. "I obey because it's the Army. They don't—often because of no reason other than they're *supposed* to."

"There's a guy sitting on top of a half truck with twenty-five other people around," commented another sergeant. "He's smoking a big joint, and nobody says anything about it. They *question* you, they ask why. We say, 'Because we're soldiers,' but that's not enough reason for them."[2]

To lifers, defiant young draftees and enlisted men of the Vietnam Generation were extraterrestrial beings run amok, destroying their carefully ordered world of command and discipline. Vietnam was the most disruptive time in U.S. military history. Never was dissent so politically oriented as during Vietnam.

Unhappiness, loneliness, family and personality problems, malaise, and war-weary bereavements had caused desertions, AWOLs, and defiance in all previous wars The Vietnam War, however, combined all these apolitical factors with the addition of a galvanizing political catalyst: it was a war universally unpopular at home in its later stages. There was mass avoidance of the war by men of the servicemen's own age. Men who entered service at that time were often reluctant draftees whose opposition to the war crystallized during training or in Vietnam. All this kindled a rebellious generational F.T.A. ("Fuck the Army") attitude. Some even painted F.T.A. on their boonie hats. The war itself "tore the fabric of the Army," one top-ranking general conceded. Although the military claims that only 10 to 15 percent of deserters were motivated by opposition to the war, the very nature of the war permeated deserters' decisions. "Every deserter chose self and family over the cause for which he was asked to fight. Had the war made more sense to him, his decision might have been different," noted Baskir and Strauss, who studied thousands of cases to prepare the final Clemency Board Report for President Ford.[3]

Real figures are hard to come by. When caught or turning themselves in, most would not risk admitting their antiwar feelings. In addition to politicized deserters like Hugh, thousands who never displayed such antipathy openly were nonetheless shaped by overriding strains, confusions, disillusionments, and shattered expectations of military life in the sixties and the war itself.

Deserters and their civilian counterparts—resisters who fled to Canada or Sweden—were marked forever for millions of Americans as true villains of the Vietnam era. American Legion and VFW Halls rang with stinging denouncements of these "gutless cowards." Only their own Watergate scandal silenced Nixon's anti-amnesty drum beaters who called deserters and dodgers "malingerers, criminals, and cowards." Charles Colson, soon to go to jail, denounced deserters as "victims of their own character deficiencies." Spiro Agnew, another Nixonian near-disgrace, suggested the Democrats could find their "future leaders in the deserters' dens of Canada and Sweden."[4]

Deserters were even more reviled than draft dodgers and have remained Vietnam's hapless permanent scapegoats—along with the more than half million veterans with "bad paper"—less than honorable discharges. In 1977 draft evaders were given an unconditional pardon. President Carter, succumbing to national outrage, however, gave literally nothing to deserters and most bad-paper veterans.

"The public confused AWOL with desertion—a technical term which means absence with the intent to remain away permanently," said David Addlestone, a lawyer who worked on legal cases in Vietnam. *"Absentee* has a more accurate, less evil connotation and in most cases was more accurate, but 'desertion' is what the public used. Desertion was hardly ever proven. The number of *absentees* was probably in the hundreds of thousands."

Once again a terrible irony concerning the Vietnam Generation is at play.

Deserters—symbolic of all cowardice—were tailor-made victims for the nation's pent-up venom about this class war. They were universally viewed as turncoats who had let their comrades do the fighting and dying. Unfortunately such rhetoric obscured the fact that nearly seventeen million draft-age men, often through scams as well as legal measures, never served in the military at all. They remain to this day largely untouched by the sacrifices of those who did serve or who publicly resisted and risked jail.

Moreover, fully one fifth of the 93,250 deserters *never* evaded the war, served their full term in Vietnam, and deserted when they couldn't stomach post-combat stateside military duty. Often they were victims of Vietnam syndrome stress, which went unrecognized until years later. And once again—like those draftees shoved into combat—deserters were disproportionately black, poorly educated, and from low-income backgrounds. Disillusioned brighter blue-collar Middle Americans like Hugh were also in the deserter brigade.

Unlike World War II, only a small number of deserters fled the field of battle. By historical standards, desertion under fire was rare in Vietnam. Only 3 percent of all deserters left from Vietnam and only 1 percent from combat.[5]

There was an obvious reason for the few in-country desertions—no place to go. Walking to Cambodia, as one GI facetiously suggested, was no answer. Some 5,000 deserted while on R and R, and another 7,000 deserted in the United States after receiving orders to report to Vietnam. "Most of those guys went over the hill to save their necks," said Frank Paquin, a strongly antiwar GI.[6]

Still almost twice that many—20,000—who served a full year in Vietnam and then deserted were never given special consideration until years later. The Ford and Carter programs did single them out and some got their discharges upgraded.

Military and government officials like to argue that Vietnam AWOL rates were lower than World War II and not much higher than Korea. Although technically accurate, this vastly understates and obscures an important difference. Only the rate of short-term AWOLs (less than thirty days) was comparable to that of earlier wars. Long-term absences peaked at higher levels than either war and corresponded directly with the war's increasing unpopularity at home. The Army rate for desertion increased nearly 400 percent—from 14.9 per thousand in 1966 to the all-time high of 73.5 per thousand in 1971. At the peak of the Vietnam War, an American soldier was going AWOL every two minutes and deserting every six. This was a total loss of roughly one million man-years of military service—almost half the total number of man-years American troops spent in Vietnam.[7]

Because deserters by and large were so disadvantaged, they were championed by no one. It served the right-wing and military officials to portray them as malingerers and criminals. (However, one Pentagon fact sheet, analyzing those who went to foreign countries, stated that only 4.5 percent left for family, financial, or other personal reasons.)[8]

Reviled by the right, deserters got little sympathy from the left. Elitists in the amnesty movement were loath to lump deserters with draft resisters. Some sympathizers tried to include in amnesty demands deserters and the more than half million veterans with bad paper (800,000 is a figure used for all veterans—those who were stationed statewide as well as those who were in Vietnam—if the years 1962–75 are considered our war years, rather than the more common 1964 to 1973 tabulation). But they had to battle the snobbism of class-biased amnesty advocates.

For the vast majority of deserters with bad paper or who are still technically fugitives at large, life remains disastrously hard, long after the war is over. Education benefits are closed to them. Some are disabled and unable to claim veterans' benefits. Most have to lie about their past to seek employment.

Personal and family problems accounted for almost half the desertions. The pay scale was so low that many returned to help families on welfare. The typical deserter had two years "good time" and left within months of discharge. The military offered Red Cross counseling, home leave, compassionate reassignment, hardship discharges, but none were administered effectively. The military was in for harsh criticism from Congress after complaints to Congress from servicemen reached a high of one-quarter of a million in one year.[9] Impatient, uninformed, discouraged by the seemingly hopeless machinery, many servicemen simply took off when personal calamity struck. Here are two such cases uncovered by the Ford Clemency Review Board: Gilly Meaks's cancer-ridden father committed suicide. His partially disabled mother was unable to work. Meaks tried to get a hardship discharge. He waited months, only to find that his papers were lost. He went AWOL to support his mother and was given a bad discharge.

Elvin McCoy was in service more than five years when two brothers were killed—one in a car accident, the other in Vietnam. McCoy was wrongly denied discharge (as a sole surviving son). He went AWOL to return to his family—and got an undesirable discharge.[10]

Of course, there were the misfits, deserters marginally fit for service in the first place, that promilitary groups like to emphasize. Yet they were the very same men shoved into service through Project 100,000 and slum recruitment, when fitness for service went unquestioned. It has *seldom* been suggested that the services bear some responsibility for the outcome.

The "bad apples" who became disciplinary and desertion problems undoubtedly should never have been taken in the first place. One salient example is Private Johnny Dee Smith. He pulled his first burglary in the first grade, served eight months in jail for burglarizing a safe, got into a knife fight with his father, was arrested for carrying a pistol and machete at fifteen, and had taken potshots at cows, children, and horses. He had used every drug known, posed nude for a homosexual photographer, and attempted suicide by slashing his wrists. He had just been released from the Modesto, California, State Hospital and went into the Army as an alternative to staying in an insane asylum. *Despite all this, the Army took him without question.* He went AWOL almost immediately. Others with unstable but not quite so bizarre backgrounds as Smith stayed in the service longer, often only adding to the Army's disciplinary problems.[11]

Largely forgotten, deserters are still castigated, but little is known about these men. Only 2 percent went to Canada or Sweden, according to the Department of Defense.[12] This is a typical Pentagon statistic that should be viewed with skepticism. How they could accurately assess the fleeing patterns of wanted military fugitives is indeed questionable. No doubt the majority of deserters had neither the knowledge, the wherewithal, nor the inclination to flee to another country, and they remained, like Hugh, underground in the States. No matter where they settled, most deserters today are among the last permanent victims of Vietnam.

Hugh puts the sleeping baby down next to him on the couch and continues his story. It would be hard to find anyone more emblematic of that generation of soldiers in revolt and the personal tragedy that followed. Hugh speaks wistfully of his Army boot camp days, when his biggest hope was to win a lot of medals and return a hero. "We had to sing these songs—how we were gonna 'kill myself some Viet Cong.' It seemed like a game. I was an excellent shot. Got medals for shooting so good." Villages were constructed and taken. "It was fun—shooting with blanks." The orders were absolute. " 'If you hear a noise, shoot. If you see a light, shoot.' They kept telling us, 'You don't know *who* is the enemy.' They were all VC, VC, VC. 'The scourge of mankind.' "

The first sights and smells of Vietnam remained with Hugh forever. When they landed at Bien Hoa, "the people looked filthy, dirty. Everything smelled bad. It was hot and muggy, and there was no sewage system. I never smelled anything like it, before or after."

Hugh was in the signal corps at Qui Nhon, "a base halfway up the coast." The first night as he lay on a mud-caked mattress gritty with sand from the sandbags stacked around to protect from incoming mortar rounds, Hugh cried silently. "I knew I was in some kind of *hellified* place." He worked inside a building that was air-conditioned for the sake of the sensitive communications equipment. "The VC always wanted to knock out the communications equipment. This created a great deal of tension."

At the time, the Vietnamese to Hugh were "still dirty people." Some of his friends who had been in-country longer already were questioning orders. "One officer—in order to get the body count up—would send patrols in to draw North Vietnamese fire so he could call in the artillery for an airstrike. Those guys just rebelled. They said, 'We're being used as bait.'

"Most of the guys treated the Vietnamese people like pigs. They felt that *all* of them were going to shoot them.

"One incident really got to me. I had a sergeant who tried to rape one of the girls who worked at the camp. I caught him—and the sergeant pushed me in the face. The next thing I know: 'The captain wants to see you.' There I was, with the bloody lip and the captain chewing *me* out. He was a friend of the sergeants. They were the 'juicers' [alcohol drinkers] and I was the 'head' [pot smoker]. I got wrote up."

Another memory: Some Vietnamese children of one village used to draw circles in the dirt roads and play a game similar to marbles. "This jeep comes roaring down the road, hits one of the kids, and splits his head open. I was on guard duty. I came out and told them to get the kid to a hospital. They were drunk—and their answer was 'He's Vietnamese. Let him take care of himself.' " Hugh picked up the wounded child and took him to the hospital.

One day Hugh's attitude toward the Vietnamese, the war, and the military began to change irrevocably.

"This really good friend, Barney, from Riverside, California, knew a lot of Vietnamese people. He brought me to a Buddhist monastery—a big marble building with polished floors, candles, and incense. There was this monk—God, he must have been 109 years old." Hugh asked the monk what he thought about the war.

"My country has always been at war and nobody ever likes. The people are tired of it," said the monk.

As Hugh listened, he "began to realize they didn't care what type of government they had. The monk said the first lady, Madame Ky, was just another word for prostitute. He said the South Vietnamese government wasn't paying the soldiers but keeping the money themselves. My friend from California taught the kids English at night, in a tiny room with one low light bulb. The kids would get all scrubbed up for this session."

Then Barney was killed in action. Hugh went to tell his students that Barney would not be coming anymore. The monk asked if Hugh would teach the class. Hugh said yes.

"I found out it wasn't true, what everyone had said. The *VC* were outlaws, but these people were just ordinary people who wanted to stay alive. They were afraid of the VC. I never worried about them killing me. I could go down to the ville and I was never afraid."

Halfway through his tour, conflicting feelings swirled in Hugh's head. He disliked the enemy, and certainly never saw the VC as saviors as did many antiwar students. But he felt deeply sorry for the civilians. Moreover, he began to hate many of his officers. Hugh went from an obedient, unquestioning teenager who once spit on antiwar protesters to a young man who questioned everything. In military parlance, he developed a "bad attitude" and a jacket of Article 15s—being written up for minor infractions. For Hugh and many others, the mere refusal to subscribe to regulations—regardless of the mildness of their rebellion—enraged commanding officers. "One time a lieutenant told me to get a haircut. I told him I wasn't going to. He pulled out his

.45 and took me at gun point to the barber." (I know two former combat captains, now in successful careers, who were threatened with courts-martial —one for wearing a mustache, another for having long hair.) Hugh was transferred several times, one of the methods used in Vietnam to break up "troublemakers." "I was sent to the most remote site, where you entered Cambodia." Hugh's bad attitude coincided with his changing view on the war. "If I was a Vietnamese, I think I'd have been for the VC, given the choice. Say Nixon hadn't left office when the country wanted him to. So he goes into another country and asks that government to send a million troops to support his regime. What would you do? You'd support the people trying to get rid of him."

Following the massive 1969 Moratorium, several GIs in Vietnam countered Nixon's battlecry that the peace movement was demoralizing to the troops. More than one hundred young draftees and enlisted men in eight different units—from I Corps in the north to III Corps in provinces around Saigon—surprised a reporter by regarding the antiwar campaign with open sympathy and let their names be used. Few bought the idea that America was stopping communism and giving the Vietnamese a better life; nearly all felt that the Paris peace talks were a "hoax" but praised Nixon for pulling Americans out of Vietnam. A sergeant spoke for the other side—the many GIs who felt that protesters who had not been to Vietnam had no right to "bitch and moan about what is going on." Still, many others like Spec. 5 Paul Torres, a medic, said, "I'll go back and carry my sign on campus. Maybe I can influence somebody." Private Jim Beck, an Italian immigrant, and his brother volunteered for Vietnam, hoping to accelerate their American citizenship. His brother was killed at Khe Sanh. "I have lost all faith," said Beck. "The war is wrong and must be stopped."[13]

Hugh recalls, "There were plenty like me. Uncooperative. Stoned a lot." Smoking pot was no different to these young draftees, enlistees, and line officers than NCOs getting tanked on alcohol at the officers' club, while older officers—men of their fathers' generation—thought marijuana a sign of certain degradation.

"Some had bad attitudes out of political beliefs, like me. Others just disliked the idea of being there, of following orders they felt were stupid. Some were refusing to fight. Refusing an order was a jailable offense. I went right up to that line but never crossed it."

Long hair and Afros, rock and soul music, beads and bracelets, peace signs and clenched fists . . . UPI photographs of Vietnam leave their impression these years later. The St. Christopher medal swings from the neck of one GI exchanging vials of heroin with another in Quang Tri province. A long string of love beads loops one combat soldier's neck, sideburns curve to his chin, a peace tattoo adorns his arm. Open rebellion surfaced in 1970; CBS News shocked the nation with a six-minute broadcast of First Air Cavalry soldiers experiencing a "smoke-in" at Fire Base Aries. GIs in boonie hats, long hair, beads, and bracelets grinned at the camera and smoked pot through the barrel of a gun.

In 1984, Addlestone recalled speaking with some of these men while they were in Saigon. "They were all reassigned and harassed."

And the most poignant picture of all is an aerial view of a patch of Vietnam, so heavily cratered it looks like the moon, the land devoid of vegetation or people. In the center, where fighting once raged, a mammoth peace sign, like some huge cattle brand, has been bulldozed into the ground by war-weary GIs.[14]

Books written by antiwar former GIs paint a picture of rampant dissent. Promilitary veterans' groups consistently downplay that image. "Only 15 percent of Viet vets identified themselves as radicals in 1973, a time when the so-called veterans' antiwar movement was at its zenith," they tell Congress.[15]

While antiwar groups exaggerated the strength of GI dissent in the sixties and early seventies, promilitary groups vastly underplayed its impact. Public dissent within the military was only for those willing to brave harsh punishment, repression, reprisal, and harassment. "Political activism within the Draconian legal structure of the military can be suicidal," wrote David Cortright, an antiwar GI, in *Soldiers in Revolt.* Public assembly, distributing literature, wearing peace symbols—political expressions that coursed through America's universities—were strictly forbidden on post. "Indeed," wrote Cortright, "there is very little a soldier can do *legally* anywhere."

Servicemen suspected of being antiwar were followed by military intelligence to such an extent that at one demonstration at Fort Sill, Oklahoma, in 1967, agents outnumbered dissenters. Lieutenant Henry Howe, Jr., in November 1965, joined an antiwar demonstration in El Paso while off duty. He got one year hard labor and a less-than-honorable discharge. In 1966 three GIs at Fort Hood, Texas, refused orders to Vietnam and got three to five years hard labor and dishonorable discharges. When two black marines simply stated in their barracks that blacks should not fight in Vietnam, one received six years and the other ten of hard labor.[16]

In 1970 twenty-five officers in the Concerned Officers movement were removed from sensitive intelligence jobs. Loss of security clearance, removal from jobs, transfer to isolated posts, less than honorable discharge, imprisonment, brutal punishment—all of this happened to antiwar GI activists during Vietnam. That resistance emerged at all, and to the extent it did, underscored the depth of disenchantment and antiwar protest among young draftees and enlisted men. To dismiss them as a fraction of the total Vietnam-era military force ignores the fact that such militant protest was *unprecedented.* It is also unfair to compare their numbers with those who served from the beginning. It is more accurate to examine their disruptive influence from 1969 on, when GI antiwar protest skyrocketed. That 15 percent *labeled* themselves *radicals* is not slight; they represented the tip of the iceberg. Thousands defied the military in less visible ways—drug abuse, fraggings (attacks on officers, usually with grenades), refusal to obey combat orders, and defying dress codes, as well as desertion. Warning threats such as tossing smoke grenades were frequent and went unreported. It was not only an antimilitary, generational abhorrence for authority; the war was at the center.

In 1972 Morris Janowitz, the dean of military sociologists, gloomily assessed in *Foreign Affairs* that the military and the ground forces were experiencing a "profound crises in legitimacy due to the impact of Vietnam, internal racial tension, corruption, extensive drug abuse, loss of command, and widespread antimilitary sentiment."

"Disgruntled GIs poured into the offices of the Lawyers Military Defense Committee by the thousands from 1970 on," said Addlestone.

Even Marine Major H. L. Seay lamented that there were "more problems today than ever before in the history of the Marine Corps." His list of problems included "an unpopular war."[17]

For the first time there were hundreds in revolt wherever there was an Army base—from Camp Lejeune to Da Nang to Frankfurt to Seoul. To dismiss dissenters as a handful of misfits cannot be done. The brightest among the GIs often led the insurrection. Resistance in the Army, labeled "RITA" by the Pentagon, led to widespread spying. In 1970 a major scandal erupted when the public discovered there were hundreds of thousands of military dossiers on military men and civilians who opposed the war.[18]

In-service conscientious objector applicants were met with intimidation—and only 17,000 GIs applied during the war. GIs had to fill out elaborate applications, collect letters of support, undergo three formal interviews with skeptical and hostile military officers. Still, C.O. application rates zoomed almost 400 percent in the Army from 1967 to mid-1971. Countless other would-be applicants, such as Hugh, never showed up in statistics because they were harassed and discouraged when they tried for C.O. status. Lawyers familiar with the process report that this was common in all services. In 1970 more than a thousand GIs a day were being shipped to Indochina. West Coast activists leafletted incoming soldiers urging them to file for C.O. discharge and delay overseas orders. In two months, 1,200 GIs had successfully delayed orders. The Pentagon was forced to send out special regulations, barring GIs from seeking C.O. status while en route. They would have to wait until Vietnam.[19]

GI newspapers—often short-lived mimeographed rags that were quickly suppressed—bore such nihilistic names as *FTA, Heresy II, Napalm, Fragging, Action,* and *Your Military Left.*

By 1971 enlisted men were evenly split as Hawks and Doves. A survey of men *on their way to Vietnam* found that 47 percent thought the war was a mistake, while another 40 percent thought America was not fighting hard enough to win. Some 87 percent of the surveyed troops soon to be in Vietnam —no matter their ideological differences—were questioning the wisdom of the war or the way it was being fought.[20]

Stories of GIs refusing combat orders *en masse* were not isolated. The first reported incident of mass mutiny was August 26, 1969, when sixty men refused to fight. Several more incidents occurred during the years. The Fire Base Pace insurrection in 1971 became well known. Six men refused an order, feeling that the patrol would be tantamount to suicide. They were threatened with courts-martial, and the next day GIs in other platoons rallied to their side and agreed not to advance. Then 65 out of 100 men signed a petition requesting Senator Edward Kennedy to protect them from what they considered needless danger.

The numbers of unreported mutinies are considered high. Field refusals (a capital offense) were frequent from 1970 on, but charges were usually dropped if the GI returned to the field. Several veterans I have interviewed told me of their troops' collective rebellion. When Fire Base Pace hit the news, returned GIs who had joined the peace movement felt it was a stunning blow to the military. Statistics tell a tale of military disarray. In 1971 a random group of Army soldiers would produce seven acts of desertion, seventeen AWOL incidents, twenty frequent marijuana smokers, ten regular narcotic users, two discipline charges, eighteen lesser punishments and twelve complaints to congressmen.[21]

Perhaps the most significant acknowledgements of trouble in the ranks were signs posted by the military at the entrance to bases such as one at Fort Ord, California: "NOTICE: Demonstrations, protest marches, sit-ins, picketing, political speeches, and distribution, display, sale of written materials, circulation of petitions for signature, and similar activities are prohibited without prior approval of the commanding general . . ."[22]

Toward the end of his duty, Hugh was at the border of Vietnam and Cambodia. "Every night we were getting rockets and mortar. We took a direct hit in a bunker one night. Blew the top off it. It gave us all a headache, I can tell you."

Hugh wanted out and spoke to both a commanding officer and a chaplain about applying for C.O. discharge. The officer sneered; the chaplain made no effort to help. By late 1969 the Supreme Court upheld far wider interpretations of what qualified for C.O. status, but the military continued to turn down most C.O. applicants, believing they were not bound by such court-imposed rules. Federal judges decided otherwise; in 1971 they held that the military had to follow civilian practice which entitled sincere pacifists to C.O. status even if not motivated by religious beliefs. The armed forces suddenly found themselves defending an unmanageable number of law suits. In 1971, two thirds of all in-service C.O. applicants were successful, but by then it was too late for Hugh. By far the most typical treatment was that afforded Hugh —antagonistic hostility. "The chaplains played a disgraceful role in the whole business," said Maury Maverick, Jr., a Texas attorney who counseled dozens of soldiers through the C.O. process. "They should have understood how a man's conscience could forbid him from fighting. Instead they invariably wrote negative reports—and that was hard for soldiers to overcome. I saw it happen again and again."[23]

Chaplains at bases like Ft. Sam Houston (in San Antonio, Texas) generally wrote negative reports because of the large number of C.O. discharge applicants they interviewed. Chaplains at bases where very few GIs applied tended to write more favorable reports. They felt C.O.'s had to be one-of-a-kind visionary loners. When whole groups of GIs started to apply, they were often viewed as insincere bandwagon followers.

One day, after Hugh had been thoroughly discouraged from trying to leave Vietnam, he was reading *Life* magazine. He started to cry. That was the day he knew he would never last his three years enlistment. Hugh was reading for the first time about My Lai.

Home from the war—but with several months of service left—Hugh took off his uniform, put on his jeans, and went to a demonstration near Jersey City State College while on thirty-day leave.

"The cops ran us into a fence." The demonstrators—the same kind Hugh had spit at, on that day which seemed so far in the past—were trapped. Now Hugh was one of them. "The cop came charging at me on a horse and hit me with a club—just for demonstrating. *Within two weeks after being back from Vietnam!* That's when I first became violently opposed to this government."

He went to a chaplain at Fort Riley, Kansas. "I *begged* him to get me out. He said, 'Son, the only way you're going to get out is in a box. Your unit is going to war games in Germany, and you're going with them.' "

Hugh's laugh holds a cutting sharpness. "I said, 'I've been to the *real* thing. What do I need with *war games?*' "

Hugh returned to his barracks and flopped down on his bunk, staring at nothing. Two other buddies, who had also been in Vietnam, came up. "Listen, this just ain't gonna work," said one. "We're leaving."

They hitched a ride in a van out of the base. An antiwar song by the Jefferson Airplane was playing on the radio. Three AWOL soldiers sat there listening. They went to the airport in Manhattan, Kansas. "We all just split. One went to Michigan, another to Texas." Hugh caught a TWA flight to New Jersey with thirty dollars in his pockets.

The one-year rotation system of Vietnam, instituted as benevolent, created another negative first. Literally tens of thousands of men returned with two- or three-year hitches to complete. They had risked death, seen friends die, lived a life of altered states, and returned with the unmistakable stench and sights of Vietnam's warfare. Dehumanized by the war, increasingly users of marijuana, and defiant of authority, they simply could not be moved by the petty standards of camp. Getting haircuts, polishing boots, standing at attention were beyond anything many could fathom. Many either deserted, went AWOL, or fought the system and received less than fully honorable discharges. Although statistically a small percentage of the 3.4 million who served in the Vietnam theater, there were still tens of thousands of these dissidents. There had been no decompression. Almost all who deserted when they returned from Vietnam did so because of severe personal problems and *mental stress arising from their experience in Vietnam,* according to studies conducted by the Ford Clemency Review Board some years later.

"You just couldn't take the boot camp mentality," sighs Hugh. "Some of us had been in *real* heavy combat; some had family problems." After the horrors of war, taking a walk from camp didn't seem like so much. "You sorta became unconcerned with the trivialities."

"I never thought *once* of leaving the country. I kept thinking that one of these days this country's going to come around to its senses about this war—and things will start all over again right."

While AWOL, Hugh did draft counseling at Fairleigh Dickinson University. He wanted to reach working-class youths like himself, but that was difficult. Astonishing as it seemed to Hugh after his experiences, "many of them were still flag wavers." In addition, Hugh didn't want to call attention to himself in unsympathetic territory. "Remember, I was an outlaw. We were wanted by the FBI."

Hugh was living at home but barely communicating with his parents. "If my father knew I was AWOL, he would have shot me himself! He was a real Archie Bunker." Hugh tried to get a job. It was May 1970, and Hugh would turn twenty that summer. Prospective employers always wanted to know what he'd been doing since high school. He told them he had just been discharged—and was waiting for his papers. He looks sad as he remembers. "That was the first time I ever lied on anything major." The lie forced reality upon him—the knowledge that he was truly a wanted criminal. Still he repeats, "I thought in my heart that this country was going to wake up and get back to normal. I felt that what I was doing wasn't *wrong.*"

For five months Hugh worked for a company that sold educational materials, books and slides, denying when asked that he was a veteran.

He sighs. "The worst thing about running is that I had to start a whole series of fabrications. I'd go home every night and start worrying about being caught. That's when I started smoking pot a lot." His mother was a probation officer, his father was doing well in his plumbing business. He wanted to leave home, but Hugh's newfound friends in the peace movement were not sympathetic about hiding a deserter. "I just wanted them to help me become a nonactive criminal. Make them stop chasing me." No matter their mutual antiwar sentiments, deep divisions remained. Students in the peace movement could not understand his metamorphosis, Hugh recalls; how he had come to his antiwar beliefs in the jungles of Vietnam. More and more he felt alone and hunted. "Every time I saw a police car, I thought they were coming for me."

Across the land in those days, the FBI carried on its task of rounding up America's young—draft resisters, evaders, deserters. They patrolled the borders between Canada and the United States, hounded relatives, and sometimes were successful. One aunt turned in a deserter I know. The FBI often found these men in their parents' home. They were not criminals, wise to criminal ways.

Hugh's story is identical to that of a Baltimore draft resister who told me of his arrest. He was nabbed while eating breakfast cereal. The front door and back door were covered by agents.

"They had on suits, sunglasses, porkpie hats." Hugh allows a thin smile. "You know, like the Blues Brothers." They asked if Hugh B—— was there. Hugh said no. They gave him a hard stare, then left.

They then went back to the local police station—and returned with the police, two squad cars, and an FBI car. A quiet working class neighborhood was alive with cops. When Hugh saw them coming up the front walk, he tried to dash out the back door. They were waiting there. "You're under arrest for desertion from the Army." They put his arms behind his back and, for the first time in his life, Hugh felt the cold metal of handcuffs clamping his wrists. "You feel like an animal." He was put in the county jail, to await the MPs. In the cell were ten men. "Me, eight blacks, and an old white wino. Four of the blacks commenced to beat my ass. They wanted my food and sexual favors from me too. So I figured I had to do something."

Hugh picked out the black who seemed to be the leader. "I started in about how, in the Army, I found out how great black people were and how I hated whites. I had hair down to my collar and looked pretty wild. Finally he said, 'He's cool, he's cool,' and they left me alone. They all talked about how many times they'd been in prison. I wasn't *about* to say I was only in for being AWOL. I told them I was in a robbery."

A few days later Hugh was rounded up with an AWOL bus load. "We were chained from the waist—so you couldn't raise your hands and beat anyone to death," Hugh says with a caustic laugh. "There were bars on the windows. The bus was always full. They made a run every Wednesday or Friday. We didn't talk. It was the first time we'd ever been chained like that. I found out later that most of the guys on my bus had been to Vietnam and deserted after they came back." Hugh was at Fort Dix where he had eagerly pursued boot camp two years before; now he was a prisoner in a huge detention center—with wire around the building—off limits to anyone on the base. Other veterans recall similar off-limits stockades. One remembers the chill he got, riding by and seeing all these men at the camp, waiting, caged.

Within the gates of military bases were thousands of prisoners who had gone AWOL or participated in political activities. The Army's 1970 MacCormick Commission found that over 80 percent of stockade inmates were charged with AWOL. An astonishing 58 percent were held in pretrial confinement; their commanders had arbitrary power to imprison pretrial without bail those considered undesirable. The commission found that every facility contained political activists and "determined dissidents."[24]

A *Life* magazine explosive exposé of Camp Pendleton's stockade in 1969 detailed 700–900 incidents of prison barbarism, torture, and degradation. In fact in a secret Marine Corps survey leaked to the press, one officer compared the Pendleton brig to the "Civil War hell hole of Andersonville."

Prisoners were exercised to the limit of endurance. Then—as guards

watched for officers—they were kicked, beaten, stomped, clubbed, and ka-
rate-chopped for refusing to obey a direct order. Guards taped prisoners'
heads like mummies to keep them quiet. Others had wrists and ankles lashed
together and were handcuffed to the ceilings of cells to hang for hours. They
were trussed in strait jackets, shackled with leg irons, and dragged painfully
by the loose string of the strait jacket pulled tight between buttocks and up
under the groin. Some were hogtied and forced to remain for hours in an
agonizing crouch. Two hundred men who refused to fall out for reveille
because of mass grievances were forced to run until exhausted, and when they
dropped many were kicked and beaten so badly they required hospitalization.
Despite doctors' complaints, the guards were not even reprimanded. As the
details, smuggled out of Camp Pendleton, became known and prompted congressional investigation, a chaplain and doctor, formerly at the camp, spoke
out to corroborate.

Some 75 percent of the Camp Pendleton prisoners were AWOL. Private
Ron Lucas went AWOL three times to visit his sick father, to see his wife, and
to avoid Vietnam. He was handcuffed to the ceiling when he yelled at guards
who refused for hours to let him go to the bathroom. When the chaplain
complained of the brutality, he was told to "stick to your preaching."

AWOLs were ordered to face a picture of the National Defense Ribbon and
scream loudly the color-coded verse: *"Red* is for the blood he's never spilled,
blue is for the ocean he's never crossed, *white* is for the eyes he's never seen,
yellow is the reason why."[25]

Such earlier exposés made stockade life easier for Hugh and others who
later went AWOL. "There was nothing to do all day except smoke pot. Everyone was into it. Nice guys who had been in Vietnam and just couldn't take the
military after Nam." The administrative discharge—used so lavishly in Vietnam—seemed tailor-made for young, naïve men like Hugh, who feared the
very words "court-martial." "You could take a court martial—but they
would tell you that you had to go to a stockade that was *worse* than where we
were. They made it very clear that if you elected to take a trial you risked
losing—and getting *convicted.* So you had your choice between a court-martial and possibly losing—or you could sign your papers and get an undesirable discharge. Which, of course, most did. In that situation, you didn't look
at the big picture. It was hard to think of the future." That hasty action
followed them the rest of their lives. Undesirable discharges were almost like
prison records when it came to getting jobs.

In the summer of 1971 after two AWOLs, Hugh was officially discharged,
with an undesirable discharge (U.D.). Of 93,250 deserters, 83,135 were discharged with undesirable, bad conduct, or dishonorable discharges. The other
10,115 remained fugitives.[26]

Hugh was just a few weeks shy of his twenty-first birthday. He could get no
GI Bill to go to college, no VA benefits, no health benefits for the partial
deafness caused when the mortar round blew off the top of his bunker. Hiding

his military record while looking for a job became an obsessive trauma. Hugh's lying days had just begun.

A double paranoia developed, from the large amount of grass he was smoking and his not being able to pursue a career. Hugh drifted, met a woman at a party, and soon married her. "I married her to have some place to go." There is no trace of emotion. The marriage was "just something to be overlooked." They divorced in 1973.

"Everytime I applied for a good job, I wouldn't get it. I wanted *desperately* to go to college but couldn't afford it." Marked for life with his U.D., Hugh finally wrote on applications that he was honorably discharged. "If they demanded to see my papers, I never showed up again. Then I stopped saying I was a veteran." When asked what he had done for those blank years, Hugh told them he traveled a lot. He laughs, remembering his journey through Vietnam. "That was not exactly a lie. I would take any old job, driving a truck, unloading, but I was resentful, nervous, and angry."

After years of this, when the Vet Centers were finally funded, Hugh went for help. "I hoped they would find me a job, but they all wanted you to tell them how rough it was in the war. There was this guy telling how he had been to a psychiatrist, how he couldn't sleep and is all messed up—mostly on account of how him and two other guys raped a young girl in Vietnam." Suddenly deep anger emerges. "That guy! *He's* got an *honorable* discharge!" Hugh slaps his right fist into his left hand. "He killed and *raped* for the government and didn't get caught, and they don't do shit for me. I was a 'troublemaker' because I was against the war, and this guy who has all these problems because he raped and killed is considered an all-right guy [for the record] with his honorable discharge."

During the mid-seventies, Hugh made a major star-crossed move. He and a friend went to Florida where they picked up odd jobs. But Hugh was getting on in his twenties and wanted something substantial. The questions were always there. "Where have you been? What have you been doing with your life?" Hugh says, "You had to make up a good story." After months like this, Hugh falsified his discharge papers, upgrading them to honorable. The FBI ran a check on him once on the job and prosecuted him. Hugh spent two years in jail in Miami.

A special affinity grew among Vietnam veterans, many of whom were in for drug-related crimes. "It was a vicious circle if they got into drugs in Vietnam. The Army just left them or locked them up. Or they'd give them a UD, let them out on the streets to fend for themselves, not cured, no benefits or anything."

Hugh became fascinated with the law and helped upgrade bad discharges for inmates who did not have the special stigma of deserter. He laughs. "I got discharge-review hearings for everybody but myself."

After jail Hugh went to the placement office of a Florida law school—and, with his newfound knowledge of the law, worked for a judge in West Palm

Beach for six months. "They said I was the best of all the ones they'd had." In order to get the job, he told them he had gone to law school. No one checked him out, but Hugh had deep guilts about lying. He worked odd jobs as well and managed to afford school part time. He met and married a dark-haired girl who had no problem with his past. She worked for a community college until the baby came.

Meanwhile, Hugh followed assiduously the ups and downs in the amnesty struggle. Not until Senator Edward Kennedy's amnesty hearings in 1972 were deserters considered in the same terms as draft resisters. A number of witnesses strongly argued that deserters were the military equivalent of draft resisters and stressed that since they more often came from disadvantaged backgrounds, they especially needed the benefits of amnesty. When Ford's limited clemency program went into effect, it was roundly—and accurately—denounced as "shamnesty" by amnesty activists.

For deserters it especially offered little. Those who were still fugitives could appear at a special clemency processing center and receive immediate undesirable discharges. After twenty-four months of alternate service they could get a clemency discharge. But, just like a UD, the clemency discharge was given in practical effect under other-than-honorable conditions and granted no veterans' benefits. The other hundreds of thousands of veterans given bad paper for offenses other than AWOL were not eligible for the clemency program.

Discharged deserters, like Hugh, could receive Presidential pardons by performing alternate service. (It was never clear what good a pardon was to someone without a court-martial conviction.) Outside the Ford program, almost all deserters were eligible to apply through normal military review procedures—with no requisite alternative service. They stood about a one-in-three chance of getting upgraded to general or honorable, entitling them to veterans' benefits. So they were better off going that route.

Perhaps the only benefit of the Ford Clemency Program was to make a few more influential citizens, those officials responsible for implementing it, aware of the real nature of most deserters. Vernon Jordan, head of the Urban League and Clemency Board member, resigned when he and other members realized the program was flawed and their recommendations to improve it were either ignored or rejected by President Ford. They argued that Clemency Discharges should be "neutral," not "other-than-honorable." Honorable discharges should be given to veteran deserters, like Hugh, with good combat records, so that they would be eligible for veterans' benefits. Such relief never happened.[27] (There were some minor exceptions. After pressure from Jane Hart, widow of Michigan Senator Phil Hart, Ford told the DOD to call up Clemency Board cases of the wounded or decorated and upgrade them.)

Amnesty was a major issue in Jimmy Carter's campaign for president in 1976. For deserters, he held out promise as he spoke of poor Georgia boys, often black, who didn't like the war but went to Vietnam anyway and were "extraordinarily heroic. They didn't know where Sweden was, they didn't know how to get to Canada, they didn't have enough money to hide in college . . . It's very difficult for me to equate what they did with what the young people did who left the country."[28]

When he became President, however, Carter went with the "young people who left the country" and shamefully ignored the deserters. During the Democratic convention, some former peace activists like Sam Brown tried to mend generational divisions by lobbying for a blanket amnesty that treated deserters and draft dodgers equally. Older Carter forces held firm, and Carter's amnesty forces settled for a "case-by-case" review for deserters. Ohio Governor John Gilligan frankly admitted that the "question of covering deserters was so controversial we walked away from it." At the convention there was a wrenching symbolic gesture to heal the generational split. Ron Kovic, the crippled Vietnam veteran, addressed the convention from his wheelchair, speaking eloquently for amnesty as he nominated Fritz Efaw, a fugitive draft resister, for vice president. Deserters—a lower class with no constituency—were left out in the cold.

Amnesty, all but forgotten now, blazed across front-page headlines when Carter issued a "blanket pardon" for draft resisters on January 21, 1977, his first full day in office.

Conservatives were furious. On the other hand, amnesty forces decried the poor treatment of deserters and other bad-paper veterans. However, Hugh, reading the news at home, felt some relief. A "Special Discharge Review Program" was announced by the Defense Department in March of 1977. Those, like Hugh, with undesirable discharges, who had completed tours in Vietnam or who had served two years of good service were virtually guaranteed automatic upgrading. Many veterans were still barred; those who deserted from Southeast Asia were automatically barred—no matter such extenuating circumstances as conscientious war resistance or combat fatigue. The program did not cover the 100,000 men (including 22,000 AWOLs or deserters) discharged by court-martial for offenses against military discipline —even though Defense Department officials privately acknowledged that their misconduct was generally no worse than those who accepted undesirable discharges as plea bargains.[29]

A major weakness in Carter's program for military offenders was that they had to apply within a six-month period. Fugitive deserters also had to apply in person. Many feared that no matter what they had heard, they would still be court-martialed and sent to prison. Congress prohibited any DOD expenditures to advertise the program; many never knew it existed. The Carter program attracted a scant 10 percent of the 433,000 eligible veterans.[30]

Carter's wish to end the war with blanket amnesty excluded a major group of men who most needed help, but Hugh was one who took advantage of the program. He was one of those decorated Vietnam War veterans whose undesirable discharge was upgraded to general, in June of 1977.

After seven long years, Hugh saw a future. *"Finally,* I think, I can get my college education. I apply, get all my papers in order, and am just waiting for my courses." Then came a final blow that ended his dreams.

In 1977, when men like Hugh had managed to get discharges upgraded, conservative veterans' groups mounted a heavy attack in Congress. And some deserters who tried to take advantage of Ford's Clemency Program were harassed out of alternate-service jobs by local veterans' groups.[31] In October, just as Hugh was off to college, Alan Cranston, a liberal who had been sympathetic to amnesty, joined with Strom Thurmond, a long-time opponent, in what Baskir and Strauss appropriately termed a "particularly vindictive" bill. It denied veterans' benefits to those who received upgrades under some of the special rules of Carter's program.

Believing he would get his benefits, Hugh had already gone into debt and taken out both government student loans and bank loans, to go to college. He was heartsick and stunned when the bill passed. Hugh struggled through some courses but was unable to complete a degree without his GI benefits. (His case was later re-reviewed, and the DOD and VA concluded that he could keep his general discharge but did not qualify for benefits.)

Hugh, his wife, and baby drifted to Washington. In 1982 Hugh was operating a laser for a company that has a government contract. No longer plagued with bad papers, he has another dilemma—a prison record from those days when he desperately forged his own upgraded discharge.

Hugh says he would like to have his name on this story because he believes in publicizing the fate of deserters. "But I simply can't. Not after I told you about those two years in jail." He knows he cannot take a job that requires a security clearance. "If I were to apply, I'd have trouble."

His interest in law continues. After researching the Consumer Protection Act, Hugh fought successfully for a $3,000 settlement with the company that was holding his condominium mortgage. If he had been a college youth with a student deferment during Vietnam, Hugh feels certain he would be a lawyer today. "I want that more than anything. But I can't. I have a record." Years after the incident, lawyers are now seeking a pardon for Hugh's prison record.

His mind continually sifts, turning over his remembrances of Vietnam and its aftereffects. The worst legacy, he quickly says, "is having to hide certain aspects of my past. The government should consider the 'undesirables' all over, considering that there is a special stigma against us. I served good and faithfully over there, except for my bad attitude. *All those years afterwards were a heavy consequence for having a moral attitude about a war that most everyone felt, sooner or later, was a bad one."*

His tone is poignant, rather than bitter, as he talks of the quirks of the ever-changing Selective Service System during Vietnam. His younger brother just missed Vietnam through the lottery. "If he had gone, who knows what would have happened to his life?" As it was, his younger brother went in after Vietnam, using the Navy in *peacetime* to become a doctor. "He's not gung ho —just very pragmatic and intelligent. The only way he could get where he is, is through government assistance. He's not in because he *likes* to be in the Navy. He's there because he likes to be a doctor."

There is a harder edge to his voice as Hugh talks of his cousin—exactly his age. "My cousin got a *student deferment* to stay out of the war, got an accounting degree, and went into the Navy *after* the war. He's got a cushy job now. It just shows you the difference between our two lives. He's making $25,000 in the Navy. Everything's behind him. He used his *GI Bill* to get a *master's.* That's all after the war. And he was just a *token* activist with his student deferment, while I was demonstrating and making a move to get out of the service *because I believed the war was wrong.*"

There is one bright side. Long alienated from his parents, Hugh is now close to them again. "They have come to see all that I was trying to say about that war. Now that I have picked myself up, we're best of friends."

Hugh looks at his sleeping son. "I don't know what the future will be for him. The world doesn't seem to be learning any lessons from the past, from Vietnam." Hugh says goodbye as he takes his son up to bed—a vulnerable-looking young father with a harsh and crippling past, caught in the chance-and-circumstance web of having been a member of the Vietnam Generation.

2 The Exiles

IN SUBWAYS AND ON BUSES, THE EVER-CHANGING FACES OF TORONTO form a rich mosaic. Hassidic Jews in rusty black coats and long sideburn curls sit next to olive-skinned Orientals. Jamaican lilts mingle with rapid Italian. Neighborhoods are ethnic oases. Turbaned East Indians wait in line for Indian movies to open. A large Chinatown teems with Orientals. Toronto has one of the largest metropolitan Italian populations outside of Rome. In a Hungarian restaurant, two turbaned Indians order goulash. Hungarians, Chileans, Vietnamese, Poles, even Tibetans, fleeing the political winds of home, have found new lives in Toronto, one of the world's most cosmopolitan cities. The heart and soul of English Canada, Toronto of course has its constant population of Scots-English descendants. Some of the earlier settlers were in fact America's first "boat people"; about 50,000 Tories, the United Empire Loyalists, fled to Canada on the heels of the revolution.

In this Toronto mix are young men in their thirties who, for the most part, look as if they were descended from English Canadians. Yet they came from New York and Chicago and Iowa and Texas and Virginia and New Jersey and Florida a little over a decade ago; the infamous draft dodgers and deserters of the Vietnam Generation. Not since the mass rush of Tories for the Canadian border has America witnessed such an exodus as during the Vietnam War.

For years, dodgers and deserters occupied a definitive niche in America's Vietnam War repertoire. No Christmas was complete without a media deluge about America's lost generation in exile. Behind the publicity, the private heartbreak of parents was often compounded by snubs and slurs of hometown neighbors.

For generations it had been the other way around; Canada consistently lost its young to the United States. Nearly 100 years ago, in 1887, the Toronto *Mail* commented, "There is scarcely a farmhouse in the older provinces where there is not an empty chair for the boy in the States." In the first century that such statistics were kept, 1851 to 1951, Canada lost nearly as many people as it gained. The "brain drain" of Canada's young was at its height in the early nineteen-sixties. Vietnam changed all that. In 1966 some 37,273 Canadians immigrated to the United States while only 17,514 Americans immigrated to Canada. By 1972 the numbers were even—23,000 leaving Canada and 22,618 *legally* arriving from the United States. No statistics were kept on America's emigrés, but the majority were safely assumed to be resisters. In all, some 67,000 Americans legally immigrated to Canada from 1968 to 1972—the peak resistance years. However, these statistics actually understate the number of resisters. Military deserters, along with drifting resisters who never landed legally, form another substantial group of unknown size.[1]

So the actual numbers of dodgers and deserters is hard to estimate. Canadian immigration officials were not permitted by their government to question potential immigrants about their military status. Estimates vary widely; one Canadian government report places the figure at a low of 15,000. The majority of estimates place the total at between 60,000 and 100,000—including those who went to other countries such as Sweden, plus the numbers of girlfriends and wives who came with them. (One estimate is that one in every four fleeing males brought a woman with him.) The Pentagon claimed that 2 percent of its 90,000 deserters were in foreign lands—a ludicrously precise number for such an amorphous underground group. Most groups who worked with deserters in Canada estimate that no less than 6,000—perhaps closer to 10,000—American deserters went to Canada.[2]

Deserters and dodgers in exile are a relatively small number of the combined 90,000 deserters and the half million who "resisted" the call to arms but never left the country. Such resisters—both those who remained in the States and those who fled to Canada—stand apart from millions of "avoiders" who took no strong moral position. Exiles, that small group within resister ranks, occupied a center of high media and political drama, however. They became convenient symbols for both the right and the left— who deflated and inflated their numbers to suit their politics. For Richard Nixon, exiles were "those few hundreds" of cowards. For some antiwar spokesmen, the number of "noble resisters" was estimated at higher than 100,000.

Yesterday's volatile words—"dodgers," "deserters," "amnesty," "resisters," "exiles"—now seem arcane phrases from another century. They—and the men they represent—have all but disappeared from the consciousness of America. Mention having interviewed deserters and dodgers in Canada, and —even from their peers, for whom the threat of Vietnam was a stark reality back then—there is an invariable response: "Oh. Are any still up there?"

This brings derisive smiles to those who are "still up there." The majority of dodgers remained in Canada in 1977—when Carter's pardon legally allowed them to come home. Over and over the response is the same. Amnesty, they say, merely gave them legal visiting privileges. By the time amnesty came, those who couldn't make it as exiles had already illegally returned.

Those who remained had grappled with almost a decade of whatever loneliness, trauma, readjustment, or depression that had accompanied their move.

Most had jobs, wives, families. Some had become Canadian citizens, so they chose to stay. Many still harbor a bitter resentment toward a government that they feel forced them to leave. Many remain intensely anti-American—as disillusioned about the American Dream in their own way as many Vietnam veterans who felt betrayed by the government. Others have a love-hate ambivalence about the United States and a wistful sense of never having given their homeland a chance as adults.

I met an eclectic lot—from a central committee member of Canada's Communist party who drives a Russian Lada, to a patrician former officer moving swiftly up a prestigious law-firm ladder. In Toronto, the United States is ever-present—Dan Rather and Tom Brokaw on nightly news, Scope and Sanka in drug stores, Linda Ronstadt and Bob Seger on jukeboxes. Yet for many of the men who have spent most of their adult years in Canada, the United States is a distant world that belonged to them when they were someone else, in the long-ago.

Although they are different in backgrounds, goals, and achievements, there are some common threads that bind these young ex-Americans. Most seem flash-frozen into sixties' attitudes regarding American politics. Ronald Reagan and his administration are viewed as if through gauze. During the sixties they often espoused hatred for corporate America and sympathy for the victims of its inequities—the oppressed, poor, blacks, and women. Such past positions are seldom matched by any intelligent criticism of existing inequities today. What is more, Vietnam is often discussed in the same "aggressor-imperialist" versus "nationalistic peasant revolt" sloganeering of yesterday; ideas caught in the rhetoric of their time. It is as if, once they crossed the border, their thinking on American politics stopped, like a smashed watch face forever telling the same time. Critics would argue that their indifference stems from not caring once their own lives were not at stake. A more sympathetic view is that those who cared deeply about remaining Americans have returned; those in Canada are the "assimilators," who care more about the life and politics of their adopted country.

Although often depicted otherwise by the right, dodgers were not America's upper class. They were privileged in the sense that most attended college, but they most often came from state universities and sometimes from community colleges. Many were of the working class, the first in their families to go to college when Vietnam touched their landscape. Ivy Leaguers didn't *have* to go to Canada. They most often found a way not to go—via doctors, lawyers, or fathers' influence with local draft boards.

Doubt and argument follow the exiles to this day. Did they act out of cowardice or commitment? Once again, Vietnam sharply divided the generation—even among those within the antiwar movement. David Surrey, a draft counselor who was saved with a high lottery number, recalls, "As a draft counselor I used to get mad when people went to Canada." He reflected the resistance movement's antipathy toward those who were not staying in their own country to "fight the system." His view has tempered with time and by surveying some sixty dodgers and deserters in 1981. "I got more sympathetic when I met them. They were not so privileged as some in the generation, but they probably could have gotten out through the lawyer route. Instead they chose to leave their country."

Many exiles today still feel that way; if they look down on anyone who did not go, it is usually on those who played along with the system and worked out some deal to avoid the draft. Some exiles go to great lengths to justify that they were making a statement—even arguing that their move was as noble as resisting and going to jail. They reason that going to jail was ineffective, since only a relative handful chose that route. However, it is hard to see the correlation; if not enough went to jail to halt the draft, it nonetheless does not follow that going to Canada would stop it either. Roger Williams gives a tortured explanation for what was in reality an oft-denied act of self-protection. Most who arrived between 1965 and 1969, wrote Williams (himself an exile), were "making the strongest statement for the good of that country [the United States] that they felt they could make commensurate with their own well-being. They weren't dying for their country or going to jail for it, but they were going into exile for it." They had "put their future on the line against a war they couldn't accept."[3]

Still, Williams has a point. Unlike others who dishonestly evaded the draft, men who went to Canada "had not permitted a man to go to war in their place without due payment, which was a costly, personal, important statement in opposition to that war: becoming an exile."

For years exiles watched with some frustration the draft-resistance movement being coopted by government changes in the draft system. Project 100,000—which lowered induction standards to take the disadvantaged—had already been a fact of life for some time, thus defusing any threat of calling up the reserves—a dodgers' haven. Switching to the lottery was a cynical move by Nixon that assured the government of sufficient manpower while destroying draft opposition. Who with a high number could get all that excited about the draft? And now younger men benefited from winds of change. The newer, relaxed definitions for C.O. status could have saved many from earlier exile. Above all, as more at home resisted, the courts were so clogged with cases that few resisters were ever going to prison. Moreover, exiles were subject to the "cop-out" invective of antiwar peers who—often safe with high lottery numbers or trick knees—were taking no personal risks. They got letters from friends saying they knew of someone who beat the draft by faking it. The unmistakable message was: "You were a fool to go." Therefore, concludes Williams, "a vast majority of war resisters tended to withdraw into their personal lives, forgetting politics or why they had left, and thereby perpetuated the notion among the left that going to Canada was a selfish act." If they had been really selfish, Williams argues, you would find them making it in

America today: "Anyone with moderate intelligence *could* get out of the draft."[4]

For those who remained activists in Canada, the war years were adrenaline-charged. The focus of exile activity in Canada was always Toronto. *AMEX* became a popular Toronto newspaper for American exiles. There were popular exile bars. Many Americans participated in antiwar demonstrations in Canada or counseled new arrivals on becoming landed immigrants (the term for living there legally). A Canadian underground bestseller, *Manual for Draft-Age Immigrants to Canada* was in its fifth edition by 1970, with 65,000 copies in print and available at any United States resistance or draft-counseling office and most U.S. campus bookstores.

Although the number of deserters is unknown, one thing is certain. Deserters received the worst of it in Canada. They were shunned as lower class inferiors by both dodgers and the Canadian government, who wanted the cream of immigrants.

Today there is no such thing as an American exile community. There is no way to find exiles except through word of mouth, out-of-date activist lists (with several changes of addresses), and fleeting contacts with an extremely loose-knit colony of former Americans. One resister was a PTA member for years before he found out that another male member was also a resister. It is a seldom-introduced subject. Sometimes there is a casual, "When did you come up?" If the date is anywhere between 1965 and 1972, the connection is usually made but not necessarily acknowledged.

Canadians for the most part welcomed American dodgers. Many have long harbored a resentment against their powerful giant neighbor, and Vietnam was not a cause championed in Canada. While Canadian enlistment posters (in both French and English) dot subway cars today, conscription was never popular in Canada. True, those dodgers and deserters who settled in the conservative Far West had more than their share of fights with "redneck" loggers and fishermen, as exiles have called them.

But even in cosmopolitan Toronto, dodgers and deserters were unsympathetically treated by conservative churches, and when unemployment worsened there was some resentment and fear of their capturing the good jobs. For years American media implied that they were a sad and lost collection. For the most part, however, that impression is not borne out among those who remain. Many in fact have flung themselves so hard into being Canadians that they assiduously affect just the right Canadian inflection or phrase: "in hospital," "on holiday," "at table," "zed" for *z*. Today exiles often refer to Canadians as "we" and Americans as "they," know all the verses to "O Canada," and sometimes affect the phrase "as *one* would say"—making many a Canadian laugh at the pretention.

Exiles in this chapter share their feelings about their lives, then and now. While patterns may emerge, there is no attempt to categorize these interviews as more than what they are—random meetings with a number of men who chose to leave their country during the Vietnam War of their youth.

Don Zimmerman sips coffee in a restaurant that brought back memories. It was around the corner from his old exile-counseling headquarters. Zimmerman says he was different from most of the exiles I would meet. He was an activist. "Most came as acts of individual conscience—alone or with a friend," he says. They soon drifted into their own worlds. He disliked the few rich he counseled, "who were used to having things done for them"—and the right-wingers. Hypocrisy knew no bounds in those days. Men who championed the war nonetheless fled when it came around to them. "Most weren't stupid enough to *admit* it, but sometimes you'd figure out a YAFer" (member of the Young Americans for Freedom). Zimmerman rolls his eyes. "The line they used to give us! 'I think the war's a *good thing*—but the government hasn't the right to *tell* me to go.'" Zimmerman says archly, "They could *volunteer,* and the government wouldn't be telling them."

He looks like a typical book-bag intellectual—slim, nonathletic, alert brown eyes behind Coke-bottle-thick glasses. The first-born in a middle-class Jewish New York family, Zimmerman had all the "my son the doctor" pressures. He rejected them. "I had no interest in blood," he says wryly. Antiwar activism, along with a general disinterest in studies, contributed to his dropping out of college in 1969. Immediately reclassified, Zimmerman never believed the Army would take him. "My vision is close to 200 without my glasses." Removing his glasses, he looks across the formica table. "From this distance, you're a blur."

The Army accepted him anyway. Zimmerman applied for C.O. status and continued across the border "to play it safe." By the time the draft board had studied his case, the lottery was on and Zimmerman was safe with a high number. After less than a year in Toronto, Zimmerman was "suddenly faced with being free, and what was I going to do about it?" He decided to stay.

To become a landed immigrant in Canada, applicants must pass with a score of 50 points. There are points for speaking English and French, age (eighteen to thirty-four is prized), education, the amount of money one could claim, job skills, and whether they correspond with jobs in demand. Dodgers were briefed to a fare-thee-well. Those with money and education could get in with the promise of a job. At the time when most dodgers arrived, Canadian rules allowed visitors to apply at any border crossing. However, if already in the country on a visitor's visa, a dodger had to go back to the United States and recross in order to apply. That ride was often nerve-racking; counselors found sympathetic Canadians who would drive dodgers in case they were stopped and questioned by American authorities.

Zimmerman talked of the price some paid. "Uprooting, insecurity, fear, turmoil, paranoia, the fact that your family may hate you. Parents were writing 'Dear John' letters to kids, disowning them. A small percentage were the 'We'll turn you over to the FBI before we'll help you' type. A higher percentage were simply disapproving. And many parents thought of themselves, asking 'How can I hold my head up in public?'

"It really ripped up families. Girlfriends or wives often couldn't stand it and returned. Some of them couldn't find work. There were pressures from parents: 'How could you live with this coward?' We did a *lot* of hand holding."

For some it was easy. They usually had family support, higher education, and found jobs. For them, Toronto was just another North American city.

Zimmerman points up the minigeneration within the generation. Dodgers who came of age toward the end of the war often had fewer problems. They were not on the cutting edge of the Canadian exiles. Their older compatriots had paved the way, and public opinion had swung against the war. "Still, it did force them to make a commitment—not as much as going to Chu Lai of course. We gave the 'worst case' lecture. The line we always pushed was: 'If you come to Canada, you have to assume you are *never* going back to the United States, come hell or high water.' "

For Zimmerman it is easy to tick off the personal pluses and minuses. Since he was free to return as early as 1970, there was no sense of forced exile, although he says that without Vietnam he would have never gone to Canada. He remains somewhat contemptuous of those who made no commitment to Canada and were "just sitting it out at the border," waiting to return if and when amnesty came. He finished college in Canada, became a social service worker, a teacher, and started a day-care center. In the fall of 1982 he was unemployed but seemed unconcerned. Like others in his generation who rejected the establishment, Zimmerman seemed to make do on little, even in a city as expensive as Toronto. More than a decade after he arrived, Zimmerman was thinking of becoming a Canadian citizen. "But as a landed immigrant with U.S. citizenship, I don't feel at all displaced." He no longer feels angry at the United States but has no desire to return. "What's so great that I haven't got here?" He remains cynical about American government. "The reaction to El Salvador has been pretty good, but five years from now I'm not sure if we will *remember* Vietnam."

As a final note, Zimmerman feels that Canada—facing unemployment problems—might not be such a "safe haven" for a new generation opposed to U.S. foreign involvement. "If we had another war like Vietnam, where moral indignation swept across the country, I don't *know* what Canada would do—but I wouldn't hold my breath waiting."

On the table are sweet potatoes that Sue Brelove is about to purée for her infant. Homemade bread is nearby. ("Our homeopath is big on a complex carbohydrate diet.") The vegetarian cookbook is open. Herbal tea is served, and classical music plays in the background of their comfortable, old row house. Her husband, Ed Kotheringer, is a well-paid community developer for the city of Toronto, and she is a freelance psychotherapist. They eagerly say they are "fully assimilated. Both our kids are legally Canadian." They are active in local politics and are, predictably, NDP (National Democratic party) members, "socialist-democratic."

Ed and Sue are classics of an era, almost clichés of a certain type of middle-class American formed by the upheavals of the sixties. Ed was at Bucknell, enrolled in ROTC, when he went to a teach-in on Vietnam. Bucknell was conservative enough; they had "no problem getting a member of the John Birch Society for the other side." Soon after that teach-in, what Ed had seen as "patriotic virtue rapidly began to burn off." He pulled out of ROTC and transferred to the University of Wisconsin, where his politicization began. There he met Sue. Both felt they had been raised in a "quite permissive" manner. In stilted language, Ed describes his parents as having "certain behavioral expectations—but no 'yes sir, no sir' rules."

At Wisconsin they found two kinds: the rabidly militant with defined political positions and others who felt they were entering a "moral crusade—a sense of indignity, rather than a thorough evaluation of the U.S. course in Vietnam."

They identified with the latter and were molded by a communal antiestablishment life-style as conformist in its way as any establishment preppie of today. Sue, fast-talking, dark-haired, with glasses, slips into the jargon of the sixties. "We were always into, like, being consistent—work in the co-op store, grow the hair long. It wasn't thought out as a political thing as much as a life-style."

"There *was* a lot of support for being antiwar," continued Ed. "It was chic for some time, but also a heavy moral crisis to face." Sue reflects. "It *was* partially a fad. There was not the pressure to think it through rigorously. I was a self-centered adolescent girl following my lover. I was down on myself for my decision to come to Canada as not really being political. But I was in love with a guy who didn't have many choices. Growing up here, an American in Canada, I came to terms with 'radical' politics. It doesn't matter if you have furniture and a house. You can be an owner of things and still be radical," she concludes—although it sounds as if they were more accurately following the status quo of their world rather than embracing radical politics.

"At that point [at Wisconsin] you couldn't *have* a house and be radical," says Ed. "That was unrealistic."

The Kotheringers were into every campus protest. "There was the black student revolt. We supported graduate students' unionizing. There was Cambodia, Kent State."

"*That* really did us in," says Sue. "Boy!"

"As much as reading about the war and the constant TV barrage, it was just seeing a whole lot of society as seamy—racist, materialistic," says Ed. "Mothers were being denied a decent working wage, blacks were denied their cultural and historical roots and discriminated against. The war was simply the most concrete of the wrongs."

Did they ever acknowledge that the poor and the blacks they championed were going to Vietnam by the jet load? Their commitment to their plight seems abstract. Ed admits that few of the college students counseled the poor and black on the draft. "There was total cultural estrangement, and also we did not think of it as a mission."

"I felt a commitment to understand the problems of civil rights. I was active in the ghetto in high school," recalls Sue. "I remember we once went to a lake, and I was the only white person on the bus, and I felt, 'This is the last time I'm going to do it. I'm a middle-class white Jewish girl. What business do I have to try to do this?'" The polarization was a tragedy of that time. "Black Panthers were saying, 'Don't you whites tell us'—and that doubled my hesitancy."

As for not examining the obvious fact that blacks, poor, and working class were going to Vietnam, Sue says, "Because of our adolescence, our heads and our guts weren't connected. I don't think, except for one guy, there was anyone in the co-op from a lower-class background."

Was there any sense of guilt about a 2-S deferment?

"Probably not an overwhelming feeling—but I was certainly aware of the fact that I had opportunities not open to minorities and the poorer class," her husband said. Ed applied for C.O. status in the fall of his senior year, 1969. The lottery came at the end of the year, and he was definite bait with a number 73. "We watched it on TV at the co-op," says Sue. Ed, six feet two, had been demonstrating unscathed. "I saw four cops holding a guy down and spraying tear gas directly on him." Now a "certain paranoia" developed about the draft. In the spring he was reclassified 1-A while still in school.

They remember landmarks: "Sue and I got married in July. They [the students] blew up the math building in August. We immigrated at the border in September." His C.O. interview came up in October. Ed didn't show. He failed to show up for induction and became a fugitive. That was December 7, 1970, Pearl Harbor Day. "I just felt there was no way our conservative Rochester Selective Service Board would hand out any C.O.'s."

Ed rejected his country. "There was so much violence," recalls Sue. "We knew what it was like to be continually harassed. After Kent and Jackson state, we saw what police in their riot gear could do. A kid got killed, shot in the back in People's Park in Berkeley. There was just that sense of violence all over."

"And Vietnam," says Ed. "I felt it was a case of civil war and a fascistic U.S.-supported regime in the South against an indigenous nationalistic following. I was more on the side of the Viet Cong."

How does he view the outcome in Vietnam? Vagueness abounds.

"I don't know enough to be either an apologist or defender. I think every time you get a transition from being insurgents to being the government, you get trapped in some bizarre situations. They were used to doing things in a very *thorough* way, and that type of thinking comes through today."

Sue says, "It was very difficult to take a position against the bad guys without siding with the other side—but certainly there is a large uncritical-ness from much of the left. It took me a long time to have sympathy for the boat people. There *was* a lot of self-righteous revolutionary stuff from kid

Maoists. Otherwise intellectual undergrads spewing forth on all this dogma. Marx claimed to be on the behalf of all people. But what do you do with the oppressors? The standard thing is you assassinate them."

In the summer of 1970, Ed decided that "there was no sense of why I should be in jail. I didn't feel I had done anything wrong." There was no "deep analysis" about Canada. Sue says, "I think we panicked. We were really scared."

The Toronto Antidraft Programme pamphlet was well-thumbed. "Someone had arranged a flat—and we had $6,000." With his college education, the promise of a job, and that much money, they became landed immigrants at the border. For a while they "lived off our bank account." By October they were codirectors of a group home for adolescents. That first Christmas, Ed faced the fact that he was a "felon" and unable to go home.

"Only one aunt made it her 'duty' to tell my parents she thought I was scum. I know my parents were really shook up by the FBI calls." Once in Canada, "I couldn't help but feel I was being penalized for not killing. We were busy with very challenging jobs, but there were times, especially around Easter, the Fourth of July, Thanksgiving . . ." Ed can't finish the sentence for a moment.

Ed is slightly contemptuous of "Harvard types who bought their way out" —until Sue protests, "But that's the end of *our* story. *We* bought our way out." By 1973 Ed finally got indictment papers as the backlog of cases reached his "failure to report for induction." They hired a lawyer who got the case thrown out on a technicality—because he was reclassified 1-A while in his last term of college, before his 2-S deferment was technically over. "We had a very sympathetic judge who didn't want to get into showcase trials putting away kids just when the war was ending."

Free to come home, Ed nonetheless was "routinely harassed and detained" every time he crossed the border. "I was always anxious. I wouldn't have put it beyond them to secrete something [dope] in the car." (This was a suspicion shared by many resisters in those days.) "I started lying and said I was born and reared in Canada."

Life has gone smoothly: post-grad education, friends with both Americans and Canadians, two babies. They are distant from American politics and like the fact that Canada "has never been an imperial power. Since World War II they've not had to take a military stance." Significantly Sue adds, "Here, you can *watch*."

Like many American exiles, they are ambivalent about the qualities of Canada and its citizens: "There is a kind of standoffishness to Canadians." There is also "a certain provincialism, and Canada is certainly not as competitive. Almost half of the industrial sector is owned by multinationalists, many of them American." There is "not as much of that energy that comes when people are politicized and looking for the truth." "Life is more genteel here." "Even the conservatives are more tolerant, in a civil-libertarian way."

Ed and Sue, like other exiles, give a passing nod to the very real racism toward the French by many Canadians and, often, toward blacks. However, most exiles conveniently ignore Canada's role in Vietnam. Canada functioned as an important supplier of hardware for the U.S. military. Under the Defense Production Sharing Agreement, Canada *sold* the United States over $500 million worth of ammunition and supplies for use in the war. Research plums were plentiful as most Canadian universities accepted money from the U.S. defense complex.[5]

Very few expressed concern—or even knowledge—of this Canadian role, even though these same Americans once marched on U.S. campuses in high dudgeon over similar roles of U.S. universities. Some were skeptical and said such things as, "Oh, you must mean that companies in Canada *owned by the U.S.* were involved." They did not want to believe that their adopted country played any role in Vietnam or that there was even the slightest hypocrisy in accepting refuge from a contributor to the war.

The distancing from America seems complete for Ed and Sue.

"We're tourists there now," said Ed.

Sue feels there is one negative aspect. "In retrospect I feel I didn't give my homeland a chance. I left as an adolescent, not as an adult.

"In a way the United States is like a parent I never really got to know."

The lawyer has blond, F. Scott Fitzgerald hair, parted in the middle, and WASP blue eyes behind steel-rimmed glasses. "Just call me Angel of the morning . . ." is crooning on the jukebox in the upscale fern-and-wood restaurant near his office in a downtown skyscraper. Tom (not his real name) drinks his Scotch-and-water. He recalls how recently he was irresistibly compelled back to his old haunt, Grossman's Bar, a grungy Toronto hangout for Americans years ago.

In Grossman's, Tom made some negative comments about the Vietnam War and was immediately shouted down by another American. "Where do *you* get off talking about it?" he asked Tom. Tom laughs. *"This* guy was a deserter! When I mentioned that, he said it was beside the point; his reasons for deserting had nothing to do with moral values. He was six months behind in his mortgage payments and just felt he had to leave. This guy was kind of tortured. Assuming he could go back to the States, he would be regarded in his world as having done wrong by deserting—and as long as he stays up here, he won't find too many sympathetic to his point of view."

Tom shakes his head. That incident had taught him, once again, that when Vietnam is the issue, "you can't make assumptions about people." I myself had just had a graphic lesson in shattered stereotypes. I had just met two hard-core militant *blue-collar* dodgers—and now I was talking with an *upper-class* deserter.

"My father was a pilot in the 'one big right war,' a good solid Barry Goldwater, Joe McCarthy Republican. A prosperous businessman. Still and all, he is a great guy." Tom went to Boston College, joined ROTC, not as a safe haven but obeying his father's wish to become an officer. "For me to say no to the war and the military would have been unthinkable. My lottery number was *eight,* so I would have gone anyway. Oh, I suppose I could have felt up the drill sergeant, but short of that I wouldn't have gotten out."

He recalls those days with measured, thoughtful pauses. There is still pain —on the one hand that he was trapped in his obedient upbringing and, on the other, that he hurt his father.

"My whole world was collapsing around me. I had been facing the war since high school. It just took me a long time to come around to the view that it was morally, politically, and legally wrong. Everybody had been telling me that, but I had to in effect say to my *father* and my country, 'Screw you.' The Cambodia invasion, about the time I graduated, shook me. The Pentagon Papers didn't come out until I was in Toronto. When I read them I remember saying, 'Holy shit, everything everybody was saying all along is true.' It especially confirmed earlier reports that the Tonkin Gulf incident was a completely trumped-up piece of theater." (Tom speaks for many in his generation who had been reluctant to buy what the left was telling them. The stark reality of the Pentagon Papers, detailing our covert war against North Vietnam long *before* the Tonkin Gulf incident, was devastating to read seven years after the fact.)

Tom was inducted, and at Fifth Army Headquarters at Fort Sheridan, Illinois, he "met a lot of guys who were supposedly 'America's finest' serving their country but who felt our involvement in Vietnam was indefensible." Tom, a commissioned officer, feels he might have gotten a cushy job, but "the more I read, the more distressed I became. I tried to speak to my father. That was very difficult. Mom had a severe health problem; I couldn't talk to her."

Years later there is a sense of being alone and alienated. He pauses. "I've always had the sense my father doesn't quite understand why his son is in Canada. He probably thinks Vietnam was an 'unfortunate mistake,' but he would never see it as a logical outgrowth of U.S. foreign policy after World War II, that this 'mess' was bound to result from our policy." For many, like Tom, the generation gap remains; their fathers still do not understand the deep cynicism of their sons.

What did your father finally say?

Long pause, the longest of the conversation. "It's your decision. He's never condemned." The ultimate Canadian horror story, not coming home for a funeral, is recalled. "I was deliberately not told about my grandfather's death until after the funeral. My brothers and sisters said there was a strange man at the funeral. Perhaps he wasn't an FBI agent. Perhaps the story is instructive in terms of family *perception.*"

When Tom left the country, he crossed into Quebec by bus, carrying his Army-green duffle bags. After four months, a Canadian neighbor drove him south across the border in an old yellow VW, and he returned a landed immigrant. Tom moved into a Toronto hostel filled with war resisters—after being scrutinized as a suspiciously short-haired possible agent—until he explained he was a deserter. "There were a lot of flawed people. We all had our own problems, but I found political and moral opposition to the war was universal. Those who had the most problems were the poor. They didn't find it easy to assimilate." Tom remained distant from the "fellow travelers, Canadian and American, who were just there hanging around, doing drugs. We all had problems making money. I delivered handbills door to door, became a cab driver, a building custodian, and survived the winter." He felt deeply homesick, a displaced foreigner. "I was leaving 'my country' behind. Americans believe no other country is worth living in. They can't understand why anyone would *want* to live anywhere else, and I was no exception."

Getting himself together "took a while," Tom says, chagrined. He did community and volunteer work with paralegals for several years, then graduated from the University of Toronto law school. He is separated from his Canadian wife. He knows rich exile clients and poor. "One deserter went back to Philadelphia. Screwed up his courage and said he wanted to report that he was AWOL. This guy at the AWOL desk with a shit-kicker drawl asks, 'How long yew been gone?' He said, 'Eight years.' This Army guy, half his age, yelled to a friend, 'Harry, come *here;* we got a guy been gone *eight years!*' Try as he might, that friend just couldn't assimilate easily. It helps if you're white and educated." He grins at his obvious description of himself. "It also helps if you look like a WASP."

Tom went back for amnesty and was given his less-than-honorable discharge. "I'm no longer a fugitive, but that's about it. I was with all kinds, from Canada, Sweden, Australia; from guys with three-piece suits to long hair. One guy had the 'Death Before Dishonor' tattoo of the 82nd Airborne. The gathering of the tribe at Fort Benjamin Harrison. They had a special camp paper for us." Tom feels he could return to the United States. "My brother would love to have me set up practice with him in Florida. If you're a lawyer, you're privileged. It's not like going to an employer who is going to screen you out because you don't have good papers."

But Tom is a Canadian citizen now and like most exiles scoffs at an American assumption that they would have flocked to the borders when amnesty came. "It's like Rip Van Winkle. Can you imagine sleeping ten years up here and coming out? Putting your life on hold? To heck with that. I think I had a little chip up here," he says, touching his tweed shoulder. "I've actually been more accepting of America in recent years. I was pissed off for a long time. I still get upset when I see mistakes repeated and lessons forgot. I view this military build-up in the United States as one of the most frightening things in history."

Tom feels he is luckier than many in his generation. "Guys who went to Vietnam and cradled dying bodies in their arms lost a definitive kind of innocence—the notion that good men can remain good by going along with the dictates of society.

"In our case, you couldn't call it a loss of innocence to come to Canada. It was a loss of *faith* and trust in an American ideal because it *was* an ideal. We were taught that the U.S. military would not be used in a bad cause . . ."

When first asked about the pros and cons of his move, Tom says that there aren't any. "Wait, that's not right. I think the whole experience has been positive. I have become a citizen of another country. I look at the world with a broader perspective. Here there is much more emphasis on 'structure.' Certain institutions have to be revered, people have 'rightful places' in the social structure. Yet there is higher respect for working men here. And there is a healthy lack of concern for military matters."

Tom recently returned to Boston for a reunion of his college roommates for the first time in ten years. Despite their very different lives, he was struck by how the sixties will "keep us close in a social way." He laughs, "One's a corporate lawyer and another is running for the state senate in Massachusetts —and *he* was the biggest antiestablishment activist."

Finally, Tom introduces a curious male longing. Untouched by battle then and now, long-distanced from war, he is imbued with unrealistic nostalgia for a kind of "noble cause" world war that since the nuclear age will never come again. "The guys who went and those who avoided all feel cheated. We missed a chance to be heroes . . . to be with your comrades. We missed a chance to fight in a 'good war.' "

Kevin Brieze refused to take his one step forward at induction. Roy Pearson did so but then deserted. By pure coincidence they met in Canada. Pearson, the deserter, happened to rent a room from Brieze, the dodger.

Pearson—trim beard, green eyes, well-cut sandy hair—retains a military neatness. College was no cushy paradise for Pearson and many other exiles who came from hard-working families. While at the University of Minnesota, he worked nights in a factory.

His life had been in turmoil for months. His father, a city housing inspector, blew the whistle on allegedly corrupt real estate deals.

"He was doing the noble thing, but at the same time it was tearing the house apart. After Dad made some threatening assaults on some men involved in the scandal, he was committed for a few months. A great deal of corruption and graft was brought out, and nothing was ever done about it."

Upset about his father, Pearson—who had made the dean's list—could no longer concentrate enough to stay in summer school and make up a credit deficiency that would assure him of a student deferment. He worked in Alaska for four months and returned to college just as he became 1-A. "I said, 'I want to fight this.' " He had worked that summer on a fishing boat with a Vietnam veteran; that made the war real to Pearson. He drew up a C.O. application, but it was before the Supreme Court decision allowing C.O. status for credible cases based on philosophical considerations. He got noncombatant status and, with several like-minded men who opposed the war, was trained as a medic. "One guy just quit eating and got out on a psychological discharge. Another feigned mental illness. Another slit his wrists, but it was a fake, superficial wound. Others, just as committed in their opposition, had no place to go. One Swede from Wisconsin thought the war morally unacceptable but had a wife and child and wouldn't think of deserting. The antiwar military left wasn't being read or listened to. In the barracks it was poor whites, blacks, and comic books."

Pearson's feelings crystallized. "I was *deeply* ashamed to be in uniform. I was *not* going to Vietnam. They made it clear we were being trained to get soldiers *back to the front.*" Out of 300, Pearson felt 5 percent were like him, C.O.'s at heart. His superior officers could never have guessed that Pearson—a model soldier honored for physical and scholastic aptitude—was thinking of deserting.

He watched training films. "They showed us a guy falling over—and then the film would cut to the intestines falling out. That part was really just a goat, but it was very realistic and you really felt it was a man and they were shoving his intestines back in."

Pearson hated it all. When he left the States, he always felt he would be able to return. He smiles sadly. "Both the war and amnesty took longer than I assumed."

One night while in the Army Pearson left the post with a soldier who was on leave to see his wife in Oklahoma. A rodeo cowboy who "just didn't want to go to war," the soldier was planning to have a friend shoot his toe off if he got orders for Vietnam. Pearson wore a stocking cap to cover his burr head, worried that he would be spotted. "I was told around Fort Bragg that they gave rewards for civilians who turned in deserters. But this was macho country, and I was treated like a king. Truck drivers thought I was military going home on leave."

Relief swept over Pearson when he reached Minnesota. Unlike many families, there was no terrible strife over his decision. His father took him across the border, pretending to be on a fishing trip. Pearson hugged his father goodbye and hitchhiked to Ottawa and got landed in two months. Meanwhile the FBI continually harassed his family. Deeply homesick, Pearson slipped across the border twice to see them but was not caught.

There was an interesting psychological twist for many exiles who set out to disprove their "coward" image. Feeling the need to prove their manhood, they took on physically arduous jobs, heading for logging camps and oil rigs and busting broncos rather than Vietnam. The grim irony was that some became physically maimed and broken by the experience.

Pearson worked in road construction in the Northwest Territories just below the Arctic Circle around Peace River, Alberta. "I was billeted with fifteen Chippewa Indians. I couldn't *believe* the racism from the bigoted cowboy machine operators." He worked from May until "freeze-up" in November and saved $10,000. He was kissed off as "just a deserter," nicknamed "Yankee Doodle," and had to defend himself in bar fights, but in the end earned grudging admiration for sticking it out. Another season he lived in a small wood-burning shack while commercial ice fishing on the Great Slave Lake at fifty degrees below zero. He worked on the Arctic oil rigs. "An absolute hellhole. Major oil exploration and no consideration for workers. Guys got maimed, frozen, slaughtered."

In the off-seasons Pearson became a well-educated man who never specialized in anything long enough to earn a degree. The wrenching life of a deserter took its toll in career indecision. Pearson is overqualified for his job as circulation technician at the University of Toronto library. "I've published about twelve papers but could not find an area in which to specialize." The end of a four-year romance left him "pretty heartbroken."

One of few deserters who bothered to go through amnesty, Pearson received his lingering punishment of a less-than-honorable discharge. He would like to upgrade his discharge but is discouraged about accomplishing this in the current political climate. He is not one who bought the assimilation dream. Although Toronto is "good for me right now," Pearson would take a job in America if a good one were offered.

Ambivalence marks his recollections of the past decade. "Looking back, I feel it would be a pity if young people had to go through what we did again. Still, I'm definitely not sorry I deserted at that point in my life." He is contemptuous of those who dodged the war through some scam and now call for a draft. "They are so morally bankrupt. They've been living in a vacuum, and they lived in one throughout that period too. *We* were the *legitimate* position in exile. We took a stand. We were freed from the guilt of those who did nothing. We wanted understanding. Instead there were just years of *forgetting*. Now there seems to be another cycle. All these people saying there was nothing to be ashamed of—'we didn't lose the war, the media lost it' and all that nonsense.

"Flag-wavers, to me, are *not* American. My father was one of the first frogmen on Iwo Jima and was also on Tarawa, Okinawa; he got the Bronze Star. He helped bury 5,000 bodies on Iwo Jima that sat in the sun for five days. You can imagine the horror. A leg here, an arm there. He served very honorably, but *he* was against Vietnam."

Pearson sighs. "But it's the flag-wavers—not men like my father—who are at it again. As one exile said, 'Uncle Sam is always there with the eraser at the blackboard of history—so that America can start another lesson.' "

Kevin Brieze, a wandering Wisconsin youth, was in a Texas Army Induction Center in 1969. So was a country boy from a Texas town with just a post office, general store, and gas station. In the interminable wait the two of them spent hours trying to put a puzzle ring together and started talking. Brieze said he wasn't going in the Army. "I honestly don't know what I'm doing here," agreed the boy. "If I'd a'knowed, I would have gone and disappeared into the hills."

When it came time, the men were told to take one step forward. Brieze took one step back. To his surprise the country boy did too. Army officers separated the two and started leaning on them heavily: "What about the disgrace to your mother? Your family?" All those who had taken a step forward plus the induction officers stood on one side. The two young men were alone in the center. They called Brieze's name. He again took a step back. Tense silence filled the room. They called the country boy's name. On the first and second call, he didn't move. His whole body was shaking. On the third he turned to Brieze, handed him his puzzle ring, and said, "At least this will be in a safe place." And took a step forward.

Brieze tells the story in a Hungarian restaurant in Toronto, light-years removed from that country boy's life. He does not know what happened to him. Brieze still has the puzzle ring.

Just a few years before induction, Brieze had seemed a likely candidate as an "officer and a gentleman." In his Baldwin, Wisconsin, farm community, three quarters of the students were bused in from the country. Brieze was second in a class of one hundred. His father was a carpenter. The family was thrilled when Brieze received an appointment from a congressman to go to Annapolis. Brieze, however, was troubled and becoming antiwar. "I sent my regrets to the congressman. That was hard. It had already been announced in the papers." Brieze, a strapping six feet tall with red hair, grew up in the Christian Reformed Church. "They instilled in me a high regard for ideals. Because of those ideals, I became what I am." He began at the University of Wisconsin and then transferred to Stout College. "The draft board got confused and sent me a 1-A. I immediately filed for C.O." After a long battle, the conservative draft board turned him down. A leading local businessman was on the board. "Years later I found out he got caught running drugs," Brieze guffawed. "I loved it."

There was long ostracism for someone who took bold measures, like Brieze —unlike many friends "who were marrying to avoid the draft." At his 1980 class reunion, Brieze was confronted by a VFW bigwig. "I don't know if I should shake your hand," said the man. "You left the country."

Brieze replied, "I was *driven* out, largely due to people like you—but I hold no grudge. I'm willing to shake your hand. *You* should be thankful." The room had grown silent. The man finally shook Brieze's hand, only because everyone was watching. "There was all that flag-waving patriotism—and yet he had nothing to say about the system with all its exemptions and avoiders."

Brieze went from being a hot Annapolis prospect to campus radical, organizing protests at several midwest schools, then he burned out. "I had been in debates with the American Legion and VFW and had had enough of the red-baiting, hassles, and threats. It no longer mattered if I was in school; my C.O. application was on file. I blasted off to California, joined a rock-and-roll band, had waist-length hair. It was a political statement. I don't wear it that way anymore because it no longer means anything."

Drifting to Texas, Brieze lost his billfold and wrote his draft board to get a new card. "If you didn't carry your card at all times, especially in the South and looking the way I did, you could be in trouble." In the meantime, his C.O. request was rejected and he was trapped.

After refusing induction, Brieze, much like the slaves going North during the Civil War, found the antidraft underground railroad. He was picked up at points all along the way—from Houston to Austin to Tulsa to St. Louis to Detroit, and finally to Windsor in Canada. His girlfriend said she would come along only if they were married. And so they were married. "Foolish boy," he said with a rueful grin.

Once Brieze was in Canada, an *AMEX* article about him was widely circulated in the States, and appeared in a local Texas paper near his mother-in-law's home.

"The KKK broke my mother-in-law's windows, slashed her tires, crank-called, and broke into her house. They literally ran her out of town." When she called the police, they responded with knowing drawls: "Nothing we can do, ma'am. If we were to advise you, we would say 'move.' There's an organization here that doesn't take kindly to draft dodgers."

This tension added to the strain of their marriage. His wife—"a small-town Texas girl who felt totally alienated with her accent"—lasted only a few months in Canada.

For the men in those days there was a support system among exiles. "There was an immediate shared history. A shared 'oppression,' if you will. You were out here on the frontier, struggling against it all, having to stick together." Going back across the border into the States to get landed was "the longest twenty minutes in my life. I had gotten the haircut. When I went through, I had to wait in Detroit for a return bus." He recalls that, with the paranoia of a fugitive, his hand trembled as he drank his coffee and ate a Danish at six in the morning. The bus came, finally, and Brieze crossed back to Canada. "The Canadian at the border asked if I had anything to *declare.* I said, 'Yes—it's nice to be back.' He welcomed me with open arms."

Despite his years of education, Brieze had no college degree and had to start over at York University. He made money as a carpenter, graduated in 1980 with a B.A. in English, a decade after he first started college in the States. In 1982, he was working on his master's part-time, working at the University of Toronto library and helping his second wife in a bakery business.

Like many in the generation, Brieze is ambivalent about his life. "Yes, I'd like to come back to the States. Why not?" And yet, "At thirty-five it's not so easy to start over again." A decade of no stateside experience is a concern to many.

Brieze retains a certain sense of displacement. Being forced into exile sets these men apart from many immigrants. "The Canadaphiles among exiles try their best not to bring up that they're from America. They'll say, 'I became a Canadian *citizen* years ago,' but they are still recognized as Americans who *became* Canadians—by everyone but themselves." Back home in Baldwin, Wisconsin, he is thought of as being partly a foreigner now.

Although Brieze emphasizes the pluses—"feeling more international in scope and an enlightened perspective"—he is wistful for lost moments. His younger brothers and sisters grew up "without my knowing them. The family had a hard time back there because of what I did. You start putting it back together, but everyone's a little older, so it takes time." He also lost a career. "Without Vietnam there is half a chance I would have been an officer at Annapolis or possibly a university professor."

In many families in America there is an avoidance of Vietnam for a very good reason. In the mix of family reunions there are sometimes veterans, dodgers, and avoiders—none of whom are yet quite comfortable with one another.

"My brother-in-law got out by paying off a doctor to fill out his medical form. That's fine," says Brieze with a shrug. "What I don't like is his *sanctimonious* pitch for the draft now. Any time he mentions it, I say, 'Richie, come *on*. You put in *your* time? I *know* what you did!' "

Once again comes the view that Vietnam made them a generation of "cynics—frustrated idealists. Veterans I know back home are bitter. They got screwed. It's really hard when they say, 'You were right—I hope you're happy.' What they've done is just as hard, and I have to tell them they were right too."

Charlie Stimac has a face worthy of sculpture: a slim, straight nose, piercing dark eyes, long drooping mustache. A member of Canada's Communist party, Stimac papers his home with colorful political posters and paintings. He is his own artist—blood-on-the-sand realism, people dragged from an El Salvadoran village and shot, the Christmas bombing of Hanoi, a poster that states, "Libertad Uraquay," and a dove-and-rainbow "workers' strike" poster.

Stimac went to Moscow one recent summer, to El Salvador another, and to Cuba as well. His den is filled with his posters, pictures of Castro, Ho Chi Minh, hammer-and-sickle buttons. There are framed pictures of toiling factory workers and a grizzled black working in a field nearby. Stimac's communism was forged by his immigrant factory-working relatives, in Detroit's ghetto, and in the hard life of northern Michigan farming. He burns with a zealot's fierceness and sees the oppressed everywhere.

Born in Detroit, the son of Yugoslavs, Stimac spent the first ten years of his life in northern Michigan. His grandmother, ninety-eight, raised her family alone as a factory worker. She was a staunch union member and among the first to sign a CIO card. When the family moved back to Detroit, Stimac went from rural northern schools to an all-black public school. "The white teachers were brutal to blacks. One kid was forced to stick out his tongue, and the teacher hit it with the side of the ruler." His antiwar views and his empathy for blacks crystallized during the 1967 Detroit riots. "The police and the Army were attacking *my* neighbors. Was I going to be a part of that Army? The likelihood of having to go back in my neighborhood and shoot down my people was just as bad as going to Vietnam and shooting a bunch of farmers.

One friend walked a pregnant woman home after curfew and was arrested. In prison he saw someone beaten to a pulp.

"There were thousands arrested and several shot. It was martial law, U.S.-style. We're tempted to think that only happens in [places like] Poland. Police and the Army stopped all food shipments to the ghetto. Two weeks! Then what do one million people do? Calm down, when you have no food, gas, liquor."

Stimac won a scholarship to Wayne State University, had a part-time job in the university bookstore, and helped to organize university workers. "We pretty much closed the university in the summer of '67. *Cafeteria workers* who really needed the money wouldn't cross the picket line—but the *professors* would say, 'I really sympathize with you, but I must cross it.' "

His activism spread to antiwar work. He went to the Chicago Democratic convention in 1968 and was tear-gassed. He worked with SDS but found the Weathermen "idiots, mostly rich kids playing at revolution. *Working* people don't romanticize poverty." He is intensely loyal to Russia, and anti-Mao and anti-China. "Bombing Hanoi in '64 or mining Haiphong wouldn't have changed the war. There was always a land link to China. But the war would have been lost by the United States much sooner if China had allowed Soviet bases in China. With that air cover for North Vietnam there would not have been the bombing of Hanoi by the United States. I'm happy Vietnam won its victory."

Stimac's doctrinaire ideology brooks no criticism of present-day oppression in Vietnam. "They'd lived through thirty years of napalm and reeducation camps and tons of bombs and tiger cages and atrocities. I think you have a much freer country today, in the same sense if you look at Cuba and compare it to any other Latin American people. It's no Utopia, but there is health care and education for all. Historically it is as much an improvement as capitalism was over feudalism. It's not perfect, but compared to Detroit? If you had to choose from the *slums* of Detroit, you would have more advantages in Cuba. Now if you're comparing it with life in the suburbs, that's different. A Cuban kid is guaranteed a quart of milk a day. Think what that would do if you had a quart of milk per child a day in Harlem."

Current Vietnam "reeducation camps" are discounted by Stimac as "not punishing for the sake of punishing but eradicating Western ways." Poland's Solidarity uprising against Russia is not seen as a fight for freedom from communist rule but dismissed as the "conservative faction of Poland. *We* have to clear up our own backyard."

When Stimac got a 55 in the lottery, he left for the north woods, built his own house, grew his own food, and took up the cause of the Chippewa Indians on nearby reservations who were "treated horribly."

A resourcefulness remains. There is a veritable truck garden in the back, huge wooden platters in the kitchen hold drying tarragon, homemade stew is brewing for Stimac and for his son Mikos and daughter Kiva (she was named for the American Indian ceremonial caves). Separated from his wife, Stimac cares for his children six months of the year.

After being a dodger fugitive at home for a year, Stimac moved to Canada, worked in an iron foundry, and went to Guelph University. He broke his back in a steel-mill accident and rails at the antiquated, American-owned factories. Stimac was unemployed at the time of this interview, receiving automatic compensation in Canada, which is three fourths of his wage. "I thought I was going to die in that lousy factory. I hope to continue with my artwork, but I have to work somewhere; the next ten years I'm going to devote to my children."

Stimac rolls up several of his "Workers unite" posters and gives them as a parting present. Brooding, intense, a man whose views were only hardened by his being a member of the Vietnam Generation, Stimac concludes, "Vietnam brushed away a lot of illusions and made us deal with the realities of American power. At the same time it was a tremendously searing experience, both for those who went and those who resisted."

David Felcher epitomizes an entirely different child of that generation—the wandering, beatnik/hippie, drug/rock, spaced-out, apolitical member of the counterculture.

"By the early seventies, the entire southern part of British Columbia, from the Alberta line all the way 600 miles over to Vancouver, was infiltrated with draft dodgers and hippies," he recalls.

"In our valley—which extended about 300 miles from the Idaho border to Golden, British Columbia—I'd say there were about 400 draft dodgers and their wives and kids." Felcher built his mud-and-log cabin in the mountains. There were no roads or electricity. Only the hard core made it through the winters that reached 40° below zero.

Felcher returns often to overcoming the "unspoken cowardice attached to being a draft dodger. The macho stance we assumed as loggers and homesteaders was to overcompensate for the fact that underneath everything we did perhaps feel we were cowards. It had nothing to do with politics, more with self-esteem. I don't think any of us had political convictions. It was a matter of being able to smoke dope, be a free guy, and not have any commitment to society. Some Berkeley types settled near us and developed suburban life-styles. They smoked dope but they had TVs. Their parents supplied them with money for appliances and washing machines and things us funky dropout hippies didn't have. Draft-dodging in Canada coincided with the blossoming or the back-to-the-land movement." Felcher hiked all day on snowshoes to go to town to do the wash every three weeks.

It was spartan isolation for a man who grew up in a five-flat walkup in the Bronx. The sixties led Felcher from New York drugs and jazz, through the briefest brush with higher education, to multiwomen relationships and sexual experiences, fathering a passel of children with names like Shasta Rose and Ethan Allen Hummingbird. Felcher's wanderings took him through San

Francisco's drug scene, occult communes, crashing in England with a famous rock star, and the mystic rituals of Indian peyote ceremonies. For years his world was ruled by the hallucinogenic haze of drugs and rock. "We were pioneers in the hippie drug world. Living on the edge . . ."

David Felcher is now a cowboy in Wyoming. He has a caressing love for the land, jarringly out of place with his casual references to *ménage-à-trois* and bizarre sex and "meth heads" (methedrine users) and junkies and giving children marijuana to lull them to sleep.

At his high school, "Dewitt-Clinton in the Bronx," he got "deep into Negro ghetto rock, listening to the Paragons and Jesters," and hung out with some "real soulful guys from Harlem." He clashed with his postal clerk father when he'd come home at 4 A.M. "with the smell of nightclubs clinging to my clothes." A post office scholarship fund paid half, and his parents paid the rest to get him out of there and into Bucknell University in 1963. "Man, all these kids were listening to Jan and Dean, and the Safaris—just the most hideous white suburban rock. I knew in the first three days I wasn't going to make it there."

After numerous girlfriends and no studying, he was thrown out that summer. He took off for Florida with Victoria, a rich girl, in her Austin-Healy Sprite. When money ran low, they "started whaling back up that road, back up into winter."

He was "rather surprised" to find a notice from the draft board. Victoria was pregnant, and they headed for New York, living in a "wino-junkie hotel. They couldn't draft me, at least until she had had the baby." He went on welfare, she to a home for unwed mothers. He worked with an "avant-garde hip clothing store and met guys using acid and methedrine." Then he was a busboy at Max's Kansas City Steak House.

"What was 'happening' all the time was methedrine." And LSD and, of course, "real heavy gold" that would keep you stoned all day. On the Staten Island Ferry at dawn, "I saw the Statue of Liberty in a rainbow color-washed spray. With my hallucinations, it looked like the city was sinking under the waves, a glimpse of the way Atlantis went down. I left New York City forever. Have never gone back."

He was heading for the coast, but *"from that day on my life was to be completely controlled by the Vietnam War.* I got a second draft notice."

Antiwar activists coached him to say he belonged to a long list of subversive organizations—"from the W. E. B. Du Bois Club to the KKK." Despite his drug use—and he gladly told them the extent and variety—they passed him. "The War Resisters League gave me my freedom and, possibly, my life. I checked ten or twelve of those groups, was considered a security risk, and borrowed time." He bummed across the country with some other long-haired freaks who, when stopped by cops, said they were Shakespearean actors on their way to Los Angeles and actually got away with it.

California meant more drugs and rock and grooving with an occult commune whose members believed in the existence of hollow mountains.

"Eating opium and making love. The hippie counterculture has always been the lunatic fringe of the revolution." He met an "old beatnik from the North Beach scene" named Leslie who shared his life for eleven years, bore some of his children, and became his wife. When Felcher got another draft notice, they sold her brass bed for a "big fat kilo" of grass, stashed it in an old hippie camper, and took off for Canada. Despite some hassles, friends along the way got them to the border where they knelt and kissed the snow-covered ground.

There were months of living in shacks. Felcher faked student enrollment to stay in the country. "The students were in Edmonton, us dopers were in Vancouver." They met a famous rock star who was into drugs and issued a vague invitation for them to visit in England. They "took in that scene," bankrolled by another dodger who "assumed the stance of a freak but was a millionaire. His father was a motor-company vice president."

Back in Canada Felcher borrowed money from a grandfather, which he needed to show solvency, and finally became a landed immigrant. Felcher logged and worked in a sawmill. By 1973 there was a large enough hippie-drug group to support a lucrative drug-smuggling operation. A half-breed draft dodger from Oklahoma taught him how to rope calves and become a cowboy, and cut him in on some of the drug action. "In return for hiding their stash, we got ours free." That eliminated a "major living expense."

But there was trouble between the "renegade" dodgers and the straighter "farmer" dodgers. Felcher, who had a foot in both camps, sided with the drug-smuggling outlaws. He speaks constantly of the casualness of sexual relationships among the hippies. Another woman moved in with Felcher and his wife. "I had lost my wife to junk. She was doing needles." Felcher became a Canadian citizen. Carter's amnesty came and went, with most in his group not even noticing.

Nineteen seventy-nine was a turning point. His half-breed friend, Jesse Blackhorse, was sentenced to seven years for international drug-trafficking. "That bust gave me an incentive to kick the drug scene. I left Canada in 1979 and haven't been back since."

Felcher cut his hair and vowed to "kick the weed. I quit cold and haven't bought a lid since. I'm using peyote, which is a whole different frame of head, more clear and alert."

His dawn-to-dusk cowboy job toughened his lean six-feet-two body. "Still can't throw a rope worth a damn but can ride with the best of them, and I'm learning how to break horses. It beats being a hippie by about a million miles."

Vietnam, however, is never far from his life. At first, his British Columbia license plates were a draft-dodger giveaway. "The other cowboys were *really* riding me—'you're yellow 'cause you wouldn't go to Vietnam.' One old boy started riding me about not having gone to Vietnam; I just spit my coffee at him, and he backed off.

"I'm now working for a guy who was in the Marine Corps in Vietnam. He seems to respect me because I did bust my chops fighting those BC winters. I know an Indian, Harvey Beartrack, Jr., who served in the Marines in Vietnam, and was real proud of it. A friend of his had a heroin habit from Vietnam. Both saw a lot of combat and made me aware of how proud they were to have been Leathernecks. Indians place a lot of value on being warriors, and it comes through with these guys. We get along real good—but there is *always* that block. I was the dodger, they the veterans."

The hippies who lived their nomadic, drugged, no-commitment life were out there just waiting for the sixties to happen, but Felcher feels that Vietnam gave them one more special excuse. He speaks almost prudishly now of drug abuse.

"There's a *lot* of drug dealing out here in the middle-of-nowhere Wyoming. I think Vietnam and Watergate made everyone so cynical. I've stayed straight, except peyote. Bought my first TV and just had a brand-new baby.

"It's hard to know what I'd be today, without having had to dodge Vietnam. The end of the Vietnam War was exceptionally messy with Kent State, riots, Watergate, and Wounded Knee. We were really glad to be in Canada, a civilized place. I think even in the eighties that the States really hasn't recovered from the attitudes Vietnam and Watergate left—about the corruption and all.

"The sixties, the mess of Vietnam, produced the America of the eighties. We prophesied Armageddon, and I think it's going to happen. I don't think the world is going to live to see 1990. Maybe that's being dramatic, but I don't really see how we can make it. The depression and the arms race. We're just all going to go to kingdom come."

Profound alienation, bitter cynicism about the government of their homeland, a sense of being forced into exile, a sense of not truly belonging, family estrangement are some of the legacies for dodgers and deserters, no matter how well they have assimilated on the surface. Their solution to the problem of Vietnam was a choice that irrevocably defined, and to an extent, scarred their lives.

No matter the strength of their conviction about the wrongness of the war. Felcher is not the only one who speaks to the whispered accusation of cowardice. Paul Steue, a writer and owner of a small Toronto bookstore, was precocious, brainy, and a 1965 Columbia graduate who had helped run a youth center in Hell's Kitchen. Today he says, "It was a Band-Aid. There's nothing for people like them in the political system." He left "profoundly alienated. You could put God, the United States government, and my father in one package. He was rigid and I was rigid." To this day, Steue has made no peace with his father.

"I've only encountered a few up here who felt we were personally cowards. I think we were, to some degree, if you see us as choosing to live rather than die." He feels that some dodgers "framed, in retrospect, a strong moral opposition to the war."

For exiles there remain complex and ambiguous responses to their life-changing choice made as youths. Accepted in Canada, they still, in some ways, stand apart. "Little things taught us how alien we were—like vinegar on potato chips," says Steue, smiling. He now speaks of "we" Canadians, but it took time to understand their "excessive politeness and reserve."

Don Zielinski, blue-collar Chicagoan, first generation to attend college, had many friends who "looked on the Marines as a rite of passage. I didn't get an invitation to my class reunion—maybe that says something. I suspect a lot of them went. It was very rigidly Catholic. Maybe I read more, maybe it's my innate cynicism, but I was damned if I would kill or be killed in that war."

An artist with a graphics company, Zielinski also did political cartoons for the Toronto *Globe and Mail* when Vietnam and other United States issues were newsworthy.

"I don't feel Canadian—but I don't feel American either. Not even when watching the World Series."

Kevin Brieze says, "Regardless of how Canadian you may act, you still are 'from the States.' Many would like to live in the States, but the feeling is 'what would we do there?'"

Above all, more than any other group of nongoers—with the exception of those who chose jail—Canada's dodgers express compassion and concern for veterans. Most accept with deep understanding why exiles are still the subject of contempt for some veterans' families. "It's easier to hate in the abstract," said one. Kevin Brieze said, "It's misplaced bitterness, but it's understandable. They were brought up to respect country and flag and all that entails. So was I. I guess they find it more offensive to question those kinds of things than to feel bitter against those who 'didn't get theirs.'"

There is an ill-defined longing to mend the divisions. They speak not in lofty tones of "binding America's wounds" but in personal, individualistic ways. What happens, however, to these men so long removed from their homes and families is what happens to veterans. No one wants to listen. And so, the papering over, the denial continues.

There is seldom overt hostility when they come home. Forgotten as political symbols, the wrenching reasons for leaving are also forgotten. When one dodger returned to the States years after amnesty and someone said, "Nice to see you," he replied, "It is nice that I was *allowed* to come back." "No one," he said, "really understood what I meant."

Avoidance, like the skirting of an ugly family skeleton, is still a principal way of dealing with the problem. Says Zielinski, "Everybody wants to forget. Families are still torn." When he returns to Chicago, there is no closure on the very different experiences of himself and his veteran friends. "It sounds odd, but no one ever talks about Vietnam. One guy was a door-gunner in a helicopter, and it is as if nothing happened. Like he'd never been to Vietnam —and I might have been in Miami."

Others recount the same awkward, unnatural dismissal of the most pivotal time of their youth. "I can't talk to guys from my class who went," says Steue. "Even my wife's relations aren't too keen on me. My wife's brother did two tours of Vietnam." He laughs. "And my wife's *sister* teaches tank maintenance at Fort Knox. Needless to say, at family reunions we have some quiet moments about the past."

Like the veterans, the exiles a decade later are getting on with their lives— slowed by upheaval and uprooting. Like the veterans, they feel somewhat apart from the rest of society, who, they feel, chose to forget the consequences of that conflict. They often feel adjusted, yet the war scarred and changed them permanently too.

Time has softened the acrimony and dissent in many families, but sadly the way of coping is, generally, *not* to cope. One victim of the war could have been speaking about America in general, when he spoke of his family. "We've got a way around my being a deserter," he said.

"We just don't talk about it."

3 The Imprisoned

MICHAEL BILLINGSLEY WAS 4-F. AT THE AGE OF THREE, HE FELL ON A rock and was blinded in one eye. Instead of living his youth with ease, knowing he would never have to face war, Billingsley burned his draft card into oblivion in a newspaper ashtray in 1968, telling a reporter that he had friends who had been killed in Vietnam. "This is a measure of empathy with those being screwed by the system," he said. After getting the publicity he sought, two FBI agents arrested Billingsley and played "good guy, bad guy," one calling him a creep and a coward, the other admonishing, "Don't be so rough on him." They wanted to find out who else was involved—but, as he had done most things all his life, Billingsley had acted alone.

Billingsley was given a year and a half probation and assigned alternate service in a children's mental hospital. "I couldn't stand it. I was locking up *kids,* many of whom shouldn't have been there. Kids picked up on the streets or those who were too much trouble for their parents. Most were being drugged by the hospital." Billingsley quit, and before his letter of explanation reached his probation officers, hospital officials had notified them. A warrant went out for his arrest. Billingsley stormed into the probation officer's, tried to explain, but was sentenced to a sixty-day psychiatric evaluation in a juvenile detention center.

(Judges can order a *pre-sentence* involuntary commitment, and there is no appeal because it is for "psychiatric evaluation.") Billingsley recalled, "I was told the judge wanted to give me a taste of jail to scare me." His "taste" of prison included transfers to seven jails where he witnessed rapes and beatings and knew personal terror.

In his first jail, Delaware's Newcastle County Correctional Institution, "people were there for life, for murder. It was a very hostile redneck environment. As they cut off my hair in the barber shop, they kept making jokes: 'Boy, are we gonna have fun with you' . . . There were about 250 black prisoners, and the white warden deliberately assigned me to the black section. A trustee later told me the warden saw me as 'one of those Commie bastards' and thought I would be killed or beaten. I was sure that I would get knifed.

At meals there would be blacks on all sides, and I would have this pocket of space around me like I was a germ. Blacks ran that jail. Short-timers were used as couriers to pass messages on the street. The jail was the nerve center for political and street action for Wilmington's black ghetto. It was after the Martin Luther King riots, and there were lots of arrests."

After three days of silent terror, the Black Muslim leader and the political leader questioned Billingsley about his politics. When they left his cell, he sat in panic. That evening the Muslim leader told Billingsley to sit at his table, his signal to all blacks that Billingsley was "not to be messed with."

The warden did not know what tipped the scales for Billingsley; it was his commitment to spread draft counseling beyond the middle class. Billingsley had done draft counseling in the black ghetto. The word passed through the prison-ghetto grapevine that he was okay.

Billingsley saw some "real bad jails" as he was transported from place to place in a system that seems as inefficient as inhumane. "If a marshall is driving from Florida to Washington, he will pick up a prisoner in North Carolina and take him to Washington—even though his destination is Chicago. Then another marshall later will pick up the prisoner and take him to Chicago. You are dropped off and picked up as it is convenient to their routing." Billingsley went from Newcastle to Hanover County Jail in Virginia, a county jail in Durham, N.C., and finally to the Ashland, Ky., Federal Reformatory for psychiatric evaluation—which ascertained that there was nothing wrong with him. On the way back, he went from Ashland to a Parkersburg, W.Va., jail to Pittsburgh and back to Newcastle for his release.

"At the Ashland youth reformatory I saw some pretty rough shit. Gangs had whole stables of younger kids they were raping on a regular basis. It was," says Billingsley, in a modulated voice that betrays no emotion now, "just horrible."

During the Vietnam War, over half a million men committed draft violations that could have sent them to prison for five years. Their cases clogged the courts. By 1969, Selective Service cases had become the fourth largest category on the criminal docket.[1]

Still, the Michael Billingsleys who served time, made up a fraction of the offenders. Fewer than half of the 570,000 who committed draft violations were reported to federal prosecutors—and only 25,000 of them were indicted. Fewer than 9,000 were convicted and just 3,250 went to prison, most of whom were paroled within a year.[2]

There were lenient jurisdictions—San Francisco led the way—where sympathetic judges handed down light probationary sentences. Antiwar lawyers, prosecutors, and law clerks—many of whom had dodged the draft themselves—dumped cases on a wholesale basis. In 1967 and 1968 more than 90 percent of all cases referred to the San Francisco U.S. Attorney's Office were dropped before indictment. In 1970 the Supreme Court issued three landmark decisions that found against draft-board practices and procedures: these decisions destroyed whatever enthusiasm remained for enforcing the law. The backlog and reluctant judges discouraged prosecutors from trying draft cases. Some offenders were even allowed to do draft counseling as their alternative service. A Buffalo musician was sentenced to give six rock concerts in Canadian prisons, and the number of dropped cases reached massive proportions. In the District of Columbia, for example, 99 percent of 1967–70 cases were never prosecuted. The national average of prosecuted cases was 11 percent.[3]

Draft resistance began in 1964, when three St. Louis men jointly promised that if one refused induction and was sent to jail the others would follow. All three served prison terms.

Muhammad Ali's conviction for refusing the draft in 1967 drew nation-wide attention to the resistance movement. Leaders set 100,000 acts of resistance as their goal after New York *Times* columnist Tom Wicker wrote: "If the Johnson administration had to prosecute 100,000 Americans in order to maintain its authority, its real power to pursue the Vietnamese war would be crippled if not destroyed." Such large-scale revolt never materialized. Few students heeded the call to drop their deferments, and inductees continued to flee to Canada rather than face jail.

At a national SDS conference, only one fifth of the mostly college-age delegates supported a plan to renounce their deferments. Antiwar leaders were, as one said, "frankly appalled" at the fear of alienating students by raising the college deferment issue. The frustrated resistance movement circulated "snowballing" petitions; signers were committed to acts of resistance only if pledges exceeded a specified number, ranging from 1,000 to 15,000. Widespread reluctance of white middle-class students to assume personal risks remained; snowballing petitions never got enough signatures to make the pledges binding.

While the resistance movement did not grind the war machine to a halt, as had been envisioned, it did give impetus to *individual* acts of defiance. Large numbers of men began refusing induction, forcing draft boards to refer their cases to federal prosecutors. This clogged the courts but did not cripple the draft system.

With so many cases being thrown out, just who *were* those few who went to prison? For the most part they fell into two groups. Many could have qualified for C.O. because of religious or philosophical objections to war but chose jail as a matter of principle. At the other end were the poor and uneducated who often unwittingly violated draft laws. Some were drifters who never notified the Selective Service of a change of address. Many would have been disqualified for the draft if they had faced induction, such as John Blass, who had a sixth-grade education and an IQ of 49. Many could have gotten off on hardship cases if they had been brighter. The public perception of convicted offenders as either radical activists or manipulative draft dodgers is incorrect. There *were* such cases, of course. The head of the Washington, D.C., Young Republican Leadership Conference was sentenced to two years for obtaining fraudulent deferments. In New York City and Cleveland, thirty-eight fathers and sons were arrested for paying up to $5,000 for false papers entitling their sons to draft exemptions. A New York City draft board official was convicted for selling deferments and exemptions for as much as $30,000. And a California orthodontist had to skip to Mexico to escape prosecution after outfitting several patients with artificial braces.[4]

Those I interviewed who went to jail were strong individualists, some with a messianic drive as well as a deep conviction that the war was wrong. Many religious or radical activists who publicly burned draft cards or destroyed draft records believed they were sacrificing themselves for a higher cause. Some acted strictly on their own, refusing induction.

In 1975 President Ford's Clemency Review Board reviewed more than 1,800 cases of convicted draft offenders and recommended outright pardons for four out of five applicants. An unexpectedly high percentage came from economically disadvantaged backgrounds. Many were blacks and Spanish-speaking. Four of every five were deeply opposed to the war, having committed their offenses as a matter of principle. Of this group, less than 1 percent had ever been convicted of other felonies. One third were Jehovah's Witnesses, Muslims, or Quakers. Although they often would have received C.O. status, many refused to have anything to do with wars—including the alternate service C.O. requirement.[5]

Willard Gaylin, a Columbia University psychologist, interviewed imprisoned draft offenders in 1968 and was shocked to find that they did not meet his naïve stereotype of political radicals. They were gentle and compassionate, with deep moral or religious principles. The men I found more than a decade later fit the same category. Almost all felt in hindsight that what they did was correct and in general that the prison experience strengthened them. Most rejected Canada as "running away." But they also knew depression, loneliness, alienation, a sense of pointlessness to their act as the war ground on and few followed their example. Like veterans, they watched in frustration as a generation of men who paid no price passed them by. Some resented their former college mates. Some never recovered from their experience. Marriages and girlfriends fell by the wayside during months of incarceration.

The impression that they sat out the war in country club prisons is for the most part erroneous. Even 'country club' prisons had their violence. All the men I interviewed, and many that Gaylin knew, witnessed prison depravity and brutality and were often the victims. They were somewhat different from the Clemency Review Board mix. Most I met were college graduates or had some college education. Some were middle class, but most sprang from working-class backgrounds. All of the men I interviewed had a deep empathy for the poor, blacks, and working class who bore the brunt of the Selective Service draft. For some, prison was the beginning of a lifelong commitment to radical causes or pacifism.

Above all, they seem the most guilt-free of their generation. There is no self-righteousness, but a calm sense of being able to face any probing, any questions about what they did in the class war. One summed it up best: "I can tell my grandchildren what I did and not feel ashamed."

Jim Harney used to be the Reverend James W. Harney—a Catholic priest who made headlines as a member of the Milwaukee 14. In 1968 they destroyed draft records in Milwaukee. Today Harney—who left the priesthood in 1973—calls himself a "religious-political person." He is deeply active in Central America, among the Catholic left who decry America's involvement in El Salvador and Nicaragua.

It was a vast conversion for Harney, the son of a Boston dockworker. In the fifties, he and his parents believed in the Red menace and Joe McCarthy. "I cried when he died." Courses offering "radical interpretation of ethical values" changed his perspective. Harney became fascinated with nonviolent civil disobedience, Gandhi, Martin Luther King, Jr., and the civil rights movement; with being able to accentuate injustice through nonviolent protest. "Noncooperation with evil," a phrase of King's, dictated much of Harney's life.

He worked among blacks with Phil Berrigan, then began activist protest after realizing that "the brunt of the war was being thrown on the poor. The government was spending thirty billion dollars a year for the war—money that could have gone to our inner cities. Blacks were being drafted heavily."

Harney is tall, earnest, and intense. He lives in a cluttered walk-up apartment in Boston filled with maps of El Salvador, pamphlets, posters, and books on revolution and resistance. In 1967, bothered by his seminarian exemption—which allowed for passive avoidance—Harney needed to get involved in an active way. At a celebrated Boston Commons draft-card-burning rally attended by thousands, Harney gave an impromptu antiwar speech. The FBI soon tracked him back to the seminary and told the rector, "You have a subversive among you bent on overthrowing the country."

"When it came time to decide whether I was going into the priesthood, the seminary was split. The rector broke the tie. He was an Air Force chaplain, but in spite of his background, my activist work, and the FBI visit, he still voted in my favor. That meant a lot to me." Later Harney found his antiwar parishioners far less accepting. "Psychic numbness was going on in this country. Destroying draft records seemed the only kind of resistance that would awaken people."

On September 14, 1968, fourteen men with satchel bags walked into the Milwaukee draft board headquarters in broad daylight. Five of them were priests. They stuck 50,000 files in their satchels and walked out. With homemade napalm they burned the files in front of the draft board and waited for the sirens of fire engines and police squad cars. In the news photo of that day, Harney's hair is close-cropped above his priest's collar. His dockworker father was having a drink in a bar when the evening news came on. He looked at the television—and saw his son burning the files. He burst out crying. The men on the docks confronted him. "If that was my son, I would have put a bullet right through his head," said one. Harney's father replied, "Well, if you're going to do that—you'll have to put a bullet through me too."

Convicted offenders who had strong family support never fail to mention this with deep gratitude. Many say that made the difference between despair and hope during their lonely imprisoned months. "My father defended me very strongly, even though he didn't agree with my breaking the law. My mother died in 1963. My father says that if she were alive *she* would have been in jail with me. She always supported me in the civil rights demonstrations."

Destroying the files was the final blow for Harney's parishioners. He returned to find his room in the rectory ransacked, his belongings stacked outside the door. "The pastor said, 'Get out. This is the end.' "

Continuing his draft resistance, Harney tried vainly to get a toehold in Catholic middle-class working communities while awaiting his trial and sentencing. "Whenever I did get in, the shit hit the fan. When parents found I was coming to the Hingham catechism class, the phone went off the hook at the rectory with complaints—'why are you bringing in this traitor?' There were 200 youths, their parents, and American flags all over the auditorium. I talked about young people having to make decisions about whether they wanted to die in Vietnam or not. Parents came up and shouted that I was a 'pinko—supporting communism.' Then one of the *kids* said, 'I'm ashamed of the people here today, the parents.' And another yelled, 'This is the first time in my life I've heard anybody speak about the draft.' " Unlike draft-wise campus counterparts, he added, "This is the first time I've ever heard there was an option."

Harney has no idea how many working-class Catholics he converted, but there is lasting sorrow that many were never reached. "Those who tried to do draft counseling in the diocese had a fight. When I *could* get to those kids, they supported me to the hilt." Harney agrees that if everyone with a student deferment had turned them in and faced the courts—if even 20 percent had—the draft system might have been in shambles. "They were against the 'imperialist' war but not for making substantive changes. Anybody who's interested in bringing about change always has to be ready to pay up personally."

Nonviolence gave way to violence in prison. For six out of eighteen months, Harney was in a maximum-security prison in Waupun, Wisconsin.

"We were in one of those Cagney-like prisons with three tiers. When we first walked in, everybody in the jail applauded us. Our story was major news in Wisconsin during 1968. It was 'Here come the revolutionaries.' The *administration*, afraid of us, sent us to different farms and minimum-security prisons. Even in a minimum-security prison, I was exposed to real violence. People were really beaten. The foreman, a real redneck, hit this old guy, about sixty-five, who got a box of auto plates out of order on the assembly line. And then he yelled at me to take his place. I said, 'You really violated him and don't expect me to cooperate.' "

Harney was taken to isolation (solitary confinement). Several security guards watched while a strip search was conducted. "You have to go through the most humiliating things, spreading your ass so that they can make sure you don't have any hidden contraband." In point of fact, the strip search was used as a psychological tool against defiant draft offenders, often in minimum security where the level of overt violence was low.

One sixties inmate named Matthew once mentioned to the warden that a guard, in ripping off a stamp from a letter written to him from Europe, ripped off half the letter. Matthew was a marked man. Punishment was malicious and psychologically sophisticated—no beatings, no marks, no physical abuse. After each visiting hour, guards searched each prisoner, routinely with a quick frisk. But for Matthew every visiting hour ended in psychological abuse. It was the same abuse Harney experienced. He was taken into a room, forced to strip, bend over, and have his rectum probed. The anticipated strip search was a constant source of anguish that destroyed the pleasure of any visits. This procedure went on for months.[6]

Harney was in isolation for six weeks out of eighteen months. "You really had to learn to stretch your imagination. I would look forward to just a bird coming to the window. I'd go back to all my creation theology and try to get in touch with that bird. I'd talk to the bird, 'Thanks for being with me and singing to me and giving me the strength to keep going.' "

Set apart by religion, education, and motivation from most in the prison population, Harney developed rapport with other political prisoners like the Black Panthers. "They immediately saw a connection between our struggles." Harney is one of those who has not the slightest regret or doubt about going to jail. "It is what I had to do." Now obsessed with the turbulence in Central America, the ex-priest cranks out political newsletters and supports himself by driving a cab.

"It's a sad commentary, but the Catholic church was totally passive during Vietnam," says Harney. "Now it's leading a lot of resistance. If El Salvador were a non-Christian country, the likelihood of the church getting involved wouldn't be as great."

Harney was in El Salvador on the day of Bishop Oscar Romero's funeral in March 1980. The priest, who worked with the people, was assassinated while saying mass. "In El Salvador demonstrations are illegal. People can't even *gather* together for any reason at all." Harney was marching with other protesters toward the cathedral when a bomb was thrown from the national palace. "People ran for their lives. I was on my stomach with a telephoto lens capturing young kids crawling across the street trying to get to the cathedral for cover. And young people were in the gutter, their arms around each other, trying to keep away from the bullets. I never heard so much firepower in my life. Back in this country, anytime I hear the slightest noise, like a firecracker, I think of that horrible scene. I don't know how in God's name Vietnam veterans ever do it. And I didn't have to kill anybody!" Harney is intense as he talks of peasants who fought and hid from the National Guard by the thousands in the hills. "An old woman took me to an occupied area, surrounded by military. I asked if she was afraid, and she said, 'Yes, but in El Salvador, either we die of hunger or we die with our people in the struggle.'"

Today antiwar activism has come full circle. Harney speaks to high school students, tying Vietnam into their future. "I tell them, 'Dammit all, I was in El Salvador and saw some of the terror that goes on. You are going to have to decide very early whether you're going to have to go to El Salvador—just like guys who sat in this same auditorium years ago had to decide whether they were going to Vietnam or not.'"

Bill Tilton is a Minnesota lawyer, a child of the Catholic middle class, the son of a Republican, graduate of a military high school, and an ex-felon. He served twenty months in prison. At the University of Minnesota, Tilton moved in several antiwar camps—the straight student-government crowd, religious groups, and "the long-haired dope smokers. You didn't *party* with the church people."

He also backed the NLF and VC. "We saw the VC as fighting for their independence. I have to admit I didn't consider how it looked to veterans at the time to see kids carrying VC flags. Hoping they won didn't mean, 'I hope my high school buddies get killed.' The North Vietnamese government has proven itself to be as vicious as any government can be. Had you told me that in 1970, I might not have believed it. But that still doesn't change the fact that we should not have been there."

After thinking about it for one year, Tilton turned in his draft card along with twenty-five others at a rally. A major flaw in the resistance, he feels, is that more students did not join in. "To equalize the Selective Service System would have unified the generation on a major scale." With the nonchalance of youth, Tilton thought he could move through activism unscathed. He and several others simultaneously raided a number of Minnesota draft boards. "At three of the locations, the FBI were waiting." To this day, Tilton doesn't know what went wrong—"whether it was a plant, phone tap, or someone in the group wanting to get arrested to make a larger statement." As Tilton was fumbling through the files, he heard, "Don't move or you're dead. This is the FBI." He froze, as if playing a game of statues. Bail was set at $50,000—"the worst thing they could have done. Those who wouldn't have done much became supporters because it was such overkill. Within hours a couple of hundred demonstrated on our behalf in one of the few violent demonstrations I ever saw."

Like many who went to jail, Tilton glosses over the details of prison life. Only after repeated questioning will they verbalize or remember much of what they have chosen to forget. Even with prodding, many have blotted out the worst details. There was a long, long pause when he was asked what was the worst thing he experienced or saw in jail.

"This guy had a woman's name—Ginger Rogers. 'She' was giving a blow job," said Tilton, reverting to the prison-slang use of the feminine gender. "I don't know if she was just angry or had been forced against her will, but she bit down real hard. The guy was lucky he didn't lose his cock." Both were transferred to prevent retaliatory mayhem.

"Another guy got forcibly 'turned out' by a bigger guy. The younger man got a job in maintenance, and little by little he smuggled out gasoline. At two o'clock one morning, he tossed this mayonnaise jar filled with gasoline into the cell." An inmate tossed a blanket to the burning prisoner, who survived but got the message. "Everybody respected the guy who threw the flame. He was a little guy and he got back."

The rules of the game—resistance and retaliation, prison leadership and prison punks, violent acts and violent retribution—were startling cultural shocks for draft offenders who came to jail nonviolent and proudly principled. No one left quite the same. Most tend to tell their stories with hard-earned distance, as if reciting something that happened to someone else. They experienced boredom, loneliness, and some shame at having to bow to the will of prison guards, and abhorred the loss of individuality. They fended off battles and sexual overtures, and they knew the loss of irretrievable years.

Their intelligence worked both ways. It often earned them a respect vital for prison survival, but it also incensed the punitive guards and "dumb hillbillies" who seemed to populate many prisons. Prisoners often viewed draft offenders as "soft," easy targets. Vincent McGee was serving time when he was asked to testify before the 1972 Senate hearings on amnesty. Jail authorities refused. McGee was allowed instead to write a statement. In it he spoke of being saddened by the change he saw among incarcerated draft offenders. "The horror of that experience for these strong men of gentle conscience and demeanor sets too many of them against the system and costs the nation years of skill and dedication to community service."

Years later, I interviewed McGee, who served ten months and twenty-five days. An organizer with a strong sense of mission, he fared well, made friends with hardened criminals, continued his antiwar work, and feels generally optimistic about his experience.

"I went to Allenwood, certainly more pleasant than most prisons," recalls McGee. "Earlier in the war, cases often were sent to maximum-security prisons." Overall the worst aspect of prison was a pervasive "loss of *any* privacy *whatever.*"

"I went through it without the negatives that others did because I had made a mark. I was one of the cases that went to the Supreme Court. I had a lot of publicity. I ran Business Executives for Vietnam Peace—comprised of 6,000 corporate executives. I could get literally any senator or congressman on the phone. I was on Nixon's enemy list." McGee liked the power and the notoriety and felt he had accomplished much through both. "I *proved* that the individual citizen who carefully figures out what he is going to do can have some effect. People paid attention to me. There may be the penalty of going to jail and the time and bother, but at least I felt it wasn't *wasted. That* was the horror for some people. A lot felt that what they did made no difference. Some were wrecked: 'We can't do anything about the war here.' 'I don't have that much of a support group on the outside.' 'It's destroyed my studies, destroyed my career.' 'I'm scared to death. Where do I go?' Many turned inward and became unreachable. They ended up bitter and alienated."

An antiwar female who knew one resister before he went to jail, recalls, "David was just a beautiful man, extraordinarily beautiful in a soft, angelic way. He came out a raving right-winger and really weird. I think he was raped or had some horrible experience." Tilton also knew David. "For him prison may have been the straw that broke the camel's back. He came out thinking women should be barefoot and pregnant and that everybody should be armed. Others came out with weird reactions. One divorced his wife and left his family and changed his name and just disappeared.

"A member of the Milwaukee Fourteen I knew never seemed to get on his feet. Created his own cult group in Oregon and was into group sex and Indian mysticism. One of my codefendants is just beginning to adjust. Another guy I knew seemed lost. Went to airplane-mechanic school, and off and on tried to be a rock-and-roll star. He was real nervous, disjointed, hard to get along with. *I* came out a little confused myself but am convinced now that I came out stronger." Tilton pauses. "I wouldn't have guessed that at the time. My family was very supportive, which helped—except they thought I was ruining my future. I didn't do hard time; I was in medium security. Luckily I learned at an early age to amuse myself by reading." After prison Tilton went to law school even though it was a gamble. Other draft resisters who served time were never able to practice. However, he was eventually pardoned. Tilton concludes that "most of us will never be the same—but most I know have learned to gain from it, rather than feel sorry for themselves."

In jail some experienced frequent dreams of escape and confinement. Psychologist Willard Gaylin found only one, Paul, who claimed it was all worthwhile at the time he was in prison. However, Gaylin concluded, he was enmeshed in one of the more primitive defense mechanisms—denial. Paul dreamed he was slowly being lowered into a huge vat of Jell-O that was chilling, and that he was stuck and suffocating in this congealing mass. Gaylin concluded that it was intriguingly symbolic of his confined, locked-up helplessness, but Paul refused to see it as a nightmare and denied his anxiety. As months wore on, however, the gentle, altruistic man became trapped and haunted. "Everything here is potentially violent or dangerous." He found it hard to be without women. "I would just love to touch a pretty face . . . The business with girls is always on our minds. You always have masturbation—even if it means staying awake until everyone is asleep . . . I don't know whether missing someone sexually is any worse or even as bad as missing people that you're terribly close to . . ."[7]

Those who refused induction as an act of individual conscience, without any supporting resistance group, sometimes never recovered from their lone battle. Thomas Marsden remembers the fights with his uncle, an officer at the Pentagon. The shouts and screams of "Commie!" Marsden had read about the war and concluded on his own that it was wrong. He remembers how scared he was at nineteen as he refused induction at Fort Holabird, Maryland. Two years of prison followed. "I was scared most of the time. It was hard putting anything in perspective."

His wife, who knew him before he went to prison, uses the same adjectives to describe the change in him as do some veterans' wives. Not as easygoing, more cynical, nervous, cranky. Marsden seems distant, as if an invisible screen protects him from others. He seldom smiles. "The only time I cried while I was in jail was the day I got out." He still thinks he was right in opposing the war but does not see himself making the same sacrifice if he had to do it over. "The next time I'd leave the country before going to jail."

Marsden was working for a graphics company. His life returned to Vietnam in 1979, when he helped make a Vietnam veterans' poster of a soldier running out of the woods, his eyes glazed in terror, gun in hand. The poster said, "Let's Finally Bring Our Boys Home." Like many former inmates, there is a strong affinity for veterans. "They went through an ordeal, and I went through an ordeal. They are having a tough time getting jobs. I'll do what little I can to help. My beef never was with them."

During the Vietnam War, homosexuality became a well-known dodge. One antidraft pamphlet gave coaching lessons on faking for the "Army shrink": "Dress very conservatively. Act like a man under tight control. Deny you're a fag, deny it again very quickly, then stop, as if you're buttoning your lip. But find an excuse to bring it back into a conversation again and again, and each time deny it and quickly change the subject. And maybe twice, no more than three times over a half-hour interview, just the slightest little flick of the wrist." San Francisco draft counselor Paul Harris recalled that "all of my clients who faked it got their exemptions—but they drafted the one fellow who really was gay."[8]

It was one thing to fake it, but years later the terror of prison rape is still recounted as the major reason for most draft resisters who ruled out going to jail for the cause.

"It was a very realistic fear," says Vincent McGee quietly. Not one man I interviewed escaped homosexual advances. Although none were violently attacked, most can recount cases of others who were not so fortunate.

One street dude and black prison leader explained the attitude of other prisoners toward war resisters. "They are seen as meek pacifists, as not being aggressive . . . This is going to be interpreted as not being too masculine." He spoke of one pacifist raped by a dozen men. "There are prisons in this country where they had a field day on the C.O.'s." The black told of a marshall who threw a new inmate, a young C.O., against the wall, "kicked him in the groin, and then turned to the inmates, saying, 'Here's a real rat. I don't think you want him in the cell with you. He's a Communist.' Then the marshall left. I told the guy to stand up, but he was afraid to. He was just lying there. I said, 'Stand up, damn it!' Finally I convinced him to stand up and I said, 'This kid is man enough to stand up for his ideas,' and that stopped things.'"[9]

Today ex-inmates are chilling in their quiet recountings of always having to protect themselves, of always being someone's prey. "You'd say, 'Bug off, bug off,' " said McGee. "But I was careful *not* to put myself in a vulnerable place. Alone on a walk. Or in a shower late at night."

To a man, they saved themselves from advances by being decidedly nonpassive. "Here you are, an alleged pacifist, but the only way to survive in prison is to make sure everyone knows you'll *fight* if cornered," says Tom Marsden. "I was really skinny—six feet and 130 pounds. There were some violent guys, lifers and murderers, and you were right with them. A shower stall is no place to try to explain you are not the violent type. I must have succeeded, because no one messed with me."

Michael Billingsley remembers one night when "I almost got raped." During a transfer to Parkersburg jail, he shared a car with a black prisoner known to the inmates. "They jumped with joy to see him. He was carrying messages from dudes in other jails. He turned out to be my salvation. This moronic-looking redneck farmer, thick-headed, practically drooling, was staring at my ass all afternoon. When it came time to get in cells for the night, the only cell I could see empty was with this moronic-looking guy. I just knew I would spend all night under assault locked in with this creep. The guard yells, 'Get in that goddamn cell,' and I was panicked. Just then friends of the black guy reached out and pulled me into a four-man cell with an empty bunk."

Billingsley was also a witness to one of the more brutal rapes. "He was as young as you could be, eighteen, real insecure, pretty, and small. He got raped and became a 'punk.' He hadn't had a girlfriend before he went to jail. When younger kids get homosexually assaulted, they can become confused about their sexual identity. Well, he got out and had a girlfriend on the street. After five months he got busted again for possession of drugs. After having a girlfriend, he was convinced he wasn't going to be a punk again. He came back resolved to fight it. Guys were leaning on him, and he wouldn't give in. More pressure—and still he wouldn't give in."

At the time I interviewed Billingsley, a Pulitzer Prize–winning Washington *Post* exposé on gang rapes and sexual assaults in Prince Georges County's prisons underscored the sordid conditions and complicity of guards. Billingsley's tale was tragically similar.

"I worked early mornings at the dairy and had late afternoons off. If I chose to be in a cell rather than the library, the guard would open it and then lock me in. This kid had a cell right across the hall from me. One afternoon he went in his cell—and the guard had been asked not to lock the cell. He didn't. About four or five guys came to his cell. They just beat the living tar out of him and then all raped him. Over the course of the afternoon, every twenty minutes or so, a new guy came down the hall, I'd say between fifteen and twenty of them, and raped him. One after the other." Billingsley's voice is strained, recalling his own powerlessness to stop the assault. "After he got beat up the first time and those five or six guys raped him and left the cell, I called for the guard to come and check him out. Nobody came. It had all been prearranged." What happened? "After that he was a punk. He didn't fight it anymore."

Why did guards do that? Were they scared for their lives or what?

"Who knows? When I was in the youth reformatory at Ashland, there was a dormlike setup with bunks. Every night some of the tougher guys would drag this one new kid out of his bed and pull him to the showers and beat him up and try to rape him, and he would fight them off. The guards would sit at opposite ends from the showers and ignore it. After two days of this, I went up to one of the guards and asked about the kid.

"The guard drawls, 'Ah sure hope he straightens out.' " Billingsley stared in disbelief. " 'What the hell are you talking about?' The guard shrugged. 'Well, he's making a lot of trouble for himself. If he would settle down and cooperate with everybody, it would be a whole lot easier for all of us.' "

It's a wonder some don't try to commit suicide, I comment.

Billingsley's voice half breaks. "Some of my friends did. One altar boy at Petersburg was also a punk. The guy who was screwing him was beating him up a lot. So he climbed the prison water tower one afternoon and threatened to jump off. I ran to the priest and told him the kid was going to jump off the water tower—but he was not going to tackle this situation of a kid about to jump.

"Finally the guy was talked down off the tower—by the same guy who had been beating up on him. He walked off with him, completely demolished emotionally. I arranged with the American Friends Service Committee to get him transferred out of there."

Jailhouse rules, with all their degradation and depravity, were not to be challenged. Most of the draft offenders experienced some roughing up but were smart enough to intimidate guards through outside connections or to form their own power groups among the regular inmate population.

Tilton, Billingsley, Harney, and McGee all used their intelligence and organizational skills to become prison leaders. Tilton became chairman of the Prisoners' Cultural Collective which controlled much inside. "Power and winning are everything. You do it through friends, intelligence, or if you're bigger and stronger than everyone," said Tilton. *"Rolling Stone* did an article about me and other resisters, and I had this notoriety which helped. Plus I didn't hang out with other draft resisters; being with bank robbers and drug people helped. I was a decent handball player, and that helped. While I was there, there was only one murder-related charge, a Mafia informer, and no one got near him. He was in protective custody."

Although the Catholic working class went to Vietnam in large numbers, a remarkable number of war protesters came from the same ranks. All felt keenly for those going to war.

Vincent Francis McGee, Jr., is the oldest of four in a lower-income Irish Catholic family—the son of a laundry deliverer who later worked for the city Department of Sanitation. At fourteen, McGee went into the seminary but later, out of curiosity, left for the secular world. He worked nights to help put himself through the University of Rochester and later studied at Colgate Rochester Divinity school. Early in 1966 McGee signed his name to an anti-war poster ad in a Rochester newspaper.

McGee was working at Eastman Kodak. The morning after the ad, an eerie silence greeted McGee as he walked the long production line. In red paint on a double-sized bed sheet hanging over his place was scrawled "Commie Pacifist—Burn Yourself or Go Back to Russia." On McGee's desk were two 10-gallon tanks of benzene and a box of wooden matches.

"I didn't quite know what to do. I pulled the sheet down, threw it in the garbage, put the benzene back, got coffee, and read the paper. Nobody said a word to me." After two days of shunning, workers gradually began to talk to McGee about the war. "Many were concerned about their grandsons and sons going to Vietnam—but the general attitude was 'the government knows best.' "

That sentiment merely fed McGee's resolve. "I decided to burn half my draft card and mail the remains in a letter to President Johnson."

At a mass demonstration in New York City, McGee was among 150 who stood in a tightly packed circle and reached into a Maxwell House coffee can filled with flammable liquid to light their cards. "I was carefully burning mine because I wanted only half of it to go up in flames. A hand came from behind me and tried to grab it as evidence. I yanked it from the FBI guy and said, 'You'll get it back sooner or later—don't worry.' " McGee mailed the charred card off to the President and "felt absolutely marvelous."

McGee always dressed FBI-uptight to stand apart from the jeans and ponytail protesters. He wore extremely short hair, black-knit tie, houndstooth jacket, and trench coat. His style captivated the press, and soon McGee was articulating his protest in *Newsweek* and the New York *Times.* When he refused induction, that move was well orchestrated—with a press release and claque of cheering antiwar demonstrators.

McGee could have qualified for C.O. but wanted to protest for those who could not. Today, like many who went to jail, he is almost completely nonjudgmental of his generation, even those who pulled some draft scam. "My twin brother nursed a hernia, got a 1-Y, and had gotten married. There were very strained times at home. My father would be ranting and raving about me, the 'draft dodger'—and my sister-in-law would point to my brother and say, '*He's* the draft *dodger,*' then would point to me and say, 'And *he's* the draft *resister.*' "

As with so many families and their buried stories, McGee is not sure what his brother thinks today about those days. "We've never talked about it directly." Of his divinity school colleagues, McGee says, "A few were just dodging and were callous about it. They kept a low profile. A lot, however, were genuinely torn. Some were conscious at some level of hiding behind the religious deferment. It was all a mix."

McGee speaks intently, "I learned in this whole process that there is no *point* in standing up if you couldn't take the strain of battling families or the legal system. Those people were useless in terms of their ability to be effective. Some who turned back their draft cards were almost catatonic. A lot of people were picked off one by one and scared to death. We never had the masses. The self-righteousness of some in college protected them from facing the contradictions of the issue. That doesn't excuse it, but the point was *not to go*, whatever way you could."

For McGee the satisfaction of success lingers. He succeeded in his goal of confronting a broad group clearly on the issues. The courts, the people, the press, the politicians paid attention to him. Priests, nuns, seminarians, and other war resisters filled his trial courtroom. McGee was sentenced to two years and served almost eleven months in 1971. With a stream of influential visitors, McGee continued his antiwar activities from jail. His contemplative seminary training served him well; prison was viewed as a quiet time to read and think. It intensified his powers as an observer. "People who don't know me well may be tempted to say I'm paranoid, but prison intensified my acuity." He knew Bobby Baker, Carmine DeSapio, Martin Sweig. "Carmen Galenti and I used to listen to opera together." The worst of jail: "mediocrity, boredom, depression." The pluses: "I had a warm relationship with many people. The blacks called me 'Teach' and the Spanish 'Maestro.'" On one anniversary of Martin Luther King, Jr.'s death, the blacks asked McGee to give the "I have a dream speech."

That remains a strong memory for McGee.

Michael Billingsley, strongly individualistic, candidly mentioned that one reason for his activism was the "power" he attained. "I felt real anger at what was happening and that people were getting badly screwed by the draft. At the same time, I was working out my own needs. I made my own statement and people listened.

"Many were working out personal psychological traumas by being in the movement—but there were also people working out personal psychological traumas by being in uniform. It's wherever you find yourself." Canadian born, Billingsley cast himself in the role of rebel early. He was "headstrong and didn't like people telling me what to do." The son of a military man, he intensely disliked the regimentation of the environment he saw. At age fourteen he refused to become an American citizen. An immigration official and his parents pressured him into signing the loyalty oath, he says. It was 1960, and Billingsley was already uncomfortable signing an oath that committed him to military service.

While in college, he realized that "most of the guys I went to public high school with were getting drafted and college kids weren't." He began draft counseling in black ghettoes and found no animosity. "I wasn't a 'college liberal,' just somebody they knew from the community. A common put-down was that the only reason guys were for draft resistance was that they didn't want to be drafted themselves. As a 4-F, with my one blind eye, I was free of that."

The violence he witnessed at the 1967 march on the Pentagon "radicalized me. Trotskyites instigated that violence, but the U.S. marshalls were making their own mistake by whacking kids and knocking some out cold. A policeman had a nightstick on a kid's throat, choking the air out of him. The crowd, seeing this, surged forward, and the marshall and soldiers were trapped by this stairwell. Then Trotskyites threw bricks and stones, yelling 'Kill the marshalls.'

"The soldiers were all real green and real nervous. *I* was nervous. I was close enough to hear the platoon leader. As things got worse, he ordered them to put clips into their M-16s and aim at the crowd. As the Trots tried to push the crowd to overwhelm the platoon, I *knew* the soldiers had loaded guns. The soldiers were really shaking—terrified—and I knew that if just one jerked on his trigger he would kill five or six people."

A two-page centerfold in a New York *Times* article at the time of the march on the Pentagon shows demonstrators facing a thin line of soldiers trapped in a corner. In the center Billingsley is screaming his lungs out. "I look like one of the prime, angry killers," he recalls, laughing. In actuality he was exhorting the crowd to find the swim mask he'd been carrying "to protect my eyes in case we got gassed." As they started looking for it, people started laughing; it distracted and defused the moment, he recalls. "I realized how powerful I could be in a group situation." He organized against ROTC at the University of Delaware. When two students who goose-stepped onto the field to ridicule ROTCs were expelled, Billingsley immediately organized a protest drawing from the left (SDS) and the right (Young Americans for Freedom)—both of whom felt the draft abrogated their constitutional rights. Billingsley remained a loner and did not embrace the SDS.

"I tended to be as manipulative with my power as anyone. Through family ties I had access to university officials and got inside information on how they were going to handle protests. I made it public. I really screwed the dean of students, a friend of the family. He felt betrayed by me, drank heavily, and left the school. I felt guilty about him, but at the same time I felt what I was doing was necessary." At one point, recalls Billingsley, snapping his fingers, "I could call a rally and 400 to 500 people would show up just like *that.*"

He worked with the poor people at Reverend Ralph Abernathy's Resurrection City in Washington, D.C., during the summer of 1968 and was incensed at the con artists who preyed on the sincere. "The Blackstone Rangers, a group of Chicago gangsters, were recruited by Abernathy to serve as camp policemen, but they were responsible for a lot of rapes and beatings. Resurrection City was the nation's worst ghetto, with tremendous amounts of drugs and prostitution. And there were these elderly black women from the South, real pitiful, who had no idea where to stay. I worked as a carpenter, building houses for them. When Bobby Kennedy got shot, what morale was left went really down."

To Billingsley, prison was "just another environment in which I could be active. I ran consciousness groups in jail. It isn't true that being in jail or in Canada meant you could not continue your activism. You can either sit on your butt, or you can keep on working."

Paul Couming served only sixteen days in prison, but it was not for lack of trying. He is an activist who didn't get sentenced. It is a good thing for Couming, noticeable for his gentleness, his gray eyes and long eyelashes, and small build. He certainly would have been prey for those who would have misread, for those who would not have seen the steel behind the softness. Couming, one of twelve children, was a Boston housing-project child. His mother was a cleaning woman and eventually a key-punch operator for the telephone company. His father was an alcoholic, but unlike many Irish males in the project, he had long ago joined Alcoholics Anonymous. Couming cannot recall his father last taking a drink. When Couming was in his early teens, they moved out of the projects into a three-decker, but Couming retained his affinity with the lower class.

His high school was a "prime target for recruiters. Most of us were learning a trade. I remember most what the recruiters *didn't* say. *There was no mention whatsoever about the Vietnam War.* It was all a job pitch. 'This is your opportunity.' Not one single teacher ever talked about Vietnam."

When some of his friends were killed in Vietnam, Couming began to have a lot of questions that no one could or would answer. He was later radicalized in his unique parish which "unlike most in the area, was not patriotic and gung ho. If I had been raised in a conservative, traditional parish, I quite easily could have gone to war." Couming applied for and got a C.O. status, floundered in college, dropped out, and joined VISTA. However, Selective Service officials determined that his C.O. status was not being fulfilled in VISTA, and he was forced to work in a Boston city hospital. "I am not a C.O. any more," says Couming, in his third-floor walk-up in a Dorchester three-decker [a row house with three-family flats]. "Then I was caught up in the idea of brotherly love." Couming had to go before the skeptical draft board twice to convince them of his sincerity. They asked the inevitable question: Would you try to stop Hitler? Couming responded, "I could do a *lot* of things [to try and stop Hitler]—but I couldn't kill anyone."

Like many jail-risking resisters, Couming was not minoring in the war, as were many college demonstrators. Couming began to plot and execute in finite detail the raiding of draft boards. In November 1969 he became a member of the "Boston Eight" who raided four draft board locations and destroyed 100,000 draft files. There were months of "casing buildings, who went in and where. I had a key to open back doors. Sometimes we went in through windows, sometimes used electric drills on locks. Many buildings didn't have guards." Couming, with short hair, would pose as a potential draftee and case the office where he was seeking information.

His most famous raid was the Camden, New Jersey, post office. "That action," says Couming, slipping into the vernacular of the times, "took longer than three months." They knew when the guard made his rounds, when the elevators were used. They backed up a truck to the loading dock. "We brought our own ladder."

Up the ladder they went, to the roof and then down the fire escape. There were usually nineteen or twenty involved in a raid, sometimes nuns and priests in religious garb. That night Couming had a walkie-talkie and was an outside relay to those inside. "We were so committed against the war that I saw the action as both symbolic and an attempt to mess up the system for a while." Couming's poor-class roots were always on his mind. "Particularly, I felt I was helping the *inner city* by trashing their draft boards and throwing the burden more equitably on the suburban kids. Two years later, at a rally in Dorchester, I was introduced as one who had ripped off Dorchester's draft board." Couming smiles shyly. "I got quite an *ovation*. I *knew* we helped the blue-collar kids by destroying Dorchester's files. Nine months later they still hadn't put it together."

Couming's greatest fear of jail was of being beaten and raped. His activism would surely lead him there, he felt, so he grilled others who had been in prison. All said that Couming, at five feet four, would have to fight inmates off. However, he only spent sixteen days in the Atlantic County jail after the New Jersey strike. Luckily for Couming there is often a strong antiauthoritarian streak among street people. They felt that what Couming was doing was right.

Couming says the Boston Eight were caught because of an informant. Couming's nickname was "the Little Man." An ex-marine known as "Big Man" turned out to be an informant who had posed as an antiwar veteran. When they arrived at the Camden, New Jersey, site, the FBI was waiting.

Couming's one severe beating took place outside of prison. Caught in a Philadelphia raid, Couming was taken, handcuffed, into the back of a police van.

"The head of the civil-disobedience squad came in—without his badge. He had removed it. He slapped me across the face, head, shoulders, legs, trying to beat a confession out of me. I remember I asked him to stop hitting me. He kept calling me a coward—which was *unbelievable*, seeing as how *my* hands were *handcuffed* behind me."

Couming's eyes still betray remembered agitation. As the man kept beating him, Couming tried to keep track of details. "His eyeglasses, noting the marking on the hinge, the thickness of frame, his complexion, a mark on his face."

As he ducked his head from the blows, Couming remembers especially "his wing-tip shoes, with a distinct nick on the side."

Couming brought up the beating in court. "They said I didn't have enough proof. I didn't have his badge number, and he had an alibi—that he had never been in the van. Still I feel the impact was made at the trial, and the judge seemed more sympathetic." The charges against Couming were dropped for lack of evidence.

All this time, Couming's parents were "fearful but very supportive. Dad didn't trust the Berrigans. He wasn't sure where they were leading his son. When we got out of jail, Dad met them, and he and Philip really hit it off well."

Couming never had much connection with college demonstrators. "Our feeling was they were not mature enough. The Catholic left had a strong element of elitism. A sense that we were more willing to take the risk, with some contempt for the rest of the antiwar movement. We didn't want to lose the image of being 'morally driven' by being overrun by a bunch of students. I could remember feeling that the students just weren't that committed." After the lottery, peasants were still being killed, marines were still killing or being killed, but antidraft enthusiasm had waned. "We filled the gym for a rally— but that was to hear Jane Fonda and folk singers. Not us."

Couming speaks with such quiet enthusiasm and deep conviction that his basic assessment about those times comes as a shock. "I don't know how to address the whole movement, but for myself, personally, it was a *mistake.*" He is obsessed by the knowledge that the people of Dorchester fought the war. "It would have been better had I stuck around here and carried on my good church connections to work from inside." He saw youths from Harvard who came down to help in a "People First" project. "It was for clothing, etc. It was very nice to care for the blacks or poor—but who did they think was fighting the war for them?"

He reflects about his actions. "It *was* effective to rip off the Dorchester draft board—but it would have been *more* effective if I could have gotten to the Dorchester boys. In a way, I took the easier way, working on the moral guilt of liberals and church people, rather than trying to organize blue-collar kids, which would have been hard."

The men who went to prison, more than any other group from the Vietnam days, remain activists. They fight fiercely against United States involvement in Central America, they give antidraft speeches in working-class high schools, they work with the poor. A gentle fierceness bred in those times remains.

Growing up during Vietnam "made me make very distinct decisions," says Couming. "I eventually saw Vietnam not as one mistake the U.S. had made but as a *pattern* of imperialism, and related it back to the profit motive." Had

Vietnam not loomed, Couming "probably would have gone into the service and learned a trade."

After the war Couming tried to hide his activism. "I basically lied when I went for job interviews. I just knew if I told them I had been arrested and for what, I wouldn't get a job." He worked desperately for loose change, rented a pick-up truck and went into the junk business, studied politics and history at a state university, and then went to nursing school.

Couming continued his fight against indignities. In the seventies he went to school by day, washed supermarket floors by night, and pushed for racial unity in Dorchester. After a black man and his son were "beaten almost to death in an all-Irish bar, Field's Corner," Couming raised money for the man's hospital expenses. He worked with whites "who were making a point that whites weren't going to tolerate that. When blacks who had moved into white neighborhoods had their houses stoned, we set up twenty-four-hour-guard defense groups. All the kids from college who had come down to help in the sixties had long gone—but almost all the working class at the meetings felt we should not have this racial trouble." Blacks left as harassment continued despite his group's effort. "I think we tried to educate too much too soon."

Men like Couming, in Dorchester's black community, and Billingsley, in rural areas of Vermont, are united in their antimilitary efforts. Tilton and other draft resisters like the Minnesota lawyer work with veterans. Tilton is intrigued by delayed stress, understands it, and has handled several veterans' cases.

Another sympathetic member of Vietnam's prison brigade, Vincent McGee, said, "That war touched me irrevocably—and I was 10,000 miles away from it. Imagine what it did to the veterans."

Today, despite their hard-earned strengths, it has not been easy for those who went to jail. McGee lost a wife during his imprisonment, just as Tilton lost a girlfriend. Both remain single. Hesitant to ascribe their workaholic commitment to prison alone, the experience nonetheless remains a factor in their singleness.

McGee, who was also pardoned, has been a vice president of colleges, a member of various foundations, a consultant to television networks. Vietnam and what it did to him is "more and more on my mind lately as I approach forty."

He angrily denounces Norman Podhoretz's book *Why We Were in Vietnam* and others as "total revisionist crap." He also has no brief for the winners, the North Vietnamese. "Some were patriots of their country, but did they do absolutely *horrendous* things for their cause? Yes. The fact *they* were doing those horrible things does not justify the horrible things *we* were doing. And had we *not* been there, they might not have been so horrible either. It was inevitable they would have won but in a more peaceable way. And had we backed them, we would have a neutralist, nominally communist country." McGee does not speak from a position of distance. In 1981 he was the United

States chairman of Amnesty International. Unlike many of yesterday's protesting students, who are now ostrichlike about the problems of the Vietnamese, McGee continues to care.

"We are very concerned about the numbers of people who are still in reeducation camps. The situation over there is very bad—but it is also bad because the United States refuses to recognize Vietnam, and therefore they're precluded from aid. The Cambodia situation is horrible. The United States, in terms of its overall policy through the whole period, has a lot of responsibility we don't want to own up to. That's why we backed the Pol Pot government, which is a horrible, political charade that has nothing to do with justice."

They are but a handful of their generation, these men who went to jail. Their subsequent optimism and continued dedication should be viewed in that context. But there is something admirable and challenging in their refusal to relinquish the battle.

The next time around, they say, things will be different. This is a questionable point of view—given the renewed popularity of ROTC in high schools and state colleges, given present political sentiment that the negative experiences of Vietnam should not control policy regarding future battlegrounds, given America's propinquity to forget—and worse—never to teach.

Perhaps in part because they wish it so, in part because it may be true, men like Billingsley and Couming see resistance coming from blue-collar wards this time. "The working class is where you'll get movement against [our going to] places like El Salvador," said Couming. "I don't think the draft is the answer to 'economic conscription' and lack of jobs for the poor. Basically, even if you instituted a 'fair' draft, you'd end up with those kids going in. I get a lot of feedback in working-class bars. There are Vietnam veterans now back in the neighborhoods who are telling the younger kids that there is no way we should support a war in El Salvador. During an anti–El Salvador rally, we had an amazing number from Dorchester."

Billingsley adds, "I'm not typical of my generation in the sense that I have retained my activism." He is now, however, contemptuous of those who have not. "Vermont attracted a lot of people who had in the sixties a 'new-age consciousness.' They have had to deal with practicality and have mellowed down to the point that rather than trying to live in a little wood shack with goats tied up to it, they, say, run a restaurant that serves foods that aren't [chemically] treated." Some compromises aren't negative. "They're making money and I'm making money. You're constantly having to make moral decisions."

A legacy of the Vietnam days is a fervid commitment to stopping another generation from going to war. The day after President Carter made his announcement about draft registration, Billingsley began organizing noncompliance in Vermont. "We got *65 percent* noncompliance in Montpelier, which is remarkable," said Billingsley in the fall of 1982. It is *déjà vu* time, as Billingsley says. "We found out the FBI had assigned an extra agent to the Montpelier area whose purpose was to deal with the new draft resistance." Billingsley's message goes to the economically depressed, to youths who see the Army as the only alternative to poverty and unemployment. "I tell them it's a horrible way to make a living, and anyone who thinks going in the Army doesn't mean going to war is naive. When they say, 'You can learn electronics in the Army,' I point out that if they need someone who knows electronics in a command post, you can't refuse. I am now fighting legally to have equal representation in high schools with recruiters."

Two Vermont men from the Vietnam era round out the circle—Billingsley and a Vietnam veteran. They go into high schools and talk with students. "I'm there because I've been in prison," Billingsley says. *"He's* there because he's been in combat. Both of us took our licks. When some kid asks, 'What if I get busted if I don't register?' I can look back and tell him some facts. There were half a million who didn't cooperate during Vietnam. Of course the federal government was able—at tremendous expense and a lot of tied-up courts—to actually convict 9,000, and some 3,000 went to prison. That represents less than half of one percent. And the average time served was eleven months. I tell them that some of those *may* have had to kill in jail to avoid being killed. I don't know. And they may have been subjected to physical abuse. But when you compare them to all the draftees—not the volunteers, but the draftees—who were killed, it is nothing. Or the veterans who died after the war because of war-related injuries or suicides. My guess is that 35 percent of the people who went to war were badly damaged in one way or another. And endless numbers were forced to kill."

Billingsley faces his audience and says that in his view, looking back down the road, "no matter how horrible jail is, it is far and away the preferred alternative."

Part VI
Women and the War

"The Young Dead Soldiers"

BY ARCHIBALD MACLEISH

The young dead soldiers do not speak,
Nevertheless they are heard in the still house.
Who has not heard them?
They say: whether our lives and our death were for
Peace and a new hope, or for nothing,
We cannot say; it is you who must say this.
They say: we leave you our deaths.
Give them their meaning.
We were young, they say.
We have died. Remember us.

1 Mothers and Fathers

ON AN EARLY SPRING MORNING IN 1968, LOUISE RANSOM CHAINED herself by the wrist to a young draft resister and seven other religious antiwar activists. To jeers of "Communists!" from the hard hats who stopped work to watch, they stood in front of New York City's Whitehall Induction Center. As Mrs. Ransom spoke, the hard hats quieted to listen. "I have come to realize—painfully—that we parents must stand behind our young men, our children, when from the depths of their profoundest convictions and from their hearts, they feel compelled to speak out against this unspeakable war . . ."

In the summer of 1976 Louise Ransom stood at the Democratic Convention podium and read from Archibald MacLeish's poem, "The Young Dead Soldiers"—up through the lines ". . . we leave you our deaths./Give them their meaning"—and called for total amnesty for war resisters, military deserters, and the 790,000 veterans who were given less-than-honorable discharges.

In the fall of 1982 Louise Ransom spoke at the dedication of the renaming of Vermont's Vietnam Veteran Memorial Highway. As she has done, every day of her life, since Mother's Day of 1968, Louise Ransom called for understanding. First it was to end the war, then to bring the dissenters home. After the war it was to help troubled and incarcerated veterans. Finally, as controversial memorials were prepared, it was to move toward *reconciliation,* not justification, of the Vietnam War.

For most, the peace movement ended with amnesty. Few in the religious community ever embraced the problems of veterans. But Louise Ransom goes on. The catalyst for her extraordinary devotion to the cause was her son, Mike. He is seldom from her thoughts. Mother's Day, in particular, holds a heartbreakingly ironic memory.

In 1968 Second Lieutenant Robert Crawford ("Mike") Ransom, Jr., died in a Vietnam surgical hospital. It was Mother's Day.

It is a slender volume, *Letters from Vietnam,* bound in burgundy with gold lettering. There is one picture of Robert ("Mike") Ransom, in profile—handsome, dark hair, thick dark brows, the field-jacket collar turned up. A sprig of some long-ago weed-flower is stuck nonchalantly behind his ear.

His parents still cannot speak of Mike without crying. Five other sons came after Mike, but as the oldest son, there was a special place for him. He was a Cub Scout, a Boy Scout, played on the high school soccer team, and sang a leading role in "Kiss Me, Kate." He was literary editor of his class yearbook, president of the Reformed Church Youth Fellowship Group, and received the church's Youth Recognition Award.

Mike was from an insulated world that seldom sent its men to Vietnam. "The draft board caught up with him. He dropped out of college." His father, Robert, Sr.'s voice is leaden. In all generations there are bright kids who need some time for roaming, but the mid-sixties were no time for such adolescent ramblings. No bumming around to make a man out of you, unless you realized that could mean Vietnam.

9 March 1968. Dearest Family, I am now headed for Chu Lai, H.Q. of the Americal Division about eighty miles south of the DMZ . . . [He indicates he was sad to be separated from a roommate who had been with him from basic training to Vietnam.] *We've both been good shoulders to each other for laughing, crying, etc. . . .* [The fighting was still remote.] *From our billets we could hear machine-gun and mortar fire from the perimeter two or three miles away. We could also see illuminating flares in the sky to light up the battlefield. Yes, I am scared. But I think it's more of the unknown than of bullets. I expect to learn a lot during the next year; I'm not sure what'll be, but I'll learn a lot.* [At this point there was still the sense of a seeing-the-world adventure. His Asahi Pentax camera, purchased for $100 less than in the United States, was recording the sights.]

The Ransoms lived for years in Bronxville, a wealthy, conservative suburb north of New York City. With their liberal views they were something of the town oddities. Robert Ransom is deep-voiced, round-bellied, with a warm, large face that crinkles into easy friendliness. "The day we learned that Mike had died, some fool told me, 'Well at least you've got the satisfaction of knowing your boy died for his country'—and I threw him the hell out of here." With a politeness welded from childhood and Vassar, Louise demurs, "Welllll, we were *very cross*—but we didn't throw anybody out."

27 March 1968. Dear Mom and Dad . . . The principal danger here is from mines and booby traps, which account for about 75 percent of all casualties . . . For the most part nobody is particularly wild with patriotic feeling . . . There are of course those who just get a real charge out of killing people. One lieutenant I talked to said what a kick it had been to roll a gook 100 yards down the beach with his machine gun. But most people generate their enthusiasm for two reasons; one is self-preservation—'if I don't shoot him, he'll eventually shoot me'—and the other is revenge. It's apparently quite something to see a good friend blown apart by a VC booby trap, and you want to retaliate in kind . . . I would love it dearly if you would subscribe to Newsweek *for me. Also, what do you think of Bobby for President? What about Westmoreland's new job? What does everything mean?*

[Mike was] . . . extremely impressed with the enemy I am about to go and fight. A captured VC said that in coming from North Vietnam down to Saigon, he walked over 200 miles completely underground. Anyone who would dig a 200-mile tunnel and who would still do it after being at war for some thirty years must be right! All love, Mike.

His father remembers Mike as a "carefree, lovable, happy-go-lucky guy, who sang in the double quartet at Colby College, in Maine, and played the piano. He was in rebellion a little bit, let his hair grow long. I still hadn't got used to that." He speaks now with the soft, sweet indulgence of a parent. "If he had a paper to write, he was always in trouble. *Always* staying up late to do it at the last minute." The Ransoms saw the swift changes of the sixties generation in their six boys—each one growing progressively more defiant of the government. Mike had his reservations about the war, but in 1966 when he entered the Army, it did not occur to him to defy the rules. By 1968, after Mike was killed, a younger brother, John, refused to salute the flag.

Mark was a senior in high school when his brother was killed, and he became a conscientious objector. He seems apolitical now, as he stops in his parents' home for dinner. "When Mike died, I felt, here he was, five years older, and he didn't do *anything* he wanted to do. I kept a lot of my feelings in. But I missed him a great deal." Mark speaks wistfully, "Mike just had a great spirit for life. For three or four years I would have dreams that he was still around."

3 April 1968. Dear Mom and Dad, . . . Our primary danger is not Charlie himself, but the mines and booby traps he sets. This morning the second platoon took fourteen casualties, including one killed, when they set off two mines . . . those booby traps are so well hidden that no matter how good you are, they'll get you . . . I heard Johnson's speech on AFVN [Air Force Vietnam] Radio last night and think it to be the best one of his career. I am heartened by his bombing reduction and pray as does everyone else here that Hanoi will respond. What do you make of it? Also, how about his not running for President? . . .

Things aren't all bad—I've got a really good company commander and a good platoon sergeant. In my job these are the most important people in the world to me. Also on the bright side, I'm getting the best suntan I've ever had. All love, Mike.

Louise looks at her husband. "Bob is different from me in that he really has a terrible lot of guilt." Bob says quietly, "I *know* I could have saved our son." Louise continues, "And he can't forgive himself, so he has to live with it."

"I could have gotten him out *legally,*" her husband says. "He had a nervous sort of blink in his eye. I think that would have been enough." The whole family spent Christmas of 1967 together in Vermont. Mike told his father, "I don't know what I'm going to do when I get out to that plane. I might not get on it."

His father's face crumples as he remembers the conversation. "This is something I'll *kill* myself for, for the rest of my life. Not being more vehement about it. I said, 'Look, whatever you want to do is fine. We'll get you the best lawyers in the country, and we'll fight it the whole damn way.' But I *never* told him, 'Don't do it.' And even by that time, I was strongly against the war."

In a burst of atonement he continues, "And to make damn sure none of my other boys and as many others that I could stop would not have to go, I became a draft counselor." He worked ceaselessly in antiwar efforts, losing six years up the career ladder as an IBM lawyer; he never recovered those years. "I literally did nothing but war work. IBM tolerated me.

"At OCS, during a graduating show for the brass, Mike wrote and sang an antiwar song. That took nerve. But he got on that plane because he genuinely felt that he could help people. He felt it was wrong, unfair that the blacks and poor were going." Robert Ransom's voice shakes with anger and sorrow. "If you know your history, March 16 [1968] was the day of the My Lai massacre. And the Americal Division was the one that did it. He joined that division just *days* after that massacre, and those bastards never told him. He got in the field about a week later. He knew nothing about it. It was very well covered up. He would have screamed like an eagle if he had known that we'd been slaughtering the people."

The realities of war were deepening Mike's perspective:

> *There is not a man over here that wants to see this war go on any longer. This is not to say that anybody shrinks from doing a job. But everyone is as confused as I as to exactly what, if anything, we're accomplishing and wants the war over ASAP* [as soon as possible].
>
> *I lost my first man last week. The squad was on night ambush and the flank man crawled away to take a leak or something, and as he was crawling back to position another man mistook him for a dink and shot him. He died on the chopper. It really tears me up to lose a man, especially like that, but I must not show any emotion over it. I've got to press on, keep doing my job . . . The concern among the team (for that is what we are) is how it will affect the man who shot him . . .*
>
> [Mike writes of an encroaching, consuming hatred for the frustrations of a war where you can't tell] *. . . the good guys from the bad guys.* [The VC

were supposed to be denied ID cards.] . . . *But about three months ago we captured a VC printing plant that manufactured ID cards. Every man we pick up says, "Me Vietnamese, numbah one, VC numbah ten"* [one is good, ten is bad], *so we have to let him go. But more than once we have captured or killed people with weapons whom we recognized as one of those smiling faces we had picked up and released earlier. It's maddening because we know damn well that they're dinks, but we can't do anything to them until we catch them with a weapon or they are actually shooting at us . . .*

His father, reflecting on those long-ago letters, said, "Naturally they were trying to kill him. Calley and crew had just wiped out hundreds of them, and yet nobody told Mike what to expect."

While Mike was learning how to hate "dinks," his father was deep in draft counseling, working with men like his son. Except that—with the luxury of being 12,000 miles removed from battle—they were often championing the other side.

Ransom counseled the sons of prestigious, often conservative lawyers, some of whom gave lip service to supporting the war. "Among 700 lawyers in one firm, there wasn't a damn one who would get out the draft regulations and tell their kids what to do. They had to ask someone else."

At IBM Ransom was the "resident peacenik"—a middle-aged man who fought in World War II and sprang from well-heeled conservative roots. Ransom would be sent out to deal with the peace groups who demonstrated against IBM and smoked pot on the company's front lawn. He tried to persuade IBM to get out of the war business. "Thailand almost sank, it was so loaded with IBM computers used to guide the bombers." His unpopular stance did little to enhance his career.

At the same time—while living through the crippling pain of his son's death—Ransom had to suffer the slings of self-righteous youths he was trying to save from the war. "Some of the guys in the peace movement said, 'How could this man have any sincerity of his beliefs? He's an IBM lawyer!' I just said, 'You *asses.*' It was that narrow, purist view."

The Ransoms remember "how terribly hard it was for someone like us to 'go public.' The only reason you *do* is that you try to turn people around. We always felt that the antiwar sentiment in the United States was as high as 40 percent at some points and that if we could only get it up to around 50 percent, we might stop the damn thing." Ransom has no illusions about many parents who intellectually opposed the war, but who, with their own sons safely deferred, were not emotionally involved. "Parents said to themselves, 'Well, it's not going to touch me for a while!' They'd just buy the kids another degree.

"How did the government finally quiet the students down?" Ransom asked rhetorically. "By stopping the draft. The war went on, but the stakes were not there. Anyone with a high lottery number was bought off."

Dear Mom and Dad,

Well I've had my baptism by fire, and it's changed me, I think . . . We jumped off the tracks [personnel carriers], and one of my men jumped right onto a mine. Both his feet were blown off; both legs were torn to shreds; his entire groin area was completely blown away. It was the most horrible sight I've ever seen. Fortunately he never knew what hit him. I tried to revive him with mouth-to-mouth resuscitation, but it was hopeless to begin with.

. . . In the month that I have been with the company, we have lost four killed and about thirty wounded. We have not seen a single verified dink the whole time, nor have we even shot a single round at anything. I've developed hate for the Vietnamese because they come around selling Cokes and beer to us and then run back and tell the VC how many we are, where our positions are, and where the leaders position themselves.

[One platoon leader told Ransom, "The people in the village he went through were laughing at him because they knew we had been hit. I felt like turning my machine guns on the village to kill every man, woman, and child in it."]

Sorry this has been an unpleasant letter, but I'm in a rather unpleasant mood.

All love,
Mike.

He wrote to a friend in an even darker vein:

. . . I'm still as opposed to the war on moral and political grounds as ever. But since I am here, and when I see the gory mess that mine made of my people, I want revenge. I want to kill every little slant-eyed I see. I just wish the hell the VC would come out and fight . . .

His mother, with her patrician features and carefully sprayed hair, had been intellectually but not passionately opposed to the war. After Mike's death, nothing was restrained. Her friend, the Reverend William Sloane Coffin, told her that anyone with such anger ought to be an activist. In 1968 her voice trembled in uncertain flight when she first began to speak that day in front of Whitehall Induction Center, her hand chained to the resister. But then it grew stronger. It had not been stilled yet.

"Bob doesn't like to hear me say this, but I think in some respects that God knew what he was doing when he took my son." There was a pause. "Because I have been *uniquely* able to say things because of that—things that very few in this whole country will say. I get the understanding from antiwar, amnesty, *and* Vietnam veterans' groups."

In her consuming attempt to bind the wounds of both sides, Louise Ransom is trying to heal her own and to find some justification for Mike's death. "In all honesty, I would like to see the poor kid *die;* have Mike rest in peace, but I feel very driven. Unless his death has something *positive* come out of it . . ." Suddenly there is a crack in the buoyancy, the detachment. Her face falls, and finally she is just a mother with her sad, sad memories. Her blue eyes swim in tears. "As long as I see there is more to do, I am very driven to do it." She has struggled through these words in a wracked, broken voice. "But I'd sure like to stop."

She has told other Gold Star mothers what many did not want to hear and still resist believing—that her son died for nothing. She didn't want to hurt them, she just did not want to see a mawkish sentimentality of "dying for one's country" being used to create any virtues out of Vietnam.

"It's the same with some of the veterans who have been wounded and want to believe it was for something. It's hard to lose your legs and feel it was for nothing. It takes a very sophisticated view to accept *total* waste. I've grown, but that growth has come from terrible *damage.* I have a horror that maybe I had to lose a son to understand the underlying injustice that the war was just a symptom of." Her children had never known any blacks but domestics until they left Bronxville. Louise now works daily with blacks in prison.

"I have friends who lost sons and don't feel the way I do." One Gold Star mother wrote to *Newsweek* protesting amnesty. "Amnesty cannot and must not be given to those who fled to escape their rightful duties while others now lie dead."

Louise Ransom wrote to the mother: "Your letter made me very sad. My son, Mike, was killed in Vietnam one month after your son, Jeff.

"He had his own reasons for serving rather than going to prison or deserting and going into exile, but he would never have been resentful of those who made other choices. He would have understood perfectly the motivation of any man who felt he would not participate in any way in the appalling things American soldiers were ordered to do in the name of patriotism and freedom . . . He knew all too well that the blame lay with those who were responsible for the war.

"Richard Nixon has said that it dishonors the dead if amnesty is granted . . . the dead have their own honor, and nothing we say or do here can detract from that . . . I know that my son and yours, and 57,000 more, had courage. But that does not preclude those who chose not to serve from having another kind of courage—or patriotism.

"The tragedy is that . . . Mr. Nixon's words have divided us here at home. It is intolerable that you and I, with our shared sorrow, should be pitted against each other for his political purposes.

"You have truly said that the empty places at our Thanksgiving tables will be filled . . . Mike would not forgive me if I stood in the way of another family's Thanksgiving reunion—in his name.

"Further, it is no tribute to those who fought and died to think they would want to have served in the name of a punitive and vengeful country."

Mike wrote his last letter on May 2, 1968:

. . . I have to tell you that ever since we hit that minefield, I am nervous all the time. My authorized strength is forty-three. I had thirty-six when I first joined the platoon and am now operating with twenty . . .

Despite losing people and being scared all the time, I find being an infantry platoon leader an exhilarating, exciting, and, yes, rewarding job . . .

[Mike asked for the small amenities of life that he never got to use: the status of his bank account, a half dozen black mechanical grease pencils to mark his maps, blue felt-tip pens with which to write his letters home.]

. . . As you can probably tell, it's a cold day in hell (or Vietnam, for that matter) when I get a chance to get to a PX.

This is all for now (both requests and deathless prose). More soon. Love to all, Mike.

[But there was a postscript. Mike Ransom's last written thoughts were of peace.]

P.S. You might tell any friends you have in Washington to get off their fat asses, quit quibbling, and start talking about ways to end this foolishness over here. Aside from being opposed to the damn war, it really gives me a case that LBJ, who claims to want peace and who says he'll go anywhere, any time, to talk peace, has taken over a month without being able to find an acceptable site. Anywhere, according to his promise, ought to be "acceptable."

For years, Louise Ransom has tried to convince people that all males in her son's generation were victims of the war, forced to make unacceptable choices.

She was a senior in Vassar, her husband in law school, when the Japanese attacked Pearl Harbor. They married before he went off to war. "I used to argue in all my speeches that I *knew* what it was like to be in college in World War II. All of our friends rushed to enlist. And then I would say," recalls Louise, flinging out her arms and raising her voice in mock stentorian tones, " 'When the young people of America feel that the kind of freedom and democracy that they believe in is truly threatened, they will *flock* to fight!' That was always my point."

Her activism, in a minor way, made casualties of her own family. Although they remained very close, the younger boys admit they knew moments of neglect. None embraced their mother's crusade about the war then or veterans now. "They think I'm engaging in futile effort, that the public could care less."

Their son, Mark, feels, "I think it's courageous now. When I was younger, I felt they were too obsessed, torturing themselves too much."

The Ransoms received official notice of Mike's award of the Bronze Star Medal:

> . . . *Second Lieutenant Ransom distinguished himself by exceptionally valorous actions on 3 May 1968 while directing a squad of men off Landing Zone Sue to establish a night ambush position. While they were moving to the night position, a mine was detonated. Although severely wounded, Lieutenant Ransom displayed outstanding professional competence as he constantly talked to his men and prevented panic. His actions prevented further injuries from additional mines. He then reorganized his element into a tight defensive perimeter until they were able to receive assistance. Despite his wounds, Lieutenant Ransom refused medical attention until the other injured men in his squad had been treated . . .*

There were desperate prayers as Mike lay dying for eight days. Recalls his father, "They were taking veins and transplanting them into his legs to create arteries and they removed his spleen . . ." His voice trails off.

The Ransoms were propelled by anguish and fierce anger to protest the rote sympathies of top brass who were hard at work justifying the war. President Johnson wrote, "I know your son is a brave man, whose honor and love for his country will continue to preserve the right of all people to be free." General Creighton W. Abrams wrote, "It is my hope that you will find a measure of solace in knowing your son gave his life for a noble cause, the defense of liberty in the free world."

Their son "wanted no part of this unspeakable war for himself or for his fellow man on either side," the Ransoms replied to President Johnson.

They particularly did not want a funeral that would make his death seem a necessary and glorious part of a struggle in a just cause. The service included readings of passages from Mike's letters denouncing the war. Seven hundred of the wealthy and protected of Bronxville overflowed the church. They heard a folksinger sing "Where Have All the Flowers Gone?"

"No one in charge of that war will ever admit that there was any wrong, and so there will be no reconciliation," Louise Ransom says today.

Fourteen years after her son's death, Louise Ransom stood on the wind-whipped highway in Vermont, dedicating it to 177 Vermonters who died in Vietnam. As some other voices in the land invested Vietnam Memorial dedications with noble cause and glory, she was, to the last, denouncing justification.

She recalled the personal pain, "The shiny buttons on their new uniforms pressing into us as we hugged them goodbye, trying to shield them with our love." She spoke for all mothers of the dead, "We remember sadly now the things that will not be: the weddings never attended; the children never born; the houses never built and the fields not ploughed; the books never written; the songs never sung . . ." Her tone shifted, and she was speaking of the anger at the government "for covering up so many truths about the war . . . for its callous neglect of the returning veterans . . ."

The families of the dead in Vermont were ignited in spontaneous applause when she spoke of a special anger at the government "for requiring such unequal sacrifices of its citizens through a system that permitted nine out of every ten men to legally avoid service—or ride out the war safely in the very reserve or guard units we pay to protect us. *If our cause was so righteous and just, how did it happen that no member of Congress lost a son or grandson there?"*

A final letter arrived from Vietnam in May 1968:

> *It is with great difficulty that I write this letter expressing my deepest sympathy over the loss of your son,* [wrote Captain Connie Schlosser]. *I have never written a letter like this before, but then in my six years of nursing, I have never met so courageous an individual as your son . . . His sense of humor and will to live made my work so much easier. Things he could no longer do for himself—like brushing his teeth—things that brought him discomfort—like turning him—brought only thank-you's, humorous remarks, a gleaming smile, or a twinkle from his eyes.*
>
> *Mike fought hard, terribly hard, to overcome his body's wounded condition. But strong as he was, his body could only endure so much. Mike was never afraid, and although I'm sure he realized what was happening, he never, never lost his smile and his courage.*
>
> *I guess I really wanted you to know that Mike did not die alone, with no one caring. I cared, we all cared . . . we all share your sorrow. Be ever so proud of Mike!*

Three other Gold Star mothers are far removed from Louise Ransom's view of Vietnam. Emogene M. Cupp is past president of American Gold Star Mothers. Her son, Robert William Cupp, was in the Americal Division at the same time as Mike Ransom. He was killed one month later, stepping on a mine. Mrs. Cupp remembers that awful day in June of 1968 when the doorbell rang. "You go to the door and there stands that military man and you *know* what he is going to say." Her only son was buried on his twenty-first birthday.

Helen Stuber's son died in Quang Tri province in 1967. Coralee Redmond's son was killed by a sniper in 1966.

In 1982 the three mothers sat in the living room of the American Gold Star Mothers national headquarters in Washington, D.C. An organization of some 6,000 now, the club's boom years were during and after World War II. Then mothers were exalted by virtue of their sons' death in service. Joining such groups was an honor in itself.

After World War II there were no more gold stars to hang in the window across the country. The government stopped giving them to mothers of the dead. Korea and Vietnam were not *wars,* remember, even though sons died just the same. A bit of doggerel sprang up, from the mud of Korea, that expressed a newer cynical, outraged view of wars. A Vietnam veteran told me it was passed down to Vietnam: "Take down your silver star mother, and hang up your gold star instead. Your son just got hit by a tank round, and it blew off his whole fucking head."

The three women in the living room of the modest townhouse in Washington, D.C., would have been understandably horrified at such gallows' irreverence. They sat near a plate with the governmental seal of the United States and a bouquet of flowers. In the arrangement, a gold paper star was purposely elevated to stand out above the daisies.

Helen Stuber's hands, like nervous hummingbirds in flight, are seldom still. Her second husband flew for the Military Airlift Command, both in Vietnam and Korea. Her son, Dan Varner, twenty-three when he died, was married and had an infant son he never knew. While in college, Varner worked part-time in a catalog store, and refused to take his student deferment. "Some of my close friends would say, '*My* son's not going, he's in college.' But Dan felt, 'Why shirk your responsibility?'"

Coralee Redmond, it seems, has known nothing but wars. Her oldest son was in World War II, another in Korea. Her youngest was in Vietnam, as well as two grandsons and a nephew. She is eighty and looks years younger. Her pierced earrings are gold stars.

Her son was thirty-two and a major when he was killed in August 1966. "He always said, 'I believe in why we're here.' He didn't want the Communists coming into our country. 'Course, as I say, he was a military careerman. He said, 'This is a job I'm trained for. I could get in a car and get killed on the way to an office job.' He had all the good ideals of a military man."

Patriotic phrases come swiftly and easily to all three women; their club is supported by the American Legion. They know no one like Louise Ransom, who says that their sons died for nothing. Louise Ransom says God had a purpose and that was to forge her antiwar activism. These three women feel it was also God's will that their sons were taken, but they do not know why and do not question it. Nor is it their place to question the war. It won't bring their sons back, they say.

"I don't think anyone can say what was right or wrong. I can't change it, no matter," says Emogene Cupp. "My son always felt if he was called he had to go."

Helen Stuber's grief was compounded by two tragedies. At the age of nine, her vibrant daughter was stricken with sleeping sickness. She lived for years in a lost state, dying in her twenties, two years after her brother was killed.

"I feel the Good Lord gave me my children and that my son was struck for a purpose and my daughter was struck for a purpose. I feel I have no right to

question the will of God. The Good Lord gave them to me for a little while."
Her eyes tear up and she can barely whisper. "You can't be bitter."

Probing about the war leads only to comments like "I have more confidence and faith in our leaders than to think they would risk the lives of young men in a political war."

Jim Webb, in dedicating a South Boston Vietnam veterans' memorial, waved a patriotic flag with his message: "Giving your life in a war is the ultimate, irretrievable gift to your culture." All three mothers live by that sentiment. They were cautious to me in their comments about Agent Orange ("I can understand how our boys feel bitter, but I don't think it was done intentionally; the government *couldn't* have known," says Emogene Cupp). They had no comment on delayed stress or whether the VA is insensitive to the needs of Vietnam veterans.

They talked often about not being bitter, but their very cautiousness, even their suspicion of being interviewed, reflects a very deep and bitter pain. Not only were veterans vilified, mothers and families also were treated with unbelievable callousness.

"I received my *first* harassment call on Saturday, the day after Dan's funeral," said Helen Stuber. "I almost went into hysterics." Her son had been "a little boy of uniforms"—Cub Scouts, Boy Scouts, Little League, Pony League, junior high band, senior high band, college band. He went to church at Easter to help Indian children on reservations. And so there had been a large funeral for a hometown son. The local paper covered his funeral. The day after, a woman snapped over the phone, "I'm glad it was your son and not mine. You got what you deserve. He had no business being there."

Coralee Redmond adds, "I *never* had anything said against my sons in World War II and Korea. Just over the one I lost in Vietnam."

"I couldn't believe it the first time, but I've been told more than once that it wasn't so bad to lose my son, *because it wasn't a declared war!*" said Helen Stuber. "That's why we have our defenses up and are very reluctant to talk to anyone. We loved our sons so much and want to protect them and their families."

Another mother, eighty-year-old Maudie Barnett, had been listening with horrified eyes. "I have always felt you should have gotten the honor that was shown us." Her son died at the age of seventeen in World War II, when his LST was torpedoed in the Mediterranean. Hometown merchants hung his picture in store windows. "The church and community gave us mothers every consideration."

Coralee Redmond worked in VA hospitals for years before Vietnam and is a member of the VA hospitals' national volunteers' advisory committee. She has visited nearly all 172 hospitals across the country and has formed some opinions about Vietnam veterans. "Even though you had basket cases out of World War II, the Vietnam veterans are more troubled because of bitterness over the way the war was fought and the reaction of the country to them. It just seems it was a more 'vicious' war—the wounds were just so vicious. They took drugs over there for relief, and I can understand it. My grandson is bitter when he talks about it, which is seldom. I almost have a feeling God did something in taking Dick. He was so military-minded that he would have been as bitter as some of these boys had he lived.

"Yes, I can understand why our boys went to drugs over there. Now the boys who stayed on the streets or went to Canada," she says a bit harshly, "I can't understand why *they* went to drugs!"

Protesters and amnesty bring the most emotional responses. Television played up the "rabble rousers" who continued antiwar protests because they were getting "recognition." Booing "our boys in uniform" was an outrage remembered vividly to this day. They are unaccepting of those who refused to serve.

"I think we have to *forgive*—but we don't forget," said Coralee Redmond. "I feel sorry for the mothers of boys who went to Canada—but I don't see how they had any *pride* or *joy*. It was the boy I couldn't understand. Who would *want* to come back after doing something like that?"

And Helen Stuber lifts her chin and says, "There's not a day that I don't thank the Good Lord that if he had to be taken, he stood *for* his country and not *against* it." She repeated that unforgiving line at the opening of the Vietnam Veterans Memorial in Washington, D.C., to cheers from many veterans and families.

The three mothers adhere to traditional concepts of womanhood—they don't discuss religion or politics. They seem not to have considered the consequences of Vietnam. Helen Stuber champions a "return to patriotism," although Emogene Cupp feels that some people "get riled up too quick" about interceding in Central America, in an attempt to reestablish some pre-Vietnam prestige. But their minds quickly close down again: "I feel we cannot live in the past . . ."; "we must have faith in our country . . ."; "we must accept . . ."

It took Maudie Barnett, the mother whose son was killed in World War II, to say something controversial. Quietly, after they had spoken so much of God, she said, "I think *men* make war. It is not God's purpose."

The others try to explain their feelings. Helen Stuber says, "Our son's *death* was God's will, not the war." ". . . I think any war is man-made," says Emogene Cupp, "but I think it's God's will my son was singled out to be killed."

"That's wonderful for you," said Maudie Barnett, shaking her silver-haired head. "I can't feel that way. I am pleased," she continued, "that the Vietnam Memorial is black; I wouldn't want to glorify it. I think we should remember what war is."

The other women refuse to talk of the controversial memorial. They are soon back to patriotism. "I feel Dan stood for his country . . ." "Dick believed in the ideal of what the country stood for . . ." "There have always been wars, and I guess there will always be . . ." "You don't have a choice but to accept his dying . . ."

The smile was pasted on Helen Stuber's face. "We like to think happy thoughts. About the good times we had with our children. The hurt will still remain—but the clock's going to tick right on. So we think happy thoughts."

An intelligence officer who returned from Vietnam with an antiwar attitude commented caustically on mothers who say they are proud their sons died for their country in Vietnam. "Good. Their younger brothers will be old enough, and they can send *them* to Central America or Beirut—and maybe *someday* they'll start to wonder *why* their sons are dying. All I know is that several mothers I met when I was an antiwar activist didn't think it was 'God's will' and were terribly bitter."

The divisiveness of Vietnam cannot be overlooked; it compounded the sorrow that any family experiences losing a son in war. Unlike the Louise Ransoms and the three American Gold Star mothers, the vast majority of parents sought no reconciliation pulpit or shared solace but went about trying to pick up the pieces of their lives. Except for the MIA and POW families who were used by President Nixon for political/emotional hype, parents were often ignored. "No one cared that he died for his country," said one mother.

Even in such blue-collar communities as South Boston, where corner gangs went *en masse* to war, parents remain divided over a confusing war that brought the death of favorite sons.

While there was fertile soil for the Vietnam-as-noble-cause viewpoint among some of Southie's Vietnam veterans, that viewpoint was not championed by some mothers.

As a band played mournful taps during a memorial dedication ceremony in 1981, Lillian Stewart stared straight ahead. In a picture in the memorial program, her son, PFC. James Stewart, resembled his mother; he had her long slim nose and the same eyes. He was killed three days after he landed in Vietnam. They named a street after him, just as they did after many of Southie's other sons—street markers for the dead. James was one of nine children. "One of the younger ones," said his mother. "I don't think we had any right being in Vietnam, but you couldn't tell the boys that. It's an awful thing to say, but if I had a boy of eighteen, I'd make sure he'd never go, if it was anything like Vietnam. James thought he was going for a cause."

Women have consistently outpolled men as doves; they can understand another mother's anguish all too deeply. Diane Sheehan, who lost a husband in Vietnam, said, "The only legacy I was left with were my eight children, who ranged in age from fifteen to two. God was very good to me. We were able to survive and sometimes with class. Nixon was the focal point for my anger and hate for a long time." She is one widow who saw justification in dodging the war. "My heart goes out to those boys who followed their conscience and went to Canada. I believe these young boys today think about it more than they did then. All people are thinking far, far more about future wars because of Vietnam."

Mostly, the families, like the veterans, are left alone with their thoughts. Robert Stone was fifteen when his brother, Edward, was killed in Vietnam. He stood by as his mother attempted a smile at the Southie dedication. "The mothers are overwhelmed that someone is finally doing something. It was always Vietnam. No one liked it then, and they still don't like it." Sonny Stone's war was among the briefest. He celebrated his eighteenth birthday on January 1, 1968, went to Vietnam in February, and died in March when he ran over a mine during the Tet Offensive.

The day they heard of Sonny's death is unforgettable. The Stones were living in a triple-decker house in Dorchester. "Mom was upstairs and I was on the couch, and I seen the priest and officer. I also had an older brother in the Marines, so I turns and says to him, 'Do you have any friends visiting you? A couple officers and a priest are coming up the stairs.' When they asked, 'Does Catherine Stone live here?' I knew right away what it was. It was heartbreaking for Mom. Last night Mom got the blues again. It's never-ending. Her thoughts of Sonny are always there."[1]

Fathers, of course, are no strangers to the never-ending sorrow of losing a son. Sometimes their grief is intensified by guilt. Patriotic and often steeped in the glories of their own special World War II, they inculcated the same sense of duty to their sons. Then, as the nature of the Vietnam War began to dawn upon them, they blamed themselves.

Shelton Clarke, a retired Virginia lawyer, had a Southern gentleman's refinement to his voice over the telephone, until it cracked with anger. He had just seen the controversial CBS special report charging that General William Westmoreland had fudged the numbers of North Vietnamese coming down the Ho Chi Minh Trail just before the Tet Offensive of 1968, reporting lesser numbers in order to make it look as though we were winning the war. Westmoreland sued CBS. The case was expected to go to trial in the spring of 1984.

"Here's the horror of it," said Clarke. "We lost our *only child* there, a marine, in 1968. Ambushed in a damn hamlet in Qui Nhon province. Let's assume he was briefed to expect *x* numbers of irregulars—and instead he was ambushed by people *Westmoreland did not think should be carried in the order of battle!* If the report is true, then the more Westmoreland reduced the order of battle, the more Americans he was killing!"

Suddenly Clarke was crying. "I *counseled* my son to go. I'll bear the burden of that for the rest of my life. I feel I killed him. When parents lose a son in war, they're supposed to be silent and lick their wounds. It's time parents became radicalized. You clutch *your* teenage son to your bosom, and don't let your government send him to Central America or the Middle East. They'll lie to you in the name of national interest.

"I'll never trust a politician again as long as I live." Clarke did not come to his pained perspective from the left. "I was gung ho as hell when our son was over there. I was a flier in World War II. I still get chills when I see the flag. But my son and all those who went to Vietnam didn't have a Pearl Harbor. They had the Gulf of Tonkin—which was a goddamn lie.

"A part of my bitterness is that the danger in Vietnam was so unevenly divided. For a very few people, Vietnam was the *deadliest* war ever fought. Most were support troops, but my son fought for his life every day he was there. He dismantled twenty-one booby traps in the dead of night with his bare hands. It took a kind of courage I can't imagine." When Clarke's son graduated from Quantico, he could have gotten a cushy officers' job but elected to go into battle. "He couldn't bear the idea of others having to have that responsibility."

Clarke's ideological odyssey changed him. "I went from hawk to dove to pacifist. My son's death destroyed me for six years. How could he have died for 'something' when Hanoi was off-limits? They never were permitted to win. It was such an Alice-in-Wonderland war. We owe those kids an accounting. It was *not* a noble cause, it was an ignoble cause." He stops for a minute. "It wasn't any cause at all."

The hawk-turned-pacifist cannot, however, bring himself to forgive the sons who didn't go. "I've been very mean to young kids because they're living. When I see these young men, thirty-five, with their PhDs and masters —well, you see the curve [the increase in graduate students deferred in the early sixties], and you know that Vietnam motivated them. It's very difficult to be nice to them."

"I don't believe the kids that went to Canada and graduate schools have enough guilt to put on the end of a pin. I've got no respect for [Jim] Fallows; he's a hypocritical little son of a bitch, writing all that stuff about guilt and championing the draft today. That's bullshit! They didn't have enough *character* to be feeling a whole lot of guilt. Tell 'em to go back to the recruiting post and get ready to go to Central America or the Middle East. They can *still* do it. They're not doing a damn thing to help veterans, to heal the rift." (Jim Fallows—who received more than 4,000 negative comments after writing about his draft dodging—remarked that it was the mothers and fathers and other relatives, rather than veterans, who were judgmental.)

Bitterness is a costly emotion and Clarke's rage is suddenly spent. Shelton Clarke would, days later, call to apologize, unnecessarily, for his outburst. The tears are in his voice. "I believe that not an hour has passed that I haven't thought of my son. I will live with that war for the rest of my life."

The anguish is not just for the parents of the dead of Vietnam. There are mothers and fathers who look at their wounded sons and remember them as they were. There are mothers and fathers who watch their sons slip into troubled nightmares and pray that nothing will trigger the depression they have known since Vietnam.

Betty Hagel Breeding is the mother of Tom and Chuck Hagel, the two brothers who fought together in the same squad for eleven months, saved each other three times, and sent five Purple Hearts home. She was protected from the war in some measure by their sugar-coated letters, but that did not of course stop the worry. Denial took over, and she did not consider the dire possibilities of their bizarre war, of their being together in a squad of eleven men. "I was just glad they were together. That they would be company for each other. Of course, if I had ever seen any Army officer walk up the front steps, I would have probably run out the back door as fast as I could."

Even when Tom wrote to his younger brother, Mike, that he was ashamed of being in the war, Mrs. Breeding did not allow herself to think of what traumas that attitude might later induce. "I didn't want Mike to go either and felt that maybe Tom was just trying to keep him from going in.

"I *hated* the war. What made me a little bitter is that I didn't know anyone from Columbus [Nebraska, a town of 12,000] whose sons had to go. Most of them ran to college. I had five sisters, and none of their sons were in. There was none of that war-effort business. From the very beginning I didn't know what we were fighting for. That's what frightens me—if something like that should start up again! We got through the war with a lot of guts on the boys' side and a lot of prayers on mine."

Mrs. Breeding, with her second husband, Charles Breeding, was visiting Chuck in Washington in the fall of 1982.

"I can't pinpoint one single way that Vietnam changed him," she says, almost in awe. "I often worry about Chuck—if he's fragile or if he isn't. Maybe he's crying on the *inside*. When he and his wife broke up, I thought that a wife will always be number two and his occupation will come first. As far as I'm concerned, for that reason, I'd just as soon he not remarry."

Tom, on the other hand, Mrs. Breeding says with a soft smile, would make a fine father if he ever settled down. A shadow of concern is in her dark brown eyes that are so similar to her son Tom's. Mrs. Breeding, who cannot explain why Tom was different from Chuck, can only describe the drastic change when he came home. "I don't think he trusted anybody when he got back. He's just now beginning to. A very, very big change was his drive. He was bound and determined. He just wanted to better himself. Without Vietnam"—she thinks a minute—"I have no idea what he would have been doing."

His depressions *"really* frightened me. When he was home for Christmas vacations, he'd rather spend time in the basement reading than be with others. It was just as if he was a frightened little boy or something. He confided in me more than anyone, but he kept so much in. Oh dear, it seemed like a holiday would be harder on him."

Were you ever upset that he might take his life?

She nods. "Particularly when he was public defender. He was always helping the down and out. One big trial was of a man who raped and killed four or five women. *That* was hard for a mother. He had these real toughies that people just felt like hanging. I always told Tom they [his clients] asked for it.

He never got any sleep. There were telephone calls day and night from those people. I saw a change as soon as he got out of that office.

"I'm so afraid something will get to him and he'll go back to his old ways. He truly loves the girl he's going with, but I think he's afraid to take a chance." She sighed. "I think something out of the ordinary may bring back memories of this or that in Vietnam. I don't think it'll ever go away. We'll never know for sure where the emotional feeling is all coming from."

Mrs. Breeding is a trim woman with black hair, who despite tragedies has a buoyancy about her life. Her husband died when the boys were young. After months of constant worry, while her two sons were in Vietnam, Mrs. Breeding felt that life was going to move forward. Then, as if playing out some horrible Greek tragedy, after all those months of worrying, death came just miles from home. One night, in 1969, only months after Chuck and Tom returned, their sixteen-year-old brother Jim, a junior in high school and the star quarterback, was speeding down a highway after a party. His car crashed into a telephone pole. A companion lived, but Jim was killed instantly. Tom had to identify his brother; after all those deaths in Vietnam, he took it very hard.

Mrs. Breeding's voice has the control of distance. "After all that happened to the boys in Vietnam, and then to have this happen to Jim. Maybe God's testing me. I'm religious—not a fanatic, but I have my certain saints. Of course, God's been so very good to us too. He's given the boys all good minds and talent. I've lost a son and a husband. My sons are grown now, but it's always the 'children,' no matter their age, that you worry about.

"I just pray that something happens to me before another tragedy. I don't think I could take any more."

Many communities in America were torn apart by Vietnam, just as those in border states were ripped by different allegiances in the Civil War. The ones who went to Vietnam and the ones who didn't often lived in separate parts of town—the working class here, the more privileged there. The parents of those who lost their sons to Vietnam or to exile were, ultimately, the last victims.

In 1972 columnist William Greider, then of the Washington *Post,* wrote a moving tale of two families in one such town—Portsmouth, Ohio. They represented the emotional extremes of the tragedy Vietnam visited upon families, the anguish of parents whose sons were compelled by their government to serve in a confusing and unpopular war.

"While the two sons chose their opposite paths," wrote Greider, "the parents came to remarkably similar grief. They both indulge in thoughts of what might have been. They share a . . . helpless feeling that these two lives may have been misspent—not by the boys themselves but by distant leaders making strategic decisions, only dimly illuminated for the people of Portsmouth."

Tim Bauer went to Vietnam and was killed by ambush in Quang Nam province in 1969. Charles Long was refused a conscientious objector status and, in 1968, fled to Canada, where he remains. For both parents, the decisions of the sixties were heartbreaking.

Tim was "so well thought of," his mother recalled in 1972. "After he got out of high school, he went down to Clark's Discount Store." His father, Bob, construction worker and former mill hand, spoke with pride of his son's job: "He was the youngest one ever to carry the key to that store." Mrs. Bauer slipped into the present tense about her son, who had died three years previously. "He's got a beautiful guitar upstairs he'd only had about six months before he went in the service."

"I asked him one day," his father said, " 'Bud, learn me how to play the guitar.' He said, 'No, Daddy, your kind of music don't sound right on my guitar.' He says hillbilly music hurts his guitar."

The parents laughed as if the joke was fresh, Greider wrote. "It seemed more valuable than the Vietnamese figurines or the medals encased in red velvet or the jade-trimmed plate, engraved with a story which nobody in Portsmouth knows how to read."

In another part of town, Mr. and Mrs. Kenneth Long used the past tense to speak of *their* son, although he was alive and well in Ottawa, and pursuing a successful career in government.

As dissent grew, the rules kept changing. If Charles had been a few years younger, the sundering of family might never have happened. Charles had refused to apply for C.O. on religious grounds. His father, an ad manager for a local newspaper, said, "He felt that would be hypocritical." His mother added, "So he applied on moral grounds only, even though we always went to church. He felt it was strictly a moral, not a religious question." Moral reasons were not enough for C.O. status when Long applied. Later the law was successfully contested, and those who then refused to fight based on ethical beliefs were given C.O. status.

The silence of community was there for the parents of exiles as well as veterans. Mrs. Long said that friends shunned the mention of Charles, as if he never existed. "They feel it's a criminal act he's done."

Tim Bauer's father, across town, with hardened voice, said in 1972, "If that Mr. Long were to walk in here right now, I'd tell him the same thing. If those boys went to Canada, let 'em stay there. If they come back, they ought to put them in uniforms, either a green one or a striped one." His wife added, "If all the boys felt that way, there wouldn't be a country very long, there really wouldn't."

Mrs. Bauer added, "I'll have to be honest, I didn't want him to go into the service." Her son argued that he had to go to help stop communism. When his younger sister was killed in an automobile accident while Tim was at boot camp, his parents arranged for hardship papers to keep him from Vietnam duty. Tim refused to sign them. "I hope you won't feel hard, Mom," her son explained, "but the way I feel about it, I'm not any better than any of the other boys that have to go." Mrs. Bauer in a slightly cross voice said, "I'll be truthful, I don't even know why we got into that war. Until Tim went into the service, I didn't even know which was the good side—North and South."

The confusion felt by many was expressed. "One minute I hate 'em all—Vietnam, our country, everybody. The next minute I'm sorry for hating them."

Both sets of parents, by 1972, agreed that U.S. intervention was a mistake—but such views were too late to save their sons. And the Bauers felt that the then-proposed amnesty would threaten the validity of their son's death.

Kenneth Long, on the other hand, had a wistful, modest proposal: let the sons in Canada come home to visit. "The way it is now, it's sort of like punishing the parents, the way the Russians punish families of defectors."

Obvious class differences, which separated the generation of goers and nongoers, separated their parents' lives: League of Women Voters versus Navy Mothers Club, construction worker versus white-collar ad man, potted poinsettias blooming in the Longs' living room and plastic forget-me-nots arranged in profusion on blond walnut end tables at the Bauers.

The Longs' scrapbook was filled with Charles's victories—National Merit Scholarship, high school valedictorian, Ohio "Class B" debate tournament second prize winner, president of the student senate at the Case Institute of Technology in Cleveland.

They were particularly anxious to prove he was not a coward. "Lots of things he did took courage and initiative," said his mother. During his junior year in college, Charles took off alone for Australia, trekking across the wilds of Tasmania, writing richly detailed letters.

Both sons were guided in their moves by idealistic reasons. The day Charles got his draft notice, he was working in an antipoverty program.[2]

A decade later, I looked up the Bauers and the Longs. The emotional confusions were still there for Ruth Bauer. "I don't know how to express it. I think the war was unfortunate—that's for sure. I don't know why we're always drawn into these things. Still, I feel my son did what was right. He said at the time that he 'would rather go over there than have them come over here.' I really feel they died for their country. My husband's still sort of bitter. He was talking about the boys in Canada, how they can get their jobs back, but veterans have been dealt with so unfairly. The President was the one that ordered them to go. But it does appear that the ones that ran away are [regarded as] heroes more than the ones who went to Vietnam and came back."

Greider's front-page story had drawn attention to an otherwise ordinary life. "There were a lot of comments, some good and some bad. A lot of people thought that he favored the ones that left more than the ones that fought. How he was telling about the education and traveling that Long boy did. But I didn't get that impression myself.

"Draft dodgers? I don't let 'em bother me. Tim felt he had to do his service and then would go to school when he came home. Of course it didn't work out that way." She seems mystified at the harsh turn in the opinion of some of the public in the sixties and seventies toward veterans and their families. "I don't understand the hostility because it wasn't our fault. I didn't feel hard at the mothers of boys who left. And my daughter now says that there's *no way* her son's going in any conflict. There was no trouble, at least, in this town. Tim was *highly* thought of. The whole town almost turned out for his funeral. The funeral director had to open another room for his flowers."

At times Ruth Bauer allows herself a few small thoughts about what Tim would be doing if he were alive, the grandchildren he may have given her. "He liked children. He sent us tapes from Vietnam, and he talked about the children being treated badly over there—how hungry they were, that's what bothered him—and how they were used as decoys."

The memory is so distant now that Tim is spoken of with ease. But Mrs. Bauer is anxious to see the national memorial. "That's what's in the back of our minds—seeing his name. At least it will be something in their memory."

Across town Kenneth Long speaks enthusiastically and with pride of his son. Charles is now a Canadian citizen, traveling and writing for magazines. Married, he lives sixty miles from Ottawa, without a phone in the home he built himself.

Charles Long answered the letter I wrote him, after the conversation with his father.

"Had I been a cynic then, or a genuine anti-American, I would not have had so far to fall. I might have rolled with the punches and stayed within the system. Perhaps gone to Vietnam, or wrangled a nice, safe desk job someplace. But I really felt betrayed."

After the disillusionment Charles Long felt toward the U.S. government, he embraced his new country. "I'm convinced I have a much better life than I ever would have had in the U.S.A.—with or without Vietnam. There was a price to be paid for dodging the draft, but I didn't pay it. My parents did. That's the pity. They even understood and accepted what I was doing, but they still were left to bear the brunt of the hate calls and the FBI watch and the small-town whispering."

Long is one of those exiles who has assimilated into the culture. Although his father has visited him and the letters flow, Charles had not been back to Portsmouth in three years.

There were family tragedies. The "enforced separation" was hard on his mother, who was particularly close to Charles. She died of cancer before amnesty was granted. Charles did not attend the funeral. "We didn't let him know. We were afraid to try it. The FBI contacted us, occasionally, wanting to know if his address had changed and so forth, so we knew they were keeping track."

According to Kenneth Long, the last years of Mrs. Long's life were hard. "Maybe I'm a little thicker-skinned, but I know it all bothered my wife—particularly the anonymous phone calls." Just as the Gold Star mothers had their hate-filled messages from those who thought their sons were wrong for going to Vietnam, Mrs. Long heard from those who branded her son a coward. "That kinda cut her."

Long remembers the arguments he had with his son about going to Canada. "We tried to talk him out of it. The older generation didn't come around till later. Of course *now* I'm very glad he did what he did. He's better off than if he were rotting in the jungles somewhere."

There is a slight sigh. Kenneth Long spoke as if families of exiles will never be free from condemnation by some whose sons died in Vietnam. "I was reading an article, not twenty minutes before you called, about the last person killed in the Vietnam War and the bitterness his family felt to those who had gone to Canada.

"I guess there will always be this latent feeling against the ones who left."

The names of Charles McMahon, Jr., of Woburn, Massachusetts, and Darwin Judge of Marshalltown, Iowa, come near the end of panel after panel of young men's names—57,661—on the Vietnam Veterans Memorial. They were the last casualties on Vietnam soil.

In the random way that men are struck down in war, McMahon and Judge, embassy guards assigned to the U.S. Defense Department attache's compound at Tan Son Nhut airport, were killed in a rocket bombardment of the airport during the final evacuation of Americans.

Neither parents are bitter that their sons were in Vietnam; they were enlisted marines who wanted to be there. "What makes you feel bitter," said McMahon's father, "are the ones who went to Canada."

At noon on April 30, 1975, after the remains of Charlie McMahon and Darwin Judge filled the last of the seemingly endless bodybags, guns fell silent across Vietnam. The American evacuation had ended. Saigon had fallen to the North Vietnamese.

Thirty years of American involvement in Vietnam was over. The cost: more than one and a half million Vietnamese civilians wounded and dead, 150 billion in American dollars, more than 300,000 Americans wounded.

And, for their families to mourn forever, 57,661 of America's young, missing or dead.

2 The Supp-Hose Five

IN THE LONG HOURS SINCE I FIRST FELT THE COLD SNAP OF HAND-cuffs on my wrists, I had added considerably to my slim knowledge of paddy wagons. It is extremely difficult to climb into one with hands cuffed behind your back. They are surprisingly low-slung; you crouch in and out. Breathing is difficult and so is bracing yourself. Curiously engineered, paddy wagons have two sidelong benches like those at the front of buses. At every stop, you jerk sideways and then are snapped back, helpless to stop the lurching when your hands are bound. One of us five women wore glasses that kept falling down, and she would hunch her face down on the shoulder of the person sitting next to her and push them up.

On a soggy summer night in Washington, D.C., we were being moved from one precinct to the central cell block for fingerprinting. The paddy wagon aroma was overwhelming—a mix of alcohol fumes, body odor, sweat, and faint traces of some long-ago disinfectant. In the lurching stench, one of the women looked stricken. "I think I'm going to be sick." It was horrible for all of us, crowded together, to contemplate. She began to meditate—and the wave of nausea passed. For the next forty-eight hours, I was to hear a great deal about putting yourself in God's hands from these deeply religious women. I envied them but didn't think I would ever quite get there.

These were the sort of women I did not know in my journalist's life—partly religious zealots, deeply dedicated. They possessed a quality the Moral Majority would do well to emulate: they were nonjudgmental of others.

At the central cell block, the two police officers did not open the doors. One of them went in the building while the other, at the wheel, ate his dinner. We peered through and watched, as an animal in a cage watches zoo tourists munching on Cracker Jacks. He sauntered to the trash can to throw the plastic away. Finally, he opened the door so that we could breathe. We waited, endlessly it seemed, to be allowed out. By then the insidious role of captor/captive had begun. We did not even think of stepping out without permission.

Three young policemen, laughing and joking, looked into our paddy wagon and saw five bedraggled women—none younger than forty, three in their fifties with graying hair and glasses. They stopped, stunned. In their world we were definitely freaks.

"What did they do," hollered one with a good-natured grin, *"raid a Tupperware party?"*

Another peered in with a comical expression. "Mom, are ya in there?" We all started to laugh.

Their shock would be as nothing, compared to that of the bag ladies, prostitutes, and drug runners with whom we would soon share our cells and several hours of our time.

The third policeman said, "It must be more of those White House protesters. What is it this time?"

"Vietnam," said Kate Litchfield, a Gold Star mother and part of a Vietnam veterans contingent that had protested the nuclear arms race in front of the White House.

"Ohhhh," groaned the young policeman, "they don't let go of that, do they? War's been over for years, and people still go on about it." I asked his age. "Thirty." Did he go to Vietnam? "No, I got out of that one."

"So did my son," Kate Litchfield said softly. "He was killed there."

His face changed instantly. "I'm sorry, ma'am. I was on the force, and I was twenty-one when I had to arrest those kids on May Day. If I knew then what I know now, I wouldn't have arrested a one."

Some more police go by. One shakes his head with a mock tsk-tsk-tsk. "Girls, girls, girls." Betty Riley, a Quaker, says crisply, "Women, women, women . . ."

This small feminine protest brings a laugh from everyone. Then the driver says, "You 'girls' aren't doing anything wrong."

By then we had formed our name. How about the "Geriatric Five"? No. We would be the "Support Hose Five"—the "Supp-Hose Five" for short.

It was the summer of 1981—before worldwide massive nuclear protest, before the polls found dissatisfaction with Reaganomics, before many had come to believe that Reagan cared little about the poor, elderly, and handicapped. Between June 2 and July 3 there were twenty-four days of prayer—and arrest—at the White House. Some 280 were arrested—among them names from a Vietnam protest past: Dr. Benjamin Spock, Phil Berrigan, Dick Gregory. For the media it was a big *déjà vu* yawn. Most gave scant coverage to the vigil protesting budget cuts and defense buildup. Spock answered the "why are you still doing this?" kind of questions. The problems are still with us, he said. Of Reagan's budget cuts, he said simply, "The kids will suffer." This was all so unfashionable in the summer of 1981. So unchic. Not like the late sixties. The smirks were there for Dr. Spock, and they were there a few days later for our group of Vietnam veterans and supporters of Vietnam veterans.

"Veterans—many of whom are the survivors of U.S. foreign policy in action—see dollars pumped into an already bloated military budget," explained a green pamphlet, distributed by the sponsoring group, the Center for Creative Non-Violence. "El Salvador threatens to become another Vietnam, and the cloud of nuclear war hangs over the survival of mankind . . . The strength of the nation is in the well-being of all its people—not in its ability to destroy others."

They came in hot sunlight, four women and six men, out of conviction and conscience. I came out of curiosity. I had not been involved in the protest movement of the sixties except to write about it and as a participant in a well-ordered candlelight march or two. Thousands of middle-class Americans, thousands of teenagers and college students, the ministers, mothers and fathers had protested. Some had been put in jail. I felt it was important to understand that facet of protest. I did not feel I could write accurately about such protesters or the conditions under which they were detained unless I experienced it. Still, I was worried about becoming less an observer and too much a participant and losing journalistic balance. While objectivity is an impossible goal (the very choosing of a lead paragraph necessitates some subjective selective process), credibility is not.

I was a very uncomfortable participant and a devout coward, prepared to step over a tiny little fence and sit on the White House grass by the driveway. There was a knot in my stomach, a sense of uncertainty, as we moved with tourists into the White House, down the marble and gilt corridors, into the Red and Green rooms. Then we were outside, by the designated "off-limits" spot where we were to kneel and pray.

In a sudden rush everyone stepped over the knee-high chain fence. I held back slightly, someone grabbed my hand, and there we were sitting. It was too late now. The White House police and the Secret Service came. This had been going on for two weeks and there were no surprises, except for the tourists who stared at us. "This is not part of the White House tour," said one officer, in a masterstroke of subtlety. "You will have to leave." Everyone prayed and bowed heads. I heard the officer say that if we didn't leave we would be charged with "failure to quit" the premises, a misdemeanor under the federal unlawful-entry statute. No one was ready to quit. The men and women felt strongly that it was their First Amendment right to sit quietly and pray. "My son died in Vietnam to keep this country free, and I can't pray on 'my' lawn," said Kate Litchfield. *"We* the people own the White House, own the lawn . . ."

After a few minutes, a policewoman grabbed me hard by the left arm— even as I was already going along peaceably. I felt a rush of anger. "Is that necessary?" She relaxed the grip. Nearby, two Secret Servicemen were talking congenially as they walked along with two Vietnam veteran protesters.

"Was it worth it?" one asked sympathetically. "Yes," said the veteran with the tattoo and old fatigues. They spoke as old buddies. *All* had been in Vietnam. Throughout the day I would find this underground network of sympathetic veterans among policemen.

Suddenly we were spread-eagled against a White House wall. My arms were pulled behind me, watch taken off, and handcuffs snapped in place. A wave of helplessness, indignation, and shame hit as I was searched—hands patting my thighs, around my breasts, at my waist. I noticed the policewoman's long grape-burgundy-lacquered nails. Quaker Betty Lou Riley's prayer book was on the ground. She asked for someone to place it off the ground, on top of her purse. Our purses were searched. The first of several mug shots were taken.

Men and women were segregated in separate wagons. We went off to spend the night in the D.C. jail. We would make a strange but quick bond with the hookers, drug runners, addicts, and bag ladies who would populate our lives for one of our longest days.

Women at the barriers. They were dragged off by police in the sixties, and they are being dragged off today, as passive civil disobedience continues. They are the housewives in Britain, the backbone of antinuclear protest there. They are the handful who marched with men and sat in front of the State Department protesting the reinstitution of aid to El Salvador in 1983. Much has been said of today's gender gap in voting and polls, as women form an alliance against Reagan and other politicians who advocate trillions for defense and nuclear arms. During Vietnam, women, as in the past, were freed from the dilemma of being drafted, yet it was not a time for the traditional female-helpmate-at-home role. In earlier wars propaganda packaging had made women feel a part of the war effort—starlets selling war bonds, Rosie the Riveter, etc. While many women felt no desire to be a part of the Vietnam war effort, they were not comfortable remaining mere bystanders in this period of growing feminism.

Many threw themselves into protest, to prove that they could be effective alongside males on the streets of America. They were joined by older, religious women who had braved civil rights sit-ins when the sixties generation was gestating in grade school, and by mothers who had been part of the World War II effort—but who then protested their sons going to Vietnam.

Arrested with me at the White House in 1981 were four diverse women. Vickie Burroughs described herself as an old sixties antiwar "rabble rouser" and a friend of a Vietnam veteran. "He was on one side, and I on the other. Now I feel he is the result of all the things we said would happen." She explained he had gone through many depressions since Vietnam.

Betty Lou Riley—plump, kind, matronly, and funny—was a Quaker "here to make witness." She was worried about what would be left for the world's children. Deeply opposed to the nuclear buildup, she shored up her argument with first- and second-strike capabilities, and other figures and statistics.

Kate Litchfield, the Gold Star mother from Dedham, Massachusetts, has a strong Irish face and an equally strong Boston accent. Her voice often filled with rage. She had been the town pariah when she first spoke out against the war. "It was only after Watergate that the phone started ringing, 'Oh Kate, what a saint you are,' " she mimicked caustically. She has six children. Her firstborn died in Vietnam. "I begged him to go to Canada, but he said, 'Mother, you always taught me to stand up and stick to things. I made a commitment.' " In the cell her eyes filled with tears. "I taught him too well."

Joanne Bruns, from Norfolk, Virginia, with Pax Christi, a religious peace organization, was a latecomer to protest. "I was too busy raising babies in the sixties." A small speck of blood on her $4.98 running shoes from Penney's was acquired when she watched the Berrigans spill blood at the Pentagon while protesting the nuclear arms race. She feels "very comfortable" with her newfound activism. "I think it's a calling I've had through prayer. When they say, 'You're under arrest,' it's like hearing, 'Have a cup of coffee.' It just doesn't bother me."

We were brought into the women's section of the D.C. jail late at night and did not meet any other women until dawn, while we were waiting to be transferred to a holding tank in the basement of Superior Court for arraignment.

The next morning a black with bleached-blond hair was curled up asleep on the only bench. Next to her was a slim, boyish-looking black with fresh Nikes, white anklets, sawed-off jeans, blue T-shirt, tennis hat, and glasses. She loaned us her comb. Somehow they had been allowed to keep their belongings while we were not. A slim bundle with long blond hair was on the floor, trembling. We were far from fastidious, but we still couldn't sit or lie on the dirty floor. Two in our group were, frankly, babbling—the talk of the momentarily dazed. Suddenly the bundle on the floor said, "Look, we're all goin' to be together for a long time, and I am deathly sick, and it would be a helluva lot better if you'd stop that motherfuckin' noise. Y'all sound like a bunch of magpies."

An old bag lady, curiously dressed in two pairs of slacks, a tunic, and a shorter top, then entered. She rummaged through a paper bag, took out a wig, placed it gingerly on her head, went over to the communal toilet—and heaved.

The paddy wagon came. Eleven of us huddled together in silence. One of the Supp-Hose Five complimented the blonde on her fine, long hair, and then asked sweetly, "And what were you arrested for, my dear?"

The blonde looked up. "For tryin' to sell a little pussy."

Welcome to 6 A.M.

The day before, we were arrested around noon and detained for six hours in a precinct cell eight feet by eight. Some of the women asked for their reading glasses and were refused. "You could break them and cut someone with them" was the explanation, although those who wore glasses all the time for distance vision were inexplicably allowed to keep them. Another asked for high blood pressure medication and was refused. "If you feel sick, we can take you to D.C. General, but no one knows what's in the pills and we are not doctors. We don't know what you could have in them." I asked for my notebook and a pencil or pen. The answer was no. Bibles and other reading material were also refused, with no explanation given. It remained an unanswered puzzle as to how all the graffiti had gotten on the cell walls, if pencils were not allowed.

There were mostly names, but some protest slogans: "No nukes, no war." And from those who had raided abortion centers: "We were arrested for saving lives."

As the Secret Service processed our papers, we talked about husbands and friends, children. Between us we had fifteen children. A central curiosity for me was these women's motivation, why they were there, and whether they felt protesting and getting arrested would do any good. I mentioned that no one paid much attention to protests these days. As I began to understand them more, I realized that in one sense this was a matter of total indifference to them. They simply were deeply dedicated and couldn't live with themselves if they did not take a stand. This fervor was the key to their ability to endure arrest and jail.

The Secret Servicemen were weary. One had been working overtime since the protest started and longed to see his young son. He brought us one cup of water to share. There was no food. We offered to send out for sandwiches, but D.C. police said no. We were let out occasionally to go to the bathroom.

The three of us who lived in Washington were asked if we wanted to apply for citation release. If approved, we would be free to go home and return the next day for arraignment. We asked if that was possible for the two from out of town. (The sponsoring group had told us they were neither financially nor emotionally able to post bond.) The five of us quickly agreed that if any stayed, all would stay. The two out-of-towners were refused citation.

There was not enough room for all of us to stretch out in the dirty cell, so we tried to rest sitting up. We shared a handful of nuts and one badly mangled banana that one woman had secretly managed to save. One Secret Serviceman gave us a mild lecture on how much our protest was costing the government. Betty Riley peppered him with statistics. "Do you know the billions that are being spent on defense, billions not being spent on people?" He looked thoughtful. After they finished processing us, we heard clanking and scraping. The men were placing a large fan in the hall to keep us cool.

With calls of "good-luck" and "good-bye," the Secret Servicemen who had been our gentle captors left for the night. Another hour droned on before we were taken to the central cell block for fingerprints and mugging. Our belongings would not go with us.

After our lurching ride to the central cell block, a slim, black man rolled the ink across the pad, then rolled our fingers and thumbs over the pad, one by one. He was slightly contemptuous. "I never asked the government for a *thing*. You get what you can in life." I explained that they weren't asking for handouts but were protesting the defense buildup at the expense of social programs. "We need the defense," he replied. But he was no longer hostile. A symbiotic attachment occurred—as it was to happen all along the way in our jail experience, with a few exceptions. He turned out to be a Vietnam-era veteran—but had not gone to Vietnam.

Kate Litchfield started an animated conversation and found out he was discharged with negative-coded spin numbers. "They said I was militant. Black power hadn't even started." (Later, we sent him an article on discharge upgrading.) I asked if he had fifteen cents for a telephone call. "You don't need fifteen cents." He let me use the office phone.

My son was away at a summer job. I had already told my then fourteen-year-old daughter that I might be in jail, and she had made plans to stay with a friend. When I called, they were out getting ice cream. I gave her friend's mother certainly the most bizarre message in her circle of acquaintances. "Just tell her I am going to be in jail overnight and everything's fine."

We mentioned to the veteran policeman that we had not had anything to eat. We had been arrested at noon, and it was now after 9 P.M. "I'll see what I can get you."

Finally, we got the reaction I had really expected all day. One policeman in the outer office stared contemptuously. His look said it all: middle-class dilettante dabblers in the prison system, kookie protesters. We started toward the sandwiches piled on the counter. "You can't have them." As we walked out the door to the paddy wagon, he shouted, "I think y'all crazy!"

The dread strip search was now on our minds. One of the earlier protesters, Phillip Berrigan's wife, had been strip-searched, with all its degrading implications, and a suit had been filed, but we were uncertain what would happen to us. Inside the D.C. jail we were greeted by a cage filled with men, mostly black, some climbing up the backs of others to stare at new arrivals. They were decidedly discouraged at the sight of us. No catcalls, whoops, or whistles for this curious caravan.

Once again doors were opening, clanking shut; keys were rattling. We were in an anteroom. Finally a large black prison matron, with her hair in a bun, a flower in her hair, and a handsome face, said sternly, "How long y'all been out here?" "About five minutes." *"Sheeeeiiiit*—why didn't you *say* something?" Then she disappeared for a long time. Kate Litchfield commented, "For a woman all bent out of shape because we didn't announce our presence, she sure is taking her sweet time."

One by one we were called in. The matron sighed and handed me a blue-flowered Mother Hubbard dress. I took my clothes off in a corner while she watched; there was, thank God, no strip search. She led me to a dirty cell with dust balls and cigarette ashes filling the corners. A bug crawled along. The walls were yellow. Two coil-spring cots were parallel, three feet apart, with a two-inch green plastic mattress on each. There were toilets in some cells but not in this one. I marked off the space with my hand; it was a little over six feet square. I shared it with Kate Litchfield.

It was now close to midnight, and we had not eaten since our noon arrest. The matron brought us food: two leathery pork chops as hard as a shoe heel, boiled potatoes, cold cabbage, and some strange chicken mixture. Gagging at the smell of the cabbage, I ate a half-slice of bread and pushed the tray under the cell door; then I apologized to the matron for not eating the food she had gone to the trouble to find. "That's all right," she said. "It's hard to get used to jail food."

They were running out of beds; street ladies were coming in as night moved on. The matron said we could make one phone call. It was late, but I called my daughter anyway. She had gotten the earlier message, and now she said, with knowledge obtained from viewing TV crime shows, "Mom, what are you doing? You're only supposed to get *one* call." She thought it all very amusing.

In the cell a huge grid of fluorescent light pounded its rays down on us. It was as bright as noon. When do the lights go out? "They don't," said the matron. "Y'all might do something, like suicide." I muttered that the lights could drive one to suicide. Then I started to laugh. They let us keep the towel from our shower, and although it was still wet, I put it across my eyes—and reflected on the fact that if I wanted to commit suicide I could do it with the towel.

As exhausted as we were, the light was still too disorienting to sleep. Kate and I talked as women do—about children, family, loves, frustrations. It was 3:30 in the morning.

At 5:30 our cells were unlocked. We changed into our clothes, ate cold scrambled eggs and scrapple, and were tumbled out into the small anteroom to meet our new friends. Inside the paddy wagon, the blonde arrested for prostitution eyed us with curiosity. She asked what we were doing there, and we told her we were arrested at the White House protest. She said, "You're crazy" and then launched into *her* night. "I was goin' by and this motherfuckin' cop says, 'How much would it be?', and I tell him and he says I'm under arrest and I start running and the motherfucker grabs me by the hair."

As we bent down to get out of the paddy wagon, she whispered, "Don't use your real name, honey. Don't tell them nothin'." I nod subserviently to this knowledgeable street veteran of, perhaps, twenty-two. "What's your name," I asked. "Ambrosia." I should have known better than to ask.

It was now seven-thirty. In the manner of prisons and other bureaucracies, we were inexplicably gathered in the holding area at dawn, even though the earliest possible time we could be arraigned was six hours later, at one-thirty.

The cells were rapidly filling. There were fourteen prisoners in ours, more clustered across the way. As in some intimate sorority meeting there were shouted greetings back and forth. "Whoeeee, Marilyn . . . Say *wha?*"

A blonde with Farrah Fawcett hair was wearing red-satin spike heels, a red bathing suit cut high up the thighs, and a see-through blouse. Catcalls greeted her from another cell, "Whooooeeee, *Cinder-ella!*"

Suddenly the cells were buzzing with street talk. I tried hard to catch the vernacular, but it was hopeless. "Motherfuck'-gets-me-for-dropping-a-ciga-rette-on-the-ground," said one, rapidly. "Littering." A prostitute snickered, "Littering? Not *loitering?*" The barbs flew back and forth like a scene in "Hill Street Blues."

One of the Supp-Hose Five looked at an athletic young girl in sawed-off jeans and T-shirt. "Do you do much running, dear?" The cell broke into laughter. The girl explained in a whisper that she runs dope to cars—a go-between who bargains with white suburbanites who line up on Washington's dope corridor. She was twenty-two and had a daughter six years old. Her mother keeps the daughter. She got hooked on heroin, wants to stop, but runs dope because she needs the money.

The hours went slowly. We were numb with exhaustion. The blonde, "Ambrosia," leaned her head on my shoulder and wove a story undoubtedly rife with fiction. Her blue eyes wobbled quick and fast, like a Kewpie doll's eyes. I wondered if this was caused by the dope she was on. Suddenly she asked, "Will you pee for me? I'm not clean, and I sure as hell *know* you are. Pardon me, but y'all look like a woman's club."

At first I didn't comprehend; then it dawned that they were about to take a urinalysis. "If they get me on drugs, I won't get out," she said. I looked around the small cell, filled with women, and at the exposed toilet toward the back. I said as noncommittally as possible that if I could I would.

Our group talked about prostitution being a victimless crime. The church women seemed amazingly tolerant. The women should not be arrested; in fact prostitution should be legal, they said. A chorus of protest came from the prostitutes. Anything but legal, they said. "We'd have to pay *taxes!*" Getting arrested was just an occupational hazard.

We had been sitting up or milling around for hours. There was nothing to read but the graffiti. "Cozy and Sam," some long-ago lovers, were united all over the ceiling in big black swirls. There were many other names, interspersed with remarks like "Fuck cops" and "Cops suck." I wondered how they ever got written. One black prostitute gave me a "Boy, are you some rube" stare, then flicked her Bic and tossed it at me. By then I'd given up trying to figure out how they all had cigarette lighters, combs, and such, and we had everything taken. I climbed up the iron bars, reaching as high as I could, and held out the Bic, trying to find a place on the wall or ceiling to emblazon "Supp-Hose Five was here." But the empty spaces were all out of reach.

The urinalysis woman came with the vials. A blonde in a see-through black dress marched over to take a vial when her name was called, but saw a male lawyer and, stalling for time, said, "I'm not gonna pee until that man is gone." The matron replied that she could wait. "We respect your privacy—and your pride."

After the man left, the blonde straddled the toilet. "What if a bitch can't pee?" The matron admonished, "Now *you're* not respecting yourself." The prostitute rolled her eyes to the ceiling in disgust at the preaching tone and slammed the empty vial down. She was warned that if she didn't give them a sample, it could go against her.

The communal life left no sense of modesty. We all urinated and handed back the vials. It was close to one-thirty.

The early afternoon passed without food. Finally we were taken out *en masse*. We passed a group of men who catcalled and whistled at the prostitutes.

One U.S. marshal stared slack-jawed at the blonde in the red bathing suit and red spike-heel shoes.

Betty Riley, the Quaker, quick-witted as ever after all those hours, didn't miss a beat as the marshal muttered, "Holy Jesus!"

"Yes," said Riley, marching primly past, "he is."

A long corridor of smaller, dirtier cells was next. They were crammed— men at one end, women at the other. As U.S. marshals and lawyers walked through, arms reached through bars and voices beseeched, "Want to see a lawyer!" There is a sense of urgency in wanting to get processed through by the close of the day, urgency in the babble and milling around of doing business in some strange marketplace. In our cell was Ambrosia, as well as a black prostitute with a corona of wigged curls, and Joanne Bruns, the Pax Christi matron with the small dab of blood on her tennis shoes. Ambrosia, skinny and trembling, stood by the bars shouting, "Scotty! Scotty!"

A disembodied voice shouted back from another cell filled with males whom we could not see. "Yeah, hon!" She pressed her face to the bars and shouted in his direction. "What do you want me to do? Pawn the car? Pawn it to post bond if I get out?" Scotty, her boyfriend, busted for violating parole, shouted, "Sell it." The business of their private life was conducted in the public arena of street people. "Who's got the baby?" Scotty asked. "I don't know." Ambrosia's voice cracked; tears were streaming down her face. "I called and got no answer. I got no money. That motherfucker got me right out, before I could turn one trick." She hustles, he deals in drugs; their baby was at home, she hoped. What a life. Joanne Bruns and I were crying. The marshal called Ambrosia's name, and she was gone. Later, they called her man, a black wearing a baseball cap, and he too was gone. As rapidly as Ambrosia passed through our very different lives, she was gone. I never knew what happened to her.

One U.S. marshal had earlier said to us, "We'll get you out soon." There is no describing how we clung to that small crumb of promise—all the more disappointing as hours went by, as cells clinked open, others were let out, and the bartering of lost souls continued. I didn't feel that I could take one more night in jail. I thought of those for whom this was a way of life. One indifferent marshal said curtly, "We're busy—and this is a *slow* day." We were quivering with exhaustion and from the waiting, waiting, waiting. And something more: the unwritten attitude that if you were arrested, you *must* be guilty of something. It pervaded the jail—captor and guilty captive—despite the moments of kindness in a degraded world of filthy cells, total lack of privacy, lack of food, confiscated books and Bibles, and interminable waits. And yet none of us had even been arraigned, much less sentenced. The harsh reality of prisons, even for just one day, remains a vivid memory.

Finally we were let out. As we passed the cells, a black man reached out, "Are you with the White House group?" We nodded. "Right on," he said. "That mo-fo [motherfucker] takin' everything away from us." It was the first year of Reagan's presidency, but the knowledge of budget cuts had rippled through this community. The young jogging drug runner, who had worked in a government jobs program, said, "There are more of us on the streets. Lots of government jobs are going." I asked her what she would be doing ten years from now. She shook her head. "I'd sure like to be doing something else." As we separated, she patted my arm in a gesture of friendship. I wished her luck.

We met with the men who were also arrested at the White House and decided to plead *nolo contendere* (no contest) and were scheduled to reappear in a month.

Fresh air for the first time in thirty hours hit me walking down the courthouse steps. I savored everything, even Washington's soggy summer night. At home I took a long hot bath and felt like burning my dress. I mixed a drink, looked around, listened to music. The next day I was still euphoric, walking down the street, seeing everything through fresh eyes. A melodramatic and excessive reaction, perhaps, for such a small time of incarceration, but as the saying goes, you had to be there. All too swiftly that appreciation for the smallest benefits of freedom would give way to the petty concerns of day-to-day life, but for the moment freedom was indescribably delicious.

We met again a month later in court. Meanwhile, the Washington *Post,* my employers, sought separate counsel for me—two uptown lawyers who were Ivy Leaguers during the Vietnam War. ("I had a high lottery number, so I was safe," said one. "I was in Europe one summer with a cousin when he got a low number, but he got out on a gimmick. Most of us felt some guilt; we were a privileged lot. But not guilty enough to give up our privilege.")

The lawyers were polite but seemed unaware and uncomprehending of why these people would protest at the White House today; they viewed them with bemused detachment. I was coached; they wanted me to say I felt sorry and that I "didn't fully realize the consequences of our act." I said I couldn't honestly say I was sorry. They asked for me to be taken separately and requested that I be handled under the pretrial diversion program—which permits a first-time offender to avoid prosecution.

Three of the other women had never been arrested before for anything, including civil disobedience, yet they all refused to ask for diversion. They were engaging in an act of protest and were proud of it. I felt awkward separating myself from the group, but they were supportive. "Just going to jail was important," they said. The amusing irony is that I was turned down for diversion; the court argued that I was willing to get arrested in order to gain some benefit—the experience to write about it. The court's position was that they might dismiss a first-time stealer; "if someone steals a watch, he's not *intending* to get arrested." The logic was lost on me. Someone who wittingly steals—which is a crime—knows that arrest might be the end result. At any event, I found myself separated from the group, listening to them and the judge.

They had brought their books of scriptures. One of the men was reading from a book on natural farming: "In my orchard there are pines and cedar trees . . ." A bizarre passage to read in this courtroom of mundane misdemeanors. A prostitute stood sullenly beside a court-appointed lawyer. A street dude insisted on representing himself in his case. The Honorable Herbert Goodrich, an older man with a kindly face, presided.

Then it was time for the White House case. "Many of these folks are Vietnam veterans, and others are supporters of the Vietnam veterans movement," said lawyer Norman Townsend, himself a disabled veteran. "It's an unlawful entry charge, a failure to quit at the White House for a pray-in after going through the tour line. They are charged with having knelt and prayed and not moved when being ordered to do so." Don Allison, Assistant United States Attorney, argued, "It is the policy of the United States Department of Justice not to consent to a *nolo* plea throughout all of the United States Attorney's offices in the country. We recognize that we can't prevent your honor from taking a *nolo* plea. However, for the record, the government does *not* consent to the entering of a *nolo* plea."

Judge Goodrich answered, drily, "At least the government is consistent in their position—because that's the same position they took in 1968 and '69 and '70, and at various other times."

Townsend explained that all the codefendants knew they could get a maximum sentencing of one year and $1,000, or both. Allison told the brief tale: "They hopped over the chain, went into an area that is restricted, knelt down, and prayed." When they refused to leave, "they were arrested." Townsend then said that most wanted to make brief remarks prior to sentencing.

Kate Litchfield opened. "My son died in Vietnam. I work with Vietnam veterans. I know the discrimination that has been placed against veterans from the VA and from the general public. We have addressed ourselves to the government many, *many* times. We have been ignored. And this was the reason I was at the White House."

John David Borgman, pilot in Vietnam and father of two, from Atlanta, Georgia, said, "I was involved in the killing and the murders over there and have a lot of guilt. We are working through being involved in a war that was unwanted—and coming back to a country not listening to our needs or the needs of the poor. I was there to pray and get some kind of response from the government for these needs."

The Quaker, Betty Lou Riley, said, "Quakers historically are against war. I was there because I support the Vietnam veterans, but I was also there making a Quaker witness because I believe that we are forcing our children today to live under the threat of a nuclear war—and we are being unfair to the children of this country when we cut the budget and take food away from them. I am an ex–school teacher, and I know that many of the children have one good meal a day, and that's the meal that they were getting at school."

Mike Caputo, with the U.S. Marine Corps in Vietnam, felt that he and his son "suffer from symptoms of the terrible defoliant, Agent Orange, which the government refuses to take action on. That's why I was arrested." Joanne Bruns, mother of three, stated: "My brother served in Korea. My husband is an ex-marine. I am a daughter of a man that served his country for thirty years. I went to pray for our President, our nation, that we would have peace and justice, that we would stop the escalation of the arms race, that our tax dollars would be spent for human needs. We are spending billions for defense, for the destruction of human life, when it should be spent for the good of human beings. So I pray that our country will have a change of heart."

Calvin Robertson, a Marine medic in Vietnam, said, "All I wanted to say is that nuclear bombs and Agent Orange are bad." The defense lawyer expressed his view: "I feel bad that our country took my generation, put guns into our hands, and told us to go kill people that we didn't want to kill and, as it turns out, shouldn't have. We are back now, but many are seeking redress."

Allison asked that the judge consider "sentencing them to a period of community service" for all the paperwork they caused the government. Townsend argued, "They have performed their community service already, many of them offering their bodies and the lives of friends and family in Vietnam—service far beyond the call of most citizens."

Judge Goodrich, who seemed close to tears, said, "I can tell you that some of the trials that take place here are extremely dull. They involve a dispute over property or money. Certain petty larcenies go on forever." His voice filled with emotion. "And then every once in a while, such as now, there is presented in this room a very dramatic and a very moving event. I recognize that you're using words to describe a deep-felt position which is based on events that took place some while back." Although the war was over, "the results of it are continuing," he said. "I assure you that I understand the position that you are describing for me very keenly . . . It's a very human case and a case that transcends just the criminal statutes alone . . . I am going to impose a five-day jail term. I am going to suspend that sentence and place you on three months unsupervised probation."

In the "thank-yous," one of the women said to the judge, "I wish there could be more like you."

I returned a month later and received the same five-day suspended sentence.

At times, all these months later, I think about those people with whom I went to jail. I am sure they are continuing with their work. I remember them fondly. Occasionally I get notes from them.

They are always signed "Peace."

3 The Women Who Went

THE STARS AND STRIPES OFFICE, NOT FAR FROM THE UNITED STATES CAP-
itol, was a sweat house of camaraderie on a rainy night in November 1982.
Finally, a long decade after Vietnam veterans came home, there was a national reunion. The media, from across the country and around the world,
recorded a week of tears and laughter among former comrades in arms, men
in fatigues and pony tails mingling with those in three-piece suits. *The Stars
and Stripes*, the national veterans' newspaper, was throwing one of the best
parties. Sixties rock and country music blared in the cavernous old ware-
house. The line was six-deep at the beer kegs. An overflow crowd stood
outside, unmindful of misting rains, telling war stories into the night.

Toward evening's end, people grabbed the mike for impromptu stream-of-
consciousness reverie. Like the antiwar movement in the sixties, they were
communing with *their* music, *their* 'love-in,' *their* self-congratulatory rhetoric.

"Think about the leaders of tomorrow," roared one veteran. "Who do you
want to lead America? Tom Hayden and Jane Fonda?" A drunk responds
from the audience, "Fuck Jane Fonda." The veteran at the mike roars again,
"The leaders of tomorrow are in this room!"

In the crowd of veterans there were politicians, including a lieutenant governor and a congressman, lawyers, businessmen, journalists, novelists, artists,
and well-known Vietnam veteran activists. A former Green Beret in fatigues
cradled his sleeping daughter in his arms. There were men in wheelchairs and
men without arms. No one, not even a silver-haired Gold Star mother, was
quarreling with the profanity-laced message of one veteran at the mike: "I got
pride for the first time in fourteen fuckin' years. I'm here from San Francisco,
and I've been getting drunk every fuckin' night. Let's hear it for the
motherfuckin' veterans and say, 'This is *our* fuckin' parade.' Excuse my language *(burp)*, but I'm pretty fuckin' drunk."

Another man shouted that he wanted everyone to give three cheers for the
nurses who were present. In the inevitable macho-raunch of the moment, he
said, "They put us back together—in my case, uh, they got the dick too

short." The mood shifted dramatically when eight nurses threaded their way through the bedlam. Men with wounded bodies stared and began to applaud. Saralee McGoran, her face beaming, said, "I met one of my patients tonight —and he is *alive* and *well!* Our government and country might have come in second [in Vietnam], but we," she said, sweeping her eyes around the room, "came in first."

By then the man with the dick-too-short joke had tears in his eyes. "Let's give these ladies who put us back together a big hand."

One of the nurses said, slightly apologetically, "This may sound corny, but I would like everyone to sing 'Oh Beautiful for Spacious Skies' and then 'God Bless America.' "

This was a room filled with the long disenfranchised—bitter veterans who felt the war was right but felt betrayed by their government, bitter veterans who felt the war was wrong, bitter veterans who saw friends die in a war that had no fixed goals for winning. There were men who wore their cynic's talismans; the "Dow Shalt Not Kill" Agent Orange T-shirts and the T-shirt with the Vietnam map that says "Participant: Southeast Asia War Games— Second Place." Many vowed a decade ago to never sing "God Bless America" again.

The nurse's quavering voice started alone. Slowly, a few began to mumble the words. Then they were joined by more and more voices. Eventually, the entire room was filled with men singing ". . . land that I love . . ." Many did not bother to wipe the tears streaming down their faces. And almost by rote, totally unself-consciously, one by one, until the whole room joined in, they gave a long-ago sign of recognition, of hail and farewell, from their Vietnam days—the thumbs-up salute.

Later, in a corner of the room, Saralee McGoran explained why she came to the reunion. She was looking for men she did not know. She knew no faces. She knew no names. She never did. They came and went too fast through the "meat factory" when she was on duty as an operating nurse in an evacuation hospital. She had no time to get to know those mangled men. But they had haunted her for years. And so she went to the Sheraton Hotel reunion suite of the Army's 25th Division and wrote her name in their book: Saralee McGoran, nurse, 12th Evac., Cu Chi.

She was trying to complete the circle.

She starts to tell her Vietnam story. "If I can get through it . . ." McGoran is a tiny, intense woman with curly graying hair, barely five feet two, who was twenty-six when she went to Vietnam. Once again, the horrors of booby-trap wounds are recalled: "A lot of times they would come in with nothing from here down," McGoran says, touching herself in midpelvis, above the crotch.

"The doctors and nurses would just cry and look at each other. We didn't know whether to work on them or not. I couldn't bear to look at their faces.

One guy couldn't have been more than seventeen. He had red hair . . . he was just blown apart. We were putting guys back together the best we could.

"About three or four days later, I walked into this long Quonset hut, and I saw this stretcher and a white sheet. All I could see under the sheet was this little bump. I walked close enough—to see the red hair. He would *live.*" The pain is in her face still. He would live, half a man. A little bump under a white sheet. "At eighteen there was not enough left of him to give him a prosthesis. His testicles were all messed up." That day McGoran walked out of the Quonset hut and sobbed and sobbed. "Then I shook my fist at the gunships in the sky and said, 'Go get 'em!' I wanted to kill everyone on their side." She was plagued by the terrible, impotent rage and helplessness which many nurses felt in a war that had so perfected its medevac operations that the bloodiest no longer died on the field of battle. The soldiers were brought to the operating table only to survive with half a life or to die crying for their assurance that they would live. In this booby-trap war the percentage of leg amputees from Vietnam was more than any other war; Max Cleland, President Carter's VA chief, who lost both legs and one arm, has said, "If I had been in World War II, I'd have died." Some amputees, like Cleland, learned eventually to find joy in being alive, but nurses, caught in the endless stream of mangled and severed bodies in an evacuation hospital, were never to know their fate. For years, McGoran was plagued with thoughts of what happened to that red-haired eighteen-year-old, wondering whether he was one of the many disabled-veteran suicides. There was the terrible uncertainty of whether they should have left him to die.

She remembers another soldier. "The only time I got to be with a guy *before* he went into the operating room. He was in so much pain and so scared, asking for his mom, wanting to know if he was going to be all right. I kept reassuring him. We got him on the operating table. His vena cava was shot, and we didn't know it. We removed a blood clot; it was the only thing that was keeping him alive. It was keeping the vena cava from collapsing. And we killed him. You never saw so much blood. It was just pouring out of him."

When McGoran returned, she was assigned to a VA hospital orthopedic ward. "I loved it. I got to take care of the ones coming back from Vietnam." Once again McGoran was trying to complete some circle, some absolving of guilt for the ones she had not been able to save. "Nobody went to that bus but *me.* I made sure they had a right welcome. We arranged to have their wives and girlfriends in the ward."

She admits to being in "some kind of shock" when she arrived in the States in January of 1968. "I hardly remember how I came back." Like so many Vietnam returnees, McGoran felt an alien displacement, like the medic who once told me he somehow felt "safer" in Vietnam than at home. "I felt totally alone," continues McGoran. "Everything was a blank. I'd been home a day and a half, in Los Angeles, when a siren sounded and I went right to the bottom of the car. We had been shelled a lot." A spaghetti dinner had been planned just before she left Vietnam. It was shifted from one night to the next. That night, mortar hit the cafeteria. "If we'd had it as originally planned, we would have all been killed."

McGoran returned to college in California for her bachelor's degree. Hers is the universal story of veterans in college who were made to feel outcasts, an experience that would scar them for years. "I was the *enemy*. All the riots were going on. I didn't tell *anyone* I was a Vietnam veteran." She was among the many nurses who hid their Vietnam past. "I didn't say *another word* about it until the boat people."

Then all of McGoran's defenses crashed. "I had a lot of depression and anger, but I didn't know why. I was in graduate school, studying to be a counselor, and everyone thought I was just trying to get sympathy. I just kept crying and crying, and it was all on account of Vietnam." She was struck by the futility of the war, the young men who died, the young men with their half-bodies. "I *knew* our country was the last to care. All those boat people, losing and leaving their country, and what the hell were we there for? We went there so that *wouldn't* happen. And we lost 58,000. For *what?*"

Her mind would not leave Vietnam. "I went to two therapists, and neither was able to help me. About that time I had my flashback. One day on the freeway, I saw an Army truck in front of me. I looked in, and I 'saw' bleeding bodies. I almost crashed."

There was a recurring nightmare. "In my dream there was a hospital on one side—and a night club on the other. All these beds, just *full* of bodies, five or six in a bed, and they all had these bleeding eyes. You know how eyes bleed in death? And on the other side, everyone was partying. And that's how it *was*. Every day there would be broken bodies and pain—and on the other hand the way we coped, not to *feel*, was to drink beer and have a party." It was echoes of "M*A*S*H." "For a few hours we blocked it off. I did it so well, I cut off all my feelings."

A year later, in college, "I couldn't relate to the guys burning draft cards. *Couldn't relate to another woman on campus*. All they wanted was short little answers. I couldn't give them short answers. I feel they may have been the smart ones. They saw what we couldn't see."

Perhaps it was inevitable, but McGoran married a Vietnam veteran. "We were both on campus on the West Coast, and you can imagine what that was like. He mentioned he was in Vietnam, and my initial reaction was to run. 'I don't want to hear anything about that.' I decided he was a creep. Our first date was for church. It was probably the only type of date I wouldn't have refused." It didn't take her long to decide that he wasn't a creep. "Today my husband doesn't get as emotional as I do." The McGorans, like many in their generation, are distanced by their different experiences. "He had a real nice war—as close as you can get to being a draft resister and still be in the war." Her husband is an attorney. McGoran is still in her serving role as a child counselor. She has two children and both have eye problems. Like many Vietnam veteran parents, when there are abnormalities in their children and no family history of problems, there is always that wonder. "At first I never thought of Agent Orange—but they were spraying where I was."

McGoran's salvation from her deep depression and crying spells was a women's veterans' rap group. "I was afraid to go but glad later. We told our stories—and it helped me to understand."

And finally, McGoran was at the Vietnam veterans' reunion in search of another bit of understanding, another bit of closure on her life in Vietnam. "I *had* to know what the men felt about what we did."

As if on cue, a crippled veteran sees McGoran's hat with 12th Evac. on it. He sobs and grabs her. "You saved my life. I was there, in Cu Chi. Thank the rest of the girls."

McGoran tells of searching for the redemptive key to dissolve those years of anguish. "I needed to know that I did a good job. Needed to know it from the guys who were there.

"In the 25th Division reunion suite, everyone was coming up and saying 'Thank you.' *For fourteen years, I needed to know that.* I went to the memorial today, and all I could do was go from panel to panel and cry for the ones I didn't know. I never knew their names."

Another veteran came up. "I got hit hard by a mortar round in '67. A little nurse, she held my hand and cried all the way to O.R. with me. Kept saying, 'I'm sorry, I'm sorry, I'm sorry.' I know she saved my life. A swell bunch of gals. They did a better job than anybody. Worked twice as hard as the doctors."

McGoran interjects, "The doctors were drafted. Didn't want to be there. We volunteered." Why? "I was single, there was a war and American boys were in it, and they needed American nurses."

The veteran can't stop praising "the girls." He has his hand on her shoulder. "They were shelled and everything. A little girl, no bigger than you are, pulled me out of bed during mortar rounds, so I wouldn't get hurt."

The hulking veteran leans down. The circle was slowly being closed. "Thanks a lot, little lady." He gives her a hug, and they rock back and forth, holding on to each other, holding on to a memory, lost in a time and place of long ago.

Lynda Van Devanter tells her story with the flair of an actress now. Since 1980, when she became a national VA spokeswoman for Vietnam women veterans, Van Devanter has told it on television shows and in congressional hearings and for journalists. To those who have heard it often, there is a staginess to the tremble, the tears, the melodramatic catch in her voice. And yet for years it was not this way. Buried deeply, locked away were her memories of Vietnam. From 1969 to 1970 Van Devanter was an operating room nurse in Pleiku. Years later Van Devanter sought psychiatric help. She never dreamed of mentioning Vietnam as a cause of any emotional problems. That, she thought, would be "overdramatizing. Vietnam was years ago. It must just be me." Today, she recalls that in those "closet-veteran" years, "I had a recurring nightmare that scared the absolute shit out of me. There are tons and tons of black, napalm-burned skin about to crash down on me. The dream always starts with this 'plop, plop, plop,' and I always think it is rain. And then I look up and everything over me is covered with black, bloody, *stinking*—I can still smell it—burned flesh. And it's all coming down and I think I'm going to drown in it. I would wake up screaming and realized I better get into therapy real fast—but I sure better not tell the doctor about *this* because he might think I'm crazy, might commit me."

Her real stories were hardly different from the nightmares. "Napalm burn just reeks—*reeks.* If you try to brush napalm off, it continues to roll down, it just oozes fire along the skin. Burning flesh smells are so beyond description. Add to that the smell of napalm, a petroleum distillate, *and* the infection, which happens with really bad burns. The infection gives off a very distinct odor, a little bit like a sewer. The combination of these three smells you will *never ever* lose the memory of."

Another memory, so a part of Van Devanter now that it is told by rote, in present tense, is of the death of one young man. "It is the largest trail of blood leading to the table that I have ever seen. I slip in it because my eyes are drawn to the gurney [a stretcher]. As they move him to the operating table, I watch in horror as the lower portion of his jaw, teeth exposed, dangles from what is left of his face." She chokes. "I have to catch myself to keep from getting sick. He is drowning in blood. I grab a tray of instruments. For the sake of speed, we perform the tracheotomy without donning gloves . . . The surgeon grabs instruments from the tray to clamp off the largest bleeders in the face and jaw. The soldier is bleeding so fast that it is necessary to start four large needles in his leg, neck, and both arms and to pump blood into all of them simultaneously." For several hours Van Devanter does this, moving around the body, continuously pumping blood into those four large needles. "During one of my circuits around the table, I kick his clothes to one side, to get them out of the way, and a snapshot falls out of the pocket of his fatigues." It is a picture of the soldier and his girl—dressed for a prom. He is straight, blond, and tall in his tuxedo. She has shining dark hair and is wearing a long pastel gown. The tears come to Van Devanter again. "Love for him shines in her eyes."

For months, Van Devanter had tried to feel as little as possible. "There had been that veneer of unreality," she says, shifting to the past tense. "Suddenly now, he was *real* to me.

"Finally, after six hours of surgery, the surgeon decided it was hopeless. He packed his head in pressure dressings and sent him to the post-op intensive care unit to die. As I cleaned up the room, I kept telling myself that a miracle could happen. I came upon the photograph again, picked it up, and stared. He was a young man who could love and think and plan and dream—and now he was lost to himself, to her, and to their future. I sat on the floor and sobbed. After making the room ready for the next casualty, I walked over to the post-op ICU to see him. His bandages had become saturated with blood several times over, and the nurses reinforced them with more rolls of bandages, and now his head was grotesquely large under the swath of white." Still, the red stains seeped through. Van Devanter held his hand and asked if he was in pain. He squeezed her hand weakly. Van Devanter called for pain medication. "I held his hand until the life just literally drained out of him. He literally bled to death . . .

"That boy has been a constant nightmare. I can see everything about him, every single blood vessel of his face. There is another nightmare. Lines and lines and lines of mothers sobbing and crying, not knowing: 'Why did he die? How did he die? What was it like for him? Who was there? Did our government really not take care of him?' "

Van Devanter's quest today is to find the thousands of nurses who came back from Vietnam with their own troubled memories, only to receive the same hostility and indifference she and many others found. These women are truly the forgotten Vietnam veterans nobody knows.

And, like male veterans, they have diverse feelings about the war. In 1983 Van Devanter wrote the first account of the war by a woman veteran, *Home Before Morning.* Her autobiography sparked an emotional debate among nurses who said she exaggerated and distorted conditions to bolster her antimilitary political views. Van Devanter denied the distortions, attributing much of the criticism to her strong antiwar tones and political activism. She was among the VVA delegation who made a controversial trip to Hanoi in 1982.

Van Devanter vividly describes grueling seventy-two-hour shifts by medical personnel "falling into an almost deathlike sleep at the operating tables," working under a barrage of rocket attacks, standing in mud and blood while tending to a "steady flow of casualties."

Colonel Mary Grace, who was a nursing supervisor in the evacuation hospital where Van Devanter worked, commented, "I certainly don't recognize that. I'd say she's been watching too much 'M*A*S*H.' " "This book makes us look like a bunch of bed-hopping, foul-mouthed tramps," blasted retired Colonel Edith Knox, a former head nurse of the 67th Evacuation Hospital in Qui Nhon. Jo Ann Webb, former Army nurse, said Van Devanter "fictionalized" the work load. "She talks about this endless flow of casualties, and official Army figures show the hospital was 50 percent full. I'm incensed that she's become a professional veteran and now she's making money off it." However, Webb's husband, James Webb, who wrote the bestselling *Fields of Fire,* is regarded as a professional veteran and a financially successful one, in many veteran circles. His wife shares Webb's view that the war was a right cause and wants to portray veterans in the best possible light. During one conversation with me, she insisted that the majority of the men on her ward had used heroin before coming to Vietnam, although official statistics contradict such anecdotal evidence.

"These people would obviously prefer that I had written a book that said we were saints and angels and everything was wonderful," said Van Devanter.

"They're trying to write revisionist history. It's absolute bullshit for Jo Ann Webb to spout these figures, which don't tell you anything about the magnitude of the casualties. This is not a book about numbers. This is also not a big sex book. I mentioned exactly two relationships in Vietnam, both of which illustrated the need to hold onto another human being in a situation of complete insanity."

Her descriptions of Vietnam are substantiated by other women veterans, including her former roommate, Army nurse Lynn Calmes Kohl. Now a housewife in Appleton, Wisconsin, Kohl, like Van Devanter, suffered a breakdown after the war.

"Actually," said Kohl, "what Lynda wrote was mild."[1]

For the public who long ignored Vietnam, Van Devanter's experiences were shocking but important revelations.

One reader, William Baffa, following one published account in the Los Angeles *Times,* wrote a letter representative of most. "I read with horror the article about the young soldier who bled to death of head wounds . . . the tiny children with arms and legs blown off . . . the pregnant woman and her child who entered the world with a gunshot wound in his belly. *It ruined my day!* My hope is that it ruined the day for many readers . . . Can anything short of ridding our civilization of the periodical insanity of war really honor the sacrifices that countless millions have made to do what remains a 'to-be-continued' cause? How long can we continue to demand this devastating sacrifice of the young and innocent?"

Kathy Gunson, who was stationed at the 85th Evacuation Hospital in Phu Bai was an emergency room nurse. She also was the evaluator of the cause of death for the Killed in Action (KIA). "One minute I had a friend, and the next minute I was determining his cause of death." She was also a triage officer, presiding over those who had been "triaged out"—left to die because they were so far gone. There were only so many nurses and doctors to work on those who might be saved.

"I desperately want my childhood back—with its innocence and ignorance. I want to go back to Vietnam and make it different," she wrote in 1979. "I want to come home to a marching band and a red carpet. I want to hear a 'thank you.' I want to hear 'I'm sorry.' " The nurse could no longer nurse. "I love nursing, but the sight of pain, suffering, and blood makes me ill, and I grieve because I can no longer cope with my feelings when I'm working." Above all, Gunson wanted to "feel at peace with myself."[2]

"What haunts me," says Van Devanter, "is that nobody knows of the contribution of these women. The major legacy study of Vietnam veterans does not include *one* woman. The mother of the boy who lost his face has no idea that somebody was standing and holding her son's hand. Even the ones who were triaged out, the 'expectant ones,' were not just shunted over to a corner. Somebody would always go and take their hand and speak to them quietly, just in case they *could* hear. The people of this country have no concept of that. Their sons might have died in vain for a cause that was horrendous—but they didn't die alone."

So little is known about the nurses of Vietnam that there are not even accurate statistics on how many were there. Official "guesstimates" range anywhere from 7,500 to 55,000. Like so many who had direct experience, Van Devanter decries Pentagon statistics, especially the DOD "official" numbers of women who served in Vietnam. "It is *absolutely inaccurate.* The Air Force doesn't even know, and the Army states 234 nurses. I know that for the one year I was in Vietnam there were a *minimum* of 500. For the years 1969 and 1970, the DOD shows a total of six in all of Pleiku! There were seven in my quarters *alone* in one year. There were a total of at least fifty-five or sixty just at my hospital, and that doesn't include any other outfits in Pleiku.

"Although animal studies show that females are more susceptible to the reproductive side effects of dioxin, not one female has been included in Agent Orange studies," adds Van DeVanter.

"In each town I visited, I've made a point of calling the VA hospital and stating clearly that I am a service-connected veteran of Vietnam and I require gynecological care. I was told by nearly every location that they did not have a GYN clinic or a GYN physician." The response of the VA is that since women comprise such a small number of veterans, it would not be feasible to provide such services—but that the women were entitled to receive government-paid service with a private gynecologist. Yet, Van Devanter claims, "In no case save one was I told that I was entitled to receive that care by contract service with a private physician—and that was only because I pushed it."

That was in 1981. Two years later, in March of 1983, for the first time there was finally a congressional hearing and a GAO report which indicted the VA for its lack of services and outreach for women.

Countless nurses did not know they had been entitled to GI education benefits. Unfortunately for most, the ten-year time period for qualification after leaving the service had expired.

Women who have served in the military have historically been ignored.

"When women tried to join veterans' groups, they were told they couldn't be full-time members," said Van Devanter. Not until 1978 did the VFW finally agree to permit women veterans to join as members. Some might surmise after such treatment, "Why would anyone want to join them?"—but women veterans should have the right to *refuse,* not be told they *can't* join.

World War II movies portrayed nurses as bravely waiting for their gallant lovers to return, with intermittent forays to the operating table. Or they were given saintly roles—epitomized in one movie where Veronica Lake walks toward a nest of hated Japs, a grenade inside her blouse, a sacrificial *kamikaze* blonde beauty who would save the rest of the hospital.

In actuality, World War II's massive mobilization brought 350,000 women into the service as well as many others who served in quasi-military support units such as the WASP, whose 800 women pilots ferried war planes around the world. They drove trucks, changed tires, repaired planes, and rigged parachutes; were gunnery instructors, air traffic controllers, naval air navigators, and nurses. The first WAC unit landed in Normandy thirty-eight days after D-Day. And sixty-five women were taken captive as POWs on Corregidor. Nurses were on the beachhead at Anzio. Studies of World War II women in the service showed that they developed psychological disorders less frequently than men, their venereal disease rate was one sixth that of men, the WAC pregnancy rate was negligible, and their disciplinary rates were much lower.[3]

During Korea, and then again during Vietnam, the unpopularity of the wars brought far fewer women into the military.

In all wars, women have been killed, maimed, disabled, and injured psychologically. No Vietnam nurses argue that they have a corner on this. However, Vietnam had its special characteristics. Nurses often suffered a more severe emotional mauling than soldiers who had respites in combat, as has been mentioned. They saw waves of the mutilated fresh from the battlefield, who in previous wars would never have been saved that long.

In this war, long on booby traps, gore was the norm.

Peggy DuVall, a New York State Vietnam veteran, remembers pumping blood into an eighteen-year-old who stepped on a mine. "Both eyes were removed, and his face was totally chewed up. He lost an arm and a leg. A shell fragment tore a hole in his trachea. When you finally saved a life," she said, "you wondered what kind of life you had saved. We could never have been prepared for that kind of nursing. We saw football-hero types with their legs blown off. We saw boys go home as vegetables because of crazy tropical diseases." DuVall repeats the words used by a remarkable number of former Vietnam nurses, "We put their bodies back together *as best we could.*"[4]

Many nurses tended to overinvest emotionally in their patients, even when the patients' chances of living were poor. DuVall, who worked in hospitals in Da Nang and Long Binh, recalls that on a 7 P.M. to 7 A.M. shift, two nurses and two medics would take care of seventy-eight men. Exhaustion and trying to build a wall around their emotions led to deep depressions for many.

"People don't want to hear about the blood and guts," said Cissy Shellabarger, "but that's all I know about, the grief. It was the first time I've ever been that frightened." In the emergency room of an evacuation hospital in Cu Chi, she worked around the clock during the Tet Offensive of 1968.

The morning in 1968 that the Tet Offensive began, mortar-rocket attacks thundered on the hospital. Still, the medical corps continued to work. Nurses saw soldiers with legs blown off who were in so much shock they registered no pain. Another Vietnam nurse, Sharon Balsey, says, "In U.S. emergency rooms you hardly ever see blast injuries. I just freaked out. Nothing prepares you for it. I never got to the point where the mutilation of bodies didn't bother me."

Many Vietnam nurses still recall how affected they were about working on men so young, in this teenage war, where the average age was nineteen.

During Tet "I've never seen so many wounded in my life. It reminded me of that scene in *Gone with the Wind* where all the wounded are lined up for miles around the railroad station," says Shellabarger. "And the rumors were so bad—that Saigon had fallen, things like that . . . Not knowing the truth was the worst."[5]

There are seven nurses' names on the Vietnam Veterans Memorial, but that small a number of dead does not fully convey a sense of the daily fear of death or injury. There were no front lines and few rear areas. Although the antiwar movement made much of American pilots bombing North Vietnam hospitals, enemy mortar-rocket attacks on U.S. hospitals were by and large overlooked in the States and formed no part of antiwar rhetoric. For nurses, mortar attacks meant the nightmare of trying to get the wounded under cots, of working in horrifying conditions, of not knowing if they would be hit.

"In the central highlands, the physical danger was there all the time. The VC would sometimes bomb the hospitals just out of harassment," said Van Devanter. "Oftentimes, they would bomb the hospitals intentionally, trying to kill a high-ranking POW who had been taken, who was injured and in the hospital. You knew if you had any NVA over the rank of major, you could *count* on rocket attacks all night long."

Many of the women went because they believed in their government, because they believed in a Florence Nightingale role, or for adventure, for the sense of helping. Many seem to have been Roman Catholics trained to believe in authority. "If our government said we were helping to stop communism," said one, "who were we to question?" Many returned pacifists; others upheld the view that the war was right but that the toll was terrible. "I was very hawkish at first, but later I was ready to say it wasn't a prosperous war. The cost in terms of life was terrible. The Vietnamese weren't willing to fight their own war. We should have left Vietnam earlier," said ex-nurse Sharon Balsey. No matter the viewpoint, disillusionment was there.

A rather typical reaction was from a nurse who cannot recall whether she was for or against the war when she went. "I just wanted to go and nurse." After her second day in the emergency room, she said, "You looked at one more of those boys, and you knew we were in the wrong place." She is still tormented. "Vietnam was really hard on me. I did not bounce well." She refuses still to confront her emergency room memories.

Certain differences separate the women from the men who served in Vietnam. First and foremost was the already mentioned ordeal of facing shattered casualties. "Medics had more in common with us than combat soldiers," said one nurse. The women often felt isolated because they were relatively so few in number. And there was a confusion of roles. On the one hand, women have been taught from childhood that it is okay to express emotions. This sometimes helped them. Together, the nurses could get drunk and cry. However, most of the time they had to negate those emotions in order to function. Most nurses recall, almost astonished, their toughness, the wall they were forced to build. However, they were also expected, as Shad Meshad explained it, "to be warm fuzzies."

A former Army psychologist in Vietnam, Meshad pioneered the Vietnam veterans psychological readjustment counseling outreach program. "Nurses had to be a wounded soldier's mother, wife, girlfriend. They saw these beautiful young eighteen- and nineteen-year-old kids, coming in every day with sucking chest wounds and ripped-off flesh, and they had to hold their hands and tell them everything was okay."

Like the soldiers who shot back, they wanted revenge.

For all the pain, nurses also recall a terrible nostalgia for the most intensely emotional time in their lives. Romances were often an attempt for a moment of closeness and tenderness; of escape, in a world gone mad.

As officers, they were not supposed to date enlisted men. However, most male officers were older and married. "I don't know how many times a doctor would tell me he couldn't bear to say goodbye to Jeannie, who was maybe twenty-two or twenty-three and deeply in love," recalls Meshad, who has, since Vietnam, counseled some 200 ex-nurses. "They'd ask me to do it for them."

"Above all," said Meshad, "the nurses, brought up to nurture and protect others, felt like failures because no matter what they did the GIs kept dying."

In some ways, the nurses' homecoming was worse than that of the men. Ignored by the VA and rejected by service organizations, they were also looked at askance by men who thought they were "combat-boot feminists" or who speculated on how many times they got laid in that world filled with men.

Van Devanter and other Vietnam-era nurses still bristle at the image of nurses in Vietnam. "To many in the States, I was either a lesbian or a hooker —the 'Did you have a good time, honey?' sneers." Later Van Devanter found out that even World War II nurses had experienced similar reactions.

However, there was a major difference. A startling majority of Vietnam nurses repeat how much they too were stigmatized for going to this war. Dean Phillips, who was a special assistant in the VA under Max Cleland, said, "Arch-conservatives often did not recognize the contributions of women because they think women shouldn't serve in the military in the first place. On the other end of the spectrum there was disdain for anyone associated with Vietnam. Where was NOW, for example, when women veterans were denied membership in VFW until 1978? Nowhere."

Like the men, many of the women had time remaining in their tour of duty. In Vietnam they were respected for their work and in crisis situations performed as associate doctors. In the States they returned to rank-and-file pettiness. "I went to Walter Reed—there was so much rank at that hospital, you could get bursitis from saluting," recalls Van Devanter. "I was sent to the hemorrhoid room!"

When Vet Centers came into existence, nurses were overlooked until persistent nurses persuaded male counselors that they too were suffering from emotional problems and delayed stress. Like male veterans, many had trouble sustaining careers, marriages, or relationships. "Walking through Vietnam" (reliving their experience) was the solution for those who finally received Vet Center therapy.

One of the few research papers on Vietnam nurses is sobering. Eighty-nine Vietnam veteran nurses were asked to complete an exhaustive survey in 1982. An astounding 97 percent complied. Approximately one third of post-traumatic stress symptoms were identified by 25 percent or more of them as *presently* occurring between ten and thirty times a month. Some 27.6 percent reported having suicidal thoughts between one and nine times a month, 19.2 percent reported feeling depressed between fifteen and thirty times a month, 16.1 percent reported feeling an inability to be close to someone they care about between fifteen and thirty times a month. And 70 percent of those who reported having experienced stress symptoms stated that those symptoms are still present today.

"It is difficult to ignore this cry for help and understanding," concluded the researcher. Still—as with most male veterans—the nurses also wished to stress positives. Many wrote that personal and professional gains were made in the harrowing but maturing year they lived through Vietnam."[6]

One former nurse exemplified an extreme case—the horror of having to wait too long for help. Like some unfortunate male veterans, before delayed stress was recognized, her preliminary, incorrect diagnosis was schizophrenia. Norma Griffiths-Boris spent nine years in a mental institution and endured forty-five shock treatments. In 1983 she told her painful story to a congressional committee after leaving the institution. She was, by then, married, pregnant, attending college, and a member of the VFW.

Vietnam veteran nurses remain isolated among women their age. An intragenerational split between the women who went and those who didn't crops up—just as it does for men. "I had antiwar female friends who persisted with 'How *couldn't* you know what we knew?' You were constantly considered stupid for going. A very dear friend ran that by me again just last year," said Van Devanter. "And I said," adds Van Devanter with a slightly caustic tone, "that not everybody had the extraordinary ability to be so perceptive and be in the right classrooms at the right time, hearing the right information from the right professors. Who the hell are you to tell me that I should have believed someone in a classroom before I should have believed my government?

"Where are the antiwar people now that we need them—the ones who were saying 'Don't send our boys?' or 'Bring our boys home'? None of them is supporting these [Vietnam veterans] projects or helping us to try to put ourselves back together again. And I was as antiwar as they were! And for better reasons. Because I *knew* what it was. They only knew what they read in books. I don't denigrate those who had a view that the other side were the good guys." Then Van Devanter adds what countless veterans have said from their first-hand knowledge, "But they were wrong. *Nobody* in that situation was a good guy."

Nonmilitary American women were in Vietnam too—volunteers who worked with Vietnamese civilians. They saw a different world than nurses or GIs, tended to be leftist, and empathized with civilian victims rather than the U.S. military.

Jackie Chagnon, earnest, intense, and in her late thirties, is still obsessed with the plight of Southeast Asians. She worked with the International Voluntary Services (IVS) in Vietnam. With her long, straight black hair and slightly almond eyes, Chagnon passed at times for a mix of French and Vietnamese. Passing as part-Vietnamese and speaking fluent Vietnamese enabled Chagnon to acquire access, friendships, and knowledge beyond the scope of most Americans.

Chagnon witnessed a form of war's destruction in Saigon that haunts her today. "Most of the prostitutes would not have been prostitutes had it not been for the war," she says emphatically. "When families lost their land, when fathers lost their livelihood, when they were shunted into refugee camps, it didn't take long for a fifteen-year-old to understand how she could make money. I fault the military greatly. If bars and whorehouses had been kept to a minimum, there would not have been an epidemic. There were five major whore districts and they made the areas unsafe. *I* was afraid of the GIs —can you imagine how a Vietnamese woman who had to go into those areas at night felt?"

Thousands of American-Asian children left behind, regarded as lost souls by the Vietnamese, is one tragic legacy. Another is the live-in Vietnamese girlfriend. "Often they were totally lost to the family after that. Many of them committed suicide. Sometimes a member of her family was fighting on the other side, and she was living with a GI, often to keep her family from starving. Many grew to love the soldiers, even though they knew it had to end. It was a tragedy for the men as well." At the time, however, she was angry at GIs who, she felt, had little interest in understanding the Vietnamese. It was an attitude fostered by institutionalized indifference. "The mere fact that the government allowed the women to be used that way proves what we thought about them as people.

"The undisciplined nature of the troops in Saigon, in terms of prostitutes, brashness, oafishness, didn't set well. Hostility between the GIs and civilians made our lives difficult, so we didn't want to be around them. The Vietnamese hated us, not because we were Americans, but because we were *there.*"

Naïve and idealistic, Chagnon was unprepared for such anti-Americanism. She had not been a part of the antiwar movement and "didn't even question our presence." After studying African affairs at George Washington University, Chagnon hoped to work in Africa. While waiting for an available job there, she took a temporary position with the Catholic Relief Service (CRS) in Vietnam. She resigned after six months because "CRS was working hand-in-glove with the U.S. government; civilian action teams were being used for political purposes. Vietnamese Catholics hated the CRS." Chagnon stayed in Vietnam with IVS, organized as a peace effort by churches in the fifties. By 1965, Hubert Humphrey called IVS "shirt-sleeve warriors." "I was shocked to learn that our classified documents were misused." (A male volunteer recalled writing an enthusiastic memo about ARVN deserters-turned-farmers that he was helping. He was horrified to find this information turned over to the South Vietnamese government, which apprehended the deserters.)

"I was not ashamed but confused about my presence in Vietnam," continues Chagnon. "I felt we exacerbated their condition. The U.S. government was pressing us to work in the refugee camps." She saw Vietnamese taken from their lands and ancestral homes to live without any means of support in camps. "It created a tremendous psychological dilemma. On the one hand, you'd say, 'My *God,* look at the conditions of these people, uprooted, in great need of help,' and yet you realized that the more you helped, the more staff the U.S. had, the more camps were being created."

When Chagnon came home, "I was no longer proud of having been there. I had this whole, lost, welling-up feeling. I had no idea how to express this—or what to do." Only then could she begin to relate to the feelings of returned GIs.

For the most part, painful empathy for innocent civilian casualties, rather than ideology, turned Chagnon against U.S. intervention. In all wars, civilians are the innocent sufferers. Pictures of staring British school children huddled in World War II bomb shelters have the same numb, old look of children being carted off to concentration camps. The faces of mothers gone mad with grief in Lebanon or El Salvador match the faces of Dresden or Guernica or Hiroshima survivors. Yet Chagnon felt there was a special brutal intensity to the destruction of civilians in Vietnam's guerrilla war.

"Napalmed children in Saigon's burn wards were *horrifying* to see." Remembering the famous indelible reminder of Vietnam, the photograph of a young girl, burned, naked, screaming down the road in pain and terror, Chagnon said, "She was one of the luckier ones—she got helicoptered out. Most of them died."

Chagnon saw Vietnamese mothers with their grotesquely deformed children—with spina bifida and cleft palates and clubfeet—now suspected to be the mutants resulting from Agent Orange poisoning. She remembers the one-legged children who had gotten too close to war. And she remembers what all this did to her. "After a year, seeing a crippled person—even a child—no longer shocked me. War scars were on every block. They no longer became horrible. That frightened me.

"There were a lot of emotional problems. At Bien Hoa Hospital there was a direct corollary—the number of people coming in with severe emotional problems would rise with the bombing. Bach Mai Hospital was really a whole area outside of Haiphong that had been leveled. I hadn't seen anything like that in Saigon."

Back in the States, Chagnon tensed every time she heard a variation on the mere gook theme of "Life is cheap to Asians." "Every day, all over the States, wherever I spoke, I heard that—or 'You must be a Communist.' It came from all ages and spectrums. 'But *those* people, they don't care about dying. Life is cheap to them.' It is a myth born of ignorance—starting with our concept of the Chinese hordes."

It also provides some comfort; such collective dismissal anesthetizes the reality of what war was doing to civilians. "I remember that scene in *Hearts and Minds* where Westmoreland is saying that, to them, life is cheap—and then they flash to a graveside. A Vietnamese mother throws herself into the grave of her child, just wailing and wailing." By then Chagnon had repressed much. She no longer cried at the sight of burned children. "Seeing that grave scene was my closest moment to a breakdown. I had totally repressed almost the exact same scene that *I* had witnessed—a mother throwing herself into her child's grave. Now I can never forget it."

Chagnon saw farmland and villages destroyed by bomb craters. "Do the American people know what the hell a bomb crater does to the country for years? Of course not."

"Tell them we are people"—that was the Vietnamese message that motivated Chagnon when she returned to the States in 1970. Chagnon and a handful of others toured the country, trying to tell Americans just that. Like many who had witnessed war firsthand, she was somewhat contemptuous of many in the antiwar movement. "We were frustrated by the way the movement patronized the Vietnamese. They too saw them as body counts, not people. We weren't talking 'Victory to the VC,' we were saying 'Look what is happening to *people.*' At Berkeley, they didn't want to hear about 'Tell them we are people.' They wanted to hear hard-core ideology.

"Some of the kids on campus were very, very torn and in the early stages had to question, 'Do I have the strength to go against my country?' By 1972 it was a different generation." Since the age of thirteen, they had been hearing it was a wrong war. "As opposed to those who came of age earlier, they knew it all and were brash and intolerant. At one meeting there was a big argument over whether the VC flag should be carried. I was with a group of Vietnamese students who were against the war but felt it was inappropriate for Americans to carry it. Why on earth were we arguing about *this?* It wasn't our flag. It was not our right to say 'Victory to the VC' or 'Victory to Hanoi.' It was for them to decide."

Chagnon was one of three in a delegation that went to Hanoi in 1974 and was asked by mystified North Vietnamese, 'Why do you Americans carry our flag?' We had to admit we didn't agree and that perhaps our young people did not understand the importance of symbols. But I remember turning scarlet."

For the most part, Chagnon was trying to reach average Americans with her message. "I found people in rural or smaller communities far more humane and reasonable about their feelings than those in college." She toured America's heartland tirelessly, talking not only to church and peace groups but facing the unconverted, the Kiwanians and Rotarians.

She agonized about making the Vietnamese experience live for Iowa farmers. "Few in America know what it is like to be completely uprooted in twenty-four hours. I would say, 'Suppose you have three, four acres at the most. That your ancestral graves are here and sacred, everything dear to your life is here, just as it is for you in Iowa. And one day a notice is suddenly dropped from the sky [as indeed, pamphlets were dropped in Vietnam] that commanded you to go to Chicago in twenty-four hours. That said your land will become a free-fire zone and anything remaining will be bombed. *That* is your option. So you make the decision to go to Chicago and you live in an encampment, vainly trying to find a place to live. There is nothing for you— no work, no way to make a living, just a squalid camp. The next thing, your son is hauled off to the draft, and your daughter ends up becoming a prostitute to support you.' "

She explained bomb craters to American farmers in high school auditoriums who had never seen one. "Imagine a 250-pound bomb in the middle of your field. You have no tractor or plow, and you have to fill it in by *hand*. It is as big around as this room and as high as this ceiling. That hole remains until you fill it in. It would take a month with ten people working *around the clock.* Now multiply that by the thousands and thousands of bomb craters in Vietnam and think how long it would take to make those fields whole again."

Chagnon felt she reached many. "They cried. They felt pain for the Vietnamese. Especially the elderly. I described the reverence with which the elderly were regarded in Vietnam, and here were these American grandparents, often away from their families, living in homes for the elderly." She told of the bond of family in Vietnam. "Most can't afford the medical care. Still, when one goes in the hospital, the *whole* family goes. They are out of work, out of school, totally committing themselves to watching over the family."

On her tours, she finally found her own bond with former soldiers. The like-minded tend to gravitate to one another, and so Chagnon's experience with veterans is far different from that of someone who supported United States intervention and finds veterans who share that view. Still, Chagnon insists that among the thousand or more veterans she met, "well over half *profoundly* felt as I did—that we shouldn't have been there. In nearly four years of speaking, everywhere I went, there were veterans who said they wished they could go back to help those people."

Going back has been Chagnon's life for years. Like many deeply affected by the war, she cannot let go. She makes frequent trips to Laos, returned to Vietnam in 1978 and 1981, and is "obsessed" with the idea of normalizing relations. Her life has been threatened by militant anti-Communist Vietnamese who settled in America, have their training camps, and dream of returning to claim their land.

Only a small number in yesteryear's peace movement have spoken out against the torture of political prisoners, the suppression of dissent existing in Vietnam today. Often those who once decried such violations of human rights now insensitively overlook them. They contend that these are the trade-offs for more food, better education, an end to warfare. Chagnon is one who obdurately brushes aside communist repression, using the familiar litany to deny the negatives: the "tension between North and South" is "not being handled properly." Reconciliation is "always a hard time." She speaks of America's ravaged South during post–Civil War Reconstruction.

"Many suffering in Vietnam are the very ones we went to 'save,'" says Chagnon, decrying our policy of no aid to Vietnam. "Not all are here as refugees, by any means. We destroyed an entire economy, displaced thousands with our bombs, necessitated a dependence on foreign aid—and then pulled out. We did that to Laos, and we did that to Vietnam.

"When I visited Vietnam, the biggest change is that they are able to return to their homes and rebuild their lives. Living where their ancestors lived is of monumental importance. The tension has greatly reduced. They are not being attacked on the roads, not being bombed."

For herself, Vietnam shattered a faith in her government. "Vietnam took me out of political diapers. It was a very hard lesson to learn—that not everybody loved us or that we were doing best for them." She worries that "we are now passing on the whole error of it all to our youth. We're doing the same thing to Central America now. We fought a 'secret war' in Laos from air bases, with bombs, and never sent the troops. Now it's the same kind of crazy intervention."

4 Women at the Barricades

UNDER THE BANGS LIES A FAINT BATTLE SCAR—THE RESULT OF thirty subcutaneous stitches that closed a gashing head wound more than a decade ago. A policeman hit her on the head during an antiwar riot at Harvard.

"It was a rite of passage. I was proud of it. I still am. It was a test of courage. 'Girls could get wounded in the cause too.' "

The woman, now in her early thirties, was speaking to the "general weirdness of being a girl in all this. Our life was never on the line; *we* weren't going to war." Since no one could accuse them of self-interest, there was a certain purity to their protest. "On the other hand, as women, we were slightly less credible."

She is a classic example of a certain woman of the sixties who embraced the antiwar movement both for its political cause and because it was *the* thing to do. Precocious, with high SATs scores, she went to Harvard at sixteen and immersed herself in that cauldron of elitist dissent.

Her father was an officer in Vietnam for eighteen months while she was in college. Her boyfriend's father was a "well-known war criminal" in the Johnson administration.

Her mother was a history teacher. Her father was in the Quartermaster Corps in charge of petroleum distribution. "He was not a militaristic type and was never very passionate about the war. By the time I got to college, being radicalized was a rite of passage. My first date was a political meeting. It created a sense of belonging.

"With the arrogance of youth," she recalls, "we just blithely threw out the past. We were enough in numbers to create our own culture. We were the beneficiaries of such wealth, and our parents beat that gratitude into us. It seems laughable now, but then we really did feel terribly, terribly guilty about the material things. That's what the blue jeans and torn clothes and living in communes were all about."

Like many of her colleagues, particularly the men who pulled some scam to get out of the service, she asks to be anonymous. She wants to be honest about her feelings at that time and yet betrays her chagrin by not lending her name to those feelings.

For her there is a guilt about her excesses in "what was in many ways, a horrible, horrible time. I still will not forgive myself for the pain and agony I caused my family. I was thoughtless, arrogant, horrible, hysterical, and unbelievably selfish." She laughs. "What spoiled brats we were!"

"We were so busy rejecting everything, we couldn't look at *anything* the way our parents did. Anything accepted by them *had* to be rejected—and in the harshest light.

"We were challenging the justification of everything—whether to have children and get married. All these things that were 'givens' to an older generation were options to us. In a way I miss that time. There was a kind of vigilant skepticism. To be against the war you had to be against the corporations profiting from it. And we really thought those companies were going to kill us."

At Harvard she was being taught a new history that did not always paint the United States as pure—from the frontier treatment of American Indians, through civil rights, to Vietnam. In this "extremely stimulating intellectual climate," her thoughts were quickly formed. Harvard represented the most avant-garde war protest. "We were among the extremes, both in attitudes and lifestyle. What I would consider liberal now, *we* considered arch-conservative. Someone who wanted to get out of Vietnam but didn't want the NLF to win was a conservative/moderate. People who disagreed weren't permitted to speak; they were shouted down." The First Amendment practitioner ruefully says of such tactics, "Somehow we managed to figure out *that* was okay too. We were all over the political lot: Marxists, Trots, Stalinists. It was *'faction du jour.'* We all thought we were there to balance out the other."

By the time she entered college, the war had become a four-year battle. Particularly at Harvard, there were no moral uncertainties, no soul searching about disobeying "God, Dad, and country" faced by those just four years older. The easy rhetoric of ills about Saigon's corrupt government and U.S. imperialist aggression made the North "by default" the group to support. It was an earnest position. Still, the intensity of war protest became a convenient catalyst for the troubled. "Not that we weren't against the war—but the ones who really went overboard were looking for a reason to go. The war was the excuse for whatever problem—'The war ate my homework,' 'The war is the reason I'm sitting in on a Saturday night,' 'The war is why I'm strung out on acid.' It was a lot easier to find oblivion in those times. It came in a lot more brands." The war, the movement, and the response to both formed a "kind of a political Rorschach. Whatever was there [inside you] came out."

Unlike some who viewed the sixties with self-righteous humorlessness, the Harvard woman has the ability to satirize the adolescent excesses during the Vietnam era. She sounds like a character in *The Return of the Secaucus Seven.*

"At cell meetings, we discussed everything from Che and Ho to 'relation-ships.' "

A particular target is the men and women then in the throes of the new sexuality and new feminism. "At one consciousness-raising session," the woman recalled, "some guy said the woman he lived with was having an affair with his best friend. He didn't say anything angrily, didn't say she was a bitch. Instead it was this gentle, 'Well, I feel kinda hurt. That's probably real terrible, but I, you know, just can't help it . . .' And then this woman got up and screamed, 'Jealousy is a *bourgeois emotion!*' and said that he had no right to oppress his woman for sleeping around. I laughed. The others didn't see the irony—that we are all fallible people, that we couldn't root out that jealousy if you really cared about someone, and here was this poor schmuck *apologizing* for it."

Another time, the feminists were asked to support a harassed radical trans-vestite—"this guy who wore tits like Nike missiles, eyelashes out to here, blond wigs. Here we all were, pallid feminists who couldn't wear *any* makeup, wouldn't shave under our arms. We were supporting not only this transves-tite's right to exist but his right to look like a 'sex-object' bimbo too. But hallelujah for it. In many ways it was a ridiculous but grand time to spend your youth."

The war was the centerpiece for much of the social change in her circle.

"We were having such a good time being young, but there *was* enough fear, especially when the lottery system came in, and you had gotten a low num-ber. I remember seeing a lot of fear drowned in drugs—pot, tons of LSD, a lot of mescaline, not too much coke. I did a lot in a relatively short period. By my senior year, I wasn't doing much at all."

She laughs and repeats, "It was a wonderful time to be young. Think how many times you got laid." Unlike some men who now feel the campus sexual revolution was a boon only for them—allowing them to treat women as sex objects while hiding behind a patina of equality—she argues that females were equally rewarded.

"Six of us pondered the best way to lose our virginity. 'Should you do it with someone you love or just friends?' There was a lot of emphasis on not associating sex with love in order not to get these two things confused."

Like all "war-time romances," the excitement and intensity of antiwar demonstrations brought heightened sexuality. They were, many felt, in the center of their own war zone. "Making love in the dean's office—there was nothing else like it." One couple were so in the throes of mad love after the ultimate triumph of helping to occupy faculty offices at Columbia that they decided to do something hopelessly bourgeois—to get married. They sent for a Jewish chaplain—who turned out to be such a liberated rabbi he didn't believe in the institution of marriage. Another was called for, who tied the knot, and the couple spent their honeymoon in one of the faculty offices.

For most, romance certainly didn't mean marriage, although the Harvard coed defends their sex as far different from the late seventies "your-place-or-mine?" casualness. "It was never with strangers but with friends."

Interspersed with the fun was the "need to feel depressed. You put on your depression when you put on your battle jacket," she said wryly. "How could you *not* be depressed when all this was going on in Vietnam, etc?

"It's hard to make a generalization, but everyone I know was marked in a way by Vietnam." Part of this effect, in their vacuum-sealed world, was a tribal togetherness. "You recognized them as 'my own.' Someone would walk in wearing jeans, flash the peace sign, and you knew a lot about them. The death knell was Kent State. It wasn't fun anymore."

By the time she was a senior at Harvard, in '72, the outsiders, the soon-to-be "next generation" were arriving. The freshmen looked at her crowd of war protesters and said, "Gee, tell us what it was like." "The very next class, Harvard tightened up. They didn't want any more rebels."

The former Harvard coed turns serious. "Our story looks silly and trendy and trite—unless you realize how *real* the anger was. We were very affected by the war and what it was doing." The surface manifestation of rebelling—clothes, sex, drugs—had to be studied within the context of politics, she says. A few years later, their counterworld had been sadly co-opted—without the purposefulness of political statement. "Our sexual freedom meant something until coldness and manipulation got transmuted into it. Without ideology and politics and a core of friendship based on that, it would have been shallow and ugly. The male ponytail was a political statement, but then long hair became 'mod' and co-opted by Madison Avenue." Everyone's mother was wearing designer jeans. Parents were smoking pot at dinner parties. It was "fashionable"—drugs without shared commitment; counterculture trappings divested of political content. "It was very sad to witness."

She was a foot soldier in the movement, a camp follower who nonetheless sincerely believed. She winces at remembrances of carrying the NLF banner but adds that nothing, even the repression in Vietnam today which she abhors, justified the United States involvement.

She was then, and remains now, untouched by personal knowledge of Vietnam veterans. The cocoon of Harvard gave way to Washington, D.C., where she joined like-minded college graduates who roamed the marble corridors of Capitol Hill and populated the Carter administration. It remains a "we, they" world.

"I wouldn't know them [the veterans] anyway. They didn't go to college with us. I don't have that sense of 'division' you talk about. I just never run across them. At Harvard I knew it was a working-class war. I felt sorry for them. The officers, I hated. They were educated and knew what they were doing. I thought *they* were criminals." The detachment surfaces as she talks of student deferments. "As a class [we felt] it was just an extension of our privilege."

Still, Vietnam "changed my life—in the way I questioned everything, in the sense of involvement in something greater than myself, and in the sense of my outrage." The experience of being on campus in that volatile time "gave me a sense of irony and humor, of just not accepting everything. Without the war I don't think journalists of our generation would question so much politically. There's precious little to show for it personally now; lately I think I'm going to want to get involved again in some cause."

She vacillates on the long-term effect of their campus upheavals and attitudes on today's society. "On up-days I feel there are a lot of lasting effects. The country is more aware, more skeptical—and we did help to generate that. There was the impetus we gave to the consumer and women's movements. We created a generation of people who went into the government as healthy skeptics. It didn't work too well under Carter, but at least we were trying. But then there are times when I think we made absolutely no difference whatsoever."

She is bitingly honest about personal growth. "We let people clean up after us for quite a long time. More so than any other generation, I feel. I think I'm rather average, and I felt like I was hostage to Peter Pan." There remains the image of herself, a young adult, "liberating" a newspaper vending machine by putting money in for one paper, opening it, and passing all the others to her friends for free. Trashing and ripping off were excused as justifiably taking from the establishment.

She regrets a lack of "intellectual discipline" today. "We were used to not having any—part of the 'spoiled-brat' routine." Although a cliché, that view is stated so often by many who did not go to war that it contains some validity.

She mentions another cost of the counterculture. At one of America's most prestigious centers of higher learning, she indeed received a partial education. "My education really suffered. We were on strike half the time. I would have loved the luxury of burying myself in books and studying." She roars with laughter as she recalls the occasional nonactivist in her midst. "There was this beautiful girl majoring in pre-med—the only thing lacking was a sense of humor." One day some of the women raced in, ready for the streets, eagerly asking, "Are you *striking?* Are you *striking?*' The beautiful one looked up from her books as if from another planet. 'I don't know. You could call me *attractive*—but I wouldn't call me striking.' "

At the opposite end were those who totally involved themselves in antiwar work or the sixties counterculture. "There were a lot of deaths—psychic deaths as well as suicides. People who went off to communes and never came back, people who burned out."

She delivers a rather common complaint of women in their thirties—most of the men their age seem selfish, immature, lacking in commitment. "There are a lot of hollow men in our generation." She dates an older man.

Still, enough of the women in her generation are marrying to produce a major change in the demographics of motherhood. For the first time, there is a decided increase in the number of births after the age of thirty-four. The women and men who bought their own rhetoric about not marrying, not having children, immersing themselves in their careers and freedom, recently have switched in droves. Sometimes they display the same maddening self-righteousness and smugness about their new roles as they once did about the former. At one time, they thought they were the first generation to *be* children—now many think they are the first to *have* them. As if reinventing the wheel, they write first-person magazine and newspaper articles about parenting and how difficult it is to combine careers and motherhood and fatherhood. Every minutiae of the experience is looked on, once again, as their special province.

"One thing I feel guilty about are some of the women older than us who *listened* to us. One I know exemplifies this. She has an idea of 'happiness' we now know to be bogus—'freedom, liberation, and therefore living life to the fullest.' She took her cue from us—got her divorce, is in her group therapy, etc. She is unhappy and filled with psychobabble. She bought what the kids told her. The older people weren't *supposed* to listen that hard.

"Out of the mouths of babes? What did we know?" She pauses. "The babes were on acid."

There is no "typical" woman of the Vietnam Generation who did not go to war or did not have a brother, lover, husband, or father in Vietnam. Some were married and mothers, and watched reports of Vietnam on TV with detachment. Others went to conservative colleges and viewed the beginning of the women's movement and female antiwar protesters with disinterest or disgust. Even among the antiwar women there were vast differences—from larky fellow travelers to dedicated full-time organizers whose education suffered. The older members of the generation, who marched and sat-in during the civil rights movement, agonized about their position on the war and came to it after serious analysis. They often felt light-years away from their brasher, younger female cohorts.

"I was in civil rights in the early sixties in east Texas—the only place that had a tacky civil rights movement. I'm going to write my memoirs, *Nobody Ever Came.* Just a bunch of uppity 'niggers' and a few of us white kids thrown in jail. It was hotter 'n' hell, and I was so fucking scared."

That is the recollection of Mollie Ivins, now a columnist for the Dallas *Times Herald.* "I was for civil rights and against the war, and people *told* me I was a liberal. Some told me I was a Communist. Of all the people I knew on the left in the sixties, I was one of sixteen who had read Marx and Lenin, and I was *no* Communist."

Ivins traveled east to Smith in 1962, studied in France her junior year, and went to Columbia's Graduate School of Journalism in 1966. The size and scope of her first antiwar march in the North astonished her. "There were thousands and thousands of people, a lot of students and teachers and *professors* in the streets, and *politicians elected to office!"* The lone liberal from

Texas was now marching along with an army of activists. "I thought I'd died and gone to heaven."

A move to Minnesota brought her in touch with more activists, including friends who went to jail rather than Vietnam. "God, we took it so seriously and worked to exhaustion." The next age group was the "straight Nam generation who didn't have a focus on civil rights and were one-tracked and angry about the war. After them came the youngsters who had no sense of history at all. They were the ones who trashed windows and were clearly angry now at a lot of other things—personal, psychological things. But the war was the catalyst. I remember older people asking me, 'What's *wrong* with the kids today?' And I'd say, 'If you end the war, it will all go away.' And when it did, so did the crazy stuff. It was a bad war."

Understanding that did not preclude anger at their antics. "There was another generation—*beyond* Vietnam—druggies, dropouts, so fucked-up. I didn't like those kids any better than the right-wingers. Those younger ones, so intolerant of soldiers and veterans, were so lacking in history. It never even *occurred* to me to blame the soldiers. All I could think was 'You ignorant little twits!' "

The sixties brought a profound searching and changing of attitudes on what it meant to be male. In antiwar circles and on most campuses, the traditional male virtue of fighting for your country without question was deeply challenged and rejected. Women played an important role in determining what were regarded as attractive male traits. Instead of the World War II song playing up the sexiness of being in the service—"You're 1-A in the Draft and A-1 in My Heart"—the sixties woman on campus bought the antidraft sexual slogan, "Girls only say yes to boys who say no."

Susan Shaughnessy, a student at Georgetown University in the late sixties, remembers the soldiers from nearby bases who used to come into a local college pub. "They'd sit around and drink beer and try to pick up girls. *Nobody* had anything to do with any guy with short hair. I used to feel sorry for them. They were the same age as everyone else and *clearly* shunned." The management took to putting them in faraway corners or a back room. The word must have passed around at camp. Shaughnessy saw fewer and fewer of them attempt to come in.

For some women there was an incredible whipsawing of emotions, depending on what circle they were in at the time. Nancy Balz was married to a man who graduated from the University of Illinois in 1968. Graduate-student deferments were dropped. So were marriage deferments. He tried to get into VISTA but was drafted just days before. The draft meant one thing to them, infantry. To be "enlisted meant [there was] some element of choice." So he enlisted and taught journalism. "The Army had one of the biggest publication systems going. We met any number of professional journalists who got in to avoid being shot at. The crunch was that Dan taught people who then went to Vietnam. He felt various guilts and relief. There was a bizarre, professional abstraction about it. In part he was torn—out of professional curiosity—maybe he should go where the action was."

By the time her husband was drafted, Nancy was deeply against the war. "I told him, 'I will go along as a person, but I will *not* live on a base.' I never shopped in the PX or visited military areas. I tried to abstract myself from being there—by physically not entering."

"Vietnam changed my life. It changed my view of the government. I consider myself a patriotic person—then and now. But I went from a naïve view that my government could do little wrong to the view that my government could do *colossal* wrong. Yet I am suspicious of people who didn't have *personal* experiences related to that period when it comes to any discussion of the military or government."

Her in-laws were "rabidly anti-Communist." Did they understand Dan's not wanting to go? "No-o-o. I don't think they knew how bad it could be." The war, more than the sixties social upheavals, affected her. "A lot of other parts of the sixties didn't have much bearing on my life. When you live in Illinois . . . ," she says with a laugh. After watching TV and seeking reasons for the war, she said, "It became so apparent to me that people were getting shot, maimed, killed, and doing it to other people for nothing. That was the horror of it."

Ricocheting from relatives who didn't understand, to an Army base she didn't want any part of, Nancy Balz found yet another explosive situation.

"Dan was out of the Army, in graduate school on the GI Bill, and we went to a neighbor's house for a drink. There were three couples and one fellow. There was a feeling of great relief on our part that Dan was out of the military. The other couples had been at the university the whole time. One person asked what the single guy had been doing lately. He responded straightforwardly. 'Seventeen days ago I was in Da Nang, watching people get shot.' He had been part of a helicopter crew.

"Well there was this gasp, and one of the women said, [and she mimics the woman's horrified tone] 'How *could* you do that?' He replied, 'How could I *not?* It was my job.' The woman launched into a tirade at him about the whole war. He slouched lower and lower and just stared at her. One of us, Dan or I, jumped in: 'The guy didn't want to do it. Hear something more about him before you condemn him as a killer.' I remember saying to Dan, 'I can't stand it here with these people jumping on this guy.' " Her husband felt he had to support the veteran and mentioned that he had been in the military too. "It turned into a heated, but general discussion, and after thirty minutes or so, we left." Her voice still rises as she recalls that incident, and others, where friends safely deferred launched into tirades about veterans and her husband being in the military.

Women in the antiwar movement became media stars—from singer Joan Baez and actress Jane Fonda to extreme radicals and anarchists who advocated violent revolution, like Weathermen Bernardine Dohrn and Kathy

Boudin. Others, less visible among the bomb throwers, like Jane Alpert, blew up their buildings, then became wanted fugitives who traveled underground and surfaced in the eighties to write about their experiences. Yet all along there were other women—nameless and faceless to the press—who threw themselves into the antiwar movement with dedicated passion. They were the reasonable, the caring, who did not make headlines. Like many veterans, some feel they were war casualties who lost time. They got off the track, but the train kept going. Curiously, while veterans feel they were discriminated against for having gone to war, many of these women feel they were also discriminated against because of their far-left credentials—especially as the country moved more to the right.

For most involved in antiwar work, writing a résumé in the mid-seventies became a game of artful dodging. "Only the top leaders landed jobs with the Carter administration. On the West Coast, the welcome mat was not out," recalls a former activist who wants to remain anonymous. "Frankly, I'm not at all anxious to portray myself as the agitator I was." She is in her late thirties and has been "trying to get legitimate for three years." Friends told her to rewrite her résumé when she came to Washington. She played up her skills—she was a superb editor of a sizable magazine—but deemphasized that they were acquired on a left-wing publication. She told her prospective bosses, "You might not agree with the content, but you have to admit I have the skills and experience." She attended both Harvard and Berkeley graduate schools but never acquired a master's, dropping out for antiwar work. She is now overqualified for her current researcher's job. "I'm doing the kind of work I used to *assign,*" she says ruefully.

In many ways, she epitomizes the best of the women of her generation. Intelligent, gentle, thoughtful, she pursued antiwar activism with passionate and sincere intensity. She uses the constant phrase of many who sided with the NLF: "We were naïve. We idealized the 'noble Vietnamese.'" She sighs. "'If America was wrong, then they *must* be right.' There was no in-between. There was a real lack of ambiguity. Still, even if we had known it would turn out *exactly* as it did, our job was to get the U.S. *out.*"

Some of her friends still work with causes. One female friend slogged through years of postwar schooling to catch up and become a doctor. Others, like herself, had not reckoned with either the shifting tides of conservatism or the heavy psychological toll of being an outsider all those years. "A lot have never left. The more their vision of the world isn't validated, the more they are convinced they are right. Getting an establishment job is still viewed as anathema to them."

During the war there had been a wrenching separation from parents and a brother in the Army. If her brother went to Vietnam and she continued to march in the streets, her mother warned she would not be welcome at home. She told her daughter, "I will never speak to you again." There was intense conflict; *she* could not understand how her mother could let a son go to Vietnam. Her brother did not go, but it took years to reunite the family.

For her, a demonstration was no Saturday-night revelry. "I took it terribly seriously." There is a touch of envy for those younger, less committed, who went on with their lives. "Even now, in their early thirties, they are young enough to start careers and families." She is approaching forty and knows that she will never have children. A marriage she has had, though not a documented one. She lived for a decade with an antiwar activist. When they parted it was, for her, like a divorce.

For women like her, Vietnam put her personal life on hold. "It didn't just interrupt your career, it could screw it up." During the early part of the seventies, she continued to speak out against the war—for a leftist radio network, newsletters, magazines, and became a foreign-policy analyst. By the late seventies, leftist views were out of fashion; few places would give her the benefit of believing she could separate her expertise from her beliefs. "Dropping out and spending ten years of your life very *actively* against the war doesn't seem the best résumé for a job."

She lacks both a strident self-promotion and the arrogance of some in her age group. "You talk about people who thought we acted superior. I'm sure we *acted* that way—but I felt I was the 'enemy.'"

They were the outsiders—the hunted, the chased, the beaten. The women would dress for demonstrations; would wear heavy work boots and jackets to catch the blows, wetted handkerchiefs to cover the face and eyes when the tear gas came. It was an experience women in the generation before and those in college now, with their designer labels and sorority pins, could never know.

Polls consistently show that demonstrators had little backing in the country. Middle America eventually tired of the war, but they disliked student demonstrators even more. Those who viewed them as troublemakers seldom saw the confrontation through the eyes of students. Some drove police to a frenzy, true, but many of the dedicated rank and file were victims of non-provoked attacks—chased into corners of alleys or buildings and then beaten. Many still recall the terror of being trapped by police swinging wildly with their clubs.

"I remember a demonstration when Dean Rusk was speaking at the Mark Hopkins [hotel]. It was the first time the police used *attack* techniques to stop us. They just started chasing us. *Anyone caught was beaten.*" The concept of free speech and assembly was gone. "They chased us into a little chapel. I knew they could get in and beat the crap out of us, and we couldn't get out. A priest came out and talked to the police, and they let us out. They shot a demonstrator in People's Park. At Berkeley, they had to rotate the National Guard constantly. They were our age, and they didn't want them fraternizing with us." The police on attack were fearsome to this woman, barely 5'2". "They wore masks, helmets, and came down fiercely."

Mollie Ivins recalls the same reaction, the unleashed rage. "I had great admiration for good cops and great loathing for bad cops. There was that whole class thing, that generational hostility. Older cops would eye these long-haired kids, certain they were 'getting a lot of pussy.' I saw some ugly stuff—cops deliberately going after women. It happened to me in a couple of demonstrations."

Being an "enemy" of the establishment provoked a sense of lawlessness in the California activist who was clubbed and chased into the chapel. "Why was I bothering to stop at a red light? Why do I obey the law when they would beat the crap out of me if they could? We were outlaws in America. We assumed our phones were tapped, assumed half our friends were agents. It affected me for a long, long time."

Reentry into the establishment world was frightening. A wariness remains. It is vastly ironic that veterans and some women who fought so hard against the war would turn up in the eighties as survivors. They lived through a searing period as unwanted outsiders.

"I'm not saying it is anything as bad as veterans who can't find jobs, but believe me it has been hard. For a lot of people, taking up your life again was not easy. *Almost no one talks about it!* Imagine what we believed! For a long time we thought and were told, 'You're all privileged. You can do this and pop back in, whenever you want.' It just wasn't true. You had to be almost irresponsible—turn away from your personal goals."

After the war, she staked everything on a nonestablishment magazine that might have remained rewarding if it had ever become solvent.

She realizes now that she "never thought through what I was going to do with the rest of my life. The movement was an all-absorbing thing. I didn't stop to think *ever* what plans I should have. *Thinking personally wasn't highly regarded.* Living in a commune, working on the war . . . There wasn't much time for yourself." Her voice gets a bit firmer. "I feel I gave a whole bunch of the best years of my life to that. Now I do not think of myself as an activist or an organizer. Now I have to put my own life together."

Jane Fonda remains the point-woman for the wrath of many veterans. The right, incorrectly, blame the whole antiwar movement for her actions. In any gathering of veterans there will always be an expletive for her. Even some who turned antiwar cannot forgive her for embracing Hanoi, for posing on one of their tanks. Dean Phillips, a much-decorated antiwar veteran, explodes, "Fonda did irreparable damage to the antiwar movement. She pissed off 80 percent of Americans not on the fringes. People needed to hear it from the guy who fought it—not those assholes at Yale whose biggest decision was getting Daddy's Mercedes and Fonda, who was not in danger of starving to death. There she was criticizing the capitalistic system—which is the hallmark of hypocrisy."

In the late seventies, Fonda further created discord by refusing to join Joan Baez and other antiwar activists in lending her name to an ad decrying the fate of Vietnam's boat people and those oppressed in Vietnam.

Today Fonda has moved on to making more millions as she deflabs the overweight women of America with her "Work-Out" books, records, and video cassettes. Most of the women who went through her regimen in 1982 have no idea that they were in fact subsidizing the political career of former SDS leader Tom Hayden. Fonda contributed handsomely to her husband's 1982 million-dollar-plus campaign for an insignificant state assemblyman seat.

When Hayden was deriving fame and power through antiwar leadership, women were discovering a cruel truth. Lip service to equality did not mean they joined the council of decision makers. Often excluded from meaningful roles at the top, many turned to the feminist movement. The civil rights and antiwar movements emphasized a heightened sense of injustice and—at least in rhetoric—created a more receptive climate for the women's movement. The rebirth of feminism was a welcome niche for those who had been burned by chauvinism in male antiwar ranks.

Margery Tabankin was a University of Wisconsin activist from 1965 to 1969 and later visited Hanoi. The first woman president of the National Student Association since 1947, she was elected on an antiwar platform. She recalls that "Hayden was my hero. We revered these guys. It was like 'what could we do for them?' When Hayden got off the plane to make a speech in Wisconsin, the first thing he handed was his dirty laundry and asked if I would do it for him. I said, 'I'll have it for you by tonight.'"

Tabankin became one of the few women organizers, joined SDS, and helped coordinate the 1969 Moratorium. "Part of being a woman was this psychology of proving I was such a good radical, 'better than the men.' We felt we were motivated by something higher because we didn't have to go to war ourselves. Most guys didn't take women seriously, however. They were things to fuck. We once did a questionnaire to check reasons why students were drawn to antiwar rallies and demonstrations. One reason frequently checked was 'to make social contacts.' You went through this intense experience, and you went back and had sex." People forget that the women's movement was fledgling at the time. "It [sex] was much more on men's terms."

Despite such aspects of second-class citizenship, the antiwar movement gave Tabankin a sense of heightened consciousness: "You had the right to have opinions about anything—including your government.

"I got beaten up badly covering one of my first civil disobedience rallies for the University of Wisconsin paper. Seventy people were hospitalized," says Tabankin. "We were protesting Dow Chemical on campus. Kids were sitting in a building, refusing to move, and the cops walked in and shouted, 'Everybody out—we'll give you three seconds.'

"They started busting heads, and everyone just totally freaked out, running to get out, clustering in panic at two doors. I got hit in the stomach with a club. Because I was injured, I was the only reporter to get into the emergency room. I ended up being the person the New York *Times* was calling in the hospital to tell them what was going on, how many were injured." Her eyes still shine, recalling the moment. "I was, like, ecstatic—but on the other hand, my friends were hurt." The experience radicalized her. "I remember saying, 'I've had it with writing about things. I'm going to *do* it.'"

Tabankin abandoned everything for antiwar work. There are great gaps in her education. "For two semesters I literally never went to classes. Borrowed notes and took the tests. We were really self-righteous. We knew a better world, and we were going to make it. That wasn't even negotiable. Our demands were to stop the war, to guarantee the poor an annual income and racial equality. We really created in our minds what the world should be like. *It was my whole reason to live.* I found a passion in my life I never knew was there. Realistically, there were about 100 major activists out of 40,000 on campus. The rest were like soldiers who marched."

Like some other women who threw themselves totally into the movement, she is somewhat envious of those who did not. "They had a much more integrated life. They still came to the demonstrations, but they were graduating and going on. The guy I was in love with—I really think one reason he would not marry me was because of my Vietnam politics—went on to law school and is with a very establishment firm. He really changed."

Tabankin recognized the less committed for what they were. "People get emotional when self-interest is at stake. Young people didn't care enough when their lives weren't on the line. I'd say 5 percent felt intensely passionate about the issue."

She recognizes the deep schisms between some antiwar leaders and the radical left. She agrees with those who view Sam Brown and Tom Hayden as pragmatic manipulators thrust into prominence by the movement. "Some were only for stopping the war, but one faction of SDS got so caught up in being against the system and for economic and racial change. They saw this as totally interrelated. Then you had crazies splitting off, anarchists, and terrorists. I was between the SDS and the student government type. Although a little more to the left of student government, I wasn't totally an SDS person. Many in the Mobe viewed Sam Brown and Al Lowenstein as sell-out pigs. We just didn't see it, the polarization, then. We were so caught up, we didn't see how destructive it was."

Tabankin was arrested seven times and finally became a burned-out casualty. She dropped out of activism and went home. "The greatest luxury was having my mother's housekeeper do my laundry." She became a community organizer for youth projects, raised money for foundations, worked on two union-reform efforts for miners, and became head of VISTA when Sam Brown became Carter's director of the Action agency. She defends the activists of the sixties and sees ongoing commitment. "The same 5 percent *then* are the same 5 percent of our generation still working for causes—toxic waste, nuclear freeze, trying to get progressives elected. Much of it is grassroots."

The attempt of some in the media to lump "the generation" as idealistic causists was a mistake. "There never *was* a 'generation' that really meant it. Many didn't give a shit, then and now. Most got caught up in the time period —but it wasn't based on ideology, it was based on events. They weren't socialized then and they aren't now."

Today Tabankin, in her mid-thirties, is herself opting for profits while working for causes on the side. In 1981 Tabankin and Bill Danoff, author of the song "Country Roads," formed Danoff Music Company. They represent twenty-four Washington-area songwriters, plugging them to Los Angeles and Nashville producers and singers. They also manage a few bands. Tabankin's biggest coup was selling a song by Jon Carroll, Washington rock musician and songwriter, to Linda Ronstadt. Carroll's "Get Closer" became the title track of an album that went gold in 1982. The single made the Top Twenty. Tabankin tries to make a vague connection between yesteryear's activism and today's entrepreneurship. You need "commonsense networking skills" in both fields, she says—who to contact and how, what will be effective. One difference, however, is the "profit motive."

Tabankin feels she acquired strength and self-confidence during the sixties and has been able to transfer organizing skills into business. The negatives? "It became my whole life, and I lost out on normal, lasting personal relationships."

The negatives for the generation? "People want to make it more than it was. Civil rights didn't change the fact that blacks still have problems, the women's movement doesn't mean women have equal rights, the antiwar movement doesn't mean our foreign policy isn't going to go totally crazy in the near future."

As women activists recall that era, it is striking how negatively they regarded American soldiers. "As we turned against the government, we turned against them as symbols," said Tabankin. "That was our biggest mistake. That was stupid tactically. The compassion wasn't there; the expressed view was that 'I don't want to get killed, and I don't think *they* should go do that.' Instead of the government, we blamed the foot soldier. If I have any regret, it's the way we treated them." At the time, reviling soldiers was part of the tactic—such as war-crime tribunals—to heighten the perception that the war had to be stopped. "You had to be for the North if you wanted the people to win."

Tabankin looks back with some chagrin at her naivety. In 1972, as part of a delegation to Hanoi, she was imbued with the concept that the war was nationalistic in origin and had remained so. "I was witnessing destruction of civilian life. I saw their hospital forty-five minutes after it had been totally demolished. The ambulance was taking out the dead and living. That was in May 1972—the scariest time of my life. There were bombing attacks at all times of day and night. We brought the first footage out of North Vietnam and sold it to '60 Minutes.'

"The North Vietnamese didn't want us to meet with POWs. We pushed and pushed and made ourselves obnoxious, and we saw ten of them," recalls Tabankin. "They looked pale but healthy. One black had heard that Wallace had been shot and was interested in that. Another asked me to go back and tell his wife he was all right."

The prisoners said little about their treatment; it did not even occur to Tabankin at the time that they would have major difficulty expressing themselves with North Vietnamese officials in the room. The accounts of torture that emerged after POWs' return demolished reports of those who had seen them under such carefully controlled conditions. We talked of Susan Sontag's ecstatic descriptions of the "gentle captors" of the North. Tabankin winces slightly, then reiterates, "It was so easy to be naive."

The range of opinions among those twenty-seven million women who came of age during the Vietnam Generation was clearly vast.

Some dropped the sixties with a vengeance, like those who populate Jerry Rubin's Manhattan mix-and-mingle salons. Rubin, yesteryear's Yippie trying to make it in the eighties as an example of the "Me" Decade Meets Wall Street phenomena, is a "networking" party giver. He talks about money, power, and "leveraged" women. "Leverage in financial terms is when a small amount of money controls a larger amount of money. Leverage is therefore power. I'm into leverage. Now Barbara Walters is leveraged. She speaks, you know, and people listen. Right? Huh? You get it? The leveraged woman."

Those serious in the movement always viewed Rubin as a member of the comic fringe, much overplayed by the media. They are not surprised that he shed his antiwar activism like an old worn overcoat and speaks without a scintilla of idealism about past motivation. "I get very nervous talking about the sixties. Who wants to live in the past?" More than anyone from the sixties antiwar, antiauthoritarian movement, Rubin epitomizes the view of one cynical observer: "Money is the long hair of the eighties." One evening incipient leveraged men and women—eager imitations of high-fashion gloss—moved around at one of his "networking" salons, handing out business cards as they used to pass around joints. Pat Frazer, who said she is a "commercial actress," spoke in a super-modulated voice and seemed to epitomize the women present. What was she doing? "Anything I can."

In the sixties, "Jerry was my ideal. At college I was involved. Now I'm involved in the eighties. You're on your own—and all of a sudden it's 'getting for yourself.' I'm interested in taxes." She had no quarrel with cutting social programs for the poor and disadvantaged. "That's okay. My priorities are now in defense and space." And in the sixties? "Then I was anti-American." Because it was chic? "Partly."

Of course there are other sixties women who wouldn't spend a minute at Rubin's mixers or embrace his values. They may be involved in careers or motherhood rather than issues—but they do not negate their past. Others remain active in causes. For some, a need for personal peace followed radical commitment. In 1983 a bright college graduate in Washington summed up the feeling of many taking time off to be a full-time mother. "I gave my *all* to the movement, but now it is time for myself."

There are a small number of men and women in the generation who came from opposite sides of the barricade and fell in love. Women who marched in antiwar demonstrations and supported men who dodged the draft have ended up marrying veterans. Generally, the men are those who also turned against the war. Occasionally, as in the case of the wife of a former West Pointer and Vietnam veteran, Tom Carhart, it is the woman who changed. Carhart led the fight against the Vietnam Veterans Memorial "black-ditch" monument. His wife feels now that she was "brainwashed" in college and didn't know the full facts of the war.

For most, a bond comes from having actively participated in an intense period; no matter their differences at the time, the veteran and a deeply involved antiwar woman can sometimes understand one another as many on the fringe cannot. In its way, the empathy is not unlike that between veterans and men who dissented and went to jail. Both groups can understand the sacrifices and dedication of the other.

Susan Shaughnessy was a Mobe marshal during the 1969 Moratorium. "There I was with my arm band; went to marshal school. October 1969. God, that was a great one! Toward the end, demonstrations became something of a 'happening'—but even just lending your presence to such a demonstration is not something to sneeze at."

She is bitter about others "climbing the ladder" while veterans were fighting. "The people who went to Vietnam lost their place in line career-wise and in many cases are still several places behind where they ought to be. We sure did a double-punch on those guys."

Her husband, Charles A. "Shaun" Shaughnessy, served with the 199th Light Infantry Brigade and then as an ARVN adviser from September 1968 to August 1969. He saw duty at Parrot's Beak, An Loc, and the Cambodian border. As an infantry platoon leader, he never lost a man in action. He returned "in time for the 1970 recession," Shaughnessy says caustically. Many veterans, job hunting in the early seventies, felt they were victims of Affirmative Action. Even those with hard-earned master's degrees felt they were shunted aside as veterans and were passed over for the magic "twofer" —black women.

Fired as the "last-hired" from a National Park Service job because of cost overruns, Shaughnessy began as a technician at the Archives of the United States and he is an archivist in the Military Archives Division. In his résumé, Shaughnessy includes a tongue-in-cheek reference. His interests list includes American wars "(particularly those where the uniforms were interesting and the issues clear-cut)."

Shaughnessy became president of the Washington Vietnam Veterans of America (VVA) chapter. He is a clear-eyed skeptic about some of the war tales he has heard. "I can't figure out where all these atrocity stories are coming from. I certainly never heard or witnessed anything."

Shaughnessy was especially disillusioned by Vietnam. "He had intended on a military career," says his wife. "Never considered doing anything else. A lot of Southern boys are like that." After the war, he no longer had that desire. Shaughnessy studied history at the University of Richmond before Vietnam and knew Susan slightly at the time. While he was in Vietnam, she transferred to George Washington University in Washington, D.C., and immediately experienced culture shock. "When I came up here, I was in rah-rah support of the war. I was a real brownie baker, letter writer—even to boys over there I barely knew. I thought all the kids protesting in the North were raving traitors." A sardonic edge comes to her voice. "I just *knew* my government was benevolent, integrity-ridden, and was presided over by statesmen of vision."

Her friends in Washington "fixed up my clothes, my hair—and my head. There were two strains of consideration—first, 'Should we be over there?' and the second was just the tremendous mismanagement. I had a sense of foreboding, listening to the guys I knew coming home about the way it was being run, that it was all misguided."

Her activism lasted until "the radical elements, like the Weathermen, repelled me. Plus we were graduating in 1971 and '72." She deadpans, "Why, we found out you had to *work* nine to five—and do it fifty weeks a year and only get two weeks vacation! I still went to demonstrations and hung out with the antiwar crowd—and I was dating Shaun."

They were in no hurry to get married and dated from 1971 to 1976. She became a speech writer for the American Petroleum Institute, worked for an advertising agency, and is now a freelance editor of trade newsletters.

Meanwhile, her husband found a vital friendship with Vietnam Veterans Against the War (VVAW) members. "There was the personal camaraderie and a sense of being sickened by the waste." After VVAW fell apart, Shaughnessy had fewer friends to talk to. When he got his job with the National Archives, his wife says, "He was called in and interrogated about his VVAW activities."

Shaughnessy kept his bitterness to himself, avoiding rather than denying his experience. When they married in 1976, Susan knew almost immediately there was trouble. "He would walk away and not address any problems. He was afraid of losing control; he might cry, might hit someone. He was *afraid* to be angry, afraid he would do something in a rage." Her tough humor got her through some bad times. She laughs as she recalls, "When a friend asked if I was going to leave him, I said, 'No—I'm going to stay—and make his life a living hell.'"

Through Vet Center counseling and active leadership in the local VVA, Shaughnessy "vastly improved" his outlook on life.

Susan learned many things about her husband. "The war itself so shook the certainties of someone who really needed those certainties. He thought of himself as an officer, a man with a purpose of high ideals—and then saw a total waste."

No matter his feelings on the war, Shaughnessy, like countless veterans, found it personally maturing. He knew the bitterness that engulfed veterans when that experience was so devalued on their return. "Leading a platoon in Vietnam is *definitely* 'management experience,'" says his wife.

The negatives of living with veterans—their inability to express their problems, their fears of unleashing anger, their inability to settle the past—are overshadowed by positives, Susan Shaughnessy feels.

"There is a difference between those who went and those who didn't. They [veterans] are people who know more of what is and isn't important. There is more depth—a lot less frivolity. Many of the men who did not go seem to be preoccupied with life's minutiae." She quotes a thought that Samuel Johnson penned to Boswell in 1777. "Depend upon it, Sir, when a man knows he is to be hanged in a fortnight, it concentrates his mind wonderfully." In many Vietnam veterans, she finds such a sense of concentrated purpose.

"And they can enjoy the smallest things of life too, in a way many cannot. Anyone who has been in combat can enjoy a clean bed and a good meal probably better than anyone I know."

The class division of the war created friction between some in the emerging women's movement and returning veterans. Leaders in the women's movement had little or no firsthand experience with anyone who went to Vietnam. For them it was simple to cavalierly dismiss veterans' preference in civil service as discriminatory. In the early seventies, when returning veterans needed all the help they could get, various women's groups, particularly NOW, opposed laws which gave extra points to wartime veterans applying for civil service jobs. For example, the Federal Women's Program Committee of the Denver Federal Executive Board questioned whether the law was consistent with equal-employment rulings—acknowledging that those who were drafted "may have suffered disruptions in their normal lifestyles." That understatement enraged combat veterans since draftees comprised 60 percent of U.S. Army dead from 1967 through 1970.

Dean Phillips, special assistant to the VA director (1977–81), said, "Women were not beating down doors to demand entrance into the armed services during Vietnam." Phillips noted that women who served did not make up the 2 percent quota then established for females. They too would have been entitled to veterans' preference if they had entered the service. "Treatises on sex discrimination often ignore perhaps the most blatantly sexist policy in our country's history," said Phillips, "the limitation of the drafting of those who will die and be crippled in combat exclusively to the male sex. At no time during the war did any women's organization file any lawsuit claiming that restrictive draft or enlistment laws injured female employment opportunities by making it more difficult for women to serve in the armed forces. After virtually ignoring the issue of the male-only draft during the veterans' preference debate in the late seventies, NOW president Ellie Smeal made a fool out of herself in 1981 by claiming that past exclusion from the draft had discriminated *against women.* Feminists, who *avoided* service during Vietnam, were now saying that their younger sisters are discriminated against by not being included in draft registration—something *they* wanted no part of during Korea or Vietnam."

Phillips, an ex-paratrooper who went on long-range patrols in enemy-controlled areas with the 101st Airborne Division in 1967–78, won numerous decorations, including the Silver Star, Purple Heart, and two Bronze Stars. During law school in Denver in the early seventies, he had a compatible relationship with NOW. He even received letters of appreciation from them for his active support of the ERA. That union was shattered when NOW refused to alter its 1971 position of opposing *any* and *all* government laws or programs giving special preference to veterans, even those badly maimed in combat. Phillips points to a letter from NOW's national headquarters confirming in 1979 that the 1971 resolution—with no modifications—was still their official position. Phillips assisted in the defense of the constitutionality of veterans' preference—which was ultimately upheld by the Supreme Court in June of 1979.

Phillips contends that NOW's opposition to all forms of veterans' preference was a tactical error that helped defeat the ERA in several crucial states. "The two-million-member VFW passed a resolution opposing the ERA in *direct* response to the NOW resolution opposing all forms of veterans' preference. Then VFW people worked effectively against the ERA through their contacts with state legislators. Sure, they would not have been *for* the ERA in any case—but they wouldn't have even gotten involved to oppose it if it hadn't been for NOW's position."

Other veterans, less active than Phillips, also felt that the women's movement should have left veterans' preference alone. "In one way I felt the government was back to pitting all of us minorities against one another in a fight for jobs," said one combat veteran, "but we felt the women didn't understand what we had been through."

Today, in urban centers like Boston, New York, and Washington, there are curious permutations of friendships from the Vietnam Generation. Ann Zill, who helps spend millions in liberal causes for Stewart Mott, had a brother who was injured in Vietnam. One of her closest friends is a Marine combat veteran who argues vehemently that the United States should have been in Vietnam and could have won. Zill herself was an antiwar activist.

Ann Broderick Zill, the oldest of four children, grew up in a small town in Maine. Her father was a "corporate mogul" who worked for Chevrolet. At Barnard College in New York, she was among the early war protesters. Zill had violent arguments with her brother, Peter Broderick, five and a half years younger, about the war, and was devastated when he joined the Army in 1968 and became an officer. Two months into Vietnam, he was "literally blown up" and spent nearly fifteen months recuperating. "He lost a whole lot of his intestines and had a colostomy for a while and has 60 percent permanent disability, and he basically does nothing with his life," Zill said in 1981. "He's a town janitor and plays a lot of tennis." For a man loaded still with shrapnel, she says, "He's in very good shape."

The wounded brother and the "knee-jerk peacenik" sister were forced to confront each other's views. There was a night in 1981 when their mother died. The Irish Catholic family had always been able to drink and fight and laugh together. The drinks came heavily that night. "Peter was sobbing and reliving the Vietnam War, and this is 1981." Did he come to a political point of view? "He views it through a very small slit of consciousness. He does not deal with the larger moral questions. Yet I suspect that if pressed to the wall now, he would be able to say some things were fundamentally wrong with the war—but he's never been able to in the past. He's scarred by the war.

"We don't fight now, but we used to back then. He was a young kid, and I could *not* believe that he believed in this war. I argued that it was stupid and wrong for us to be involved."

All the time her brother was in Vietnam, all the time he lay in the hospital, Zill marched and worked for peace. "I felt very conflicted. I watched this man of six feet two, who now weighs 190, go to something just over 100 pounds. Skin and bones and could barely walk. He kept getting pneumonia." His agony reinforced her feeling that the war was wrong. "But I couldn't talk about that with Peter. He didn't want to hear that. He liked to tell war stories and make us laugh, and I had to laugh at the damn fucking war stories whether I wanted to or not. I will *always* believe that war was senseless."

Her brother tells a story of a marine whose injuries were so overwhelming that he was encased in a plaster cast. For nights he kept begging for a knife. Broderick was convinced the man wanted to commit suicide. Then one night the marine, whose face was bandaged except for his face and mouth, yelled, "I can't see, I'm caught in a net and can't get out." Broderick felt "deep elation. He *didn't* want to kill himself." He was trying to see. "I sensed a great pride in that marine; he hadn't given up. He didn't let my faith down. He was a fighter . . . never quitting the struggle or relenting an inch . . . I never saw him again, although he remains with me forever."

It is this emphasis on personal bravery and courage that fill the memory of many veterans, not the ideological rights and wrongs of the war. Ann Zill, unlike many women in the movement, was able to broaden her perspective through her brother, to understand the motivation of some who went. "He was a very good antidote for my overall sense that if you were for the war, you were crazy. He forced me to realize that a lot of perfectly reasonable people had been trained to believe it was your patriotic duty to defend your country—and that they believed this war was about protecting Vietnam from the Communists."

Zill is now divorced from the husband who "used to joke that he made love, not war, because that's how he got out. By having babies." As a father he was deferred. In 1981 she was dating a Mexican American who was too young for Vietnam and now organizes against the draft, arguing that blue-collar and lower-class youths would still be the ones to go. "The inequities would still be there."

Zill loved growing up in the sixties. "The spirit of liberation and of questioning authority. Vietnam shaped my life. One of my closest friend's lifework grew out of war protest. She now does analytical think-pieces about Indochina and Southeast Asia. And I haven't changed my basic view—although I like to think I'm more effective now. I work for a man who gives away about a million a year, and his first interest is to prevent nuclear annihilation. Trying to prevent another going-to-war exercise is a very sobering, humbling exercise. The peace movement today is *meshuggina*. It's a terrible failure, completely inadequate. The selling of the Pentagon was brilliant. They played to the psychological needs of this country to be strong and protected after Vietnam—even as life is crumbling all around." Zill was talking in 1981, before public sentiment had shifted to some degree against the government's excessive defense budget.

She is asked to assess the sixties movement.

"I'm somewhat critical by nature. There were a lot of arrogant kids. Sam Brown so turned me off that I have never been able to like him to this day, and I used to run into him at the same parties when he ran Action." Like many dedicated antiwar activists, she tried to overlook personalities. "My allegiance remained with the people who were trying to stop the war. And my efforts in that regard got more sensible as time went on. It never occurred to me to side with the North, but I can't blame those who did. Still, that is part of my brother's story. He was really rejected when he showed up on campus in his Army outfit one day because he had to wear it to get some discount on the cost of something—I've forgotten what. But how vilified he was!" She points up an important psychological reaction of many veterans in similar situations. "That made him cling to the *need* to defend that war longer, I think, than he would otherwise have done. And so that's an example of one of those great ironies about how much campus condemnation exacerbated and helped polarize an already tough situation. Yet I understand those people who did it."

Zill is not too optimistic about generational reconciliation. "You need to bring the extremes together, and I'm not sure that can happen. I doubt that I would ever be able to say that my sympathies are with my brother, who believed in it as he did. On the other hand, I will defend to the death his right to think that way. Maybe if more people can understand someone like I can my brother, there *will* be a coming together."

One of the problems of the Vietnam Generation was a tendency to stereotype, to divide into monolithic clumps of "them" and "us." Vestiges of that thinking remain. One female antiwar activist enjoys a close friendship with a veteran—but irreconcilable differences cloud it.

"We all viewed each other back then as some faceless mass. To the veterans, we were a faceless mass who treated them like shit. Just as I criticize people for not seeing *us* as individuals, we didn't see *soldiers* as people. We just wanted to stop the war. We felt so defensive, a minority of college kids clustered together. I remember being angry at the soldiers. It was good to say, 'Fuck you,' to let them know people didn't like it—that there were people who passionately *did not want this war*. We had a real macro view—do anything to stop it. We were more oblivious than arrogant about the classness."

She pauses to reflect. "We were lucky to live in a time when there was a social movement. As a generation it set us apart in an irreconcilable way—even as it caused huge divisions within the generation. Maybe as time goes by, and people don't know where Vietnam is once again, maybe it will bring us together. The fact that we lived through it, on one hand, is all of our touchstone with reality. For us it will always be—and for the veterans it will always be. And yet on another level, we are on opposite sides."

She sighs. "I'm still emotional about it, and so are they. One friend thinks he's better because he faced death and we haven't. I think there is something more important to life than being on a battlefield—I don't see it as the highest value of life, and yet I appreciate his feeling.

"People who fought and people who fought against the war were at loggerheads—but it changed our lives forever." She sighs. "Still, there is no settling of accounts.

"No one can lay it to rest."

Part VII
Vietnam Kaleidoscope

"Goodnight, Saigon"

BY BILLY JOEL

We met as soulmates on Parris Island,
We left as inmates from an asylum . . .
And we were so gung ho
To lay down our lives . . .

We passed the hash pipe
And played our Doors tapes . . .
And we held on to each other
Like brother to brother . . .

Remember Charlie, Remember Baker
They left their childhood on every acre
And who was wrong?
And who was right?
It didn't matter in the thick of the fight . . .

And we would all go down together
We said we'd all go down together
Yes we would all go down together.

1 Atrocities

"WHAT DID MY DADDY DO? HELL, HE WARN'T NOTHIN' BUT A WHORE-hoppin' drunk." Kenny sprawls on the chair, cowboy boots crossed. A USA belt buckle digs a furrow in his flabby belly; a Cat tractor hat is slung low on his brow. Red-tinged hair covers his arms, matching his beard. He looks past —not at—anyone. Kenny is doped beyond the beyond on the good grass he has cultivated in his lone garden in Alabama country wilderness.

He tells hard stories. Hard stories to listen to, undiluted in his fuzzy haze of drugs. He is a Southern kid who never had anything. Whose life, for good or bad, began and ended in Vietnam.

"Killin' goddamn gooks. That's the ultimate goal I ever achieved. When they put me in Vietnam, they got a damn zero to start with."

Kenny tells his story of atrocities and seems borderline crazy. It is disturbing, after all these months of being in sympathy with veterans, of liking so many of them, to meet someone who fits a "killer" stereotype. Kenny for years has sought relief through drugs and counseling—relief from the awful knowledge that he took pleasure in killing.

"I was a head man," Kenny drawls. "Cut a man's head off with an ax. It's not an easy task. I cut off twenty-one heads. We sold 'em to doctors and sech as that. They'd let 'em decay and have an actual skull they could use . . . ."

Atrocity stories are staples of all wars, a blend of fact and fable, legendary embellishments and folklore. Vietnam's guerrilla war—fought in the midst of civilians and in deep jungles where booby-trapped deaths left soldiers aching for revenge—created its own special brutalities, rules and ethics.

One former intelligence officer, skeptical of some of the stories, finally shrugged and said, "It's really hard to separate what happened from what didn't. Anything *could* have happened there."

Some would have you believe that My Lai was commonplace. Others vehemently contend that most of the stories are concoctions of those who never saw combat.

Vietnam critics produced a first in war: American soldiers recanting in front of war-crimes tribunals. For many Americans, no matter their revulsion to the war, there was something galling about Englishmen and Frenchmen (such as Bertrand Russell and Jean-Paul Sartre) calling tribunals to denounce America's role in Vietnam, given their countries' age-old record of brutal colonization. Sartre, for example, never suggested that France be brought before such a tribunal during *its* Vietnam War. Lord Bertrand Russell was, to be sure, a pacifist, but U.S. black writer James Baldwin—in general, a supporter of the war-crimes debate—wrote, "It might be considered more logical for any European, and especially any Englishman, to bring before an international tribunal the government of South Africa or the government of Rhodesia."[1]

Still, worldwide outcry over our presence in Vietnam underscored the fact that no matter what we could have won militarily, a large portion of the world would see no political or moral victory. And it underscored the differences about Vietnam once again—why the sense of censure pervaded many veterans. For some participants, the war-crimes tribunal brought cleansing identity. Others, caught up as media "war-crimes heroes," testified far beyond their personal knowledge. "We found one guy who would have had to have been in nine places at the same time for his stories to be true," said one veteran who participated in the tribunal.

No one could listen to Larry Mitchell and not be engrossed. He was a lieutenant in the Special Forces, he said. In 1982 Mitchell told me how he would sneak into camps and slit people's throats, including that of a young female Viet Cong sympathizer. Mitchell was captured, beaten, tortured; his ankles were shackled and bent so he could not sit or stand. One day following an escape attempt, his captors told him and another prisoner that they were going to be executed. "I and an Air Force colonel had to dig these graves. Then they bound our hands and the executioner stood behind us and I heard the click of the gun. I heard the shot. I was still alive. The colonel was not. They walked over and shot him again. They made me cover the grave. They didn't shoot me, for some reason."

The main reason was that none of it seems to have happened. Mitchell, as a member of Vietnam Veterans of America (VVA), was interviewed by national news magazines and television reporters; spoke at national Vietnam seminars. When a member of the MIA-POW became curious and checked the lists, Mitchell was not on any. The VVA confronted Mitchell—who had shown them a Xerox of discharge papers—and demanded that he verify his POW record and other stories. Mitchell never showed up again. "Believe me, we are a lot more careful now," said Rick Weidman of VVA. "We demand their Army record and keep it on file. It has a chilling effect on bullshit war stories." Mitchell is probably just one of countless hundreds who feel a sick need to exaggerate their role in the war. In their own way they demonstrate some need to belong to the most cataclysmic event of their time.

Kenny, therefore, is naturally viewed with suspicion, although the Vietnam veteran therapist who works with him feels his story is true. Kenny says he was in Vietnam during Tet 1968 on reconnaissance missions, roaming the jungles with small packs of soldiers.

He starts to tell in graphic detail of lifting an ax heavy with blood, after cutting off a man's head. *"That* affects me, lady.

"It was just a wild, mayhem thing. We had a guy in our outfit, Davis. Didn't smoke, didn't curse, didn't go after the whores. A guy you had to respect because he had so much will power." Kenny's head is low on his chest. "Davis kicked open a door of this old French building and was cut in two. When he was found, they had cut his head off and put it at his feet. And they had his penis in his mouth. The boys come back and said, 'Oh hell, Davis is a fuckin' *mess.'* The platoon sergeant, it really freaked him out. He just started screamin', 'Let's track 'em *down.'* We knew then he meant to kill anything—men, women, children, goddamn dogs, water buffalo. So we found 'em and killed 'em. I said to the sergeant, 'Bobo, what do we do now?' Tears was rollin' down. 'I want their goddamn heads,' he said. 'Just like they did to Davis. People in this area will *know* who we were when we get through.' "

I sigh. Another gonads-in-the-mouth story. Did *all* best buddies die that way? It is a legendary ultimate atrocity, described frequently, no matter when or where you were or how much action you saw. That and the pregnant woman shot in village firefights. When it came time for the body count, you turned over this body and discovered it was not only a woman, but a pregnant one. So you counted the baby.

After a while, both stories call for suspension of belief. Could there *really* be that many pregnant women shot, that many gonads-in-the-mouth executions? Yet they made the rounds of Vietnam then and in the States now. One reason for this is that they exemplify the two extremes of war's inhumanity. All those buddies mangled and mutilated, often booby-trapped after death by the VC, are distilled into the gonads-in-the-mouth atrocity. True certainly in some cases, apocryphal in others; a barbarous act made so commonplace in the telling that it could justify murderous mayhem as retribution. On the other hand, the pregnant woman "twofer" body count is usually told with revulsion for the U.S. government body-count obsession. "We" and "they." Committing atrocities together.

Kenny is mumbling. "Sometimes, sittin' down by my brook, I'm back in that country. I can see them damn *faces,* and I wonder, well, did that son of a bitch I cut a head off of have a family like I do? I have woke up screamin' to the top of my damn voice. Woke up chokin' my wife. I think about it, layin' there. I don't sleep much. I bet you don't run into too many guys that was up at 2 A.M., smokin' dope, watchin' 'Bonanza' till it burns out on the TV."

Kenny says he sought help from the VA years ago. "Them psychiatrists just tole me, 'You gonna have to get a *holt* of yourself.' I took them goddamn downers they give me and waited to pass out. Finally a doctor put me in a hospital. All they could tell me was 'You gonna have to get over it yerself.' I tried to tell 'em what was botherin' me, only it never was anything they could understand."

Talking through his war with one nonjudgmental Vet Center counselor has helped. "I can talk about gettin' behind an M-16 and just eatin' them sons of bitches up. It's the biggest rush you ever had in your life. I remember killin' this dude and knowin' the first round did it but still just goin' at it, goin' at it."

Suddenly Kenny lifts his head and demands, "Hey, lady, look me in the eye. I was taught to kill and I *loved* it." He stares, waiting for the reaction. I try to keep a passive expression. "You get a dude blowed away, and you see one of them slopes, and *goddamn! Revenge!*"

A man of no accomplishments before or after Vietnam, a man who wistfully fondles in his memories the power he once had, Kenny continues, "It was truthfully the highest point in my life—bein' successful in combat." Kenny was awarded the Bronze Star with oak-leaf clusters, the V for valor, and the Purple Heart; he says, "They give you a twenty-five-cent medal for *executing* those people. Calley, he did not do a damn thing we didn't do. We executed hundreds."

I argue that his experiences seemed very different than those of most combat veterans. He insists his are true.

Today Kenny sits on his front porch and shoots at cans. "Drive my neighbors crazy. They call me the 'Doper.' "

Do you feel you're crazy?

"No, ma'am. I'm *different.* I bet you think I sound like a dumb old hillbilly. Well, God, I'm proud to be a Southerner. My daddy tells me, 'Son, yer a fuckin' nut. They always pick us poor dumb sons of bitches to get shot up, and when they send you back, they laugh at you and don't want to have nothin' to do with you.' Now my daddy, he's *country.* Used to make moonshine. Never ever carried a Social Security card."

His reading consists mainly of *Soldier of Fortune,* the hardcore military magazine with its ads for mercenaries that sells well among a certain veteran subculture. "Oh God, I could imagine having a goddamn time now in El Salvador. You damn better believe we should be there. Here you got Cuba settin' ninety miles off the coast! I got a son of fifteen, and if he took off to Canada, Uncle Sam wouldn't have to worry about bringin' him back. I'd go get him and bring him back—in a pine box. I don't give a damn if it's a right war or not. I thought we was over there to kill Communists, and I feel like we shoulda never left."

It is one thing to fight and another to commit atrocities, but it seems all the same to Kenny. The thin line between civilization and barbarism endemic in wars seems embodied in Kenny.

How do you make it through the days?

"I rely heavily on drugs. Pot, Quaaludes, Seconals, amphetamines. I never heard of marijuana till I went to Vietnam. Hell, I'd never heard of *Vietnam* till I went to Vietnam."

He is a loner. "I don't have no friends. Me and my son have a good relationship. I've had a couple instances—these spells. One time I just shook him up against the wall, and I believe if I hadn't got a holt, I would have kilt my own son." There are tears in Kenny's eyes, and he lapses into silence. Kenny has a hard time living in the present for long. "I ain't had a thrill since I been home."

Finally, after all the protestation of loving the killing, Kenny says, slowly, "The worst part, I guess, was the senseless mutilation, senseless killing." The ambivalence is not overlooked. "I *loved* it, but I still realize a lot of it was senseless." Then, in a flat voice, "It was murder."

Do you hate yourself for doing it?

"Maybe not hate myself—but I think I'm *odd* for *loving* it. To most people, that's voodoo. Very few will tell you they enjoyed it. I *enjoyed* cuttin' the slopes' heads off. It was power."

He was seventeen and his wife eighteen when Kenny married her, before he went to war. His wife is waiting in the parking lot to take Kenny home. Her face is as pale as vanilla cream; hers is a washed-out prettiness, with curly blond hair and eyelashes so light they look dusted with powder. The look in her blue eyes is a combination of embarrassment and pain, as if she has tried to explain Kenny to herself and others for a long time now. Her Southern politeness made her carry on a reluctant conversation.

I ask her how she felt about his stories of atrocities, of killing with an ax, of liking it; whether she felt they were true. Her eyes, like some stray animal's, plead for comprehension. "When he first come home, it was hard to accept. But I know he was telling the truth. He had so many nightmares. He'd jump up, all in a sweat, and tell me till I knew it wasn't made-up. I try to understand. I've seen how he's suffered over the years."

Her voice is whisper-soft when she answers the question of whether she could understand her husband saying he enjoyed killing.

"It's hard to understand, but hearing him talk over the years, it's just something . . ." Her voice trails off. "It's been hard for him to get along, to control his temper. For just a few minutes, he really goes insane. His nerves has always been extremely bad since he come back. This is a main reason why we don't have any more children."

She speaks of the changes in Kenny since Vietnam. Before, he managed some small-town theaters, the last picture shows in town. He was gentle, she says. Now he occasionally works odd jobs and sells his homegrown marijuana. She is a cashier for a grocery store.

Kenny's wife fiddles with her sunglasses and says that for the first time there is some hope. She insisted that he come to the Vet Centers. "He never liked to talk about this to *anybody*. I'm surprised he comes down here every week, but it seems to help. I think he understands himself better. Even in the South we still have a lot of people who look down on Vietnam veterans. They just think they're off their rocker."

There were tears in her eyes. "I left him quite a few times." Her eyes plead once more. "I really don't think he liked it as much as he says. I think that's a cover-up. He's always felt like people looked down on him because he went to Vietnam. For some reason he wants them to look at him as though he is *really* bad. It isn't enough to just do it—he has to say he *liked* doing it. That way he tries to cover up his guilt feelings.

"You probably don't understand. He's just a wonderful person. He really is."

"History is a bath of blood. The *Iliad* is one long recital of how Diomedes and Ajax, Sarpedon and Hector killed. Greek history is a panorama of jingoism and imperialism—war for war's sake . . . It is horrible reading, because of the irrationality of it all." In ancient times, wars were waged solely for the sake of the ideal harvest ". . . To hunt a neighboring tribe, kill the males, loot the villages, and possess the females was the most profitable as well as the most exciting way of living." William James, the noted turn-of-the-century Harvard professor of philosophy, mused thus in 1910 about ancient man's inhumanity to man.[2]

As civilizations progressed, mere plunder no longer seemed sufficient justification for war. The moral quotient of the "cause" was added—as bloody excesses continued. Civil and religious wars through the ages are replete with unspeakably brutal tortures and atrocities. In modern times, since Vietnam, the Khmer Rouge have obliterated millions of Cambodians, "death squads" in El Salvador have wiped out whole villages, and the 1982 massacre of 900 Palestinians in Shatila showed the world once again those familiar forms— babies and women, arms and legs splayed in contorted, bloated death.

It has been said that America lost its virginity in Vietnam. A protective cloak of morality and mysticism made defensible whatever was done in World War I, World War II, and Korea. Propaganda always played a vital role in how Americans perceived war. One difference between World War II and Vietnam is that the brutality took place in a different context. A *Life* magazine photo is proudly displayed in a coffee-table anthology; a Japanese skull, like some exotic hood ornament, rests on a World War II tank. A PBS documentary on packaging American wars shows a World War II film clip of a bombed-out town. Stirring music accompanies the voice-over, proudly explaining that the destroyed town was caused by "American firepower—*your* firepower—so that no American town will ever look like this." There was no mention of whether the town was inhabited when that firepower descended, if children and women were there.

The savagery of the Pacific war is recalled by historian Paul Fussell, author of *The Great War and Modern Memory.* "One remembers the captured American airmen locked for years in packing crates, the prisoners decapitated, the gleeful use of bayonets on civilians . . . And the savagery was not just on one side. There was much sadism and brutality—undeniably racist—on ours. No marine was fully persuaded of his manly adequacy who didn't have a well-washed Japanese skull to caress and who didn't have a go at treating surrendering Japs as rifle targets."[3]

During America's Civil War, Yankee and Southern prisoners were starved by their captors. Who could forget Andersonville, where systematic starvation amounted to torture; where 40,000 Yankees died in subhuman living conditions.

With Vietnam, the elitist opinion and later the mass opinion came to be that we were the aggressors, at worst, or that we were mired in a hopeless war, at best. Therefore the brutality was *perceived* differently; we were visiting atrocities upon innocent peasants. In the field, the gray reality was that some of those "innocent peasants" *were* the enemy. Children were not to be trusted. One Army doctor recalls pumping the stomachs of two GIs who bought beer from Vietnamese urchins. The "beer" was battery-acid fluid. Children set booby traps and led the enemy to their positions. A 1968 Associated Press report tells of the North Vietnamese using children and women as shields in at least one battle—with Americans losing lives because they resisted shooting at them.[4] Veterans often tell their own stories of individual civilian attacks. Trained to kill the enemy, it was not long before they were indiscriminately responding. And in such an uncensored war, Americans at home witnessed much of it. Atrocities on the other side, however, were often difficult to uncover and report.

James Lawrence, a lieutenant who saw fierce fighting against the NVA regulars, says, "It really used to gall me when Jane Fonda went on about the horrible things Americans were doing after seeing some of the things the North Vietnamese did. They would souvenir-hunt; take weapons, clothes, boots. And they would mutilate bodies. The men who went back after the battle found Sergeant J——. (I would prefer you not use his name; I don't know if his family knew about this.) But they found him hung in a tree by his ankles and skinned, like you would a deer. Maybe they'd never seen a black before. I just don't know. We identified him by his gold teeth."

The ultimate North Vietnamese atrocity that we know of was the mass killing of hundreds at Hue during the Tet Offensive of 1968. Ours was My Lai.

No matter what the enemy did to our soldiers, My Lai punctured the pristine myth of American "goodness" in war; GIs were not handing out bubble gum, they were slaughtering babies. Color photos confirm the undisputable horror. A barefoot woman grimacing in terror, another clinging to her, a child cowering with wild eyes.

"Guys were about to shoot these people," photographer Ron Haeberle remembers. "I yelled, 'Hold it,' and shot my picture. As I walked away, I heard M-16s open up." In another photo, two boys, the oldest perhaps eight, are still alive, although crawling, wounded. "The older one fell on the little one, as if to protect him," said Haeberle. "Then the guys finished them." On the road, the bodies of nearly two dozen women and babies lay grotesquely toppled in their blood.[5]

Millions of words have been written about My Lai. Lieutenant "Rusty" Calley was defended by some on the right as "doing what he had to do" and by some on the left as a pawn in a systematic policy of genocidal warfare. For some it became necessary to show that "the other side did it too." Depending on the ideology of the writer or historian, the discussion of atrocities became a mental-gymnastics battle of words and statistics that continues unabated.

For many on the left who championed the North Vietnamese, *willing* them to be nicer somehow made it so—an attitude that was exasperatingly dense. Susan Sontag, for example, "loved the deep sweet silence of Hanoi" and felt that the "North Vietnamese aren't good enough haters"—a view the boat people just might not share. In a cloying essay, the North Vietnamese were described as virtuous and unflawed: "The North Vietnamese genuinely care about the welfare of the hundreds of captured pilots and give them bigger rations than the Vietnamese population gets—'because they're bigger than we are,' as a Vietnamese Army officer told me, and 'they're used to more meat than we are.' "[6]

American prisoners, when they returned, had their own stories, like that of Alabama Senator Jeremiah Denton. Two guards "began roping one arm from shoulder to elbow. With each loop, one guard would put his foot on my arm and pull, another guard joining him in the effort to draw the rope as tightly as their combined strengths would permit . . . The first pains were from the terrible pinching of flesh. After about ten minutes, an agonizing pain began to flow through the arms and shoulders as my heart struggled to pump blood through the strangled veins . . . Pigeye laid it (a nine-foot-long iron bar) across my shins. He stood on it, and he and the other guards took turns jumping up and down and rolling it across my legs. Then they lifted my arms behind my back by the cuffs, raising the top part of my body off the floor and dragging me around and around. This went on for hours . . . I began crying hysterically . . . My only thought was the desire to be free of pain . . .

". . . He pulled me to my feet and hit me several times . . . he indicated that I must rise whenever he entered. Bound as I was, that was no easy matter. The next time Smiley entered, I began pushing myself against the wall until I was on my feet. He beat me anyway, slapping me hard across the face and hitting me in the stomach . . . On the seventh day, I decided to give them something [biographical information]. I cried for help. Dried blood streaked my chest. Feces clung to the bottom of my pajamas, which were completely stained with urine . . ."[7]

At a 1981 reunion, former POWs glistened with prosperity, looking so healthy that it was hard to imagine that most had spent seven years in prison. There were occasional, brief clouds. Asked about his children, one stopped, smiling. "I lost them when I was over there. They don't know me." Ron Bliss, a Texas lawyer, looked at another former POW, Jack Fellows, and said, "He was my first roommate." He was not referring to a military academy.

They were together for nearly a year in the prison dubbed the Hanoi Hilton. "He was tortured so badly he couldn't move his arms for months." As Bliss moved off, Fellows said, "He saved my life. When I couldn't move my arms, he fed me, bathed me, clothed me . . ."

Daniel Ellsberg remains an outspoken critic of America's role in Vietnam, yet he recalls VC atrocities toward villagers, and the massacre of hundreds of Vietnamese in Hue. "Most of us never promised a rose garden if the North won. That was naive."

Such leftist naivety, creating Robin Hoods out of the VC and North Vietnamese, unfortunately fueled the right to tote up enemy atrocities as if to exonerate ours. Author Gunter Lewy attempted to cast the United States strategy of warfare in a favorable light and stated that "statistics for the years 1968–72 indicate about 80 percent of the [VC] terrorist victims were ordinary civilians . . ."[8] Critics of Lewy's book, noting that he documented from military records, caution that Vietnam was a war long on misinformation, subterfuge, questionable and corrupt Vietnamese intelligence gathering, and inflated body counts. Lewy states that a total of 38,954 civilians were reportedly assassinated by the VC.

Jeff Stein, an Army intelligence case officer who controlled a net of agents throughout Quang Nam and southern Thua Thien provinces from 1968 to 1969, recalled, "I never saw any after-action reports of civilian massacres in my fairly detailed summaries of what happened. The general VC methodology was to attack village military forces and assassinate the village chief. In point of fact, villagers were often absolutely complicit in the VC attack. It was strategy," not humanitarian dictates for holding back, stressed Stein. "You don't kill people you need as your friends in guerrilla warfare."

Lewy wrote that VC selective assassination, "occasionally carried out by disembowelment with the villagers forced to be in attendance," took place well hidden from Western journalists, "whose reports on wartime atrocities therefore inevitably lacked an element of balance. The killing of noncombatants through VC terror was "systematic and intentional," while civilian casualties from American warfare were an *incidental byproduct* [emphasis added] of general military tactics," he argued. Lewy conveniently overlooks the systematic and intentional Operation Phoenix assassination program of the CIA. His defense completely misses the point. However "legal" the military tactics, such as "H and I" (harassment and interdiction) and free-fire zones, an incredible number of civilians tragically became "incidental byproducts."

Lewy apparently feels there is some justification in pointing out that Vietnam civilians were killed on a par with civilians in Korea. Other historians decry the indiscriminate use of firepower in Korea, including napalm, which served as a terrible precedent for Vietnam. Korea was a war "unlike any in modern history. Over the last two years of the war, the United States dropped six times the tonnage used during the first year. Half the South Korean population was homeless by early 1951; over one million South Korean civilians died, many of them from disease and starvation in guarded camps. Several years later, from 1965 to 1969, the Vietnam War produced over three million refugees, the majority seeking to escape free-fire zones and America's rain of fire. The formerly neutral sided with the VC. "They say this village is 80 percent VC supporters," one American officer commented in 1969, as his men combed a village. "By the time we finish this, it will be 95 percent."[9]

The quantity of air ordnance dropped in January–October 1969 reached 1,388,000 tons. From 1965 to 1969, six and one half times the tonnage employed in Korea pummeled Southeast Asia. Added to that were ground munitions—well over a million tons in the first eleven months of 1969—and cluster bombs and fléchette rockets, defoliants, anticrop chemicals. "In an air and mechanic war against an entire people . . . barbarism can be the only consequence of American sledgehammer tactics," stated Gabriel Kolko, historian and analyst of American foreign policy.[10]

Even Gunter Lewy wrote, "There is reason to believe that the suffering inflicted upon large segments of South Vietnam's rural population during long years of high-technology warfare contributed to the spread of a feeling of resignation, war-weariness, and an unwillingness to go on fighting."

Turning Vietnam into a sea of fire from above, however, never had the same impact for the American, safe and distanced at home, as did stories of face-to-face brutality.

Daniel Ellsberg wrote of the contrasting moral values placed on "high" and "low" technology warfare—"a tendency to confine the applicability of the war-crimes concept just to such crimes of low technology" [as My Lai's face-to-face killing]. "This tends to absolve our use of high-technology weapons—such as B-52s, carrier aircraft, helicopter gunships, CBU bombs—which are our main implements of death" and are "regarded very highly by our culture." It would be politically difficult, he conceded, to include such firepower triumphs against civilians as Dresden, Tokyo, Hiroshima—"and the free-fire zones of South Vietnam"—in the notion of "crimes against humanity." Yet "it would be shocking and perverse to condemn only rape and murder in wartime while continuing to tolerate the strategic bombing of noncombatants." Ellsberg called for taking the war-crimes inquiry up to the highest military ranks and civilian government strategists."[11]

With elaborate charts, Lewy, on the other hand, proposed to make sense of noncombatant casualty statistics, although no statistics were officially gathered on civilian casualties until 1967. He estimated that the percentage of World War II and Korean civilians killed were higher than in Vietnam. (Lewy warned that his numbers dealt with estimates and extrapolations, nonetheless stating that the broad picture is "probably" valid.)

Such statistical cataloguing of noncombatant victims, like so many pieces of machinery, obfuscates a considerable imbalance. A brutal disregard for civilians was woven into the war tactics in Vietnam—where the enemy was so indistinguishable from the innocent. South Vietnamese officials, often corrupt, were relied on to point out the enemy. Vietnamese province chiefs gave permission to burn villages and reportedly extorted money from villages by threatening to call air strikes. They designated whole chunks of South Vietnam as free-fire zones, often in populous areas, and that meant Americans could bomb and kill everything.[12]

Individual responsibility for participating in atrocities should not be swept aside in "following orders" rhetoric, but in some ways My Lai and other isolated incidents were an extension of this overall policy. My Lai was a free-fire zone, and the men were told to destroy everything in it. GIs—described as "depressingly normal" and who in their Middle American hometowns would never have thought to strike a child—would not have so slaughtered had U.S. war policy shown any recognition of the value of Vietnamese peasant life. "You can't just blame Calley's platoon—you've got to blame everyone," said a soldier at My Lai. "It was a free-fire zone. And, you know, if you can shoot artillery and bombs in there every night, how can the people in there be worth so much?"[13]

It is grossly unfair to tar the majority of Vietnamese veterans with the brush of My Lai. Most were not wanton or even wittingly accidental killers of civilians. Yet I am struck by the individual accounts of the disregard for human life that recur in interviews. Every combat veteran seems to remember at least one wild soldier.

Johnny, a former Green Beret: "We were goin' down this narrow road, and an MP beeped the jeep horn and bumped a motorcycle off, and these Vietnamese on it fell down. The third time he hit two young kids who worked on the military base. One of 'em died. I can still see his head hit the side of the jeep. The MP told me if I'm questioned to say he was only going thirty miles an hour and lost control. I told what I saw, but I don't know if anything happened to him. He was a career soldier."

Eddie, from South Boston: "War makes you *accept* violence. After one buddy was killed, a guy was torching a hootch when an old woman pleaded with him to stop. In a fit of madness, he set her on fire. Back home, he tried to commit suicide. He's dead already. He died that day in Vietnam."

Tom Vallely, now a member of the Massachusetts legislature: "I saw maybe three or four incidents of people going crazy, but My Lai was an aberration. It could never happen in my unit. They would have shot Calley. One guy shot up a villager after his friend was killed by a booby trap. Everyone grabbed him and kept him from shooting more."

Others remember atrocities on the other side. A white Army infantry sergeant from Atlanta: "Two five-year-old boys were killed because they had associated with our units. While we were there, they gave us a lot of information, and one night a Viet Cong or NVA woman came into the village and killed both of them." A white marine from Westchester: "The ARVN brought in a woman whose husband was a Viet Cong. They stripped her to the waist and took a generator . . . and they took one wire and put it to her left breast, the other to her right, and started to crank it . . . ." Another veteran reported Viet Cong treatment of Americans. "They didn't believe in taking prisoners . . . They tortured our men, cut them up, and hung them in trees." A Los Angeles veteran: "They [VC sympathizers] were selling Zippo lighters, and the second time you would strike it, it would blow up in your hand . . ." And once again, back to our side—a Brooklyn Army veteran: "The back door of our vehicle was grated, and hot air from the engine comes out and that back deck gets to be 600 degrees after a while. It will burn through your shoes. That is where we would put our prisoners. Rope them, tie them, just throw them down there like a piece of cattle."[14]

There were rapes and pot shots at buffalo with people riding on them, the indiscriminate blitz of helicopter fire and tossed grenades. Ears were being taken as souvenirs to such an extent that Westmoreland was forced to issue a directive denouncing the practice.

On the other hand, there were countless individual acts of moral courage. Men like Marine Colonel Michael Yunck, who refused to call an air strike on an enemy village filled with women and children. Instead, he took his helicopter low to pinpoint VC positions and got his leg shot off by a VC machine gun for his compassion.

Kit Lovell, a San Diego real estate broker with a master's degree in urban planning, was an ace Navy pilot in Vietnam. He flew close air support in propeller-driven airplanes in the only land-based Navy squadron in Vietnam. By 1971 Lovell had "grave reservations about the war" and struggled to psych himself up for duty, not having the luxury of distance from the gore, as did jet pilots. "I had a lot of respect for the helicopter pilots, but the way that war was fought was truly surrealistic. There were a lot of free-fire zones." What saved Lovell and many combat soldiers who felt the war was wrong was the sense of helping others to survive. "I knew guys on the ground who could say I saved their lives. That was important, to justify my participation. The ARVNs, if they knew only two words of English, they were Black Pony, our squadron." One day a call came from support for ground troops taking fire. "We were watching, and for the life of me I couldn't see what the military target was. I knew these villages were considered friendly. The helicopters came in and started raising hell. I saw people running from hootches. *They killed everybody and every animal.* The radio talk was just incredible. I mean the laughter and talking. I knew they were taking no fire. I remember one guy saying, 'Get that one over there.' I got my radio onto a different frequency and said, 'Let's go home.' We had made our decision not to participate. When they called us to 'finish the job,' I just said, 'Well, we're running low on fuel and have to return to base.' " That incident bothered Lovell for years.

The decision not to participate. In battle, men fight, not for lofty principles but survival, sometimes for revenge, and sometimes to remain a part of the unit. In World War II, the American Army undertook the first systematic study of human combat behavior. The "remarkable revelation" was that soldiers do not think of themselves, in life-and-death situations, as subordinate members of a military organization, but as equals within a *very tiny group.* They fight and continue to fight for personal survival, which is bound up with group survival—and because of the *fear of incurring, by cowardly conduct, the group's contempt.*[15]

Many Vietnam veterans who hung back from participating in unnecessary violence still refrained from stopping others or reporting what they saw; group mentality is strong in battle. Others—caught up in the chaotic fear, excitement, revenge, and mayhem—participated. Violence was sanctioned when officers strongly implied that everyone they would see was a Viet Cong or a VC sympathizer.

Lieutenant Kenneth W. Boatman, a forward artillery observer assigned to Bravo Company, recalled for the Peers Panel investigating My Lai, the orders leading to another massacre that took place in a nearby hamlet, Me Khe 4, on the morning of My Lai. "We were informed to clean the damn place out. He [Captain Earl R. Michles] said that we were going to take care of them, get rid of them . . . I think everybody was enthusiastic . . ."

My Lai 1, 2, 3, and 4 hamlets were part of the village of Son My, known as Pinkville—heavily VC in the fiercely contested province of Quang Ngai. Larry G. Holmes of Peru, Indiana, summed up many GIs' recollections when he testified: "They told us they had dropped leaflets, and everybody was supposed to be gone. If anybody is there, shoot them."[16]

Within minutes of their approach, a mine was tripped, and the men of Bravo Company heard screams. One was killed and four GIs were seriously wounded. Frustration reached a fever pitch. More than 90 percent of the American Division's combat injuries and deaths in early 1968 resulted from booby traps and land mines. Another booby trap was tripped. Screams and smoke again. The unit was in disarray. When they "heard about" a grenade being thrown, "that was good enough," Homer Hall told the Peers Panel.

At Me Khe 4 "it was sort of like being in a shooting gallery . . ." One ex-GI later told Seymour Hersh, author of *Cover-Up,* about several incidents. "He told of a machine gunner who with a blaze of bullets methodically tore one woman in half at the waist," wrote Hersh. "And he told of a tiny infant, barely of crawling age, who became the object of a marksmanship contest." A rifleman took aim at the infant with a .45-caliber pistol, from ten feet away, and missed. " 'We all laughed,' the GI said." He got three feet closer and missed again. " 'We laughed. Then he got right on top of him and plugged him.' "[17]

Mrs. Nguyen Dhi Bay, one massacre survivor, recalled how she was raped by two soldiers. One soldier hit Bay and several other women a few times with the butt of his rifle. After this the two soldiers raped Bay—she does not remember how many times . . . She was two-months pregnant and lost her baby the next day.[18]

The precise number of murdered will never be known. The Army later charged Lieutenant Thomas K. Willingham, the platoon leader, with murder, but the charges were never pressed. Between 40 and 100 innocent Vietnamese civilians were murdered "with impunity," wrote Hersh.

My Lai 4, unlike Me Khe 4, became the massacre that will be forever synonymous with the Vietnam War. Out of the ordinary in its magnitude, My Lai was a confluence of disasters—inexperienced, unintelligent line officers; edgy troops who expected to engage the fierce 48th Viet Cong Battalion; higher-ups who covered up and eventually got off scot-free; inept intelligence reporting about supposed VC troops; and an endemic, pervasive feeling in the military that wasting "mere gooks" was of no great consequence.

In a morning's rampage at My Lai, 347 Vietnamese civilians were ruthlessly murdered. Rounded up and shot, flung into a drainage ditch and shot. Mowed down by "Machine Gun" Calley in clusters. Women and girls were raped, then murdered. Smoke over My Lai could be seen for miles. The pilots saw it, but the commanders claimed they did not. Major General Samuel Koster testified that he had not seen a burning hamlet when he flew over, nor had he witnessed anything out of the ordinary.

There were some men of conscience. A black soldier shot himself in the foot so that he would not have to participate. Warrant Officer Hugh C. Thompson, Jr., witnessed the murders from his helicopter and complained over the radio "that if he saw the ground troops kill one more woman or child, he would start shooting [the ground troops] himself." Finally, viewing about ten women and children huddled in terror as Lieutenant Calley and his men came toward them, Thompson landed his craft and ordered his two machine gunners to train their weapons on Calley. He said he was going to fly the civilians out. "The only way you'll get them out is with a hand grenade," Calley replied. Thompson and two crewmen made three trips, the last time to save a wounded Vietnamese boy, the only person who Thompson could see still alive in the huge ditch of bloodied bodies.

In rage and frustration, Thompson and a few other pilots described the scene to his company commander, Major Frederic Watke. Thompson continued to speak out about My Lai—to his chaplain, to other officers—but the denials and cover-up had begun. In official reports, massacred civilians were miraculously transformed into sixty-nine VC killed in action. One can only wonder at the pressure placed on Thompson during the disillusioning months of cover-ups, but somewhere along the way, he apparently decided to become "one of the boys." He later changed his testimony to say he could no longer recall if he had made a statement to Colonel Oran K. Henderson two days after the massacre. Thompson also accepted a Distinguished Flying Cross Medal; the citation noted the he rescued Vietnamese children "caught in the intense crossfire."[19]

Whistle blowing is never popular. The modern-day method of putting to death the messenger bearing bad news is to vilify and impugn. My Lai was common knowledge and gossip for months, but if ex-GI Ron Ridenhour had not written his famous letter, and had not Seymour Hersh followed up on the tale, a central part of Vietnam's history might have died in its murky jungle.

The four-page, single-spaced bombshell arrived a year after My Lai on thirty congressmen's desks. It is still grisly and gripping, from the opening paragraph describing "something rather dark and bloody" that had occurred at My Lai. Ridenhour had not been there but was to hear the tales from many GIs who could not keep the awful secret. In the letter he recounts one soldier's memory of a three- or four-year-old boy "clutching his wounded arm with his other hand, while blood trickled between his fingers. He just stood there with big eyes, staring around like he didn't understand; he didn't believe what was happening. Then the captain's radio operator put a burst of 16 [M-16 rifle] fire into him."

Calley was not the famous name it would shortly become, and Ridenhour wrote that a "2nd Lieutenant Kally (this spelling may be incorrect) had rounded up several groups of villagers . . . then machine-gunned each group." Ridenhour told of two soldiers who couldn't eat their lunch because some in the Vietnamese heap were still alive and moaning. The soldiers got up and went over to the pile. "I guess we sort of finished them off," said one. One GI recounted to Ridenhour that they had been ordered to destroy the village, and he was hesitant, "as if it were something he didn't want to do but had to do." Three times Calley set up a machine gun and mowed down groups of Vietnamese. When one private refused to man the machine gun, "Kally didn't bother to order anyone" after that. "He simply manned it himself." PFC Michael Bernhardt, who flatly refused to participate, told Ridenhour that Captain Ernest Medina told him "not to do anything stupid like write my congressman."

Today, Ron Ridenhour, now a freelance writer, recalls Vietnam and the aftermath of My Lai. He was with the Americal Division, 11th Brigade, as a door gunner. "We flew pretty low. You could really see what was going on. You could see expressions, what people looked like."

Did you feel that Vietnam was more prone to atrocities than other wars?

"I didn't see other wars. I didn't see *that* much of Vietnam. I saw nothing like My Lai. I saw a lot of individual one-on-one murders—at least that's how I would term what I saw. Some guys on patrol come across some Vietnamese farmers or villagers and they don't speak English, and there is some confrontation and the Vietnamese ends up dead. But there was confusion in everyone's mind; it was real hard to tell one side from another."

The anger bubbles up after all these years. "My Lai was a result of policy. A result of direct orders. Top commanders ordered it, wanted it to happen. The commanders, the general of the Americal were flying overhead all morning!" says Ridenhour, his voice rising. "They could tell the difference between an adult and a child! It was presumed that they [the villagers] hated all Americans, and they had a good right to, but the point is you don't go in and mow them down in a line like sheep. I think it was deliberate policy to drive them out of the countryside and into the cities—to get the guerrillas out of the countryside. They had to make the area uninhabitable." (Westmoreland acknowledged "it was necessary on some occasions *intentionally* to raze evac-

uated villages or hamlets . . . to remove the people and destroy the village."
That "removal" was not always bloodless.)[20]

Ridenhour heard about My Lai a month after it happened. Participants
transferred to his outfit seemed haunted and compelled to confess. "My first
thought was disbelief. It was the extraordinary few that resisted, but I didn't
think any of those I knew were weird. Some I felt could have been involved,
but others I felt could *never* have, and they were." For seven months he
collected as much information as possible, then waited until he returned to
the States to write his letters. "I was turning over names and specific information. It was a real tough situation. I had to make a choice—to betray the
victims and a certain set of principles or my friends. I came down on the side
of victims and principle."

A repeated theme—that it was policy—threads through Ridenhour's conversation. The gory pictures were taken by an Army photographer who came
along for a routine mission and roamed through the carnage at will.
Ridenhour believes that a great many participants were troubled after My
Lai, "and Hugh Thompson was a real hero, risked his life and career, and
filed a complaint and demanded an investigation."

Anyone who has seen combat can understand the urge to "blow 'em all
away" after a friend has been booby-trapped into oblivion. "You see enough
horrible things to understand the sense of loss and anger, the frustration and
fear. Anytime anyone dies in front of you, it's a horrible thing. Atrocity
became part of your daily life out there in line companies. I don't mean lining
up a village and shooting them every day, week, or month. A lot *never* lined
up a village at all, but boy there was a lot of day-to-day stuff. With the body
count, it didn't take very long before it didn't matter who was killed—just as
long as there were a lot of them."

Added to that "kill 'em and count 'em" policy was a special hype about
going in for the kill at My Lai. Many testified that their orders left no doubt
that *all* were enemies to be "wasted." "They were given a pep talk the night
before—which programmed them," said Ridenhour. "These things don't
happen by coincidence. Calley was a witting victim—but he was a victim, in
an act of policy. The guy was a fifteen-watt bulb. It's pathetic."

Ridenhour came from a blue-collar family, left home at sixteen, and was
working his way through college when he fell a few credits short and was
drafted. "It was suggested I doctor my medical reports, but I decided not to."
He emphatically says, "It was an *immoral* war. If I had known before what I
was going to be involved in, I might have taken some way out. There is no
real . . ." He pauses. "No real release from that *ever*—being involved in a
war like that. Some guys who had simply horrible experiences don't admit to
being traumatized by guilts, but they are really just messes. They're still
fighting the war and always will be. It is something that should not be forgotten but has to be gotten past. I'm still trying to get there. For a while I was
obsessed by it. Really violent films would give me the shakes."

How do you view the fact that veterans were stamped "baby killers" largely as a result of the My Lai massacre that you exposed?

"I met some absolutely wonderful guys over there who returned wonderful guys. But there still were My Lais, and we still killed a lot of people unnecessarily. I don't know how it balances out. What bothers me is that people are not facing the realities of what a shitty policy it was. I have great sympathy for all the people who went and had their minds twisted and will never be completely whole again. We'll never be the same. We've been messed with seriously."

Vietnam and My Lai would trail Ridenhour for years. When he came home, in March of 1969, he sat at his parents' kitchen table, "and poured out this horrible story. I told them and wept, and it was pretty horrifying."

How did they react to your plan to write the letter?

"There was a split in my family—like in most of America. My dad told me to mind my own business. He felt I was exposing myself to government harassment. Mom said to do what I think is right."

Did your father morally feel you would be doing the right thing?

"It never came up."

When his letter became public, vicious hate mail confirmed Ridenhour's gut feelings that "it was not a real popular thing to do." He heard from "a lot of Bible Belt folks" who felt there was every justification for "killing Communists." One of them wrote that Ridenhour was a " 'traitor who had betrayed our boys and, more specifically, my friends.' I knew when I wrote the letter that some people I felt really close to might be publicly exposed and ultimately go to jail. I felt bad about it. Still do."

When he received the letter, Congressman Morris Udall moved quickly, but according to sources at the time, there were right-wingers on the Hill who sought to dismiss My Lai by trying to discredit Ridenhour and Thompson.

So many top-command My Lai principals were exonerated that Ridenhour's legacy is deep cynicism. "It made me *see* that there are some policymakers in this country who are willing to do anything if they believe it is necessary. It taught me a lesson about the nature of power and reality."

When My Lai became an international metaphor for all that was wrong with Vietnam, Ridenhour began to hear from soldiers of other wars. After his lectures, they would come up. "One guy told me how they were moving a bunch of POWs during World War II, and there was a 'take no prisoners' policy. Another told me about wiping out a bunch of civilians in a German hamlet. 'Nobody ever said it was wrong. We were never confronted by something,' they told me. 'Everybody thought we were right. I knew we were wrong—but nobody ever questioned us. There was no way for us to complain or tell anyone.' "

In the end, My Lai resulted in the conviction of only Lieutenant William Calley, and that was shortlived. In a war that had crowned few heroes, Calley, a convicted mass murderer, strangely enough became one. Whole draft boards resigned in protest. The "Ballad of Rusty Calley" played in country bars. The public clamored for his release, and after *15,000* letters and telegrams, President Nixon responded. While seventy-five to eighty men served time in Fort Leavenworth, Kansas, on murder charges which originated in Vietnam, while still more were imprisoned at the Naval Prison in Portsmouth, New Hampshire, Lieutenant Calley was famous and confined to his quarters, not a cell.

Comparisons are necessary: An enlisted man in 1970 was sentenced to five years in prison for pushing a warrant officer. The Air Force sent a colonel away for three years for smoking marijuana. Howard Levy, the celebrated doctor who refused to train soldiers bound for Vietnam, was sentenced and served two years for disobeying an order.[21]

The verdict of murder rendered by six combat veterans—who knew firsthand that there is killing and then there is killing—brought a life-imprisonment sentence. It was quickly reduced to ten years, and Calley was granted parole effective in November 1974. The Peers Panel Inquiry listed thirty men implicated in various "commissions and omissions," some constituting criminal offenses. Charges were preferred against sixteen; twelve were dismissed for insufficient evidence. Four others, besides Calley, were tried by court-martial, but none were found guilty. Captain Ernest L. Medina was acquitted —and there is general agreement today that the instructions of the military judges were wrong.[22]

Administrative action for substandard performance of duty was taken against the commanding general of the Americal Division, Major General Samuel W. Koster—who allegedly failed to report a serious criminal offense to higher headquarters. By 1970 Koster was superintendent of West Point, when coverup charges were raised. He received a letter of censure, his Distinguished Service Medals were withdrawn, and he was reduced in rank from major general to brigadier general.

The leniency of the findings prompted Rep. Samuel S. Stratton to charge that "the ground rules of the mythical WPPA, the West Point Protective Association, have taken precedence . . . never mind what happens to the Army or to the country, just make sure we keep our paid-up members out of embarrassment and hot water."[23]

With some on the right clamoring that Calley was a simple boy doing his job and others on the left clamoring that he was but a part of the overall atrocity of this war, the middle ground was not considered. "The idea of assuming collective national guilt for My Lai—a notion which may be satisfying to people who opposed the war anyway—does not settle anything," wrote William Greider, who covered the Calley trial for the Washington *Post.* "When you say we are all guilty for My Lai, that has truth in it, but it is also another way of saying no one is guilty."[24]

To find Calley guilty of cold-bloodedly herding women and children and babies into clusters and murdering them should not have, in any way, absolved generals for the devastation of village after village by aerial bombardment or burning huts and shooting livestock "just for sport," wrote Greider. But there was an international covenant the Army attempted to uphold; even in combat, soldiers do not shoot defenseless people who are captured and unarmed.

What My Lai did to the country remains, to some extent, buried among the many denials about Vietnam. At the time, public response to My Lai ranged from shock to denial to an acceptance of the "war is hell" cliche. Many sought comfort in the "these things happen in war" generalization. Journalists, "if they were now reporting on the Spanish War of the thirties instead of Vietnam, would not . . . have the strength to stay indignant about isolated atrocities," wrote Stephen Francis.[25] "Atrocities are the basic irregularity of war, and the Spanish War . . . was a long series of My Lais."

Others spoke of the "high-technology" systematic obliteration of such towns as Hamburg in World War II. Well over 2,200 British and American aircraft dropped more than 7,000 tons of high explosives and incendiaries on Hamburg, a city the size of Detroit . . . with inhabitants of 1,800,000. A German radio announcer gasped, "Terror . . . terror . . . terror . . . pure, naked, bloody terror."[26]

The larger picture of morality in My Lais and other atrocities holds endless fascination. The issue of legal and illegal killing gets terribly confused, particularly in guerrilla warfare. To this day veterans claim that they too killed civilians in the heat of it all. But ask them if they herded people together, unarmed and unresisting, and put them in a ditch, then stood over them and fired. The ones who say no—the vast majority—are typical. Most infantry men barely saw who they shot at, much less killed. Calley's was one of those rare clear-cut cases of mass murder.

Still, *denial* of *that basic fact* prompted thousands upon thousands of America's "good citizens" to write the President asking for Calley's freedom. Some 65 percent of 1,608 surveyed by *Time* magazine denied being upset at reports of the massacre. Americans reacted to reports of My Lai atrocities as Germans did to the "Final Solution" Holocaust. As one woman viewed photographs of the mangled bodies and contorted faces of those about to die at My Lai in *Life* magazine, she trembled and shut the pictures out by closing her eyes. Then, quickly recovering, she said, "When people are taught to hate, it doesn't surprise me how they react, particularly when they are given a weapon." Another said, "I can't take the responsibility of the world on my shoulders . . ." George Wallace said he couldn't believe an American soldier would purposely shoot any civilian . . . "Any atrocities in this war were caused by the Communists." Once again, the media was blamed. One man said, "Newspapermen get a little bit wild."[27]

Strong doubts served the same blotting-out purpose as denial. Skeptical questions were raised about the people of the village. "These little bastards are devious. Had the women set booby traps?" "Following orders" became a principal justification even from some of the more dovish respondents: "What

would their punishment be if they had disobeyed? They had no choice . . ."
When asked what they would have done if ordered to line up people and kill
them, 74 percent of women in one survey said they would have refused, but
only 27 percent of men agreed. Emotional detachment, above all, seemed
vital to distance My Lai from their lives. Both hawks and doves argued in one
way or another that no massacre happened. Hawks tended to justify My Lai.
Doves tended to comfort themselves with the thought that My Lais occur in
every war.[28]

In all the psychobabble of the time, people tried to ignore the fact that
normal American boys, trained to kill, went beyond the bounds in My Lai. In
1969 *Time* was flooded with letters ascribing to a myriad of feelings: A
woman from Idaho asked, "How is it possible to wage a 'humane' war? Is
there a nice way to slaughter people?" A Vietnam veteran from South Carolina, on the other hand: "Calley should be fined $2, given a carton of ciga-
rettes, promoted to captain, and reassigned to the Pentagon . . . Charlie
Cong is not a conventional soldier, but a toothless old woman, a goateed old
man or a mine-setting little boy. Lieutenant Calley and his men just did their
job—staying alive in a rich man's war but a poor man's fight."[29]

"Why the hell all that noise about My Lai?" wrote one man. "The story of
humanity is a long, uninterrupted list of atrocities . . . the Spanish War,
Lidice, Babi Yar, Korea, Algeria, the Congo, Mozambique, day after day—
children murdered in my generation. We are only human beings, and the
fittest will survive." Another writer from California: "Let's have that line
again about Saving South Vietnam from Communism . . ." One veteran,
Harry McDaniel, wrote, "Nineteen years ago today I was captain in frontline
combat in Korea, with orders to shoot anything that moved after dark. We
did, and we won. So it has always been and will ever be, until some power
stops war." Newspapers around the world refrained from judgment. Typical
was Milan's *Corriere della Sera,* which realistically noted: "Every country on
the old continent has a fine collection of skeletons in the cupboard."[30]

The particular conviction in America, however, is that we believe America
is always on the side of democracy and liberty, that we are unusually innocent
and generous in our relationships with others. The dark underside of American history—massacring American Indians, enslaving blacks, annihilating
the people of Hiroshima—is always glossed over in Memorial Day platitudes.
My Lai was a painful message—that America is capable, like other nations,
of evil in war.

General Eugene "Mike" Lynch, who fought in World War II, was an aide
to General Matthew Ridgway in Korea and served in Vietnam but opposed
our presence there. "You had the whole chain of command trying to keep My
Lai quiet—CYA—cover your ass." He feels that atrocities are part of the
arsenal of a losing side. "Atrocities normally take place when the loser is
pulling out—when he has nothing to gain by keeping the terrain or people.
There were military victories, but the economic, pyschosocial, and political
war we were losing every day. It all goes back to a false standard. If you

measure performance on body-count justification, you would have the total debacle we did. In any war where you lose so much, soldiers will want revenge. Anytime you have a losing situation, you've got a potential My Lai. That is when it is up to the commander to set the tone, to halt it."

It is debilitatingly depressing to hear the stories. Those of us who have never known what it is like to kill or see friends killed, who have not lived through the madness of combat, have difficulty listening nonjudgmentally to what often remains incomprehensible. How to explain a youth who had been a choirboy one year, a killer the next. Many veterans recount stories with an air of unreality, as if they cannot believe they were once like that. Countless tens of thousands, of course, never participated and often reported incidents that offended them morally. Still, those who saw the worst of combat often remain disgusted by the Calleys but are nonjudgmental. "We were like animals," recalls one marine.

The unanswerable question is why some behave one way and others not? Why does war unleash a side long checked by civilized restraints—and why are participants often, years later, driven by unrelenting guilt? And why do other participants profess no guilt?

There are probably no adequate answers, but there are, unfortunately, stories.

A Baltimore veteran and his wife sip wine in their living room. There is a desire to edit out his atrocity, to erase it from notebook and mind. I too want to believe American boys don't do such things—men who, no matter how unstable, for the most part would have lived out their lives untouched by such violence without the triggering experience of war.

In their living room is a valentine "to the most wonderful wife in the world." He gently strokes their dog. Then he tells me how he and seven buddies gang-raped two North Vietnamese nurses, then murdered them. "You could tell they were nurses by their clean hair and hands." The rapes were a combination of evening the score ("we had lost a lot of men") and lust —"five months without a woman. We pointed our guns at them. We were probably the grossest-looking things they'd ever seen. We roamed that country like nomads."

We talk of "unnecessary violent acts." "In every company you have about five or six guys who do it all. Others wouldn't even fire their weapons." The men repeatedly raped the nurses. After one of the nurses started to run, one of the soldiers shot her. "And then we had to shoot the other." His words are toneless. He asks the question asked often by those who try to explain, seeking some absolution in the answers of others. His eyes are full of tears. "Do you understand?" I cannot answer yes.

Ground troops faced hostile peasants in many VC strongholds; the atrocities of VC or NVA regulars against Americans often roused little sympathy from these peasants, which only compounded GI hatred. The desire to avenge dead buddies was a staple of court-martial testimony. One Marine lance corporal killed four young Vietnamese captured and suspected of alerting enemy troops to the presence of Americans. He was charged with four counts of premeditated murder. Pressure for a high body count was apparently a factor for a lieutenant and sergeant who shot a prisoner and were charged with murder. Records are replete with several cases of mistreatment and torture of prisoners—dragging them behind APCs, [armored personnel carriers] giving them "water treatment," applying electric shocks to genitals. American correspondents at times took pictures of Americans standing by as the South Vietnamese abused prisoners.

Westmoreland wrote a letter in 1965 to Third Marine Division Major General Louis Walt stating that U.S. troops should try to "moderate" the conduct of the South Vietnamese troops but noted that the United States had "no command authority" over them. In any case Westmoreland wrote, "We should attempt to avoid photographs being taken of these incidents of torture and *most certainly in any case try to keep Americans out of the picture.*"[31] [Emphasis added.] But the pictures emerged. In January 1968 the Washington *Post* published a picture showing an American soldier pinning a Vietnamese to the ground while two other Vietnamese placed a towel over his face and poured water into his nose. The soldier was tried for the offense.

Between January 1965 and March 1973, 201 Army personnel in Vietnam were convicted by court-martial of serious offenses against Vietnamese; from March 1965 to August 1971, 77 marines were convicted of serious crimes against Vietnamese. Offenses included murder, rape, mutilation of corpses, and negligent homicide. Many other acts went uncovered or unreported. No central file for allegations of atrocities and war crimes or the deposition of these allegations exists. The *Legacies of Vietnam* study previously points to many observances of "unnecessary violence." Others escaped trial because no law provides for the trial of discharged servicemen accused of offenses committed while in the service. MACV, critics charged, did not adequately investigate alleged war crimes, and courts-martial often brought excessively lenient treatment. For example, two incidents where the subjects scalped and cut the fingers and ears of two dead enemy soldiers resulted in fines of $100. Once again in this class war, officers received more lenient treatment than enlisted men—61 percent of officers were either acquitted, had their charges dismissed before trial, or got off with administrative action only—the corresponding number for enlisted men was 34 percent.[32]

Class distinction in conviction is rife in the case of PFC Samuel G. Green, Jr., a marine from a poor background charged with the unpremeditated murder of sixteen civilians in Son Thang village, Quang Nam province, on February 19, 1970. He was convicted as an aider and abbetor on all sixteen counts, and petition for review was twice denied. The patrol leader who gave the orders was acquitted. James Webb, decorated ex-marine, author, and lawyer, appealed to reverse the decision, citing his "personal experiences with the difficulties of operating in enemy-controlled civilian areas."

Green was part of a "killer team" that searched out the enemy in a roaming, random manner. In intensely hostile areas, they were ordered to "get some," wrote Webb. Green had been in Vietnam only eleven days. A Private Herrod, [Webb does not include first names of Herrod, Schwarz, and Boyd in this account] who had recently been recommended for the Silver Star, was appointed patrol leader. Herrod and a Private Schwarz dragged four unarmed civilians, two women and two boys, into an open area. When the woman, about fifty years old, began to run, Herrod knocked her to the ground with a buckshot blast from his M-79 grenade launcher, then ordered Schwarz to finish her off. He did so. "I want these people killed because I had orders from the lieutenant to do it," Herrod told the patrol. Herrod and Schwarz fired several more times, and then Green and PFC Boyd fired their M-16s. They moved on to other hooches, Herrod giving the same order, and all members participated. Herrod, Schwarz, Boyd, and Green were all tried separately for the murder of the sixteen. Herrod, the active perpetrator and leader who *gave* the orders, was acquitted of all charges, as was Boyd, whose situation was similar to Green's. Once again, as with My Lai, Americans at home came to the defense of such killing in warfare. Herrod and Boyd were represented by civilian counsel—made possible by donations from citizens of their hometowns totaling nearly $40,000 and $20,000, respectively, Schwarz and Green had no financial resources and were represented only by military counsel. Both were convicted.[33]

Webb argued that Green was following orders no matter how wrong; "when should a 'boot' venture to disobey the orders of a highly seasoned and respected leader? Green had no experience on which to base a refusal to obey." Webb argued that local inhabitants of Quang Nam province, including women and children, were not "innocent civilians" in the traditional sense of the word but were a tightly knit, essential element of the VCI (Vietcong Infrastructure). Five days before, an unarmed woman apparently yelled a warning to hidden VC soldiers and was promptly killed. The morning of the incident, young children attempted to draw the company into an enemy ambush. "In Green's short experience there was no moral sanctity evidence to him regarding the life of a woman and child," wrote Webb.[34]

While his superiors escaped conviction, Green, a poor black from Detroit, was found guilty. He later committed suicide. After his death, his discharge was upgraded to under honorable conditions by the Board for the Correction of Naval Records.

Rapes often involved complicity of participants. One case became a vivid account in *The New Yorker* by author Donald Lang. PFC Sven Eriksson (not his real name) returned home with unrelenting memories of a Vietnamese peasant girl in a remote hamlet in the Central Islands. She had a prominent gold tooth and particularly expressive dark eyes. And she was wearing dusty earrings made of bluish glass. He never knew her name or spoke with her, and he knew her only in her last twenty-four hours of life.

At the court-martial, events unfolded of her rape-murder in November of 1966. Sergeant Tony Meserve was the first to enter the hooch holding the captive girl, who was later identified as Mao. Soon, Eriksson said, a high, piercing moan of pain and despair came from the girl, to be repeated in waves. "She was real good—pretty clean," said Meserve, appearing a half hour later. The next man found Mao naked, lying on a table, hands bound behind her back. In all, four raped her; Eriksson did not. Later, as he guarded her, the soldier "thought of letting her go, but what would I tell Meserve when he got back?"

After several hours, Mao's fate worsened. A fever and cough had reduced what allure she had had for the soldiers. The girl's murder was plotted. Three, including Eriksson, refused any involvement in the murder. According to testimony, Ralph Clark, a corporal from near Philadelphia, took her in the woods, a hunting knife in his hands. Soon the sound that Eriksson remembered from his Minnesota childhood, that made by gutted deer, was heard. Clark told Meserve he had just finished the job when the girl, like a wounded apparition, crawled rapidly downhill, then disappeared into the thick foliage. Clark raced after her and blasted the bush with his M-16. "You want her gold tooth?" he called over his shoulder.

Eriksson reported the murder and was repeatedly told by commanding officers that "everything was being handled." Eriksson was eventually transferred but not before any number of GIs rallied to the patrol's defense and took a dim view of Eriksson "throwing good lives after bad." The familiar argument was that the VC also kidnapped, raped, and murdered. Eriksson himself took pains to tell that the kind of behavior he described was by no means limited to Americans. Much of the evidence of enemy atrocities, he said, came from the Vietnamese themselves, constantly reporting rapes and kidnappings. None of this, however, could right the rape-murder of the Vietnamese peasant girl to him. In frustration, Eriksson went to the chaplain. As the murder report went through channels, Eriksson was placed in confinement for "protection." The court-martial trial was another study in disillusion. Court records show that defense lawyers made a studied effort to depict Eriksson as a "coward" whose veracity would therefore somehow be questionable. Clark was convicted of rape and premeditated murder and given a life sentence. Meserve was found innocent of rape but guilty of premeditated murder and given a ten-year term. Eriksson returned haunted by the ordeal, and, his wife said, with a deeper kindness. He was still ostracized by those who thought him wrong for reporting the rape-murder.[35]

On February 10, 1970, Norman Ryman, Jr., mailed a package home to himself from Vietnam. It contained one photo album, one mirror, one pair of rubber sandals, two tiger fatigue shirts, one hat, one camouflage ascot, one brown shirt, one fatigue jacket, four pairs of tropical combat trousers, three tropical combat coats. And three human ears. Ryman, in a sworn statement, explained that two of the ears he took from a dead NVA soldier he had killed.

"I then kept the ears as souvenirs. I got the third ear from a soldier that was assigned to the 101st Airborne. I paid five dollars for the ear. He had a large jar of ears that he was selling. He was a white guy with a mustache. I haven't seen him since."

Ryman's photo album contained pictures of mutilated "gooks."

Ryman was not alone in his practice of collecting ears. As Michael Herr wrote in *Dispatches:*

> There was a reedy little man in the circle who grinned all the time but hardly spoke. He pulled a thick plastic bag out of his pack and handed it over to me. It was full of what looked like large pieces of dried fruit. I was stoned and hungry, I almost put my hand in there but it had a bad weight to it. The other men were giving each other looks, some amused, some embarrassed and even angry. Someone had told me once, there were a lot more ears than heads in Vietnam; just information. When I handed it back he was still grinning, but he looked sadder than a monkey.[36]

In a letter to all commanders in October 1967, Westmoreland called the practice of cutting ears and fingers from the bodies of dead enemies "subhuman." Some crackdowns in the souvenir hunting led to soldiers being court-martialed. Some, like Kenny, cut off the heads of corpses; evidence was gained when soldiers posed for photo remembrances with the dead.

Norman Ryman was in the States on leave when the package arrived. He was returning for his third tour of Vietnam, he loved it so. Although court-martialed, his case was mysteriously dismissed due to "lack of a speedy trial."[37] Within days he was out of the Army by reason of a hardship discharge under honorable conditions. My Lai was on every news show, in all the front pages; Ryman's ear collecting would no doubt be a minor embarrassment. Ryman would later charge that he was rushed out of the Army and onto the streets in a psychotic state and should have been detained for treatment.

Ryman was the oldest of five children born to a trash collector. He has said that he hated his father, who would on occasion beat Ryman and his four siblings as punishment, using rubber hoses, paddles, belts. Ryman hated his father for "letting Mother stamp down the garbage."

After the ninth grade, Ryman quit school to help in the trash-collecting business and joined the Army as soon as he was old enough. "When I went to Vietnam, I drummed up a lie that my father had medals from World War II. He wasn't in it. He was chickenshit."

Norman Ryman was one of those misfits who never should have been allowed in the Army. Unsurprisingly they sometimes make vicious soldiers. He desperately sought something to build his nonexistent self-esteem. "The Army was like heaven, the officers my gods." Rage and revenge guided his actions in combat, and when he was on his rampages the rest of the troops, acknowledging his craziness, called him "Normal Norman."

He was a LRRP (pronounced "lurp"—for "Long-Range Reconnaissance Patrol") with the Airborne Rangers, called by some the "Animals of the Army," due to their ferocity in combat. For the first time, Ryman was feeling a part of a close-knit team, as they roamed in packs of five.

"Early one afternoon my company walked unknowingly into an NVA ambush. Two of my close friends were the first to get hit. I could hear screams coming from my brothers as they cried in pain. I tried to get to them, but the fighting was so intense. By the time I finally did get to where my brothers were lying, one was dead, the other was going into shock from his severed arm. We were all in our late teens and scared half to death. I remember I was crying so hard that I could hardly see as we worked to save my comrades in shock."

Then, says Ryman, "I vowed to kill ten gooks to every one of my comrades who got hit, and even more for the ones who died." From that day on, Ryman declared his "own personal war" against "every damn gook in Vietnam."

"I don't believe I could really ever explain the horror that runs through one's mind as he searches for an arm or a leg that belongs to the very same guy who showed you some pictures of his wife and kids just before . . . to help load his body onto a chopper . . ."

After listening to the screams of his wounded friends, and after the dust-off chopper took them away, Ryman completed his rituals. "I went over to the bodies of the dead NVA soldiers and began pumping more bullets into their dead, mutilated corpses. I was sealing the bond of personal declaration of war against the Vietnamese as I watched those bodies bounce and disembowel right in front of my eyes to the pace of my automatic weapon, until my other brothers pulled me away, screaming that they had had enough."

In his rambling account, written in 1976 while he was incarcerated for rape, Ryman dwells constantly on vengeance: "Each time one of our boys was hit and/or killed, their bill went up."

He reveled in reconnaissance missions. "We were quite effective and very professional, and I'd grown to love every damn minute of it. Although I must admit *that there were times that I would be forced to stay sober long enough to realize just how insane I had become. I continued to grow more and more insane with each breath without any feeling of remorse because I had an excuse to be hostile and aggressive and I also had a license to kill without prosecution which made my actions enjoyable and my insanity bearable.*" [Emphasis added.]

After ten NVA walked into a trap set by Ryman's team and were killed, Ryman "decided to have myself a little fun" with one of the NVA soldiers. "I took out my survival knife and began to stab the bastard in the head. I must have punctured his skull at least forty times before my arm got tired. After that I took my weapon and blew his entire leg off; then I took pictures of his mutilated body. To complete one of these accomplishments I would feel magnificent."

With another wounded Vietnamese, "I pumped twenty rounds into his face and head while I held onto his hair."

"I was only twenty at that time, and I was starting to stand out among my brother comrades . . . [who] admired me for my ability to kill without feeling. I was *receiving the wrong type of decoration; what I really needed was a straight jacket and a padded cell, but I sure didn't think so at the time.*" [Emphasis added.] With masterful understatement, Ryman continues, "I guess I should have noticed something, especially since I would mutilate bodies and I would feel great. If I didn't get a chance to kill and mutilate, I would suffer with aggression and fall into a state of despair until I could go back out and make up for my failure."

A very major question is where was the Army during all of this? At the time of his court-martial, one commanding officer wrote an assessment that clearly should have been made months before.

"Spec. 4 Ryman's character was questionable even before we knew of the alleged severing of ears," wrote First Lieutenant Joseph F. Brand, on July 29, 1970. "I was the Executive Officer of Company N (Ranger) 75th Infantry for sixty days before he went home on leave. I had the chance to observe him from time to time and formed the conclusion that he did have a mental problem. His reputation in this unit was one of a madman." The judgment of his fighting ability was another matter. "His professional ability . . . as an infantry soldier was outstanding, and his courage went without saying."

That apparently kept the Army satisfied. After battle, Ryman drank himself into oblivion—so often, he contends, that "I began experiencing something called DTs, or delerium tremens, which landed me in the hospital for alcoholism four or five times. However, not once was I interviewed by a psychologist or psychiatrist to determine what was torturing me inside. I was merely nursed back to health each time and returned to combat."

Ryman was on thirty-days leave before he was to join a Special Forces team where he would "really get into some steady action, which would enable me to get all the kills I wanted."

About that time, his package from Vietnam was wending its way through the postal service. The Army Criminal Investigations Division (CID) called Ryman in northern Virginia. Only when they asked him about the friends he had seen killed or wounded did Ryman break down and cry . . . "histeria *[sic]*, my hands shaking and wet with sweat. This is when I finally started screaming that I had taken the ears and photographs—that I had been getting even with those bastard gooks." Ryman states that he was free to return home. "No treatment, no charges at that time, nothing except neglect." They told him they would get back to him.

During the next two weeks of leave, Ryman's parents convinced him that he should apply for a hardship discharge. It was approved in two days, but "a blanket was thrown over my records. Word came down that I was to be court-martialed for war crimes. I was never placed on any kind of restriction, house arrest, or anything.

"I wanted my honorable discharge. I felt that I had deserved it."

After a one-hour pretrial examination, Ryman states, "I was never to see anyone else for treatment and/or examination." His case came to trial in September 1970. His attorney made a motion for dismissal due to a lack of a fast and speedy trial. The lawyer argued that Ryman should be cleared to be discharged as soon as possible. The motion was immediately approved, and Ryman was discharged the next day. "I must have been one of the most rapidly discharged individuals ever to separate from the U.S. Army. Discharged without even a physical exam."

With only a high school equivalency test-diploma, Ryman was out in the world. "The Army dropped me like a hot potato; they got rid of me before they were embarrassed by yet another case of war crimes. *I was released back into society without any type of treatment or even any acknowledgment of any such need for treatment.* [Emphasis added.] I can't help but wonder just how many veterans have received similar treatment, [have been] discharged with a severe psychological problem. Just released to maintain my own problems and disorders all alone. I never received psychiatric treatment or was even seen by any more than one Army psychiatrist, who merely said I was sane but a very definite walking time bomb."

The pretrial psychiatric evaluation, dated May 18, 1970, stated that Ryman was "quite cooperative, coherent, relevant, oriented, and logical. There was no evidence of a paranoid delusional system or a paranoid trend. He did seem to be preoccupied with 'the Communists and their taking over the world.' " However, he was judged "mentally responsible and able to distinguish right from wrong. Apparently [Ryman] was operating under a great deal of stress while in Vietnam, and this might account for some of his *inappropriate* behavior." While he was described as "neither physically nor mentally deficient," the report did send strong warning signals: "He does manifest inadaptability, ineptness, poor judgment and social instability, and lack of physical and emotional stamina at times. His way of dealing with his emotional conflicts is by drinking alcohol."

And what were the recommendations, given such facts? Nothing except "as indicated by Command."

It is hard to know whether Vietnam created new pathologies or simply aggravated old ones in Ryman, but the Army took no time to find out, nor any responsibility for the man they returned to society.

Thirty days after discharge, Norman married a high school girl he had known for six months, "the most wonderful woman alive." He wanted her to have "all the good things in life." He worked a minimum of fourteen hours a day in the sanitation business. Then, in 1973, without a "dime in my pocket," he borrowed to start his own sanitation business, developed a good business, but was deeply in debt. His wife spent what he made, he was overextending himself, working seventy to ninety hours a week, keeping his rage inside. In the military, he learned three things: "how to hate, how to kill, and how to stay alive. But the one thing I was best at doing was useless to me in society, because that was the ability to kill and torture other human beings. I was scared to death that if I allowed myself to express myself I might do something to hurt someone I loved." Ryman became withdrawn and drank heavily.

Meantime, his wife ridiculed and insulted Ryman publicly, making him feel inadequate and undeserving. Ryman felt she used sex as a weapon, depriving him of satisfaction for months at a time.

In 1975 Ryman had started night school and was suffering from severe headaches. He had a deep-seated fear that he might start to mutilate people again. Finally, he was arrested and charged with the rapes of four women. Following the advice of his attorney, Ryman withdrew the plea of temporary insanity and pleaded guilty. He was sentenced to life imprisonment plus forty years. The judgment was based on the assumption that he was legally sane and thus responsible for his actions—although psychiatrist Brian Crowley contended that while Ryman's "memory, orientation, and intellect are intact, the patient's judgment, impulse control, and sense of social realities *are all obviously grossly defective.*" (Emphasis added.) Another doctor, Veena Kapur, wrote that Ryman was "out of touch with present-day reality and lacking in the capacity to appreciate the criminality of his conduct in regard to the alleged offenses."

From jail, Ryman wrote long tracts, blaming the Army for everything. "I am simply a family man who has gone haywire because the Army failed to treat a problem six years ago. This is the first time in my life I have even been in trouble with the law, with the exception of [the military] trial. I have a legitimate problem. I want and need treatment. During the whole time I was committing those insane crimes, I would continue to repeat to myself that I was sane—the Army said so."

Unquestionably, the Army was grossly negligent in keeping a psychotic killer in the field, and Ryman should have received psychiatric help before his military release. Even now, psychiatric treatment, rather than imprisonment, seems more constructive. If a delayed-stress disorder had been acknowledged at the time of his trial, Ryman no doubt would have been considered an extreme case needful of prolonged institutionalized care. His ability to place blame elsewhere, not uncommon among the convicted, is noticeable for its incoherent inconsistencies. He blames the Army for all his problems, for having let him loose. Yet he contends at another point that his rapes were demented attempts to find a compatible lover after being spurned by his wife.

Known as the "midday rapist," Ryman typically would knock on doors, try to gain access under pretext, such as borrowing an aspirin, and then force intercourse. According to one psychiatrist, "Apparently he never seriously injured any of his victims." Ryman writes remorsefully, "The main thing that bothers me is that I have always been so set against crime all my life. Yet I

committed a crime far worse than robbing or stealing will ever be. I was on
the border line of insanity. I had become a rapist, the scum of the earth."

Ryman quickly returns to blame the Army. "All this happened to me and
my undeserving family merely because the United States Army had neglected
to provide the proper care and treatment of one of their veterans."

Veterans such as Ryman, who committed atrocities and remained in combat, cannot totally blame the military for their excesses. Yet Ryman does
epitomize the tendency that sometimes did exist to overlook the insanity of a
"good killer" in the field.

Today, Norman Ryman, Jr., is serving a life term.

Some may question the point of rehashing the worst of the war at this
distance. It is important to speak of it at some length because atrocities and
acts of unnecessary violence remain one of the unspoken, awful legacies. Time
muted the outrage. As there was more understanding of the kind of war
young men had been asked to fight, Americans experienced yet another ambivalence—abhorrence for the acts, mingled with tolerance for the conditions
of guerrilla warfare. The denial of collective national involvement must also
be addressed. Atrocities are inevitable in wars, but Vietnam's frustrating war
fought against civilians merely heightened that inevitability. If nothing else,
this should be understood and examined as a caution for possible similar
involvements in the future. Some people still argue the callous and inaccurate
concept that "Orientals think very little of life." Because it has not come to
grips with the kind of war we fought in Vietnam, America continues to hold a
mixed bag of remembrances and confusion.

As for veterans who either participated in or witnessed acts of unnecessary
violence, the *Legacies of Vietnam* study indicates a lingering trauma. Veterans
remain deeply troubled. The study at first theorized that combat itself caused
delayed stress. After reexamining the data, new analysis placed far greater
emphasis on acts of unnecessary violence and atrocities as a major cause. The
helplessness of being unable to control their environment in a guerrilla war
"significantly contributed to the prevalence of abusive violence," often stemming from "rage, fear, and/or anxiety." The sample included 226 whites, 100
blacks, and 24 chicanos. About 29 percent of black vets were exposed to
abusive violence and 32 percent whites; 14 percent of black vets actually
participated in these acts and 8 percent of white vets. Yet they responded in
different ways. Whites and blacks were equally troubled by exposure to abusive violence—in other words by events that they *witnessed*. Blacks were
much more greatly troubled if they participated, feeling in retrospect that
they had committed crimes against another racial group. Said a black infantryman from Chicago, "I raped a [Vietnamese] girl one time and prayed. God
forgive me for doing that because I knew I was losing my mind." Whites who
committed such acts remained, surprisingly, less stressed—as compared with
those who only witnessed abusive violence. *Legacies* experts surmised that
they belonged to a group who not only thought war was right, but had an

abiding hatred for Vietnamese. They "denied the traumatic quality of their experience. Instead they numbed themselves to the toll of human misery they encountered," the study concluded. They subscribed to the "mere gook syndrome" and were more revenge-filled over the death of close buddies. One quote summed up this view: "Killing a gook was nothing really. I could have butchered them like nothing really. I had no feelings."

Yet, for many among that small percentage of the total combat force who committed atrocities, there is little rest. For Kenny, the "head man" of Alabama, for the veteran in Baltimore who raped the nurse, for those who participated in lesser My Lais, for the marine who recalls a time "when we were like animals," even for "Normal Norman," and for others who keep their dark secrets close, they remember and remain haunted.

2 The Reluctant Warriors

AFTER TET, AFTER MY LAI, AFTER NIXON WAS ELECTED SAYING HE HAD a "secret plan" for peace, after Nixon promised that thousands of troops would soon be home, after Kent and Cambodia, after the Pentagon Papers' disclosure of blatant lies, after massive protest in the land—after all that, troops were still being sent to Vietnam.

This peculiar and sordid paradox, of being asked to fight a war most of the country could no longer condone, left many GIs trapped. These were the reluctant warriors—who had rejected Canada or jail or didn't even know of such options. They went with varying degrees of dissent, low morale, and an abiding sense of frustration and anger. The last years of the war were fought by whole cadres of reluctant soldiers.

"There comes a time in some wars when the killing, or just the manner of dying, appears so senseless that even the obedient soldier who is 'not to reason why' begins to question the meaning of his sacrifice," wrote Neil Sheehan of the New York *Times* in *Harper's* in 1969. That August, a company of the 196th Light Infantry Brigade refused an order to attack. In A Shau Valley, the battle for a ridge that came to be known as Hamburger Hill —for the fifty-five paratroopers who did not survive the eleven consecutive assaults—exemplified the rebellion of the reluctant warrior.

Why were American youths still being killed for such godforsaken ridge lines, asked Senator Edward Kennedy, when the diplomats were supposedly negotiating a peace in Paris? A week after the paratroopers gained the summit, the ridge was abandoned, just as countless others had been before. It had "no tactical significance," said Major General Melvin Zais, the commander of the 101st Airborne Division. It was still a "gallant victory," however; 55 dead paratroopers had been traded for 629 North Vietnamese corpses. The letters of praise Senator Kennedy received from men who participated in the assault on Hamburger Hill were from the articulate as well as the barely literate. A kind of infantryman virtually nonexistent in Vietnam in earlier years—a college-educated soldier who reflected the antiwar movement at home—had joined the ranks. Ironically, the abolition of graduate-student deferments produced this rebel who could find no cause in Vietnam. In the fiscal year ending 1969, approximately 45,000 college graduates, more than double the 20,000 of two years previously were drafted into the Army or enlisted because they faced the choice of conscription or jail.[1]

The ambivalence of being in a war they wanted no part of created problems, guilt, and anger—then and now. Many of them are like Paul Barnicle, a medic in Vietnam with a genius IQ who became a cop on the beat. He is typical of a certain type of veteran—a gallant coper—yet not able to fully utilize his potential.

Barnicle is Boston Irish and shows a certain intrigue with the mores of Irish Americans. "There's this self-destructive acceptance. As my mother used to say, 'God works in strange but wonderful ways.' It's a denial of self-will. The Jews will push you to become a doctor or lawyer, whereas the Irish would say, 'That's not your lot in life.' So you get a job as a fireman. It's screwy."

The pivotal incident in Barnicle's childhood was the death of his father. Paul was twelve. They buried his father on Christmas Day, and Paul could not cry at the funeral. During the wake he sneaked back into the funeral parlor and cried alone in front of the casket.

"I felt unsure, deserted. I reacted by becoming a little old man."

That statement seems ludicrous now. Slim, red-bearded, good-looking, Barnicle today is easy with the quips.

"Wit and humor make everyone like you," he says with a shrug. "At the same time it keeps people at arm's distance. After Vietnam, for a while I was a buffoon. I was saying, 'Don't ask these questions, because if you do I'm simply going to make a joke out of it and disarm you.' But at that point as a teenager, I was a little old man. I had my future planned out." Paul got a scholarship to Assumption Prep, finishing second out of 900 in the admissions' examination. "I thought that's my ticket to Princeton."

Barnicle rolls his eyes, remembering his short time at Assumption. He was unprepared for the *"tremendously* regimented spartan life. The brothers would hit you if they caught you talking." He graduated from public high school in 1967 and that summer started smoking grass. With his poor record at Assumption, Princeton was a faded dream. Still, he had very good SATS scores, 1300. He went to Boston College but was a "total fuck-up. Never studied, lasted a year and half."

Weren't you worried about the war?

"It scared the hell out of me, but I didn't do much about it." There was a small politicized minority at B.C. "There was a demonstration against Dow, but I really didn't understand what Dow Chemical did."

Instead of protesting, it was more pleasurable to smoke dope, in the closet with a towel stuffed at the door, drifting off on the Doors, Buffalo Springfield, or the Rolling Stones. A particular song by the Doors, "Strange Days Are Coming," foreshadowed much for him.

After flunking out, Barnicle read Bernard Fall's books on the French fiasco in Vietnam and Senator J. William Fulbright's *Arrogance of Power*—and pumped gas. "I got called for my physical; B.C. immediately sent a letter to the draft board informing them I was no longer a student," he says caustically. The bus to South Boston Naval, in the spring of 1969, was "filled with working kids. They gave you a checklist of about 200 symptoms, and I checked off about 60 percent. If I had thought of it, I would have worn lace panties. The doctor looked at my list and said, 'You've checked off insomnia.' 'Yes, *sir.*' 'You've also checked off you *walk in your sleep.* Could you explain that?' 'Yes, *sir.* I toss and turn, and I toss and turn—but once I *get* to sleep, I walk.' It went over just swell," he adds drily. Barnicle saw no superpatriots in his blue-collar group. "We were like rats trying to get out of the maze, but most of us didn't have the money or the presence of mind to get out."

Barnicle decided that if he was drafted he'd be killed in Vietnam. "I had a recurring dream of a figure running across a distant knoll in silhouette, and a rifle appears in the lower left field of vision and emits smoke, and the figure falls. I was *convinced* that was me. So I enlisted—which meant a whole *extra year*—to avoid the infantry. I signed up for clerk school. How dangerous can that be? Tet had a big effect on me. There's Westmoreland talking about the light at the end of the tunnel, and then you could see on TV civilian employees at the *embassy* running around firing .45s. You just *knew* there was 'no light at the end of that tunnel.' I swear, *every* kid by then had a gut feeling that the war was fucked-up."

Instead of infantry, Barnicle, with his clerk MOS, became a medical records specialist. They posted the list, and there was Barnicle leading the list for RVN (Republic of Vietnam). As the GIs read the list, the room was filled with collective murmurs of "Oh shiiiiit." Barnicle smiled, recalling his reaction. "I became very Irish. I decided it was in the cards for me; I was going to die." On the way to the airport, Paul gave his brother burial instructions.

Paul Barnicle was leaving for Vietnam just after Cambodia and Kent State —amidst massive protest and violence at home. The "incursion" into Cambodia rejuvenated the Vietnam Moratorium Committee, which had closed its offices for lack of support. From all over the country, Senator George McGovern received about $100,000 in contributions to buy television time to reply to Nixon. One third of American colleges and universities closed or were disrupted by protest.[2] Four students were killed and nine wounded at Kent State, and then two more were shot dead protesting Nixon's actions at black Jackson State College in Mississippi. Nixon, as disassociated as always from antiwar reality, asked the Jackson State president, "Look, what are we going to do to get more respect for the police from our young people?"[3]

Importantly, Nixon was losing not just the people on the streets but more and more of the academic elite who helped shape foreign policy and top-level military who helped carry it out. Several members of the National Security

Council quit in protest, and 250 foreign-service officers signed a petition. An Army man like Major Hal Knight, who knew the true story of the secret bombing of Cambodia, which had occurred a full year earlier, was by then so disillusioned that he resigned and later revealed the secret bombing.[4] The division of consensus at the top was ever widening.

"The whole populace was questioning what the hell we were doing over there!" exclaims Barnicle. "I told my brother that if I died, I didn't want to be buried in any *uniform,* and I wanted them to tell the papers *why*—because I had died in an immoral war. I thought of deserting, but the word 'deserter' didn't set very well in my mind. I passed out leaflets at Fort Sam [Houston], rationalizing that I was fighting the system from within. The antiwar coffee houses were like therapy for us—until the last day when we got our orders."

One of the last nights before Vietnam, *Midnight Cowboy* was shown on the base. "They cut out the scene where Jon Voight beats the guy with the telephone. I asked, 'Sarge, why did you cut that scene?' He says, 'It was too violent!' Here we're fuckin' going off to kill, and it's too *violent!'*"

The plane ride was uneventful until they started their approach to Saigon. "They turned the lights *off* as we started to descend." The ominous message was clear. "You don't do that on *domestic* flights. Everyone got real quiet. A nineteen-year-old warrant officer sitting next to me started saying, 'What the fuck have I done?' His life expectancy was shit."

From his first day in Chu Lai, Barnicle saw nothing but gore. "I was supposed to be admissions clerk to the hospital, but they were short on help and they made me a medic in the emergency room."

The horrible irony is that Barnicle, who wanted to avoid the infantry, saw *more* death and dying and human waste as a medic than as a grunt. "A private came in with his best buddy on the dust-off. We got his buddy into surgery. I was mopping up the blood. The guy just looked at the blood, at me, and said, 'Man, you keep your job and I'll keep mine.' My very first day, I'll never *ever* forget," Barnicle says quietly. "Four WIA's (wounded-in-action) coming in. They had gone over a command-detonated mine in an armored personnel carrier. This guy, what was left of him, all the skin was penetrated by sand. His entire body was a flesh wound. The first lieutenant, the son of a general, had one arm and both legs blown off, the second guy had two legs blown off, the third had an arm blown off and two pieces of shrapnel entering his head in a downward angle with so much pressure his eyes were bulging out. The fourth had a leg blown off. The guy with the eyes popping out was just screaming, *nothing* but screaming." Two of the four died.

"Since I wasn't a full-fledged medic yet, I had to bag the dead bodies." They were supposed to put the identification tag on the toe. "If he'd lost his legs, you taped it to his chest and another identification on his thumb." After he bagged the bodies, Barnicle went outside and sat on a bench. "I just cried and cried and cried. And I realized I had about 360 days left there. I told myself, 'If you act this way every time you see this, you're going to be a basket case.' No one prepares you for it." Barnicle got so hardened he didn't recognize himself. "I just told myself I could *not* care."

But there was one story he could not forget, one incident he could not take calmly, then or now. "Are you up for my horror story? My *best* horror story?" he asks, caustically. "There was this suicide attempt. I had to pump his stomach. I asked his deros date and he was so short. Just weeks left. And I asked, 'Why would you do this? You're so short.' He was Jewish. Daniel . . ." Barnicle starts to tell his last name, then stops. "I don't know if his family ever knew how he died. He was from Massachusetts. A Jewish grunt. *That* was rare! He started talking: 'I've been in artillery for ten and a half months, and I've done everything they've asked me to. I've killed people. I'm just sick and tired of the killing.' I told him I'd been burying men for a long time, and I felt that they just couldn't send him back to fight. I said, 'I'll send you to a shrink who will give you a profile that will exempt you from certain kinds of duties.' The last thing I said was 'I'll look you up back in the world.' I sent him out with great confidence.

"A few days later I got a DOA [dead on arrival]. They handed me a poncho. It was 150 pounds of body parts." Barnicle tells the story with a stony face, as if compelled to tell it without emotion, except for the telltale pain in his eyes. "The only recognizable part was half of a flank of a right buttock. The only distinguishable *part.* I told another medic to find the dog tag. He got sick." By then Barnicle, who had sobbed and sobbed his first night, appeared a hardened robot. "I had earned a reputation of being so damn cold, so I put my hand in and fished around and found dog tags. It was Daniel. He had taken a claymore mine and cradled it in his arms and detonated it."

Barnicle's voice grows hard, reliving the anger. "I called that goddamn shrink. 'This is Sergeant Barnicle at 91st. Remember the kid I sent to you two, three days ago? What was his disposition?' The son of a bitch says, 'Oh, he was a *malingerer!*' " The cold rage flowed. " 'I want to tell you something, *doctor.* Daniel ——'s body parts are lying outside my office right now.' " Barnicle was crying for the first time in months. With tears streaming down his face, he started phoning to find a rabbi. "There was no rabbi in Chu Lai. I had to get a rabbi flown down from Da Nang."

Once again Barnicle tried to engage an outsider in the horror of it all. "I said, 'Rabbi, don't you want to see this?' I just couldn't stand it all alone anymore. He kept saying, 'Oh no, no,' in a 'that won't be necessary' tone. I opened up the poncho. After he looked in, he turned to me with total disgust. He kept saying, 'What is wrong with *you*—what is wrong with you that you could do this? You're an *animal!*' "

God forbid that the war's ghoulish realities should be shown to others. Those who faced it daily often resorted to dope, including heroin. "It became a nice high. You'd lace a cigarette. So strong, so pure. I'd smoke it. You could get it for two bucks, the size of a contact-lens case; 95 percent pure smack." Heroin-laced cigarettes meant a Russian roulette chance of getting hooked, a consequence few soldiers considered at the time, when tomorrow seemed ages away.

"I had a friend; he was from rural Missouri. A farmer. The kid was a rube, a *real* rube, and *he* got hooked on smack! At one time, one third of the guys in my unit (out of a 150 hospital staff) were heroin addicts, and 90 percent of the smack freaks had never tried it back in the world."

Barnicle's tale is supported by an unknown white medic—speaking from another time, on a tape that is a decade old. He was in the Long Binh jail, detoxing on heroin. His Vietnam experiences startlingly point up the dramatic change—from his first tour in 1969 to his next in 1971; from no heroin to rampant use, from no fragging to a constant hostile tension and threat of fragging. His voice is deep, sensitive, and ranges from an unemotional monotone to tears when he speaks of the dead and wounded.

Sometimes he stayed in the field three weeks without a break. On his first tour there were a lot of booby traps in the area, a lot of men being blown up every day. "You could see 'em be blown up, and there was no way you could do anything about it. I had two or three close friends . . ." His voice begins to shake. He fights for control. "When the enemy hit us, we never had a chance. In six months I saw eighty-two men turn over—that's how many were killed or wounded. I can remember times," he says, his voice shaking again, "having to carry my dead friends for two or three days at a time because they couldn't come to pick them up . . . A friend and myself actually tried to injure ourselves to get out of the field. I pulled a grenade on myself, but it flew behind a rock. Later on, *X* shot himself to get out of the field."

When the medic returned to the States, he was supposed to be a medical instructor for the remainder of his term of service. "Preparing them for Vietnam, many times I was told what to say and *censored.*" Like many GIs, he was unable to adjust to the spit-and-polish of home base, the harassment. "That's why there are so many second-tour men [in Vietnam]. Besides, I had helped a lot of people when I was over here. In a way I was *proud* of my service, although I can't condone killing."

He received the Silver Star for saving seven men. "I got a dust-off job" [picking up the wounded]. "Every day it scared me to death, worrying about being shot down. We were pulling secret missions into Cambodia, which the Army was hushing up. In one incident two helicopters were shot down, which is when I got my Silver Star. Here were four *dead* Green Berets. I had just extracted seven *wounded* men, and here was this officer, walking in, taking pictures." The voice is filled with disgust.

"I just sat back and cried," he responded in a broken voice. "My job is to *save* people. There was this old 'mama-san.' She was just kicking and everything else. Because of the language barrier, I didn't know what was wrong with her. I could see age, *years,* in this old lady's eyes. Now she was flying on a chopper. She was deathly scared of it. She just died on me. I gave her

mouth-to-mouth. Heart massage. Everything. I just sat back and wept because, you know, this old lady had been through so much. She really tore me
up. I thought that I had failed."

Like a broken record, his unfinished story ends ten years ago, with him still
in Vietnam. I tried in vain to find him in the States, through people who once
knew him. But like many veterans, the medic had simply disappeared.

Paul Barnicle returned with a year and a half of service left, violently
opposed to the war. He applied for C.O. status. "I told them that I was
violating my ethics every day." After eight months, he was granted a C.O.
discharge. "I became a free man five days before my twenty-third birthday."

He has great understanding for veterans with problems and feels lucky he
is less troubled. "I just lay it to my constitution." Barnicle points up that
peculiar paradox, apparent in so many surveys; men who loathed the war yet
who would do it again. "Yeah, I would. I can't figure out any other circumstance where I could have tested myself, my limits to such an extent. In one
year I had twenty years of life, and I came through that. I knew then that I
was a tremendously strong person. I still get scared and everything. I'm a
cop. Like if I get a call on a hold-up, I'm *scared,* Jesus—but I'm also confident."

It took well over a year to adjust. "Coming back was like being an ex-con.
The veterans got screwed. I was going to school full time at B.C. and also had
to work twenty-five hours a week, the GI loan was so bad." The climate of
the time is seared into his mind. He wanted a job in an intensive care unit. On
the application, he left blank the question "Are you a *veteran?*" When asked
about it, Barnicle replied that he was a *medic.* The personnel manager asked
if he was in Vietnam. Barnicle replied yes. "I could just *see* in his eyes that I
didn't have the job. I was, clearly, either a stoned junkie or a psychotic. So I
ended up driving a cab at night."

For a while Barnicle worked in a Roxbury drug clinic. He was following
that pattern of veterans who became motivated to help others although he
remained distant, detached. "It was interesting for a year, and then all the
stories started to sound alike. Most of them were full of shit. They thought I'd
just fallen out of an apple tree, but I'd been around the block too long. They
were getting off on being poor, black addicts. There were some legitimate
guys I had empathy for. The rest were just thieves."

Why did you become a cop?

"A lot had to do with Vietnam—the camaraderie, the sense of danger."

Do you need that?

A long pause. "I don't know. A lot of my preconceptions of cops had
changed. They weren't all pigs. I saw that they could really help people."

Another disillusion was in store for the liberal-minded Barnicle. "I've become . . . I feel I'm very racist. Ninety-five percent of the people I lock up
are black. I see people doing *incredible* things to others. Robberies where they
cut people when they don't have to. Vicious gang rapes. In Southie, the Irish

steal cars and do B and E's [breaking-and-entering]; they might stick up a store, or get involved in some organized crime or drug dealing. The Italians are similar, but [with them] there is no such thing as cutting you when you mug, or raping. I'm worried about myself. I don't *like* being a racist. Shouldn't we be good to each other? I used to think, 'Well, these blacks are committing these crimes because of economic and social deprivation. Just letting out their anger. Then, when I find a woman vaginally, rectally, and orally raped and then cut up, by five people at gunpoint, I just can't believe it anymore. I don't want to generalize, but the really vicious, *vicious* rapes I have seen happened to be blacks against whites. I never thought I'd say it, but rape deserves the death penalty. No—it really deserves castration."

There are long thoughts about how his life would have been different if he had not gone to Vietnam. "I wonder about that all the time. I think I would probably be a lawyer, have a wife and one-and-a-half kids, and drive a VW Rabbit, and donate to all the right causes." Barnicle laughs.

"I'm not unhappy anymore, but I want to do more with myself. I don't want to be trapped as a cop at fifty-five flirting with the high school waitress behind the counter at Dunkin' Donuts. This woman I was living with said I had to get a straight job. 'Use your brains,' she kept saying."

Suddenly there is an outpouring I have heard so many times that I have lost count from so many of the brightest veterans. They live daily with the knowledge that few people in their crowd understand what they went through—first in Vietnam and then in the seventies, being "branded" a veteran. "I've seen a lot go into high-risk occupations, I've seen so many Vietnam veterans take shitty jobs—way beneath them. My girlfriend hates for me to be a cop. She is a social worker at the VA, and she works with veterans in therapy. She broods a lot. There are guys in the spinal-cord unit; some have been in there, severed, for a decade."

"You can't blame everything on Vietnam, but there are a lot of guys who came back so *angry* that they cannot function to full potential. Maybe I'm one of them. Look, I have a 148 IQ, for what that's worth. I should be writing a book or be a lawyer. We're so angry at just the way we've been treated. *That people don't want to understand that Vietnam ever existed in your life really angers me.* There's a lot of anger that I would have not had otherwise. A lot of anger at everyone for not realizing the specialness of that war and what it did to us."

The following are four of the least stereotypical Vietnam veterans. Had this been the Korean War, they would have been the kind who stayed student-deferred but upon graduation, without question, become young officers. They went to Vietnam far more reluctantly than their Korean War counterparts, questioned their presence there constantly, and ultimately opposed our intervention. Still, they were propelled by a residual childhood sense of duty. They returned to worlds and careers filled with those who didn't go. Three are writers. One, a graduate of Georgetown's Foreign Service School, took prominent Capitol Hill jobs, including being an assistant to the House Judiciary Committee's Impeachment Inquiry. All are antiwar still. Their complex and ambiguous feelings about Vietnam and those students who didn't go nonetheless distance them from those in the exempted world. Only one saw combat, but all three were affected and changed by Vietnam.

John Peterson led a squad in Vietnam, and that was as much a fluke as his being drafted.

In 1967, just before the magic age of twenty-six, he was drafted after graduating from Georgetown University's Foreign Service School. Peterson is uncertain how he got picked up in a Project 100,000 sweep whereby many of those who had gotten 4-F and the once-married–now-divorced were being reexamined and reclassified. Peterson felt an important ambivalence, unknown to younger members of the generation nurtured in total cynicism about the war. "I was against the war as a political mistake. But my doubts about the morality of that war never led to any *pro*–Viet Cong or *pro*-NVA position, and that's one reason I had problems with some of the antiwar Vietnam veterans, who marched with the VC flag-carriers. I felt that some of the antiwar people were right, and yet I wondered what's my responsibility? I didn't see that it merited resisting the draft to *not* go, which would rip you out of the context of your family. My family weren't gung ho, but they certainly did not think it righteous not to go."

Peterson also thought he would never have to make a choice about killing. "I never thought I'd *ever* be in the infantry," he says, with a reticent, soft laugh. He made 'instant' NCO (noncommissioned officer) and urgently tried to transfer into interpreter courses, until he found out he would have to extend for three years.

NCO school delayed his arrival in Vietnam six months. "Otherwise I would have arrived a week and a half *before* Tet, when your odds of making it were approximately 50-50."

Like many others, Peterson uses the word "absurd" to describe his condition—hitting the field of battle as the shape of the peace table was being thrashed out. "I remember thinking that if I die for something I don't believe in—that two weeks later will be over—that is going to be the *ultimate* absurdity. No matter the level of education, grunts would say, 'Why are we here? It's all bullshit. F.T.A.' The actual rank-and-file infantry comprised about 10 percent of the total forces in Vietnam. I think a lot of this macho stuff comes from rear people or West Pointers or Annapolis types. If you *really* had to risk your life, then you have to isolate the major question—is it worth it? *Most of the line infantry were draftees.* The support troops enlisted."

There is an incredibly upper-class look to Peterson—even white teeth, cleft chin, lock of brown hair with a shock of gray. As an instant NCO, he found himself in limbo—alienated from the regular NCOs, "who didn't like us because we got ranked too fast," and the regular GIs, "who knew we were just draftees who had received accelerated promotions to sergeant and had a 'what have you got that I haven't got?' attitude."

Despite his class and education, Peterson's affinity was with the GI because Peterson felt that he too was treated as expendable cannon fodder. "We were the instant NCOs, put in as squad and platoon leaders to *save their career staff people,*" he says with uncharacteristic harshness.

When Peterson went on R and R, he returned to find a new man in his squad. "I hear you read books," said the soldier who had been a philosophy major. They spent the first night on guard duty talking about Sartre. Yet Peterson was being changed by the war. "My intellectual affinity with this guy became less important. He turned out to be the least willing to share food and the least willing to risk himself for the group. A lot of guys were, class-wise, less educated but with native brainpower, and that comes out when you're finding a trail or tracking an enemy. That became more important."

Peterson and company developed an intuitive, time-immemorial grunts'-eye sense of the ridiculous conditions of battle. "I heard of the majors with their pins in their maps—the '200 NVA spotted and go there' bullshit. *The total intelligence was all fragmentary and all wrong.* Stuff we paid for from corrupt South Vietnamese. Some fat-ass deadbeat son of a bitch is sitting there saying, 'Just move that pin,' and away with the troops. I was talking with my radio operator and told him that a colonel got killed, which is extremely rare. Rich just said, 'Good. Hundreds of GIs are getting killed; I'm glad this thing's being spread around.' "

An attitude found in all wars, to be sure, but Vietnam's peculiarities invited low morale and an extreme we-they, grunt-officer division. There were all those phrases—H and I (harassment and interdiction), search and destroy, body count, and rachet (McNamara's term for incrementally slight escalating). "All became an extension of Pentagon statistics, all bureaucratic formulations. There's a limit to which people were willing to carry out that stuff," says Peterson. "The GIs never believed that, bought it, or fought for it. And I don't think *officers* believed it—if they were in the field for a while—but we were committed to a structure." In addition, the one-year tour created a contemptuous caste system, regardless of rank. "The shorter you were [the less time you had left on your Vietnam tour of duty], the more ignorant the new people were considered. *It was very hard to tell somebody what to do if you knew they knew more than you.* A general rule of thinking was that a greenhorn 'would get my ass killed.' "

Peterson was hardly bucking for stripes; the war's absurdity prompted an evasive, not a glory-seeking, approach. "It wasn't really a war; nothing was toward a total effort. I always looked for the most secure place to be for my squad. That's one reason I was successful. I knew one of their concerns was 'How safe are you going to keep us?' " Still the sense of war and battle and competing for the kill "comes out in everybody. It's atavism—100,000 years of it. You do get into it. We were once told that our platoon got *three* kills and the next platoon had only *two,* and I said, 'Good.' It was just automatic."

On the wall in Peterson's townhouse bedroom are his Purple Heart, an autographed picture of Robert Kennedy, a note from Sam Ervin, and a long-ago picture of his mother and dad—she in a long gown, he in a starched World War II officer's uniform. His living room is a blend of fine oriental rugs, dark-stained floors, and hundreds of neatly stacked books—Camus, Stilwell, Adlai Stevenson, and Talleyrand, Kenneth Clark, *Pilgrim's Way* . . . It is in remarkable contrast to his old Vietnam scrapbook. A street-smart GI friend, who looks twelve, sits talking, a cigarette dangling out of his mouth. There are tattoos on the arms of others. A Snoopy cartoon says "Happiness is heading home." Like some new-wave movie, those starkly different worlds fade in and out and overlap in his mind's eye. He has been pushed and pulled by the two extremes. Peterson experienced something to-tally out of his class experience—not trained to it through ROTC or military academies, but brought to it through happenstance. On the one hand there is loathing for it. "Just going and going and putting in two years for nothing—*worse* than nothing. Something I didn't agree with and didn't want to do at all. I really *hated* the Army. The Army in peacetime *truly* is awful. *Vietnam* was better than that! And I *really* hated Vietnam." Peterson considers himself lucky to have no delayed stress. "It was partly luck. No real close friends were killed. Nobody in my squad was killed when I was squad leader. There was never that guilt that something I did wrong got somebody else killed. Some kids got into drugs—purely an escape mechanism. One guy totally cracked up. He believed that he had killed another guy by accident on patrol. He was totally gone for the rest of the year. Totally destroyed mentally. The Army kind of hushed it up."

Age was a big factor, as well as class. Peterson specifically planned, as a psychological motivation, something he could look forward to on his return —a trip to Europe. He also held no illusions. "I knew the terms on which I was there—to save my life and others."

For all the hates, paradox intrudes. "In some ways it was a growing, hu-man experience. The camaraderie, being close to people in a common en-deavor. That was hard to sort out when I got back. You know you hated it, and yet it was a great personal experience." He is struck with the profound sense of sadness at the farewells to GIs leaving Vietnam. "We absolutely did not know how to deal with it. The last day should have been a *happy* occa-sion, but *everyone* was sad. We knew we'd probably never see each other again."

If there is a scar in all this for Peterson, it is that veterans were denied an emotional binding. They were denied the reception or acknowledgment of society, yes, but also something else. "This is *very* important," he says em-phatically. "For the first time there is no unifying veteran hall where we can talk over experiences." He echoes the view of many Vietnam veterans. "World War II was a camp reunion for many for the rest of their lives. If you abstract Vietnam out of the negatives and the politics, it was the most vivid experience we had—and no one is sharing it."

His career progressed restlessly but well. Peterson thrust Vietnam from his mind, started on Capitol Hill in a research job, and then became an aide to the Senate Watergate Committee. "I was an old California Democrat from way back, and when impeachment loomed, I of course was interested." He worked on the Senate Intelligence Committee until 1976, held a scheduling job on the Carter campaign, was a Schedule C appointee at the State Department, and became a special assistant to the assistant head of AID. Later, Peterson, long intrigued by history, looked for something new. He is with the historic preservation program of the National Park Service. An avocation now is military history.

For years he spoke little of Vietnam. He sighs. "Vietnam is a very complex thing. There is no simple answer. That's one reason conversations are so long. I really hate to get into it." Peterson rejected the simplistic thoughts of both the right and left. "Staying had to be based on the people doing it themselves. There's no way we could have stayed on a permanent basis. That was what was so complicated about Tet." In recent years, many books have argued that the press had not perceived that Tet—with its massive enemy casualties—was a military victory for the United States and that the failure to recognize this turned the country against the war. However much the United States won it militarily, Tet still was not a *victory* in any psychological sense. The VCI (Viet Cong Infrastructure) remained. "We won in one sense, and they won in another. They showed us on a massive basis that they would never give up, no matter the casualties. And the fact that we won *proved* that we were necessary for the South Vietnamese. There was no hope for them on their own."

Complexities aside, Peterson avoided the subject of Vietnam when he returned, in part because the conversations would have been with people who did not go. "They are most of my friends. I knew I'd get into resentment, such as 'Why do you say *I'm* wrong [for going] if you didn't really have to *make* the same choice?' " The feelings are convoluted "because they are my intellectual friends by choice. I had a lot of attitudes similar to those who were out—and yet I didn't agree with them; you just can't get out of certain societal decisions. It is impossible to explain to them.

"I was very touchy for years about little reminders of Vietnam, although I appeared fairly detached. While in Europe, I met this girl. We were off on a weekend, with a group, and somehow we got on the subject of Vietnam. One of my friends teasingly said, 'Tell us something about shooting the nun, John.' " Before John could respond, the girl piped up, matter of factly, "Oh, John, what about that?"

"I was just *horrified*. Here I'd opened up enough to consider her a friend, and she was willing to believe I had *shot a nun!* It was just a horrifying experience." He can still see her: "Tell me, John, *tell* me. I really *want* to hear it."

Now Peterson sees Vietnam as an intensely important experience that will permeate most veterans' lives. "In spite of all the rotten experiences, for all the absurdity, fear, and danger, there was some transcending personal worth —friendships, nobility, whatever . . ."

Tom Fiedler turned eighteen in 1964 when there was little awareness of Vietnam. Green Berets were seen as glamorous soldiers of fortune. Fiedler received a federal congressional appointment, and followed the romantic lure of going to sea by becoming an officer in the Merchant Marine. He recalls how little he could relate to the liberal arts students he occasionally met. The upperclassmen in *his* academy carried a dinghy into the quadrangle, raised the sail, and shouted, "Ding dong, kill the Cong."

In 1968 Fiedler attended his first big antiwar demonstration. He came into Washington with his close-cropped hair and the scruffiest jeans he possessed —which meant they were starched and creased. "I felt out of place, and I *resented* the fact I was *made* to feel out of it. There was very much of a confrontational atmosphere."

Later, as a third officer on a Merchant Marine freighter heading for Vietnam, Fiedler "knew my generation was going through something and I was missing it. My main motivation for going was curiosity." Robert Kennedy was shot the day before. An admirer of Kennedy, Fiedler was beginning to question the war but felt that "the only way to settle it for myself was to take a look."

Disillusion was immediate. "My first negative experience was when we arrived in Cam Ranh Bay. Here we were carrying materials the South Vietnamese needed to 'help fight back the North Vietnamese aggressors'; we were *loaded* with trucks and jeeps, and the harbormaster wouldn't let us in unless we paid a *bribe* to him and his brother-in-law, who owned the only barge that provided fresh water!

"Had they treated us like 'liberators,' that would have confirmed my idealistic image." Intellectually, Fiedler could understand that after decades of colonial oppression, *any* white person was viewed with suspicion and/or hate, but he resented it. "Part of the ethic became to rip off whoever the most recent intruder happened to be." Danger was not the norm, except one time when his ship was part of a convoy up the Nah Be River, "very winding and shallow in some parts. The VC controlled the delta, and they would shell, and I felt just like a sitting duck, scared to death. The ship behind us took mortar fire that killed five people." It was then that he thought, "What the hell are we doing? The whole concept that we were protecting them from communism was absolutely ridiculous. Most had no concept what communism was.

"I think we may have exacerbated the boat-people problem. We destroyed and divided things so badly that when reunification came, that sort of situation was inevitable. Had we *never* been there, there would never have been the polarization. Whether they are worse off is a valid question, but it still doesn't justify us being there. It was a war of self-determination. I thought I ought to register a protest by resigning my commission and applying for C.O. status. Maybe I now rationalize what I did, but I decided not to. One, it was not the military's fault—the wrongdoing was done by politicians. And two, if I did ask for C.O., I wouldn't be true to myself because I *wasn't* a C.O. It certainly was the first crisis of conscience I had ever gone through."

Vietnam forged a career in writing. Fiedler is now an editor with the Miami *Herald.* "I thought a newspaper was one place where you could raise ideas about politics and force people to be accountable for their positions."

His feelings about those who didn't go are ambivalent. "On one hand I think it was elitism and arrogance for those self-centered people to whom it was 'just an inconvenience.' Yet I give many of them credit for knowing more about themselves at eighteen than I did. I have a lot of contempt for the ones who went out and yelled, 'Hell no, we won't go,' threw blood on the Pentagon steps, and maintained deferments. I feel intellectually they were frauds. That's what bothered me—how could they have been so *sure?* If they wanted to register protest accurately, they should have gone *not* for ROTC, but the *political science* building, because that's where the system got fouled up." Struggling, as always, for balance, Fiedler adds that he is also uncomfortable with the hawk warrior veteran "who is just as sure on his side as those who never went and are convinced that everyone who did not go was evil."

Fiedler is like many of the generation who regret, in part, having gone along with the flow. "It still tears me up that I didn't resign my [Merchant Marine] commission, make some symbolic gesture. I'm free of guilt—but I'll probably *never* know whether I should have done anything."

Bill Nack was a University of Illinois graduate who could write well. Jeff Stein was a college dropout, playing with a rock-and-roll band in Martha's Vineyard when the Army drafted him. He too had potential.

After a year and a half of training he arrived in Da Nang in 1968—the rock-and-roll singer had become a Vietnamese-speaking agent for U.S. Army Intelligence. Nack and Stein belong to an elitist corps, sometimes viewed with collective contempt by combat veterans. Although both returned, never having experienced battle, they were deeply influenced by their year in Vietnam.

Nack was in college during the early stages of the war, when all things Kennedy were romanticized and college men still thought going to war was something you did. Men joined ROTC at the University of Illinois and wore Bermudas and led panty raids. There had been Selma and Vietnam was still just an echo somewhere and John Kennedy was killed and Martin Luther King, Jr., was a new name. Nack was sports editor of the *Daily Illini,* and just before he graduated in 1965 he wrote an unsigned editorial against the war. "I was under the influence of Walter Lippmann and was hanging around with what were called the campus 'radicals.' We'd sit around drinking coffee, and the resident Communist would come in. SDS was just getting started."

Nack's parents were politically conservative and had some measure of influence, as well as Walter Lippmann. Still, the dread of serving in Vietnam overcame the duty to one's country. One day in ROTC class, "I remember raising my hand and asking, 'Does it look like we will have to go—or will it always be voluntary?' "

By the time Nack graduated, "I was *scared.* I knew I was going into the service as a lieutenant." Nack is big, with a broad body and face, and looks a little like Stacy Keach. He looked the perfect specimen for war. "There I was, prime grade A beef, stamped with blue. I remember some doctor asking, 'Lieutenant, do you have any clotting problem?' and I felt like saying 'Well, yessir, there's this yellow streak.' " He recalls a Pattonesque soliloquy from a gung ho officer: "A lot of you are concerned you'll chicken out under fire. Don't worry about it. When you put your hand in a bunch of goo that a moment before was your *best friend's face,* you'll know what to do." It all seemed unreal.

When Nack was called up in 1966, "I was the only dove in the entire troop." Nack argued without much success with other young officers from Harvard, Notre Dame, or Temple University.

Jungle Warfare School meant "learning how to rip a chicken's head off to eat it, running around in the jungles of Panama getting chased by Green Berets, and watching one guy get electrode shock on his genitals. Most of the Green Berets were decent, but some were inhuman. We were trying to simulate the experience of being POWs, and one of the rules was you weren't allowed to talk to your captors. If you did talk or were out of line, they would put electrodes on your nuts."

Nack's wife had just had a baby, and he remained stateside for one year. By then the war was "eating officers alive." When Nack got his orders, he, like Paul Barnicle, made many symbolic gestures preparing for death. He got a life insurance policy and had his picture taken. With melodramatic flair, he envisioned his wife taking out this faded picture fifteen years later and saying, "Your father was a great man."

He also went from dove to hawk as a denial process took over. "I said, if I'm going, I'm going. No more of this antiwar bullshit. I can't *afford* it. I really psyched myself but good! I stopped watching Eric Sevareid, stopped reading Walter Lippmann. I was a hawk!"

Three days after landing in Vietnam, assignments were posted. A friend, Geoffrey, came up to Nack. "Jeesus, Nack, how did you do it? Did you see the board?" Next to Nack's name was MACV (Military Assistance Command, Vietnam). "Geoffrey's mouth was dry. He wasn't getting any spit. His face was ashen. I saw these guys run and get on choppers. All red dust and noise, and then they'd disappear. Talk about whim of fate. I was the only one left in Bien Hoa. I didn't feel guilty—I felt lucky. I took a bus to Saigon. Geoffrey died in May."

Nack was a desk jockey, a writer for the Army, and had an easy time of it. "Tet [1968] was my *goodbye* party. Only time I really felt threatened. The night before, the colonel gave me his motorbike, 'the Blue Goose.' I felt free, and I got drunk at the Continental Hotel." The morning of Tet, Nack took off on the Blue Goose, from downtown Saigon, bound for Tan Son Nhut Air Force Base. "I was driving for five minutes and there was not a soul. No little kids. No old men pissing on corners. It was eerie. And *then* all of a sudden I heard helicopters and the noise of guns. A helicopter gunship and rockets and all sorts of noise. I saw an MP up ahead and raced up and said, 'What the hell's going on?' He looked at me in absolute amazement. 'Lieutenant, *what* are you doing?' I told him I was going to work. *He* said, 'You just drove through a VC battalion.' I had taken a shortcut. If I had driven the normal route, I would have been dead."

Nack adamantly refuses to buy the Tet victory argument. "It psychologically destroyed us. We lost the war that day. It was not *supposed* to happen. I drove through a VC battalion we didn't even *know* was there! I don't care how many they eventually lost. We were the biggest war machine—and they came in!"

The VC were walking in mortar rounds on the runway as Nack's airplane left Tan Son Nhut in March. Engines screaming, the plane took off in one of those abrupt vertical escapes. Everyone was pressed back in his seat by the ascent. Finally the pilot announced in his *Right Stuff* voice as calmly as if he were pointing out the Potomac River on approach to Washington, D.C.: "The VC, uh, were walking in some mortars back there. Don't know if you saw it or not. I apologize for such a rough takeoff."

"Apologize?" recalls Nack. "It was one of the greatest moments of my life."

There were adjustments, even for those not in combat. "The first job interview, I had on different-colored socks and was so nervous the guy didn't hire me. I couldn't hold anything down for three weeks. I was embarrassed about being in Vietnam. The antiwar sentiment was so puerile. There was no red badge of courage out of that place. It was just something you tried to hide." Nack got a job on Long Island *Newsday.* Although the mood was jocular, there was a slight rubbing-your-nose-in-it texture to the assignment. "The first KIA [Killed in Action] story, you're doing," said the editor. Nack recalls, "I used to dread to go to work. They were getting killed at a rate of 400 a day. One day the editor said, 'Nack, guess what? I have Private so-and-so. Here's his parents' address.' I said, 'Can't I do it on the phone?' 'No.' So I did my first KIA. Had to listen to the parents cry." They were always so young, always the former baseball player, the ones who could jump three feet in the air, the Boy Scout . . . They asked if I had been in Vietnam, and I said, 'Yes, I am just out.' And I felt guilty I was *alive.*"

As with so many, Nack is "still sorting out my feelings after all these years." Now a writer for *Sports Illustrated,* Nack feels he would have found the same career regardless of Vietnam. "But Vietnam hurt my marriage. I couldn't relate to the family. It just divided us for a long time."

How do you feel about not being in combat? "A *lot* of ambivalence. A little guilty that I wasn't out in the boonies. My greatest fear was of what would be done after being captured. They told us about beheading, and I used to wonder what it was like. Was it like a chicken who flops around? Do you still see, for a second, when the head is off?" The reporter in Nack is somewhat envious of writers like Michael Herr *(Dispatches):* "He saw more than I did. Yes, I wish I'd gone on a couple of patrols."

As for that generation of men, Nack sees no large-scale coming together. "Only in the individual conscience will the rehabilitation and reconciliation be made. My first thought when I find out someone didn't go is 'Is this guy genuine or a coward?' I think a lot were genuinely concerned."

If you had been six years younger, would you not have been right with them?

"I don't know. I don't think I would have resisted the draft. I'm the conventional middlewesterner. I have begun to believe that, despite what we all thought ten years ago about the war, that our presence cannot be judged accurately, maybe, for another twenty or thirty years."

He feels some pride in having served—but quickly begs off trying to examine the origins of that pride extemporaneously. "It is too complex." Instead, he thought about it and later wrote about his feelings:

"I don't know what to call it. Pride, perhaps, or something akin to it. But some time during the last few years I stopped being embarrassed at the fact that I had served in Vietnam, stopped feeling vaguely guilty about my involvement, and actually began to feel good about it. I began to talk about it more openly. As time went on, people no longer regarded me suspiciously when they found out I had served there. And there was one other thing: I began to realize—and I really believe this today—that I was at least a part of probably the most dramatic and ambitious, if ill-fated, enterprise that this country had ever gotten itself involved in. Nothing in our time has ever so consumed this land, so divided its people, so made of it one theater. Twisted and tragic, yes, but colossal and dramatic too. And I was *there*, you know. I was there. I like the thought of that."

To Jeff Stein getting drafted was a little like getting caught playing hooky to go to the Red Sox opener, which he also did. "You get caught, you have to stay after school. I accepted the punishment. In my time you obeyed the rules. When you were thrown out of college, the version of 'staying after school' was that you got drafted. In post-'67, people began to say, 'Fuck it. Break the rules. Puke on deans' desks, break into the files.'"

"I went to church, came from a conservative Republican family, have a certain class background. All those things add up when you make decisions, and a lot of it isn't within your control. I'm kind of existentialist in that way."

But he was not existentialist enough to go with the flow into the infantry. With his draft notice coming down, he enlisted.

The Army sent him to an intensive Vietnamese language course. His basic intelligence qualified him for spy work. Espionage training was a Le Carre-like romantic adventure. They learned to write in invisible ink, how to make dead drops (messages left in trees), and how to ferret out and train an agent.

"With my two years of college, I had the least education of everyone in my intelligence-school class. I was surrounded by guys who'd gone to Harvard and Yale. If we questioned the war, it was in a humorous way. 'It's kind of dumb.' Reporters who covered the antiwar movement got a sense that everyone of that ilk was against the war, but I don't think that's true. First of all, those of us in the Army were institutionally captured. And many of us were operating along the lines of 'If you're caught, you go and make the best of it.'

"VVAW [Vietnam Veterans Against the War] *never* would have happened if the goddamn war hadn't gone on and on and on. If Korea had gone on, you would have had the same thing."

Vietnam intelligence operations quickly became the theater of the absurd. The first night in Da Nang, Stein went to a party at the consulate and was asked what he did. Stein responded with his cover—that he was part of a civilian refugee care unit—whereupon the questioner casually replied, "Oh, you're a *spook!*" Late that night, the nervous novice agent complained about this to his fellow undercover operatives. "Oh, that's nothing," one casually told Stein with a cynical laugh. "The Green Berets captured a VC map of Da Nang with an *X* on our house." The words "Nha Dac Biet," meaning "special intelligence house," were beside the *X*.

"I had a beer halfway to my mouth," recalls Stein, "and I said, 'Holy shit! What are we doing here? Everyone knows who and where we were!' I then got a different cover—a civilian working for the Navy personnel office. I actually worked there—and as a joke I was given an award. Years later I met Admiral Elmo Zumwalt and reminded him of that."

From November 1968 to November 1969, Stein was a case officer under deep cover, controlling a net of agents based in Da Nang and spread throughout Quang Nam and southern Thua Thien provinces. He collected mostly order-of-battle intelligence and occasionally political intelligence, which was forwarded to the Operation Phoenix program coordinator. "I eventually learned that my agent and his subagents were members of a right-wing Vietnamese militarist party. He had this world fascist allegiance and wanted to *overthrow* the Vietnamese government—*from the right!*

"I tried unsuccessfully to fire my agent because he passed me much retreaded and fabricated information. A friend of mine had a net of agents in Quang Nhi, and he called them 'Ali Baba and the Forty Thieves.'"

Stein's experience should be heeded by those revisionists who attempt to reconstruct a winning or laudable Vietnam War based on unquestioning studies of military documents. "One night the proverbial light bulb went on in my head. I had been reading through *pages* and *pages* of intelligence reports of these agents, as well as CIA, Navy, Air Force stuff, reading Vietnamese newspapers, really getting a feel for the situation. The pattern of information made me realize, 'Oh my God, we're being used by this political party to wipe out *their* opponents on the left.' The people they were naming as Communists were left-wing Buddhists, and that information was going to the Phoenix program. We were being used to assassinate their political rivals.

"At the same time I was trying to get him fired, my commanding officer wanted to raise my agent's reliability rating because, in my opinion, it would make my officer look good. He was a former West Point instructor and a real jerk-off. I got into an incredible struggle with him. He began to collate the reports and *skew* them to make this agent look better than he was. I told him about my agent's political affiliations but to no avail. I became resigned to it. The first thing you learn in the Army is not competence, you learn corruption. And you learn 'to get along, go along.'

"I suddenly became aware that if I lost my agent, there'd be nothing for me to *do* there anymore," he says caustically. "That was fraught with all sorts of exciting possibilities—like getting sent to the infantry or back to the States to paint rocks at Fort Bragg. I remember a new team chief came over from the States and asked me what I thought about the war. I said, 'We don't *think* about the war here, because if we really *thought* about it, we couldn't stay here anymore.' For us intelligence officers, there weren't too many options. We could've defected—and gone on the talk-show circuit in Moscow—or we could've quit. We thought that meant being thrown into the infantry."

In spite of his scheming agent, Stein won awards for having the best intelligence operation in northern South Vietnam. "It's like [being] a reporter; after a while you sense what's true and what isn't." And he was evolving a view that has hardened in time. "It was a stupid, and I would go so far as to say, a criminal war. I think it's a criminal war in El Salvador right now. We're financing *death squads.* Vietnam was a criminal war. We were clearly foreign oppressors, and I am ashamed that I participated. That I wasn't smart enough to figure it out before I was drafted—or call a press conference in Saigon and say, 'I am a military intelligence officer, I run agents, and I know what's going on, and it's a crime. And on top of that, we can't win.' "

Back home Stein completed college and then earned his M.A. in Southeast Asian studies on a fellowship at the University of California at Berkeley. "I wanted to understand intellectually what I had just experienced personally." In 1970 "a deep guilt set in. I recognized the participation of U.S. intelligence agents in the overthrow of Sihanouk [in Cambodia]. I became increasingly frustrated." Stein organized against the war and wrote tracts while at Berkeley.

Like many veterans, he had little empathy for those in the student left who persisted in casting the VC as romantic saviors. "It pissed me off—to be *against* the war, they had to *elevate* the other side. The right wing has a legitimate bitch: the movement and the mass media collaborated on the notion of the VC as a romantic force. Yet on the other hand the Communist Party *did* by 1945 capture and articulate and put into action the desire of the masses of Vietnamese to free themselves from colonial oppression. Then it was a very broad-based movement. It was a form of socialism—now shoved out by what can only be considered Stalinists from Hanoi, with a very harsh, punitive approach. There are hardly any VC with influence anymore."

The fate of Vietnam—the repressive "reeducation" camps, the boat people, etc.—is being used by those who argue that our presence was just and we should have "fought to win"—no matter that we *did* destroy more than a million civilians with our firepower. For the soldier in the field—no matter the political restraints—the military restrictions on this war makes him, understandably, a believer in the "they wouldn't let us win" theory.

"They're right in their own way," says Stein. "There *were* limits—but the limits were placed out of larger geopolitical and domestic considerations. Our leadership was terrified about wider Chinese and Soviet intervention. So it's such a big *if* that it doesn't count. Wars are fought with political constraints. Nuking Hanoi was not acceptable—any political aims would have been defeated so greatly, and we would have been so roundly condemned internationally, it wouldn't have been worth it. So drop it down a scale. Try to assure conventional victory? *We were doing it!* There's no question who the aggressors were, and it was us. So they say, 'Why didn't we mine Haiphong Harbor early on?' At that time the Chinese were absolutely allied with the Vietnamese. They were in the midst of the cultural revolution, the hardliners were in power, and they would have *loved* to have drawn the United States deeper into a land war. If we had bombed Haiphong, then we would have had to pay another penalty, maybe 100,000 Chinese, into the war and get our asses kicked when we were already losing it the way we were going."

It is indeed too great a simplifier to say 'what if?' and then relive the war in speculatively military glory.

"It's much easier to say we could have won than that we *couldn't* have won because we were on the wrong side—one not supported by its own people. Politically we couldn't win because the policy became known to be illegitimate by too many people in America and in Vietnam. And there were national and international stakes beyond Vietnam—SALT and detente for example—which remained the festering sore. Still, there remains the question whether we could have won anyway, notwithstanding those political restraints—without totally killing all the people. Good God, look at the firepower we used. We couldn't destroy the VC infrastructure *any way*. It was impossible—for military, political, and moral reasons."

Stein's personal Vietnam legacy is similar to Paul Barnicle's. Although he became an activist against the war, that moral stance was not a total catharsis; it did not save him from the same emotion engendered in so many veterans who said or did little on return. His thoughts are identical to many, including Barnicle, as he speaks intensely about his anger. "No one wants to listen to what we have to say—especially those of us veterans on the left: A bunch of guys who ducked Vietnam now think El Salvador and Lebanon should be "pushovers" and want to send their younger brothers off. It makes me *very, very* angry."

Myth shattering remains an uneasy course.

Cynicism, the one shared reaction of that generation, was graphically addressed by William G. Pelfrey, when he returned from combat in 1970. "I am speaking of those who *were* politically aware but were also faced with the draft after graduation. The complex issues debated on campus dissolved into three choices for us: go to jail, duck out of the country, or become a part of the military . . . After serious and tormenting thought, we chose to accept conscription, and less than a year after the end of student deferments, our class rings were glistening against the Asian sun from the open side of a helicopter as we made our first combat assault," he wrote.

It was no longer a matter of cocktail debate and campus rally. "My bitterest memory of Vietnam is the inevitable chaplain's visit whenever we suffered a killed-in-action . . ." The cynicism is not missing in Pelfrey's comment. "He would play taps on a portable tape recorder and then comfort us with thoughts on how our dead comrade had willingly lain down his life in defense of our country and all its cherished ideals."

Pelfrey, on return, remained in a vacuum watching the GI being reduced to little more than an abstract, paternalistic figure of speech. ". . . After Vietnam, the confident righteousness and boisterous tone of the undergraduate ring with a marble hollowness . . . Communication with our former peers becomes almost as distant as with the grandfather who volunteered in 1918 . . .

"We too want to forget the mess. Yet there will always be some stigma, positive or negative, at having been a physical part of it." Pelfrey ended his thought with a hope that the bitterness and emptiness felt by veterans would wear off with time. But then, in 1970, cynicism was the abiding theme. He recalled the popular engraving on cigarette lighters in Vietnam:

"When I die, bury me face down so the whole world can kiss my ass."

"Perhaps in thirty years the popular image of the Vietnam GI will be one of an unthinking subhuman machine blindly submitting to the state," reflected Pelfrey. He added, "Even more repulsive is the image of some future patriot rising to national power with a chest of Asian medals and the bellicose slogan, 'Proud to have fought for America and Freedom in Vietnam.' "[5]

3 The Warriors

DEAN FELT THE MAN'S BOOTS SLOWLY GRIND THE POLISH OFF ONE *spitshined toe, then the other. "Your shoes look like shit."*

Dean stood silent in his tight attention, the uncomfortable denigrating "brace" reserved for plebes . . .

He had just told the older man that his squad leader "seemed quite pleased with the way he looks." The older man had retorted, "You never talk to an upperclass that way, you slimy smack," and then proceeded to grind off ten hours of spitshining.

"Do you think Mister Swenson will be 'quite pleased' when he sees your shoes now?"

"Sir, no sir."

The man wiped his mashed nose with a thick hand and casually rubbed sweat and snot onto Dean's shined belt buckle. "Your brass is tarnished too. Oh, you are a mess, Dean. A real mess."

From *A Sense of Honor* by James Webb.

James Webb: Annapolis graduate; first lieutenant of Delta Company, First Battalion, Fifth Regiment, U.S. Marines, in the An Hoa Basin of Vietnam in 1969; three times wounded and many times decorated; lawyer and author. A man who planned a military career until his Vietnam wounds left him with a torn leg and a slight limp. Webb was taking time out from his word processor in the spring of 1983 to talk of war and peace, Vietnam-style. He tamps his pipe and leans back in his chair in his private office near the Pentagon. His laugh is a characteristic sudden, staccato burst as I question the "discipline building" of military schools that seems to border on the sadistic. Dean, the plebe in Webb's novel, for example, is hounded by the officer for months with extreme punishment and harassment.

"A lot of people don't understand. You've got for one year a guy [plebe] who thinks he's the smartest, greatest valedictorian, high school athlete, whatever. You're teaching that guy humility. You're saying, 'Okay, you've been cool all your life. Now *you* are going to have command of fifty people in four years. You better have humility in front of your men.' And you denigrate somebody in sort of a constructive way because eventually they are going to be officers. To me, it's perfectly permissible to act that way to a plebe. But *never,* ever, ever to an enlisted man. I wouldn't give you a dime for an officer who touched an enlisted man." His vehement comment about breaking a code of conduct sounds almost condescending; never demean your servants or underlings. Officers should remain, above all, officers.

I ask if Webb ever saw discipline and "humility teaching" reach sadistic proportions.

"The plebe system was investigated during my plebe year. It probably went as far as it had ever gone in the three years ending that year. It wasn't sadistic, but it was beyond the point of being constructive. I had four guys who spent some time telling me 'pain was irrelevant.' I started out with three M-1s—thirty-three pounds. I was holding them straight out in front of me. Then you can't hold them anymore, and they give you two, then one, then seven books, six, five, four, three, two, one. Your muscles just completely go dead from lack of circulation. And all the time they're saying, 'What is pain? Does it hurt? Does it matter?' And after, they just started beating me with a cricket bat. They were telling me they would *stop*—if I told them it hurt.

"And I'm thinking, 'Now wait a minute. They just spent a half hour telling me that pain was irrelevant. I'm not going to tell them it hurts—or they'll start all over again.' Finally, they split the bat longitudinally on my butt." He had deep welts, could barely walk. "I was just beat to death."

What could that possibly do constructively?

"That went beyond the point," Webb conceded. "One thing it did do, I have to admit—although it is not something 99 percent of the people in the world need—I got to the point where I could completely disassociate personal pain. I was watching them from another place when they were beating on me. Now when I have problems with [my leg], I just turn it off. But it was not worth doing that to 1,300 people to make sure that four eventually may have to use it. *That* was out of control. But the 'stress-indoctrination system' is pertinent if you're trying to figure out whether you're going to allow someone else to have responsibility for other people's lives."

James Webb was a trim man of thirty-six in the spring of '83. After hours of writing, a roomful of exercise equipment in his office dekinks the wound-stiffened leg. He has a boyish face and a Southern softness in his voice. Both mask an abrasive terrierlike tenacity; the gut fighter who once boxed, the warrior who "took care of his men." The former first lieutenant who speaks witheringly of campus protesters that dodged the war. A Vietnam-veteran spokesman for those who decried the Vietnam Veterans Memorial as a black ditch for the dead. Webb was regarded by some as a national authority on Vietnam with the success of his *Fields of Fire* in 1978. It was a powerful war saga of emotion and description, not politics. Since then, his ideological stance has crystallized; his political beliefs have become solidified about a war he experienced as an unquestioning young man bound by honor and duty. Now he speaks for a certain segment of Vietnam veterans who embrace the revisionism of the right—the cause was noble, and moreover the war could have been won, a view which ignores the political ramifications of the time. Webb feels, judging from the response to his writing and speeches, that the numbers of veterans who agree are vast—perhaps a majority. I do not know. Others with opposing views find their *own* vast audience among veterans. (In one poll, nearly half of the veterans felt the war was a mistake.) There is some danger and certainly distortion in making any one veteran a spokesman for the more than three million who went and returned ambiguous and divided. Webb no more speaks for all than does a soldier who feels it was a mistake. In his vehemence Webb often leans to absolutes. At times he seems flatly to dismiss the possibility that other veterans genuinely feel otherwise. They are, he believes, merely led along by left-leaning interviewers or sociologists to profess antiwar sentiments or guilt.

Moreover, Webb is viewed by many activist veterans who do not share his ideology as a destructive element who worked against the design of the memorial and against VVA, which seeks to improve the benefits and image of veterans. Still, because of his prominence, he is often regarded as *the* spokesman for all veterans.

We tangled once after I wrote an article on the reasons for the Vietnam Veterans Memorial and the 1982 Vietnam veteran week of observance. He called to say it was a "terrible" piece—fighting words for an ego-injured writer. His gracious apology ("my personality is basically abrasive anyway") brought a mutual desire to talk about our differences. Webb disliked the article because "the totality of it expressed the view that we had no business being in Vietnam. That it was an overwhelmingly negative experience. That was my objection to it."

Other veterans had found a different message. I had tried to convey the pride many had in their own service, despite their feelings about the war. At any rate, we proceeded to go on from there . . .

Through the ages, every society has had its warrior class; honed to fight its battles, to protect its people. The lure of the military—camaraderie, *esprit de corps*, idealized or romanticized concepts of heroism, as well as a darker atavistic side—has pulled at young men from time immemorial. War is the romance of history. "We inherit the warlike type; and for most of the capacities of heroism that the human race is full of, we have to thank this cruel history . . . Our ancestors have bred pugnacity into our bone and marrow, and thousands of years of peace won't breed it out of us."

The author of such thoughts also wrote that doubt had crept into public thinking. "The military instincts and ideals are as strong as ever, but are confronted by reflective criticisms which sorely curb their ancient freedom.

Innumerable writers are showing up the bestial side of military service . . ." "We" and "they" motivations are ascribed. America and its allies are solely for "peace"; the enemies are bent on loot and glory. " 'Peace' in military mouths today is a synonym for 'war expected' . . . Every up-to-date dictionary should say that 'peace and war' mean the same thing."

This could have been written during the Vietnam War—or it could be present-day reflections on Reagan's justification for a show of force as he sees an East-West showdown in most global hotspots. It was, however, written by William James, professor and pacifist, many, many decades ago.[1]

James was writing of an 1898 war, "our squalid war with Spain," as he put it. Decades later, the sour Vietnam years sorely tried both our involvement in Southeast Asia and the ethos of militarism—but many youths still dreamed of being warriors. They were often first and second generation, steeped in gratitude to the country that gave their ancestors a home. American Indians, reared on tribal dictates, viewed fighting for their country as a matter of course. Their fathers asked one another as a matter of course, "Has your son done his service yet?"

"The whole history of my family is that way," says Webb, the Southerner. "My grandfather's name was Robert E. Lee Webb. What stuck in my mind, from Annapolis, was 'Don't ever abandon your values.' They didn't say, 'Be warriors'; they said, 'Take care of your men.' "

This was at the time of Tet, 1968, "the only time in its history that the Naval Academy didn't make its quota of marines." Some who entered the military with the same values as Webb later joined the "Concerned Officers" organization, denouncing the war as a misguided and, to some, immoral venture. Such views are foreign to Webb, who speaks of "old, traditional values." Like many other military men, Webb feels Vietnam was both winnable and justifiable. They are haunted by their visions of "what might have been—if only . . ."

Webb champions revisionist hawk talk: If only we had bombed Hanoi in 1965, we could have won. If you have any doubts that we should have been there, look at Vietnam today. If only the media had not been "duped" in the analysis of what the North was waging—a protracted invasion masked as a civil guerrilla war. If only Lyndon Johnson had set clear-cut goals and explained them adequately, the country would have backed him and the antiwar movement would have had less significance. If only the media had been censored—limited in its access to the war. Such points are debated coast to coast these days in symposia. Charitably labeled the "new scholarship" by some, other scholars and journalists see many recycled old arguments.

Webb attended a Wilson Center seminar in 1983 and came away embracing Douglas Pike's pronouncements. "If we had gone in 1965, bombed Hanoi— and also mined Haiphong Harbor—the way Nixon did in 1972, we would have had a negotiated settlement in six months," Webb avowed. Don Oberdorfer, an award-winning journalist, acclaimed for his book *Tet!*, listened to Pike at that conference and said, "He must be smoking something

I'm not. There is no way they would have given up if we had bombed them then." Such scholars and journalists argue that the North Vietnamese will to win was so strong that they would have overcome temporary setbacks. Others argue that any military win would have been a Pyrrhic victory with the United States needing a massive force to keep the peace for years after.

Webb vehemently disagrees. The United States' bombing of the North as early as 1966 obliterated its industrial centers, railyards, hundreds of bridges, power transformers, ammunition dumps, and other objectives near Hanoi and Haiphong as well as three quarters of the country's oil-storage facilities. Still, the North Vietnamese kept coming down the Ho Chi Minh Trail; if anything, their will to fight was galvanized by the bombing raids.[2]

Webb argues that "those targets were totally inappropriate to the kind of war we were fighting. We should have done as we did in 1972—make them *feel the rumble in Hanoi.* That would have forced a political settlement and [we would have] had occupation forces in there like we did in South Korea." Arguments and ideological battles over Vietnam will not be settled now, in this book, or any other, and they will not be settled fifty years from now.

Yet, with a lost war, suppositions never die. Theorizing, rewriting, rethinking history is a fascinating exercise—which cannot, of course, change the outcome. But it serves the purpose of one group saying, "See, we are right," to an equally certain other group—both groups hoping to implant the "right" lessons about Vietnam in society.

Webb certainly hopes that revisionism will prevail. Strongly anticommunist, he says, *"I believe the war was probably the most moral effort we have ever made.* We fought for purely ideological reasons and we blew it. This is one reason I am such an absolutist in some of the things I say." Webb says he has learned tolerance for those who believe otherwise; however, he condescendingly dismisses antiwar veterans as succumbing to reentry "recanting." "You had to bad-mouth the war in order to be accepted when we returned. The veterans who felt futility always had a microphone in front of their faces if they wanted it."

I ask him about the belief that America's mistake was in not accommodating Ho Chi Minh years before, when he had popular support against the French; the belief that we created and backed a corrupt South Vietnamese regime with little following.

"Ho Chi Minh was a dedicated Leninist! It was true that Vietnam should have ceased to be a colonial object. They should have been *allowed* to become a nation. *Now,* should they have been *allowed* to become a Leninist nation? To be free as a nation does not mean to be under a totalitarian state."

But was it *our* position to prescribe a future, to say, "We are giving you this government that you ought to back"?

Webb brushes that argument aside. "The irony to me is that all the people who were saying eight years ago that it was an immoral, unjust war are now saying, 'Well, yes, it *was* moral, but it was unwinnable.' That's sort of the last defense of people who opposed the war."

I point out that many still feel it was immoral. "Look at what we *lost!*" He contends, "You have Communist Indochina under a Leninist state. You now have Russian bases in Cam Ranh Bay and Da Nang." Unlike veterans who profess guilt for "what we did to the people of Vietnam," Webb feels there should be another guilt. "We made a moral and political commitment. We believed it was worth something that those millions of people have the same opportunities as a culture that we have."

There are many who argue that as repressive as the system may be, the poor of Vietnam are better off now. They are able to return to their homes, to be with their ancestral graves, to farm, to live without being trapped between our bombs and napalm, and the NVA and VC.

"Look," sighs Webb, "into the mid-thirties or later, people were going into the Soviet Union and saying, 'I've seen the future and it works.' It is just *so* incredible to me that we can be so gullible. This is a Leninist state. The first thing they do very closely is control the access of journalists who are allowed in. During the war, dissenters threw up a red herring, 'Thieu is corrupt. He's taking political prisoners.' VC and North Vietnamese prisoners were being treated roughly the same as our American POWs in the North. But this 'Thieu's government' became the focus of the media. And yet look what's happening now? How many boat people did you see during the Vietnam War? Bombs, anything else, as bad as the war was, they stayed. No one was trying to get into *North* Vietnam. No one is trying to get *in* to North Korea or *in* to East Germany now. You've got Vietnamese reeducation camps, Vietnamese slave labor working on the Russian pipeline. People liquidated. What kind of system does that?"

I present the views of other scholars and journalists, who suggest that the "bloodbath" never materialized, that people do walk out of the reeducation camps, that many of the current troubles were exacerbated by the war, that the very people we were "saving" now live in an impoverished economy because the millions pumped in during the war were withdrawn. "I wouldn't give that government one dime." He sighs in disgust. "I wish I could hear someone from the left responsibly deal with the fact that the reason that country is Communist now is that the North Vietnamese created a massive violation of the cease-fire agreement. If they would have honored that, there would have been $32 billion for Vietnam. We're supposed to reward them for having created a Leninist state?"

Their argument was that they were reunifying the country.

"That's why there are no former VC officials in responsible positions in the South," Webb says drily. "Most of the VC leaders have fled."

As for not wanting United States intervention, Webb argues with quiet rage, "I think it's unfortunate that *you* can't take a poll of South Vietnam now to see how many of them wish we were back. I think it would be an overwhelming majority."

Isn't it disturbing to see only Communists as a threat, while excusing and supporting far-right authoritarian repressive regimes in such countries as El Salvador?

That is the lesser of evils, Webb feels. "Countries on the edge of worldwide conflict between totalitarianism and a free society cannot be totally free. But consider the alternative."

Attitudes of former combat soldiers are, to say the least, varied. William Mattson, another marine in Vietnam at the same time as Webb, returned to become a headmaster of a small New England school. "I do not like to face the conflict of what is happening over there now because it does make me question whether we should have been there. However, what I always come back to is the deep suffering I witnessed while we *were* there. I can't see how there could be more suffering now. Repression, yes, but destructions are not occurring as they did on a personal level. I worked at an orphanage in Kim Lam, and I never saw such devastation to children, before or after. They were left bereft, homeless! That kind of suffering was *absolute*. I don't know what could have been worse," says Mattson emotionally. "I was a coordinator of a village outside of Hue, and every night whole families had to leave because we were there to fight. When whole groups have to leave their homeland in droves in order to survive—that's suffering."

Webb has many more theoretical views on Vietnam, but it is important to return to the war *as it was*—how Webb experienced it and what he thinks it did to his generation.

For years, Vietnam and his homecoming—when he was an alien in law school, taunted by an antiwar law professor—were seen through wellsprings of deep emotion. *Fields of Fire* was written as a catharsis. He was driven to give honor to the men who went. In so doing, he also had to justify the war. The novel became many things to many people. Some saw it as a reaffirmation of honor and courage in battle; others, such as *John Barkham's Review,* saw "the suicidal, inescapable, *debasing* character of combat in Vietnam."

Some veterans rile at Webb's biases and point out that the one character who questioned the morality of the war was portrayed as a sissified Harvardite and combat misfit. Some black veterans felt that prejudice against blacks and sixties black nationalism permeated Webb's depiction of black-white friction in the rear.

There is no mistaking Webb's vision of himself—"Lt. Robert E. Lee Hodges, Jr.: Bred to it, like a bird dog. The last of a family of American samurai, who fought not because of Vietnam, but for honor." Hodges is constantly portrayed as a strong leader who could be "one of the boys." He still speaks of those who served with him as "my men."

Mike McGarvey, who served under Webb, still calls him the "Skipper." A long-haired, overweight Harley-Davidson motorcycle mechanic in Nashville in 1978, McGarvey has one arm. Webb "cried like a baby" when McGarvey was wounded—a nineteen-year-old kid with an arm gone. Mike looked up and said, "Knock off that shit. It's only an arm." McGarvey recalled of

Webb, "You'd go out on a patrol unarmed if he told you to. He'd rather be in the hootch playing Back Alley [a card game] with the guys than talking with a bird colonel [full colonel rather than lieutenant colonel]. His loyalty went down, not up."[3]

One of the compelling questions of Vietnam is why so many men, especially marines, willingly chose to fight in the unpopular and—to many—purposeless war. Webb cites the John Wayne, all-American image as one reason, but he also in his book refers to an "anomalous insanity. The terrors and miseries are so compelling, and yet so regular, that I have ascended to a high emotion that is nonetheless a crusted numbness. I am an automaton, bent on survival, agent and prisoner of my misery," says his alter-ego, Lieutenant Hodges. "How terribly exciting."

Killing was an inevitable part of the bloody post-Tet landscape. "We killed people all the time. That was our *job*. We didn't get a [body count] reward. We didn't give kills unless a guy *touched* a body."

The absurdity of the body count was the media's fault, says Webb. "The process became perverted because of pressure from the government and media, demanding a measure [for victory]. You got a lot of enthusiastic unit commanders who would do things like pop flares and have guys pull a sweep in the middle of the night to count the bodies after an attack. That is unnecessarily exposing your people to get a count."

Webb gets emotional at the thought of unnecessarily sending troops into death. The hardest thing, he says, is not killing but giving an order that might bring the death of somebody under you. He points out that his Silver Star and Bronze Star citations emphasize his actions on behalf of the safety of his men.

Some veterans are deeply haunted by the killing of civilians, and Webb quickly says that "my saddest feelings from Vietnam are [about] things that happened with civilians." However, he just as quickly rattles off statistics of death to civilians as an inevitability of war. "Some 28,000 people died in the battle on Okinawa, and well over half were civilians. The hard thing as unit commander in Vietnam was that it was a *small-unit* war. If I had been on Okinawa, it would have been hard, but you were more of an instrument moving on. It does not affect you emotionally like it does when you're a squad leader and you're having to do this day to day without momentum."

He defensively recollects the tactics of the other side. "The worst thing I ever went through as far as turning your stomach was the way the VC operated. Quang Nam and Quang Ngai provinces were the strongest VC infrastructure in the country. The way they operated with the peasants was, 'We want you to like us—and if you *don't,* we will *kill* you.' That's how they controlled! It wasn't sitting around with a guitar playing songs. The district chief lived in Da Nang. We used to make fun of him—'Look at that asshole!' —but the point was if he came back to the ville, he was a dead man. Our company commander said, 'Hearts and minds. We've got to get the district chief back to the village. We're going to get thirty people, and he's going to talk about what his government is doing.' The commander puts a fire team on the other side of this hootch, the chief comes in, and thirty people are trundled in from the village to a hootch about half the size of this room.

"I was just coming in from a patrol. All of a sudden we heard *boom, boom, boom, crack, crack, crack,* and a three-man Communist assassination team killed nineteen people in that hootch. They threw grenades up in the thatch, got airbursts off 'em, and greased 'em, swish, right through the middle. We caught one guy running out. I'll never forget it, having to clean out that hootch with nineteen dead and everybody else screwed up [injured]. Ankle-deep blood. Now *that* [such an assassination attack] was never reported."

What about our Operation Phoenix?

"We didn't kill anyone who was not associated with the Communists," says Webb—a view directly contradicted by some former Phoenix participants. "The Communists would kill *anyone* associated with the government for the sake of discipline."

I mention the account of a former intelligence officer whose Vietnam agent was deliberately fingering members of his rival political factions who were not Communists. No after-action reports, this officer said, indicated such rampant random killing as Webb mentions.

"I can't speak to that."

Some veterans cannot forget their personal involvement and anguish over killing civilians. Webb has an ugly memory too, but it is told without emotion —in marked contrast to those who haltingly, tearfully, walk through such tales today.

"After pushing a North Vietnamese unit through a village, we fragged bunkers. If you didn't frag them [the family bunkers] as you went through, they would wait until you swept through and come up behind you. We'd sweep through and yell, 'Lai Day! Lai Day! Lai Day!' ('Come here') three times, and if there were civilians in the bunkers, they'd come running out. It was an established procedure. We fragged a bunker, moved through, and started to search the village. Well, there was an older guy, and he had cradled a little boy inside one of those bunkers. And the boy was still alive. And I knew he was gonna die. It was really hard. It's funny how something small like that can really get to you." The child was around four years old.

"Here I am, twenty-three years old, and my corpsman [medic] comes up to me and says, 'If he doesn't get out of here in thirty minutes, he's going to die.' I called a routine evac. It was my decision to make."

Why routine evacuation?

"Because no Vietnamese civilian could get an emergency evacuation, particularly when your units are in contact [under enemy attack]. It's like anything else. It's a 'space available' basis when you're a civilian. We just laid that little kid on top of a table right in front of me, and I just sat there and waited for him to die."

Such destruction of the people we were trying to "save" would have been lessened if the strategy had been different, Webb feels. "The sad thing is we did in the South what Johnson never had the courage to do in the North. I *don't* think China would have come in if we had used airpower."

Airpower on the level of Dresden? "Yeah. We had the technological ability to not do what we did at Dresden. The targets were carefully marked. In 1972 we bombed Hanoi for twelve days, and after the eighth day they did not have any antiaircraft capability at all. If Kissinger had pushed it right, he could have gotten almost anything he wanted." Webb's "what-if's" ignore a crucial point of domestic and geopolitical dynamics: we did not have the popular support in 1965—*or* in 1972—for such an invasion.

As for veterans who had horrifying face-to-face encounters with civilians, Webb feels that many are less guilt-ridden by the experience than they are by how they were received at home.

"Post-traumatic stress is a lack of *catharsis.* If just one civilian was killed—in a situation that was totally justifiable—[the memory of] it is not going to leave you, but you could *assimilate* it as a tragedy and go on *if* there was catharsis.

"Veterans came under such a microscope. People didn't say, 'Look, you were nineteen years old; you did the best you could handling an ethical situation every day that most people in your age group will *never* have to experience even once! Sometimes you didn't get it all the way right, but consider what you were trying to do.' If they had been dealt with that way, they could have handled it. But if you say, 'Did you ever kill a civilian? And how are you dealing with it now?' it's like saying 'You bastard'—and 99 and 44/100 percent were not.

"One of my best men on earth cut a woman in two [with gunfire], and it just about demolished him. I don't know why she was out of her bunker, but he just cut her in two. You're not allowed to go back to your dormitory room and think about it; you've got to go on. So he goes on, and two hours later he's saying 'Oh, my God, I just never thought that would happen.' And as a friend and commander you have to say, 'Look, you didn't search her out. It just happened.' "

Do you think he still might be having troubles?

"I'm sure he might. It's not something you throw away like a napkin. But he needs to understand he was nineteen years old and had responsibilities that few his age had, and he dealt with those responsibilities and not always 100 percent [correctly].

"Vietnam *was* a different war and required *more* catharsis. It required a sensitivity that wasn't there [on the part of Americans]. The average veteran served longer in a period of 'future-shock' syndrome than veterans of other wars. He should have had *more,* not less, readjustment benefits than World War II veterans [had] to let him walk through that mine field. Burying Vietnam erodes you from within. It's like drinking Drāno. I bet just about anyone who was in heavy combat—who didn't go back to a rural community or to a blue-collar job where a lot of his contemporaries were veterans—went through some stress. But I don't think we do anybody justice by *magnifying* it. Labeling it a psychological disorder that affects 700,000 is just not true. The bottom line is that most got through it and were made stronger. *Much stronger than others their age."*

Webb's feelings about the ones who didn't go surface in little flash floods of anger.

"For every guy who went to Canada, four guys died in Vietnam." Webb feels sociologists, many of whom did not go, seek to find guilt in veterans for personal purposes. "It's in their interest to find people who are guilty. They are driven to justify the fact that they didn't go." As if dictating a story, Webb firmly enunciates his words, *"The major unspoken problem in our generation is that too many of these people who didn't go have transferred their guilt on the people who did!* 'Don't tell me to feel guilty! Examine yourself.' How many people are doing studies on what these guys who didn't go feel about it?"

The numbers of troubled veterans are inflated by those "who work in the area," Webb avows. "You become an expert, you want to perpetuate your expertise. They look at the high side. All social scientists do that. This is not to minimize the problems a *relatively* small number of these guys have, but it's a small number." The *Legacies* study, headed by a Vietnam veteran, Dr. Alan Egendorf, and the most comprehensive study to date, lists approximately one fourth of Vietnam combat veterans as having problems. Webb dismisses it as "not a complete study." "There's a wish on the part of the media to *believe* all these negatives. Certainly they happened to some percentage—but that's not the story. Vietnam veterans are less likely to be in jail now than nonveterans. I saw more drugs at Georgetown Law [School] than I ever saw in the Marine Corps. And where are those guys now? A lot of them are out prosecuting drug cases."

Webb repeatedly turns to the split in the generation. He clings to the view that guilt fueled nongoing males, who thus needed to make the veteran a scapegoat.

"The overwhelming majority of veterans are not political. If I push them, they'll say, 'Yeah, man, we should have gone.' If you push them, they'll say, 'Yeah, it was lousy.' But putting on a uniform *is* a formative political act. People who say this is 'blind patriotism' misread the visceral nature of doing that."

I argue that there are veterans who are not pushed but who *volunteer* their disenchantment, their sense of guilt and doubts, their sense of betrayal that their government lied to them. "You and I could argue that one too."

Webb is fond of saying that "giving your life in a war is the ultimate irretrievable gift to your culture." The country, in return, *"must* nurture the people who have gone through the experience of war, must give them dignity. You talk to Tom Martin, this guy in the wheelchair," says Webb, pointing to his picture on the wall. "He'll say 'I *won*—because I found out about myself.' "

Do you feel some veterans practice denial? That they bury the horrors of war or a belief that it was wrong because they can't bear to say their wounds, loss of friends, and nightmare memories were all for nothing?

"That *may* exist. But the main thing a person troubled by his experience is going to want is acceptance by his peers. Veterans who have been troubled, who believed 'it was for nothing,' have *always* had a receptive audience. When you said, 'This was a worthwhile thing we were attempting,' you were not making many friends. If you go to any vet center, you'll find people with problems. If you go to the VVA [Vietnam Veterans of America], you'll find [antiwar] ideologues. So I go with the polls. People say *they* don't show you anything. But they do show something—that 90 percent of Vietnam veterans were proud to serve." Webb uses that statistic frequently—but ignores a vital point. The *lowest* percentage of those who felt the phrase "glad I served my country" closely mirrored their feelings were veterans smack in the Vietnam Generation—twenty-five to thirty-four years of age at the time of the 1980 survey. Only *64 percent* of them—vastly smaller than the overall 90 percent—agreed. (The highest, 97 percent, were fifty-five and over, obviously career military or retirees).[4]

In addition, it is possible to be proud of that service yet deeply ambiguous about the overall experience, but Webb does not look to such shadings.

Webb had intended a lifelong military career. When it was cut short by his wounds, Webb joined the thousands of veterans who returned to America's campuses during the antiwar upheaval. His Vietnam experience immediately came under fire. His eyes flash as he recalls his Georgetown University criminal law professor. Webb says his name with contempt. "Heathcoat Wales. Antiwar. The same age group. The whole bit. Never been out of a school environment."

Early in the year, Wales taunted Webb: "Well, you were in Vietnam—you know how guys are in Vietnam. You get a little horny, so you go down in the ville and you point a finger at some girl, and she sees your weapon and knows you're going to kill her if she doesn't come across. Does she consent—or is that considered rape?"

Still, Webb was unprepared for the question on his final exam—which would be his full grade for the year in that class: " 'You're in Vietnam, your name is Sergeant Jack Webb. You take a platoon out, and you screw up somehow and two guys get killed.' It was all supposed to be humorous, ha-ha-ha," recalls Webb. " 'So you bought some jade on the black market, and you stuff it in their wounds.' . . ."

I stare incredulously. "There's *more,* believe me," says Webb. "After a whole year this is my grade!" He continues with his account of the exam question. " 'You stuff it into their wounds, and you bribe two guys out of your platoon who are going to be body escorts to take the bodies back and unload the jade and give it to your girlfriend,' and so on and so forth."

What was the point?

"Search and seizure, federal authorities intercept the coffins. I couldn't reconstruct the point, it's been so long."

Webb recalls that he ground his teeth and finished the exam. Afterward, he walked up to his professor and told him, "Vietnam was *not* funny!" He got a C plus in the course. "There was a principle involved. Do I scream about the grade or do I scream about Wales? I talked to the dean and told him what the exam was. He said, 'Well, you cannot take it over.' I said, 'I don't *want* to take it over. I would like Wales talked to.'"

Wales came up for tenure the next year, and Webb—who belongs to the 'don't get mad, get even' school of encounters—wrote a letter to the tenure committee. "Basically, I said that had he done that about World War II, he would have been hung by his thumbs. At a minimum it was a horrible error in judgment, and no one with that kind of judgment deserved to be professor. It got him denied tenure for one year. That guy," Webb spits out vehemently, "he'd preached sensitivity and 'personal rights' all year.

"Unlike those who went back to a receiving and receptive community, people who went back to college—it depended on when and where—had the hardest time emotionally. As well as those who entered professions populated by those who didn't go."

A slight sigh escapes. "I went to Vietnam because I was a lieutenant and that was the war and I trusted my government. I still trust my government. I didn't fight in Vietnam because I thought the war was right. I fought in Vietnam because I was a unit commander. I felt I was the best they were going to get, and that's where I belonged. Even after I was wounded, I didn't come back thinking I'd fought a war for democracy. I didn't examine this war clearly until the last two years." When Webb did, it was to embrace profoundly all the old themes of containing communism.

Webb acknowledges that there were well-intentioned, committed war protesters and principled journalists. However, he dwells on the most radical in the movement and thinks censorship should have prevailed in Vietnam.

"You had a free media on our side and a controlled media on the other. Because the North Vietnamese could control the information, we never really knew what they were doing. It was not a war of liberation but of aggression and subjugation. The whole world knew the North Vietnamese had troops in the South beginning in 1964—and they were saying, 'It's not true.' The problem was so many American journalists were *duped!* It was just demonstrable. We'd kill a North Vietnamese, and he'd have an I.D. card [identifying him as a South Vietnamese civilian] on him!

"The media had too much access," says Webb flatly. "That was *wrong.* That is not so much censorship . . . well, call it what you want. But when a guy from the Dallas *Shopping News* can walk out to any unit and say, 'Will you be the last guy killed in Vietnam?' you don't need that. You're trying to fight a war."

The real Vietnam War villain, in his mind, was Lyndon Johnson, whose "greatest failure was not requiring a full debate before he went in. He tried to sneak us in, on the cheap. As a result, the dissent movement started the debate after the war had begun. We ultimately failed because of that. Point number two: Johnson screwed things up so bad because he never articulated to the American people what we were doing militarily. The confusion so many troops have today about taking a piece of territory and then *leaving* it stems from that. It didn't do any good to 'freeze' your units in a particular spot because we didn't have that many people. Most were at support bases. The North Vietnamese had fifteen out of sixteen divisions in the South and could move anywhere they wanted. In a war of attrition, we were at their mercy. We could only 'stop' them until it could be negotiated. That put us behind the eight ball.

"If it had been explained properly, had the people understood our commitment, we could have possibly done something about it."

Webb ignores one salient point. Most of America's publishers and some executive editors and columnists not only backed the war, but bent over backward in its early years to portray the venture as noble and to explain our strategy. I argue that Middle America did stay with the commitment until after Tet, 1968, years after the war had begun. When disaffection came, it was often not for "moral" reasons, not because of media coverage, but because they were tired of their sons and neighbors dying in a war that was perceived as unwinnable. Webb's familiar military rejoinder is that Tet was a military victory, but press coverage conveyed that it was a psychological defeat. Both points happen to be true. No matter that the enemy was slaughtered in vast numbers in Tet, their presence in Saigon—not the press coverage—convinced most Americans that the light was indeed not at the end of the tunnel.

Webb feels that the antiwar movement did nothing to halt the war. "I think it *extended* it. They were irresponsible in the way they conducted dissent. There is a principled place for dissent—it should be done in a context that *embraces* our value system. I'm thinking of the Chicago Seven and Jerry Rubin, the march on the Pentagon, all that. If you push the institutions of a free society far enough, you *create* the conditions of fascism."

Webb has a different view than those—women, for example—who were in the fray and were clubbed by unleashed police. He blames the movement for provoking the police "so the cameras could catch them clubbing heads. Those guys were the provocateurs. You create the wrong kind of strain, confront the people who are in authority, encourage the North Vietnamese, and the war drags on. *They* had no need to negotiate. The negotiating was being done for them on the streets of Washington. When the Indochina Peace Campaign began in 1973, Jane Fonda was in *Hanoi*. That's why, in my opinion, the war went on. Lord knows how many . . ." Webb chokes. "I don't want to put a number on it."

On what? The number of men who died because of the protest? "Yeah." At one seminar, Webb stated flatly that the peace movement resulted in the death of several thousand more Americans. "And the Indochina peace campaign succeeded in getting funds cut off to South Vietnam in '74, '75. They were surviving on three rounds per day per gun! They had no beans, bullets, or Band-Aids because we cut off the money. The fall of South Vietnam was inevitable after that."

Webb also smarts at the loss of upper-class leadership in Vietnam. "I honestly believe the ultimate responsibility for Calley is Lyndon Johnson. Not because he conducted an immoral war, but because he conducted it on the cheap and did not *require* the better, talented people to go in the military. Why did a guy like Calley, who had flunked out of college, almost all F's after one semester, become an officer in the military? Because the other people *weren't there.* The whole population base of officers in the Army became skewed. Based on historical experience the upper middle class would have been *there* as officers. Yet Calley was there." (Other veterans, who do not share Webb's justification of the war, however, frequently mention the same thought about the lack of middle or upper class officer leadership.)

Calley wasn't alone at My Lai, I protest. Reading the Peer Inquiry and *Cover-Up,* one can't help but be appalled by the high-ranking commanding officers who flew overhead and did nothing to halt My Lai.

"It is very confusing to try and view it [ground action] from the air," defends Webb. "One time I was moving a platoon forward, and I had a spotter plane telling me I was hitting North Vietnamese bunkers. What it was, however, was a *village.* All the villages had family bunkers. We caught it in time—but the view from the air is different than from the ground. You see a lot of confusion, smoke, and people moving. So the fact that the guy was up there [over My Lai] doesn't necessarily mean he knew what was going on, on the ground. Now perhaps he should have come *down* on the ground . . ."

Webb sees a lasting generational schism between those who went and those who didn't. Asked if he has made friends with any draft dodgers, Webb replies, "It took me a long time." Webb once dismissed the concept of sacrifice even among those who went to jail: "There weren't any VC at Allenwood." Today he says, "It depends on how honest the person is. Rick Hart, the sculptor on the Vietnam Veterans Memorial statue [which was added to the memorial grounds after Webb and others denounced the memorial design], is a very good friend of mine now. Ask Hart what he did during Vietnam, and he'll say, 'I was under the bed.' He's honest about it. At the same time, he's a principled guy, and we have bitter arguments about it."

Still, Webb feels, "I don't think it will ever be healed *inside* our generation. But there will be ways to patch it up and go on. Pete McCloskey, one of my favorite congressmen, was as liberal on the war as you can get, but he did it in the right way." (McCloskey won the Navy Cross, Silver Star, and Purple Heart during the Korean War.)

Webb, skeptical that anyone of fighting age truly believed Vietnam was an immoral war, contents himself with the thought that they have the most guilt. "A lot of them, I think, are working off a continued *insecurity* about not having gone. They embraced a moralistic statement that became less and less moral as we see what happened to Vietnam. This is the hardest group to deal with when you start talking about the war.

"In the larger sense, they've got the *most* to lose—if this is ever put into perspective."

To the end, Webb was fighting the design of the Vietnam Veterans Memorial. "It's a nihilistic statement. You get the emotion off the names, but the names of the dead were to be on *any* design, so that *was* going to remind you of the cost of war. But you're saying that wall is an appropriate, affirmative tribute to people who did a very difficult thing. I don't think it is. And I don't think many will look at it and say that it is either.

"The memorial was supposed to recognize and honor the people who served." It was supposed to be a proper heroes' edifice, says Webb. "It was *not* supposed to be the Vietnam *Dead* Memorial. It was not supposed to be the Vietnam *War* Memorial. There are appropriate places for that reminder [of death and destruction]. I go to Arlington Cemetery all the time. Every year, May 9, I go to Snake's grave [a soldier who became one of his men in *Fields of Fire*] and drop a Marlboro on it [Snake's dying request]. That is a proper place. The Vietnam Memorial is an open grave! Art is metaphor, and the metaphorical statement of it is absolutely negative. The great contrast is the Iwo Jima Memorial. I always come out of there really uplifted. I think how proud I am to be living in the same country as those seven guys. If I went there and saw a *wall,* I would feel nothing."

How do you feel about the decision to place the statue and American flag away from the wall at the entrance?

"Ahhhh, that was just dumb. Yet I'm glad there's going to be a flag and sculpture. But that [battle] is over with," he says as if trying to resign himself. "That wall is going to be there forever."

I said there are many who cherish the memorial, like a Vietnam veteran who left a daisy-festooned note at the wall that stated: "I love the Vietnam Memorial. If it will keep more people from being killed, I will love it even more." For men like him, the wall is an appropriate message of remembrance and caution. But that is the incorrect message for Webb, who deeply believes it was our honor to go into Vietnam.

That anger is in his eyes still. "All I can say is that there are some things worth dying for."

Not all veterans with a military mentality were soldiers. One doctor plays back the war as if caught in a time warp. Dr. Homer "Butch" House was a Green Beret in Vietnam from 1966 to 1967. He reenlisted for another tour. "I was more comfortable, felt fulfilled in the Army. I didn't feel comfortable being a civilian.

"I worked with amputees and paraplegics at Walter Reed—and I just couldn't believe those peace demonstrators. A 'vocal minority' made it impossible to stay and defend the borders and eliminate infiltration. The draft dodgers and those who went to Canada were chicken, okay?

"Look, our prisoners were atrociously treated—beaten, tied up for weeks. Using napalm? Dealing in an underground war, how do you get people out of a tunnel? You burn them out. There were six-year-olds wheeling bombs into our areas!

"Look at those dumb sons of bitches now. Fighting another war. They're totally incapable of governing themselves. There's no question in my military mind they were much better off when we were there."

House speaks bitterly of the public reaction to Vietnam veterans. "It's a terrible thing when a guy comes back and nobody's proud of him."

Fred Reed, a journalist covering the military for the Washington *Times*, smarted at Hollywood's penchant for playing veterans as either witless dupes or ruthless killers. He wrote of the many reasons marines—"the ones I knew best"—enlisted. "Some joined for adventure; if they were dupes, so were Columbus and Alan Shepard. Some went simply to see the war. Some to fight communism, which they understood with different degrees of sophistication. The ones who would volunteer to be door gunners, went to prove themselves, and some were the born samurai who joined the elite outfits."

Reed says he met "only one veteran who felt guilty about the war." Most of those he knew who felt the war was a mistake held no moral reasons—it was either that we couldn't or didn't win it. "The phrase 'immoral war' has little meaning in a rice paddy. For a surprising number, it was just the war: not everyone analyzes." Reed denigrates the delayed-stress concept. He spent a year in a Bethesda Naval Hospital ward full of wounded marines. Badly hurt and survivors of the most ferocious fighting, "none was subject to wild irrational rages. They weren't bitter. None had 'flashbacks.'

"Were the veterans ruthless killers? Killing, alas, is not so repugnant as we would like it to be. The awful truth is that soldiers—anybody's soldiers— quickly get used to it. Military training doesn't make men into killers. It just shows them how."[5]

Some of the young military men are not so absolute as Jim Webb about Vietnam. James Lawrence, a lieutenant in Vietnam, feels many ambiguities. He went to the Citadel as a "poorly disciplined young man" and came out with "glorious dreams of being a career soldier." He saw fierce fighting in An Khe, in 1965, against hordes of North Vietnamese regulars. His best friend was killed and mutilated, and Lawrence was wounded by a shot that caused temporary paralysis. He has many of the same military feelings as Webb does. "I think it was the Citadel and the discipline that helped keep me alive." While recuperating in a hospital, Lawrence had second thoughts of returning to battle. "This doctor just chewed my ass. He said, 'You are an *officer!* It is your obligation to go back—and *my* obligation to send you back.'" And Lawrence agreed. "People find it very square to talk about flag and country, but I don't have any problems with that. I can tell you why I went. And I can justify it. Because my country asked me to go."

At one point, Lawrence said, "I guess I was a bad officer. I had a recon platoon, and I was more concerned about my men than great military victories. That was one of my weaknesses."

That was a weakness?

"To a general it's a weakness."

Lawrence returned to a receptive homecoming. "George Wallace was governor, and they were looking for a local hero." The American Legion lavished awards on Lawrence, and as part of a "big P.R. reaction to the antiwar movement," Lawrence made countless speeches, "justifying why we were there." He reflects. "Back then I would give a flag-waving, rah-rah 'let's go get 'em' speech. A lot of it was to make me sound pretty big.

"The naivety went away, and I saw that it was a no-win war. I don't think we tried to win it or could have. We certainly had the military power, but had we just bombed them off the map, it would have been an even more unpopular war than it was. The ground that I fought for and that my friends died for, right now, is in their hands," he says grimly.

There is a depth to Lawrence's perceptions today that allows for ambiguities. He recognizes the flawed arguments of the past on both sides. "I came back and was mouthing the words that I thought a good soldier should mouth. The antiwar guys were doing the same thing, mouthing the words a good liberal, a good hippie should be shouting. There was no difference—except in the words. Today, I'm a bit disappointed in the country because I tend to believe that it was a political war, an economic war, and the people at the top did not have my best interests at heart. That disappoints me but not enough to denounce America."

Lawrence resented the VVAW members he saw on stage with Jane Fonda at the University of Alabama when he was in graduate school. "The auditorium was packed, and Fonda goes on about enlisted men fragging officers. She started naming units and dates, and she named *my* unit and the date I was there. And none of it happened! I'm saying, 'Now wait a minute'—and there are 5,000 eighteen-year-old freshmen going crazy, saying 'Right on, Jane,' and 'Down with America!' One veteran got up and said, 'Lady, you're full of shit,' and spun around and walked out. I felt if I had said anything, she would have said, 'Well, of course you would say that. You're an officer.' "

Filled with military pride, yet disillusioned about the war, Lawrence says he no longer "puts so much faith in our government. El Salvador? We've been through one of those. Until we know what we're involved in, we've got to keep our young men out of it."

There are many conflicts. "If they called me today, I'd go," says Lawrence. At that point, Lawrence's son, six years old that day, walks in with a birthday-party present. Lawrence hugs him close, and suddenly a trembling passion touches his voice. "My son is maybe the first person I love more than myself. I'd go a *long way* to keep him out of a Vietnam—maybe even so far as

Canada. I don't want him to know the agony, number one, of what I went through; and, number two, I don't want my agony while he is going through it."

What if we are honestly threatened?

"I don't know how to define that. Who says we all ought to have automobiles? I'm not sure we want gas enough to give the Saudis a fight! I think of my son, and I'm already asking, where can we be in the year 2000? Vietnam turned out to be a really costly lesson." Lawrence says he would be an activist against another Vietnam if his son were asked to go. "I'm a flag-waver, and I believe in loyalty, so I would have a hard conflict. But I *would* protest." He hugs his son even more protectively. "We've just *got* to look at alternatives to war."

4 The Blacks

It is Sunday, and little girls in patent-leather Mary Janes and ribboned pigtails, mothers holding their hands, are coming to see their fathers. They walk into the gray-stoned, forbidding fortress. One by one gates open, then close; they are finally in the visiting room of the Atlanta Federal Penitentiary. The room is a torrent of English and Spanish and hugs and kisses. In this spring of 1981 the room is filled with Cuban refugees who had been detained since their entry to America.

A small number of American inmates remain. One of them, sitting in a corner, is Eldson McGhee—a compact, 5'8" mid-thirties black, an arresting streak of gray running through his hair. For nine years he has been incarcerated, convicted in federal court as an accessory to a bank robbery and a kidnapping. Although McGhee was not at the site at the time, the kidnapping charge became crucial to his sentencing. He was given life-plus-five. In those nine long years, McGhee became a "jailhouse" lawyer who, until 1982, fought unsuccessfully to overturn his sentence and to reduce the time required for parole eligibility.

If delayed stress had been a known defense ten years ago, McGhee might have been in a drug rehabilitation and readjustment program, rather than in jail. He had never been arrested before Vietnam. Afterward, he participated in robberies to support a service-connected drug habit—first morphine and then heroin—that went undetected when he was released from the Army. In prison he learned all those skills—how to make car mechanics out of ex-cons. But he also earned an associate arts degree in management from DeKalb Community College, a bachelor of science degree in human services administration from Mercer, and a master's degree from Georgia State for a training program in interpersonal communications.

In progress reports McGhee was consistently lauded as an excellent library aide and clerk in the staff training office. Officials requested that he remain in the Atlanta area after parole for his "valuable assistance and skill" in helping them in their task of closing the Federal Penitentiary institution, which was being phased out. McGhee was cofounder and president of an NAACP chapter in prison and cofounder of its crime-prevention program, an organizer of incarcerated veterans and leader in a drug-abuse program. He served as a witness before the U.S. Senate Committee on Veterans Affairs regarding drug abuse and counseling for veterans.

McGhee's exemplary prison record matched his teenage dreams of making something of himself. But unfortunately Vietnam came between.

When McGhee returned from Vietnam, he was among the many black soldiers caught up in the sixties black-nationalism movement. McGhee had four months left in the service. He was given two miserable choices. "I could have been assigned to riot control. It was actually 'civil disobedience' control. Many blacks did *not* want to do that. It would be our own people we would have to arrest! There were so many riots that summer . . ."

McGhee's voice drifts off. He then recalls the other assignments, the "funeral detail," the weeks of hell that only extended the effect of Vietnam on his life. He starts slowly, then talks rapidly of the memories that will never leave. "You can imagine having a son in *Vietnam* and then seeing a military car coming to your house! What *else* could it be coming for?"

Mothers would peer out windows and race to the streets as if to halt the terrible news. They would beat on the doors and sob as an officer who had lost his leg in Vietnam hobbled out of the car. McGhee drove the officer through ghettoes and down country roads—to "do the telling." Once he and the captain broke the news, they had to arrange the funerals. "You couldn't help but break down," recalls McGhee. "You just had to keep reliving Vietnam over and over."

McGhee evokes the worst of war—never taught in basic training or eulogized in memorial dedications. Many black soldiers, having a "choice" of funeral detail or riot control, where they would be pitted against their own people, experienced a kind of pain seldom remembered in discussions of Vietnam and the sixties.

McGhee was the last to predict such sorrow when he proudly entered the service. Like many poor blacks, McGhee, "unable to pursue the American Dream through a college degree," saw the Army as his Harvard. When he left for Vietnam, everyone gave parties in his honor. "My dating opportunities flourished beyond description, and rest became an impossibility," he says wryly. "I could never recall such fussing over me, such kissing, crying, and other carryings-on, even in my childhood."

He took one last spin in his cherished new car, and a policeman clocked him doing 100 m.p.h. McGhee explained he was driving it one last time before going to Vietnam. The policeman escorted McGhee home to make sure he parked the car and did not give him a ticket. McGhee was off to Vietnam with an unblemished record—not even a speeding ticket.

McGhee's dream of success in the Army followed a traditional pattern. Black leaders have urged young males to "prove yourself worthy" in military service ever since Benjamin Banneker rallied for black support of the colonial

rebellion. American wars were inextricably intertwined with black develop-
ments. The Civil War deconstitutionalized slavery and in its Reconstruction
phase established the dynamics of modern black-white relations. The imperialism of the Spanish-American War formed a background to legalize segregation and a plunge into oppression. World War I brought a new self-image
among some blacks and fresher stereotypes among some whites. In World
War I, poor blacks from the South often went to war in disproportionate
numbers. Fifty-eight percent of those mustered into service in one Georgia
county were black. The treatment of black soldiers in World War II forced the
nation to examine the ideology if not the practice of desegregation. Black
Power and black nationalism arose naturally and not casually during Vietnam.[1]

Despite the racism and segregation of Army life, fighting in the country's
wars was generally viewed by the black male as an opportunity and a chance
to secure "justice for his folk," as W. E. B. Du Bois wrote.[2] Black leaders did
not speak as one, however. A. Philip Randolph strongly opposed black participation in World War I, just as Martin Luther King, Jr., and Stokely Car-
michael would decry the black "cannon fodder" role in Vietnam.

Nonetheless the appeal of the military to blacks was—and remains—unmistakable. Today, with unemployment at an all-time high for black youths,
joining the volunteer Army is often simply economic conscription. During
Vietnam, for some, it was the Army or jail; for others it was the Army or
unemployment. Boredom and the lack of a future on ghetto streets played a
part. Many volunteered for elite fighting units. As one eighteen-year-old
black marine said in Vietnam, "The brother is here, and he's raising hell.
We're proving ourselves."

Yet Vietnam also collided with black resistance. In a collection of essays on
black protest and the war, professor and black historian Clyde Taylor wrote:
"Faced with American wars, black people have been caught and continue to
be caught in the cycle of hustles with the implicit promise, 'This time, it'll be
different.' This time it *was* different, in that many didn't swallow the Vietnam
hustle at all."[3]

When Muhammad Ali refused to fight, saying "No Viet Cong ever called
me Nigger," he spoke for many young blacks all over America. Overall, one
third of blacks who enlisted volunteered for combat. However, many who
were drafted spoke out with all the militancy of their black-pride counterparts stateside. Vietnam in its later years, particularly in the rear ranks,
seethed with racial tension, discrimination, and rebellion.

As one veteran told me, only half in jest, "Our company was one third
Black Panther, one third KKK—and the rest of us ducked a lot."

All of that was in the future when Eldson McGhee landed in Vietnam in
December 1967. He could not wait to "find Charlie" and "get my Congres-
sional Medal of Honor." He was stationed in An Khe, the 173rd Airborne
Brigade base camp.

In a short time, McGhee changed; he became a twenty-year-old who wanted to leave Vietnam "more and more every day." His first known kill haunted him—shooting two armed villagers, finding one collapsed in bloodied death. "I was in the field day in and day out until wounded. At first, and even until I was wounded, I thought it was the right thing to do. Later, in the rear, I was indoctrinated into the idea of the war being lousy from a lot of disgruntled peers. I began to rethink my position."

He saw "too many brothers dying." Hanoi Hannah would interrupt Armed Forces Radio with communist propaganda aimed especially at black soldiers. Her pitch was "Why were we blacks fighting in Vietnam when we had our own war at home?" McGhee recalls, "It was *very* effective. You'd see another black buddy wounded, or friends would write about our people being attacked viciously in the streets of America, struggling for equal rights. You *had* to begin to question what was going on at home—and whether you would receive that chance for upward mobility that you were in Vietnam for."

On March 25, 1968, McGhee was hospitalized with wounds in the hand, left arm, face, and head. His platoon was all but annihilated. His weapon had been completely destroyed in his hand, his steel helmet smashed by shrapnel from rocket fire, but he only needed sixteen stitches in his scalp. Still, McGhee "could not get the pain in my head to cooperate with the doctors' diagnosis." He was placed on morphine and was well enough to work cleanup detail.

Then came the day that enraged black soldiers. There was so much noise in McGhee's camp that he thought they were under attack. Instead it was a riot. "A guy called 'Preacher'—a brother of many fire fights who was later killed in action—raced in, tears running down his face. 'Brother man,' he bellowed, 'these rednecks have got to be *stopped;* they have murdered Dr. King and declared war on our people . . .'"

McGhee reflects, "There was a whole change of attitude. Even among those, like me, who were *committed* to the war. You began to wonder, 'What am I really fighting for?' After Dr. King's death there was a greater sense of being black. Some of us perceived that there *was* an attack on blacks. It's kinda hard not to feel that when you're in a company that's got a lot of blacks, and you go back into the rear and it's a different story altogether."

McGhee's ambiguities mounted. Unlike many blacks, he did not quarrel with the concept of fighting Third World peasants. "I never felt the war was wrong, and I don't now. I think the way we *fought* it was wrong." Still, he smoldered over the disproportionate numbers of blacks killed or wounded, the riots back home, the death of Dr. King. On top of this, McGhee learned while in the hospital that his best friend, Theodore Roosevelt Johnson, was killed. "I guess it's a natural tendency to think that your friends are a bit better than you. I always thought that if he could've come back and not me, he may have made better contributions than I have."

McGhee returned to the field "mad, anguished, and frustrated. I wanted to *kill* for Theodore Roosevelt." Morphine had put him in a "utopia state, and I didn't want to get out of it."

He became a zombie who fought unnaturally, dangerously. "I did a lot more killing—*unnecessary* as I look back. I had reached the point where I did not want to take anyone alive. I went beyond my job. That causes me a lot of anguish yet. The morphine made me feel like I was bullet-proof—a supernigger. Someone had to always scream at me, making sure I kept low during fire fights. The medic protected me, made sure my drug problem wasn't detected by the Old Man [company commander]. Finally, the medic knew I had to go in or I was going to get killed or get someone else killed. He recommended I be put on light duty at the support station until taken off medication."

Duty at the support station was "worse than death—seeing the dead and wounded coming in from all four companies in my battalion. Every day it seemed that someone I knew was getting killed or seriously mangled." When McGhee was taken off medication, he found relief and heroin in one of Vietnam's many "soul cities" that catered to black GIs ostracized from white hangouts. McGhee, who wouldn't even touch marijuana his first two months in the country, now snorted heroin, put it on grass or regular cigarettes. Like most GIs who used heroin in Vietnam, McGhee was under the tragic delusion that he could not get hooked because he "never shot it."

The strength of the heroin in Vietnam was legendary and lethal. "Many guys got sores on parts of their bodies if they kept heroin in fatigue pockets for a few days without being wrapped in some strong plastic bagging. A few guys mainlined and died from overdoses like roaches from Raid. The brothers I hung out with, in the supposedly hipper set, never shot drugs."

McGhee left for the States when his tour was up, his drug addiction undetected. (The urine test to detect drugs was not instituted until 1971.) As the plane started off the runway for home, McGhee felt tears running down his face for the first time since he was a child.

Approaching Atlanta, facing the world again, McGhee almost went into hysterics. "I knew something was terribly wrong. I could not let my mother know that I had deserted the faith she had in me. The hero they awaited was a junkie now." McGhee was a stranger in his own home. "Thoughts of building up my neighborhood, buying my mother the kind of house she always dreamed of having, all of my dreams of becoming a prominent figure were leaving me faster than blood from a body shot full of holes with an AK-47. I was having problems just coping with being on the *streets.* I would hear Jimi Hendrix, and I would think about the guys back there. I couldn't *stand* to have someone touch me when I was asleep. You develop such sensitivity to noise in Vietnam." The paranoia was being fed by his heroin addiction.

Desperately trying to leave the military with an honorable discharge, McGhee went to great lengths to hide his drug problem. "I just told them I was having trouble sleeping."

He slid farther into depression during the funeral detail. "I don't believe *any* combat veterans came back untouched," says McGhee. "[Those] that were able to adjust came back to people that were prepared to deal with them as individuals. I always had a close relationship with my mother, but I was always [expected] to be a 'man'—whatever that is. Like many blacks, I grew up not knowing my father. I thought it would be 'unmanly' to complain about what I had gone through."

In addition to being a veteran, McGhee was a young black caught in the upheaval of black nationalism. Many black veterans report similar experiences, "The riots, the protests—I was with them. Finally, I felt I was being used by one pseudomilitant group. They wanted me to train guys for guerrilla-type operations against the establishment. They were interested in media attention. The 'black power' thing—with no plans whatsoever for replacing the system they wanted to destroy."

McGhee was honorably discharged. "I am still trying to understand how the Army, with all its medical and technical know-how, allowed me to be discharged without a thorough check-up." McGhee got a job but could not hold onto it. "I got involved in a drug ring, running drugs to maintain the habit, but refused to do anything directly involving violence. I'd seen too much in Vietnam. I planned robberies, and that eventually led to this," he said, waving his hand around the locked penitentiary room filled with armed prison guards.

"People in the underworld are constantly looking for people who have the skills—veterans, police, anyone who can help get the job done. So veterans are good marks for criminal activity. Especially veterans who are mad, like a lot of us were when we came out."

McGhee's life as a junkie was "one long, continuous nightmare. All of my hangouts were places the police raided, or they constantly stopped and frisked anyone in the area at random. I stayed in the streets at night and nodded all day."

McGhee was first arrested and placed in jail for eight months, from November 1970 until July 1971, for aiding and abetting in a robbery. There his addiction took a step up. "You can get drugs in this country's jails and prisons easier than on any street corner in Saigon. I also learned how to use a hypodermic needle without any assistance."

Once out, McGhee sought help in the first VA drug-abuse program in Atlanta. "I thought it would be safe for me to go there—but that feeling was not long-lived; the bureaucracy and the daily feeling of being *followed* upon leaving the drug center were too intense. If they had had Vet Centers, then I feel I would have been helped."

His $100-a-day habit had to be fed. In September 1972 McGhee was convicted as an accessory to a bank robbery and kidnapping. McGhee was not at the scene and claims there was no evidence of his aiding and abetting, except the testimony of one of the robbers who turned government informant and testified that McGhee was "supposed" to drive the getaway car. McGhee was picked up ten miles from the robbery. He could not afford expensive counsel.

In prison, he was forced to quit his habit cold turkey. McGhee still shudders at that memory.

"*All* pain. Nose runnin', eyes runnin', aching of the bones, knots in your stomach. I was unconscious for two days. I'm not making any excuses for them not giving me any treatment. I think that pain was the shock I needed. It's ironic, but it's the best thing that happened to me."

McGhee was bitter for years over his sentencing. Finding and organizing other veterans was a salvation. "We set goals beyond this place." At that time, among 2,000 federal prisoners there were 300 known Vietnam veterans —15 percent of the prison population. McGhee worked at upgrading discharges. He pushed for a review process for all incarcerated veterans. "That is the only justice for anyone who lost his sense of self-direction upon returning from combat and being rejected for his sacrifice. When I was president of the NAACP [chapter in the prison], we set up a prerelease program that helped a lot of veterans. You don't have the high recidivism with veterans that you do with others. It don't take but one time for us to realize this is the wrong road."

Chalking up his degrees is McGhee's way of "hoping to erase the stigma of a record." McGhee was paroled in the depression days of September 1982. He hoped to get into a community counseling program. No matter what happened, McGhee swore with a soft smile that he wouldn't go back to drugs. "Oh no. It *can't* ever get that bad!"

After his release, McGhee said, "I am free in spirit and faith. I've used this suffering, this adversity to perfect my capacity to put 'mind over matter' and excel."

More and more Eldson McGhee was bothered about the future. "El Salvador is very much a concern for all parents who have sons and daughters eighteen to twenty-five years old, but there can only be another Vietnam if we permit it. At the risk of sounding facetious, if America has to go into military conflict, then let those who made the decision to do such a thing fight the enemy. If this country must resort to military action, let it be with men between ages twenty-six and fifty. The American people in general and American politicians *in particular* must be held fully accountable for sending kids off to military combat and for caring for the readjustment of those who return bearing scars. This must be the demand of the Vietnam veterans and all of our supporters. I, personally, have decided to live the rest of my life as a pacifist."

Not all incarcerated veterans are as motivated or caring as Eldson McGhee, nor of course are they all black. Still, blacks comprised a disproportionate percentage of McNamara's Project 100,000 'subterranean poor," who often got into trouble during and after Vietnam.

To understand the special problems of some black veterans, it is important to return to their history in Vietnam. No one has to be a whiz at math to realize that Project 100,000—instituted in 1966 and billed as a Great Society program—was a vehicle for channeling poor, mostly Southern and black youths to Vietnam's front lines. Military standards were lowered to recruit and "rehabilitate" 100,000 underprivileged youths annually who previously had been rejected for failing to meet the armed services mental or physical requirements. The concept was to teach them new skills and self-confidence. Service would enable them to receive veterans' benefits. The project would also reduce domestic unemployment. Senator Patrick Moynihan, then an assistant secretary of labor, effusively argued that the advantages for blacks would be great. The Army was a "world away from women" which would be beneficial to blacks "given the strains of the disorganized and matrifocal family life" in which so many lived, Moynihan said. Such patronizing beneficence was underscored by the Army's recruiting message: "In the U.S. Army you get to know what it means to feel like a man."

In reality, Project 100,000 turned out to be one of the most shameful aspects of our Vietnam policy. Seldom mentioned was the fact that a disproportionate number of Project 100,000 men entered combat. Their combat force helped stave off the politically nettlesome possibility of dropping student deferments or calling up the reserves.

The much touted training skills were seldom taught. The program sent several hundred thousand men to Vietnam and several thousand to their deaths. The most volatile aspect of the program was race. Four out of every ten brought into the armed forces through Project 100,000 were black.[4]

A 1970 Defense Department study disclosed that *41* percent of the Project 100,000 men were black, compared with *12* percent in the armed forces as a whole. What is more, *40* percent of Project 100,000 men were trained for combat, as compared with *25* percent for the services generally.[5]

Moynihan praised the government in its effort to "eradicate poverty" and noted that in 1965 blacks were underrepresented in the armed forces. They comprised only 8 percent of the military. He neglected to mention, however, that it looked far different in Vietnam's fields of fire. Although underrepresented in the armed services as a whole, blacks still accounted for 16 percent of combat deaths from 1961 to 1966. In 1965, the year of Moynihan's report, *23.5* percent of all Army enlisted men killed in action were black.[6]

Veterans who belong to the Reagan administration's Vietnam Veterans Leadership Program gloss over such Department of Defense statistics and point out that overall, in the entire period of the war, blacks suffered 12.5 percent of the deaths in Vietnam. However, they do not point out the inequities—such as the higher numbers of blacks killed before the armed service in later years changed its tactics and began to send proportionately fewer blacks into combat.

Moreover, that 12.5 percent does not reveal the disproportion. "While blacks averaged about 9.3 percent of total active-duty personnel in 1965–70, they suffered 12.6 percent of the deaths—30 percent in *excess* of their presence in Indochina. (During the Vietnam fighting, blacks comprised 10 percent of U.S. armed forces in Southeast Asia.) Disproportionately high casualty rates for Spanish-surnamed soldiers have also been reported.[7]

McNamara labeled Project 100,000 men the "subterranean poor," as if they lived in caves. In a way they did, in their teeming ghettoes unseen by whites or in Appalachian hill country. Noticeably omitted in the voluminous statistics compiled by the Pentagon on Project 100,000 were casualty rates and combat deaths. Pentagon officials denied that casualty rates for these men were disproportionately high. Given their percentage of men in combat, however, that must mean they were somehow miraculously better at dodging bullets and booby traps.[8]

In one 1969 sampling of Project 100,000 men, the Department of Defense put an attrition-by-death rate at 1.1 percent and noted "the largest single cause of death is battlefield action." For all Vietnam-era veterans, the killed-in-action rate was less than 0.6 of one percent.[9]

In all 354,000 men were taken in under the program. For many, the service exacerbated their problems and bitterness. Even members of the "moron corps," as they were sometimes called, could figure out that more from their ranks were dying. They also got into trouble more frequently; they received 50 percent more nonjudicial punishment than others in Vietnam and were court-martialed twice as frequently.[10]

Discrimination began with the draft board; the Selective Service System was the guardian of the status quo. Blacks comprised only 1.3 percent of all 16,632 board members in 1967, with no blacks on the boards in Alabama, Arkansas, Louisiana, Mississippi, Kansas, Indiana, or New Jersey. After adverse publicity, the number of blacks on draft boards rose to 6.7 percent. Needless to say, few boards questioned the large numbers of blacks drafted.[11]

After Project 100,000 was instituted, recruitment in the ghettoes rose to an art form. Previously, the minimum passing score on the armed forces qualification test had been 31 out of 100. Under Project 100,000, those who scored as low as 10 were taken if they lived in designated "poverty areas." Black recruiters were carefully assigned to black neighborhoods, striving to let dropouts and drifters know there was a place for them in the military. The response was great—the excess from poverty areas in many cities compensated for the decline in volunteers from more affluent neighborhoods. "President Johnson wanted these guys off the street," recalled Colonel William Cole of the Army's Sixth Recruiting District in San Francisco. The Marine Corps dipped heavily into the pool. In 1969, of 120 Oakland Marine Corps volunteers, nearly 90 percent scored under 31, almost *all* had police records, and *more than 70 percent* were black or Mexican American.[12]

Black Marine Corps recruiters often hung around street corners, hamburger joints, and basketball courts to "rap with the brothers." Even a white Marine sergeant noted, "We use their language. You know, we say *'man.'* We even call the cops 'pigs.' " The pitch was that everybody starts out *even* in

Boot Camp—the delinquent as well as the exemplary high school graduate. Recruiters visited shabby slums where mothers were often fair game. Recruiters told them that if their sons were *drafted,* nine times out of ten they wouldn't get the job they wanted. But if their sons *enlisted* in the Marines, they would get "valuable training." The recruiter realized, however, that their sons' low scores made them unlikely training candidates for much more than combat.[13]

Just how many Project 100,000 men wound up in jail after Vietnam is impossible to gauge. However, those who work with incarcerated veterans feel that a large number went that route.

"I think McNamara should be shot," said Herb DeBose, a former black first lieutenant who works with incarcerated veterans and is director of a New York City discharge-upgrade and employment program for veterans. "I saw him when he resigned from the World Bank, crying about the poor children of the world. But if he did not cry at all for any of those men he took in under Project 100,000, then he really doesn't know what crying is all about. Many weren't even on a fifth-grade level. And the Army was supposed to teach them a *trade* in something—only they didn't.

"Some were incorrigible, always fighting, and *did not belong there.* They brought their mentality with them. I had people who could do things only by rote. I found out they could not read. No skills before. No skills *after.* Disciplinary problems while in the military. Like any other guy in that war, they began to ask *why,* and when *they* asked why, it was often viewed as a discipline problem."

Louise Ransom, who also works with incarcerated veterans said, "The right-wing veterans who wish to ignore these men in prison want to say they were predisposed to get in trouble. Well, they should not have been taken in that case! The number of bad discharges among Project 100,000 men is really high because these guys should *never* have been in the military. There is definitely a causal relationship, between bad paper and incarceration."

One survey turned up an alarming post-Vietnam mortality trend. Some 500 men comparable in background to Project 100,000 men—but who did not serve—were studied. Only two in that category were dead. In sampling 500 Project 100,000 veterans, however, *16* were dead. Two died of disease, four in automobile accidents, three were murdered; five died of "unknown causes," and two committed suicide. A Pentagon analyst hypothesized that such statistics lent "anecdotal support" to "post-service psychological adjustment problems."[14]

For the most part, Project 100,000 men slipped back into the world of the "subterranean poor," once their usefulness was over. Today most people—some who even work on the Hill in veterans' affairs—scratch their heads at the mention of the name. It is a page from the past. These men are seen from time to time by veteran activists who report that many received less-than-honorable discharges. Perhaps the most surprising, and positive point is that the majority, despite all odds, performed well in service, doing the dirtiest and deadliest of jobs. Where they are today is unknown. Government statisticians no longer keep track, now that their usefulness is long over. They are, once again, among the forgotten.

Racism was a minor problem in frontline combat, where the saying went, "Same mud, same blood." In the rear it was a different story. After Martin Luther King, Jr.'s assassination, after black nationalism swept through the service, after the war was pretty much perceived as a lost cause, after drugs became prevalent in the rear, racism escalated to incendiary proportions. Blacks fought to wear ballooning Afros and black-power bracelets, woven, it was said, from the shoelaces of dead comrades.

They would give each other the dap—an elaborate, finger-popping, hand-slapping ritual with African origins that could take several minutes, depending on how many blacks were together. White officers, viewing this as a mutinous rebellion, sometimes punished or arrested black GIs. There was self-imposed segregation—eating together, living when they could in all-black hooches, where white pin-ups were replaced by black. "I don't want no stringy-haired beast broad with 'hidden beauty' on my wall. Black is beauty," one black marine said in "The Little Ghetto" hooch in Da Nang. Near riots would start over blaring soul music vying with hillbilly music. When Martin Luther King, Jr., was murdered, crosses were burned at Cam Ranh Bay and Confederate flags were flown at Da Nang. After appearing on the cover of *Time* magazine for the story of "the Negro in Vietnam," Army Airborne Sergeant Clyde Brown found a cross burning outside his tent.[15]

Blacks who were in Vietnam during the earliest days report a whole different war and attitude. Later many blacks, who had bought the recruitment pitch that there was less discrimination in the armed forces, felt bitterly ripped off in Vietnam. Enlisted men and the few black officers alike greeted each other with the black-power clenched fist. Black flags were flown on boats that swept the Mekong Delta. Some whites today agree that there was obvious discrimination. Others recall feeling intimidated by menacing "brothers" who stood together against "chucks" and "white rabbits." Whites were often deeply resentful of black hostility aimed at them merely for being white. Ron Karenga's Swahili-speaking U.S.-based movement spread to at least four Marine and Army bases in I Corps. The Ju-Ju's and Mau-Mau's, black protective clubs, found ready recruits. One member warned whites, "Mess with one of us, and you mess with all of us."[16]

In 1969 journalist Wallace Terry surveyed 833 black and white soldiers in Vietnam. He found that a large majority of black enlisted men felt blacks should not fight in Vietnam because of discrimination back home. This was a striking change from the more gung ho, complacent black soldiers Terry interviewed in 1967. Of 392 black enlisted men, 64 percent believed their fight was in the United States, not in Vietnam. Some 32 percent of the blacks and 11 percent of the whites felt withdrawal should be immediate because the United States had no business in Vietnam in the first place. The white student movement drew more support from black GIs than whites. Perhaps because of the disparate number of blacks in combat, 12 percent of blacks but less than 3 percent of the whites wanted the war to end because the loss of American lives was too great.

The vast majority—83 percent of the blacks—believed America was in for more race violence, and only 38 percent of black enlisted men agreed that weapons have no place in their struggles for their rights in the United States. Nearly half, in fact, said they would use weapons in that cause. Many said they would not participate as soldiers in a riot. More than 45 percent said they would refuse an order to put down rebellious blacks at home. Despite the military's contention that life for blacks is better in the service than out, fewer than three black GIs in ten said they get along better with whites in Vietnam than they did back home.[17]

Mistrust and hostility spilled over into dangerous, ugly incidents time and again in Vietnam—beatings, killings, fraggings, cross burnings, and racial slurs from both sides escalated as the war continued.

Studies revealed that blacks' sense of discrimination and military injustice were not imagined. A 1971 Defense Department survey of Air Force units in Southeast Asia found minority-group frustration so high that many men found it difficult or impossible even to articulate their complaints. They were bitterly resentful of the many commanders who tried to enforce discipline by banning such symbolic acts of racial identity as dapping and the clenched-fist salute. For militant blacks who challenged fighting in the "white man's war," prison terms were sometimes imposed. A 1971 Congressional Black Caucus study discovered that half of all soldiers in confinement were black. An NAACP study also learned that a white first-offender was *twice* as likely to be released without punishment as a black first-offender. A 1972 Defense Department Task Force on military justice reported what black soldiers had felt for years—blacks of comparable education and aptitude who committed offenses of comparable seriousness received much harsher punishments than whites. Blacks received a disproportionate share of the less-than-honorable discharges awarded during the Vietnam era—a fact that led the Equal Employment Opportunity Commission to hold that requiring job applicants to have honorable discharges constituted racial discrimination in employment.[18]

One of the best accounts of racism came from lawyer David F. Addlestone and legal worker Susan Sherer, who witnessed military justice in Vietnam. "Racism manifested itself with discouraging regularity in almost every phase of the military," they concluded. They cited a candid soliloquy of a Long Binh stockade guard: "The Human Relations Council asked if I was prejudiced. I said, 'Hell, yes!' I hate these swine. They call *me* swine. Once a prisoner set his mattress on fire, and we beat the shit out of him. He said we tried to poison him, but all we did was beat the shit out of him. There are some others I want to beat the shit out of."

The Department of Defense Task Force found disproportionate punishment of racial minorities in every category of discipline. As of March 21,

1971, blacks made up 12.3 percent of the enlisted men in Southeast Asia and only 2.7 percent of the officers. The Lawyers Military Defense Committee found that stockade populations were consistently 60 percent black, with disproportionate numbers of blacks in maximum security—they had been labeled "militants."[19]

Tension was so high that commanders wanted to break "troublemakers" quickly. Often this meant that blacks were in pretrial confinement for the slightest offense—for example, the refusal to take a poster off the wall.

Once in the stockade, GIs often accepted an undesirable discharge (U.D.) in lieu of a court-martial, particularly true with blacks who had little faith in what to them was a lily-white system of justice. Their U.D.'s followed them through life, hindering them in post-Vietnam employment. Those who went to court found themselves defended and prosecuted by white captains and lieutenants before white judges and juries made up of white officers. Token black career officers did appear on many juries, and there was one black judge in Vietnam—for one year.

By 1970 suspicion and alienation were beyond repair, and blacks had gained a subtle power. They simply refused to go in the field or, in many instances, to work. "What are they going to do—send me to Vietnam?" was the derisive comeback. At Camp Baxter near the DMZ, an investigation of murder following a race riot revealed that vast numbers of GIs carried illegal handguns. The word "nigger" resulted in a brawl in January 1971 at Phu Loi near Saigon; the huge American base at Da Nang was in a state of open racial war for nearly a week in early 1970.[20]

Although many blacks report that they felt more at home in villes with Vietnamese than at base camps, the Vietnamese had their own sense of discrimination. Prostitutes who serviced black soldiers were generally considered inferior by prostitutes who serviced whites. Blacks complained about Vietnamese knowing the term "nigger"—someone had to teach them that, they said.

Racism—perceived as well as tangible—led to fiery outbursts. Enlisted men's clubs were a constant source of tension. One incident at Cam Ranh Bay led to a fragging in which thirty-one were injured.

Fraggings, for real or imaginary slights and slurs, increased enormously from 1969 to 1970. In 1969 there were 96 documented assaults, in 1970 there were 209. Halfway through 1971 there had already been 154 assaults, and the figures were climbing.[21] Many "warnings"—smoke grenades or grenade pins left by the door—were not reported.

By 1970 black unrest had begun to hinder the fighting effort. White soldiers openly feared blacks, feeling that some would not hesitate to "shoot at whitey." Two white majors were shot and one killed when a fight broke out after they had tried to get blacks to turn down a tape recorder blasting soul music.[22] A general in Germany in the early seventies was told by a black that all whites, including him, were pigs. "I burned buildings in Chicago and shot

Whitey, and it doesn't bother me one bit," said the black. "I'd just as soon shoot at Whitey as the VC."[23]

Blacks spoke of fragging then—and do so now—with a casualness that is chilling. "I'll tell you the way it went," said Herb DeBose. "Lieutenant Kennedy was about to be fragged one night. He was really one of those persons who deserved what he was going to get," said the former black officer. "The men had gone offpost to visit some women in the ville. These men weren't even under his command. He followed them, called in the MPs, had the guys busted in rank and given Article 15s (nonjudiciary punishment). I didn't consider any of them troublemakers. That night, my men asked me, 'How far you live from Lieutenant Kennedy?' I told them, 'We share the same room.' So they said, 'Well, don't you want to come down and play cards?' I understood what was going on. So I went down to play cards. And he was fragged. He didn't get killed or injured—they threw a tear-gas grenade to let him know they could do something else."

As a civilian attorney in Vietnam in 1970, David Addlestone interviewed whites and blacks about the case of a black who shot and killed two white soldiers while heavily drugged. Listening to the tapes that still haunt Addlestone a decade later, there is a Rashomon quality to the incident. Two MPs talked about how the soldier, Johnson (not his real name), was "ranting and raving" as they arrested him and dragged him into a helicopter. Did he threaten to shoot you? asked Addlestone. "Well, *everybody* threatens to shoot an MP, so that didn't mean a whole lot. He threatened to shoot anybody that was white."

Blacks said the MPs did more than drag him into the helicopter, that Johnson was beaten on arrest and a cigarette was put out on his face near his eye.

Friends said Johnson was heavily drugged. "He shot [heroin] that morning; I seen him twice. He snort too. Had ten jays. He smoke all of them. And then them BTs [benoctols—a French pill regularly available without prescription in Vietnam until 1971]. They make you violent. Like somebody ax you a question, you cuss 'em out. He was crying. I told him the best way to get sober was to get down to tox [the detoxification unit]. He talk about how whites all mess with him, how he tired of it, how he do a good job, and they don't give him credit. Said he couldn't stand for it no more. All of us tole him he was outta his mind to kill. I think he was goin' crazy. He isn't the same bro' I know. Brain just snapped. Dope, I guess. I seen that quite a few times."

The soldier on tape continues. "We would take our problem back to our sergeant and try to get him to tell our company commander what was going on, but they wouldn't even take care of it," he complains. "We found relaxation in the ville because of the girls. They treat us just like human beings, you know. It got to the point where we felt safer in the ville than in our own compound."

The black was in the stockade for "giving the power. I see you and I give you the power." A hand slap is heard on the tape, as he demonstrates the greeting of one black slapping another's palm. "All the ones in maxumum security? They the ones that say, 'Well, you can't take my principles from me, after I already went out there and fought for you. I can shake my brother's hand, do the dap.' In the rear they'll put you in jail for that."

Addlestone asks what it is like to be black in Vietnam.

"Well, it seems like you're here for nuthin'. I just have to break all the principles. Everything my mother taught me about not killing and stuff like that. Go out in the field and sacrifice my life for *them*. A brother feels after being here he hasn't accomplished anything material-wise. Or rank-wise."

His story is filled with bravado, anger, resentment, hate and self-hate, insecurity, and a sense of having been wronged. He is, of course, by no means representative of all blacks in Vietnam, but he fits one category, the streetwise urban black. "I couldn't get a rear job. *Nothin'* but white guys work in the orderly room. I type faster than any of them, and yet I was in the field.

"My mother kept saying, 'Why don't you go to Vietnam? Just like all these other guys are doing? You can get some money and come back and get your own house.' I ran away from the hassle to come here and try to make something out of me. And then, hump, you find out, hey *this* not it. And you stuck.

"In jail you eat the slop that the dogs wouldn't eat. They beats you up at night. But they still don't kill my mind. We brothers in jail together. We layin' back, enjoyin' it, gettin' our minds together." He laughs and contents himself with a sly observation about how the whites have to wait on him in the stockade at Da Nang. "And these people that are guardin' us, they in jail *every day with us*. They gotta bring our food to us! They gotta go and bring us water when we calls for it. That's almost like bein' in a hotel. I even drew on the walls to make me feel I was on the outside. I drew me a tree. I just go sit under that tree I drew. Get the shade." He laughs at his behind-bars make-believe world. "The sun is out."

That particular black soldiers' brigade seemed either especially unruly or more punished than others. Addlestone interviewed a white captain about disciplinary problems. "Perhaps half the time the brigade has led all units in Vietnam in courts-martial and Article 15s. I've seen the statistics on AWOL and desertion rates, and we again lead almost every month," said the captain. "The CO told me since he's been here, which has been eleven months, there have been forty-five fraggings, attempted shootings, or shootings."

Herb DeBose, a first lieutenant, was in Vietnam in 1971 with the Army's 26th Support Group at Phu Bai. He went the ROTC route. "Out of fifty-six officers, I was the only black at adjutant-general school."

Did white officers discriminate against blacks who served under them?

"Oh yes. I grew up in the South, and that prepared me for the military. I had to be a 'supernigger' to do my job at a level that would be beyond reproach. In '71 the specific idea was to clean the guys up and bring them home. Regulations kept changing in regards to sideburns and hair, for example. The war between the races at the time I was there was *not* exaggerated. I venture no one will tell it exactly as it was."

As one of the few black officers, DeBose was in a lonely world. He didn't feel at home with whites, but black enlisted men viewed him as an Oreo—black on the outside and white on the inside. There was constant emphasis on the black-power salute and "Brother, give me the dap." "If I didn't want to, I was labeled an Oreo. They said they did not want to fight the white man's war, and we black officers were a part of it. But I got the guys to work for me. I explained *why* I was doing certain things, disciplining a person, etc. A lot of whites just gave orders that many of the guys felt were wrong. 'The Old Man is a racist,' they'd say, and yes, the Old Man *was* a racist. The only thing ineffective officers could resort to is 'I'm an officer, and you do as I say.' That was in the rear. I only saw one other black lieutenant in the rear. I wasn't out in the boonies where you saw the interplay of people putting their lives on the line for each other."

Black officers indeed were scarce in Vietnam. The Navy, traditionally the most racist, as recently as 1971 had fewer than 5 percent black—and below 1 percent among officers.[24]

By October of 1971, 14.3 percent of Army enlisted men were black, yet only 3.6 percent of the officers were black.[25]

Barracks room griping is endemic to all wars, but the depth of hostility and rebellion went much deeper in Vietnam. In 1971 one of the few black majors, Tyrone Fletcher, stated that "confrontation between whites and blacks was the Army's most serious problem." Fort Benning, Georgia, home of the U.S. Infantry, developed special seminars to help Army officers cope with the crisis of race, crime, rebellion, and antimilitarism. In one session, a black officer told the class to think about the white soldier who comes from a background where "NIGGER is a household word." As he shouted the word "nigger" at the officers, many of them blinked. Sensitizing them to the mind-set of young blacks included such recommended reading as *Black Power* and the *Autobiography of Malcolm X.*[26]

Finally, all services began compulsory education on racial sensitivity, although most observers felt it was too little, too late.

Of course, not all blacks felt the same about Vietnam. Herb Denton was a black soldier who was also a reporter and public relations specialist for the Army in Vietnam from June 1967 to 1968. "If we were fired on, I put down my notebook and picked up an M-16."

In the field he saw little emphasis on race. "I spent very little time in the rear. Idleness and boredom there caused people to do mean and crazy things. I remember hearing about a poker fight and how one guy got a .45 and threatened to kill someone." Denton was drafted from Washington, D.C., and "there was not *one* white guy on the bus." At Fort Holabird, Maryland, "out of 300 there were only two of us who had graduated from college."

Denton found that blacks he kept in contact with after Vietnam have done well. "From everything I hear, it was a much different war in the later years, and the attitudes of blacks were vastly different. I've heard how they came back really resentful and messed up. I hate to sound Pollyannish, but the guys I was drafted with, the military settled them down. It settled *me* down in a very similar way. These are 'no fixed address' guys, and the military gave them something. When we graduated from basic, one said to me, 'I've never graduated from anything before in my life.' They are now truck drivers, bus drivers, cops. One's a liquor distributor. The sense of mortality and two years of confinement settled them down.''

Many in the sixties, including black writers, predicted that black soldiers returning to the United States with their refined killing skills would merge with black radicals with frightening results. This did not happen.

Black militant organizations were suppressed and destroyed. As the black nationalist movement fragmented and dissipated, so did overt manifestation of black veteran militancy.

Still, the concept of radical black veterans taking up arms lingers in mainstream America. After the rioting in Miami in May of 1980, law enforcement officials suggested that black veteran guerrillas were active revolutionary participants. However, all available evidence for the assertion that black veterans have become urban guerrillas is circumstantial and flimsy.

Lee Sloan, associate director of the Vietnam-era research project at the Center for Policy Research, argued that such "sensationalist" charges diverted attention from the underlying social and economic conditions that made Miami riot-prone. It also buried the special problems of black veterans, who, in the main, seek the same interest-group political solutions as do white activist veterans—obtaining upgraded discharges, action on Agent Orange, veterans' benefits, assisting fellow veterans in prison, employment, and so forth.[27]

What little insane veterans' militancy surfaced in post-Vietnam America came from the handful of far-right mercenaries and KKK veterans who want to lose themselves in the fire drills of yesteryear. In Texas, Vietnam veterans led raids on immigrant Vietnamese fishermen in 1981. The KKK exchanged white sheets for fatigues to train in the hills of Alabama in 1980 at a "special forces" camp named My Lai for the "race war that's coming."

Considering the number who fought, blacks seem far less visible at Vietnam veteran functions. They were noticeably absent in numbers at the weeklong catharsis for veterans in Washington in November of 1982 at the dedication of the Memorial. Those I spoke with who did attend were in Vietnam in the earlier days. They were indignant about their treatment at home but supported the war.

As darkness descended outside the Sheraton-Park suite of the 25th Division reunion, a black gave an extemporaneous pep talk to the mostly white veterans. His rhetoric held the inevitable hyperbole of such reunions. "No matter what units you were in, what you did, you did *not* run off to Canada!" he shouted. "You did *not* put on a pair of panty hose." Cheers greeted that message. "For fifteen *years* I waited to not bow my head in shame—and I refuse to live one more day in shame. We are as good as anyone who *ever* put on a uniform!" More stomps and cheers. "Millions died since we left; that will tell you we were *right!* Sixty thousand Americans *died* for so many damn freedoms that the ones who didn't go can enjoy."

The main question is what, if any, differences separate the black and white veteran? The *Legacies of Vietnam* study showed that while *nonveterans* in general are *better* educated than Vietnam veterans, there is a different breakdown among blacks. Despite the Project 100,000 men, black veterans tended to be better educated than black nonveterans—but *white veterans* were better educated than black veterans. Once again, while nonveterans are markedly more successful than veterans overall, black veterans held better jobs on the average than did black nonveterans.

Black veterans tended to hold low-level white-collar jobs rather than unskilled and laboring jobs. This may seem to cast a rosy employment picture for blacks, but this is not the case. The unemployment rate of black veterans was *three times* that of white veterans. Unemployment was especially high among those who served in Vietnam (22 percent). Career unemployment was especially high among black Vietnam veterans.[28]

This study found no disproportion as to the numbers of whites and blacks who *went* to Vietnam. Once in Vietnam, however, there were major distinctions. Twelve percent *more* blacks were involved in heavy combat than whites —37 percent to 25 percent.

For many reasons, blacks returned home with more problems that were more persistent. A higher preponderance of blacks came from very unstable families, regardless of class controls, the study found. They were lacking in coping skills and support systems. Especially those who served in Vietnam were convinced that they had "paid their dues" and felt racial justice their due. Such heightened expectations contributed to adjustment problems when they returned to economically depressed and, often, segregated situations.

In addition to heavy unemployment, those who found jobs earned approximately eighteen dollars less per week than white veterans. Many were too old for the Affirmative Action programs of the late sixties and early seventies that concentrated on black teenagers.

The study indicates that an enormous number of black veterans are troubled. Almost 70 percent of blacks who were in heavy combat were classified as stressed in the late seventies. And 40 percent of *all* black Vietnam veterans, as compared with 20 percent of white veterans, are currently stressed. Just being in Vietnam, the study concluded, was as stressful for blacks as being in combat was for whites. Blacks who were stressed after the war remained 12 percentage points more likely than white veterans to remain stressed. And blacks who participated in atrocities, rape, or acts of random violence were more greatly troubled than whites—in retrospect, they felt that they had committed crimes against another racial group.[29]

A need for strong social support was indicated. While all married Vietnam veterans were better off than unmarried, having spouse support was of more help to blacks and combat veterans than others.[30]

In Vet Centers, black team leaders report a lingering animosity about talking to white counselors and suspicion about revealing drug problems.

The strong perception of racism in Vietnam remains, for many, even successful blacks, a visceral and bitter memory. It seems particularly so for blacks who fought side by side with whites, gave them mouth-to-mouth resuscitation, were looked on gratefully as gallant comrades in arms, only to find an abrupt schism back in the rear. The words "we" and "they" still slip easily into conversations when black veterans talk about white soldiers.

Phil Bidler, a white combat veteran and a professor at the University of Alabama, described the dilemma of fighting in Vietnam. "We realized collectively we had nothing to fight for, that nobody cared about us, and we didn't give a shit about them. Our sense of motivation was a buddy system: 'we are in this and nobody cares, but at least we can care about each other.' *Blacks had even another kind of microcosm—they cared for each other. I felt the whites were explicitly bigoted."*

A black Tuscaloosa attorney, John Bivens, volunteered for Vietnam, became a sergeant and item-records specialist in the supply division of the Air Force. He bristles still at the way many whites treated the Vietnamese who worked for them. They "told them their music was a piece of shit and made insanely vulgar jokes about the way they would squat rather than stand. They had to listen to the word 'gook' and never be able to do anything about it. Attractive Vietnamese girls got propositioned all the time."

However, others who were in Vietnam recall, as did Addlestone, "Blacks ridiculing the Vietnamese was plentiful; it wasn't just the whites. It's a strange irony, but the natural pecking order reaction of the underclass."

For Bivens the service was a plus and "eliminated a lot of insecure feelings I had about my ability." He returned to work in the antiwar movement on campus but with a black's wariness. "You know that movie on Kent State, where the young white girl leans over a body and says in astonishment that the guns really were loaded? This black kid turns to her and says, 'The guns are *always* loaded.' *There is no sequence in that movie that more symbolized the difference between white and black cultures.* We *know* the damn guns are loaded. Whenever it was close to the time for things to break loose, we left the white kids there. 'Cuz you couldn't tell them that the police were not our friends. Couldn't tell them that police would raid their community, abuse their constitutional rights, and beat the shit out of them. They had to experience it."

Bivens worked for the Health, Education and Welfare Department in Washington after graduating from law school but then returned to fight injustice in the South. "There are no black attorneys in the seven counties surrounding Tuscaloosa County, with the exception of this county. And here there is only one other black attorney. Our mere presence advances something, has a tremendous impact on the legal system. They can no longer do things without a challenge. I say, okay, this damn system is here, let's keep kicking that sonofabitch until it starts working."

Bivens says, "The direct cause of black veterans not getting a fair shake is the fact that they are black. They got a fair shake when it comes to fighting Viet Cong, but when we got on that plane coming home, it was back to black versus white." John McClusky, a white poverty lawyer in Alabama, agrees. "Now, with all the cutbacks in this administration, it's 'open season on niggers' again."

Forest Farley, Jr., a 6'1½", 230-pound former marine, works with black as well as white veterans in a Florida Vet Center. He notices an endemic disillusionment among blacks that differs from whites. Their residual resentment has its roots in the initial belief in the military as a haven of opportunity. In one 1965 survey, nearly 40 percent of the blacks gave self-advancement as their reason for enlisting—close to twice the proportion of whites, who were mostly motivated to avoid the cannon-fodder draftee status. That dream of advancement was all the more disillusioning when shattered.[31]

"They found it was mainly a myth," says Farley. The unrealized promises of the sixties jarred them on their return. "The racial problems that were going on when they left were still going on when they came back." Even death in antiwar protest did not receive its due. Black veterans often point out the disparity in outrage over Kent State, as compared to the relative silence when two blacks were killed at Jackson State during that campus's Cambodia protest.

Farley remembers his own list of grievances: bitterness because of the small number of black officers, anger that so many black friends "died for a corporate war," disgust at the callousness of Project 100,000. Like Eldson McGhee, he recalls the gut-effective sting of Viet Cong propaganda: "Black soldier do not fight us, we're people of color too."

"Most of the blacks I've come in contact with wouldn't do it again," says Farley. "They had pride in their individual service, but they're also dealing in a lot of guilt. Many feel they have two strikes—being black *and* a Vietnam veteran."

Life has gone full circle for so many desperate black veterans. The Oakland Vet Center—where recruiters so eagerly sought their Project 100,000 quotas over a decade ago—is filled with blacks as Oakland reports record unemployment.

Blacks who have surfaced as successes represent that number fortunate enough to make it up and out via Vietnam. But for every one of them, there are an unknown number who have drifted back to their hidden, subterranean America, a world of "no fixed addresses."

5 Drugs, Bad Paper, Prison

CONSERVATIVE ACTIVIST VETERANS—PREACHERS OF VIETNAM AS A noble cause and often right wing when it comes to questions of current military intervention—like to present the rosiest of Vietnam veteran statistics. There is undeniable laudatory value in pointing out that the majority of veterans are honorably discharged, not on drugs, not in jail, and have moved —often through difficult periods of readjustment—into successful lives. However, there is danger in such representation, which generally seeks to bury or minimize these who have not yet made it out of Vietnam. These activists often leave the impression that the others are a mere handful of "dregs" to be found in any army—too insignificant a number and too unsalvageable with which to concern ourselves. As one colonel said, "We do society a favor by spotting and labeling the undesirables."

Their point of view was an understandable backlash to the negative stereotypes perpetuated for years. Drugs were irrevocably intertwined with Vietnam veterans. One particular arrest photo stands out in my mind, months later. A paraplegic veteran in a wheelchair is flanked by policemen. He was, the caption said, a decorated Vietnam veteran, arrested for trafficking in cocaine. That kind of labeling—"Vietnam Veteran Arrested"—enrages many veterans.

On the other hand, many who work with troubled veterans, feel an urgent need to point out that Vietnam was often the *cause* of their downhill slide.

The widespread use of drugs in Vietnam was reported, analyzed, and examined in great detail at the time. Although heroin was indeed a serious problem in the later years of the war, many veterans, surprisingly, never became addicted or were mildly enough addicted to kick the habit when they returned to the States.

Whatever statistics are used to quantify their numbers, however, cannot possibly be meaningful. For example, the conservative Vietnam Veterans Leadership Program, headed by Reagan's Vietnam veteran Action director, Tom Pauken, states categorically, "Of the minority of GIs who were dependent upon narcotics in Vietnam, the number who remained addicted after the war represented only 1.3 percent of all Vietnam theater veterans."[1]

If they are "only" 1.3 percent of the more than three million men who served in Vietnam, that still represents some 40,000 drug-troubled veterans, who should not be swept away as statistically irrelevant.

Moreover, such glossing over with statistics ignores the most salient point: *Vietnam was the direct cause of their heroin use.* A large majority of heroin users never touched the drugs before they went to Vietnam. Many of them were white rural youths. Only 11 percent of the users had ever touched heroin before Vietnam, according to Pentagon statistics.[2] For many, heroin was self-medication in a violently oppressive setting, in a war that had lost all meaning.

In addition, statistics on those currently addicted are meaningless because the numbers of addicted soldiers, like Eldson McGhee, who slipped through cannot be estimated.[3] Nor is there any way of knowing the numbers who sought help from private drug centers rather than the VA and never disclosed their veteran status. Nor the men who are simply "out there," addicted and unhelped. The biggest flaw is in stating that the addicted represent only a portion of all who served in Vietnam from 1964 on. Heroin was not even prevalent in the country until 1970. The number of users should be compared with those in the country from 1971 on. There never was any way of accurately detecting the number of users then, nor the number of addicted now.

What is important is to examine the reasons why. In addition to racial conflict, another barometer of the military morale crisis toward the end of the war was the widespread use of drugs.

Officers—confronted with a new breed of antiauthoritarian soldiers—were as ill-equipped to handle them as were the deans faced with their like-minded peers on campus. The armed services went through a stage of denial on marijuana, followed by a crackdown on pot smoking. Many observers of that period felt that the punitive, confiscating attack on marijuana in fact led to the use of heroin. (Heroin smoked with tobacco could not be smelled: hence it was not "as loud"—GI lingo—as grass.) Later, the stated armed service policy was to finally confront and aid the drugged wrecks they had largely ignored. In practice, however, once soldiers drifted into hard drugs they were mostly regarded by unit commanders as "criminals" to be punished.

Old myths die hard. A major myth is that anyone on heroin in Vietnam had to be a hard-core, street-smart addict—even though the facts first rocked the military and civilians at home thirteen years ago. In the spring of 1971, two congressional investigations confirmed that large numbers of American soldiers in Vietnam had been using heroin. One study estimated the numbers were as high as 10 percent; the other ranged from 10 to 15 percent.[4]

Not only did these facts underscore pervasive alienation, collapse of discipline, and low morale. They showed that some among our so-called friends—highly placed Laotians, Thais, and South Vietnamese—were making a killing in drug trafficking. Several American pilots were convicted of importing opium from Thailand.[5]

Although one Army study showed substantially higher rates of heroin addiction among minority group soldiers, the *use* of heroin in Vietnam was widespread among whites—some 68 percent who used heroin in Vietnam were white, according to Defense Department data.[6]

Although controversy always surrounded the numbers of users, the Department of Defense's "best estimate" of heroin addiction among all Army enlisted men was 7 percent in 1971, called at the time "perhaps the gravest disease epidemic in modern military history" by Dr. Richard Wilbur, Assistant Secretary of Defense for Health and Environment. "If an epidemic were to reach such drastic levels in the population of the United States, ten to fifteen million victims would be involved." (These figures do not include the others who used speed, opium-laced grass, barbiturates, and alcohol.)

"These kids are a cross section of what the Selective Service was picking up throughout America," said one general, Michael Davison. "And this is what really shatters you." Unlike the typical heroin user at home, a deviant "loner" from a deprived background . . . The "typical Vietnam user would fit many people's idea of the healthy, all-around American boy . . . often from a small town, in good physical condition, has used virtually no drugs before joining the Army, and shows no evidence of character disorder,"[7] stated Dr. Norman Zinberg, a psychiatrist in Vietnam in 1971.

In Vietnam, using heroin became a "social activity." It was very cheap (a typical 250-milligram vial was about two dollars) and very strong (96 percent pure, compared to 3 to 10 percent in the United States). The majority, like Eldson McGhee, smoked or sniffed it (only 5 to 10 percent injected it, according to one congressional report).

Unlike the unmistakable smell of grass, heroin left few detectable traces. "A guy could be on it [heroin] with light to moderate addiction, and you'd never tell because he could still fly an airplane or do a complicated task. It's very insidious," said General Davison.[8]

There have been eruptions of widespread drug use among today's post-Vietnam military. For the men in Vietnam, who blazed this dubious trail, there were often shattering repercussions. These remain to haunt their lives today.

The number of soldiers discharged for drug abuse rose steadily each year. Drug-related criminal investigations, mostly for marijuana, rose 80 percent from 1968 to 1969. Still, the number of new users climbed faster—and soldiers banded together to thwart the military strategy of intimidation and suppression. Since punishment and scare tactics didn't work, the "amnesty" program was introduced. Soldiers could ostensibly seek rehabilitation without threat of punitive action. The exemption applied only when possession was the sole offense. A soldier turning himself in could still be prosecuted for a variety of drug-related offenses such as the sale of drugs. He could still receive a general discharge on the basis of his drug use. He could lose security clearance, job classification, and flying status—and in-patient treatment time would only be added to the length of his tour of duty. Pay would be docked, and medical records could be made available to the FBI. Moreover, he was often harassed by superiors as a "junkie" and assigned to menial tasks upon rehabilitation. The most frightening aspect was that a soldier could seek exemption only once. The amnesty program left him totally exposed; if one attempt to shake the habit failed, he was marked and subject to the full range of punitive actions the next time.[9]

When urinalysis testing or "trial by urine" was instigated, soldiers claimed they were treated "like animals." The detoxification center at Cam Ranh Bay seemed like a prison to many, and a major riot erupted over conditions there in 1971. Conex boxes, about six feet high, five feet wide, and eight feet long were sometimes used for confinement and punishment.[10]

When rehabilitation or often brutal "cold turkey" detoxification did not work, soldiers were often discharged. They returned home, sometimes addicted and almost always with "bad papers."

It took several years before the courts overturned the awarding of bad-paper discharges under the urine-test program.

"Bad paper," that childish-sounding phrase, is loaded with all the negative connotations of leaving the military with anything less than an honorable discharge. Veterans could not use the GI Bill or obtain free VA medical care without at least a general discharge, and often could not find jobs with any kind of bad paper. There were five categories of discharge—honorable, general, undesirable, bad conduct, and dishonorable. The last two are issued by court-martial, the others administratively—often without a right to counsel or hearing. Although 93 percent of all who served, stateside or overseas, during the Vietnam War were honorably discharged, thousands of men in that other 7 percent carried the stigma of bad papers. Although only a fraction received bad conduct and dishonorable discharges, *anything* less than a fully honorable discharge carried a negative meaning that amounted to a life sentence for unemployment and a lack of veterans' benefits. While most with general discharges ("under honorable conditions") can get benefits, general— and even some honorable discharges—held their secret, often lethal messages for employers.

Estimates of the number of less-than-honorable discharges given vary, depending on the dates used for the Vietnam era. One study indicates that more than half a million men (563,000) out of more than nine million Vietnam-era veterans received less than honorable discharges.[11]

Yet another, using 1961 to 1975 as the Vietnam era, put the total at more than three quarters of a million (790,000).[12]

Moreover, an insidious code of numbers on the honorable discharge often penalized veterans. After 1952, the military began using three-digit Separation Program Numbers (SPNS), referred to universally and accurately by veterans as "spins." The spin these numbers created in their lives could be devastating. These numbers corresponded to 446 capsule reasons for discharge. For example, 46A meant "unsuitability, apathy, defective attitudes, and inability to expend effort constructively." There were spins for bed wetting, inadequate personalities, passive-aggressive reaction, immaturity, and homosexual tendencies. Depending on command whim and caprice, a soldier could also get an even more impairing "general" discharge with similar "spins" for the same things.

Lists of the codes were given to the VA and were used for deciding benefit claims. *More injurious, employers soon had their copies and used them to evaluate job applicants.* One marine veteran encountered nothing but rejections when he applied for California state-government jobs. He always proudly showed his honorable discharge. Finally someone asked why he was a homosexual. For the first time, he found out about his spin number.[13]

The furor over spin numbers in the early seventies resulted in their prohibition in 1974. By then the damage for Vietnam veterans was often irrevocable. The Pentagon stated that those discharged to that date could exchange discharge papers for "spin-free" certificates, but the Defense Department refused to notify veterans directly. Only a few thousand knew enough to ask for new certificates. Even those who did sometimes learned that their old discharge paper was there for the record on file in many personnel offices. No official tally was made of bad spin numbers, but one Defense Department sample suggests some 200,000 Vietnam-era veterans may have spin-code blackmarks on their *honorable* discharges.[14] This group, added to the several thousand with bad papers, left nearly a million veterans vulnerable in the job market.

Courts-martial of the Vietnam era produced 31,800 bad conduct and 2,200 dishonorable discharges. However, tens of thousands of Vietnam soldiers accepted undesirable discharges in lieu of a court-martial trial, not understanding the destruction this would mean to their life after Vietnam.

Just as there were many other negative firsts in Vietnam, the use of the "administrative" undesirable discharge rather than going through the judicial court-martial process was escalated. The administrative process was a "whole circumvention of the Uniform Code of Military Justice," claims David Addlestone, who was a JAG officer (a military lawyer) before going to Vietnam as a civilian lawyer and has worked for years on discharge upgrading.[15]

In 1972 general and undesirable administrative discharges amounted to almost 10 percent (9.2 percent) of *all* discharges that disruptive year, and increased each year through to the end of the war. It often took little. Using drugs, even to a minor degree, getting drunk, developing a personality conflict, being rebellious, not handling the work effectively. One self-help guide for discharge upgrading made this central point: "You may even think what you did was 'wrong,' but to be labeled 'undesirable' or have a suspicious 'general' discharge for the rest of your life is too much to pay."

Despite efforts of interested groups to contact veterans with bad paper, the DOD estimates that only 60,000 were upgraded, most only to general. "In the Reagan administration, there is absolutely no climate for upgrading," said Addlestone.

After the war, back home and struggling for jobs, many bad paper veterans tried to upgrade their discharges. There were often two-year backlogs of discharge-upgrade applicants waiting for review hearings. Once again, the smarter or more privileged of the generation were favored. Those veterans who had the time, money, or legal representation to fight and show up before a board overwhelmingly were upgraded, compared to those who tried only in writing.

By 1981, time had run out for many veterans. Those who had served before 1966 were no longer eligible for upgrade hearings before the Discharge Review Board. Those veterans still carrying bad papers by 1981 became just more flotsam-and-jetsam victims of Reagan's budget cuts, and the new "get tough" spirit at DOD filtered down to the review boards. Many veterans with bad papers won't admit it and feel they are penalized for life. It takes hard outreach effort to get to them. Community-based organizations that worked tirelessly on upgrade discharges were no longer funded. The already meagerly funded programs that worked with incarcerated veterans—fighting for their benefits and to upgrade discharges—lost vital Labor Department money and were forced to limp along with some state and local assistance. For those who work with troubled veterans, such budget cuts and indifference were especially galling, as they witnessed Reagan at his patriotic best, with choked voice, periodically mouthing platitudes about noble Vietnam veterans.

In its usual bureaucratic swiftness, it took the VA years to develop any programs specifically for drug patients. It belatedly opened five drug-treatment centers in 1970. Public criticism erupted six months later (Senator Alan Cranston disclosed that the VA was treating a total of 219 drug patients), and the VA was forced into a stepped-up program. This only brought chaos. Most drug users got general discharges and thus were eligible, but it took several years before legislation made treatment available for those with undesirable discharges. Moreover, many with general discharges did not know they were eligible for the drug program.

After years of neglect or harassment, veterans responded to drug programs with deep skepticism and stayed away from VA facilities in droves. In the late seventies, community-based organizations tried to help those with drug-related problems. The Vet Centers of the early eighties—twelve to fifteen years after soldiers returned from Vietnam—were still seeing those who continued to have drug-related problems. In visits to several facilities, I found some veterans on heroin. However, the majority with drug problems seemed to have a severe psychological dependency on marijuana—remaining in a pot-induced haze—or were anesthetizing themselves with alcohol. In fact, alcoholism has become an increasing problem among troubled Vietnam veterans. "For Vietnam veterans with post-traumatic stress disorder [PTSD] high use of alcohol is associated with attempts at self-medication of the disorder," said Dr. John Wilson, a delayed stress expert.

For years there has been considerable conjecture regarding the Vietnam-veteran prison population. Did they come disproportionately from the ranks of the bad-paper brigade? Were they more often Project 100,000 misfits? Were veterans overly represented in prison? Did Vietnam cause their problems?

Searching for facts about incarcerated Vietnam veterans means endless frustration. There simply are *no* reliable statistics. "I *know* there aren't," says Bill Brew, Vietnam veteran and associate minority counsel on the Senate Veterans Affairs Committee. "I tried very hard to get numbers for hearings and simply could not. On both federal and state levels there is *no* interest, either among the prisoners or the prison officials in knowing the numbers."

Finding out if an inmate is a veteran depends on self-reporting. There is a lot of denial about service participation if they have bad paper. They, like their counterparts outside prison, try to hide their negative veteran status in hopes of getting a better break at jobs.

"In addition," says Brew, "prison officials and wardens very often don't want to know. They feel that any differentiation among the prison population can only cause trouble." A general view is that Project 100,000 men dispro-portionately received bad papers. There *is* a direct corollary between bad papers and unemployment. Whether that unemployment translates into more criminal activity is an unknown. The assumption—suggested by anecdotal evidence of several who have worked with incarcerated veterans—is that "bad paper" Project 100,000s and others with bad discharges may well be incarcerated in greater numbers, but there is no conclusive evidence. There is, in fact, no evidence that the Project 100,000s left the military with a dispro-portionate number of bad discharges. It seems logical—given the fact that they received 50 percent more nonjudicial punishment than others in Viet-nam and were court-martialed twice as frequently. However, the Department of Defense—in spite of its seemingly endless statistics—has no records.

What remains are individual studies and random surveys. The comprehen-sive *Legacies* study of random interviews turned up a widely used statistic—one fourth of all those in combat in their sample self-reported that they had been in prison at some time following service.

In 1980 this led to a widely held assumption that combat soldiers engaged in more violent or criminal activities—which was challenged by a later report to be examined in this chapter.

No matter the confusion on the numbers of veterans in prison, there were some positive universal findings in institutions where Vietnam veterans have been identified. In earlier studies—in the mid-seventies—veterans seemed to have greater rehabilitative potential than other prisoners and more positive characteristics. Eldson McGhee—with his stack of degrees and laudatory reports—may be more exemplary than most, but many show a longing and striving to make it outside prison that is lacking in the regular prison population. As one state official said in 1976, incarcerated veterans are the "cream of the crop—at the bottom of the barrel."[16]

This is both encouraging and depressing to the handful of dedicated—often Vietnam veterans themselves—who work with incarcerated veterans. They see them caught in a maze of confusion over veterans' benefits or treated with hostility by wardens who resist anything that smacks of special favors for any group.

"I felt really bad after interviewing these men," said Dr. Daniel P. LeClair, who supervised a Massachusetts study of imprisoned veterans. "They just didn't look or act as ordinary inmates. They were among the better behaved, moved very quickly through the various stages of security. They seemed to move into medium- and minimum-security institutions as soon as they were eligible. They made stupid mistakes—but big ones."

The warden of a maximum-security prison at Somers, Connecticut, Carl Robinson, agrees. "By and large they are easier to deal with. Even those who cause disciplinary problems are not the assaultive kind. He isn't that hard, con-wise guy." Dr. Robert L. Carr, chief of psychological services at Lewisburg, estimated in the mid-seventies that veterans represented about one third of the federal inmate population. "But they represent *far less* than one third of the problem. Veterans in general and Viet vets in particular adjust well," said Dr. Carr, crediting the standard and values and discipline taught in the military for that group ability to adjust.[17]

However, veterans languished in prison with no special programming, helped only by the dedicated few to secure benefits, discharge review, counseling, or job training. "It's far cheaper for the government to pay veterans benefits for education and training than to keep a man in prison," argues Gold Star mother Louise Ransom, who spent twelve months directing a Department of Labor–funded National Council of Churches Incarcerated Veterans Project. When Reagan came into office, the project was not refunded. At the time, Ransom found that the $500,000 grant could not stretch to aid enough veterans. A General Accounting Office report in 1974 estimated 125,000 veteran inmates, most of them Vietnam veterans, one fourth of the prison population in federal, state, and local prisons and jails. "There is a need far beyond our capacity to serve," said Ransom. One solution was to urge the men to organize themselves into veterans groups.

At the maximum-security prison at Walpole, Massachusetts, Vietnam veterans are on both sides of the bars—as prisoners and guards. Sometimes an empathy and bond is established as they talk about Phu Bai or Da Nang or Pleiku or I Corps. One day five men sitting around a table sounded like any Vietnam veterans as they talked of their military history. Three are ex-marines—two were decorated; one holds the Silver Star for bravery. Yet they are different from the vast majority of veterans. When they returned, three of them ran up a body count of six confirmed kills in Massachusetts. One is serving a term for armed robbery. All are officers of American Veterans in Prison, a small group at Walpole. Like most veterans, in and out of prison, they repeat the now-familiar litany: no decompression, Vietnam on Monday, Roxbury on Wednesday, no appreciation or interest from folks back home, watching buddies die in your arms in a war thought to be a mistake. Those who work with Vietnam veterans are hardened to the simple dodge of blaming Vietnam solely for their problems. The post-Vietnam syndrome is an easy cliché to borrow. "We sold the Viet vets a bill of goods that said they were 'funny,' " says psychologist Carr. "We told 'em they were peculiar, and by God they bought it."[18]

Still, for those who saw heavy combat, the returning adjustment period was unquestionably hard. Dr. John Wilson sampled 346 combat and noncombat Vietnam-era veterans in Cleveland for his Forgotten Warrior Project in 1977 and found enormous problems among combat veterans. Unemployment among black combat veterans was 48 percent; among whites, 39 percent. Nearly one third of black and 22 percent of white combat veterans were divorced. A high number, 41 percent of black and white combat vets had alcohol problems. Thirty-seven percent of black combat veterans and 28 percent of the whites had negative attitudes about themselves.

Among those trained to kill—who already had horrific readjustment problems and possibly unstable backgrounds—resorting to violence in those early returning years became a lifetime mistake. Many imprisoned veterans talk about those days as if they belonged to someone else. Some complain that they were miserably served by society—but for most there is an attempt to put Vietnam in some perspective.

"Vietnam isn't the only reason I'm here," said a Walpole inmate in for armed robbery. "It's my own ignorance. That's why I'm here. But Nam did have somethin' to do with it. It did. From my neighborhood, to go in the service was 'nix,' you know? You was a fool. You come back, and you're still trying to find yourself. You say, 'What did I go over there for?' You went to save the country. Cool. People on this side of the country don't even recognize the fact that you were there. All right. Now you apply for a job.

" 'You a veteran?'

" 'Yeah, I'm a veteran.'

" 'Were you in Vietnam?'

" 'Yeah.'

"Now they get skeptical of you.

" 'Was you in combat?'

" 'Yeah.'

"Now they figure, well, this guy's liable to go off any minute. We don't want to hire him. What if a crisis comes up? They don't really want to hire you. You can't keep doin' that every day, lookin' for a job, losin' a job, lookin' . . ."

Some of the most deeply affected by combat lived a schizophrenic existence in their first months home. "When I came back, the first thing I did, I went and got me some weapons. Some carbines, shotguns, and pistols," said a Walpole inmate. "I was still at war. We used to get on the bus with jungle fatigues and go into downtown Boston. *With jungle fatigues on!* Any citizen in their right mind would say, 'Hey, this ain't right. Here's a group of men goin' around in Army fatigues, doin' their boots the same way they did in the service, and then goin' to buy C rations and then campin' out and eatin' the C rations the same way as they did in Vietnam.' I swear before God. Right there, in Cambridge, that Army surplus store, you used to go there and buy cases of C rations, and you'd go out there, set up the stove, just like in Vietnam—the tent, bayonets, canteen with water, ammunition pouch, first-aid pack, the whole thing. We were still at war. At one time we had fifteen guys, a *whole squad.* Back in the United States physically, but our orientation was still Vietnam."[19]

The love of the dramatic, inevitable in most prison hyperbole, pervades this recollection of readjustment blues. However, statistics consistently point to little involvement with even juvenile crime before Vietnam and far less recidivism for veterans, many of whom participated in a once-only crime rather than crime as a way of life.[20]

Although lack of pre-Vietnam crime could be explained away by the fact that the military does not accept recruits with criminal records, that rule was often bent in collecting Project 100,000 and other street youths. Sometimes military service became a sort of plea-bargaining; it was that or jail.

Although there is considerable controversy over whether Vietnam contributed to veterans' crime, an obvious inequity is irrefutable. The majority of incarcerated veterans never received the benefits legally entitled to them by virtue of previous military service. And many of them had bad papers that kept them unemployed—no doubt a contributory factor in some criminal actions.

Despite the rehabilitative potential of veterans indicated in surveys, little was done to develop model programs to use the GI Bill in probation, incarceration, or parole plans. Special training to ensure jobs was proposed by activist groups, but little came of this. (After a 1974 GAO investigation chastising the VA was sent to Congress, the VA stepped up its prison counseling services. Nearly 20,000 incarcerated veterans received individual counseling, and 9,428 participated in group orientation, according to the VA. However, individual studies show VA involvement was spotty and uneven.)

A vast majority of veterans in prison were unaware they were entitled to any benefits. One disabled veteran was falsely told by a correctional officer that his disability stopped once he was in prison. "I took his word for it and let it go." Georgia prison officials found some years ago that only three of the seventeen Georgia inmates attending DeKalb Junior College received benefits to which they were entitled. Over and over, from state to state, in survey after survey it was the same story. Only a handful of those eligible were receiving GI Bill benefits. Guards and administrators—many of them veterans themselves—opposed government benefits going to criminals. "If I were a prison warden and lost a son in Vietnam, I'd be damned if I'd give these SOBs a break as Viet vets," was the blunt comment of a Washington VA official.[21] A Michigan VA regional representative told Louise Ransom, "These men are *not* veterans." "It didn't matter whether they had previous combat service, Bronze Stars, or whatever," sighed Ransom.

By 1980 that attitude had sufficiently filtered back to Congress; benefits for incarcerated veterans convicted of a felony were severely slashed. GI Bill benefits were reduced to costs for tuition or books; subsistence was dropped. Some corrections officers argued that subsistence money was used to finance illegal drug operations, although most did not. Most prison systems in fact disallowed cash benefits sent directly to the prison; instead the money had to be sent home or to outside savings accounts. One warden said, "We haven't had any problem managing money. Commissary limits hold down the problem. You have GI Bill checks, yes, but you can also have a guy in the hobby shop putting out a product that sells for $500 or $600."

Some state corrections departments required GI Bill recipients to use some of the subsistence money to pay for educational courses—and many eagerly did so. Darryl Kehrer, Pennsylvania's Chief of Programs to Advance Veterans Education (PAVE) at the time said, "In 1977 veterans at Pittsburgh and Rockview correctional institutions paid $18,800 of their own tuition costs and showed a sense of financial responsibility."

With the subsistence portion of the GI Bill benefit gutted, many incarcerated veterans were unable to support their families; that money had gone to housing and food for wives and children.

Imprisoned veterans peculiarly became the victims of the public's rage over Son of Sam (David Berkowitz, who shot and killed random victims in New York in 1976 and 1977). "This [cutting of benefits] all started with Son of Sam—when it was revealed that he was getting social security benefits," said Bill Brew.

Not only were education benefits cut, disability compensation was greatly reduced. If a veteran in prison is more than 10 percent disabled, he only gets compensation payment for 10 percent disability. The current difference between 90 percent disabled and 10 percent disabled is $667 per month. An incarcerated veteran rated 10 percent disabled gets only half of that benefit.

"I volunteered when I was seventeen and fought in the Marine Corps for my country," says a Walpole inmate. "I was wounded, got hit with shrapnel in the head. Had two serious operations. I've got a steel plate in my head! I feel that any money the VA is allowing I should get. No one should tell these men who served in Vietnam that they shouldn't get that money because they're in a prison."

Some conservative Vietnam veteran activists are using more recent data to indicate the numbers of veteran inmates are insignificant. The Vietnam Veterans Leadership Program of Reagan's Action agency, for example, consistently touts the 1981 Department of Justice statistic that only 4.5 percent of all state prison inmates served in Vietnam. "In other words, a miniscule 0.38

of 1 percent of [Vietnam theater] veterans are behind bars," is how they put it in a Vietnam veteran fact sheet.

This ignores the numbers in federal prisons; an estimated 20 percent of federal inmates are veterans, but there is no available breakdown by war. In addition, the flat use of that statistic ignores the caveat of the Department of Justice when it released its findings: *"It is impossible to know how many Vietnam-era veterans were imprisoned and released before the survey took place."* The survey was a "snapshot at a moment of time, November 1979," a stratified random sample of 12,000 prisoners across the country, in state facilities only. It also ignores the revolving-door cases in county jails.

The Bureau of Justice (of the Department of Justice) findings indicate that the veteran state-prison inmates in their survey were more hard-core criminals than incarcerated veterans in earlier studies. For example, previous studies showed that most veterans were in prison for less serious crimes than nonveterans; the majority of veterans had committed only one crime, and recidivism was markedly low. However, the Bureau of Justice findings differ greatly. Violent crime was the principal offense of 60 percent of inmates, regardless of their veteran status. Veterans were *more* likely than nonveterans to have been convicted of murder, rape, or assault. While this study once again found that veterans in prison were much better educated than nonveteran prisoners, they found lower percentages of honorable discharges than did previous studies.

Both bad discharges and previous military criminal record added to unemployment problems prior to incarceration. About 14 percent reported no income for the year prior to arrest. One fourth were without jobs at the time of their arrest. (At the time the 1979 unemployment rate for veterans in the general population was 3.4 percent.)

A reversal of the tendency noted in earlier studies was found in the degree of prior incarceration. Some 60 percent of the Vietnam-era veterans had served time before, while earlier studies showed little prior record among veterans. Some 25 percent of the Vietnam-era veterans used heroin, compared to only 10 percent of post-Vietnam-era veterans in the Bureau of Justice survey. Large numbers of veterans reported that they were heavy daily drinkers (33 percent among Vietnam-era veterans).

There is one obvious reason for grimmer crime statistics in the 1979 study of incarcerated veterans as opposed to earlier studies. No doubt those who were in prison for lesser crimes and who seemed disposed to get on with life have done so. *There are no statistics on veterans out on parole or reintegrated into society.*

Since the acknowledgment of veteran status depends on self-reporting, it is not uncommon to find studies that vary widely. Take, for example, the Justice Department estimate of the number of prisoners who served in combat as compared to the *Legacies* study, which revealed that one fourth of their sample of *combat* veterans had served time. The total Bureau of Justice sample was 65,500 veterans in state prisons—comprising one fourth of the total of all state prisoners. Well over half, in fact closer to two thirds, (39,500) served in the Vietnam era (again, a fraction of the more than nine million in the military at that time). But only 13,000 had been on duty in Southeast Asia. "This is surprising, since it had been assumed that this combat group would have felt most acutely the difficulties of transition to civilian life," theorized the study.[22]

Perhaps those combat veterans who did indeed have difficulty readjusting had, like Eldson McGhee, served their time and been paroled. In any case, while such statistics are a reassuring boon to combat veterans—plagued for so long with the walking time-bomb image—the men in prison should not be forgotten. Yet even when previous statistics indicated that Vietnam veterans were far more in number, they received no help from traditional service organizations. Both the Veterans of Foreign Wars, with 10,000 posts, and the American Legion, with 17,000 posts and a collective membership of more than three and a half million, had no programs for incarcerated veterans (in 1979). There are only a handful of posts within penal institutions. Even the Junior Chamber of Commerce has 495 chapters inside U.S. prisons.[23]

Instead, veterans behind bars must generate most programs themselves and depend on the committed few on the outside.

Two such men are Robert Jackson, who served twelve years in Angola, Louisiana, penitentiary and started one of the most successful incarcerated veterans organizations there, and Herb DeBose, a lawyer with New York's upgrade center.

One raw, gray spring day we three drove through New York's countryside. We were going, as they used to say in James Cagney movies, upriver to Sing Sing. New York's state prison, renamed Ossining, situated on the bluffs of the Hudson, is a hulking stone and iron fortress. Guns were manned by guards in the towers. In the courtyard, soul music blared. After several doors were unlocked, we were in a classroom, with a bulletin board, surrounded by black and white veterans.

Some of the men in the room heatedly argued for their benefits. Their leader wanted to sue the VA and Congress over the latest budget cuts. One man asked me to call his girlfriend and tell her that he still loved her. I later tried several times but got no answer.

Herb DeBose and Robert Jackson never asked the standard question of curious reporters: what are you in for? They know that such queries are not appreciated and that the chance of getting an unloaded answer is slim. All Jackson and DeBose cared about was the here and now and what they can do to make sure veterans get whatever benefits are coming to them, whatever helpful education and training programs, whatever post-parole help on the outside. My attempts at personal history met with little success. The prisoners had more important concerns. They had but a few hours of time with their Vietnam veteran representatives from outside, and talk between them was long and earnest.

As we left, soul music rocked the prison. The men stared as we left and said nothing.

6 Agent Orange

"WHEN JOE AND I GOT MARRIED, WE DIDN'T WANT A HELL OF A LOT. Three kids, a dog, a house, the white picket fence, two cars. We only wanted *one* color TV set," says Eleanor Zuccaro, with a laugh, "and it didn't have to be *big*. Just your average, normal next-door life."

It took the Long Island housewife four years to get pregnant. During delivery, she had a spinal block which left her awake but free of birth pains from the waist down. "I heard the nurse say, 'Did anybody see his penis?' and I asked, 'What's wrong?' They never answered me. After he was born, they handed him to me. He was totally clothed—and then I knew something was wrong." Zuccaro and her husband, Joe, sat together and cried. "He had extrophy of the bladder [meaning that it had formed outside his body], and you know how you take a hot dog and cut it down the middle? That's how his penis was. The testicles were floating, not in a sac. If he had been born ten years ago, they would have removed the bladder and he would have had a colostomy with a bag on his hip for the rest of his life." Over the years, doctors at Johns Hopkins performed a series of operations on her infant son. "They put the bladder back inside, closed the pelvis, and sewed him up. Later, they sewed his penis up. He'll have a bladder like everyone else and will be able to pee like any other normal boy. We are uncertain whether he will be able to ever father a child." In the summer of 1983, at six years of age, her son was still having to undergo more surgery. "One doctor told me the normal ratio statistics for extrophy of the bladder and genital complications was one in 50,000; another said one in 30,000. But besides us, four other families on Long Island have children with similar problems. Susan's boy was born with one kidney, and his anus had to be reconstructed. Some are born without testicles. All four of us on the island have one thing in common: we all have husbands who are Vietnam veterans."

Another Long Island mother, Diana Hackett, drily uses scientific jargon to describe her four children. "We have our own little 'control group.' Our seventeen-year-old daughter was born a year before my husband went to

Vietnam. She is completely normal. After he returned, we had a child who has multiple problems. We divorced, and I married another veteran. After nine miscarriages, I gave birth to a set of twins with multiple problems. The three youngest of my children have severe allergies—but all the tests came back negative except to chemicals. Any time anyone sprays fields around here, they are flat on their backs for three weeks with allergies. All have mixed seizure disorders. One son is legally blind, severely allergic; one has an enlarged spleen, the daughter has a 59-degree curve in the spine. Any liver-function tests come back abnormal. There are neurological impairments."

Louise Nachsen gave birth to fraternal twins. "One with problems and one *without,* so it couldn't have been me. One has spina bifida." Spina bifida is a limited defect in the development of the vertebral column. In the relatively common spina bifida occulta, the vertebral arches fail to develop or do not fuse in the midline, so that the spinal cord and its coverings are unprotected by bone. While minor defects may go undetected for life, severe spina bifida can cause varying degrees of paralysis. Hydrocephalus (water on the brain) is often associated with spina bifida.

Today, treatment by installation of a shunt to carry away excess fluid is frequently successful. Nachsen's son is paralyzed from the knees down. Says his mother, "In one spina bifida organization, 75 percent of the fathers in our age group were Vietnam veterans."

A fourth couple, Heather and John Harper, have lived under great emotional strain since his return from Vietnam. Their daughter had been born with two club feet, "one of the worst cases" according to specialists. In 1979 Harper formed an organization of Vietnam veterans who either had children with birth defects or were themselves suffering from severe skin rash, insomnia, depression, violent mood swings, headaches, loss of sex drive, liver ailments, or cancer. Like other veterans and their wives, the Harpers found hundreds who shared their illnesses, problems, and concerns. The Harpers and their group are not Americans. These are Vietnam veterans of *Australia.*[1]

In the hospital lay children with massive limb deformities, stunted growth, cleft palates, diseased eyes. After examining 700 married veterans, a scientific study concluded that those who were in contact with Agent Orange are more than *twice* as likely to have children suffering from congenital defects than fathers in the general community. These fathers were not American veterans who had fought in Vietnam. The children were in the hospitals of Saigon, and their fathers were former Vietnamese soldiers.[2]

The children of America, Australia, and Vietnam—with club feet, cleft palates, skeletal anomalies, holes in their hearts, and kidney ailments—may well be the most tragic and innocent victims of Vietnam. The men who made it alive out of the jungles of Vietnam fear that they and their children are the hapless inheritors of a sinister legacy—Agent Orange. This defoliant was highly contaminated with dioxin, the most toxic of all manmade substances. A single drop of dioxin, if it could be divided equally among 1,000 people, would kill them all. Agent Orange—laced with this deadly toxin—was sprayed from American planes, raining for years on Vietnam, turning fields and jungles into cracked-earth wastelands, killing fish and fowl. Peasants in heavily sprayed areas died, and still-born births and miscarriages increased; then came Vietnam's pitifully deformed babies. For several years, such reports from Vietnamese scientists were dismissed as propaganda. Finally, in 1970, after nearly a decade, after five million acres were repeatedly doused with 12.8 million gallons of the highly toxic herbicide, the planes sprayed no more. The Department of Defense decision to halt the spraying of Agent Orange was, in part, due to pressure stemming from reports of frequent birth defects in South Vietnamese areas where it had been used.

In Vietnam, in America, in Australia, the types of birth defects are often eerily the same: cleft lips and cleft palates, shortened limbs, hydrocephaly, spina bifida, club feet, enlarged livers, sight and hearing losses, missing digits on hands and feet, kidney and heart abnormalities, and intestinal and testicular alterations.

And the symptoms of those veterans exposed to the defoliant are startlingly similar: severe chloracne (a skin eruption of painful and ugly sores); piercing migraine headaches; recurring attacks of nausea; vomiting; dizziness and diarrhea; violent rages; memory lapses; aching and numbness in the limbs; kidney and bladder ailments; and colonic and testicular cancers. Wives sometimes try to joke about their husbands' severe depressions and mood swings. "It's like some women get when they go through menopause."

Agent Orange was so named for the orange-colored stripe that circled the huge drums that stored the herbicide. It is only one of a chemical rainbow used in Vietnam—Agents Pink, Purple, Red . . . a "chemical cocktail" with a lethal aftertaste.

For years, Vietnam veterans claimed Agent Orange caused their cancer or nausea or violent rages or numbness in limbs or deformed children. They were treated shabbily by the U.S. government. Pleas for testing, treatment, and compensation continued to be ignored. As late as 1981, the then VA director, Robert Nimmo, dismissed their complaints, saying that Agent Orange created nothing more than a condition similar to "teenage acne." The VA stalled so long on a major epidemiological study that Congress finally demanded in 1983 that it be turned over to the Centers for Disease Control in Atlanta. Bills for compensation have been rebuffed repeatedly by Congress. By early 1984 over 19,000 veterans had filed claims for adverse health effects from Agent Orange exposure. The vast majority were turned down. Of some 1,525 claims allowed, 1,456 were for skin conditions, but none of them were cited as Agent Orange–connected.

Moreover, veterans are barred by federal law from taking final VA benefit decisions to court.

Chemical companies, fearing the loss of billions of dollars in lawsuits, continued through the years to fire salvos in an attempt to counter Agent Orange "hysteria." In 1983 veterans finally had their own vital breakthrough when a Long Island federal district judge—who is hearing a multibillion-dollar lawsuit by 20,000 Vietnam-era veterans against several chemical companies—released damaging Dow Chemical Company documents. Dow—the largest supplier of napalm and Agent Orange to the government during the war—knew as early as the middle 1960s of evidence that exposure to dioxin might cause people to become seriously ill and even die. However, the company withheld its concern from the government and continued to sell herbicides contaminated by dioxin to the Army and the public, according to the documents. For the first time, the documents, released by Judge George Pratt, Jr., provided a detailed look at what the company knew about dioxin dangers and when. In 1965, when the government was purchasing millions of pounds of Agent Orange, Dow's toxicology director wrote an internal report that dioxin could be "exceptionally toxic" to humans, and the company's medical director warned, "Fatalities have been reported in the literature." This is in stark contrast to the public posture of Dow, whose herbicide research has long been relied on by the government. The company has maintained that, aside from chloracne, the company did not know of any harm to humans from dioxin. When the papers were released, company spokesmen said that references to fatalities must have been referring to other substances. They also contended that the government knew as much as the companies did about dioxin. Meanwhile, lawyers for Vietnam veterans charged Dow with "outright conspiracy" to mislead the government on dioxin dangers.[3]

The trial was expected to reach court in mid-1984, and promised to be heated and well publicized. Dow and six other smaller companies stood to lose billions. By 1983, the lawsuit was already four years old. If Judge Pratt had dismissed the case, it would have been all over. Pratt said a trial was merited because there was enough evidence that Dow, along with six other chemical manufacturers, might have withheld crucial information on the dangers of Agent Orange.[4] This decision was crucial to the case because the government itself cannot be sued. In order to have a legitimate claim against the chemical companies, the veterans had to demonstrate that the companies knew more about the dangers than the federal government. Since 1948 the Supreme Court has consistently held that soldiers do not have the right to sue the government. "If a military officer tells you to jump off a cliff because he doesn't like your hair style, you can't sue the government," says Ron Simon, a lawyer active in the veterans' Agent Orange battle. "It's medieval, based on the assumption that if you could sue the government, how could you ever have a military?"

In early 1984 Judge Jack B. Weinstein took over the case from Pratt, sped up the trial, and indicated that the government should be included. Weinstein changed the direction of the case to deal more directly with this critical question: is Agent Orange really to blame for the veterans' illnesses?

Simon remained skeptical about the prospect of 20,000 veterans and their families collecting from the chemical companies. "They resolved the question of whether they could sue them—now they have to go back and prove the birth defects and illnesses were caused by the dioxin. That's a rough row to hoe."

Within the veteran community, the Dow documents came as no surprise. For years they had been charging that Dow and the government knew what dioxin could do. Judge Pratt echoed their sentiments when he said, "The record demonstrated that the government and the military had a considerable amount of knowledge about dioxin and its health hazards going back to the 1940s." Pratt also said that then Secretary of Defense Robert S. McNamara attended a mid-1960s meeting discussing human health hazards of dioxin and that the DOD had a study commissioned in 1967 which reported the health dangers of the herbicide.[5]

Such disclosures seemed late in coming to these families living for years with the spectre of Agent Orange. Many middle-American veterans and their wives, who would never have thought of protesting against their government, were turned into frustrated militants. They showed up at Agent Orange conferences across the country in their bright orange T-shirts, emblazoned, "Dow Shalt Not Kill." Wives who used to meet for Tupperware parties now meet to discuss the latest scientific reports in hopes of proving cause-and-effect in their husbands' illnesses and their children's deformities.

Like a neglected Greek chorus, Vietnam veterans tried to involve other Americans—pointing out that it was everyone's concern, that herbicides containing dioxin are still being used domestically. In 1979 the Carter administration's Environmental Protection Agency (EPA) temporarily banned the use of the dioxin-contaminated herbicide 2-4-5-T for most domestic use, but under Reagan's administration EPA moved in 1983 to ease those restrictions. In general the Agent Orange sprayed in Vietnam was *twenty times more* contaminated with dioxin than that banned by EPA.[6] EPA still lets chemical manufacturers sell dioxin-ridden herbicides for use on rangeland and rice— 1.3 million gallons were sprayed on rangeland in 1982.[7]

Not until 1983 in Times Beach, Missouri—when the government evacuated the residents exposed to dioxin—did veterans have an incident at home to give a psychological boost to their claims. The release of the Dow Chemical documents a few months later came at a time of growing public debate over dioxin dangers. There is general agreement that dioxin can cause death and serious injuries in laboratory animals, that exposure can cause chloracne in humans, and that dioxin is highly toxic if swallowed. Beyond that, there is still great dispute over its effects on people. Scientists point out that it is extremely difficult to extrapolate what a substance can do to human beings from experiments on laboratory animals—although that is the accepted type of research on everything from studying the harmful effects of cigarettes and asbestos to saccharine. Still, the figures do chill. In all, *11 million* gallons of Agent Orange sprayed in Vietnam contained perhaps no more than *370 pounds* of dioxin in all. However, a dose of *one part* of dioxin *per 20 billion* ingested by a young, male rhesus monkey killed it in twelve days.[8]

Most knowledge of the effect of dioxin on humans comes from industrial accidents or exposure. In 1964 a major outbreak of chloracne at Dow's Midland, Michigan plant afflicted fifty workers, none fatally. "In extreme exposures to certain chlorinated compounds, a general organ toxicity can result," wrote Dow's medical director, Dr. B. B. Holder. "This is primarily demonstrated in the liver, hematopoietic [the body's blood-forming system], and nervous systems." In extreme exposure there may come the onset of "psychopathological and other systemic findings." As early as 1949, 228 workers at a Monsanto 2-4-5-T plant in Nitro, West Virginia, developed chloracne as the result of an industrial accident. Other symptoms included "severe pains in skeletal muscles, shortness of breath, intolerance to cold, palpable and tender liver, loss of sensation in the extremities, nervousness, irritability, insomnia, and loss of libido."[9] Through the years, other accidents caused similar afflictions in chemical workers.

In April of 1983 David Burnham reported in the New York *Times* a closed meeting attended by Dow senior scientists and officials of four rival chemical companies nearly twenty years before. (Excerpts of corporate memorandums about the session just began to surface in 1983 as a result of the veterans' lawsuit.) One executive in attendance noted that Dow did not want its findings about dioxin made public because the situation might "explode," cause panic, and generate more government regulations for the chemical industry. Dow officials revealed at that 1964 meeting a study showing that dioxin caused "severe" liver damage in rabbits, one scientist noted.[10] Over the years, other cases and studies pointed to circumstantial, if not conclusive evidence, that Agent Orange could indeed be harmful to your health.

Those members of Congress who sympathize with Vietnam veterans and their Agent Orange claims decry the government tactic of holding out for scientific proof-positive studies, which most scientists admit will never come. "I'm personally convinced soft-tissue cancer [a rare form] is related to dioxin exposure," said Ryan Krueger, legislative assistant to Representative Tom Daschle (D-South Dakota) in charge of veterans' affairs. "There's a substantial amount of evidence on that." The scientific community remains divided. (Dr. Samuel Epstein, a cancer researcher at the University of Illinois, states categorically, "The evidence is overwhelming that dioxin is carcinogenic in humans." However, Dr. Matthew Meselson of Harvard, a pioneer in dioxin research, says it has not been proven yet whether there is or is not a "clear and present danger.")

Daschle, and others who had long sought legislation to compensate for at least "the most indisputable" illnesses, urged the government to take action, particularly after "the decision to compensate the residents of Times Beach."

Dioxin—the toxic substance that made Times Beach, Missouri, unfit for its 2,400 inhabitants—was found in that town at levels far *less* than the mean level of dioxin tested in samples of Agent Orange. Daschle's bill, introduced in March of 1983 with 200 sponsors, would compensate a small number of Vietnam veterans suffering from soft-tissue cancers, a specific liver condition, and, possibly, a few thousand with chloracne claims depending on the VA diagnosis. Compensation for these three illnesses would not break the bank, would not mean untold billions, as some VA officials have claimed, and unfortunately would leave many Vietnam veterans with other complaints as uncompensated as before. Still, Congress has taken a long time to act. By early 1984 it appeared that the bill would pass the House, but Senate prospects were uncertain. Daschle said that the government's decision to purchase the Times Beach property "implies an acknowledgment that dioxin is dangerous enough to pay for the evacuation of an entire community. If this government is willing to accept this responsibility, it has even more of a responsibility to provide compensatory relief to individuals it was directly responsible for exposing to the very same chemical in Vietnam." Pointing out that over 1,110 studies and reports on the chemical have been published, Daschle called for action. "The social policy implications of Agent Orange poisoning have been ignored too long."[11] Predictably, the VA immediately went on record opposing the bill, citing once again, "insufficient evidence" to warrant such relief— even though some scientific studies have made a strong correlation between these three illnesses and dioxin exposure.

The government's "out" always has been that scientific evidence does not conclusively link exposure to Agent Orange with illnesses and deformities that plague veterans and their children. Therefore, it has washed its hands of responsibility.

Peter C. Kahn, a scientist testifying before Congress, blasted the government for its lack of political and moral courage and for passing the buck to the scientific community. "I think that there is an abundance of circumstantial evidence to suggest such a connection [that Vietnam veterans' medical problems are the result of exposure to noxious materials during the war], but that is not rigorous proof. We are asked to produce evidence sufficient to 'convict beyond reasonable doubt.' Science cannot do that. There is always 'reasonable doubt' in the evaluation of research, particularly biological research. In shifting the burden onto science, you shift it away from its proper place—which is on you and on the rest of the government. The issue is not primarily scientific; it is *political* and *moral.*"[12]

Veterans or their wives with deformed children who seek Agent Orange answers rarely seem to have a history of congenital defects in their families. In several personal interviews, I have found none. This is one reason why they hold firm to the belief that Agent Orange is the cause of their sorrow and tragedy.

The one place that could have catalogued the complaints to see if patterns emerged was the VA. Not surprisingly, it kept no records for years that could have established a linkage of illnesses. The families instead collect their data, go to meetings, find other veterans with the same problems, and become even more convinced. They pour out their detailed personal stories. The scientific community calls these stories "anecdotal data" that contain no hard-core facts. However, veterans and their families feel there are insidious and peculiar patterns.

At one conference of 200, Margaret Driscoll was the third woman to mention that she had had amniocentesis, that no birth defects were detected, that there was no family history of abnormalities. "We went all through the genetics, and the doctors still haven't given us an answer." Her husband, Larry Driscoll, was a medic who began getting severe headaches in Vietnam. "They continue to this day. Nothing helps. All I can do is lie down and wait." Driscoll had a job in the computer field but left to do manual labor, unloading trucks, "just in case my headaches were caused by the mental stress of the job." His problems grew. Headaches, severe skin rash, "and now my joints kill me. I was on the swimming team before. Now I can't throw a ball ten feet." In 1969 his wife Margaret had a still-born, badly deformed baby. "A very rare defect. She was born with only half a brain. They couldn't give me any reason." (Other veterans have reported the same terrible deformity. In 1953, there was no recorded evidence that a child without a brain had ever been born in Vietnam. In 1967, one in every 100 children suffered this fate, according to evidence compiled by North Vietnamese doctor Ton That Tung.) The Driscolls held off on children, and then, eight years later, a daughter was born healthy. The next year, a baby was born with a cleft palate. "You look down at your newborn and you see this. She had only two chambers to her heart, a displaced spleen," said Margaret. "She died three days later."

The grisly stories seem endless. Kerrie Ryan was fathered by Michael Ryan who feels his Agent Orange exposure caused him severe weight loss, migraine headaches, skin rashes. Kerrie has eighteen birth defects including missing bones, twisted limbs, a hole in her heart, double reproductive organs, and no rectum. John Woods was a Green Beret whose weight dropped from 200 to 139 pounds after his exposure to Agent Orange. He has suffered severe chloracne, migraine headaches, temporary blindness. Before Vietnam, he fathered two normal children; his two sons born since his return suffer skin rashes, muscle cramps, spasms. The youngest was born with a tumor on his face. Victor Yannacone, the lawyer for the Vietnam veterans lawsuit, mentions six children with the very same defects. Each one is missing one eye and one ear; each has a cleft palate and a club foot. The only thing they have in common is that their fathers were marines who served in the heavily defoliated DMZ.[13]

As anecdotal data piles up, everyone remembers some bit of evidence, hardly even regarded at the time. I, for example, happen to remember an interview with a Green Beret doctor some years ago who casually mentioned in passing that whenever he had the time he was forever fixing the very common cleft palates of Montagnard children.

Veterans in different lands, thousands of miles apart, tell their similar stories. Ron DeBoer is a tall, dark-haired veteran. He remembers bathing in streams where the defoliant had left the landscape barren. Then came severe headaches that plagued him while in Vietnam. DeBoer returned to the States, went to college, and started his own business. Then he discovered he had testicular cancer—a form so rare it affects only 6 out of every 100,000 males between the ages of eighteen and twenty-four. Laboriously, DeBoer began trying to find out "what happened to the other men in A Troop, Seventh Squadron, 17th Air Cav." He called Kevin, a New York City cop. His first child was born dead and his second deformed. Kevin put him in touch with another from his troop who told DeBoer, "My first child was born with a deformed leg, and my second was born mentally retarded." Next was Alan, a California mailman. He had developed hypertension, severe headaches, skin problems, and "never felt well a day since I returned." Five out of the six he contacted had "hard-core Agent Orange problems"—dead or deformed children, cancer, gastritis, hypertension, and liver problems.

In Sydney, Australia, when a group of veterans first met to discuss their physical problems, "it was like an Alcoholics Anonymous meeting," recalls Jim Wares. "They were all saying, 'Well, this happens to me,' and 'Yeah, I get that too.' " Wares's son was born with no fingers on his left hand. For weeks before the meeting, Wares had been compiling cards on symptoms and family health of every veteran who had contacted him. Sorting through the cards of fifty men, he found that one in four said they had fathered a deformed child— including three cases in which all the fingers of one hand and half a thumb were missing, two cases of deformed legs, four cases of club feet. While too small a group to be statistically significant, Wares's findings caught the attention of physicians who studied deformities. The types of deformities he listed normally affect only one Australian baby in a thousand. One Australian research biochemist on fetal deformities said, "There's obviously something wrong. At this stage we can't say whether it is linked with Agent Orange."[14]

In Australia, as in America, there was another similarity. The government gave short shrift to veterans' Agent Orange concerns and dismissed the data Wares had compiled. Not until 1983 did the Australian government agree to set up a commission to examine the effect of chemicals and herbicides on Australian servicemen who fought in the Vietnam War.

Birth defects from toxic agents usually mean that the mother, not the father, is exposed. Unfortunately for veterans, the birth-defect link to the exposure of fathers is quite weak. The few studies examining males in this area reveal conflicting or inconclusive results. For example, two herbicide studies conducted abroad reached opposing conclusions on whether Agent

Orange caused birth defects in children of troops who fought in Vietnam. One study by Vietnamese scientists reported an increase in abnormalities in children of North Vietnamese women whose husbands served in South Vietnam and were exposed to Agent Orange. (The mothers were not exposed.) But a study of Australian veterans of Vietnam found "no evidence" that service in Vietnam relates to the risk of fathering a child with a birth defect. American scientists were unclear why the studies reach opposite conclusions. American scientists attending a 1983 symposium in Ho Chi Minh City were "very much impressed" with the Vietnam findings but stopped short of endorsing them. "There is no precedent for it in the international literature," said Arthur H. Westing, an American ecologist.[15]

Many scientists say the state of the geneticists' art does not permit flat conclusions one way or the other. Scientists in Australia are looking into one theory in which genetic damage can be transmitted, which could provide the link to males. "The male stem cells from which the sperm are produced are a bit like the egg cells in females. They are the stem cells from which, years later, sperm cells are produced. The genes in stem cells can be damaged by mutagenic effects in exactly the same way as egg cells. The effect of that damage will only appear when that particular stem cell is called on to produce sperm. And that can occur at any time in the reproductive life of the male," said Australian geneticist Donald MacPhee, "possibly years" after the initial damage to the stem cell. A soldier in his teens has his stem cells for sperm already produced and lying dormant in his body. If he absorbs chemical mutagens in herbicides, the damage can show up years later. The theory is that the damaged stem cell produces a damaged spermatozoan, which produces a damaged fetus. There is no established case where the theory has been proved. It is difficult to study humans directly, MacPhee points out and adds, "Mutagenic chemicals are not specific—a particular chemical can't be said to always attack a specific gene. Thalidomide always interfered with normal limb development, so the babies born to mothers taking that drug looked pretty much the same. The cause-and-effect relationship was easy to establish. With the herbicides (like Agent Orange), it's tremendously more complicated. Mutagens act on the genes at random, so you can't say that Agent Orange acts on this particular gene and therefore it will cause all babies to be born blind." Another Australian biochemist, Dr. David Walsh, agreed. "Trying to trace the effects of mutagenic chemicals on our mammalian gene pool —it's like looking for a needle in the Pacific Ocean or at least Sydney Harbor."[16]

Scientists at the University of Wisconsin have discovered one male-related effect. High doses of dioxin can reduce the sex hormones produced by male rats and cause their reproductive glands to shrink. The experiments, financed by the National Institutes of Health, are believed the first to link dioxin to reductions in the male sex hormones which can lead to loss of sex drive, sexual dysfunction, and impotence—some of the effects veterans claim they have suffered because of Agent Orange exposure. Scientists warned against extrapolating their test results to humans, but the tests could explain why several men reported temporary loss of sex drive after being exposed to high amounts of dioxin during industrial accidents.[17]

Where there is a known quantity some conclusions can be drawn. For example, scientists have found that if you look at the reproductive histories of cigarette-smoking fathers, you find indications of increased frequency of defects in children born to them. Also, an increase in sperm abnormalities because cigarette smoke contains mutagens which get into the blood and circulate into the tissues, said Dr. MacPhee.[18]

A long-awaited five-year CDC study on birth defects is due this year. CDC scientists explained the enormous variables in attempting to chart the cause and effect of such birth defects. First was the task of tracking down 13,000 children born in the Atlanta area with birth defects as indicated by attending physicians between 1968 and 1980. They were hoping to locate 70 percent of them. One of the major questions is whether the fathers of those deformed babies were veterans exposed to herbicides in Vietnam. If birth defects occurred at an increase of 20 percent among veterans, scientists are "70 percent confident we would find it. If there is a 50 percent increase, we're 90 percent confident we would find it," said CDC's Dr. Vernon Houk.

The chilling anecdotal data of similar birth defects compiled by veterans around the world does not mean all that much to scientists. Dr. Houk said, "There are many problems in working with birth defects and miscarriages. Some 20 percent of all pregnancies end in miscarriages. Close to 5 percent of all live births have some structural defect. The March of Dimes says 10 percent." Dr. J. David Erickson, who is working on the CDC birth-defect study, adds, "Unfortunately, birth defects are not all that uncommon. Say three million men went to Vietnam, and let's suppose that each one fathers one baby apiece and that just 2 percent of their wives' pregnancies get into the later stages with serious structural malfunctions. There would be 60,000 with deformities in the *normal course of events.* You'd expect to hear about several reports of spina bifida and a couple of thousand with cleft palates in the normal course of events. Cleft palate and spina bifida are fairly common deformities. Now, if you find among nonveterans, say, *one* in every thousand of their children has spina bifida and among Vietnam veterans it is *five* in a thousand, there might seem to be an increased risk in having been in Vietnam." But does that prove cause and effect? "Not necessarily."

Dr. Erickson sympathizes with the parents faced with the uncertainty of what caused their children's deformities. "I understand that every person who has a child with a problem wants to know why—and focuses in on it. I have a child who is mentally retarded."

Many mysteries remain. For example, in recent years there has been a marked increase in the recorded number of birth defects, and no one knows why. Some increase may simply be due to better record keeping and to health practices that bring such babies to full term. Toxic substances, an ever-increasing menace in our society, are not ruled out, but the consensus is that the exposure comes from the mother. "My opinion is that there has been no evidence that Agent Orange is the cause of the problem in birth defects through the male," said Dr. Erickson, adding, "but nobody has looked very hard either. In humans, what little we know about birth defects points to the exposure of the fetus. On the other hand, nobody looks at the father. Down's syndrome was always associated with the age of the mother. Most people say, 'It has got to be through the mother.' In recent years it has been made fairly clear that the extra chromosome that causes Down's syndrome can come from the father."

The problem with Agent Orange, however, is that there is no clear factor like thalidomide or German measles that can be isolated. Even seeming correlations can be discounted. For example, Dr. Houk explained, in the county of Midland, Michigan, home of Dow Chemical, there are more cleft-palate deformities than in other counties. "But, there are also more [cleft-palate deformities] in twenty some other counties in the country that had nothing to do with chemical manufacturing. There are thousands of counties in the country—and only a few of those show an increase in cleft palates—so the fact that Midland is one of them proves little.

"That is one of the difficulties, particularly in the hospital in Saigon where they treated nothing but birth-defect children. A lot of anecdotal information comes from such situations, where you see the same deformities in fairly large numbers day after day but don't compare that with the rest of the population."

For the veterans and their families, who search the family genes and find nothing, but then look at their deformed children, such variables and uncertainties do little to relieve their pain. Like Tom Vallely, a Massachusetts state representative and a Vietnam veteran who received the Silver Star for bravery, they cannot help but blame the war. "This is the first war that reached into our maternity wards," said Vallely. "The Vietnam experience does not belong to the past. The warfare we saw in Vietnam is the warfare of the future. Vietnam was a *laboratory*. Our own men were the guinea pigs. Our men got caught in a crossfire of bullets and chemicals."

On the surface it seems relatively simple to have conducted an epidemiological study involving the men who went to Vietnam, who were exposed or not exposed to Agent Orange, as well as peers who remained stateside. Veterans requested it for years. Finally, the study Congress turned over to the CDC—after the VA stalled on it for months—got underway in 1983. It will not be completed until the end of the decade. The study is in three parts and involves 30,000 men. A Defense Department Agent Orange task force has plotted areas where the herbicide was sprayed, and has calculated wind drifts and speed in an attempt to determine areas of exposure. "They think they've picked up about 80 percent of the herbicide use," says CDC's Dr. Houk. CDC will study 6,000 Vietnam veterans documented to have been exposed and another group that most probably was not exposed and will try to eliminate compounding factors. The second part of the study is to examine whether the Vietnam experience *per se* is any different. Vietnam veterans will be studied against a random sampling of men in the same age group who were in the military but did not go to Vietnam. The third part is a case control study of soft-tissue sarcomas, using a cancer register supplied by the National Cancer Institute, to see if the Vietnam experience indicates any difference in the incidence of such soft-tissue cancers.

After years of testing, will they be able to figure out whether Agent Orange caused something?

"Epidemiological studies don't prove cause and effect," says Dr. Houk. "What they do is to establish an association in two things. You try to remove as many confounders as you can so that later reasonable people can make reasonable judgments."

It seems obvious that even after these two major studies, there will still be enough room for doubt for the government to duck any responsibility of testing, compensation, or treatment to Vietnam veterans. There also will be room for disagreement. For example, the preliminary 1983 initial mortality results of an Air Force study on participants in Operation Ranch Hand—the men who flew the planes that sprayed Agent Orange—was both hailed and criticized. The study of 1,200 pilots and crew members who had been exposed to the herbicide indicated that these men were not dying in unusual numbers or from unusual causes. They, in fact, had a lower death rate than other men their age in the general population. The Air Force said this was because men inducted into the armed services tended to be in better health.

The Air Force, in its press release of the ongoing study, however, played down the fact that a subgroup of *enlisted* men had a higher mortality rate than officers. The Ranch Handers showed a relative decrease in cancer among comparison subjects—but a marked *increase* in liver disorders. Deaths caused by nonalcoholic cirrhosis were five times higher than the comparison group. The study, however, concluded that the findings were statistically insignificant.[19]

However, at a Pentagon press conference, Colonel George D. Lathrop, a medical doctor from the Air Force School of Aerospace Medicine at Brooks Air Force Base in Texas, said there was "mild concern" that former Ranch Hand enlisted men were statistically not living as long as officers. "We're concerned about that because that conforms to a self-perception of the Ranch Hand groups themselves—because they view the enlisted personnel as being far more exposed [to the herbicide] than the officer personnel."[20]

The National Veterans Law Center, a Washington group battling for servicemen exposed to Agent Orange, sharply criticized the report, saying that no "meaningful conclusions" could be drawn from a study of only 1,200. The center also said the study had not addressed itself to whether Agent Orange might cause nonfatal skin diseases and internal ailments, or whether it might cause fatal or nonfatal ailments that do not manifest themselves until two decades or more after exposure. The Air Force agreed that there could be adverse effects in the future and that further analyses were intended in the study population annually for the next twenty years. (Biologists now believe that dioxin accumulates in the body fat and liver, in much the same way as DDT, and may remain dormant for years.)

One of the medical mysteries is why some people exposed to a harmful substance are adversely affected and others are not. The world now knows that cigarettes categorically cause cancer—but a large number who do smoke do not get lung cancer. We know absolutely that asbestos causes cancer—but not in everyone who is exposed. Those who believe Agent Orange causes fatal and nonfatal illnesses are understandably annoyed that the government seems to demand a higher percentage of incidences as "proof" than what was needed to acknowledge the harmful effects of such substances as cigarettes or asbestos.

After a decade of publicity, after a decade of hearings where the deformed children are paraded in front of legislators and veterans reveal their skin rashes, after a decade of young men dying of liver disorders, the major result is an almost manic emphasis on testing.

By 1984 the federal government had commissioned twenty-six human health studies including five cancer studies, a study of identical twins (cases where one served in Vietnam and the other didn't), a mortality study of 60,000 deaths of Vietnam-era veterans, and the CDC birth defect and epidemiological study. The cost is in millions. The American Legion is conducting its own independent epidemiological study with a team of highly reputable scientists, Jean and Steve Stellman. There are numerous state-sponsored tests.

For the veteran who thinks he is dying of cancer or for his wife who bears a catastrophically deformed child, these tests simply mean more delays on the part of government. The results of most of these tests are months and years down the road. "By the time those SOBs finally complete their belated studies, most of us will be dead," said Dean Phillips, who has endured four major cancer operations, chemotherapy, and radiation treatment on his neck since returning from Vietnam. (Phillips obtained a medical waiver for other Vietnam injuries and is currently serving in the Army Reserves as a company commander with the 11th Forces Group.)

I met Steve Zardis in 1979. By then, scientists had known for years that dioxin causes birth defects and tumors in animals. Animal tests showed that dioxin causes cancer, especially of the liver. By 1979 there were already a number of veterans who had died of liver cancer. Their widows were joining in the Agent Orange battle. And so was Steve Zardis. He used his disability checks to finance his Agent Orange International "office"—a table filled with growing files. He sold his car to help with expenses. It took Zardis two hours to dress himself. Eight months before, Zardis put in a claim at the regional office for a nurse. It was rejected—even though he had the highest disability rating.

"In Vietnam I was in a forward air-control unit, and we used to clear the flight pattern for spray planes. I remember daily spraying. My unit was called the Lepers because we were on sick call all the time. We were throwing up, we had high fevers, and once my throat became paralyzed for a week."[21]

Still, Zardis thought he'd made it back whole from Vietnam. Then, one December day in 1975, he felt a numbness in one hand. Then both hands and feet went numb. Six months later he was walking very clumsily. Neurological tests proved nothing. In the spring of 1977 multiple sclerosis was diagnosed for Zardis. By September he was using two crutches and a brace. On his thirtieth birthday, in January 1978, he got his wheelchair. The speed with which MS was wasting his body puzzled doctors. So they called it "atypical MS."[22]

By 1981 Zardis had been hospitalized twenty-one times since returning from Vietnam in 1969. The pain was so excruciating that in 1981 he had the nerves severed from his spinal cord to his legs.

His plaintive question, as Zardis lay a wasted young man, was "How many veterans have to die before they pay attention?"

Zardis asked that question in 1979. It still applies. It should always be remembered that Congress had to mandate the VA study of Agent Orange—and *then* had to turn it over to the CDC after months of stalling by the VA. A group of veterans even tried to raise money from foundations for an independent epidemiological study. There could hardly be a sorrier spectacle—veterans turning to private philanthropy for help when the responsibility is clearly the government's.

No matter the outcome of the veterans' lawsuit against Dow and six other chemical companies, the industry's disgraceful public avowals of the safety of their herbicides are mocked in those secret meetings and private documents concealed for twenty years.

One of the most telling lines in the 1965 memos was that dioxin could be "exceptionally toxic" to humans. So much for the flat assertion made eighteen years later, in 1983, by Paul F. Oreffice, president of Dow, that "there is absolutely no evidence of dioxin doing any damage to humans except for something called chloracne."[23]

Dow counters that they are not alone in their hidden knowledge that the government knew about Agent Orange's toxicity in the sixties—and still sprayed its millions of gallons on Vietnam. The veterans are in the middle as the two giants, the chemical industry and the government, slug it out.

There are a lot of uncertainties—but there can be no uncertainty as to the debt the government and the chemical companies owe the thousands of men who feel they and their children are Agent Orange victims. The companies will spend millions on lawyers to disabuse the jury of their culpability. Instead, they would do well to heed a request of the suing veterans. They want the chemical companies to establish a tax-exempt trust fund against which the veterans, their widows, and children can draw to cover their medical expenses. Some attorneys involved in the lawsuit speculated that if the government were willing to share in a benefit fund for the veterans this could lead to an out-of-court settlement.

The government cannot be sued. But it—and its shameful treatment of veterans—can be taken to task. It should assume the cost of the medical care for these families—not force them into some litmus test of proof, not haggle for months over their compensation requests. The government should not force the impossible—a specific connection between exposure and illness. It should not stall for yet one more scientific test.

Agent Orange is a ghastly metaphor for all the things that were wrong about the most unpopular war in American history. The men who served in that combat zone, the soldiers who were exposed to the deadliest toxin known to man are owed a special obligation.

They should not have to become the next generation, the sons of "Atomic Veterans"—men who participated decades ago in the early testing of atomic weapons in the western states and in the Pacific. Now, years later, thousands of them are filing disability claims—often in vain—for illness they blame on exposure to radiation. Broad rules can be written and presumptions made in favor of both groups of veterans.

The time is long overdue. In 1963, as the first troops were moving into Vietnam, an explosion at a Dutch chemical plant making 2-4-5-T left part of the building contaminated with dioxin. It was considered so dangerous that the plant was encased in concrete and buried at sea. Today, we have our Times Beach, Missouri, and Love Canals and hazardous-waste dump sites. A 1981 review for the EPA concluded that effects are likely to occur from exposure to dioxin in dump-site soil. The effects include the possibility of cancer and fetal birth defects. Dioxin's evil effect is ironically, perhaps one of the few things the rest of us can share with veterans, whether we like it or not.

In 1978, a twenty-seven-year-old veteran, Paul Reutershan, died of a type of stomach cancer rare for a man of his age. The day before he died, Reutershan pleaded with his friends not to let the Agent Orange issue die. He became a martyr as well as a victim of what many veterans now feel is the most awful, lingering legacy of Vietnam. His words echo as a fearful reminder of their own past—and possible horrible future: "I got killed in Vietnam—and didn't know it."

Epilogue

Requiem for a Generation

"With God on Our Side"

BY BOB DYLAN

I've learned to hate Russians
All through my whole life
If another war starts
It's them we must fight
To hate them and fear them
To run and to hide
And accept it all bravely
With God on my side . . .

So now as I'm leavin'
I'm weary as Hell
The confusion I'm feelin'
Ain't no tongue can tell
The words fill my head
And fall to the floor
If God's on our side
He'll stop the next war.

The mothers and fathers of the dead, the buddies who had been there when they died stood in the wet, cold mud, listening patiently to the platitudes and hollow rhetoric of dedication speeches for the Vietnam Veterans Memorial. As the last politician droned to an end, real feelings began. The crowd surged to the black granite wall with its 57,939 names of the dead and missing.

A young man knelt in the mud in his jeans. The fingers on his left hand gently stroked the indentation of Richard V. Knight, Jr.'s name, almost as a blind man fingers Braille. In his right hand was a last letter from his fallen friend. He read it aloud to the name on the wall: "Oh well, at least I will be home by Christmas." Richard Knight had written this from somewhere in Vietnam more than a decade ago. "I bought a camera in Saigon. It will last a lifetime . . ." The man's voice trembled slightly, and then he said the Lord's Prayer, stroking Richard's name, giving it a soft pat at the end. The wall had become an icon for the heart.

Tucking the letter into his pocket, he moved quickly, head down, through the crowd. I started to pursue him, the inevitable questions burning in my mind: Who was Richard Knight? Was he called Dick or Richie? Who was this man here now? A brother, a buddy who was there with Richard in the jungle? Was he perhaps standing in for Richard's mother, who couldn't make it to the dedication? Was he like the marine passing through Shreveport, Louisiana, on his pilgrimage to Washington, who encountered a sixty-two-year-old waitress in a restaurant? She begged him to take a picture of her son's name inscribed on the wall and send it back, just in case she never got there herself. I came close to the man, then stopped. I could not bring myself to ask him anything, to break the spell.

I have been to the memorial many times since that November day in 1982 and am always struck by the hushed reflection it provokes. Tourists still their talk and laughter as they do at no other shrine in monument-clogged Washington. Single roses are stuck in the crevices of the panel, next to someone's special name. Relatives take rubbings of the names home with them.

Critics of the memorial decried its "nihilistic," "black ditch" funereal message of war. They called it a wailing wall. In that respect they were right. In Jerusalem the alabaster wailing wall is worn smooth by the daily touching of thousands of hands. Stuck in the crevices are pieces of paper, millions of them, paper prayers to God—often asking for peace. And, like that wall, so has the Vietnam Veterans Memorial instantly become a peoples' monument. Its base was strewn with flowers and flags and hand-scrawled messages to the now silent soldiers: "To Stevie, from the guys . . ." On the dedication day, medals, even Purple Hearts, were taped next to the names. And countless pictures gave faces to those names—youthful, long-ago faces; long-ago polarized grins next to studio-stiff smiles in elaborate gilt frames.

Hands touched the names, parents huddled by volunteers searching through directories for their sons' names . . . "tenth panel, fortieth row . . ." A veteran read from the Bible, and a mother next to him sobbed as she said, "Oh, thank you, thank you." Men in wheelchairs were pushed close to the wall. Men in faded fatigues and boonie hats stood with veterans in expensive tweed overcoats. They cried. Together.

The afternoon sky darkened, blurring the images of faces mirrored in the black granite, blurring the surrounding trees, November-black stick-figure trees denuded of leaves. A lone veteran in fatigues stood on the grass above the center of the memorial where the two sloping walls meet, at the point where the memorial is ten feet high—inch after inch filled with name after name after name . . . He looked down at the crowd below and put a bugle to his mouth. He slowly played the haunting notes of "Taps."

All during that reunion week there were drunken midnight visits to the monument. Stumbling they came, with the aid of flashlights. One midnight two marines held each other and sobbed. One had saved the other in Vietnam, giving him mouth-to-mouth resuscitation. For the first time since they had come home, veterans were given warm greetings from strangers. Bartenders bought them drinks and cab drivers refused their money.

A sense of betrayal is strong—among those who thought it was right to be in Vietnam, among those who thought it was wrong, and among those who still don't know. At the reunion were defiant bikers in jungle boots, head bands, and ponytails with their "don't mess with me" saunters. One patch on a jacket said, "I'd rather be killing Commies." Another said, "Viet Cong Hunting Club" with a silhouette of an Oriental with a conical hat in the gunsights. There were antiwar vets too, but there were few flare-ups, few arguments. One former VVAW member, a veteran in a business suit, smiled tolerantly at the patches. "They don't mean anything by that." Mostly there was a "what the hell" attitude that every veteran here had earned his viewpoint on the war.

"The Vietnam combat veterans drew this lesson: you are alone, no one else shares your experience or cares about you—no one except your 'buddies,'" wrote William Broyles, Jr., a former Vietnam combat veteran, for *Newsweek* in 1982. The sense of love and commitment they felt for each other welled up over and over again at the dedication and reunion.

Toward the end of the week, a few marines liberated a hotel's American flag and flagpole. They lit matches and shone flashlights on it at the monument, and they took turns holding the flag up through the night. At dawn the crowds started to return. The wind began to blow, and a few drops of rain fell. The flag billowed, then whipped back and forth. Whenever a veteran came up, Terry McConnell, a marine from Cleveland, told him to touch the flag.

And each time, wrote Broyles, he said the same thing, "Welcome home."

Broyles ended his article the same way:

"Welcome home. The war is over."

Only it is not over. As much as we yearn to put it behind us, we cannot get over all the pain and divisions it caused. Vietnam is there in the memories of the generation asked to fight it. Men in wheelchairs and on crutches, or those who remember the war too well in their nightmares, live with Vietnam daily. So do mothers and fathers who keep their dead sons' pictures on their pianos. Its effect is felt throughout our country, whose economy and faith in government were shaken. It is there in the actions of our commander-in-chief, who sends troops to die in Beirut and to invade and die in a tiny island called Grenada. It is there in the military's fierce determination to keep the press out during last fall's secret invasion of Grenada, so convinced are they that media coverage of Vietnam cost them the war. It is there in the zealousness of some in the government and the military to "win one" after years of impotency.

Capturing the euphoric mood of the country over finally winning something, a character in Mark Alan Stamaty's political cartoon *Washingtoon* quipped, "Gosh! If a small-scale invasion feels this good, imagine how great a war would feel!"

As time blurs the awful tragedy that was Vietnam, militarism is once again alive. In the fifties and early sixties, "the trend toward unshakled presidential power in foreign affairs was spurred by congressional, academic, and media liberals whose minds were molded during the Roosevelt era," wrote Stanley Karnow in his *Vietnam: A History*. "They believed World War II could have been averted had we moved earlier to stop the Nazis." And so, with a vow of "No more Münichs," they applied that same logic to the Communist threat. Today, nearly a decade after Saigon fell, the ideological support is different, but intervention marches on. Cheers for Reagan's unshackled military moves come from conservatives and the far right, now bent on erasing the defeat of Vietnam. The specter of Vietnam looms behind bellicose yearnings to stop the Reds, from Central America to the Middle East; behind the need to define the mess in Lebanon as an East-West crisis; behind policies of confrontation that could have disastrous consequences, once again, for the young of America.

The danger in remembering Vietnam wrongly, or in remembering it only as our defeat, is that this propels many—including some men in the Vietnam

Generation who wallow in guilt at not having gone there—into a false patriotism, repeating the same errors that marked our Vietnam experience.

Healthy skepticism and caution gripped the country for several years after Vietnam, yet the country seems to be moving inexorably into very troubled waters again. Meanwhile, the level of high anxiety and high paranoia, in Washington *and* Moscow, created a deepening crisis in Soviet-American relations as the superpowers continue to fight their surrogate wars of bluff and bloodshed in tiny countries around the world.

I had hoped by the end of this long journey through the Vietnam Generation that I could concisely tie all the emotions and experiences and beliefs into a tidy conclusion of what Vietnam meant then—and what it means now and for the future. This was not to be; a seeming absolute, once examined from another person's perspective, always took on less certitude. Confusion-free conclusions may be the reward for only the doctrinaire on the right or left. Vietnam was an ambiguous war that left us with ambiguous moral, political, and personal conclusions—not just about the war, but about the generation asked to fight it.

Still, after listening to the voices of the generation, particularly the veterans, there is one lesson we *must* learn. Sending young men into combat on the basis of nothing but the most abstract threats to national security is folly. Worse still is leaping into impossible situations where young men get killed for symbolic reasons—which is what happened in Vietnam. The explanation for being there was that we were containing communism, primarily the Chinese. After all the bloodshed, the destroyed land, the millions dead, the crops ruined, the Vietnamese are fighting the Chinese and the Chinese are our allies.

Revisionists never make it clear what we would have "won" had we beaten the North—a victory that would have necessitated keeping a large occupation force there endlessly, with the probability of the fiercely determined North Vietnamese breaking out in warfare again.

Today, we are once again back in the business of recording the grief of bewildering wars. We see the tear-reddened eyes of fathers, holding their dead sons' pictures to the TV cameras. We see mothers, waiting for the polished military car and the knock on the door from the officer come to tell them they will never see their sons again. There is one difference this time. Some say their sons died for their country, but others already show an anger that did not surface until we were years into the Vietnam War. The 241 servicemen in the peacekeeping force who died in the terrorist bombing of Beirut—the largest number on a single day since Vietnam—were "sacrificed for nothing," as one father said tersely on the nightly news. And a mother echoed the lament of mothers who watched their sons die fifteen years ago: "Why are we there?"

Once again, a President was making our young soldiers pawns in a complex diplomatic and political struggle—this time in a country with an ancient history of civil and religious warfare. One of the bravest voices in Congress speaking out against Reagan's Lebanon buildup was Representative John McCain of Arizona, a white-haired Republican, retired Navy admiral, and former Pentagon lobbyist. He knows about war. For six years he was a prisoner of war in North Vietnam. He spoke passionately in favor of enforcing the Constitution's commandment that Congress, not the President, has the power to declare war. Congress heeded not the voices of those who remember Vietnam, however, and gave Reagan nearly everything he wanted, including the right to keep the troops there for eighteen months. The bluffs of yesteryear in Vietnam were implicit in McCain's question: "Are we prepared to use this power? I do not think so, nor do I believe the Syrians think so." He sounded an ominous echo of Vietnam, "The longer we stay in Lebanon, the harder it will be for us to leave. We will be trapped by the case we make for having our troops there in the first place." McCain knew the immediate cost of withdrawing would be some embarrassment but tried to sell Congress on the long view. "What can we expect if we withdraw from Lebanon? The same as will happen if we stay. I acknowledge that the level of fighting will increase if we leave. I regretfully acknowledge that many innocent civilians will be hurt. But I firmly believe this will happen in any event."

Senator John Stennis (D-Miss.), in his eighties now, spoke with anguish about how he had stayed too long with his leaders on Vietnam. This time he could not "go for it." The people of America were the ones who would have to "put up the boys and the blood to fight a war if we get into it now or later. Let us just look it right in the face and tell them the truth."

The truth. General Maxwell Taylor learned one lesson from Vietnam—guidelines for vital conditions that must be met before sending American troops into foreign lands: The objectives must be explainable to the man on the street in one or two sentences. There must be clear support from Congress and our allies. And finally there must be a clear national interest at stake.

And that is why people who remember Vietnam were able to ask why we were moving into Lebanon.

If we are to continue to approach war as mindless "get tough" first strikes rather than as the final measure to be used only when all else fails, then we are going to have to start facing one major cost. It is a cost never written in the defense budget—the cost of creating new veterans. And for the lesson of what happens to veterans of wars that cannot be adequately explained, we can look to our Vietnam veterans. The President gets very emotional when he fires off a sure-winner about Vietnam and its veterans, "We will never again ask young men to fight and possibly die in a war our government is afraid to let them win."

Behind the ceremonial flag waving, however, it is hard to find anything constructive that either Reagan or Congress has done for Vietnam veterans. It was Reagan's administration that tried to gut the Vet Centers. It was his VA administrator who stalled a congressional order to study the effects of

Agent Orange. By 1982 congressmen were ready to publicly salute the Vietnam veteran—although Congress's shabby history of ignoring veterans continues. For a decade Congress refused to appropriate adjustment-counseling funds. A bill introduced in 1981 called for VA reforms in helping veterans with problems. The agency is woefully ill equipped to locate and treat the 500,000 to 700,000 veterans who by its own estimate may need professional help. The bill called for a larger staff of mental-health workers trained in treating post-traumatic stress disorder (PTSD). It also proposed that veterans who are understandably skeptical of the VA would be allowed to seek private therapy and bill the agency. Both provisions died in committee. The miserly GI Bill for Vietnam veterans through the mid-seventies made it impossible for many to complete their education when they came home. Congress repeatedly ignored pleas to extend the bill. For many who still need the bill, time has run out. In 1982 the House dismissed a proposal to lengthen the eligibility period to twenty years after discharge.

Frustrated Vietnam veterans by the thousands have filed benefit claims. There are several strikes against them from the start. VA decisions are virtually unchallengeable—there is no judicial review; veterans cannot sue. The only appeal is within the VA itself, and to add to this insult, a statute dating from the Civil War forbids a veteran to pay more than ten dollars to a lawyer handling his case. The Senate passed bills, both in 1979 and 1982, that would have permitted judicial review and would have eliminated the ten-dollar ceiling on lawyers' fees. Both bills died in the House Committee on Veterans' Affairs.

The private sector was little better. Businessmen finally spent lavishly for the memorial granite—but frustrated veterans tried in vain for years to get businessmen to hire veterans. The monument came about through the hard work of veterans, who were left to raise the money to pay tribute to themselves; it was not a gift from a grateful nation.

Reagan was cochairman of the National Salute to Vietnam Veterans, but he skipped the dedication ceremony. (He was attending memorial services for his father-in-law, who had died three months previously.) Countless congressmen skipped it too. The names on the memorial tell you a lot. There are no names of the sons and grandsons of policymakers who planned that war, no names of sons or grandsons of congressmen who voted the appropriations to keep it going. The names speak to that: José K. Brown, Witold J. Leszczynski, Salvatore J. Piscitello, Thomas L. Little Sun, Bobby Joe and Donnie Lee and Richie . . . Lopez and Salinas and Murphy and Garcia . . .

The war is the common denominator for everyone in the Vietnam Generation, no matter how deeply it divided them. It was an ill-conceived, ill-advised, ill-planned tragedy, and it caused all kinds of reactions, good and bad. It turned aimless teenagers into heroes who found a bravery they never knew they had. It turned nice, normal college boys into dodgers. It crippled some who went—and gave others a chance to find a direction in life. It took some young men of promise to their deaths and gave other young men a chance to find strength in resisting to the point of jail.

Just as attitudes were locked into polarizing rhetoric in the sixties, there remains a freezing of attitudes. Many on the left who dreamed a different dream for Vietnam have long given up their subjective history lesson on Southeast Asia and refuse to acknowledge the boat people, the repression, the re-education camps that came with communism. On the other hand, the right uses the outcome to validate our presence there—not accepting the fact that we helped create the seeds for nationalistic rebellion long before the first American soldier stepped foot in Vietnam. By backing French colonialists who were starving the peasants, by creating and propping up leaders that the South did not want, and then by carrying on our long, ruinous war, we contributed greatly to the continuing sorrows of Vietnam.

Todd Gitlin, one of the early leaders of Students for a Democratic Society (SDS), brilliantly analyzes the antiwar movement, its strength and weakness, its success and failure. The movement battered the knee-jerk acceptance of the anticommunism of the fifties. Today may be our chance to get past what Gitlin calls the "knee-jerk *anti*-anticommunism of the sixties."

Says Gitlin, "The movement sloppily squandered much of its moral authority. Too much of the leadership, and some of the rank-and-file, slid into a romance with the other side. If napalm was evil, then the other side was endowed with nobility. If the American flag was dirty, the NLF flag was clean." The worst became "mirror images of the absolutist authority they detested. Even today we hear voices on the left conjuring rationalizations for crimes committed by left-wing guerrillas. Why is it necessary to keep silent about the shutting down of newspapers in Managua in order to oppose American intervention on behalf of death squads?"

The antidote is not to revert to the simplistic reasoning of Cold Warriors— the inevitable backing of right-wing dictators and despots, which hardens revolutionary resolve, ups the ante, and creates dependency on the Soviets. Like many moderates in the movement—who in the end became the appalled silent majority of the left, as the Weathermen and their ilk trashed the cause with senseless violence—Gitlin argues for a different lesson from Vietnam. Take a hard view of the left, he suggests, but realize that "revolutionary change is often the superior alternative to hunger and massacre in the Third World and that American support might soften the most repressive features of revolutionary regimes." Note that he says "might." In the aftermath of Vietnam, tentative assessments are better than arbitrary, know-it-all solutions. As America still sifts the legacy of Vietnam and the peace movement on foreign policy, one lesson is that intervening is a much more complicated matter than merely siding with "good guys" or "bad guys." Another lesson is the need to give up our delusions of omnipotence—that it is not in our power to shape countries as we would want them. Rather than intervene on ideological grounds, humanitarian concerns would be better served if we asked ourselves: "Will it work?" "Can we make life better for the country?" "Is it really in our national interest?"

The villains of the antiwar movement were not the students who on cue sometimes delivered revolutionary rhetoric from bourgeois mouths, but the violent bomb throwers. Magnified by the media out of all proportion to their numbers, they nonetheless succeeded in alienating and massively demoralizing the far larger numbers of moderate students and adults in the movement.

Above all, Vietnam was a war that asked everything of a few and nothing of most in America. While the country turned its back on veterans for a decade after the defeat, the tendency today seems to be a swing back to a visceral dislike of the ones who didn't go. In a country that buys the myth of egalitarianism, residual loathing exists. It is fashionable to deride the entire generation of nongoers as vain, selfish, and hypocritical six-figure lawyers and executives who have discarded any "alleged" sixties altruism. And confessions come from those who say they really were just wimps after all. I have succumbed to that temptation myself. There *was* an arrogance about the actions of nongoers (to their credit, this was readily acknowledged by everyone I interviewed) that still burns deep in many who shared their beliefs on the war but not their insensitive self-righteousness. And so the tendency is to pigeon-hole them as sellouts, or as people who were never committed in the first place.

But the blame rightly belongs with the misbegotten war itself and the politicians who cynically judged the self-interest that abides in everyone—particularly adolescents. The government made it easy to avoid war with deferments and legal loopholes: there were so many men in that generation; why not give the most vocal an out? Nixon even more cynically knew that if he turned the draft into a lottery, many of those clamoring voices in universities would be stilled.

Some in the antiwar movement feel it was a failure, that nothing worked. By retreating into inactivity, they send a "why bother?" message to today's young. Gitlin argues that failing to end or slow down the war did not mean total failure. "To choose political passivity today is to succumb to all-or-nothing petulance." The movement can be truly faulted for closing ranks, for not broadening its middle-class base to bring in blacks, antiwar veterans, and many in Middle America who had turned against the war not for moral reasons, but because it wasn't working. Gitlin's message is not to give up monitoring the government, not to give up protesting, but to "do it smarter and better the next time."

What the movement *did* is exactly what the right said it did. It kept Johnson and Nixon from waging a more aggressive, intensely escalated war that would have widened the conflict, with God only knows what kind of global consequences. Seymour Hersh, in *The Price of Power,* points out that Nixon had a plan in 1969 to launch an unprecedented assault on the North that did not exclude the possibility of nuclear weapons. In utter secrecy, once again a

President made plans that would have horrified a sizable portion of America's population had they known. For the first time since the Cuban missile crisis, a President kept American B-52s on full nuclear alert. Protest, in part, kept him from carrying out plans to destroy Hanoi and Haiphong Harbor. Nixon later wrote, "After all the protests and the Moratorium, American public opinion would be seriously divided on the war."

However, few in the movement felt they were making an impact, since Nixon made a public show of ignoring their protest. Earlier, in 1966, Johnson resisted the military clamorings to bomb Hanoi and Haiphong. David Halberstam points out in *The Best and the Brightest* that a sighing Johnson asked how long it would take for "five hundred thousand angry Americans to climb that White House wall . . . and lynch their President if he does something like that?"

For those who felt such monumental escalation would have disastrous consequences, the movement was, as Gitlin wrote, "history's most successful opposition to a shooting war." For those who are convinced that the North would have caved in under such aggression, the movement caused us to lose a "noble victory."

And so it goes. Just one more reason why Vietnam is not behind us.

The men of this generation teach us that myths die very hard. One such myth is the belief that the ultimate way to prove one's manhood is on the field of battle. I have dwelled on a recurring theme—the concern of many in this generation about what it takes to be a man—because of the continued prevalence of the myth that being bloodied in battle, *no matter the lack of justification for the cause,* is the penultimate rite of passage. There are other ways to show bravery and courage, not the least of which is doing for others and making unselfish commitments in life.

Vietnam will continue to have a profound impact for the next several decades as the generation moves into positions of leadership. The largest generation in the history of America holds certain beliefs that were set by the Vietnam War. There are those like Jan Skruggs, the veteran who dreamed of a memorial, who says, "Some of those attitudes may be dangerous to the country and the free world. A lot have a real bad attitude toward the military—that we should never interfere anywhere. If we lived in a perfect world, that would be fine, but we don't." Lately there seems to be a rebirth of jingoism among some who didn't go, and that could be equally dangerous.

It is important to note that there never will be a generation quite like that of the sixties again. The reason for some postadolescent guilt among nongoers, the reason for the incredible rift between some fathers and sons during the sixties, the reason so many other sons went to Vietnam as a patriotic duty—all this is rooted in World War II. They can never forget that they were the sons of men who served in the "good war."

There is an old maxim that those who never saw bloodshed are among the quickest to send the young into battle. In World War II Reagan made training

films and also put on a uniform for the feature film *Hellcats of the Navy.*
Historians point out that Joe McCarthy—the anticommunist zealot of the
fifties who successfully intimidated dissenting voices in Congress—may have
been overcompensating for the fact that he did not have a distinguished
combat record in World War II.

There is a Republican senator now on Capitol Hill, Paul S. Trible, Jr., of
Virginia who came from the Vietnam Generation. He laced his campaign
speeches with conservative slogans and patrotic homilies. He is a staunch
supporter of Reagan's foreign policy. While others were being shipped off to
Vietnam, Trible flunked his preinduction physical because of a "slight malfor-
mation" in his right arm. It is a ticklish subject in this heartland of the
Pentagon. The Defense Department is Virginia's biggest employer, and military service has long been considered a virtue. While campaigning in 1982,
Trible refused to talk to some reporters about whether he was relieved to get
his medical deferment. "I was hoping to go to law school," was his answer.

The citizens of Virginia, however, had ample opportunity to deduce that he
had indeed served his country. To symbolize his strong defense posture, one
campaign ad showed Trible decked out in an Air Force pilot's flight suit,
complete with helmet, sitting in the open cockpit of a jet fighter—although he
never served in the military or piloted a plane. He was giving the thumbs-up
salute with the same right arm that had kept him out of the service. Virgin-
ians picked the bogus hero over the genuine one. His Democratic opponent in
the Senate race was Richard Davis, who participated in numerous World War
II battles as a marine. Trible's opponent in an earlier race for a House seat
had been Lou Puller, son of the legendary warrior "Chesty" Puller. Lou
Puller sits today in a wheelchair. He lost both legs in Vietnam while leading
his men against North Vietnamese troops. Having lived through the real war,
Puller has a more tempered view of resolving conflicts through battle. So do
many veterans. Jan Skruggs worries about a generation that might advocate
too much caution, but on the other hand he too has learned that "people's
lives are more important than a piece of territory."

In a personal way both those who went and those who didn't have similar
legacies—alienation and cynicism about American politics, ambiguity and
doubts about their youthful decisions or about the war.

"In every veteran I've ever talked with," says combat veteran and psychologist Jack Smith, "there is this incredible conflict [over] 'what did it mean,
what was it for, what a waste'—coupled with 'we tried to act with honor, and
we were acting on the beliefs of our country.' Or '*I* never saw anything like
My Lai.' And so on. In order to be true to the experience, they have to hold
on to that point—that they had integrity."

And the vast majority did. Holding on to their integrity takes all forms.
Sometimes it's an elaborate justification of the war that brooks no dissent.
Often it is fierce clinging to the idea of 'if only they would have let us win
it.' "

Veterans who try to turn Vietnam into a winnable, noble cause do not have the framework, along with many others in the country, to understand the coexistence of both nobility of service *and* the inevitable misguidedness. These are extremely difficult and complex strands to tie together, and the country is still groping toward that conclusion.

The memorial captures that confusion, that ambiguity. It is not a symbolic military monument like Iwo Jima, which instantly captures the heroics of war in the struggle of those men putting the American flag in place. The Vietnam Veterans Memorial forces everyone to confront his or her feelings. The names of the dead are listed without mythic meaning. No matter how wrenching it is to view the names of their dead friends, "veterans who have come to grips with the war can be at ease with it," Smith says. "Those who have not find that it adds to their conflict and are incredibly torn."

As the fiercest memories of Vietnam fade, polls show that Americans are more willing to use troops overseas. This is particularly true if they are to be used to protect Western Europe and Japan from Soviet invasion. American *leaders* are far more ready and willing to send troops than the public, however. By 1982 a willingness to use troops still had not led to a change in public response about the rightness of our presence in Vietnam. Seventy-two percent of the public sample concurred, in 1982, that "the Vietnam War was more than a mistake; it was fundamentally wrong and immoral." This was the same result as that of polls taken in 1976. (Only 45 percent of our political leaders felt that way, however, in 1982.)

But nothing is static about Vietnam, and as 1984 approached, shifts were occurring. "It's a changing dynamic," says Bobby Muller of the Vietnam Veterans of America (VVA). "That's what revisionism is all about."

In a long-ago photograph, Bobby Muller is seen arching gracefully through the air as he pole-vaults, his legs in perfect position for landing. That was Bobby Muller in high school. Today he sits in a wheelchair, immobilized from his waist down, paralyzed by a bullet in the spine. A man of relentless energy, Muller talks nonstop and has worked tirelessly to give veterans a public forum. The VVA recently became the first veterans' organization in a generation to be formally recognized by the VA.

Muller has been attacked by some veterans for his personal antiwar stance —particularly after he visited Hanoi and laid a wreath on Ho Chi Minh's tomb. Muller argues, "We [the VVA] have *never* taken a position on any issue in foreign policy or defense. We have stayed within the boundaries of aggressively fighting for Vietnam veterans' concerns and benefits." In the past two years, divisions among veterans have widened. "The country has moved distressingly to the right under Reagan," says Muller. "Everyone in combat I found was against the war when we came back—so I thought Vietnam vets were like me and my friends. I felt if we could bring us all together, we'd have something. It's a hard lesson to learn after I've traveled across the country that perhaps one third are like us, but a whole lot buy the conservative line. They can only relate to the one little patch they fought over, and they want to feel good about 'killing gooks.' A number of [VVA] chapters are strongly pro–nuclear freeze and anti–El Salvador, but the factionalism is growing."

America's decade of ignoring the sixties has resulted in an unfortunate ignorance about Vietnam among today's young. To them, the war is ancient history, seldom studied. Muller went to thirty-eight colleges in 1983. "I am constantly asked by students, 'What side did we fight on—the North or the South?' 'I've heard about napalm, but what actually is it?' I swear, the first college I went to, they asked, 'What's My Lai, and who is Lieutenant Calley?'

"I ask them if America were to set up a draft to send them somewhere, *for whatever reason,* would they go? Overwhelmingly they say yes. Given what happened in Vietnam, these kids cannot give a blank check to the government anymore. When nobody understands Vietnam, and it's as if the sixties never happened, Reagan and his ilk can play their old games."

Some of today's marines, who were in diapers during Vietnam, are getting a strong message about that war from their officers. Reporters in Grenada were startled to find nineteen-year-olds asking, "How does this [invasion] play back home?" They were defensive and very wary of the press and resented the scrutiny of congressmen. Some officers who had lived through Vietnam were giving them their version—nothing they did was appreciated back home, we had every right to be there, and the media were the villains.

But there are other voices sending a different message. It comes from the top and it comes from the bottom in the military. This year high-ranking active-duty and retired military officials harshly criticized Reagan's policy in Lebanon. This unusually blunt Department of Defense report warned that the marines' role had been escalated almost unthinkingly. The commission urged the pursuit of diplomatic alternatives and chastised the Reagan administration for an emphasis on "military options." These military men remember all too well how Vietnam started—and how it ended.

A few months before the commission released its explosive report, a group of much younger veterans gathered in Washington for a VVA conference. This is by and large a blue-collar organization of some 20,000 men, and their regional officers had come to Washington from such small-town places as Chippewa Falls, Wisc.; Belfontaine, Ohio; and Prescott, Ariz.

Many of them had been radicalized by their Vietnam experience, and they, too, are not forgetting.

David Evans, the son of a West Virginia coal miner, went unquestioningly to Vietnam. He fought well and courageously as a marine. Today he moves around the room in blue jeans and loafers, looking physically untouched by war. Evans is prepared for the shocked stares of strangers when they find out he lost both of his legs in Vietnam.

"I work for a prosthetic company," he says, laughing. "If I don't walk good, they'll fire me."

Evans was among the many Vietnam veterans in the room who opposed America's presence in Lebanon and Central America. "When I read of Lebanon, I feel sick. I see those pictures, and I look into the eyes of a nineteen-year-old marine, and when I look real close, it's me—it's myself. We must never let another generation go through the pain and suffering we have! We are the working-class guys. We are the people whose children are going to die."

Tracing the social currents of what it means to have grown up in the sixties is far from easy. Everything from Vietnam to the sexual revolution shaped members of that generation in a variety of ways. However, a theme that recurs with great frequency is a sense that they lack commitment. Many veterans and nonveterans alike feel this.

While there are far too many of them to ever be a "lost generation," many keenly feel a loss of innocence. "A lot of what we believed in *did* get shattered. Many on both sides are lost," says Muller. "Those who were seriously antiwar or veterans who tried to change society when we came back took a lot of time to sort things out. We've got a generation right behind us, climbing over us. They were plugged into succeeding from day one. They get their MBAs and think nothing of first-year salaries of $35,000."

Others feel that those in the middle, who participated not at all in the most significant event of their time, are the ones who will eventually feel a loss.

Unlike the fifties generation and the young of today, the Vietnam Generation was made to feel it had to *believe* in something, that it had to take a stand. This bred fierce polarization. To this day many remember having to remain silent on the war. A conservative at Yale and a long-haired antiwar liberal at the University of Virginia were equally isolated and ostracized. Traditional concepts of what it meant to be a male were challenged. For many, to be against the war meant you had to be against all things macho, and so the hair came down to the shoulders, football games were only for dumb jocks, the "right stuff" preadolescent hero worship of astronauts gave way to a ho-hum attitude about such scientific wonders as men walking on the moon.

Many men found a sense of relief in being able to return as grownups to such simple pleasures as cheering on their alma mater in football.

Still there is wistful nostalgia for their campus years, when they felt "special" and "powerful" in their cocoon of togetherness. For those men and women who embraced the antiwar movement, no matter how superficially, there was a bonding unlike anything they have known since. For veterans there was a bonding in the jungles of Vietnam unlike anything they have known since.

In some ways this was not the best training ground for going out in the world, for learning to live life alone. At universities, they had collective power, something previous generations never experienced. The media, professors, manufacturers catered to the largest generation ever of "kids." One exile in Canada says, "I have this vision of being eighty years old and having some interviewer come up and ask me, 'What do you *kids* think about Vietnam now?' " That power was as fleeting as their youth. It was deflating to become an adult, and many found themselves growing older—but not up. Veterans often had other problems, but they had at least learned the hard way that going it alone was a part of life.

A celebrated lack of commitment is the staple of media reports from the sexual and marital homefront—and the stuff of psychiatrists' couches. Dr. Richard Restak, who wrote a book about the narcissism of *The Self-Seekers,* found that a preponderance of his examples came from this generation. Unmarried women in their thirties moan that the biological time clock is ticking away, but that they can't find men who can get past the fear of trying to build something lasting. Journalists write frequently of a generation of Peter Pans, men who don't want to grow up or cut their options by settling down with one woman, one job.

This has been viewed both positively and negatively—as a healthy freedom from the stifling traditional concepts of early marriages and settled careers, and as no freedom at all. Without commitment there is often no sense of inner development. "Being a spouse, a parent, a lover, a friend, having a job of some concreteness—in other words making commitments—defines who you are," says Dr. Restak.

Some psychiatrists speculate that those who made no commitment, either to the war or the antiwar movement, carried that lack of commitment into their adult lives. Others think that the problems of today were caused more by other upheavals of the sixties. Some men feel the women's movement so "liberated" the women of their era that it is easy for them to avoid commitment. They can have casual, sexually active relationships without the responsibility.

Interestingly, while more and more of them are settling into marriage and child rearing as they move into their late thirties, the rebellion of the sixties has left its stamp on other generations. That the family is in a significant state of flux and "the uncertainty reverberates throughout society" was the conclusion of a massive National Science Foundation study of "American couples." The term "couples" can refer to a variety of arrangements today—platonic couples, same-sex couples, working wives who support house-husbands, dual-career couples remaining "child-free" by choice, and the traditional couples of the nuclear family.

There are quiet legacies of the most flamboyant aspects of the sixties. The movement has become institutionalized in the country in ways that many antiwar people who have gone about their lives do not even understand. A network of independent thinkers are still active. You find them in everything from the nuclear-freeze movement to the environmentalist movement.

Young women today see films of yesterday's feminists and view them as strident anachronisms—not realizing that they are now able to enter medical and law schools in unprecedented numbers because of these older women. They can wear the silk blouses and high heels and *still* be taken seriously in business because of the women activists of the sixties.

The winds of freedom that came with the sixties may seem dormant, but they are alive in changed patterns of thinking and living around the country.

Reconciliation is a word used often when anyone takes the time to think about Vietnam and the sixties generation.

One spring morning in 1983, a Vietnam veteran stood up in an Episcopalian church filled with the good citizens of an elite and fashionable Washington suburb. No one left feeling as comfortable as when they had arrived. "Here we were, thinking good and lofty thoughts, and then the bombshell of Vietnam exploded," recalled one parishioner.

R. Christian Berg, the Vietnam veteran, came to the church to "act as an interlocutor between those who went and those who did not. The need for reconciliation over Vietnam constitutes a political and moral imperative of the first order." He felt the need to "come out of the closet and end the drift of ambivalence. Many of us who went have been going through this kind of transition."

And then Berg started in. "Who are we? We are from and in all walks of life. You will find one of us on occasion sleeping, on a cold night, on the heating-duct ventilators outside the State Department wearing his medals. Three of us also founded and built a little company called the Federal Express. My sense is that the vast majority of us have escaped the fate of that poor fellow outside the State Department."

He asked them to raise their hands if any had witnessed real shooting between real people, not on television or in the movies; to raise their hands if they knew anyone who had been in Vietnam, or knew anyone who was killed or missing over there, or if they had ever been shot at. And finally he asked, "Do you know for a fact that you have killed another human being?" The vast majority remained silent on all questions.

"We are anguished," he said. He asked the parishioners to remember the most terrifying experience they had, then to add memories of "a dominant sense of complete paranoia" known in Vietnam. "You dare not even give a spare cigarette to a begging urchin because someone told you that as he or she runs off, your reward will be a live hand grenade between your legs. Add to the scene the constant presence of death. Not the death that most of you are probably familiar with—the body in peaceful repose in a casket. No. It is the image of a piece of shrapnel entering into the chest of a friend lying next to you and emerging through the back, dragging entrails behind. Day after day, week after week, month after month. Consider your state of spirit when in that environment you shot a sniper out of a tree," Berg continued, "and then you realized that probably she had not reached puberty."

All of this was a "piece of the anguish or one source of it. Now not everybody had that much. For some it was hours and hours of boredom punctuated by moments of sheer terror. But nobody got out of there without a piece of it."

The parishioners squirmed as he told of a shattering homecoming for most.

"This leads me to the second quality which we all bear. We are angry. You will see this quality of anger displayed in a variety of ways. We are, I'm told, in your perceptions, arrogant, judgmental, full of anger and hostility, difficult to work with, self-righteous. We think we are more prescient and stronger—we know what is important—than those who have not seen and done and had done to them what has occurred with us. One thing that really upsets us is petty game playing. We are impatient. But then we too play our games with each other up to a point. We are very gentle with each other when we first meet . . . And then the game begins. It turns on things like how much mud did you sleep in, how many times did you get shot, and how many medals did you bring home? It's part of the transition you go through when you're full of yourself and full of anguish. Some of us are quick to remind you that the first two letters of the word 'coward' are 'C.O.' Some of us are quick to tell you [that there's] no way any son of ours will ever be used the way we were . . . We risk consumption by self-pity. Our fullness of self is our defense against those whose insensitivity brings on our anger. I have often felt like a mute trying to converse with a world full of people who are both deaf and blind."

They were listening quietly now. "So what is this thing called reconciliation? . . . We don't want your pity . . . Whether our involvement as a nation in that place was good, bad, moral, or not is beside the point . . . I say that the offer of more VA benefits, the thank-you's, the statements like 'you are a hero'—these are all *evasions.* Reconciliation is not an exercise in which we take our picnic basket off to the country on retreat in order to search for the collective guilt. It is not, in the words of Henry Kissinger, an exercise in self-flagellation. Reconciliation can begin only with a search for our own individual spirit and the stuff of which it is made."

Christian Berg, who survived three combat tours in Vietnam, had been to the Vietnam Veterans Memorial a few days before he stood up in that church. "A substantial number of veterans find the monument an extraordinarily moving place," he said. "It is a place in which we find a piece of the affirmation we were denied upon our return and which, in quiet desperation, we still seek."

He suggests it is a place where veterans and "fellow citizens can at long last find reconciliation. One need only stand quietly at the apex of the walls to see it happen. Gentle volunteers help the confused find the name they seek. The young assist the old. Adolescents find the father they never knew. Widows find tangible connection with the best of fading memories."

To reach reconciliation we as a country must get *beyond* the politics of Vietnam, beyond the rancor, beyond the debate. This must come from the veteran who is corroded with anger at the ones who didn't go. It must come from those who still smugly say, "I don't know anyone who ever went to Vietnam."

Berg tried to convey that to those who had never known Vietnam. He told them to witness what he had seen at the memorial. "In this place there is no rancor, no debate; not even bygones are raised. There is only reconciliation on basic human terms, strangers spontaneously hugging each other in tears. Consider whether you might go down there sometime. Take a friend, take your spouse, take the child you yelled at this morning.

"Stand there and watch what happens."

Perhaps it is only tragically fitting that a war so divisive should end in a battle over the monument. It was a small group on the right who opposed the design, but the media chose to overplay this. The memorial always had the backing of the American Legion, the VFW, William Westmoreland—as well as those on the left, like George McGovern. All that rancor seems in the past now, with the compromise statue of veterans and the American flag about to be erected near the wall.

In less than a year two million had passed by the monument. They come at the rate of 10,000 a day on some sunny days. They come and they stare, and war's destruction is staggeringly brought home in panel after panel of names. There is a hushed gentleness as workmen polish the names. Jack Cavanaugh, with his weather-beaten face and eyes near tears, has come from nearby Gaithersburg. "Holy cow," says Cavanaugh, as if comprehending for the first time that "so many boys died. I can't think of anything better. It shows what war means." In the shadowing of the sun, the granite becomes a massive mirror, catching the reflection of the Washington Monument and the Capitol, superimposed on the names of the dead. Staring at the wall, seeing your face mirrored there, forces a painful conclusion that many still do not want to face. We, as Americans, were *all* involved in Vietnam. It is, finally, only that knowledge that will bring reconciliation.

One sunny day Jan Skruggs stood in front of the monument as he has so many times, his long lean face still full of wonder at what he had managed to do since that day in 1979 when he spoke to a reporter about wanting a memorial for veterans, and a two-paragraph item appeared in print.

Skruggs, an infantry corporal with nine pieces of shrapnel in his back, came back with his adjustment problems and saw other veterans who felt the same. For years he pushed both for readjustment counseling and the memorial. He fought stupidity, narrow-mindedness, and indifference, and he raised six million dollars, and finally there was the memorial. It is on ground where war protesters marched. "It is," says Skruggs, the son of a milk deliveryman and a waitress, "our turn on the mall."

Now, as he looks at the wall and at the people filing by, Skruggs knows a contentment beyond measure.

"If I never accomplish anything else in my life," he says, "I have this."

John Binder, a retired Coast Guard captain, stands with the directory in his hands, helping people find their special names. "I've assisted 5,000 to 6,000 people in finding names. I think the monument's gorgeous. Nobody is neutral. About two percent violently object to the point of ending up and shouting at *me* for the memorial. But there is a great feeling of shared sorrow with this. It had been a private sorrow up until now. Now the country has acknowledged the cost."

Veterans come to the wall remembering only one name, and they find that one name and then names of other buddies come back to them, listed in the order in which they fell. One veteran, whose platoon had been nearly wiped out, took picture after picture from his pocket, then gently brought his children close to the wall. One by one he matched the pictures to the name and tried to tell his young sons why these men still meant so much to him.

The notes are there, always changing: "Happy birthday to a special son." A note next to a picture taped to the wall: "This is my father. I never knew him. If anyone knows him, please write me."

I ask why John Binder devotes so much of his time to the memorial.

"I had a son who was there. He was wounded several times and survived— and I'm grateful for that. This is the least I can do."

He speaks to the larger, finally most important message of the Vietnam Veterans Memorial.

"It doesn't say whether the war was right or wrong. That's for everyone to decide on his own," said Binder. "It just says, 'Here is the price we paid.' "

As I left the memorial grounds that afternoon, I looked back at the parents who came to hold their silent communions with their dead sons, at the children who do not yet understand why their fathers and mothers cry at this wall. I saw a single red carnation stuck in a crevice of the panel and I thought of a long time passing.

I looked back at the wall of names.

Here is the price.

Glossary

AK-47 Infantry weapon of the North Vietnamese and Viet Cong.

ARVN Army of the Republic of Vietnam. A South Vietnamese soldier.

Boonie hat An olive-drab or camouflage-colored cotton cap which matched army fatigues but was not part of the official uniform. It was not allowed in rear areas but became popular with GIs in the field. Now frequently worn at veterans' reunions.

Boonies Short for boondocks. Remote field areas. "Bad boonies" meant either very remote or very dangerous areas.

Charlie Radio terminology for the enemy, using words that represent letters in radio communications, such as Alpha for A, Bravo for B, Charlie for C. VC (Viet Cong) were called Victor Charlie, shortened to Charlie.

Chinook A large transport helicopter used to move men and equipment. Holds approximately thirty men with combat gear.

Chopper Helicopter.

Cobra A small, lightweight helicopter gunship.

Coordinates Numbers that indicate specific place in the field when a unit needs to identify its exact location over the radio; used when calling in artillery, helicopters, mortars, medevac helicopters.

DEROS Date of expected return from overseas service. Sometimes used as a word: "I was going to be Deros (pronounced "de-rose") in May . . ." Or, "When was your Deros?"

Deuce-and-a-half A two-and-a-half-ton truck.

DMZ, the Z Demilitarized Zone. The border between North and South Vietnam, running from Laos to the South China Sea along the 17th Parallel, "demilitarized" by the 1954 Geneva Accords. Scene of many of the major set battles with the regular North Vietnamese Army.

Frag A grenade; stems from "fragmentation grenade."

To Frag or Fragging To wound or kill someone, using a grenade. Also used when referring to any sort of attack by soldiers on an officer.

Freedom bird Passenger airliner returning troops from "the Nam" to "the World."

Gook Slang for an Oriental—often derogatory—passed down from Korea to Vietnam.

H & I (fire) Short for Harassment and Interdiction. An Army policy to fire artillery shells on a regular basis at sporadic locations such as trail junctions, sites of previous enemy sightings, etc., as opposed to firing at actual or suspected live military targets. (This policy was responsible for over 95 percent of the artillery fired on South Vietnam.)

Heads Pot users.

Hooch Any dwelling, but usually a Vietnamese peasant's home.

Huey (UH-1) All-purpose helicopter, used in Vietnam for regular transport between rear areas and the field, for medical evacuation, and as a gunship. Usually carried a pilot, copilot, one or two M-60 machine gunners, and up to eight troops with grear.

Incoming Enemy artillery, mortars, rockets, or grenades coming into a troop location. Used also as a shouted warning to take cover.

In-Country Term to denote being in Vietnam.

Juicers Alcohol drinkers, as opposed to dopers or heads.

Jungle boots Specially designed Army footgear for Vietnam, of lightweight canvas construction, with vent holes to let water out, and metal plates in the soles to resist punji stakes.

Klicks Kilometers.

Lifer A career officer or long-term enlistees (sergeant majors, master sergeants, first sergeants, etc.).

LP Listening post. A fire team located outside the perimeter to give advance warning of attack.

Lurps LRRP (pronounced "lurps"), short for Long-Range Reconnaissance Patrol. A very small team operating independently, frequently behind enemy lines. "Recon patrol" or "reconner" is the Marine version.

LZ Landing zone.

MACV (pronounced "mack-vee") Military Assistance Command, Vietnam. American military, air, and naval headquarters for Vietnam, commanded by General William Westmoreland and, later, Creighton Abrams.

Medevac To medically evacuate the wounded, usually by helicopter.

M-16 Standard American infantry rifle.

NCO Noncommissioned officer.

NVA North Vietnamese Army.

On Rock 'n' Roll Slang expression for putting the M-16 on fully automatic rapid-fire mode, as compared to one bullet at a time. Typical phrase: "I put it on rock 'n' roll and let it go."

Point man The soldier out in front of a unit traveling in a single file. The most exposed position, especially to booby traps.

PTSD Post-traumatic stress disorder. Stress that continues after the traumatic event, such as combat or harsh treatment of returning Vietnam veterans.

R and R Rest and recreation leave. One week during year's stay in Vietnam.

Sapper A soldier with special training in explosives and mines. VC and NVA troops trained to infiltrate and attack American bases from within.

Tracer A bullet or artillery round designed to light a red path along its trajectory. Used at night to mark locations and fire zones.

Triple canopy Dense jungle cover of trees and vines, preventing visibility from airplanes or helicopters.

Trip wire A wire or string, placed across a path or trail, which would set off an explosive charge. (Booby traps could also be buried and set off by pressure from above or could be "command-detonated"—i.e., controlled by someone exploding it from an observation point.)

VVA Vietnam Veterans of America, a service organization comprised of several thousand Vietnam veterans.

VVAW Vietnam Veterans Against the War. A group of antiwar veterans active in the early seventies.

Willy Peter From the initials for white phosphorous. A chemical in some artillery and mortar rounds which emits white smoke on impact. Used to mark the location of targets before actual explosives were fired.

The World The United States.

Backnotes

I: Prologue
1. *Myths and Realities: A Study of Attitudes Toward Vietnam Era Veterans.* Reprinted by the Veterans Administration, July 1980.
2. Woolf, Virginia. *A Room of One's Own.* New York: Harcourt, Brace, 1929.
3. Terkel, Studs. *Hard Times.* New York: Pantheon, 1970.

I/2: The Generation
1. Baskir, M. Lawrence, and Strauss, William A. *Chance and Circumstance: The Draft, the War, and the Vietnam Generation.* New York: Alfred A. Knopf, 1978.
2. Ibid.
3. Lipset, Seymour; and Raab, Earl. "The Non-Generation Gap." *Commentary,* August 1979.
4. Ibid.
5. Mueller, John E. *War, Presidents, and Public Opinion.* New York: John Wiley, 1973.
6. Karnow, Stanley. *Vietnam: A History.* New York: Viking Press, 1983.
7. Baskir and Strauss.
8. Ibid.
9. Ibid.
10. *Newsweek.* October 6, 1969.
11. Baskir and Strauss.
12. Mailer, Norman. *The Armies of the Night.* New York: New American Library, 1968.
13. Johnston, J., and Bachman, J. G. *Youth in Transition.* 1972.
14. Figley, Charles R., and Leventman, Seymour. *Strangers at Home.* New York: Praeger, 1980.
15. Keegan, John. *The Face of Battle.* New York: Viking Press, 1976.
16. Ibid.
17. *Myths and Realities.*
18. Fallows, James. "What Did You Do in the Class War, Daddy?" *Washington Monthly,* October 1975.
19. *Life.* November 28, 1969.
20. American Legion Archives, National Headquarters, Indianapolis, Ind.

21. Lifton, Robert J. *Home from the War.* New York: Simon and Schuster, 1973.
22. *Newsweek.* October 6, 1969.

I/3: A Different War

1. *Myths and Realities: A Study of Attitudes Toward Vietnam Era Veterans.* Reprinted by the Veterans Administration, July 1980.
2. Ibid.
3. Ibid.
4. *Playboy.* January 1982.
5. *Myths and Realities.* Seventy-seven percent of those who served in Vietnam *saw* Americans wounded or killed; 43 percent of those in Vietnam killed or thought they had killed someone; 23 percent of those veterans suffered war-related wounds. Furthermore, the study states that these statistics obviously "understate the actual impact of combat on those troops who fought in Vietnam. Only the survivors are represented in this sample."
6. Horne, A. D., ed. *The Wounded Generation, America After Vietnam.* A Washington *Post* Book. Englewood Cliffs, New Jersey: Prentice-Hall, 1981.
7. U.S. Army official statistics, Division of the Office of Comptroller of the Army.
8. Figley, Charles, and Leventman, Seymour, eds. *Strangers at Home.* New York: Praeger, 1980.
9. Keegan, John. *The Face of Battle.* New York: Viking Press, 1976.
10. *Playboy.* January 1982.
11. Kerry, John. *The New Soldier.* New York: MacMillan, 1971.
12. *National Journal.* August 15, 1970.
13. *Playboy.* January 1982.
14. *Myths and Realities.*
15. *Playboy.* January 1982.
16. *Myths and Realities.*

I/4: Southie and the Rebels

1. Lumpkin, Katherine Du Pre. *The Making of a Southerner.* Athens, Ga.: University of Georgia Press, 1981.
2. Suid, H. Lawrence. *Guts and Glory, Great American War Movies.* New York: Addison-Wesley, 1978.
3. Herr, Michael. *Dispatches.* New York: Alfred A. Knopf, 1977.
4. *Newsweek.* November 9, 1970.

II/1: Draft Board Blues

1. *Life,* May 15, 1970.
2. McCague, James. *The Second Rebellion: The Story of the New York City Draft Riots of 1863.* New York: Dial Press, 1968.

3. Murdock, Eugene C. *One Million Men: The Civil War Draft in the North.* Madison, Wisc.: State Historical Society of Wisconsin, 1971.
4. Ibid.
5. Ibid.
6. Ibid.
7. Baskir, M. Lawrence, and Strauss, William A. *Chance and Circumstance: The Draft, the War, and the Vietnam Generation.* New York: Alfred A. Knopf, 1978.
8. Ibid.
9. Halberstam, David. *The Best and the Brightest.* New York: Random House, 1972.
   Baskir and Strauss.
10. Reedy, George E. *Who Will Do Our Fighting for Us?* New York and Cleveland: World Publishing, 1969.
11. Baskir and Strauss.
12. Ibid.
13. *U.S. News and World Report.* March 1, 1971.

II/2: The Chosen

1. Kelman, Steven. *The Escalation of Student Protest: Push Comes to Shove.* Boston: Houghton Mifflin, 1970.
2. Jones, Landon Y. *Great Expectations: America and the Baby Boom Generation.* New York: Ballantine, 1980.
3. Ibid.
4. *Life.* March 21, 1969.
5. Gitlin, Todd. *The Whole World Is Watching.* Berkeley, Calif.: University of California Press, 1980.
6. Baskir, M. Lawrence, and Strauss, William A. *Chance and Circumstance: The Draft, the War, and the Vietnam Generation.* New York: Alfred A. Knopf, 1978.
7. Ibid.
8. Sale, Kirkpatrick. *SDS.* New York: Random House, 1973.
9. Gitlin.
10. Ibid.
11. Sale, Kirkpatrick.

II/6: The Reserves and National Guard

1. *The New Republic.* February 1970.
2. Baskir, M. Lawrence, and Strauss, William A. *Chance and Circumstance: The Draft, the War, and the Vietnam Generation.* New York: Alfred A. Knopf, 1978.
3. Ibid.

II/7: Game of Chance

1. *Time.* December 12, 1969.
2. *Newsweek.* November 9, 1970.
3. *Time.* December 12, 1969.

II/8: Confessions

1. New York *Times*. January 11, 1981.

II/9: Impressions

1. Polner, Murray. *When Can I Come Home? A Debate on Amnesty for Exiles, Antiwar Prisoners, and Others*. Garden City, N.Y.: Anchor/ Doubleday, 1972.
2. *Playboy*. January 1982.
3. *Myths and Realities: A Study of Attitudes Toward Vietnam Era Veterans*. Reprinted by the Veterans Administration, July 1980.
4. Sale, Kirkpatrick. *SDS*. New York: Random House, 1973.

III/1: Post-Traumatic Stress

1. Lifton, Robert J. *Home from the War*. New York: Simon and Schuster, 1973.
2. Polner, Murray. *When Can I Come Home? A Debate on Amnesty for Exiles, Antiwar Prisoners, and Others*. Garden City, N.Y.: Anchor/ Doubleday, 1972.
3. Figley, Charles, and Leventman, Seymour, eds. *Strangers at Home*. New York: Praeger, 1980.
4. Ibid.
5. Ibid.
6. *Time*. October 9, 1972.
7. *Legacies of Vietnam: Comparative Adjustment of Veterans and Their Peers. A Study*. Conducted for the Veterans Administration, 5 vols. New York: Center for Policy Research, March 1981.
8. *Playboy*. January 1982.
9. *Legacies*.
10. Ibid.
11. *Playboy*. January 1982.
12. Harrington, David, and Jay, Jeffrey. "Value Issues in the Treatment of Vietnam Veterans." *The Family Therapy Networker*, Vol. 6, No. 3, May–June 1982.

III/2: The Afflicted

Notes 1–17: A Review of 120 Years of the Psychological Literature on Reactions to Combat from the Civil War through the Vietnam War, 1860–1980. A major area paper submitted for the degree of Doctor of Philosophy in the Department of Psychology of the Graduate School of Arts and Sciences of Duke University, 1981, by psychologist John Russell Smith, who has graciously given me permission to quote extensively from his work. I have used the original sources as Smith has indicated.

1. "Great Britain Army War Office Committee of Enquiry into Shell Shock," 1922.

2. Bailey, Pearce W. "War Neurosis, Shell Shock, and Nervousness." *Journal of the American Medical Association,* 1918.

3. Ibid.

4. Hastings, D., Wright, D., and Glueck, B. *Psychiatric Experiences of the Eighth Air Force.* New York: Macy Foundation, 1944.

5. Bailey.

6. Yealland, Lewis. *Hysterical Disorders of Warfare.* London: MacMillan, 1918.

7. Ibid.

8. Hurst, Arthur F. "Hysteria in the Light of the Experience of War." *Archives of Neurology and Psychiatry,* 1919.

9. Lidz, T. "Nightmares and the Combat Neuroses." *Psychiatry,* 1946.

10. Major General Paul Hawley, Chief Surgeon, U.S. Army, 1944 report, Med. Dept., U.S. Army, 1974.

11. Med. Dept., U.S. Army, 1974 report.

12. Archibald, H. C., Long, D. M., Miller, C., and Tuddenham, R. D. "Gross Stress Reaction Following Combat: A Twenty-year Follow-up." *Archives of General Psychiatry,* 1965.

13. Office of the Surgeon General, 1968 report.

14. Allerton, W. S. "Army Psychiatry in Vietnam," in P. G. Bourne, *The Psychology and Physiology of Stress.* New York: Academic, 1969.

15. Wallen, V., in P. G. Bourne, op. cit.

16. Wecter, Dixon. *When Johnny Comes Marching Home.* Cambridge: Riverside Press, Houghton Mifflin Company, 1944.

17. Marshall, S. L. A. *Men Against Fire.* New York: William Morrow, 1947.

18. Strayer, R., and Ellenhorn, L. "Vietnam Veterans: A Study Exploring Adjustment Patterns and Attitudes." *J. Soc. Issues,* 1975.

19. Wecter. *When Johnny Comes Marching Home.*

20. Ibid.

21. *Playboy.* January 1982.

III/3: The Criminals

1. Peter Krutschewski case, pages 210–16: Compiled from personal interviews with Krutschewski, lawyer Joe Zengerle, and the following periodicals: Washington *Post,* January 3, 1982; The Boston *Phoenix,* April 14, 1981; *Time,* March 29, 1981; Boston *Globe,* September 10, 1980; Boston *Herald American,* September 10, 1980; Boston *Globe,* August 27, 1980; New York *Times,* March 10, 1982.

2. Lewis Lowe III case, pages 216–19: Birmingham (Alabama) *Post-Herald,* October 27, 1981, October 28, 1981, October 29, 1981, October 30, 1981, November 1, 1981; *Newsweek,* November 23, 1981; Birmingham *News,* October 26, 1981, October 28, 1981, October 29, 1981; Miami *Herald,* October 30, 1981.

3. Charles Heads case, pages 219–26: Compiled from a personal interview with Heads's lawyer, Wellborn Jack, Jr.; a lengthy account by Jack

detailing the introduction, history of the case, attorney-client relationship, PTSD, Heads's Vietnam experience, picking the jury, the trial and its aftermath, reprinted in *Criminal Defense,* Vol. 9, No. 1, January–February 1982, "The Vietnam Connection of Charles Heads's Verdict"; and articles in the Shreveport *Times* by Lynda Farrar and Shreveport *Journal* by Mary Durusau, October 4–15, 1981.

III/4: The Vet Centers
1. *Newsday.* September 25, 1979.
2. *Vet Center Voice* newsletter. May 1983.
3. The Arizona *Republic.* April 20, 1981.
4. *Newsday.* September 25, 1979.
5. Ibid.

III/5: The Disordered
1. *Newsday.* September 25, 1979.
2. *U.S. News and World Report.* December 1970.
3. *Newsweek.* January 12, 1970.
4. Ibid.
5. Ibid.

III/6: The Significant Others
1. *Legacies of Vietnam: Comparative Adjustment of Veterans and Their Peers. A Study.* Conducted for the Veterans Administration. 5 vols. New York: Center for Policy Research, March 1981.
2. Ibid.
3. Ibid.
4. "Post Traumatic Stress Disorder of Vietnam Veterans." *DAV Manual,* 1980.
5. Stanton, M. Duncan, and Figley, Charles R. *Stress Disorders Among Vietnam Veterans.* New York: Brunner/Mazel, 1978.

IV/1: Successful Veterans
1. *Legacies of Vietnam: Comparative Adjustment of Veterans and Their Peers. A Study.* Conducted for the Veterans Administration, 5 vols. New York: Center for Policy Research, March 1981. More than one third who were in heavy combat remain stressed to some degree today. In addition, a high percentage in the "stable" group examined in this study are denying their problems through avoidance.
2. Ibid.
3. Ibid.
4. Ibid.
5. Ibid.
6. "Discriminant Analysis of Post-Traumatic Stress Disorder Among a Group of Vietnam Veterans." J. Stephen Frye and Rex A. Stockton. *American Journal of Psychiatry,* January 1982.

7. *Legacies of Vietnam.*
8. *The New Republic.* August 30, 1982.

IV/2: From Losers to Winners
1. *U.S. News and World Report.* March 29, 1982.

IV/3: The Wounded
1. Washington *Post.* April 10, 1978.

V/1: The Deserters
1. Baskir, M. Lawrence, and Strauss, William A. *Chance and Circumstance: The Draft, the War, and the Vietnam Generation.* New York: Alfred A. Knopf, 1978.
2. Johnson, Haynes, and Wilson, George. *The Washington Post National Report: Army in Anguish.* New York: Pocket Books/Simon and Schuster, 1971.
3. Baskir and Strauss.
4. Ibid.
5. Surrey, David. *Choice of Conscience: Vietnam Era Military and Draft Resisters in Canada.* Praeger Special Studies. South Hadley, Mass.: J. F. Bergen, 1982.
6. Baskir and Strauss. "In contrast, almost all of the 100,000 deserters still at large at the end of the Civil War were front-line troops. And more than 20,000 soldiers were *convicted* for desertion in combat in World War II. (Forty-nine were sentenced to die, although only one, Eddie Slovik, was executed.) Only 24 men were convicted for deserting in combat in Vietnam; of 14 Army GIs tried between 1968 and 1972, only 6 were found guilty."
7. Ibid. "During the five peak years in Vietnam, desertion rates jumped three-fold—from 8.4 to 33.9 per thousand. The Army's 1971 rate was *three times* as great as the highest Korean War level and surpassed World War II's maximum of 63 per thousand during 1944.
8. Cortright, David. *Soldiers in Revolt.* Garden City, N.Y.: Anchor/Doubleday, 1975.
9. Ibid.
10. Baskir and Strauss.
11. Sherrill, Robert. *Military Justice Is to Justice as Military Music Is to Music.* New York: Harper and Row, 1970.
12. Baskir and Strauss.
13. *Life.* October 24, 1969.
14. Johnson and Wilson.
15. "Vietnam Veterans Leadership Program Fact Sheet." *Congressional Record.* October 1, 1982.
16. Cortright.
17. Ibid.
18. Baskir and Strauss.

19. Cortright.
20. Baskir and Strauss.
21. Cortright.
22. Waterhouse, Larry G., and Wizard, Marian G. *Turning the Guns Around.*
    New York: Praeger, 1971.
23. Baskir and Strauss.
24. Cortright, David. *Soldiers in Revolt.*
25. *Life,* October 10, 1969.
26. Baskir and Strauss.
27. Ibid.
28. Washington *Post,* March 1976 editorial board conversation.
29. Baskir and Strauss.
30. Ibid.
31. Ibid.

V/2: The Exiles
1. Surrey, David S. *Choice and Conscience: Vietnam Era Military and Draft
   Resisters in Canada.* Praeger Special Studies. South Hadley, Mass.:
   J. F. Bergin, 1982.
2. Surrey. *Choice and Conscience.*
   Williams, Roger Melville. *The New Exiles: American War Resisters in
   Canada.* New York: Liveright, 1971.
   Baskir, M. Lawrence; and Strauss, William A. *Chance and Circumstance:
   The Draft, the War and the Vietnam Generation.* New York: Alfred A.
   Knopf, 1978.
3. Williams. *The New Exiles.*
4. Ibid.
5. Surrey. *Choice and Conscience.*

V/3: The Imprisoned
1. Baskir, M. Lawrence, and Strauss, William A. *Chance and Circumstance:
   The Draft, the War, and the Vietnam Generation.* New York: Alfred A.
   Knopf, 1978.
2. Ibid.
3. Ibid.
4. Ibid.
5. Ibid.
6. Gaylin, Willard. *In the Service of Their Country: War Resisters in Prison.*
   New York: Viking Press, 1970.
7. Ibid.
8. Baskir and Strauss.
9. Gaylin.

VI/1: Mothers and Fathers
1. Washington *Post.* September 15, 1981.
2. Washington *Post.* January 30, 1972.

VI/3: The Women Who Went
1. Washington *Post.* May 23, 1983.
2. *The Oregon Veterans' Forum,* March 1979. Vol. 2, No. 5.
3. "Use of Women in the Military." Office of the Assistant Secretary of Defense, Manpower, Reserve Affairs, and Logistics, May 1977. Background study.
4. Dallas *Times Herald,* January 25, 1981.
5. Ibid.
6. Testimony of Jenny Ann Schnaier before the Committee on Veterans' Affairs, Subcommittee on Hospital and Health Care, March 3, 1983. Research for University of Maryland master's thesis.

VI/4: Women at the Barricades
1. Chapter by Dean Phillips. In *Strangers at Home,* edited by Charles Figley and Seymour Leventman. New York: Praeger, 1980.

VII/1: Atrocities
1. Taylor, Clyde, ed. *Vietnam and Black America: An Anthology of Protest and Resistance.* Garden City, N.Y.: Anchor/Doubleday, 1973. Essay by James Baldwin.
2. Wasserstrom, Richard A., ed. *War and Morality.* Belmont, Calif.: Wadsworth, 1970. Essay by William James.
3. Washington *Post,* Outlook, August 23, 1981.
4. Associated Press, September 6, 1968.
5. *Life,* December 5, 1969.
6. Sontag, Susan. *Trip to Hanoi.* New York: Farrar, Straus and Giroux, 1968.
7. Denton, Jeremiah. *When Hell Was in Session.* Pleasantville, N.Y.: Reader's Digest Press, 1976.
8. Lewy, Gunter. *America in Vietnam.* New York: Oxford University Press, 1978.
9. Knoll, Erwin, and McFadden, Judith Nies. *War Crimes and the American Conscience.* New York: Holt, Rinehart and Winston, 1970.
10. Ibid.
11. Ellsberg, Daniel. *Papers on the War.* New York: Simon and Schuster, 1972.
12. *The New Republic.* December 20, 1969.
13. Ibid.
14. *War Stress and Trauma: The Vietnam Veteran Experience.* A study conducted for the Veterans Administration. New York: Center for Policy Research. Additional paper of *Legacies* study, January 1983.
15. Keegan, John. *The Face of Battle.* New York: Viking Press, 1976.
16. Hersh, Seymour. *Cover-Up.* New York: Random House, 1972.
17. Ibid.
18. Ibid.

19. Ibid.
20. Lewy.
21. Greider, William. Washington *Post,* April 5, 1971.
22. Lewy.
23. Hersh.
24. Greider, William. Washington *Post,* April 5, 1971.
25. *The New Republic,* August 29, 1970.
26. Wasserstrom, Richard A., ed. *War and Morality.* Belmont, California: Wadsworth, 1970.
27. *Life,* December 19, 1969.
28. Opton, Edward M. and Duckles, Robert. "Mental Gymnastics on My Lai." *The New Republic,* February 21, 1970.
29. *Time,* December 26, 1969.
30. Ibid.
31. Lewy.
32. Ibid.
33. Webb, James. *Ras Ipsa Locuitur Law Review.* Georgetown University Law Center, Fall 1973.
34. Ibid.
35. Lang, Daniel. *Incident on Hill 192.* London: Secker and Warburg, 1970.
36. Herr, Michael. *Dispatches.* New York: Alfred A. Knopf, 1977.
37. Information on Norman Ryman, Jr.'s case was obtained through official Army documents, psychiatric reports, and an account of his life penned by Ryman while in prison.

VII/2: The Reluctant Warriors

1. *Harper's,* November 1969.
2. Shawcross, William. *Sideshow.* New York: Pocket Books/Simon and Schuster, 1979.
3. Evans, Roland, Jr.; and Novak, Robert D. *Nixon in the White House.* New York: Random House, 1971. As quoted by Shawcross in *Sideshow.*
4. Shawcross, and the Bombing in Cambodia congressional hearings.
5. *The New Republic,* July 18, 1970.

VII/3: The Warriors

1. Wasserstrom, Richard A., ed. *War and Morality.* Belmont, Calif.: Wadsworth, 1970. Essay by William James.
2. Karnow, Stanley. *Vietnam: A History.* New York: Viking Press, 1983.
3. Washington *Post.* September 7, 1978. Paul Hendrickson's profile on Weber.
4. *Myths and Realities: A Study of Attitudes Toward Vietnam Era Veterans.* Reprinted by the Veterans Administration, July 1980.
5. Washington *Times.* September 11, 1979.

VII/4: The Blacks

1. Taylor, Clyde, ed. *Vietnam and Black America: An Anthology of Protest and Resistance.* Garden City, N.Y.: Anchor/Doubleday, 1973.

2. Ibid.
3. Ibid.
4. Starr, Paul. *The Discarded Army: Veterans After Vietnam.* New York: Charterhouse, 1973.
5. Barnes, Peter. *Pawns: The Plight of the Citizen-Soldiers.* New York: Alfred A. Knopf, 1972.
6. Starr.
7. Phillips, Dean. "The Case for Veterans' Preference." Chapter in *Strangers at Home,* ed. Charles Figley and Seymour Leventman. New York: Praeger, 1980.
8. Starr.
9. *National Journal.* April 15, 1978.
10. Ibid.
11. Surrey, David. *Choice of Conscience: Vietnam Era Military and Draft Resisters in Canada.* Praeger Special Studies. South Hadley, Mass.: J. F. Bergin, 1982.
12. Barnes.
13. Ibid.
14. *National Journal.* April 15, 1978.
15. Taylor, Clyde, ed. *Vietnam and Black America: An Anthology of Protest and Resistance.* Essay by Wallace Terry, "Bringing the War Home."
16. Ibid.
17. Ibid.
18. Baskir, M. Lawrence, and Strauss, William A. *Chance and Circumstance: The Draft, the War, and the Vietnam Generation.* New York: Alfred A. Knopf, 1978.
19. Addlestone, David F., and Sherer, Susan. "Race in Vietnam." *Civil Liberties,* February 1973.
20. Taylor, ed. Essay by Wallace Terry, "Bringing the War Home."
21. Johnson, Haynes, and Wilson, George. *The Washington Post National Report: Army in Anguish.* New York: Pocket Books/Simon and Schuster, 1971.
22. Addlestone and Sherer.
23. Johnson and Wilson.
24. Cortright, David. *Soldiers in Revolt.* Garden City, N.Y.: Anchor/Doubleday, 1975.
25. Johnson and Wilson.
26. Ibid.
27. New York *Times,* Op Ed page, September 14, 1980.
28. *Legacies of Vietnam: Comparative Adjustment of Veterans and Their Peers. A Study.* Conducted for the Veterans Administration, 5 vols. New York: Center for Policy Research, March 1981.
29. Ibid.
30. Ibid.
31. Baskir and Strauss.

VII/5: Drugs, Bad Paper, Prison

1. *Congressional Record,* October 1, 1982.
2. Starr, Paul. *The Discarded Army: Veterans After Vietnam.* New York: Charterhouse, 1973.
3. Ibid. "The first 4.5 percent caught through urinalysis on the way home represented only the tip of the iceberg; most were able to abstain long enough to escape detection."
4. Ibid.
5. Ibid. "Much of the opium grown in Laos was produced by the CIA-equipped and CIA-trained tribesmen."
6. "Profile of Drug Abusers in Vietnam." DOD Office of Health and Environment, December 1971. Information in *The Discarded Army.*
7. Dr. Norman Zinberg, Harvard Medical School psychiatrist in Vietnam in 1971, under the auspices of the DOD and Drug Abuse Council. Information in Starr, *The Discarded Army.*
8. Starr.
9. Ibid.
10. Ibid.
11. Baskir, M. Lawrence, and Strauss, William A. *Chance and Circumstance: The Draft, the War, and the Vietnam Generation.* New York: Alfred A. Knopf, 1978.
12. Addlestone, David F. "Background Paper on Less than Fully Honorable Discharges Issued During the Vietnam War." Rev. ed., April 27, 1979.
13. Baskir and Strauss.
14. Ibid.
15. Much of the material in this chapter came from David Addlestone, National Veterans Law Center director. He is the principal author of a detailed manual on how to obtain an upgraded discharge, *The Military Discharge Upgrading and Introduction to Veterans Administration Law,* which may be obtained through the Veterans Education Project (P.O. Box, 42130, Washington, D.C. 20015).
16. Pennsylvania Secretary of Education John C. Pittenger—cited in Senate Committee on Veterans Affairs testimony, July 11, 1979.
17. *Corrections,* March 1979.
18. Ibid.
19. Ibid.
20. A 1975 Pennsylvania survey found that three fourths of inmate veterans were discharged under honorable conditions. Massachusetts and Georgia surveys discovered similar results: veterans were more likely to be first-offenders, more likely to be involved in drugs, better educated than other prisoners. Fewer had been jailed for juvenile offenses and as adults had been convicted less often and of less serious crimes.

    Data collected on 1,521 inmates in eight Pennsylvania state prisons in the mid-seventies showed that approximately one fourth of this group were veterans and a little over one fourth (26 percent) of veteran inmates received less than honorable discharges. On average, 64 percent of all veterans had *no* prior offense, 14 percent had one prior offense, and 22 percent had two or more prior offenses. The average age of veteran inmates was 33.6 years. (The average age of the total inmate population was 25 years.) Some 52 percent of the veterans were black.

Studies consistently show a higher educational level among veterans—10.7 years versus 8 years for the total inmate population. The Massachusetts study found that 36 percent of veteran inmates had completed high school—as compared to only 19 percent of nonveteran inmates. The Massachusetts study found that only 12 percent of veterans had prior adult incarceration as compared to 39 percent for nonveterans. Some 15 percent of veterans had prior juvenile incarcerations versus 33 percent for nonveterans. One Illinois study, in 1973, reported a recidivism rate among veterans of only 10.6 percent, compared to an overall recidivism rate *five times as high.* Testimony before the Senate Committee on Veterans' Affairs of Darryl K. Kehrer, Chairman of the American Association of Minority Veterans Program Administrators (AAMVPA), July 11, 1979.

21. *Corrections Magazine,* March 1979.
22. *Department of Justice, Bureau of Justice Statistics Bulletin,* October 1981.
23. *Corrections Magazine,* March 1979.

VII/6: Agent Orange
1. Dux, John and Young, P. J. *Agent Orange: The Bitter Harvest.* Sydney, Australia: Hodder and Stoughton, 1980.
2. Ibid.
3. New York *Times,* July 6, 1983.
4. New York *Times,* May 13, 1983.
5. Ibid.
6. *New Republic,* June 27, 1983.
7. Washington *Post,* February 27, 1983.
8. *New Republic,* June 27, 1983.
9. New York *Times,* July 6, 1983.
10. New York *Times,* April 19, 1983.
11. *Congressional Record,* March 8, 1983.
12. Testimony of scientist Peter C. Kahn before the Subcommittee on Compensation, Pension, and Insurance of the House Committee on Veterans' Affairs on behalf of the New Jersey Agent Orange Commission.
13. *New Republic,* June 27, 1983.
14. Dux and Young. *Agent Orange: The Bitter Harvest.*
15. New York *Times,* March 18, 1983.
16. Dux and Young. *Agent Orange: The Bitter Harvest.*
17. Washington *Post,* May 30, 1983.

18. Dux and Young. *Agent Orange: The Bitter Harvest.*
19. Ranch Hand Mortality Study: Department of the Air Force, presentation to the House Committee on Veterans' Affairs subcommittee on Compensation, Pension and Insurance, July 12, 1983.
20. Washington *Times,* July 4, 1983.
21. Texas *Observer,* September 25, 1981.
22. Washington *Post,* June 1, 1979.
23. New York *Times,* July 6, 1983.

Epilogue

Information for the epilogue came from articles by Todd Gitlin in *Mother Jones,* November 1983; William Greider in *Rolling Stone,* November 24, 1983; Harry Maurer in *The New York Review of Books,* February 3, 1983; Seymour Hersh's *The Price of Power;* and a report from the Chicago Council on Foreign Relations regarding public information on defense spending, current foreign policy, and the Vietnam War.

Acknowledgments

Those who have given encouragement and advice during the three years of research and writing this book are both invaluable and too numerous to mention by name. Friends, acquaintances, and strangers all graciously offered suggestions because they cared that the story be told of what it meant, then and now, to have come of age during the Vietnam War.

A special thanks goes to my editor, Lisa Drew, who saw the possibility of a book after reading a two-part series of mine in the Washington *Post*—and whose enthusiasm and talent kept it on track. Also to Ben Bradlee and Shelby Coffey III of the Washington *Post,* who encouraged the book when it was just a two-page memo and then granted me the time to pursue it. A host of editors, friends, experts, and/or participants in Vietnam and other wars read the manuscript and offered vital suggestions, among them: Jeff Stein, Jeffrey Frank, John Peterson, Ed Fouhy, James Dickenson, Shelby Coffey, Dean Phillips, Joe Zengerle, Bob Healy, Art Blank, Ryan Krueger, David Addlestone, Tom Alder. Bruce Martin and Adoreen McCormick, of the Library of Congress, were especially helpful in extending the use of its research facilities. I also thank the Washington *Post* library staff, copy aide supervisor Nancy Brucker, and dictationists Olwen Price, Lynn Elmehdaoui, Susan Kelly, Carol Leggett, Diane Saenz, who typed the manuscript, and *Post* style reporter Richard Harrington, who assisted in song selections for section headings in this book.

I am most grateful to the Jack and Ruth Eckerd Foundation for providing me with a grant to assist in my research.

A major debt of gratitude goes to those whose serious studies on Vietnam veterans and the generation provided an essential foundation and context for my research and interviews. These include Charles Figley, who edited *Strangers at Home* and encouraged me with my book; Robert Laufer and all others who contributed to the *Legacies of Vietnam* study; Lawrence Baskir and William Strauss, who compiled *Chance and Circumstance,* their landmark compendium of facts about the Vietnam Generation. The chapter on the history of war traumas could not have been written without John Russell

Smith's detailed *Review of 120 Years of Psychological Literature on Reactions to Combat from the Civil War through the Vietnam War.*

Above all, I can never thank enough the men and women of the Vietnam Generation who gave of their time, their hearts, and their minds to tell me their stories—especially those who went to Vietnam. Putting it down on paper is an attempt to explain what they went through over there and on their return, although it can never do justice to their experiences, emotions, or their thoughts, which are now a part of me forever.

Bibliography

Periodicals

America National Catholic Weekly Review. Vol. 124, January 9, 1971–June 26, 1971.

Atlantic Monthly. January–December 1975.

Congressional Record. October 1, 1982; March 8, 1983.

Corrections Magazine. March 1979.

Dallas *Times Herald.* June 25, 1981.

Department of Justice, Bureau of Justice statistical bulletin, October 1981.

Fortune. October–December 1970.

Harper's Magazine. July–December 1969.

Life. January–February 1969; March–April 1969; May–June 1969; November–December 1969; May–June 1970.

Mother Jones. November 1983.

Nation. January–June 1970.

New Republic. December 20, 1969; February 21, 1970; July 18, 1970; August 29, 1970; June 27, 1983.

Newsweek. April–June 1970.

New Yorker. March 2–30, 1968.

New York Review of Books. February 3, 1983.

New York *Times.* March 8, April 19, May 13, July 6, 1983.

Oregon Veterans Forum. March 1979 (Vol. 2, No. 5).

Rolling Stone. November 24, 1983.

Texas *Observer.* September 25, 1981.

Time. October–December 1969.

U.S. News and World Report. January–March 1971.

Washington *Post.* April 5, 1971; September 7, 1978; June 1, 1979; August 23, 1981; February 27, May 23, and May 30, 1983.

Washington *Times.* September 11, 1979; July 4, 1983.

Reports, Studies

Addlestone, David F. "Background Paper on Less than Fully Honorable Discharges Issued During the Vietnam War." April 27, 1979.

Addlestone, David F., and Sherer, Susan. "Race in Vietnam." *Civil Liberties,* February 1973.

Post-traumatic stress disorder of the Vietnam Veteran: Observations and recommendations for psychological treatment of the veteran and his family. DAV (Disabled American Veterans) Manual, edited by Tom Williams, 1980.

"Ranch Hand Mortality Study." Department of the Air Force, July 12, 1983.

"Use of Women in the Military." Office of the Assistant Secretary of Defense, Manpower, Reserve Affairs and Logistics. May 1977. Background study.

Books

Adelson, Alan. *SDS.* New York: Charles Scribner's Sons, 1972.

Alpert, Jane. *Growing Up Underground.* New York: William Morrow, 1981.

Arlen, Michael J. *Living-Room War.* New York: Viking Press, 1966.

Barnes, Peter. *PAWNS: The Plight of the Citizen-Soldiers.* New York: Alfred A. Knopf, 1972.

Baskir, M. Lawrence, and Strauss, William A. *Chance and Circumstance: The Draft, the War, and the Vietnam Generation.* New York: Alfred A. Knopf, 1978.

Blumenthal, Michael. *SYMPaTHETIC MaGIC.* Huntington, N.Y.: Water Mark Press, 1980.

Bryan, C. D. B. *Friendly Fire.* New York: Putnam, 1976.

Carey, Alex E. *Australian Atrocities in Vietnam.* Sydney, Australia: R. S. Gould, n.d.

Cortright, David. *Soldiers in Revolt.* Garden City, N.Y.: Anchor/Doubleday, 1975.

Davies, Wallace Evan. *Patriotism on Parade: The Story of Veterans and Hereditary Organizations in America 1793–1900.* Cambridge, Mass.: Harvard University Press, 1955.

Decter, Midge. *Liberal Parents, Radical Children.* New York: Coward, McCann, and Geoghegan, 1975.

Denton, Jeremiah. *When Hell Was in Session.* Pleasantville, N.Y.: Reader's Digest Press, 1976.

Dux, John, and Young, P. J. *Agent Orange, The Bitter Harvest.* Sydney, Australia: Hodder and Stoughton, 1980.

Ellsberg, Daniel. *Papers on the War.* New York: Simon and Schuster, 1972.

Emerson, Gloria. *Winners and Losers.* New York: Random House, 1976.

Ensign, Tod, and Uhl, Michael. *G.I. Guinea Pigs.* Wideview Books, 1980.

Fall, Bernard B. *Street Without Joy.* Harrisburg, Pa.: Stackpole, 1961.

Ferber, Michael, and Lynd, Staughton. *The Resistance.* Boston: Beacon Press, 1971.

Figley, Charles, and Leventman, Seymour, eds. *Strangers at Home.* New York: Praeger, 1980.

Fitzgerald, Frances. *Fire in the Lake: The Vietnamese and the Americans in Vietnam.* Boston: Little, Brown, 1972.

Franks, Lucinda. *Waiting Out a War: The Exile of Private John Picciano.* New York: Coward, McCann, and Geoghegan, 1974.

Fussell, Paul. *The Great War and Modern Memory.* New York and London: Oxford University Press, 1975.

Gaylin, Willard. *In the Service of Their Country: War Resisters in Prison.* New York: Viking Press, 1970.

Gitlin, Todd. *The Whole World Is Watching.* Berkeley, Calif.: University of California Press, 1980.

Halberstam, David. *The Best and the Brightest.* New York: Random House, 1972.

Halstead, Fred. *GIs Speak Out Against the War: The Case of the Ft. Jackson 8.* New York: Pathfinder Press, 1970.

Heath, Louis G. *Vandals in the Bomb Factory: The History and Literature of the Students for a Democratic Society.* Metuchen, N.J.: The Scarecrow Press, 1976.

Herr, Michael. *Dispatches.* New York: Alfred A. Knopf, 1977.

Hersh, Seymour M. *Cover-Up.* New York: Random House, 1972.

———. *The Price of Power.* New York: Summit Books, 1983.

Hodgson, Godfrey. *America in Our Time.* New York: Vintage Books/Random House, 1976.

Hofman, Margret. *Vietnam Viewpoints: A Handbook for Concerned Citizens.* Published by the author, 1968.

Horne, A. D., ed. *The Wounded Generation, America After Vietnam.* A Washington Post Book. Englewood Cliffs, N.J.: Prentice-Hall, 1981.

Johnson, Haynes, and Wilson, George. *The Washington Post National Report: Army in Anguish.* New York: Pocket Books/Simon and Schuster, 1971.

Jones, Landon Y. *Great Expectations: America and the Baby Boom Generation.* New York: Ballantine, 1980.

Just, Ward. *Military Men.* New York: Alfred A. Knopf, 1970.

———. *To What End.* Boston: Houghton Mifflin, 1968.

Karnow, Stanley. *Vietnam: A History.* New York: Viking Press, 1983.

Keegan, John. *The Face of Battle.* New York: Viking Press, 1976.

Kelman, Steven. *The Escalation of Student Protest: Push Comes to Shove.* Boston: Houghton Mifflin, 1970.

Kernan, Michael. *The Violet Dots.* New York: George Braziller, 1978.

Klein, Robert. *Wounded Men, Broken Promises.* New York: Macmillan, 1981.

Knoll, Erwin, and McFadden, Judith Nies. *War Crimes and the American Conscience.* New York: Holt, Rinehart and Winston, 1970.

Kovic, Ron. *Born on the Fourth of July.* New York: McGraw-Hill, 1976.

Kunan, James S. *Standard Operating Procedure: Notes of a Draft-age American.* New York: Avon, 1971.

———. *The Strawberry Statement—Notes of a College Revolutionist.* New York: Random House, 1969.

Lang, Daniel. *Incident on Hill 192.* London: Secker and Warburg, 1970.

Levy, Charles J. *Spoils of War.* Boston: Houghton Mifflin, 1974.

Lewy, Guenter. *America in Vietnam.* New York: Oxford University Press, 1978.

Lifton, Robert. *Home from the War.* New York: Simon and Schuster, 1973.

Liston, Robert A. *Greeting: You Are Hereby Ordered for Induction . . . The Draft in America.* New York: McGraw-Hill, 1970.

Lukas, Anthony J. *Don't Shoot—We Are Your Children.* New York: Random House, 1968–71.

Lumpkin, Katherine Du Pre. *The Making of a Southerner.* Athens, Ga.: The University of Georgia Press, 1981.

Mailer, Norman. *The Armies of the Night.* New York: New American Library, 1968.

McCague, James. *The Second Rebellion: The Story of the New York City Draft Riots of 1863.* New York: Dial Press, 1968.

McGill, Ralph Emerson. *The South and the Southerner.* Boston: Little, Brown, 1959.

Mueller, John E. *War, Presidents, and Public Opinion.* New York: John Wiley, 1973.

Murdock, Eugene C. *One Million Men: The Civil War Draft in the North.* Madison, Wisc.: The State Historical Society of Wisconsin, 1971.

Patti, L. A. Archimedes. *Why Vietnam? Prelude to America's Albatross.* Berkeley and Los Angeles, Calif.: University of California Press, 1980.

Pike, Douglas. *The Viet-Cong Strategy of Terror.* n.p., 1972.

Podhoretz, Norman. *Why We Were in Vietnam.* New York: Simon and Schuster, 1982.

Polner, Murray. *No Victory Parades: The Return of the Vietnam Veteran.* New York: Holt, Rinehart and Winston, 1971.

———. *When Can I Come Home? A Debate on Amnesty for Exiles, Antiwar Prisoners and Others.* Garden City, N.Y.: Anchor Press/Doubleday, 1972.

Reedy, George E. *Who Will Do Our Fighting for Us?* New York and Cleveland: World Publishing, 1969.

Reich, Charles A. *The Greening of America.* New York: Random House, 1970.

Remarque, Erich Maria. *All Quiet on the Western Front.* New York: Fawcett-Crest, new edition, 1975.

Richardson, Frank M. *Fighting Spirit.* London: Leo Cooper, 1978.

Sale, Kirkpatrick. *SDS.* New York: Random House, 1973.

Salisbury, Harrison E. *Behind the Lines—Hanoi: December 23, 1966–January 7, 1967.* London: Secker and Warburg, 1967.

Sartre, Jean-Paul. *On Genocide.* Boston: Beacon Press, 1968.

Shannon, William. *The American Irish.* New York: Macmillan, 1963.

Shawcross, William. *Sideshow.* New York: Pocket Books/Simon and Schuster, 1979.

Sheehan, Neil; Smith, Hedrick; Kenworthy, E. W.; and Butterfield, Fox. Edited by Gerald Gold, Allan M. Siegal, and Samuel Abt. *The Pentagon Papers.* Toronto: Bantam, 1971.

Sherrill, Robert. *Military Justice Is to Justice as Military Music Is to Music.* New York: Harper and Row, 1970.

Sontag, Susan. *Trip to Hanoi.* New York: Farrar, Straus and Giroux, 1968.

Stanton, M. Duncan, and Figley, Charles R. *Stress Disorders Among Vietnam Veterans.* New York: Brunner/Mazel, 1978.

Starr, Paul. *The Discarded Army: Veterans After Vietnam.* New York: Charterhouse, 1973.

Suid, H. Lawrence. *Guts and Glory, Great American War Movies.* Reading, Mass.: Addison-Wesley, 1978.

Surrey, David S. *Choice of Conscience: Vietnam Era Military and Draft Resisters in Canada.* Praeger Special Studies. South Hadley, Mass.: J. F. Bergin, 1982.

Suttler, David. *IV-F: A Guide to Draft Exemptions.* New York: Grove Press, 1970.

Taylor, Clyde, ed. *Vietnam and Black America: An Anthology of Protest and Resistance.* Garden City, N.Y.: Anchor/Doubleday, 1973.

Terkel, Studs. *Hard Times.* New York: Avon, 1970.

Uhl, Michael. *Vietnam: A Soldier's View.* Wellington, N.Z.: New Zealand University Press, 1971.

Unger, Irwin. *The Movement: A History of the American New Left 1959–1972.* New York: Dodd, Mead, 1974.

Wasserstrom, Richard A., ed. *War and Morality.* Belmont, Calif.: Wadsworth, 1970.

Waterhouse, Larry G., and Wizard, Marian G. *Turning the Guns Around.* New York: Praeger, 1971.

Webb, James. *A Sense of Honor.* Englewood Cliffs, N.J.: Prentice-Hall, 1981.
———. *Fields of Fire.* Englewood Cliffs, N.J.: Prentice-Hall, 1978.

Wecter, Dixon. *When Johnny Comes Marching Home.* Cambridge, Mass.: Riverside Press/Houghton Mifflin, 1944.

Weigley, Russell F. *The End of Militarism.* n.p., n.d.

White, William W. *The Confederate Veteran.* Alabama: Confederate Publishing, 1962.

Williams, Roger Melville. *The New Exiles: American War Resisters in Canada.* New York: Liveright, 1971.

Wilson, John P. *Forgotten Warrior Project Report.* Funded under grant from Disabled American Veterans, September 15, 1976–September 15, 1977.

Woolf, Virginia. *A Room of One's Own.* New York: Harcourt, Brace, 1929.

Index